Price Guide to
FLEA MARKET
TREASURES

Second Edition

Harry L. Rinker Jr.

Wallace-Homestead Book Company · Radnor, Pennsylvania

Designed by Arlene Putterman
Manufactured in the United States of America

ISBN 0-87069-671-8 (pbk)
Library of Congress Catalog Card Number 92-50670

1 2 3 4 5 6 7 8 9 0   2 1 0 9 8 7 6 5 4 3

Contents

PART TWO   FLEA MARKET TREASURES

Foreword

Over eighteen months have passed since I sat down and wrote the foreword to the first edition of *Price Guide to Flea Market Treasures*. While cautiously optimistic that I would eventually be writing a foreword for the second edition, I now confess that I had my doubts.

The project was full of risks. A number of new and well-established general antiques and collectibles guides were already on the market, including my *Warman's Americana and Collectibles*. Many provided strong coverage of the traditional flea market categories. The flea market environment also had changed. The arrival of antiques and collectibles malls, the enormous growth of the indoor show circuit, and the corruption of the outdoor flea markets by non–antiques and collectibles material raised questions about the validity of a price guide devoted exclusively to flea market categories.

Harry Jr., my son, was the biggest risk of all. It took all my effort to persuade Harry Jr. to agree to prepare the first edition. Think of a mule driver trying to persuade a stubborn mule to get off his butt and move. He was in college and had trouble understanding why learning and writing about flea market material was more important than doing the art projects that were part of his course work.

If you have children, I do not have to explain that the time-honored "Father knows best" argument holds little sway with modern youth. Harry Jr. has been known to be quite vocal on occasion, his decibel level often surpassing my own—no mean accomplishment. He never hesitates to tell me what I can do with my arguments. Fortunately, my ears are as deaf to hearing what I do not want to hear as are his; but, I blame his problem on the volume at which he listens to music.

Harry Jr. finished the first edition of *Price Guide to Flea Market Treasures* with a great deal of help from the Rinkettes and myself. In truth, we all had so much fun doing the book that none of us would have been heartbroken if Harry Jr. did not want to do a second edition. Volunteers were lined up and willing to step in. Harry Jr. guaranteed himself a second shot at the flea market book when he joined the staff at Rinker Enterprises, Inc., in January 1992. We agreed to try working together on a two-year trial basis. It has been a trying experience: I try, and he is trying.

In order for there to be a second edition of this book, the first edition had to be a success. It was. Far beyond my wildest expectations and, I suspect, those of the publisher as well.

One of the keys to this success was Harry Jr.'s acceptance of my challenge to make his book "different." *Price Guide to Flea Market Treasures* pioneered new ground. Part One, "A Flea Market Education," was written from the point of view of the flea marketeer, not the flea market dealer—a first for a major price guide. Numerous categories appeared that simply could not be found in other price guides, including my own.

There is more of Harry Jr. in this second edition of *Price Guide to Flea Market Treasures* than there was in the first. Slowly he is discovering that joy can be found not only in writing about the collecting categories you like but also in sharing the excitement and enthusiasm of sellers and buyers regardless of the collecting category. He still deals with some categories grudgingly, but so did I when I was his age.

This past year has been a struggle for Harry Jr. He went to college to become an artist and wound up primarily working for me as a photographer and an occasional writer. Over the next year, examples of his photography will appear in over a dozen different books in the antiques and collectibles field. He continues to draw in his spare time; although, I must confess that in my opinion he should not have any free time. Like any son who works for his father on salary, he feels he is grossly underpaid for the work and time he devotes to the business. Since he wants so badly to be an artist, I keep telling him that he needs to experience a "struggling period" and that I am more than willing to provide him with one.

Harry Jr. has a year to go on our agreement; and, Wallace-Homestead has decided to publish *Price Guide to Flea Market Treasures* annually. Harry Jr. will do a third edition; and, I will write another foreword. If all goes well, it will be my last, with the possible exception of anniversary editions. At some point you simply have to cut your children loose and let them sink or swim on their own.

Harry L. Rinker
Vera Cruz, PA
February 1993

Preface

Some people have suggested that I voluntarily commit myself to a mental institution for agreeing to work for, and ostensibly in the shadow of, my father. More often than not, I agree with them. However, there are those days when being around Dad makes it all worthwhile.

Clint Eastwood's famous "make my day" phrase became reality for me the time Dad came storming into the office after a visit to a local K~Mart store. He always checks a store's book racks no matter where he goes. In his humble opinion, his books deserve to be sold everywhere. When he checked the K~Mart book racks, there prominently displayed among the romance novels and other popular paperbacks were copies of my *Price Guide to Flea Market Treasures*. His price guides were nowhere to be found.

If Dad were a reasonable person—and I am not saying he is—he might have assumed that K~Mart had sold out of his books and was stuck with my meager effort. Not good old, competitive Dad. He was on the telephone immediately to Chilton asking why K~Mart would have the audacity to carry my book instead of his. I think his scream could be heard at least twenty miles away when he learned that K~Mart felt my book was more appropriate to their clientele.

As Kevin of *Home Alone* fame would say, "YESSSSS!!!!"

Sales of *Price Guide to Flea Market Treasures* mounted and eventually challenged those of Dad's baby, *Warman's Americana and Collectibles*. For my part, I learned the true meaning of the phrases "discretion is the better part of valor" and "keep your mouth shut." Dad can discuss matters of editorial content quite calmly, not sales.

Actually, the initial success of *Price Guide to Flea Market Treasures* has done a world of good for Dad. It has ensured that he will never become complacent about his own titles. He currently is in the process of doing a major overall of *Warman's Americana and Collectibles. Warman's Antiques and Their Prices* will follow. It sure feels good as a son to be able to kick your Dad in the pants once in a while.

While working on the first edition, Dad kept telling me about the new friendships I would make. "Sure," I told him just to keep him quiet. Well, he was right. I now correspond with flea marketeers around the world. I look forward to traveling to Australia someday to go flea marketing with R. W. French of Burnie, Tasmania. Hint, hint, Dad.

Do not tell Dad, but some of his messages are getting through to me. I had much more fun doing the second edition of *Price Guide to Flea Market Treasures* than I did the first. It is quite an experience to watch and record one's childhood as it moves from junk to secondhand to collectible. I have learned to appreciate a broader range of material, even things I do not personally collect.

Finally, I discovered that no one in the antiques and collectibles field survives on his or her own. An individual's success relies heavily on a host of supporting individuals. With this in mind and in appreciation for all that it took to make the first edition of *Price Guide to Flea Market Treasures* a success, I acknowledge and express my appreciation to the following individuals and groups.

No book has a chance for success unless it is made available for purchase. A special thanks to the sales and marketing staff of Chilton Book Company, parent company of

Wallace-Homestead Book Company, and its sales representatives for their sales and promotional efforts. Their results were spectacular, creating a mark that will require a concerted effort to surpass. I have done my best to provide them with a product that exceeds the quality of its predecessor, hopefully making their task a bit easier.

Next, I want to thank those individuals who purchased the first edition of *Price Guide to Flea Market Treasures*. I suspect that you found the information that I provided helpful and financially rewarding or you would not be reading the Preface of this second edition. If I have done my job, you will find even more reasons to applaud yourself for investing in my latest effort.

For those who are purchasing this book for the first time, I thank you for providing me with an opportunity to show you the fun of flea marketeering. You will laugh as you learn. I have tried my best not to allow any stuffiness to work its way into these pages.

Any book prepared at Rinker Enterprises, Inc., is a team effort. Dad's Rinkettes are one of the most talented antiques and collectibles research staffs available. I am proud to be part of this group. Besides, they needed a tenor. All kidding aside, without the efforts of Ellen L. Schroy, Terese Oswald, Dana Morykan, Nancy Butt, Jocelyn Mousley, and Diane Sterner, this book would not have been possible. I look forward to the day when I can help them as much on their projects as they have helped me on mine.

As with my first effort, this edition was written only with continued strong support from antiques and collectibles flea market promoters, managers, workers, and dealers. Collectors who regularly participate in the flea market circuit also have shared their thoughts with me. My sincere thanks for the advice, criticism, and encouragement.

Finally, there is my dad, Harry L. Rinker, who, unwilling to admit that he is becoming a true old fart, continues to refrain from using "Senior" behind his name. I like to kid with him that he taught me little or nothing throughout the years. I would tell you his reply, but it would never clear Chilton's manuscript editors. He is everywhere in this book as am I—independent and opinionated.

One thing Dad continually emphasizes is that no product is ever perfect. Improve, change, be the leader. God, I hate Type-A personalities. Yet, he is right. Therefore, I welcome your comments and criticisms. There is going to be a third edition; and, I want it to be better than this one. Send your thoughts to: Harry L. Rinker Jr., *Price Guide to Flea Market Treasures*, 5093 Vera Cruz Road, Emmaus, PA 18049.

Harry L. Rinker Jr.
Vera Cruz, PA
February 1993

Introduction

Harry L. Rinker, my dad, always claims that the third edition of any book is actually the book that the author really would have written in the first place if he or she would have had all the time in the world to prepare it. As I worked on the second edition of this book, I began to understand the reasons behind his premise.

In this enlarged second edition of *Price Guide to Flea Market Treasures,* I corrected the few minor miscues that slipped into the first volume, fine-tuned a number of categories to more accurately reflect their market importance and the variety of items available, and added over a dozen new categories to give the book greater depth and strength. As a result, this second edition is more responsive to the needs of its user than the first. Not that I feel the first edition was inadequate. Quite the contrary. What I have done is make a good product better.

The success of the first edition of *Price Guide to Flea Market Treasures* provided ample proof that a major new approach was needed for flea market price guides. Combining basic information about flea marketeering with price listings by category appears to be just what the doctor ordered. Why tamper with success? This second edition follows the same format as the first.

Price Guide to Flea Market Treasures is divided into three principal parts.

The first part is a guide for flea marketeers. It helps you identify a "true" flea market, tells you how to find and evaluate flea markets, provides a list of the top twenty flea markets nationwide, gives tips for surviving the flea market experience and honing your shopping skills, and provides in-depth analysis of the current flea market scene.

Much of the information is a repeat of that which appeared in the first edition. You will find minor changes in the sections dealing with general guides to flea market locations, trade papers, and top twenty flea markets. Chapter 6, "The Flea Market Scene Today," has been totally rewritten to reflect the impact of the current economic recession upon flea markets.

In talking with many of the individuals who purchased the first edition of this book, I was surprised to learn how many "experienced" flea marketeers had skipped this first part. They made a mistake. Even the most experienced flea marketeer will find something of value. One of the worst mistakes you can make in the antiques and collectibles field is to assume that you know all you need to know.

The second part is devoted to price listings by category. First-edition users are advised to thumb through the categories and not rely on the assumption that they know what the book contains. This second edition of *Price Guide to Flea Market Treasures* contains an additional thirty-two pages and over twenty new categories.

You will make a serious mistake if you assume this book is just another general antiques and collectibles price guide. Not true. This book was prepared using the premise that everything imaginable turns up at a flea market—from the finest antiques to good reusable secondhand items. "Dearly Departed" and "Secondhand Roses" categories are not found in any other antiques or collectibles price guides.

In a few categories you will not find specific priced items. Instead you are provided with general information that allows a broad understanding of the category. Occasionally, you are referred to specialized books on the subject.

One of the great joys about working on the categories in this book is that so many are supported with collectors' clubs, newsletters, and periodicals. You will find full addresses for these listed in the appropriate category before the price listings.

Just like Dad, I am one of those "wild and crazy guys." Unlike Dad, whose books tend toward the conventional, my book allows me to express this aspect of my character. As a result, you will find that the category introductions range from serious to humorous to sublime. If the key to a great flea market is that it evokes these emotions and more within you, why should this book do any less?

Although I am not certain why, the third part of this book, which contains reference material for flea marketeers, including the "Flea Marketeer's Annotated Reference Library" and a list of "Antiques and Collectibles Trade Papers," was used least by those who bought the first edition of this book. I strongly recommend that you become familiar with this section. The information not only helps you become highly proficient as a flea marketeer but serves as your introduction to the other wonderful areas of the antiques and collectibles field.

It is time to honor the cry of the Circus ringmaster: "On with the show." Take a moment and read the program (the first section) before you watch the acts in the center ring (the second section) and then relive the memories (the third section). Most of all, don't forget—the entire purpose of the performance is for you to have fun.

Part One
A FLEA MARKET EDUCATION

What Is a Flea Market?

1

It is difficult to explain the sense of excitement and anticipation felt by collectors and dealers as they get ready to shop a flea market. They are about to undertake a grand adventure, a journey into the unknown. Flea markets turn the average individual into an explorer in search of buried treasure. The search is not without adversity—conditions ranging from a hostile climate to intense competition as one waits with other collectors and dealers for the gates to open may be encountered. Victory is measured in "steals" and bargains and in stories that can be shared at the end of the day over dinner with friendly rivals.

Flea markets provide the opportunity for prospective collectors to get their feet wet in the exciting world of antiques and collectibles and for novice dealers to test their merchandise and selling skills at minimal expense. Many first contacts, some of which last a lifetime, are made between and among collectors and dealers there. More than any other aspect of the antiques and collectibles trade, the flea market is the one forum where everyone is on equal footing.

Before you learn how to find, evaluate, and survive flea markets, it is important that you understand *exactly* what a flea market is, how it fits into the antiques and collectibles market, and the many variations of it that exist. This is the first step to identifying the flea markets that are most likely to provide the greatest opportunities for you.

Defining a Flea Market

Few terms in the antiques and collectibles field are as difficult to define as *flea market*. If you visit the Rose Bowl Flea Market in Pasadena, California, you will find discontinued and knock-off merchandise, handmade crafts, clothing (from tube socks to dresses), home-care items, plants of all types, and specialty foods more in evidence than antiques and collectibles. On the other hand, if you visit the Ann Arbor Antiques Market in Michigan, you will find primarily middle- and upper-level antiques and collectibles. Both are flea markets, yet they are light years apart from one another.

The flea market concept is generations old. As it spread throughout the world, each country changed and adapted the form to meet its own particular needs. Regional differences developed. In New England, the Mid-Atlantic states, and throughout the Midwest, the term generally is used to describe a place where antiques and collectibles are sold. In the South and Southwest, the term is more loosely interpreted, with the emphasis on secondhand and discounted goods.

It is not hard to see where the confusion originates. Check the dictionary definition for *flea market*. *Webster's Ninth New Collegiate Dictionary* (Springfield, MA: Merriam-Webster, Inc., 1984) defines a flea market as "a usually open-air market for secondhand articles and antiques." Individuals involved with antiques and collectibles make a big distinction between secondhand (recycled or reusable) goods and antiques and collectibles. Although the dictionary may lump them together, collectors and dealers clearly differentiate one from the other. The flea markets described in this book fit a much more narrow definition than the dictionary definition.

When collectors use the term *flea market*, they mean *a regularly scheduled market, held either indoors or outdoors, in which the primary goods offered for sale are those defined by the trade as antiques or collectibles.* Occasionally, you will find some handcrafted products and secondhand goods among the offerings, especially in the seasonal and roadside flea markets, where professional flea market dealers mix with individuals selling on a one-shot basis.

The problem with trying to define *flea market,* even when limited to the antiques and collectibles perspective, is that a multiplicity of flea market types exist. There are the great seasonal flea markets such as Renninger's Extravaganza (Kutztown, Pennsylvania) and Brimfield's (Brimfield, Massachusetts), the monthlies such as the Metrolina Expo (Charlotte, North Carolina), and numerous weeklies scattered across the country. Personally, I feel that Atlantique City, held in Atlantic City, New Jersey, in March each year, is really a flea market rather than the "show" it purports to be.

One of the best ways to understand what an antiques and collectibles flea market encompasses is to discuss how it differs from three other closely related institutions in the antiques and collectibles trade: the mall, the garage sale, and the show. While the differences may appear subtle, they are significant to collectors and dealers.

Prior to the arrival of the mall, there was a clearly defined ladder of quality within the antiques and collectibles community which progressed from garage sale or country auction to flea market to small show to major show or shop. This is how most goods moved through the market. This is the route many dealers used to establish themselves in the trade. Two things changed the equation: (1) collectors recognized the role flea markets played as the initial source of goods and actively participated in flea markets in order to eliminate the "middleman" and (2) the antiques and collectibles mall came into existence.

The 1980s was the decade of the antiques and collectibles mall. Malls resulted because many flea market and weekend dealers wanted a means of doing business on a

daily basis without the overhead of their own shop. They also needed an indoor environment free from the vagaries of weather. Additionally, the buying public wanted to find as many sellers as possible in one location when shopping for antiques and collectibles. Antiques and collectibles malls bring together a number of dealers—from ten to hundreds—in one location. Malls differ from flea markets in that they are open for business on a daily basis (a minimum of five and often seven days a week), the display and sales process is often handled by a manager or other representative of the owner of the items, a more formal business procedure is used, and the quality of material is somewhat higher than that found at flea markets. The main drawbacks are that the buyer generally has no contact with the owner of the merchandise and price negotiation is difficult.

Garage sales are usually one-time events, often conducted by people with no pretensions of being antiques or collectibles dealers—they are merely attempting to get rid of used or damaged goods that they no longer find useful. While it is true that some antiques and collectibles enter the market through this source, most individuals conducting garage sales have enough good sense to realize that this is the worst way to sell these items. Emphasis in a garage sale is on secondhand merchandise, often in heavily used and partially damaged condition.

A recent development in the garage sale area is the annual or semiannual community garage sale. A promoter rents a large hall or auditorium and sells space to any individual wishing to set up. Usually there is a rule that no established antiques and collectibles dealers are allowed to take part. However, many dealers sneak in with friends or simply use a different name to rent a space in order to "pick" the merchandise during the setup period. Although community garage sales fit the dictionary definition of a flea market, the large volume of secondhand merchandise distinguishes them from the flea markets discussed in this book.

An antiques or collectibles show consists of a number of professional dealers (weekend, full-time, or a combination of both) who meet in a fixed location on a regular basis, usually two to three times each year, to offer quality antiques and collectibles primarily to collectors, interior decorators, and others. Once an antique or collectible reaches the show circuit, the general assumption is that it is priced close to book value. Flea markets thrive on the concept that merchandise priced for sale is significantly below book value. While this concept is more myth than reality in the 1990s, it still prevails.

Confusion arises because a number of monthly flea markets have dropped the term *flea market* from their titles. They call themselves *shows* or *markets*. They do not use *flea* because of a growing list of problems, ranging from unscrupulous dealers to an abundance of unmarked reproductions, that plague flea markets in the 1990s. Calling yourself something else does not change what you really are. Most monthly markets and shows are nothing more than flea markets in disguise.

Seasonal Flea Markets

Seasonal flea markets are those held a maximum of three times a year. Theoretically, they are held outdoors. However, many sites now provide either indoor or pavilion shelters for participants, especially those whose merchandise is expensive or susceptible to damage by weather. Most have clearly established dates. For example, Renninger's Extravaganza is held the last weekend in April, June, and September.

If there is a Mecca in the flea market world, it is Brimfield. The name is magic. You are not an accomplished flea marketeer until you have been there. Actually, Brimfield is not a flea market, it is an event. For the first full week in May, July, and September over

fifteen separate flea markets open and close. On Fridays the dealer count exceeds 1,500. Area motel rooms are booked over a year in advance. Traffic jams last hours.

For the past several years Renninger's has been promoting seasonal markets during the winter months at its Mount Dora, Florida, location. They are an important stop on the Southern winter circuit. Although there are a few seasonal markets in the Midwest, none are on a par with the Renninger's Extravaganzas and the Brimfield weeks.

Monthly Flea Markets

The monthly flea market's strength rests on a steady dealer clientele supplemented by other dealers passing through the area, a frequency that allows dealers enough time to find new merchandise, and a setting that is usually superior to the seasonal and weekly flea markets. The monthlies range from the upscale Ann Arbor Antiques Market to the mid-range antiques and collectibles show copycat (for example, the Fairgrounds Antiques Market in Phoenix, Arizona) to the something-for-everybody flea market (like the Kane County Flea Market in St. Charles, Illinois).

Most of the monthly flea markets have some outdoor spaces. The Kentucky Flea Market in Louisville, Kentucky, and the Fairgrounds Antiques Market in Phoenix, Arizona, are two exceptions. Flea markets with outdoor space operate only during warm weather months, generally April through November. A few of the larger operations (e.g., the Springfield Antiques Show & Flea Market in Springfield, Ohio) operate year-round. Double-check the schedule of any flea market you plan to visit between November and April, with the possible exception of those located in the Deep South or the Southwest.

Another strength of the monthly flea markets rests is the fact that they attract a large number of dealers who appear on a regular basis; hence collectors and dealers have time to cultivate good working relationships. A level of buying trust is created because the collector knows that he or she will be able to find the seller again if questions develop.

Weekly Flea Markets

The weekly flea markets break down into two types: those held on a weekday and those held on a weekend. The weekday markets are primarily for dealers in the trade. Monday flea markets at Perkiomenville, Pennsylvania, and Wednesday flea markets at Shipshewana, Indiana, are legends. These markets begin in the predawn hours. The best buys are found by flashlight as participants check merchandise as it is being unpacked. Most selling ends by 9:00 A.M. These markets are designed primarily for individuals actively involved in the resale of antiques and collectibles. Most collectors prefer something a bit more civilized.

Renninger's #1 in Adamstown, Pennsylvania, shows the staying power of the weekend flea market. Within driving distance of several major population centers, yet far enough in the country to make the day an outing. Renninger's combines an ever-changing outdoor section with an indoor facility featuring primarily permanent dealers. Renninger's #1 has survived for years by opening only on Sundays, except for Extravaganza weekends. However, because buyers like to shop for antiques and collectibles on Saturdays as well, Renninger's Promotions created Renninger's #2 in Kutztown, Pennsylvania.

Weekend flea markets are now a fixture across the country and constitute the largest segment of the flea market community. It is not unusual to find several in one location as each tries to capitalize on the success of the other. However, their quality varies tremendously.

The biggest problem with weekend flea markets is merchandise staleness. Many dealers add only a few new items each week. Most collectors shop them on a four- to eight-week cycle. The way to avoid missing a shot at a major new piece is to maintain a close working relationship with the dealers at the flea markets who specialize in the category of items you collect. Most weekend flea market dealers do get to shop the market. They can be your eyes when you are not there.

As with the monthly flea markets, you can buy from indoor dealers knowing that you are likely to find them if a problem develops later. You must be much more careful when purchasing from the transient outside dealers. The key is to get a valid name, address, and phone number from anyone from whom you make a purchase at a flea market.

One of the things I like best about large weekend flea markets is that they feature one or more book dealers who specialize in antiques and collectibles books. I always stop at these booths to check on the latest titles included in the large stock of privately published titles carried by these dealers. In some cases, I find a book I never saw advertised in the trade papers. Some of the dealers offer search services for out-of-print titles. Spending time getting to know these book dealers is something I never regret.

Roadside Flea Markets

I have ignored roadside flea markets up to this point because the merchandise they offer is more often than not secondhand and of garage sale quality. This is not to say that I have not experienced some great finds at roadside markets at which I have stopped. However, when I consider the amount of time that I spend finding these few precious jewels, I quickly realize I can do much better at one of the more traditional flea markets.

Chances are that you collect one or two specific categories. If so, not every type of flea market is right for you. How do you find the best markets? What type of evaluation can you do in advance to save the frustration of coming home empty-handed? These questions and more are answered in the next chapter.

Finding and Evaluating Flea Markets

2

In order to attend a flea market, you have to locate one. It is not as easy as it sounds. In order to thoroughly research the available markets in any given area, you will have to consult a variety of sources. Even when you have finished, you are still likely to spot a flea market that you missed in your research along the way. I told you there was a strong sense of adventure in flea marketeering.

Flea Market Guides

There are three national guides to United States flea markets: *Clark's Flea Market U.S.A.: A National Directory of Flea Markets and Swap Meets* (Clark's Publications, 419 Garcon Point Road, Milton, FL 32583), *The Great American Flea Market Directory* (21st Century Marketing, PO Box 692, Abington, PA 19001), and *The Official Directory to U.S. Flea Markets,* third edition (House of Collectibles, Division of Random House, New York, NY). Buy them all.

Clark's, issued quarterly, lists over 2,000 flea markets and swap meets. The guide is organized alphabetically by state. The secondary organization is city or town closest to the flea market within the state. You will find information on name, address, days and occasionally hours of operation, and telephone number. Information provided about each market varies greatly. Completely missing are directions for hard-to-find markets. Do not be fooled by the fact that this guide appears to be produced using an old manual typewriter. The information is helpful. I buy an issue every year or two as a safety check against my regular sources. A one-year subscription is $25.00. Single copies are available from the publisher at $7.50 plus postage and handling.

The *Great American* guide, published twice a year, lists approximately 2,500 markets using the same format as *Clark's.* Much of the information is vague—a Ft. Myers, Florida, listing reads "Northside Flea Market. U.S. Highway 41." The lack of detailed locations is particularly unhelpful. The guide is now under new ownership, which hopefully will correct many of these problems. A single issue is available from 21st Century Marketing for $10.45, which includes shipping and handling.

The *Official Directory* guide covers fewer markets—slightly more than 500. (It lists a few annual markets that technically, by our working definition, are not flea markets, which raises the number of listings to over 600.) However, it provides quality information about the ones that are covered. Detailed comments about merchandise and operating practices are extremely helpful. You can purchase a copy of this guide in most larger bookstores. It is a bargain at $5.99.

I am not quite certain how to classify *Swap Meet USA* (Swap Meet USA, PO Box 200, Grover City, CA 93433). Some of the listings are flea markets; others are community garage sales. This seventy-two–page publication covers 1,800 markets in approximately forty pages (the balance of the pages are devoted to advertising), using small type and a triple-column format. Of special interest to flea marketeers are the advertisements for market merchandise and equipment.

Antiques and collectibles flea markets are not unique to the United States. In fact,

the modern antiques and collectibles flea market originated in Paris. Flea markets play a vital role throughout Europe, especially in France, Great Britain, and Germany. Accordingly, Travel Keys (PO Box 160691, Sacramento, CA 95816) has published a separate flea market price guide for each country. Peter B. Manston is editor of *Manston's Flea Markets of Britain, Manston's Flea Markets of France,* and *Manston's Flea Markets of Germany.* The introductory material, especially the section on export laws and regulations, should be read carefully.

Regional Shop Guides

A number of specialized regional guides for locating antiques and collectibles flea markets, malls, and shops exist. Most are published by trade papers. A few are done privately. None focus solely on the flea market scene.

The *Antique Week Mid-Central Antique Shop Guide* (Antique Week, PO Box 90, Knightstown, IN 46148) is typical. Organization is by state, region, and alphabetically by city and town within a region. Brief listings for each business are supplemented by display advertising. The Mid-Central edition (there is also an Eastern edition) covers more than 3,000 flea markets, malls, shops, and shows. One of the features I like most about the guide is that it designates businesses selling new gift and reproduction items. The principal problem with the guide is that you have to pay a fee in order to be listed. As a result, coverage is limited to those willing to pay. It is a great starting point for the region it covers, but it is not all-encompassing.

When planning to visit a new area, contact some of the trade papers that serve the region and ask if they publish a regional guide or know of such a guide. Regional guides are inexpensive, ranging from $4.00 to $10.00. Many of the businesses listed in the guide sell it across the counter. I always pick up a copy. The floor behind the front seat of my car is littered with road maps and regional guides, most of which show signs of heavy use.

Trade Newspapers

The best source of flea market information is advertisements in trade newspapers. Some papers put all the flea market advertisements in one location, while others place them in their appropriate regional section. Most trade papers' events calendars include flea markets with the show listings.

Once again, the problem rests with the fact that all advertising is paid advertising. Not all flea markets advertise in every issue of a trade paper. Some advertise in papers outside their home area because the locals know where and when to find them. Flea markets that operate between April and September usually do not advertise in December and January. The only way to conduct a complete search is to obtain a four- to six-month run of a regional paper and carefully scan each issue. When doing this, keep your eyes open for reports and features about flea markets. As advertisers, flea markets expect to get written up at least once a year.

The following is a list of national and regional trade papers that I recommend you consult for flea market information. You will find their full addresses and phone numbers (when known) in the listing of trade newspapers at the back of this book.

NATIONAL TRADE PAPERS

American Collector, Southfield, MI
American Collector's Journal, Kewanee, IL
Antique Monthly, Atlanta, GA
Antique Trader Weekly, Dubuque, IA
Antique Week, Knightstown, IN
Antiques & the Arts Weekly, Newtown, CT
Collector News, Grundy Center, IA
Maine Antique Digest, Waldoboro, ME

REGIONAL TRADE PAPERS

New England
Cape Cod Antiques & Arts, Yarmouth Port, MA
MassBay Antiques, Danvers, MA
New England Antiques Journal, Ware, MA

Middle Atlantic States
Antique Country, Berryville, VA
Antiquer's Guide to the Susquehanna Region, Sidney, NY
Antiques & Auction News, Mount Joy, PA
Eastern Seaboard Antique Monthly, Burtonsville, MD
The New York Antique Almanac of Art, Antiques, Investments & Yesteryear, Lawrence, NY
New York–Pennsylvania Collector, Fishers, NY
Renninger's Antique Guide, Lafayette Hill, PA
Treasure Chest, New York, NY

South

The Antique Press, Tampa, FL
The Antique Shoppe, Bradenton, FL
Antiques & Crafts Gazette, Cumming, GA
Cotton & Quail Antique Trail, Monticello, FL
MidAtlantic Antiques Magazine, Henderson, NC
The Old News Is Good News Antiques Gazette, Baton Rouge, LA
Southern Antiques, Decatur, GA

Midwest

The Antique Collector and Auction Guide, Salem, OH
Antique Gazette, Nashville, TN
Antique Review, Worthington, OH
Buckeye Marketeer, Westerville, OH
Collectors Journal, Vinton, IA
Michigan Antiques Trading Post, Williamstown, MI
Yesteryear, Princeton, WI

Southwest

Antique & Collector's Guide, Beaumont, TX
Arizona Antique News and Southwest Antiques Journal, Phoenix, AZ

Rocky Mountain States

Mountain States Collector, Evergreen, CO

West Coast

Antique & Collectables, El Cajon, CA
Antique & Collectible Marketplace, Huntington Beach, CA
Antiques Today, Carson City, NV
Antiques West, San Francisco, CA
Collector, Pomona, CA
West Coast Peddler, Whittier, CA

This list is by no means complete. I am certain that I have missed a few regional papers. However, these papers provide a starting point. Do not be foolish and go flea marketeering without consulting them.

Which Flea Market Is Right for You?

The best flea market is the one at which you find plenty to buy at good to great prices. This means that most flea markets are not right for you. Is it necessary to attend each one to make your determination? I do not think so.

I am a great believer in using the telephone. If long distance rates jump dramatically as a result of the publication of this book, I plan to approach AT&T and ask for a piece of the action. It is a lot cheaper to call than to pay for transportation, lodging, and meals—not to mention the value of your time. Do not hesitate to call promoters and ask them about their flea markets.

What type of information should you request? First, check the number of dealers. If the number falls below one hundred, think twice. Ask for a ratio of local dealers to transient dealers. A good mix is 75% local and 25% transient for monthly and weekly markets. Second, inquire about the type of merchandise being offered for sale. Make a point not to tell the promoter what you collect. If you do, you can be certain that the flea market has a number of dealers who offer the material. Do not forget to ask about the quality of the merchandise. Third, ask about the facilities. The more indoor space available, the higher the level of merchandise is likely to be. What happens if it rains? Finally, ask yourself this question: Do you trust what the promoter has told you?

When you are done talking to the promoter, call the editor of one of the regional trade papers and ask his or her opinion about the market. If they have published an article or review of the market recently, request that a copy be sent to you. If you know someone who has attended, talk to that person. If you still have not made up your mind, try the local daily newspaper or chamber of commerce.

Do not be swayed by the size of a flea market's advertisement in a trade paper. The Kane County advertisement is often less than a sixteenth of a page. A recent full-page advertisement for Brimfield flea markets failed to include J & J Promotions or May's Antique Market, two of the major players on the scene. This points out the strong regional competition between flea markets. Be suspicious of what one promoter tells you about another promoter's market.

Evaluating a Flea Market

After you have attended a flea market, it is time to decide if you will attend it again, and if so, how frequently. Answer the following nineteen questions yes or no. In this test, "no" is the right answer. If more than half the questions are yes, forget about going back. There are plenty of flea markets from which to choose. If six or fewer are answered yes, give it another chance in a few months. If seventeen or more answers are no, plan another visit soon. What are you doing next week?

YES	NO	
———	———	Was the flea market hard to find?
———	———	Did you have a difficult time moving between the flea market and your car in the parking area?
———	———	Did you have to pay a parking fee in addition to an admission fee?
———	———	Did the manager fail to provide a map of the market?
———	———	Was a majority of the market in an open, outdoor environment?
———	———	Were indoor facilities poorly lighted and ventilated?
———	———	Was there a problem with the number of toilet facilities or with the facilities' cleanliness?
———	———	Was your overall impression of the market one of chaos?
———	———	Did collectibles outnumber antiques?
———	———	Did secondhand goods and new merchandise outnumber collectibles?
———	———	Were reproductions, copycats, fantasy items, and fakes in abundance? (See Chapter 5.)
———	———	Was there a large representation of home crafts and/or discontinued merchandise?
———	———	Were the vast majority of antiques and collectibles that you saw in fair condition or worse?
———	———	Were individuals that you expected to encounter at the market absent?
———	———	Did you pass out fewer than five lists of your "wants"?
———	———	Did you buy fewer than five new items for your collection?
———	———	Were more than half the items that you bought priced near or at book value?
———	———	Was there a lack of good restaurants and/or lodging within easy access of the flea market?
———	———	Would you tell a friend never to attend the market?

There are some flea markets that scored well for me, and I would like to share them with you. They are listed in the next chapter.

Top Twenty U.S. Flea Markets

3

Selecting twenty flea markets from the thousands of flea markets throughout the United States was not an easy task. Everyone will have regional favorites that do not appear on this list. I wish I could list them all, but that is not the purpose of this price guide.

In making my choices, I have used the following criteria. First, I wanted to provide a representative sample from the major flea market groups—seasonal, monthly, and weekly. Since this price guide is designed for the national market, I made certain that the selections covered the entire United States. Finally, I selected flea markets that I feel will "turn on" a prospective or novice collector. Nothing is more fun than getting off to a great start.

This list is only a starting point. Almost every flea market has a table containing promotional literature for other flea markets in the area. Follow up on the ones of interest. Continue to check trade paper listings. There are always new flea markets being started.

Finally, not every flea market is able to maintain its past glories. Are there flea markets that you think should be on this list? Have you visited some of the listed flea markets and found them to be unsatisfactory? As each edition of this guide is prepared, this list will be evaluated. Send any thoughts and comments that you may have to: Harry L. Rinker Jr., Rinker Enterprises, Inc., 5093 Vera Cruz Road, Emmaus, PA 18049.

NAME OF FLEA MARKET

Location
Frequency and general admission times
Type of goods sold and general comments
Number of dealers, indoor and/or outdoor, and special features
1993 Admission Fee
Address and phone number (if known) of manager or promoter

Seasonal Flea Markets

BRIMFIELD

Route 20, Brimfield, MA 01010.
Six days, starting on the Tuesday before the second full weekend in May, July, and September and ending on that Saturday.
Antiques, collectibles, and secondhand goods.
Over 3,000 dealers. Indoor and outdoor.
1993 Admission: Varies according to field, ranging from free admission to $3.00. Average parking fee: $3.00.
More than ten different promoters: Brimfield Acres North/The Last Hurrah, PO Box 397, Holden, MA 01520, (508) 754-4185; Central Park Antiques Shows, PO Box 224, Brimfield, MA 01010, (413) 596-9257; The Dealers Choice, PO Box 28, Fiskdale,

MA 01518, (508) 347-3929; Faxon's Treasure Chest/Midway Shows, PO Box 28, Fiskdale, MA 01518, (508) 347-3929; Heart-O-The-Mart, PO Box 26, Brimfield, MA 01010, (413) 245-9556; J & J Promotions, Route 20, Brimfield, MA 01010, (413) 245-3436 or (508) 597-8155; May's Antique Market, PO Box 416, Brimfield, MA 01010, (413) 245-9271; New England Motel Antiques Market, Inc., PO Box 139, Sturbridge, MA 01010, (413) 245-9427; Shelton Antique Shows, PO Box 124, Brimfield, MA 01010, (413) 245-3591.

You can subscribe to the *Brimfield Antique Guide* from Brimfield Publications, PO Box 442, Brimfield, MA 01010. Phone: (413) 245-9329. Five issues for $14.95, first class mail.

RENNINGER'S EXTRAVAGANZA

Noble Street, Kutztown, PA 19530.
Thursday, Friday, and Saturday of last full weekend of April, June, and September. Thursday opens 10:00 A.M. for pre-admission only ($40.00 per car carrying one to four people). Friday and Saturday, 7:00 A.M. to 5:00 P.M.
Antiques and collectibles.
Over 1,200 dealers. Indoor and outdoor.
1993 Admission: $4.00 on Friday, $2.00 on Saturday.
Renninger's Promotions, 27 Bensinger Drive, Schuylkill Haven, PA 17972. Monday through Friday (717) 385-0104, Saturday (215) 683-6843, and Sunday (215) 267-2177.

Monthly Flea Markets

ALLEGAN ANTIQUES MARKET

Allegan Fairgrounds, Allegan, MI 49010.
Last Sunday of the month, April through September, 7:30 A.M. to 4:30 P.M.
Antiques and collectibles.
Over 170 dealers indoors, 200 dealers outdoors.
1993 Admission: $2.00.
Larry L. Wood and Morie Faulkerson, 2030 Blueberry Drive N.W., Grand Rapids, MI 49504, (616) 453-8780 or (616) 887-7677.

ANN ARBOR ANTIQUES MARKET

5055 Ann Arbor–Saline Road, Ann Arbor, MI 48103.
Third Sunday of the month, April through October, 5:00 A.M. to 4:00 P.M. November market usually occurs second Sunday of month.
Antiques and select collectibles. The most upscale flea market in the trade.
Over 350 dealers. All under cover. Locator service for specialties and dealers.
1993 Admission: $3.00.
M. Brusher, Manager, PO Box 1512, Ann Arbor, MI 48106.

BURLINGTON ANTIQUES SHOW

Boone County Fairgrounds, Burlington, KY 41005.
Third Sunday of the month, April through October, 8:00 A.M. to 3:00 P.M.

Antiques and collectibles.
Outdoor.
1993 Admission: $2.00.
Paul Kohls, PO Box 58367, Cincinnati, OH 45258, (513) 922-5265.

CARAVAN ANTIQUES MARKET

The Fairgrounds, State Route 86, Centreville, MI 49032.
One Sunday per month, May through October, excluding September, 7:00 A.M. to 4:00 P.M.
Antiques and collectibles. All merchandise guaranteed.
Over 600 dealers.
1993 Admission: $3.00.
Humberstone Management, 1510 N. Hoyne, Chicago, IL 60622, (312) 227-4464.

DON SCOTT ANTIQUES MARKET

Ohio State Fairgrounds, Columbus, OH.
Saturday 9:00 A.M. to 6:00 P.M. and Sunday 9:00 A.M. to 5:00 P.M., March, April, May, June, November, and December. Weekend dates vary. Check Scott advertisements in the trade papers.
Antiques and collectibles.
1,500 booths. Indoor and outdoor.
1993 Admission: Free.
Don Scott, PO Box 60, Bremen, OH 43107, (614) 569-4912.
Note: Don Scott conducts a second monthly flea market: The Don Scott Antique Market, Atlanta Exposition Center (I-285 to Exit 40 at Jonesboro Road, two miles east of Atlanta airport), second weekend of every month.

FAIRGROUNDS ANTIQUES MARKET

Arizona State Fairgrounds, 19th Avenue & McDowell, Phoenix, AZ 85009.
Third weekend of the month, year-round, except March (second weekend) and December (first weekend). Saturday 9:00 A.M. to 5:00 P.M. and Sunday 10:00 A.M. to 4:00 P.M.
Antiques, collectibles, and crafts. Antique glass and clock repairs.
Approximately 200 dealers. All indoor.
1993 Admission: Free.
Jack Black Shows, PO Box 61172, Phoenix, AZ 85082-1172, (800) 678-9987 or (602) 943-1766.

GORDYVILLE USA FLEA MARKET & AUCTION

Rantoul, IL 61866. On Route 136 or 7½ miles east of I-57 on Route 136.
Second weekend (Friday, Saturday, Sunday) of each month. Friday 4:00 P.M. to 9:00 P.M., Saturday 9:00 A.M. to 6:00 P.M., and Sunday 9:00 A.M. to 4:30 P.M.
Antiques, collectibles, vintage items, arts, crafts, and other unique items.
Indoor and outdoor.
1993 Admission: Free.
Gordon Hannagan Auction Company, PO Box 490, Gillford, IL 61847, (217) 568-7117.

(KANE COUNTY) ANTIQUES FLEA MARKETS

Kane County Fairgrounds, Randall Road, St. Charles, IL 60175.
First Sunday of every month and preceding Saturday. Year-round. Saturday 1:00 P.M. to
     5:00 P.M. and Sunday 7:00 A.M. to 4:00 P.M.
Antiques, collectibles, and some crafts. A favorite in the Midwest, especially with the
     Chicago crowd.
Combination indoor and outdoor. Country breakfast served.
1993 Admission: $3.00.
Mrs. J. L. Robinson, Mgr., PO Box 549, St. Charles, IL 60174, (708) 377-2252.

KENTUCKY FLEA MARKET

Kentucky Fair and Exposition Center (take Exit 12B off Interstate 264), Louisville, KY.
Three- or four-day show first weekend of most months. Friday 12:00 P.M. to 8:00 P.M.,
     Saturday 10:00 A.M. to 8:00 P.M., and Sunday 11:00 A.M. to 5:00 P.M.
Antiques, collectibles, arts and crafts, and new merchandise.
Approximately 1,000 booths. Indoor, climate-controlled.
1993 Admission: Free.
Stewart Promotions, 2950 Breckinridge Lane, Suite 4A, Louisville, KY 40220, (502) 456-
     2244.

LONG BEACH OUTDOOR ANTIQUES & COLLECTIBLES MARKET

Veterans Stadium, Long Beach, CA.
Third Sunday of each month, 8:00 A.M. to 3:00 P.M.
Antiques and collectibles including: vintage clothing, pottery, quilts, primitives, advertis-
     ing, etc.
Over 700 dealers.
1993 Admission: $3.50. No early admission charge; stalwarts can get in at 6:30 A.M.
Americana Enterprises, Inc., PO Box 69219, Los Angeles, CA 90069, (213) 655-5703.

METROLINA EXPO

7100 North Statesville Road, Charlotte, NC.
First and third weekends of every month, year-round. Friday, Saturday, and Sunday,
     8:00 A.M. to 5:00 P.M.
Antiques and collectibles.
Indoor and outdoor. First weekend approximately 1,500 dealers; third weekend be-
     tween 800 and 1,000 dealers. Metrolina hosts two Spectaculars yearly—April and
     November—which feature more than 2,000 dealers.
1993 Admission: First weekend $2.50 per day, third weekend $1.50 per day, and
     spectaculars $5.00 per day.
Metrolina EXPO Center, PO Box 26652, Charlotte, NC 18221, (704) 596-4643.

SANDWICH ANTIQUES MARKET

The Fairgrounds, State Route 34, Sandwich, IL 60548.
One Sunday per month, May through October, 8:00 A.M. to 4:00 P.M.

Antiques and collectibles.
Over 600 dealers.
1993 Admission: $3.00.
Sandwich Antiques Market, 1510 N. Hoyne, Chicago, IL 60622, (312) 227-4464.

SPRINGFIELD ANTIQUES SHOW & FLEA MARKET

Clark County Fairgrounds, Springfield, OH.
Third weekend of the month, year-round, excluding July. December market is held the
    second weekend of the month. Saturday 8:00 A.M. to 5:00 P.M. and Sunday 9:00 A.M.
    to 4:00 P.M. Extravaganzas are held in May and September.
More than half the market is antiques and collectibles.
Over 400 dealers indoors and 900 dealers outdoors for monthly market in warm
    weather.
1993 Admission: $1.00. $2.00 for Extravaganza.
Bruce Knight, PO Box 2429, Springfield, OH 45501, (513) 325-0053.

Weekly Flea Markets

ADAMSTOWN

Route 272, Adamstown, PA 19501.
Sundays.
Antiques, collectibles, secondhand material, and junk.
1993 Admission: Free.
Three major markets.

> **Black Angus,** 8:00 A.M. to 5:00 P.M., year-round, indoor and outdoor; Carl Barto,
>   2717 Long Farm Lane, Lancaster, PA 17601, (717) 569-3536 or (215) 484-
>   4385.
> **Renninger's #1,** 7:30 A.M. to 5:00 P.M., year-round, indoor and outdoor;
>   Renninger's Promotions, 27 Bensinger Drive, Schuylkill Haven, PA 17972.
>   Phone on Sunday: (215) 267-2177.
> **Shupp's Grove,** 8:00 A.M. to 5:00 P.M., April through September, indoor and
>   outdoor; Shupp's Grove, 1686 Dry Tavern Road, Denver, PA 17517. Informa-
>   tion: (215) 484-4115; dealer reservations: (717) 949-3656.

ATLANTA FLEA MARKET

5360 Peachtree Industrial Boulevard, Chamblee, GA 30341.
Friday and Saturday, 11:00 A.M. to 7:00 P.M. and Sunday 12:00 P.M. to 7:00 P.M.
Antiques, collectibles, and gift items.
150 dealers. Indoor.
1993 Admission: Free.
Atlanta Flea Market, 5360 Peachtree Industrial Blvd., Chamblee, GA 30341, (404) 458-
    0456.

LAMBERTVILLE ANTIQUES FLEA MARKET

Route 29, 1½ miles south of Lambertville, NJ 08530.
Saturday and Sunday, 6:00 A.M. to 4:00 P.M.
Antiques and collectibles.
150 dealers. Indoor and outdoor.
1993 Admission: Free.
Mr. and Mrs. Errhalt, 324 S. Main St., Pennington, NJ 08534, (609) 397-0456.

RENNINGER'S ANTIQUES CENTER

Highway 441, Mount Dora, FL 32757.
Saturdays and Sundays, 8:00 A.M. to 4:00 P.M. Indoor opens at 9:00 A.M. Extravaganzas
    on third weekend of November, January, and February. Friday 10:00 A.M. to 5:00
    P.M., Saturday 8:00 A.M. to 6:00 P.M., and Sunday 8:00 A.M. to 5:00 P.M.
Antiques and collectibles.
Over 500 dealers. Indoor and outdoor.
1993 Admission: Free. Extravaganza admission: three-day pass $10.00, Friday $10.00,
    Saturday $5.00, and Sunday $2.00.
Florida Twin Markets, PO Box 939, Zellwood, FL 32798, (904) 383-8393.

SHIPSHEWANA AUCTION AND FLEA MARKET

On State Route 5 near the southern edge of Shipshewana, IN 46565.
Wednesdays, 6:00 A.M. to dusk from May through October, 7:30 A.M. to dusk from
    November through April.
Antiques, collectibles, new merchandise, and produce. In fact, you name it, they sell it.
Can accommodate up to 800 dealers. Indoor and outdoor.
1993 Admission: Free.
Shipshewana Auction, Inc., PO Box 185, Shipshewana, IN 46565.

Thus far you have learned to identify the various types of flea markets, how to locate them, the keys to evaluating whether or not they are right for you, and my recommendations for getting started. Next you need to develop the skills necessary for flea market survival.

4

Your state of exhaustion at the end of the day is the best gauge that I know to judge the value of a flea market—the greater your exhaustion, the better the flea market. A great flea market keeps you on the go from early morning, in some cases 5:00 A.M., to early evening, often 6:00 P.M. The key to survival is to do advance homework, have proper equipment, develop and follow a carefully thought-out shopping strategy, and do your follow-up chores as soon as you return home.

If you are a Type-A personality, your survival plan is essentially a battle plan. Your goal is to cover the flea market as thoroughly as possible and secure the objectives (bargains and hard-to-find objects) ahead of your rivals. You do not stop until total victory is achieved. Does not sound like you? No matter. You also need a survival plan if you want to maximize fun and enjoyment.

Advance Homework

Consult the flea market's advertisement or brochure. Make certain that you understand the dates and time. You never know when special circumstances may cause a change in dates and even location. Check the admission policy. It may be possible to buy a ticket in advance to avoid the wait in line at the ticket booth.

Determine if there is an early admission fee and what times are involved. It is a growing practice at flea markets to admit collectors and others to the flea market through the use of an early admission fee. In most cases the fee is the cost of renting a space. The management simply does not insist that you set up. Actually, this practice had been going on for some time before management formalized it. Friends of individuals renting space often tag along as helpers or assistants. Once inside, the urge to shop supersedes their desire to help their friend.

Review the directions. Are they detailed enough to allow you to find the flea market easily? Remember, it still may be dark when you arrive. If you are not certain, call the manager and ask for specific directions. Also, make certain of parking provisions, especially when a flea market takes place within a city or town. Local residents who are not enamored with a flea market in their neighborhood take great pleasure in informing police of illegally parked cars and watching the cars get towed away. In some cases, I have found locating parking to be more of a problem than locating the flea market. Avoid frustration and plan ahead.

Decide if you are going to stay overnight either the evening before the flea market opens or during the days of operation. In many cases local motel accommodations are minimal. It is not uncommon for dealers as well as collectors to commute fifty miles each way to attend Brimfield. The general attitude of most flea market managers is that accommodations are your problem, not their problem. If you are lucky, you can get a list of accommodations from a local chamber of commerce. The American Automobile Association regional guidebooks provide some help. However, if you attend a flea market expecting to find nearby overnight accommodations without a reservation, you are the world's biggest optimist.

If possible, obtain a map of the flea market grounds. Become familiar with the layout of the spaces. If you know some of your favorite dealers are going to set up, call and ask them for their space number. Mark the location of all toilet facilities and refreshment stands. You may not have time for the latter, but sooner or later you are going to need the former.

Finally, try to convince one or more friends, ideally someone whose area of collecting is totally different from yours, to attend the flea market with you. Each becomes another set of eyes for the other. Meeting at predesignated spots makes exchanging information easy. It never hurts to share the driving and expenses. Best of all, war stories can be told and savored immediately.

Flea Market Checklist

In order to have an enjoyable and productive day at the flea market, you need the right equipment, ranging from clothing to packing material for your purchases. What you do not wear can be stored in your car trunk. Make certain that everything is in order the day before your flea market adventure.

CLOTHING CHECKLIST

_____ Hat
_____ Sunglasses
_____ Light jacket or sweatshirt
_____ Poncho or raincoat
_____ Waterproof work boots or galoshes

FIELD GEAR CHECKLIST

_____ Canvas bag(s)
_____ Cash, checkbook, and credit cards
_____ Wants lists
_____ Address cards
_____ Magnifying glass
_____ Swiss Army pocket knife
_____ Toilet paper
_____ Sales receipts
_____ Mechanical pencil or ball-point pen
_____ *Warman's Antiques and Their Prices, Warman's Americana and Collectibles,* and this price guide

CAR TRUNK CHECKLIST

_____ Three to six cardboard boxes
_____ Newspaper, bubble wrap, diapers, and other appropriate packing material
_____ Sun block
_____ First aid kit
_____ Cooler with cold beverages

The vast majority of flea markets that you attend will either be outdoors or have an outdoor section. If you are lucky, the sun will be shining. Beware of sunburn. Select a hat with a broad rim. I prefer a hat with an outside hat band as well. First, it provides a place to stick notes, business cards, and other small pieces of paper I would most likely lose otherwise. Second, it provides a place to stick a feather or some other distinguishing item that allows my friends to spot me in the crowd. Some flea marketeers use the band as a holder for a card expounding their collecting wants. Make certain that your hat fits snugly. Some flea market sites are quite windy. An experienced flea market attendee's hat will look as though it has been through the wars. It has.

I carry sunglasses, but I confess that I rarely use them. I find that taking them on and off is more trouble than they are worth. Further, they distort colors. However, I have found them valuable at windswept and outdoor markets located in large fields. Since I usually misplace a pair a year, I generally buy inexpensive glasses.

The key to dressing for flea markets is a layered, comfortable approach. The early morning and late evening hours are often cool. A light jacket or sweatshirt is suggested. I found a great light jacket that is loaded with pockets. Properly outfitted, it holds all the material I would normally put in my carrying bag.

You must assume that it is going to rain. I have never been to Brimfield when it was not raining. Rain, especially at an outdoor flea market, is a disaster. What is astonishing is how much activity continues in spite of the rain. I prefer a poncho over a raincoat because it covers my purchases as well as my clothing.

Most flea markets offer ponchos for sale when rain starts. They are lightweight and come with a storage bag. Of course, you have to be a genius to fold them small enough to get them back into their original storage bag. The one I purchased at Kane County has lasted four years. Mrs. Robinson, being a shrewd promoter, just happened to have them imprinted with information about her flea market. I had a great time there so I have never objected to being a walking bulletin board on her behalf.

The ideal footwear for a flea market is a well–broken-in pair of running or walking shoes. However, in the early morning when the ground is wet with dew, a pair of waterproof work boots is a much better choice. I keep my running shoes in the car trunk and usually change into them by 9:00 A.M. at most flea markets.

Rain at outdoor flea markets equals mud. The only defense is a good pair of galoshes. I have been at Brimfield when the rain was coming down so fiercely that dealers set up in tents were using tools to dig water diversion ditches. Cars, which were packed in the nearby fields, sank into the ground. In several cases, local farmers with tractors handsomely supplemented their income.

I always go to a flea market planning to buy something. Since most flea market sellers provide the minimum packaging possible, I carry my own. My preference is a double handled canvas bag with a flat bottom. It is not as easy an item to find as it sounds. I use one to carry my field gear along with two extra bags that start out folded. I find that I can carry three filled bags comfortably. This avoids the necessity of running back to the car each time a bag is filled.

If you are going to buy something, you have to pay for it. Cash is always preferred by the sellers. I carry my cash in a small white envelope with the amount with which I started marked at the top. I note and deduct each purchase as I go along. If you carry cash, be careful how you display it. Pickpockets and sticky-fingered individuals who cannot resist temptation do attend flea markets.

Since I want a record of my purchases, I pay by check whenever I can. I have tried to control my spending by only taking a few checks. Forget it. I can always borrow money on Monday to cover my weekend purchases. I make certain that I have a minimum of ten checks.

Most flea market sellers will accept checks with proper identification. For this reason, I put my driver's license and a major credit card in the front of my checkbook before entering the flea market. This saves me the trouble of taking out my wallet each time I make a purchase.

A surprising number of flea market sellers are willing to take credit cards. I am amazed at this practice since the only means they have of checking a card's validity is the canceled card booklet they receive each week. They wait until later to get telephone authorization, a potentially dangerous practice.

I buy as much material through the mail as I do at flea markets. One of the principal reasons I attend flea markets is to make contact with dealers. Since flea markets attract many dealers from other parts of the country, I expand my supplier sources at each flea market I attend. The key is to have a wants list ready to give to any flea market seller that admits to doing business by mail. My wants list fills an 8½″ × 11″ sheet of writing paper. In addition to my wants, it includes my name, post office box address, UPS (i.e., street) address, and office and home telephone number. I also make it a point to get the full name and address of any dealer to whom I give my list. I believe in follow-up.

Not every dealer is willing to take a full-page wants list. For this reason, I have an address (business) card available with my name, street address, phone numbers, and a brief list of my wants. Most take it as a courtesy. However, I have received quotes on a few great items as a result of my efforts.

I carry a simple variety-store ten-power magnifying glass. It is helpful to see marks clearly and to spot cracks in china and glass. Ninety-nine percent of the time I use it merely to confirm something that I saw with the naked eye. Jewelers loupes are overkill unless you are buying jewelry.

Years ago I purchased a good Swiss Army pocket knife, one which contains scissors as part of the blade package. It was one of the smartest investments that I made. No flea market goes by that I do not use the knife for one reason or another. If you do not want to carry a pocket knife, invest in a pair of operating room surgical scissors. They will cut through most anything.

I am a buyer. Why do I carry a book of sales receipts? Alas, many flea market sellers operate in a nontraditional business manner. They are not interested in paper trails, especially when you pay cash. You need a receipt to protect yourself. More on this subject later.

I keep a roll of toilet paper in the car and enough for two sittings in my carrying bag. Do not laugh; I am serious. Most outdoor flea markets have portable toilets. After a few days, the toilet paper supply is exhausted. Even some indoor facilities give out. If I had five dollars from all the people to whom I supplied toilet paper at flea markets, I would be writing this book in Hawaii instead of Pennsylvania.

I carry a mechanical pencil. When I pick up someone's business card, I note why on the back of the card. Use the pencil to mark dealer locations on the flea market map. I do not always buy something when I first spot it. The map helps me relocate items when I wish to go back for a second look. I have wasted hours at flea markets backtracking to find an item that was not located where I thought it was. A ball-point pen works just as well. The mechanical pencil is a personal preference.

Anyone who tells you they know everything about antiques and collectibles and their prices is a liar. I know the areas in which I collect quite well. But there are many categories where a quick source check never hurts. *Warman's Antiques and Their Prices* and *Warman's Americana and Collectibles* are part of my field gear. I could tell you that I carry them out of loyalty to my dad, who edits them. The truth is that I carry them because I have found them more helpful and accurate than other general price guides. I have also scored some major points with dealers and others when I offered to share some of the information found in the category introductions with them.

My car trunk contains a number of cardboard boxes, several of which are archival file boxes with hand inserts on the side. I have them because I want to see that my purchases make it home safe and sound. One of the boxes is filled with newspaper, diapers, and some bubble wrap. It supplements the field wrapping so that I can stack objects on top of one another. I check the trunk seals on a regular basis. A leaking car trunk once ruined several key purchases I made on an antiquing adventure.

A wide-brim hat may protect the face and neck from the sun, but it leaves the arms exposed. I admire those individuals who can wear a long-sleeved shirt year-round. I am not one of them. In the summer, I wear short-sleeved shirts. For this reason, I keep a bottle of sun block in the trunk.

I also have a first-aid kit that includes aspirin. The most used object is a Band-Aid for unexpected cuts and scratches. The aspirin comes in hand when I have spent eight or more hours in the sun. My first-aid kit also contains packaged cleaning towelettes. I always use one before heading home.

It does not take much for me to get a flea market high. When I do, I can go the entire day without eating. The same does not hold true for liquid intake. Just as toilet paper is a precious commodity at flea markets, so is ice. I carry a small cooler in my trunk with six to a dozen cans of my favorite beverage of the moment. The fastest way to seal a friendship with a flea market dealer is to offer him or her a cold drink at the end of a hot day.

How to Shop a Flea Market

After attending flea markets for a number of years, I would like to share some of the things that I do to bag the treasures found in the flea market jungle. Much of what I am about to tell you is no more than common sense, but we all know that this is probably one of the most ignored of all the senses.

Most likely you will drive to the flea market. Parking is often a problem. It does not have to be. The general rule is to park as close to the main gate as possible. However, since most flea markets have a number of gates, I usually try to park near a secondary gate. First, this allows me to get closer than I could by trying for the main gate. Second, I have long recognized whatever gate I use as "my" main gate, and it serves well as home base for my buying operations.

As soon as I arrive at the flea market, I check three things before allowing my buying adrenaline to kick into high gear—the location of the toilets, the location of the refreshment stands, and the relationship between outdoor and indoor facilities. The latter is very important. Dealers who regularly do the flea market are most likely to be indoors. If I miss them this time around, I can catch them the next. Dealers who are just passing through are most likely set up outdoors. If I miss them, I may never see them again.

I spend the first half hour at any flea market doing a quick tour in order to (1) understand how the flea market is organized, (2) spot those dealers that I would like to visit later, and (3) develop a general sense of what is happening. I prefer to start at the point farthest from my car and work my way to the front, just the opposite of most flea market shoppers. It makes trips back to the car shorter each time and reduces the amount of purchases that I am carrying over an extended period of time.

Whenever I go to a flea market to buy, I try to have one to four specific categories in mind. If one tries to look at everything, one develops "antiques and collectibles" shock. Collectors' minds short-circuit if they try to absorb too much. They never get past the first aisle. With specific goals, a quick look at a booth will tell me whether or not it is likely to feature merchandise of interest. If not, I pass it by.

Since time is always at a premium, I make it a practice to ask every dealer, "Do you have any ——?" If they say "no," I usually go to the next booth. However, I have learned that dealers do not always remember what they have. When I am in a booth that should have the type of merchandise that I am seeking, I take a minute or two to do a quick scan to see if the dealer is right. In about 25% of the cases, I have found at least one example of the type of material for which I am looking.

I eat on the run, if I eat at all. A good breakfast before the market opens carries me until the evening hours when dusk shuts down the market. I am at the flea market to stuff my bag and car trunk, not my face.

When I find a flea market that I like, I try to visit it at least once in the spring and once in the late summer or early fall. In many flea markets the same dealers are located in the same spot each time. This is extremely helpful to a buyer. I note their location on my map of the market. When I return the next time, I ask these dealers if they have brought anything that fills my needs. If they say "yes," I ask them to hold it until I return. In most cases, a dealer will agree to hold a piece for one to two hours. Do not abuse the privilege, but do not hesitate to take advantage of it either.

There is an adage among antiques and collectibles collectors that "if you bought something at a flea market, you own it." I do my best to prove this adage wrong if I am not happy with a purchase. I am successful most of the time.

I try to get a receipt for every purchase that I make. Since many individuals who sell at outdoor flea markets are part-time dealers, they often are unprepared to give a receipt. No problem. I carry a pad of blank receipts and ask them to fill one out.

In every case, I ask the dealers to include their name, shop name (if any), mailing address, and phone number on the receipt. If I do not think a dealer is telling me the truth, I ask for identification. If they give me any flack, I go to their vehicle (usually located in their booth) or just outside their indoor stand and make note of the license plate number. Flea market dealers, especially the outdoor group, are highly mobile. If a problem develops with the merchandise I bought, I want to reach the dealer in order to solve the problem.

Whenever possible, the receipt should contain a full description of the merchandise along with a completeness and condition statement. I also ask the dealer to write "money back guaranteed, no questions asked" on the receipt. This is the only valid guarantee that I know. Phrases such as "guaranteed as represented" and "money back" are open to interpretation and become relatively meaningless if a dispute develops.

I always shop around. At a good flea market, I expect to see the same merchandise in several booths. Prices will vary, often by several hundred if not several thousand percent. I make a purchase immediately only when a piece is a "real" bargain, priced way below current market value. If a piece is near current market value, I often inspect it, note its location on my map, and walk away. If I do not find another in as good condition, at a cheaper price, or both, I go back and negotiate with the dealer.

I take the time to inspect carefully in natural sunlight any piece that I buy. First, I check for defects such as cracks, nicks, scratches, and signs of normal wear. Second, if the object involves parts, I make certain that it is complete. I have been known to take the time to carefully count parts. The last two times that I did not do this, the objects that I bought turned out to be incomplete when I got them home.

I frequently find myself asking a dealer to clean an object for my inspection. Outdoor flea markets are often quite dusty, especially in July and August. The insides of most indoor markets are generally not much better. Dirt can easily hide flaws. It also can discolor objects. Make certain you know exactly what you are buying.

I force myself to slow down and get to know those dealers from whom I hope to make future purchases. Even though it may mean that I do not visit the entire flea market, I have found that the long-term benefits from this type of contact far outweigh the short-term gain of seeing every booth.

Flea Market Food

Flea market food is best described as overcooked, greasy, and heartburn-inducing. I think I forgot to mention that my first-aid kit contains a roll of antacid pills. Gourmet eating facilities are usually nonexistent. Is it any wonder that I often go without eating?

Several flea markets take place on sites that also house a farmer's market. When this is the case, I take time to shop the market and eat at one of its food counters or buy something that I can eat while sitting in my car. I make a point to spot any fast-food restaurants in the vicinity of the flea market. If I get desperate, I get in the car and drive to one of them.

I do make it a point to inquire among the dealers where they go to have their evening meals. They generally opt for good food, plenty of it, and at inexpensive prices. At the end of the day I am hungry. I do not feel like driving home, cleaning up, and then eating. I want to eat where the clientele can stand the appearance and smell of a flea marketeer. I have rarely been disappointed when I followed a flea market dealer's recommendation.

The best survival tactic is probably to bring your own food. I simply find this too much trouble. I get heartburn just thinking about a lunch sitting for several hours inside a car on a hot summer day. No thanks; I will buy what I need.

Follow-Up

Immediately upon returning home, at worst the next day, unpack and record all your purchases. If you wait, you are going to forget important details. This is not the fun part of collecting. It is easy to ignore. Discipline yourself to do it. Get in the habit. You know it is the right thing to do, so do it.

Review the business cards that you picked up and notes that you made. If letters are required, write them. If telephone calls are necessary, make them. Never lose sight of the fact that one of your principal reasons for going to the flea market is to establish long-term dealer contacts.

Finally, if your experiences at the flea market were positive or if you saw ways to improve the market, write a letter to the manager. He or she will be delighted in both instances. Competition among flea markets for dealers and customers is increasing. Good managers want to make their markets better than their competitors'. Your comments and suggestions will be welcomed.

Honing Your Shopping Skills

5

Earlier I mentioned that most buyers view flea markets as places where bargains and "steals" can be found. I have found plenty. However, the truth is that you have to hunt long and hard to find them, and in some cases, they evolve only after intense bargaining. Shopping a flea market properly requires skills. This chapter will help shape and hone your shopping skills and alert you to some of the pitfalls involved with buying at a flea market.

With What Type of Dealer Are You Dealing?

There are essentially three types of dealers found at flea markets: (1) the professional dealer, (2) the weekend dealer, and (3) the once-and-done dealer. Each brings a different level of expertise and merchandise to the flea market. Each offers pluses and minuses. Knowing with which type you are dealing is advantageous.

So many flea markets developed in the 1980s and 1990s that there are now professional flea market dealers who practice their craft on a full-time basis. Within any given week, you may find them at three or four different flea markets. They are the modern American gypsies; their living accommodations and merchandise are usually found within the truck, van, or station wagon in which they are traveling. These individuals survive on shrewdness and hustle. They want to turn over their merchandise as quickly as possible for the best gain possible and are willing to do whatever is necessary to achieve this end.

Deal with professional flea market dealers with a questioning mind; i.e., question everything they tell you about an object from what it is to what they want for it.

Their knowledge of the market comes from hands-on experience. It is not as great as they think in most cases. They are so busy setting up, buying, selling, and breaking down that they have little time to do research or follow trade literature. More than any other group of dealers in the trade, they are weavers of tales and sellers of dreams.

The professional flea market dealer's circuit can stretch from New England to California, from Michigan to Florida. These "professionals" are constantly on the move. If you have a problem with something one of these dealers sold you, finding him or her can prove difficult. Do not buy anything from a professional dealer unless you are absolutely certain about it.

Judge the credibility and integrity of the professional flea market dealer by the quality of the merchandise he or she displays. You should see middle- and high-quality material in better condition than you normally expect to find. If the offerings are heavily damaged and appear poorly maintained, walk away.

Do not interpret what I have said to imply that all professional flea market dealers are dishonest. The vast majority are fine individuals. However, as a whole, this group has the largest share of rotten apples in its barrel—more than any other group of dealers in the flea market field. Since there is no professional organization to police the trade and promoters do not care as long as their space rent is paid, it is up to you to protect yourself.

The antiques and collectibles field works on the principle of *caveat emptor*, "let the buyer beware." Just remember that the key is to beware of the seller as well as the merchandise. It pays to know with whom you are doing business.

Weekend flea market dealers are individuals who have a full-time job elsewhere and are dealing on the weekends to supplement their income. In most cases, their weekday job is outside the antiques and collectibles field. However, with the growth of the antiques mall, some of these weekend dealers are really full-time antiques and collectibles dealers. They spend their weekdays shopping and maintaining their mall locations, while selling on the weekend at their traditional flea market location.

In many cases, these dealers specialize, especially if they are in a large flea market environment. As a result, they are usually familiar with the literature relating to their areas of expertise. They also tend to live within a few hours' drive of the flea market in which they set up. This means that they can be found if the need arises.

Once-and-done dealers range from an individual who is using the flea market to dispose of some inherited family heirlooms or portions of an estate to collectors who have culled their collection and are offering their duplicates and discards for sale. Bargains can often be found in both cases. In the first instance, bargains result from lack of pricing knowledge. However, unless you are an early arrival, chances are that the table will be picked clean by the regular dealers and pickers long before you show up. Bargains originate from the collectors because they know the price levels in their field. They realize that in order to sell their discards and duplicates, they will have to create prices that are tempting to dealer and collector alike.

The once-and-done dealers are the least prepared to conduct sales on a business basis. Most likely they will not have a receipt book or a business card featuring their address and phone number. They almost never attempt to collect applicable sales tax.

There is little long-term gain in spending time getting to know the individual who is selling off a few family treasures. However, do not leave without asking, "Is there anything else you have at home that you are planning to sell?" Do spend time talking with the collector. If you have mutual collecting interests, invite him or her to visit, and view your collection. What you are really fishing for is an invitation to view his or her holdings. You will be surpised how often you will receive one when you show genuine interest.

What Is It?

You need to be concerned with two questions when looking at an object: What is it? and How much is it worth? In order to answer the second question, you need a correct answer to the first. Information provided about objects for sale at flea markets is minimal and often nonexistent. In a great many cases, it is false. The only state of mind that protects you is a defensive one.

There are several reasons for the amount of misidentification of objects at flea markets. The foremost is dealer ignorance. Many dealers simply do not take the time to do proper research. I also suspect that they are quite comfortable with the adage that "ignorance is bliss." As long as an object bears a resemblance to something authentic, it will be touted with the most prestigious label available.

When questioning dealers about an object, beware of phrases such as "I think it is an . . . ," "As best as I can tell," "It looks exactly like," and "I trust your judgment." Push the dealers until you pin them down. The more they vacillate, the more suspicious you should become. Insist that the sales receipt carry a full claim about the object.

In many cases misidentification is passed along from person to person because the dealer who bought the object trusted what was said by the dealer who sold the object. I am always amazed how convinced dealers are that they are right. I have found there is little point in arguing with them in most cases. The only way to preserve both individuals' sanity is to walk away.

If you do not know what something is, do not buy it. The Warman guides that you have in your carrying bag can point you in the right direction, but they are not the final word. If you simply must find out right that minute, consult the listing of references in the Warman guides and then check with the antiques and collectibles book dealer at the market to see if the specific book you need is in stock.

Stories, Stories, and More Stories

A flea market is a place where one's creative imagination and ability to believe what is heard are constantly tested. The number of cleverly crafted stories to explain the origin of pieces and why the condition is not exactly what one expects is endless. The problem is that they all sound plausible. Once again, I come back to the concept upon which flea market survival is founded: a questioning mind.

I often ask dealers to explain the circumstances through which they acquired a piece and what they know about the piece. Note what I said. I am not asking the seller to reveal his or her source. No one should be expected to do that. I am testing the openness and believability of the dealer. If the dealer claims there is something special about an object (e.g., it belonged to a famous person or was illustrated in a book), I ask to see proof. Word-of-mouth stories have no validity in the long run.

Again, there are certain phrases that serve as tip-offs that something may be amiss. "It is the first one I have ever seen," "You will never find another one like it," "I saw one a few aisles over for more money," "One sold at auction a few weeks ago for double what I am asking," and "I am selling it to you for exactly what I paid for it" are just a few examples. If what you are hearing sounds too good to be true, it probably is.

Your best defense is to spend time studying and researching the area in which you want to collect before going to flea markets. Emphasis should be placed equally on object identification and an understanding of the pricing structure within that collecting category. You will not be a happy person if you find that although an object you bought is what the seller claimed it was, you paid far more for it than it is worth.

Period Reproduction, Copycat, Fantasy, or Fake

The number of reproductions, copycats, and fantasy and fake items at flea market is larger than in any other segment of the field. Antiques and collectibles malls run a close second. In fact, it is not uncommon to find several stands at a flea market selling reproductions, copycats, and fantasy items openly. When you recognize them, take time to study their merchandise. Commit the material to memory. In ten years when the material has begun to age, you will be glad that you did.

Although the above terms are familiar to those who are active in the antiques and collectibles field, they may not be understood by some. A period piece is an example made during the initial period of production. The commonly used term is *real*. However, if you think about it, all objects are real, whether period or not. *Real* is one of those terms that should set your mind to questioning.

A reproduction is an exact copy of a period piece. There may be subtle changes in areas not visible to the naked eye, but essentially it is identical to its period counterpart. A copycat is an object that is similar, but not exactly like the period piece it is emulating. It may vary in size, form, or design elements. In some cases, it is very close to the original. In auction terms, copycats are known as *in the style of*. A fantasy item is a form that was not issued during the initial period of production. An object licensed after Elvis's death would be an Elvis fantasy item. A Chippendale-style coffee table, a form which did not exist during the first Chippendale period, is another example.

The thing to remember is that reproductions, copycats, and fantasy items are generally mass-produced and start out life honestly. The wholesalers who sell them to dealers in the trade make it clear exactly what they are. Alas, some of the dealers do not do so when they resell them.

Because reproductions, copycats, and fantasy items are mass produced, they appear in the market in quantity. When you spot a piece in your collecting area that you have never seen before, quickly check through the rest of the market. If the piece is mint, double-check. Handle the piece. Is it the right weight? Does it have the right color? Is it the quality that you expect? If you answer "no" to any of these questions, put it back.

The vast majority of items sold at any flea market are mass-produced, twentieth-century items. Encountering a new influx of never-seen-before items does not necessarily mean they are reproductions, copycats, or fantasy items. Someone may have uncovered a hoard. The trade term is *warehouse find*. A hoard can seriously affect the value of any antique or collectible. All of a sudden the number of available examples rises dramatically. So usually does the condition level. Unless the owner of a hoard is careful, this sudden release of material can drive prices downward.

A fake is an item deliberately meant to deceive. They are usually one-of-a-kind items, with many of them originating in shops of revivalist craftspersons. The folk art and furniture market is flooded with them. Do not assume that because an object is inexpensive, it is all right. You would be surprised how cheaply goods can be made in Third World countries.

It is a common assumption that reproductions, copycats, fantasy items, and fakes are of poor quality and can be easily spotted. If you subscribe to this theory, you are a fool. There are some excellent reproductions, copycats, fantasy items, and fakes. You

probably have read on more than one occasion how a museum was fooled by an object in its collection. If museum curators can be fooled, so can you.

This is not the place for a lengthy dissertation on how to identify and differentiate period objects, reproductions, copycats, fantasies, or fakes. There are books on the subject. Get them and read them. What follows are a few quick tips to put you on the alert:

1. If it looks new, assume it is new.
2. Examine each object carefully, looking for signs of age and repair that should be there.
3. Use all appropriate senses—sight, tough, smell, and hearing—to check an object.
4. Be doubly alert when something appears to be a "steal."
5. Make a copy of any articles from trade papers or other sources that you find about period, reproduction, copycat, fantasy, and fake items and keep them on file.
6. Finally, handle as many authentic objects as possible. The more genuine items you handle, the easier it will be to identify imposters.

What's a Fair Price?

The best selling scenario at a flea market is a buyer and seller who are both extremely happy with the price paid and a seller who has made sufficient profit to allow him or her to stay in business and return to sell another day. Reality is not quite like this. Abundance of merchandise, competition among dealers, and negotiated prices often result in the seller being less than happy with the final price received. Yet the dealers sell because some money is better than no money.

Price haggling is part of the flea market game. In fact, the next section discusses this very subject in detail. The only real value an object has is what someone is willing to pay for it, not what someone asks for it. There is no fixed price for any antique, collectible, or secondhand object. All value is relative.

These considerations aside, there are a few points relating to price and value that the flea marketeer should be aware of. Try to understand these points. Remember, in the antiques and collectibles field there are frequently two or more sides to every issue and rarely any clear cut right or wrong answer.

First, dealers have a right to an honest profit. If dealers are attempting to make a full-time living in the trade, they must triple their money in order to cover their inventory costs; pay their overhead expenses, which are not inconsequential; and pay themselves. Buy at thirty cents and sell at one dollar. The key problem is that many flea market dealers set up at flea markets not to make money but simply to have a good time. As a result, they willingly sell at much lower profit margins than those who are trying to make a living. It is not really that hard to tell which group is which. Keep the seller's circumstances in mind when haggling.

Second, selling is labor- and capital-intensive. Check a dealer's booth when a flea market opens and again when it closes. Can you spot the missing objects? When a dealer has a "good" flea market, he or she usually sells between fifteen and thirty objects. In most cases, the inventory from which these objects sold consists of hundreds of pieces. Do not think about what the dealer sold, think about what was not sold. What did it cost? How much work is involved in packing, hauling, setting up, and repacking these items until the objects finally sell. Flea market sellers need a high profit margin to stay in business.

Third, learn to use price guide information correctly. Remember the prices are guides, not price absolutes. For their part, sellers must resist the temptation to become greedy and trap themselves in the assumption that they deserve book price or better for every item they sell. Sellers would do better to focus on what they paid for an object (which, in effect, does determine the final price) rather than on what they think they can get for it (it never sells as quickly as they think). They will make more on volume sales than they will trying to get top dollar for all their items.

Price guide prices represent what a *serious* collector in that category will pay provided he or she does not already own the object. An Elvis Presley guitar in its original box may book for over $500, but it has that value only to an Elvis Presley collector who does not already own one. What this means is that price guide prices tend to be on the high side.

Fourth, the IRS defines fair market value as a situation where there is a willing buyer and seller and both parties are equally knowledgeable. While the first part of this equation usually applies, the second usually does not. There is no question that knowledge is power in the flea market game and sharing it can cost money. If money were the only issue, I could accept the idea of keeping your mouth shut. However, I like to think that any sale involves transfer of information about the object as well as the object itself. If there were a fuller understanding of the selling situation by both sides, there would be a lot less grousing about prices after the deal is done.

Finally, forget about book value and seller's value. The only value an object has is what it is worth to you. This is the price that you should pay. The only person that can make this judgment is you. It is a decision of the moment. Never forget that. Do not buy if you do not think the price is fair. Do not look back if you find later that you overpaid. At the moment of purchase, you thought the price was fair. In buying at a flea market, the buck stops in your heart and wallet.

Flea Market Haggling

Few prices at a flea market are firm prices. No matter what anyone tells you, it is standard practice to haggle. You may not be comfortable doing it, but you might as well learn how. The money you save will be your own.

In my mind there are only three prices: a bargain price, a negotiable price, and a ridiculous price. If the price on an object is already a bargain, I pay it. I do this because I like to see the shocked look on a seller's face when I do not haggle. I also do it because I want that dealer to find similar material for me. Nothing encourages this more than paying the price asked.

If the price is ridiculous, marked several times above what it is worth, I simply walk away. No amount of haggling will ever get the price to where I think it belongs. All that will happen is that the dealer and I will become frustrated. Who needs it? Let the dealers sit with their pieces. Sooner or later, the message will become clear.

I firmly believe it is the responsibility of the seller to set the asking price. When an object is not marked with a price, I become suspicious that the dealer is going to set the asking price based on what he or she thinks I can pay. I have tested this theory on more than one occasion by sending several individuals to inquire about the value of an unmarked item. In every case, a variety of prices were reported back to me. Since most of the material that I collect is mass-produced, I walk away from all unpriced merchandise. I will find another example somewhere else. This type of dealer does not deserve my business.

I have too much to do at a flea market to waste time haggling. If I find a piece that is close to what I am willing to pay, I make a counter-offer. I am very clear in what I tell the seller. "I am willing to pay 'x' amount. This is my best offer. Will you take it?" Most dealers are accustomed to responding with "Let's halve the difference." Hard though it is

at times, I never agree. I tell the dealer that I made my best offer to save time haggling, and I intend to stick by it.

If the flea market that I am attending is a monthly or weekly, I may follow the object for several months. At the end of four to five months, I speak with the dealer and call attention to the fact that he or she has been unsuccessful in selling the object for the amount that had been asked. I make my counter-offer, which sometimes can be as low as half the value marked on the piece. While the dealer may not be totally happy selling the object at that price, the prospect of any sale is often far better than keeping the object in inventory for several more months.

In Summary

If you are gullible, flea markets may not be for you. While not a Darwinian jungle, the flea market has pitfalls and traps which must be avoided in order for you to be successful. The key is to know that these pitfalls and traps exist.

Furthermore, successful flea marketeering comes from practice. There is no school or seminar where you can learn the skills you need. You fly by the seat of your pants, learn as you go, wing it. The tuition that you pay will be the mistakes that you make along the way. Never get discouraged. Everyone else you see at the flea market has experienced or is experiencing exactly what is happening to you. When you become a seasoned veteran, you will look back upon the learning period and laugh. In the interim, at least try to smile.

The Flea Market Scene Today

6

This section is written based on the premise that "honesty is the best policy" and "forewarned is forearmed." I acknowledge in advance that many flea market owners, managers, and dealers are not going to be enamored by some of the points that follow. I also am aware that it is easier to find fault than to praise.

What follows is my analysis of the flea market scene today. Read it in full. What you need to remember most are its final three paragraphs.

The economic recession of the early 1990s has profoundly affected flea markets, perhaps more than any other sector in the antiques and collectibles field, with the possible exception of the major New York auction houses. Some effects proved positive. Unfortunately, the vast majority did not. Rather than function to correct existing problems, the current recession accentuated and compounded them.

Ideally, the two most positive effects of the recession should have been the reduction in the number and frequency of flea markets and a general reduction in the number of dealers. Neither occurred. In fact, the opposite happened. The number of flea markets and flea market dealers increased.

Flea market owners and managers are the big winners in the current recession. Dealers desperately seeking cash flow have increased, not decreased, their flea market commitments. Many dealers who thought they had graduated from the flea market to the antiques show circuit found themselves back in the flea market arena in search of immediate cash and a broader customer base. It was all too apparent from the mood of several such individuals that they were none too happy about finding themselves in this position.

Flea market owners and managers, realizing they had a potential cash cow, held to established space rental fees or, in a few cases, raised them. Many expanded their facilities to accommodate the increased demand for space. Some even increased the frequency of their markets or the number of days the market was opened. "Get it while you can" has been the prevailing sentiment. In a country where free enterprise is encouraged and lauded, far be it from me to blame these owners and managers.

Increased dealer participation at an ever-expanding number of flea markets also increased merchandise exposure. The end result was twofold. First, a "haven't I seen that before" attitude quickly spread throughout the field. Merchandise staleness is one of the worst things that can happen in the antiques and collectibles field. Flea markets do best when there is a steady diet of new existing finds at bargain prices. Second, dealers did not have time to acquire sufficient amounts of replacement stock. Instead of working auctions, garage sales, or a string of pickers, they devoted the bulk of their efforts to moving from show to show. What buying of new merchandise they did, and it was precious little, was done during flea market setup. At some antiques flea markets, dealer buying during setup is virtually nonexistent. Actually, it is nice to find dealers in their booths during setup rather than watching them race around the field like chickens with their heads cut off.

Likewise, the sale of early admission tickets to buyers is down drastically. More and more buyers are willing to take their chances at the official opening of business, rather than taking time out of their schedule or paying a premium to buy during the setup

period. Gone is the "I have to be there or miss the chance to buy it" attitude that influenced many buyers of the 1980s and early 1990s. The early admission ticket will not disappear. It is found money for antiques flea market owners.

Rather than decrease the number of flea market dealers, the recession actually served to greatly increase their number. Many individuals who found themselves in a financial crunch saw the flea market as a way to make a quick buck. They did not need an education or have to pass a licensing test to become a flea market dealer. All they needed was a car load of merchandise that they could tout as old, a gift of the blarney, and a mixture of greed and larceny.

One has to be careful when painting with a broad brush. Not every new flea market dealer who entered the marketplace in the early 1990s fits this description. The tragedy is that the vast majority do.

The recession saw only a limited number of dollars being spent in the flea market sector. The arrival of this host of new dealers meant available dollars were spread thinner and thinner. Established dealers and competent new dealers were hurt. Cut-throat competition became commonplace. A number of old timers, sickened by these developments, simply gave up and left the market.

Perhaps the most damning effect of these "get while the getting is good" individuals is the arrival at flea markets of recent store stock that is sold at two to ten times the shelf price on the premise that it is a good investment. Of course, none of the sellers promise to return your money in ten years if the item fails to increase in value. In fact, it is highly unlikely that these sellers will still be in business in ten years.

In some cases, the situation is so bad that material is being offered at antiques flea markets that can be bought at the local discount store for ten to fifty cents on the dollar. Several dealers are capitalizing on regional collecting differences. They acquire items that have limited regional distribution, take them to a different area, and sell them at premiums ranging from two to five times the initial cost.

The 1990s' economic recession continues to chop away at the purity of the flea market. In the 1980s many flea market owners policed the "antiques" quality of the goods sold on their sites. In 1993 the key concern seems to be to sell space rather than control merchandise.

The "Flea Market Scene Today" in the first edition of this book warned about the growing number of "crafts, reproduction and copycat wholesalers, discontinued merchandise, new merchandise, clothing, plants, produce, and food" that had made their appearance at antiques flea markets. The number of booths devoted to this merchandise increased in the early 1990s. The situation appears almost irreversible. If this is the case, the days of the pure antiques and collectibles flea market are numbered.

Worth noting is the decline in the amount of reproduction and fake folk art at the flea markets of the early 1990s. Do not interpret this to mean that these fakes have vanished. Far from it. The amount of it has simply lessened. The good news is that most buyers have recognized this material for the junk that it is and are shying away from it. This is a trend well worth continuing.

Unfortunately, reproductions, copycats, and fantasy items have continued to increase in number. Their quality also has improved, thus making them harder than ever to spot. A number of publications are attempting to track the new arrivals, but these efforts have about as much effect as a teardrop in the ocean. It really is "buyer beware" in today's flea market scene.

Given this gloom-and-doom picture, is there anything positive that can be said about the flea market scene today? The answer is "yes."

First, many established dealers and the more competent new dealers have recognized that customer service is the major key to survival. As a result, they have become much more customer-oriented. They now actively solicit collectors' "wants," keep these wants in mind as they travel, and sell long-distance via mail and telephone. They also take time to know their customers better.

Second, quality dealers are insisting on carrying only quality merchandise in fine or better condition. Good and very good merchandise is no longer acceptable merchandise to today's sophisticated buyer. The smart dealers emphasize quality and condition, and the booths of these dealers easily stand out from those of the flea market junk merchants. Provided these quality-oriented dealers resist the temptation to overprice their merchandise, they manage to sell well at most flea markets.

Third, there are rewards for the person willing to invest time in the hunt. The wealth of new dealers, the vast majority of whom have very limited knowledge about antiques and collectibles, continue to misprice much of their merchandise. Often, they overprice. However, there are plenty of instances when their merchandise is priced significantly enough below market to make it a genuine bargain.

Fourth, prices are far more negotiable than they were two years ago. It is not uncommon to hear of discounts ranging from 20% to 50% or more. There is a danger here. Better dealers work on a much tighter profit margin. Their prices do not allow this level of discounting. It is not safe to assume that because one dealer is willing to discount deeply, the same holds true for the other dealers.

Fifth, in a few instances, local government has stepped in to check the growth in the selling period of flea markets. The best example is Brimfield, Massachusetts, where the time available for local flea markets has been cut back to six days from the ten plus days into which each of the three annual sessions had expanded.

Sixth, new and improved facilities have been constructed at a number of the more established flea market sites. The principal result is that more merchandise is being offered for sale under cover. This is very positive. Many dealers with quality material are unwilling to risk exposing their goods to the elements. Who can blame them? When proper facilities exist, they are willing to consider participating in the flea market scene. Many do. However, do not deceive yourself. The primary force pulling them back into the flea market arena is the need for cash. Proper facilities have simply made the move back a little more palatable.

Do these positives outweigh the negatives? The answer is a tentative "no." Antiques flea markets remain a risky place to do business. They are the wild-west frontier of the antiques and collectibles field. Survival remains a matter of strapping on your guns and drawing faster than your opponent. The good news is that this book and others have clearly identified the opponent that you face. Knowing the strengths and weaknesses of the current flea market environment greatly enhances your chance for survival.

The flea markets of 1993 remain at the crossroads. Flea market owners and managers remain unorganized. As a result, standards of operation and ethics for owners, manager, and sellers have not been formulated, let alone implemented. There is little point in getting frustrated over what most likely will never be. However, one can always hope.

In searching for a way to end this analysis, I reread the final three paragraphs that ended "The Flea Market Scene Today" chapter in *Price Guide to Flea Market Treasures*, first edition. The advice given remains as meaningful in 1993 as it was in 1991. Instead of rephrasing it to show how clever a writer I am, I have simply decided to repeat it. Here goes:

> Permit me one final thought. The key to having an enjoyable experience at a flea market does not rest with the manager, the dealers, the physical setting, or the merchandise. The

key is you. Attend with reasonable expectations in mind. Go to have fun, to make a pleasant day of it. Even if you come home with nothing, savor the contacts that you made and the fact that you spent a few hours or longer among the goodies.

As a smart flea marketeer, you know the value of customers to keep a flea market alive and functioning. When you find a good flea market, do not keep the information to yourself. Write or call the regional trade papers and ask them to do more stories about the market. Share your news with friends and others. Encourage them to attend. There is plenty for everyone.

Happy Hunting from my dad, the Rinkettes, and me.

Part Two
FLEA MARKET TREASURES

Price Notes

Flea market prices for antiques and collectibles are not as firmly established as those at malls, shops, and shows. As a result, it is imperative that you treat the prices found in this book as *guides*, not *absolutes*.

Prices given are based on the national retail price for an object that is complete and in fine condition. *Please Note: These are retail prices.* They are what you would expect to pay to purchase the objects. They do not reflect what you might realize if you were selling objects. A "fair" selling price to a dealer or private collector ranges from 20% to 40% of the book price, depending on how commonly found the object is.

Prices quoted are for objects that show a minimum of wear and no major blemishes to the display surface. The vast majority of flea market objects are mass-produced. As such, they survive in quantity. Do not buy damaged or incomplete objects. It also pays to avoid objects that show signs of heavy use.

Regional pricing is a factor within the flea market area, especially when objects are being sold close to their place of manufacture. When faced with higher prices due to strong regional pricing, I offer the price an object would bring in a neighboring state or geographic area. In truth, regional pricing has all but disappeared due to the large number of nationally oriented antiques and collectibles price guides, magazines, newspapers, and collectors' clubs.

Finally, *you* determine price; it is what *you* are willing to pay. Flea market treasures have no fixed prices. What has value to one person may be totally worthless to another.

Is it possible to make sense out of this chaos? Yes, but in order to do so, you have to jump in feet first: attend flea markets and buy.

Happy Hunting! May all your purchases turn out to be treasures.

Abbreviations

These are standard abbreviations used in the listings in *Price Guide to Flea Market Treasures*, second edition.

3D	three-dimensional	mfg	manufactured
adv	advertising	MIB	mint in box
C	century	mkd	marked
c	circa	MOP	mother of pearl
circ	circular	No.	number
cov	cover or covered	orig	original
d	diameter or depth	oz	ounce or ounces
dec	decorated or decoration	pc	piece
dj	dust jacket	pcs	pieces
emb	embossed	pgs	pages
ext.	exterior	pkg	package
ftd	footed	pr	pair
gal	gallon	pt	pint or point
h	height	qt	quart
hp	hand painted	rect	rectangular
illus	illustrated, illustration, or illustra-	sgd	signed
	tions	SP	silver plated
imp	impressed	SS	sterling silver
int.	interior	sq	square
j	jewels	vol	volume
K	karat	w	width
l	length	yg	yellow gold
lb	pound	yr	year
litho	lithograph		

Categories and Prices

ABINGDON POTTERY

Over the years, Roseville and Weller pottery, favorites of old-time traditionalist collectors of mass-produced pottery wares, has become more and more expensive. In the 1970s and 1980s collectors with limited budgets began concentrating on firms such as Gonder, Hall, Hull, McCoy, Stangl, and Vernon Kiln. Now this material is going up in value. Stretch your dollar by concentrating on some of the firms that still have limited collector appeal. Abingdon Potteries, Inc., J. A. Bauer Pottery Company, Haeger Potteries, Metlox Potteries, and Pfaltzgraff Pottery Company are a few suggestions. I'll bet you can think of many more.

The Abingdon Sanitary Manufacturing Company began manufacturing bathroom fixtures in 1908 in Abingdon, IL. In 1938, they began production of art pottery made with a vitreous body. This line continued until 1970 and included over 1,000 shapes and pieces. Almost 150 colors were used to decorate these wares. Given these numbers, forget about collecting an example of every form in every color ever made. Find a few forms that you like and concentrate on them. There are some great ones.

Bookends, pr
  Cactus, 6" h. 60.00
  Sea Gull, 6" h 40.00
Bowl, low, blue, 12" d, flower decals,
  #518. . . . . 25.00
Candlesticks, pr, pink, double, #575 . . . . 20.00
Cookie Jar
  Daisy, 8" h. 30.00
  Little Girl, 9½" h. 40.00
  Pineapple, 10½" h 70.00
  Sunflower. 15.00
Cornucopia, blue, #474 . . . . 15.00
Planter
  Cactus, 7" l, bookend type, pr 55.00
  Scroll and Leaf pattern, 9 × 3½", yellow. 6.50
String Holder, mouse, 8½" d 80.00
Vase
  Cactus, #669 . . . . 15.00

Scroll, soft green, flared, 9" h. 5.00
Sea Horse. 18.00
Wall Pocket
  Book 40.00
  Calla Lily 20.00

ACTION FIGURES

Action, action, action is the key to action figures. Action figures show action. You can recognize them because they can be manipulated into an action pose or are modeled into an action pose.

There is a wealth of supporting accessories for most action figures, ranging from clothing to vehicles, that are as collectible as the figures themselves. A good rule is the more pizazz, the better the piece.

This is a relatively new collecting field. Emphasis is placed on pieces in mint or near-mint condition. The best way to find them is with their original packaging. Better yet, buy some new and stick them away.

Periodical: *Action Figure News & Review*, 39 N. Hillside Lane, Monroe, CT 06468.

A-Team, Galoob, 3¾" h, set of four,
  1984. . . . . 30.00
Bruce Wayne, Kenner, #63180, quick
  change Batman costume, 1990 . . . . . . 15.00
Carey Mahoney, Police Academy, Kenner, 1990. . . . . 6.00
Charon, Clash of the Titans, Mattel,
  3¾" h, 1980 . . . . 15.00
Dick Tracy, Playmates, #5701, 1990 . . . . 5.00
Hawkeye, M.A.S.H., Tri-Star, large size,
  1970. . . . . 35.00
Hoss Cartwright, Bonanza, American
  Character, 1966 . . . . 100.00
Illya Kuryakin, Man From U.N.C.L.E.,
  Gilbert 200.00
Incredible Hulk, Toy Biz, #4809, 5" h,
  with crushing arm, 1990 . . . . 12.00
Indiana Jones, Kenner, #46010, field
  outfit with whip, 1982 . . . . 80.00
Johnny West, Best of the West, Marx,
  quick draw, 1965 . . . . 75.00

Juggernaut, X-Men, Toy Biz, #4909, 5″ h, power punch action **10.00**

Moon McDare, Gilbert **150.00**

Officer Bowzer and Blitz, C.O.P.S., Hasbro, #7687, 1988 . . . . **15.00**

Robocop, Kenner, 1988 . . . . **8.00**

Sheriff of Nottingham, Robin Hood Prince of Thieves, Kenner, #05850, with sword, 1991 . . . . **6.00**

Starbuck, Battlestar Galactica, Mattel, 1978 . . . . **20.00**

Starship Troopers, Robert Heinlein, Avalon Hill, 1976, MIB **20.00**

Star Wars Star Warriors, West End Games, 1987, MIB **25.00**

Woman & Man: The Classic Confrontation, Psychology Today Games, 1971 . . . . **12.50**

ADVENTURE GAMES

Adventure games have been played for hundreds of years. In an adventure game, each player is asked to assume the role of a character. The character's fate is determined by choices that he or she and other players make. The rules are often very complex; games can last for days, even months.

There are many different game scenarios, ranging from sports and entertainment or war and conflict to finance and fortune. The principal marketing source for current games is the comic book shop. Some comic book shops are also starting to handle discontinued games.

Collectors fall into two groups: those who buy discontinued games to play them and those who buy them solely for the purpose of collecting them. Both groups place strong emphasis on completeness. Many of the games contain more than one hundred different playing pieces. Few take the time to count all the parts. This is why adventure games tend to be relatively inexpensive when found at garage sales and flea markets.

A small group of individuals have begun to collect playing pieces, many of which are hand painted. However, rarely does the price paid exceed the initial cost of the figure.

Dungeons & Dragons, Gygax & Arneson, Tactical Studies Rules, orig set, three volumes: *Men & Magic*, Book 1, *Monsters & Treasure*, Book 2, and *The Underworld & Wilderness Adventures*, Book 3; 1974, MIB **150.00**

Gettysburg, Avalon Hill, 1958 . . . . **30.00**

High-Bid: The Auction Game, 3M (Minnesota Mining and Manufacturing Company), 1965 . . . . **7.50**

Management, Avalon Hill, 1960 . . . . **15.00**

ADVERTISING ITEMS

Break advertising items into two groups: items used to merchandise a product and items used to promote a product. Merchandising advertising is a favorite with interior decorators and others who want it for its mood-setting ability. It is often big, splashy, and showy. Promotional advertising (giveaways) are primarily collector-driven.

The thing to remember is that almost every piece of advertising is going to appeal to more than one collector. As a result, prices for the same piece will often differ significantly depending on who the seller views as the final purchaser.

Almost all advertising is bought for the purpose of display. As a result, emphasize theme and condition. The vast majority of advertising collectibles are two-dimensional. Place a premium on large three-dimensional objects.

Clubs: Antique Advertising Association, P. O. Box 1121, Morton Grove, IL 60053; The Ephemera Society of America, P. O. Box 37, Schoharie, NY 12157; Tin Container Collectors Association, P. O. Box 440101, Aurora, CA 80014.

Pinback Button, Experts Use Peters Cartridges, bullet, light green ground, celluloid, ⁷⁄₈″ d, $25.00.

Newspapers: *National Association of Paper and Advertising Collectibles*, P. O. Box 500, Mount Joy, PA 17552; *Paper Collectors' Marketplace* (PCM), P. O. Box 128, Scandinavia, WI 54917.

Ashtray, Barbasol, 3½" d, 3" h, eight-sided clear glass jar on metal tray **15.00**
Bag Rack, Honey Bread **165.00**
Banana Hook, Jacko, boy with banana hair illus. **18.00**
Bank
    Blue Bonnet Sue **25.00**
    Kool-Aid, 7" h, plastic, mechanical, red, yellow base, slogan decal, orig box, 1970s **50.00**
    Norge Refrigerator, 4" h, metal, painted, white, black base, 1930s... **40.00**
    Pillsbury Doughboy, MIB........... **40.00**
Beater Jar, Wesson Oil **72.00**
Bill Hook
    Ceresota Flour.................... **45.00**
    Peacock Roasted Coffee, diecut, full color cardboard, wire hook. **22.00**
Blotter
    Beech-Nut Gum, color graphics, 1937........................ **22.00**
    Blue Coal, The Shadow illus. **18.00**
    Holstein Milk. **9.00**
    Royal Corona Stoves, range illus **10.00**
Book
    Eveready Flash Light Batteries, *Book of Radio Stars*, illus, includes Groucho Marx, Jack Benny, and George Burns, 1930................... **38.00**
    Kellogg's, *Storybook of Games*, 1931.... **35.00**
Booklet
    Colgate, *Jungle Pow-Wow*, 1911 ...... **18.00**
    Ringen Stove, Buster Brown, c1905....................... **30.00**
Bookmark, Acorn Stoves **6.00**
Bowl
    Sample From The Strong Mfg Co, Sebring, Ohio, 3½" d, porcelain enamelware, green and white, inscription int. **40.00**
    Use Jaxon Soap, 6" d, cast iron, bail handle **75.00**
Box
    Baker's Chocolate, wood, dovetailed, 1900....................... **45.00**
    Dr Baker's Condition Powders, cov, wood, dovetailed. **45.00**
    Fairy Soap, five bars, unopened...... **65.00**
    Imperial Peanut Butter, wood, dovetailed **35.00**
    Uncle Tom's Chewing Gum **135.00**
Broadside, Pure Milk, "New System" illus, c1885 .... **32.00**
Broom Rack, Blu-J Brooms, two multicolored signs **495.00**
Butter Tub, Willow Farm, LaGrange, IL, stoneware **88.00**

Can, Dutch Cleanser, unopened, 1940s......................... **15.00**
Christmas Card, Breyer Ice Cream Company, c1920..................... **20.00**
Cookbook
    Alaga Syrup, 15 pgs, 1920s **5.00**
    Maxwell House Coffee, 22 pgs, 1927....................... **7.00**
    Sleepy Eye Bread Loaf **250.00**
Cookie Jar
    Blue Bonnet Sue **50.00**
    Keebler Elf, sitting. **75.00**
    Mr Peanut, MIB **40.00**
    Pepperidge Farm, cookie bag, MIB ... **60.00**
Condiment Set, creamer, sugar, salt and pepper shakers, Ken-L-Ration Dog CJ......................... **225.00**
Crock, Germ Proof Water Filter, Pasteur Chamberland, Dayton, OH. **175.00**
Cabinet, Putnam Dye **95.00**
Charm, Ideal Dog Food, metal **12.00**
Clipboard, 4 × 5¾", Ludlow-Saylor Wire Co, St Louis, 75th Anniversary, brass, 1931.......................... **26.00**
Dispenser, Smith Brothers Cough Drops......................... **225.00**
Display, counter top
    Eveready Flashlight Batteries, litho tin, 1930s **75.00**
    Monarch Range Golden Jubilee, 1896–1946, 14 × 14", double gold coin, orig mailing envelope **40.00**
    St Joseph's Aspirin, tin **75.00**
    West Hairnets, 6" sq, litho tin, 1918.......................... **150.00**
    White Horse Whiskey, 15" h, horse shape **85.00**
Doll
    Chiquita Banana.................. **20.00**
    Del Monte
        Shoo Shoo Trudy **15.00**
        Sweet Pea, 12" h **10.00**
    Jack Frost, 19" h **12.00**
    Wurlitzer Fun Maker **12.00**
Door Push
    Colonial Is Good Bread, 3 × 22", adjustable, double-sided, blue and black paint.................... **75.00**
    Fleischmann's Yeast, porcelain **250.00**
    Red Rose Tea..................... **350.00**
    Salada Tea, porcelain **250.00**
Figure
    RCA Victor Nipper, chalk, logo **45.00**
    Regan's Holsum Bread, 9½" h, cardboard, pudgy little girl............ **25.00**
Flyswatter, Wittman's hardware, wood handle, 1930s **4.00**
Game, checkers, Standard Oil **60.00**
Glass
    Welch's, cartoon scenes, boxed set, 1974......................... **45.00**
    Wilson Tennis Balls, set of 6 .... **25.00**
Hatchet, Art Stove Co, 4" l **50.00**

Jar, Lik-Em Nuts, counter top, clear glass, hexagonal, raised lettering, ribbed dec, metal screw lid **75.00**

Ledger, pocket type, Chicago Stove Works, heaters and ranges illus, c1900 .... **10.00**

Match Holder

J C Stevens **225.00**

Juicy Fruit **145.00**

Matchsafe, pocket type, Buffum Tools, Louisiana, Mo **75.00**

Mirror, Consolidated Ice Co, polar bear and Eskimo scene **150.00**

Needle Threader, Prudential Insurance, tin **6.50**

Paper Clip, Venus Pencils, brass **23.00**

Paperweight

Diamond Tool & Horseshoe Co, horse-shoe shape **30.00**

Star Biscuits, metal, figural mouse and biscuit **85.00**

To Forge Our Relationship, King Sales-Memphis, TN, brass, anvil shape, emb **25.00**

Pen, Winchester, rifle shaped **10.00**

Pie Plate, Coon Chicken Inn **140.00**

Pinback Button

ABC Soda Crackers, parrot illus, 1896 .... **35.00**

Dandee Bread, tan, black, and white, early 1900s **20.00**

Sunbeam Bread, litho, Sunbeam girl, red, white, and blue, 1930–40 ..... **15.00**

Pot Scraper

C D Kenny Teas, Coffees, Sugars, cast iron, S-shape handle, raised letter-ing **50.00**

Sharples **145.00**

Reamer

C D Kenny Co, Teas, Coffees, Sugars, 3″ d, side handle, emb bottom **50.00**

Sunkist, 6″ d, milk glass, block let-ters **30.00**

Ruler, Old Hood Ice Cream, 12″ l, wood **28.00**

Salt and Pepper Shakers, pr, Green Giant **12.00**

Sharpening Stone, Bull Brand's Feeds, cow litho **16.00**

Shoe Buttonhook, The Savings Store, Kalamazoo, MI **12.50**

Shot Glass, Adlerika Bowel Cleanser **15.00**

Sign

Adam's Express Co, reverse painted glass **375.00**

Bell System Public Telephone, round, porcelain **80.00**

Breidbach & Sons, Mfgs of Fine Colors, brass **65.00**

Butter-Nut Bread, tin, loaf and bakery kid illus **75.00**

Cranford Dairy, 4 × 9″, cardboard, Charles Twelvetrees illus **12.00**

Drink Krim's For Health, porcelain ... **75.00**

Forthoffers Soda, counter top, color li-tho, c1905 .... **35.00**

Keen Kutter, tin, hardware adv **48.00**

Kraft Kraylets, tin, diecut pig **195.00**

Pellegrino Water, porcelain, two bot-tles illus **385.00**

Polarine, wood, painted, 1910 .... **290.00**

Red Man Chew, tin **35.00**

Standard Red Crown, wood, painted, 1910 .... **290.00**

Southern Bread, tin, loaf and child illus **65.00**

Southwestern Bell Telephone, 19 × 5½″, porcelain **290.00**

Vigorator Hair Tonic, tin **45.00**

Western Union Telegraph & Cable, porcelain **135.00**

White Eagle Beverages, 19 × 3½″, tin **10.00**

Spoon

Banner Buggies, tablespoon, buggy in spoon bowl **35.00**

Heinz, child's, silver plated, raised de-sign, early 1900s **15.00**

Towle's Log Cabin, child's, silver plated, early 1900s **12.00**

Stick Pin

Doe Wah Jack **20.00**

Dr Bell's Pine Tar Honey **12.00**

Tip Tray, Globe Wernicke, couple illus, 1930s **65.00**

Toy Truck, Campbell's Soup, product logos on trailer **45.00**

Tray, Jersey Creme Soda **100.00**

Watch Fob

American Snow Plows & Wings **25.00**

Butler M C, Kansas City, scales, pumps, and water supplies **30.00**

Chicago Business Men's Association Insurance **15.00**

Duenning Construction Co, Slinger, WI, enameled **10.00**

E C Atkins Silver Steel Saws, saw dec **38.00**

Galion Iron Works, three machines dec **28.00**

Manitowoc Speed Shovel, nickel and enamel **28.00**

Richards Wilcox Hardware Specialist, Aurora **28.00**

Whistle, Butter-Nut Bread, c1920 ...... **18.00**

Wristwatch, Charlie Tuna, silvered metal, full color dial, blue vinyl straps, 1973 copyright, Star-Kist Foods **75.00**

AFRICANA

The bulk of what you see out there is junk—either souvenirs brought home by tourists or decorative pieces sold by discount or department stores. The problem is twofold. First, modern-day African craftspeople continue to work in centuries-old traditions, making pieces with the same tools and in the same form as did their ancestors. Second, telling the difference between a piece made a century ago and a piece made a few months ago requires years of study. The only safe assumption is that most flea market dealers do not have the slightest idea which is which.

When buying African art at flea markets, be cheap about it. Never pay more than you can afford to lose. Buy primarily for decoration. When you think that you have found the real thing, have it checked by a museum curator.

Many pieces of African art involve the use of animal hides and tusks. Be extremely cautious about buying any object made from animals that are on the endangered species list.

Quality African art does show up at flea markets. The listings show some possibilities, provided you spot the real thing.

Bowl, 29" h, cov, carved woman sitting on top, geometric edges, three legs, flat base, c1920 . . . . **350.00**
Door Lock, 19 × 19", carved man, cross bar handle, dark brown stain, Mali, 20th C **270.00**
Figure
    Ibiji, 12" h, male effigy, punch hole eyes, Nigeria, late 19th C **125.00**
    Senufo, 39" h, female, relief facial dec, brown and black paint, Ivory Coast, 1940s **350.00**
Grain Scoop, 16¼" l, dark wood, handle tip carved with Dan style face, Liberia, 1930s **175.00**
Helmet, 15" l, wood, engraved geometric triangular, Bobo, 1920s **170.00**
Knife, 22½" l, iron blade, wood handle, engraved snakeskin pattern, late 19th/early 20th C **145.00**
Mask, wood, carved
    Dan, oval-shaped face, dark brown paint, Liberia Border **300.00**
    Guro Bird, 13½" h, bird atop head, Ivory Coast **120.00**
    Horned Guro, 16" h, curved horns, Ivory Coast **175.00**
Staff, 15" l, wood, head-shaped finial, varnished, Yaka Tribe, Zaire, 1940s . . . **125.00**
Stool, 12" h, 17" l, wood, U-shaped seat, brown, openwork dec, 1930–1940 . . . **425.00**

AKRO AGATE GLASS

When the Akro Agate Company was founded in 1911, its principal product was marbles. The company was forced to diversify during the 1930s, developing floral ware lines and children's dishes. Some collectors specialize in containers made by Akro Agate Company for the cosmetic industry.

Akro Agate merchandised a great many of its products as sets. Full sets that retain their original packaging command a premium price. Learn what pieces and colors constitute a set. Some dealers will mix and match pieces into a false set, hoping to get a better price.

Most Akro Agate pieces are marked "Made in USA" and have a mold number. Some, but not all, have a small crow flying through an "A" as a mark.

Club: Akro Agate Art Association, P. O. Box 758, Salem, NH 03079.

Powder Jar, Apple, opaque pumpkin color, $165.00.

Ashtray
    Ellipsoid, dark jade **5.00**
    Westite, gray and brown marble, rect playing card, recessed spade **10.00**
Basket, marbleized orange and white, two handles **28.50**
Bowl
    5" d, marbleized orange and white, emb leaves **35.00**
    6" d, Westite, marbleized brown and white **18.00**
Children's Dishes
    Cereal Bowl, Interior Panel, transparent amber **20.00**
    Cup
        Concentric Rib, blue-green **10.00**
        Houzex Opaque, blue **45.00**

Interior Panel, lemonade and ox-
blood **35.00**
Pitcher, Stacked Disc, blue **15.00**
Plate, Concentric Rib, green **3.00**
Saucer, Concentric Rib, white **3.00**
Set
5 pcs, Stacked Disc, bright blue
and white, pitcher and four
tumblers. **25.00**
8 pcs
Interior Panel, pink, orig box **100.00**
Stacked Disc & Panel, transparent
blue, orig box **200.00**
16 pcs, Concentric Rib, green and
white, orig box **85.00**
Sugar, cov, Houzex Opaque, blue **55.00**
Teapot, cov, Interior Panel, lemonade
and oxblood **85.00**
Tumbler, Raised Daisy, yellow **25.00**
Cigarette Box, Mexicali **28.00**
Demitasse Cup and Saucer, orange and
white **12.50**
Flower Pot
4" d, Single Dart, blue and white **15.00**
5¼" d, Westite, brown and white **15.00**
Jardiniere, 4½" h, Westite, marbleized
green and white **17.50**
Nasturtium Bowl, 6" d, Graduated Darts,
pumpkin, ftd **15.00**
Planter, 4½" d, Hexagon, opaque,
green **15.00**
Powder Box, Colonial Lady, blue. **55.00**
Powder Jar, Scottie, pink **75.00**
Urn, 3¼" h, orange and white, ftd **6.50**
Vase, 4½" h, marbleized orange **6.50**

ALADDIN

The Mantle Lamp Company of America,
founded in 1908 in Chicago, is best known
for its lamps. However, in the late 1950s
through the 1970s, it also was one of the
leading producers of character lunch
boxes.

Aladdin deserves a separate category because of the large number of lamp collectors who concentrate almost exclusively
on this one company. There is almost as
big a market for parts and accessories as for
the lamps themselves. Collectors are constantly looking for parts to restore lamps in
their possession.

Club: The Mystic Light of the Aladdin
Knights, R. D. #1, Simpson, IL 62985.

LAMPS
Bracket
Model 12 . . . . **80.00**
Model B, Alacite font, ring foot **150.00**

Caboose
Model 21C, shade **55.00**
Model B, shade **90.00**
Floor, model B, #1254 . . . . **175.00**
Hanging
Model 2, 203 shade **350.00**
Model 6, 215 shade, harp with chim-
ney tube. **250.00**
Model 12, four post, parchment
shade **165.00**
Model B, tilt frame, 716 glass shade. . . **200.00**
Parlor
Model 3 . . . . **750.00**
Model 4 . . . . **450.00**
Shelf, model 23, drape font
Clear, 1975–1982 . . . . **65.00**
Ruby, no oil fill, 1979 . . . . **90.00**
Student
Model 4 . . . . **3,500.00**
Model 23, replica, 1983 . . . . **350.00**
Table, kerosene
Model 1, emb foot. **500.00**
Model 9 . . . . **95.00**
Model 12
Brass, slanted sides **65.00**
Crystal, vase, 1243, green Venetian
Art-Craft, 10¼" h, 1930–1935. . . **85.00**
Model 23, aluminum font **35.00**
Model A, 100, Venetian, white, 1932–
1933. . . . . **75.00**
Model B
106, Colonial, amber crystal,
1933 . . . . **135.00**
108, Cathedral, green crystal, 1934–
1935. . . . . **70.00**
B-25, Victoria, decorated china,
with oil fill, 1947 . . . . **325.00**
B-29, Simplicity, green foot, 1948–
1953. . . . . **65.00**
B-39, Washington Drape, round
base, clear crystal, 1939 . . . . **55.00**
B-90, Quilt, white moonstone font,
black moonstone foot, 1937 . . . . . **200.00**
B-100, Corinthian, clear crystal,
1935–1936 . . . . **55.00**
B-121, Majestic, rose moonstone
font, 1935–1936 . . . . **225.00**
B-134, Orientale, bronze, 1935–
1936. . . . . **110.00**
B-138, Treasure, nickel, 1937–
1953. . . . . **90.00**
Model C, Brazil, quilted font, steel
foot. **85.00**
Practicus **185.00**

PARTS AND ACCESSORIES
Burner
Lumineer. **50.00**
Model 21C **18.00**
Ceiling Extension Hanger, No. 3 . . . . . . **65.00**
Chimney, ball style, logo **85.00**
Flame Spreader
Model 4A **135.00**
Model 11 . . . . **10.00**

Gallery
  Model 4 . . . . **70.00**
  Model 23 . . . . **8.00**
Mantle, Welsbach **8.00**
Shade
  Glass
    21C, English cased, red, 10" d **65.00**
    203, plain, opal, hanging lamp **70.00**
    401, fancy, satin white, table
      lamp **110.00**
    616F, decorated, poppies, hanging
      lamp **500.00**
    681, decorated, dogwood, satin
      white **45.00**
  Paper
    Aladdinite Parchment, 17½" d, vase
      lamp, 1929–1933 . . . . **125.00**
    Alpha, plain, 14" d, table lamp,
      1960s **4.00**
    Whip-o-lite Parchment, Coach and
      Four design, 14" d, table lamp,
      1933–1960 . . . . **60.00**
Tripod, model B, 14" w **5.00**
Wall Bracket **40.00**
Wick, orig box
  Model 6 . . . . **12.00**
  Model 12A **5.00**
Wick Raiser, model B **5.00**
Wick Trimmer, brass **4.00**

ALBUMS

The Victorian craze has drawn attention to the Victorian photograph album, which enjoyed an honored place in the parlor. The more common examples had velvet or leather covers. However, the ones most eagerly sought by collectors are those featuring a celluloid cover with motifs ranging from floral designs to Spanish American War battleships.

Most albums housed "family" photographs, the vast majority of which are unidentified. If the photographs are head-and-shoulders or baby shots, chances are they have little value unless the individuals are famous. Photographs of military figures, actors and actresses, and freaks are worth checking out further.

Cardboard albums still have not found favor with collectors. However, check the interior contents. In many cases, they contain post cards, clippings, match covers, or photographs that are worth far more than the album.

Daguerreotype, gutta percha, baroque
  motif cover **45.00**
Cabinet Cards, Victorian
  Embossed "Album" and floral design

Victorian Family Photo Album, emb "Album" and floral dec on celluloid front cover, orange, red, and green velvet back cover, brass closure, 8½ × 10¾", $60.00.

  on celluloid front cov, green and or-
    ange floral pattern on velvet back
    cov **65.00**
Floral motif on celluloid front cov, red
  velvet back cov **65.00**
Leather cover **30.00**
Plain red velvet covers **25.00**
Raised floral design and gold highlights
  on red velvet covers **45.00**
Spanish-American War battleship mo-
  tif front, celluloid front and back . . . **200.00**
Young maiden dec on celluloid front
  cov, red velvet back cover **85.00**

ALIENS

IEEEEKK!! As the scream goes up for extraterrestrials, their collectibility also rises. Arriving from such sources as *War of the Worlds* and *My Favorite Martian,* aliens have been landing in our collections with some frequency. Aliens have gained in popularity with the influence of television and the advances made in movie special effects. The *Mork and Mindy* show, starring comedian Robin Williams as a fun-loving extraterrestrial, and the *Star Wars* trilogy, with its strange alien creatures, are just two prime examples of alien familiarity.

So what is an alien? An alien is any creature, character, or being that is not of this planet. Aliens appear in many shapes and sizes, so be careful: you never know where an alien will turn up.

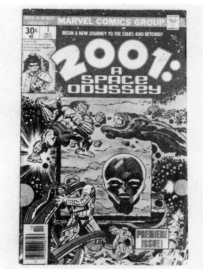

Comic Book, **2001: A Space Odyssey,** *Marvel Comics, Premiere Issue, Dec, 1976, $2.00.*

CLOSE ENCOUNTERS OF THE THIRD KIND
Figure, alien, Imperial, 1977 . . . . **12.00**
Pinback Button, alien illus, ''CON-
   TACT'' **1.50**

DUNE
Model Kit, Sandworm, Revell, unassem-
   bled, orig box **20.00**
Pinback Button, Sandworm illus **1.50**
Poster, Sandworm illus **3.00**
Vehicle, Sandworm, LJN, battery oper-
   ated, 1984 . . . . **18.00**

E. T.
Action Figure, wearing robe **3.00**
Address Book, E. T. and ''Addresses'' on
   cov **1.00**
Finger Light, plastic, battery operated . . . **5.00**
Glass, Pizza Hut promotional, ''Phone
   Home'' **2.50**
Keychain, plastic disc, E. T. face illus **1.50**
Lunch Box, Aladdin **10.00**
Stickers, puffy, E. T. engaged in various
   activities, set of 9, orig pkg . . . . **.75**
Tee Shirt, E. T. illus **9.00**
Wristwatch, Melody Glow Alarm Watch,
   Nelsonic. **12.00**

ALIEN
Board Game
   Alien Game, Kenner, copyright 20th
     Century Fox Film Corp, 1979 . . . . . . **35.00**
   This Time It's War, Leading Edge,
     1990 . . . . **35.00**
Comic Book, *Aliens,* #4, Dark Horse, Sec-
   ond Series, 1989 . . . . **4.00**
Figure, Alien, Kenner, 1979, 18" h **500.00**
Game, Alien Blaster Target Game, H G
   Toys, 1979 . . . . **140.00**
Halloween Costume, Alien, Ben Cooper,
   1979 . . . . **60.00**
Jigsaw Puzzle, Alien illus, H G Toys,
   1979 . . . . **20.00**
Model Kit
   Alien Face Hugger, Halcyon, 1991 . . . . **70.00**
   Alien with teeth, MPC, unassembled,
     orig box **80.00**
   Queen, Kaiyodo, 1987 . . . . **300.00**
Movie Viewer, Kenner, 1979 . . . . **90.00**
Mug, plastic, logo **5.00**
Note Pad, ''Trust Me I'm the Boss'' **4.50**
Poster, Alien Warrior, multicolored, GS,
   72" h, 1988 . . . . **18.00**
Shirt, Alien Chestburster, 3D, Distortions
   Unlimited **250.00**
Trading Cards, Topps, 1979, set of 84 . . . **30.00**

BATTLESTAR GALACTICA
Chair, inflatable, Cylon **15.00**
Costume, Cylon **20.00**
Helmet Radio, Cylon **25.00**
Stuffed Toy, Daggit, plush **15.00**

ALUMINUM, HANDWROUGHT

With increasing emphasis on post-World War II collectibles, especially those from the 1950s, handwrought aluminum is enjoying a collecting revival. The bulk of the pieces were sold on the giftware market as decorative accessories.

Do not be confused by the term *handwrought.* The vast majority of the pieces were mass-produced. The two collecting keys appear to be manufacturer and unusualness of form.

There is an enormous difference between flea market prices and prices at a major show within driving distance of New York City. Handwrought aluminum is quite trendy at the moment among the ''arty'' community.

Newsletter: *The Alumist,* P. O. Box 1346, Weatherford, TX 76086.

Ashtray, Rodney Kent, 5½" d, tulip design, three cigarette rests curve to form
   feet **5.00**
Basket, Farber & Shlevin, china insert
   with Indian Tree pattern and gold border, aluminum frame and handle **20.00**

Silent Butler, Chrysanthemum pattern, Continental Silverlook, 7½" d, 12" l, $15.00.

Beverage Set, 5 pcs, World Hand Forged, hammered, pitcher with square knot handle, four tumblers with flared lip 60.00

Bowl, Arthur Armour, 11½" d, sundial and zodiac signs, inscribed "Grow old along with me, the best is yet to be". 55.00

Buffet Server, Keystone Ware, 10 × 14½", rect caddy with wrapped handle, six square ribbed glass inserts with fruit design on lids, No. 606 . . . . 25.00

Butter Dish, cov, Buenilum, glass insert, beaded, double looped finial, castle mark 20.00

Cake Basket, Canterbury Arts, 12" d, floral spray design, twisted handle, helmet mark faces left. 28.00

Candy Dish, Wrought Farberware, round divided glass dish with sunburst pattern, aluminum lid with camellia and leaf design, wood knob finial 12.00

Casserole, cov, Cromwell, hammered, glass liner, ftd 12.00

Chafing Dish, Rodney Kent 25.00

Cigarette Box, Arthur Armour, pine bough dec 32.00

Cocktail Shaker, Continental, 12" h, cork lined top, No. 530 . . . . 40.00

Creamer and Sugar, Everlast, hammered, open mark, No. 5018, pr 12.00

Crumb Tray, Wendell August Forge, zinnia design, No. 705 . . . . 28.00

Ice Bucket, Canterbury Arts, 8" h, hammered, double walled, rubber seal 45.00

Lazy Susan, Everlast, 14½" d, 7" d recess, Rose and Forget-Me-Not pattern, open mark, No.5063 . . . . 15.00

Meat Platter, Everlast, rect, oval center well with tree, grape leaf dec in corners, two handles 42.00

Napkin Holder, Rodney Kent, hammered, decorative floral bands and feet. 10.00

Nut Bowl, Continental, 11" d, Wild Rose pattern, No. 1011 . . . . 12.00

Pitcher, Cromwell, 2 qt, hammered, looped ice guard 25.00

Relish Dish, Everlast, 7¾" d, glass bowl, aluminum underliner, Bali Bamboo pattern, open mark. 10.00

Sandwich Tray, Wendell August Forge, 11" w, eight-sided, dogwood design 20.00

Silent Butler, Buenilum, 6½" d, hammered, mkd "Handwrought" 15.00

Tidbit Tray, Hammercraft Hand Hammered, 7½" d, grape cluster design, looped finger hold. 5.00

Tiered Tray, Wrought Farberware, two circular tiers with beaded edges, flower, stem, and cascading stamen design handle and stand 14.00

Waste Basket, Arthur Armour, dogwood and butterfly dec. 135.00

AMERICAN CHINA DINNERWARE

There is a growing appreciation for the thousands of dinnerware patterns that graced the tables of low-, middle-, and some upper-income families during the first three-quarters of the twentieth century. Some of America's leading industrial designers were responsible for forms and decorative motifs.

Collectors fall into three groups: those who collect the wares of a specific factory or factories, often with a strong regional emphasis; individuals who are reassembling the set they grew up with; and those who are fascinated by certain forms and motifs. The bulk of the books on the subject appeared in the early 1980s. Prices stabilized in the mid-1980s and remain so today.

Several of the companies have become established collecting categories in their own right. This is why you will find companies such as Blue Ridge and Hall elsewhere in this book.

Franciscan, Apple pattern, compote, marked "Franciscan Hand Dec Oven Safe," 8" d, 4" h, $24.00.

COORS

Coors Pottery was manufactured in Golden, CO, from 1920 to 1939.

Rosebud
Baking Pan, 12¼ × 8¾"	20.00
Bean Pot, cov, yellow	22.00
Cake Plate	18.00
Cereal Bowl, 6" d, yellow	12.00
Custard Cup, blue	12.00
Mixing Bowl, handle, orange	25.00
Plate	
6" d, bread and butter	10.00
9" d, dinner	12.00
Teapot, rose	50.00
Utility Jar, cov, yellow	25.00

CROOKSVILLE

The Crooksville China Company, Crooksville, OH, was founded in 1902 for the manufacture of artware including vases, flowerpots, and novelties. Dinnerware soon became its stock and trade. Manufacture continued until 1959.

Pantry Bak-In Ware, 1931
Bean Pot	20.00
Cake Plate	6.00
Custard Cup	2.50
Leftover, 6" d, round	7.50
Pie Baker	7.50
Tray, 9" sq	5.00

Petit Point House
Berry Bowl, small	4.00
Bowl, 6" d	5.00
Cup	4.50
Plate	
6" d	4.00
7" d	5.00
9" d	8.00
Saucer	2.00

EDWIN M. KNOWLES CHINA COMPANY

Dinnerware was produced by this company in East Liverpool, OH, from 1900 to 1963.

Deanna, 1938
Butter	10.00
Coaster	8.00
Creamer	5.00
Cup and Saucer	5.00
Egg Cup	5.00
Pickle Dish	3.00
Plate, 9" d	4.50
Soup, lug handle	4.00
Sugar	8.50

Yorktown, 1936
Bowl, 5½" d, yellow	3.75
Casserole, cov	15.00
Creamer, rust	4.50
Cup and Saucer	4.50

Plate, 10" d	4.00
Sugar	6.00

FRANCISCAN

Produced by Gladding McBean and Co, CA, 1934 to the present.

Apple
Bowl	
6½" d	9.00
8½" d	20.00
Butter Dish, cov	17.50
Chop Plate, 13" d	50.00
Compote	80.00
Creamer	25.00
Cup and Saucer	10.00
Egg Cup	12.50
Fruit Bowl	6.00
Pitcher, 9" h	40.00
Plate	
6½" d	5.00
7½" d	7.00
10½" d	10.00
Platter, 12" l	30.00
Relish	20.00
Sherbet	9.50
Spoon Rest	12.00
Sugar, cov	35.00
Teapot, repaired lid	35.00

California Poppy
Creamer	22.00
Cup and Saucer	25.00
Plate, 10" d	25.00
Sugar, cov	35.00

Desert Rose
Butter Pat	12.00
Casserole, cov	85.00
Coffeepot, cov	75.00
Creamer and Sugar, cov	35.00
Cup and Saucer	12.00
Demitasse Cup and Saucer	45.00
Gravy, attached underplate	35.00
Mug	15.00
Plate	
Bread and Butter	5.00
Dinner	6.50
Salad Bowl, 9" d	30.00
Salt Shaker, rosebud	10.00
Soup Plate	7.00

Duet Rose
Ashtray, individual	12.00
Creamer	6.00
Cup, green rim	2.00
Gravy, underplate	15.00
Plate	
Bread and Butter	5.00
Dinner	12.00
Salad	9.00
Platter, 15" l	16.00
Relish, 7" l, handle	9.00
Salt and Pepper Shakers, pr	12.00
Saucer	1.50
Sugar, cov	8.00
Vegetable Bowl, divided	22.00

El Patio
- Cereal Bowl, yellow gloss 5.00
- Creamer, Redwood Brown 8.00
- Cup, Redwood Brown 5.00
- Gravy, yellow gloss 20.00
- Vegetable Bowl, divided, green gloss 15.00

Meadow Rose
- Cereal, ftd 28.00
- Platter
  - 13" l 42.00
  - 14½" l 55.00
- Vase, bud 95.00
- Vegetable Bowl, 8" l 38.00

Pebble Beach
- Cereal Bowl, 6" d 9.00
- Coffee Pot, cov 45.00
- Creamer 12.00
- Gravy, liner 35.00
- Vegetable Bowl, large 15.00

Strawberry Fair
- Creamer 25.00
- Cup and Saucer 25.00
- Plate
  - 8" d 20.00
  - 10" d 25.00
- Sugar, cov 32.00

METLOX

Metlox Potteries was founded in Manhattan Beach, CA, in 1927 and is currently still producing artware, novelties, and Poppytrail dinnerware.

Antique Grape
- Bread and Butter Plate 6.00
- Cup and Saucer 15.00
- Platter, 14" l 22.00

California Ivy
- Coaster 5.00
- Creamer 6.50
- Cup and Saucer 6.50
- Gravy 12.00
- Mug 8.00
- Plate, 8" d 6.00
- Salad Bowl, 11¼" d 12.00
- Vegetable, 11" d, divided 17.50

Provincial Fruit
- Bowl
  - 5" d, tab handle 4.00
  - 6" d 4.00
- Butter Dish, cov 25.00
- Coffee Pot 45.00
- Creamer 7.00
- Cup and Saucer 8.00
- Plate, 10½" d 8.50
- Platter, 14" l 20.00
- Soup Plate, 8½" d 8.00

Sculptured Grape
- Cereal Bowl, 6" d 15.00
- Creamer and Sugar, cov 18.00
- Cup and Saucer 22.00
- Relish, two part 20.00
- Salad Plate 9.00

- Soup, flat 18.00
- Vegetable Bowl, divided 45.00

PURINTON

Purinton Pottery was founded by Bernard Purinton in Wellsville, OH, in 1936. The pottery ceased operations around 1959.

Apple
- Berry Bowl 6.50
- Canister, cov 22.00
- Casserole, cov, oval 20.00
- Coffeepot, cov 25.00
- Cookie Jar, cov 35.00
- Creamer 10.00
- Cup and Saucer 6.00
- Honey Pot, 7" d 10.00
- Plate, 9" d, dinner 6.00
- Relish, divided 20.00
- Salt and Pepper Shakers, pr 15.00
- Sugar, cov 18.00

Fruits
- Casserole, crimped cov 30.00
- Relish, three part, clover shape 30.00

ROYAL CHINA COMPANY

Royal China Company began production of dinnerware in Sebring, OH, in 1934 and continues to the present.

Colonial Homestead
- Bowl
  - 5½" d 3.00
  - 6¼" d 5.00
- Casserole, cov 30.00
- Creamer and Sugar 12.00
- Cup and Saucer 4.00
- Gravy, underplate 18.00
- Plate
  - Bread and Butter, 6¼" d 1.50
  - Dinner, 10" d 3.50
  - Salad, 7" d 2.50
- Salt and Pepper Shakers, pr 10.00
- Serving Plate, 10" d, tab handle 12.00
- Soup, flat 3.00
- Teapot, cov 35.00

Currier & Ives, blue and white
- Ashtray 10.00
- Berry Bowl 3.00
- Cake Plate, 10½" d 6.50
- Creamer 5.00
- Cup and Saucer 3.00
- Gravy 8.00
- Pie Plate, 10" d 15.00
- Plate, dinner 3.50
- Platter, 13" l 12.50
- Salt Shaker 6.00
- Soup, flat 4.00
- Sugar, cov 8.00

Memory Lane, pink and white
- Berry Bowl 4.00
- Cake Plate, tab handle 12.00
- Creamer 4.00

Cup and Saucer	3.50
Plate	
6″ d, bread and butter	2.00
10″ d, dinner	4.00
Soup, flat	4.00
Sugar, cov	5.00
Tumbler	
Old Fashioned glass	4.00
Water, 5½″ h	4.00
Old Curiosity Shop, green and white	
Bowl	
5½″ d	1.25
9″ d	6.00
Creamer	3.00
Cup and Saucer	3.00
Plate	
Bread and Butter	2.00
Dinner, 10½″ d	5.00
Salt and Pepper Shakers, pr	8.00
Soup	3.50
Sugar, cov	6.00

AMUSEMENT PARKS

From the park at the end of the trolley line to today's gigantic theme parks such as Six Flags Great Adventure, amusement parks have served many generations. No trip to an amusement park was complete without a souvenir, many of which are now collectible.

Prices are still modest in this new collecting field. When an item is returned to the area where the park was located, it often brings a twenty to fifty percent premium.

Box, Goff's Atlantic City Salt Water Taffy, blue tones, woman in orange swimsuit, 8⅞″ l, $6.00.

Ashtray, 7½″ d, Disneyland, ceramic, brown, green marbleized recessed center section, raised images of Haunted Mansion, Monorail, Sleeping Beauty Castle, Jungle Cruise, Mark Twain, c1960 .... 25.00
Baggage Tag, silvered brass, emb "Coney Island," numbered "1904," c1920 ... 25.00
Book, *Walt Disney's Guide to Disneyland*, 8 × 11½″, 28 pgs, 1960, full color 30.00

Butter Dish, cov, Lancaster Fair, ruby stained glass, Button Arches pattern, 1916 .... 150.00
Game, Disneyland Riverboat Game, Parker Bros, 8 × 16 × 1½″ box, minor use wear, c1955 .... 50.00
Hat, Disneyland, Mouseketeers, stiff black felt, large black plastic ears, white, blue, and orange "Disneyland/ Mickey Mouse" patch, c1960 .... 25.00
Lunch Box
Disney World, orig Aladdin cardboard tag, thermos, c1972 .... 40.00
Ludwig Von Drake in Disneyland, emb steel, orig thermos, Aladdin, 1961 copyright, slight use wear 100.00
Magazine, *Disneyland Vacationland Summer 1970*, 8½ × 11″, 20 pgs, light general wear 18.50
Medal, Coney Island, steeplechase face, orig ribbon, 1924 .... 90.00
Pennant
Coney Island, 24″ l, maroon felt, white title, yellow, green, orange, and white scene of Steeplechase Pool, amusement rides, Luna Mill Sky Chaser building, c1930 .... 20.00
Hershey Park, felt, brown ground, white letters, c1950 .... 25.00
Photograph, 8 × 10″, Coney Island, glossy, park scene, orig 50.00
Pinback Button
Asbury Park, 1¼″ d, black and white, bathing beach scene, c1900 .... 10.00
Coney Island
1¼″ d, multicolored, bathing beauty center, rim reads "Citizens Committee of Coney Island," c1915 .... 35.00
1¾″ d, multicolored, Brooklyn, Coney Island, Arverne, center scene of ladies swimming, rim reads "Swimming Taught In Six Lessons By MacLevy Quick Trolley System," c1900 .... 150.00
Dreamland Park, NY, white lettering, red ground, 1900s 5.00
Hershey Park, multicolored, child emerging from cocoa bean, c1905 .... 35.00
Luna Park, Washington, DC, multicolored, six adults on park ride, 1910s 35.00
Post Card
Coney Island, 1920 scene of entrance gate 10.00
The Great Allentown Fair, Allentown, PA, Dan Patch race horse illus, 1906 .... 75.00
Poster, Coney Island, 1911 Mardi Gras 450.00
Salt and Pepper Shakers, pr, Disneyland, orig 2 × 4″ tray with raised name, white metal, silver and gold metallic

finish, fit together to form castle, orig cork and "Japan" sticker, c1950 . . . . . 35.00

Sign, 36" l, Coney Island, porcelain, arrow shape 350.00

Stereograph, Asbury Park, NJ, 1870s . . . 10.00

Sweater Guard, Disneyland, cardboard case, clear plastic slipcover, bright brass chain, two brass star-shaped charms with pink glass stones, "Disneyland" spelled out in brass, c1960. . . . . 40.00

Ticket

Coney Island, Steeplechase 30.00

Disneyland, paper, black and purple illus, $4.75 adult admission ticket, checklist of attractions on back, c1960. . . . . 15.00

Toy, windup

Double Loop-the-Loop Roller Coaster, McDowell, figural man driving car, 1920s, MIB 425.00

Ferris Wheel, Chein, 1930s 350.00

Mickey Mouse Ferris Wheel, Chein. . . 450.00

View-master Reel

Disneyland/Fantasyland, 4½" sq color envelope, three reels, sealed package, Sawyer, c1960 . . . . 30.00

Mickey Mouse Club Circus Visits Disneyland, color envelope, three reels, #856-A-B-C, 1956 Disney copyright 35.00

ANIMAL DISHES, COVERED

Covered animal dishes were a favorite of housewives during the first half of the twentieth century. Grandmother Rinker and her sisters had numerous hens on nests scattered throughout their homes. They liked the form. It did not make any difference how old or new they were. Reproductions and copycats abound. You have to be alert for these late examples.

Look for unusual animals and forms. Many early examples were enhanced through hand painted decorations. Pieces with painting in excellent condition command a premium.

Cat, lacy base, glass eyes. 120.00

Chick and Eggs, 11" h, emerging chick, Atterbury, white milk glass 185.00

Dog, patterned quilt top, white milk glass, sgd Vallerystahl 175.00

Duck, 6" l, Mama Quack, Jeannette Glass Co, crystal, hp eyes and bill, 1950s. 15.00

Eagle, on nest, banner reads: "The American Hen," white milk glass 85.00

Elephant, Jumbo

4 × 7", reissue, Indiana Glass Co, crystal, 1981. . . . . 20.00

Reclining Cat, milk glass, ribbed base, imp "3" on base int., 5⅜" w, $65.00.

6 × 13", Co-Operative Flint Glass Co, ruby glass, 1920s–30s 200.00

Fish, 8¾" l, walking, detailed scales, red glass eyes, white milk glass 175.00

Frog, sitting, Co-Operative Flint Glass Co, green glass, 1920s–30s 85.00

Hen

6½" l, blue, frosted, quilted base 75.00

7½" l, Atterbury, white and deep blue marbleized glass, lacy base 165.00

Lovebirds, blue milk glass 55.00

Rabbit

4½" l, rect, narrow stylized head, emb features, footed, pink frosted glass, underside emb: Dermay-Fifth Avenue-New York-970. . . . . 225.00

6" l, white frosted glass. 70.00

ANIMAL FIGURINES

Animal collectors are a breed apart. Collecting is a love affair. As long as their favorite animal is pictured or modeled, they willingly buy the item. In many cases, they own a real-life counterpart to go with their objects. My personal zoo includes a tarantula, lovebird, two rabbits, a Golden Ball python, and three tanks of tropical fish.

Clubs: Canine Collectibles Club of America, 736 N Western Ave, Suite 314, Lake Forest, IL 60045; Cat Collectors, 31311 Blair Drive, Warren, MI 48092; Equine Collectors Club, Box 4764 New River Stage II, Phoenix, AZ 85027; The Frog Pond, P. O. Box 193, Beech Grove, IN 46107; The National Elephant Collectors

Society, 380 Medford St, Somerville, MA 02145; Russell's Owl Collector Club, P. O. Box 1291, Bandon, OR 97411.

Dog, Goss Crested Ware, Arcadian China, England, 2⅝" h, $20.00.

Bird, 12" h, ruby, head pointing down, long tail, Viking Glass, c1960 . . . . **30.00**
Cat, Persian, white, Royal Doulton #2539 . . . .**150.00**
Dog, Whippet, Morton Studios, c1940. . . . . **80.00**
Duck, 5" h, vaseline, Viking Glass, c1960. . . . . **20.00**
Elephant, 6½" h, Oriental jar on back, Cliftwood **60.00**
Frog, reclining, wearing jacket. **15.00**
Goose, 2" h, white, gold dec, Midwest Pottery. **6.00**
Horse, Percheron, dapple gray, Breyer **50.00**
Kitten, 3" l, white kitten on brown shoe, Japan. **9.00**
Owl, carnival glass, Mosser **18.00**
Pheasant, ringneck, 11½" h, crystal, K R Haley, 1947 . . . . **20.00**
Pig, sitting in Dutch shoe **35.00**
Pony, ceramic, Wade, Tom Smith artist **15.00**
Pouter Pigeon, 2½" h, light blue frosted glass, Westmoreland Glass, c1970 . . . . **25.00**
Puppy, aqua, Red Wing **15.00**
Reindeer, celluloid, pink accents, Occupied Japan. **12.00**
Rooster, 9" h, amber, head down, Kemple **30.00**
Swan, 3¾" h, Occupied Japan **10.00**
Unicorn, black, Vernon Kilns. **180.00**

APPLIANCES, ELECTRICAL

Nothing shows our ability to take a relatively simple task, e.g., toasting a piece of bread, and create a wealth of different forms to achieve it. Electrical appliances are viewed as one of the best documents of stylistic design in utilitarian form.

Collectors tend to concentrate on one form. Toasters are the most commonly collected, largely because several books have been written about them. Electric fans have a strong following. Waffle irons are pressing toasters for popularity. Modernistic collectors seek bar drink blenders from the 1930s through the 1950s.

Clubs: American Fan Collector's Association, P. O. Box 804, South Bend, IN 46624; Electric Breakfast Club, P. O. Box 306, White Mills, PA 18473.

Toaster, Challenge, two slice, Art Deco design, chrome plated, $20.00.

Broiler, Royal Master Appliance Co, Miriam, Oh, 1930s **25.00**
Butter Churn, Mixmaster, stainless steel, wood paddles, clear glass jar, 4 qt **35.00**
Coffee Grinder, Kitchen Aide. **65.00**
Coffee Maker
  Dripolator, Silex, 13" h, 2 pcs, glass, Bakelite holder, 1930s **18.00**
  Percolator, Royal Rochester, 10" h, nickel plated copper, black wooden handles, #366 B-29, 1920s **15.00**
  Sunbeam Coffee Master, 12½" h, 2 pcs, chrome, Bakelite handles and base, 1939–44 . . . . **25.00**
Drink Mixer, Made-Rite, Weining Co, Cleveland, OH, 1930s **20.00**
Egg Cooker, Hanskcraft Co, Madison, WI, 5¼" d, cream china base, aluminum top, late 1930s **15.00**
Fan
  General Electric
    Brass blade, steel guard. **80.00**
    Steel blade, steel guard, 12" h **45.00**
    Whiz, brass blade, steel guard. **90.00**
  Polar Cub, A C Gilbert, brass plated blades, steel guard. **60.00**

Starrite, brass plated blades, steel guard 50.00

Westinghouse
Brass blades, brass guard 115.00
Brass blades, steel guard 80.00
Whirlwind 50.00

Flour Sifter, Miracle Electric Co, ivory metal body, push button above blue wooden handle, decal label, unused, 1930s 35.00

Hot Plate, Edison/Hotpoint, New York, Chicago and Ontario, copper heat control, 1910s 25.00

Iron, Sunbeam, "Iron Master," 2¾ lb chrome body, steam attachment, orig box, unused, #52, 1940s 40.00

Mixer, Handy Hannah, natural wooden handle, single shaft, quart jar base, Cat #495, late 1930s 22.00

Popcorn Popper, Knapp-Monarch, oil type, aluminum body, wire base, domed glass lid with vented sides, walnut handles, measuring cup, Cat #12A-500B, 1930–1940 . . . . 20.00

Tea Kettle, Mirro, aluminum, 4 qt, nickel chrome domed body, Bakelite handle, 1930s 20.00

Toaster
Electrahot Mfg Co, Minneapolis, c1934 . . . . 20.00
Hotpoint Model 115T1, marked "Royal Rochester," 1919–23 . . . . . . 65.00
Manning Bowman, nickel body, double wire mechanical turnover doors, Bakelite knobs, #1225, 1926 . . . . . . 35.00
Star-Rite Extra Fast Toaster, Fitzgerald Mfg Co, Torrington, CT, 1925–30 . . . . 20.00
Thermax, No. 1941, Economy model, black painted base 35.00

Waffle Iron, Universal, horizontal type, 8 × 4½" rect top, nickel, black wooden handles, two-headed cord 75.00

Whipper
Kenmore, Sears, Roebuck & Co, Chicago, IL, cream metal dome top, dark blue Bakelite knob, clear glass bottom, 1940s 15.00
Knapp Monarch, 9½" h, red plastic handle, mid 1930s 25.00

AQUARIUM COLLECTIBLES

You don't have to be all wet to collect aquarium-related items. Old filtering systems, heaters, and decorative accessories as well as the containers themselves provide an overwhelming array of collecting possibilities.

Aquariums aren't just for fish. They also provide a home to air-breathers such as lizards and snakes. Terrariums, with their animal habitats, rock heaters, and strange plants, are reminiscent of a prehistoric tropical forest—a wonderful environment for any collector.

Accessory
Dragon, ceramic, three parts, Japan 2.00
Sunken Ship, plastic, bubble stone . . . 3.00

Air Pump, Second Nature Whisper 600, 10–15 gal. 3.00

Aquarium Heater, Aquarium Systems, 20–30 gal. 15.00

Goldfish Bowl Stand
Ceramic, television lamp, black cat, sitting with front paw raised, green tree stump base, 1920s 45.00
Chalkware, 9½" h, cat sitting on haunches, peering into bowl, 1930s 65.00
Pottery, white cat, sitting, looking in bowl, "Wistful Kitten," Camark Pottery 25.00

Reptile Heater, Hot Rock, stone 5.00

Tank
10 gal 5.00
20 gal 20.00

Tank Hood, Perfecto, iridescent light, 10 gal 7.00

Water Filter System, Whisper Second Nature Power Filter, 15–20 gal 20.00

ASHTRAYS

Most price guides include ashtrays under advertising. The problem is that there are a number of terrific ashtrays in shapes that have absolutely nothing to do with advertising. Ashtrays get a separate category from me.

With the nonsmoking movement gaining strength, the ashtray is an endangered species. The time to collect them is now.

Advertising, Federal Pumps, blue pump, tan base, Huekel China Co, El Monte, CA, 8 × 6⅛ × 3", $28.00.

Advertising
BF Goodrich Silvertone, tire form,
    green insert 30.00
Cliff House, San Francisco, shell, li-
    tho 15.00
General Electric Motor 15.00
Kelly Springfield, tire form, green in-
    sert, heavy duty 30.00
Mountain States Telephone & Tele-
    graph, granite 85.00
Moxie, ceramic, white, Moxie man
    dec 25.00
Old Judge Coffee, tin 90.00
Penn Rubber Co, tire shape 12.00
Salem Cigarettes, tin, emb 8.00
Sombrero Tequila 8.00
Winston Cigarettes, tin, emb 8.00
Airplane, chrome 35.00
Bird, chrome, Art Deco, figural 18.00
Black Cat, open mouth, Shafford la-
    bel 20.00
Cloisonne, 5" d, blue, covered match
    holder 70.00
Cowboy Hat, lusterware 15.00
Devil Head, bronze, open mouth 75.00
Fiesta Ware, green 25.00
Fish, Frankoma Pottery 15.00
Frog, 4½" h, porcelain, sitting, Japan . . . 20.00
Glass, 3½" h, sq, blue, Fire King 8.00
Hand, leaf dec, yellow, McCoy Pottery,
    1941 . . . . 6.50
Hat, figural, blue 7.50
Playboy, 1960 . . . . 15.00
Saddle on Fence, copper 15.00
Scottish Terrier, 4½" h, 5¾" w, figural,
    glass insert 25.00
Skillet, Griswold #00 . . . . 22.00
Spade, 4½" d, dark blue, white cupids
    dec, marked "Wedgwood" 30.00
Tire, amber insert, cigarette rests 35.00
Triangle Shape, 3½" d, apple blossom
    dec, marked "Town/Hand Made Alu-
    minum" 4.00
Vargas Girl, tin, 1950s 10.00
Wagner, round 45.00

AUTOGRAPHS

Collecting autographs is a centuries-old
hobby. A good rule to follow is the more
recognizable the person, the more likely
the autograph is to have value. Content is
a big factor in valuing autograph material.
A clipped signature is worth far less than a
lengthy handwritten document by the
same person.

Before spending big money for an autograph, have it authenticated. Many movie
and sports stars have secretaries and other
individuals sign their material, especially
photographs. An autopen is a machine
that can sign up to a dozen documents at
one time. The best proof that a signature is
authentic is to get it from the person who
stood there and watched the celebrity sign
it.

Clubs: Manuscript Society, 350 Niagara
St, Burbank, CA 95105; Universal Auto-
graph Collectors Club, P. O. Box 6181,
Washington, DC, 20044.

PIA ZADORA

Pia Zadora, black and white glossy, personal-
ized, 8 × 10", $10.00.

Abdul-Kareem Jabbar, and Julius Irving,
    first day cover 45.00
Anka, Paul, 8 × 10" black and white
    glossy photo 10.00
Brothers, Joyce, first day cover 10.00
Buchwald, Art, first day cover 10.00
Bush, George, 8 × 10" black and white
    glossy, inscription, sentiment and sig-
    nature on lower white border 450.00
Chamberlain, Wilt, 8 × 10" black and
    white glossy photo 30.00
Crosby, Cathy Lee, 8 × 10" black and
    white glossy 10.00
Diller, Phyllis, 5 × 7" black and white
    glossy 5.00
Farrow, Mia, 5 × 7" black and white
    glossy 5.00
Ford, Gerald, 11 × 13" color photo, bust
    pose 75.00
Glenn, John, Alan Shepard, and Deke
    Slayton, plain 5 × 3" light green
    card 65.00
Hoover, Herbert, 11 × 12" color Sunday
    supplement picture, seated at desk on
    87th birthday, signed on desk area . . . 125.00
Kroc, Joan, 5 × 7" color photo 20.00

Lawford, Peter, black and white snapshot	65.00
Lee, Stan, 2 × 2" color collector card	10.00
McDowell, Roddy, 5 × 7" color photo	5.00
O'Brien, Hugh, 8 × 10" black and white glossy photo	10.00
Pavarotti, Luciano, 8 × 10" black and white glossy photo	25.00
Perot, Ross, 5 × 3" white plain card	75.00
Price, Vincent, 5 × 7" black and white glossy	5.00
Quayle, Marilyn, 8 × 10" color photo	45.00
Rashad, Phylicia, 8 × 10" black and white glossy photo	10.00
Russell, Jane, 8 × 10" black and white glossy photo	10.00
Sarandon, Susan, 5 × 7" color photo	5.00
Slayton, Deke, 8 × 10" color NASA photo of Shuttle Enterprises on launch pad, huge signature	25.00
Snead, Sam, first day cover	50.00
Vinton, Bobby, 8 × 10" black and white glossy photo	10.00
Welch, Racquel, 5 × 7" color photo	5.00

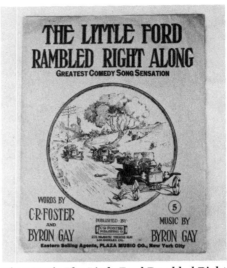

Sheet Music, **The Little Ford Rambled Right Along,** *words by C. R. Foster and Byron Gay, music by Bryon Gay, published by C. R. Foster, $15.00.*

AUTOMOBILE COLLECTIBLES

AUTO PARTS AND ACCESSORIES

An automobile swap meet is twenty-five percent cars and seventy-five percent car parts. Restoration and rebuilding of virtually all car models is never-ending. The key is to find the exact part needed.

All too often, auto parts at flea markets are not priced. The seller is going to judge how badly he thinks you want the part before setting the price. You have to keep your cool.

Two areas that are attracting outside collector interest are promotional toy models and hood ornaments. The former have been part of the craze for 1950s and 1960s Japanese tin. The latter have been discovered by the art community, who view them as wonderful examples of modern streamlined design.

Periodical: *Hemmings Motor News*, Box 100, Bennington, VT 05201.

Ashtray, Buick, dash type	20.00
Carburetor, Buick, 1924–1925	25.00
Clock, Motor, "Luna," 8-day, luminous dial, brass and bronze, 1914	120.00
Engine	
Maxwell, 1914	200.00
Packard, 1935	800.00
Gearshift Knob, glass swirl, blue and white	15.00
Grill, Packard, 1941	125.00
Headlamp, 12" d, bull's-eye, Marchal	700.00
Hood Ornament	
Dodge Ram, 8" l	35.00
Lion, dated 1924	30.00
Rolls Royce, sgd, 1926	500.00
Horn, Pierce Arrow, 1915–1920, cowl-mounted, correct bracket	175.00
Hubcaps, Plymouth, 1939–1940, set of 4	250.00
License Plate, North Dakota, orig wrapper, 1933, pr	7.50
License Plate Emblem, Mobil flying horse, unused	15.00
Owner's Manual, Ford, Model T, 1914	15.00
Radiator Ornament	
Buick, front grill emblem, 1934	30.00
Hubmobile Nash	25.00
Plymouth, 1933	45.00
Pontiac, feather headdress, 1958	15.00
Reo, colorful	30.00
Willys Knight	25.00
Radio, Cadillac, 1937	250.00
Reference Guide, 1931 Buick	15.00
Trunk, Packard, 18 × 36", pre-WWII, metal	450.00
Shop and Parts Manual	
Cadillac, 1941	110.00
DeSoto, master, 1936	45.00
Tube Patcher, Cameo	10.00
Visor, 1932 Ford, full length	125.00

SALES AND PROMOTIONAL ITEMS

Ashtray	
Chrysler, 4" d, brass, emb name and lightning bolts, raised rim, 1930s	20.00

Goodyear, tire, amber glass wheel center. **30.00**
Pontiac-Chief of the Sixes, 3 × 5½",
brass, raised image, 1930s. **25.00**
Blotter
Goodyear Tires **5.00**
Kelly Tires, 1910s **28.00**
"Smooth as a '47 Ford," nude baby,
bottom up **20.00**
Book
Ford at Fifty, 106 pgs, Simon &
Schuster, 1903–53 50th anniversary **20.00**
Starting, Lighting, Ignitions, Harold
Morley, 800 pgs, leather bound,
c1920. . . . . **50.00**
Booklet, Chevy, Soap Box Derby Rules,
illus, 1939 . . . . **20.00**
Brochure, dealer, fold out
Buick
1933, Series 90, orig photos, 8 × 10",
black and white **7.00**
1957. . . . . **24.00**
Chevrolet
1937, prices shown for. several
models **40.00**
1949. . . . . **25.00**
Chrysler, Town & Country, 1946. . . . . **26.00**
DeSoto, 1957. **20.00**
Dodge, 1957 . . . . **20.00**
Ford, color pictures, nine different
models, prices, 1929 . . . . **85.00**
Franklin Car, 1921 . . . . **45.00**
Plymouth Valiant, 1970 . . . . **10.00**
Studebaker **35.00**
Calendar, 14 × 22", 1986 Century of the
Automobile, chronological photos of
classic automobiles with historical
news photos, 12 pgs **16.00**
Candy Container, car, glass, paper closure, includes candy **35.00**
Catalog
American Gear, 256 pgs, auto parts,
1925. . . . . **45.00**
Auburn, 9 × 16", part color, 16 pgs,
1935. . . . . **35.00**
Kissel Kar, 10 × 13", 36 pgs. **125.00**
Magazine Advertisement, Wayne Cut
278, 1912 . . . . **85.00**
Match Holder, Exide Battery & Goodyear
Tire, orig box **35.00**
Pinback Button
Buick, "Looking Fine For 39". **45.00**
Chevrolet, 1¼" d, black and white,
1930s **22.00**
Pocket Mirror, Studebaker Vehicle
Works, South Bend, IN, 2¾" oval,
1910. . . . .**125.00**
Post Card, DeSoto, full color, one with
four-door sedan, other with two-door
sedan, 1939, pr **8.00**
Poster, Buick, "Kansas City," 25 × 38",
black and white, 1921–1922,. **85.00**
Program, Indy 500, 1953 . . . . **40.00**

Routing Chart, 10", movable, orig envelope, 1936 . . . . **25.00**
Shoulder Patch, Oldsmobile Service, emblem, c1940. **23.00**
Sign, dealer's
Ford, neon. **750.00**
United Motor, neon outline of
early auto **1,250.00**
Tie Tack, 1953 Chevrolet, gold colored
metal, Chevrolet form, orig card **15.00**
Viewer, Chrysler with the Hundred Million Dollar Look, 2" l, plastic,
keychain loop, inscription on one side,
c1955. . . . . **15.00**

AUTUMN LEAF

The Hall China Company developed Autumn Leaf china as a dinnerware premium
for the Jewel Tea Company in 1933. The
giveaway was extremely successful. The
"Autumn Leaf" name did not originate
until 1960. Previously, the pattern was
simply known as "Jewel" or "Autumn."
Autumn Leaf remained in production until 1978.

Pieces were added and dropped from the
line over the years. Limited production
pieces are most desirable. Look for matching accessories in glass, metal, and plastic
made by other companies. They also made
Jewel Tea toy trucks.

Club: National Autumn Leaf Collector's
Society, 120 West Dowell Road, McHenry,
IL 60050.

Bowl
6½" d, cereal. **8.50**
8½" d, soup. **10.00**

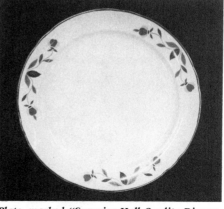

*Plate, marked "Superior Hall Quality Dinnerware, Tested and Approved by Mary Dunbar
Jewel Makers Institute," 9¼" d, $12.00.*

Cake Plate	20.00
Canister Set, sq, 4 pcs	125.00
Casserole Dish	25.00
Coffeepot, electrical	240.00
Cookie Jar	90.00
Creamer	8.00
Cup	7.00
Custard Cup	6.50
Drip Jar	20.00
Fruitcake Tin	5.00
Gravy Boat	18.00
Jug, ball	30.00
Mixing Bowl, nested set of 3	40.00
Mug, ftd	75.00
Pepper Shaker, handle	10.00
Pie Baker	19.00

Plate
6" d, bread and butter	4.00
8" d, salad	8.50
10" d, dinner	9.00
Platter, 11½" l, oval	15.00
Salad Bowl	17.00
Saucer	4.00
Sugar, vertical lines	20.00
Tablecloth, 54" sq, sailcloth, slight damage	40.00
Tea Towel	20.00
Tidbit Tray, three tiers	40.00
Toaster Cover, plastic	20.00
Tray, metal, oval	50.00
Vase, bud	150.00
Vegetable Dish, divided	55.00

AVIATION COLLECTIBLES

Now is the time to get into aviation collectibles. The airline mergers and bankruptcies have produced a wealth of obsolete material. There were enormous crowds at Eastern's liquidation sale in spring 1991. I have a bunch of stuff from Piedmont and Peoples, two airlines that flew off into the sunset in the 1980s.

The wonderful thing about airline collectibles is that most of them initially were free. I try to make it a point to pick up several items, from bathroom soap to playing cards, each time I fly. Save the things most likely to be thrown out.

Club: The World Airline Historical Society, 3381 Apple Tree Lane, Erlanger, KY 41018.

Ashtray, Convair B-36, chromed metal, military bomber, chrome base, lift-out black glass tray, inscribed "Convair B-36/Consolidated Vultee Aircraft Corporation" ... 100.00
Book
Principals American Technical Society ... 15.00

Plaque, 100,000 Mile United Airlines, 1955, 6½" w, 8½" h, $25.00.

Heroes of Aviation, Laurence LaTourette Driggs, dj, 1927 ... 20.00
Booklet, *Man Has Learned To Fly,* 4 × 6", Monarch Food Products, copyright 1929, 24 pgs ... 25.00
Calendar Plate, 6½" d, biplane, 1912 ... 35.00
Figure, 4" h, tin ... 25.00
Flatware
Flagship, fork and spoon, silverplate, streamlined propeller plane handles, 1930s ... 25.00
United Airlines, fork, knife, and spoon, 1950–60 ... 25.00
Folder, 4 × 6", Beech-Nut Autogiro ... 45.00
Jacket, stewardess, American Airlines, navy, seven insignia buttons, designer's label, 1950s ... 15.00
Necklace, emb aluminum charm, airship "Akron," enameled beige and black background, 1930s ... 75.00
Pen, Allegheny Airlines ... 5.00
Pilot Wings, US Air Force, senior, wing with star, SS ... 35.00
Pin
Flight Commemorative, Spirit of St Louis, New York to Paris, May 21, 1927, emb, brass ... 25.00
Stewardess, Eastern Airlines ... 25.00
Western Airlines Jr Stewardess, silvered metal, totem style wing feathers and Indian symbol, 1960s ... 12.50
Pinback Button
American Airlines, wing, lead, 1940s ... 125.00
British Overseas Airways Corps Junior Jet Club, brass, wings, blue enameled symbol, 1960s ... 15.00

Northwest Airlines, US Airmail Official
Carrier, half wing, 1950s **75.00**
TWA Junior Pilot, brass, red accented
initials, 1960s **12.50**
Plate, 7½" d, hot air balloon dec, Li-
moges, set of 4.................... **75.00**
Post Card, set of 12, Dirigible &
Lakehurst, Lakehurst Naval Air Sta-
tion in NJ and USS Los Angeles She-
nandoah Dirigbles scenes, numbered,
unused, 1930s....................**200.00**
Propeller, 32" l, wood, marked "Kroeh-
ler" **50.00**
Puzzle, American Airlines, 707 jet in
flight, frame tray, Milton Bradley,
1960 copyright **15.00**
Shot Glass, Eastern Airlines **2.00**
Tapestry, 19 × 52", Charles Lindbergh,
New York City skyline, Spirit of St
Louis center, and Paris skyline,
France **175.00**
Toy, adv, Eastern Whisper Jet, 7" l,
Aero.......................... **18.00**
Tray, Pan American Airlines, tin litho. . . **30.00**
Umbrella, Capital Airlines **100.00**
Watch Fob, 1¼ × 1½", silvered white
metal, raised illus of single-wing pas-
senger plane, c1920 .... **18.00**

AVON BOTTLES

Back in the late 1960s, my mother worked
briefly as an Avon lady. If only she had
saved one example of every product she
sold! I am not certain that she would be
rich, but she would have one heck of a
collection.

Avon products, with the exception of
California Perfume Company material, are
not found that much at flea markets any
longer. The 1970s were the golden age of
Avon collectibles. There are still a large
number of dedicated collectors, but the
legion that fueled the pricing fires of the
1970s has been hard hit by desertions.
Avon material today is more likely to be
found at garage sales than at flea markets.

Clubs: Bud Hatin's National Avon Collector's Club, P. O. Box 9868, Kansas City,
MO 64134; Western World Avon Collectors Club, Box 23785, Pleasant Hills, CA
93535.

American Belle, Sonnet cologne, 1976–
78............................ **5.00**
Baby Grand Piano, Perfume Glace,
1971–72 .... **8.00**
Betsy Ross, white, 1976 .... **12.00**
Cable Car, green, 1975 .... **7.50**
Calculator, black, 1979............. **5.00**

*Dagger, Windjammer After Shave Lotion, gold,
red jewels, 1968, orig box, 10" l, $18.00.*

Caseys Lantern, Island Lime After Shave,
1966–67 .... **30.00**
Country Kitchen, Moisture Hand Lotion,
1973–75 .... **4.50**
Dutch Girl Figurine, Somewhere, 1973–
74............................ **8.00**
Eight Ball, black and white........... **2.50**
First Class Male, Wild Country After
Shave, 1970–71 .... **3.00**
Flower Maiden, yellow paint, 1974..... **7.50**
Golf Cart, green, 1973 .... **4.50**
Leisure Hour, Charisma Bath Oil, 1970–
72............................ **4.50**
Library Lamp, gold plated base, 1976 ... **5.00**
Little Girl Blue, Cotillion, 1972–73 ..... **7.00**
Looking Glass, hand mirror shape,
1970.......................... **3.00**
Partridge, Occur, 1973–75............ **4.50**
Pheasant, brown, green plastic head,
1972.......................... **7.50**
President Lincoln, Tai Winds After
Shave, 1973 .... **6.50**
Rainbow Trout, 1973 .... **5.00**
Royal Coach, Bird of Paradise, 1972–
73............................ **4.75**
Santa **35.00**
Sea Trophy, Windjammer After Shave,
1972.......................... **4.50**
Snail Perfume, Brocade, 1968–69...... **8.00**
Spirit of St Louis, silver paint, 1970 ..... **12.00**
Stage Coach, brown **7.50**
Strawberry Bath Foam, 1971–72 ...... **3.50**
Swan Lake, Charisma, 8" h, 1972–
1976 .... **5.00**
Treasure Turtle, Field Flowers Cologne,
1971–73 .... **4.50**
Twenty-Dollar Gold Piece, Windjammer
After Shave, 1971–72............. **4.25**
Victorian Fashion Figurine, Field Flowers
Cologne, 1973–74 .... **22.00**
Western Boot, Wild Country After
Shave, 1973–75 .... **2.50**

BADGES

Have you ever tried to save a name tag or
badge that attaches directly to your cloth-

ing or fits into a plastic holder? We are victims of a throwaway society. This is one case where progress has not been a boon for collectors.

Fortunately, our grandparents and great-grandparents loved to save the membership, convention, parade, and other badges that they acquired. The badge's colorful silk and cotton fabric often contained elaborate calligraphic lettering and lithographed scenes in combination with celluloid and/or metal pinbacks and pins. They were badges of honor, often having an almost military quality about them.

Look for badges with attached three-dimensional miniatures. Regional value is a factor. I found a great Emmaus, Pennsylvania, badge priced at $2.00 at a flea market in Florida; back home, its value is $20.00 plus.

Bicycling, Thistle Cycling Club, link badge, 1¼ × 2¾", engraved hanger with thistle bloom surrounded by wreath of leaves, gold plated connecting bar inscribed "Sept 15–95," enameled brass disk inscribed "2nd Annual Century/Elgin-Aurora-Chicago," second bar inscribed "Aug 2–96," 1895 .... **85.00**
Convention
  Grain Dealers, brass, 3½" h, Minneapolis name and skyline on hanger bar, red, white, and blue ribbon, pendant inscribed "24th Annual Convention, 1920" **10.00**
  Republican National Convention, celluloid insert on brass bar inscribed "Ass't Sergeant At Arms," red, white, and blue ribbon, celluloid insert on fob inscribed "Republican National Convention, Phila, PA, June 18, 1900" **15.00**
Military
  Grand Army of the Republic (GAR) Commander Staff Aide, bronzed metal, raised portrait of I. N. Walker, Commander In Chief GAR, inscribed "Walker National Staff, St Paul 1896," unmarked gold fabric ribbon **15.00**
  GAR Veteran, 1¼" d brass pendant, red, white, and blue flag ribbon, brass hanger bar of eagle, crossed cannons, cannonballs, and saber, GAR symbol on pendant and serial number, c1890 .... **20.00**
Occupational
  Deputy Constable, silvered brass, 2½" h, embossed design, spring clip metal fastener, 1930s **20.00**

Fireman's, silvered brass, 2¼" h, fire symbols surrounded by inscription "Allison H. & L. Co. 12, Harrisburg, Pa," 1920s **25.00**
Pennsylvania State Police Force, brass, emb, 4½" h, state symbols over starburst shape, early 1900s **45.00**
Special Police, silvered brass, 2½" h, star shaped, black lettering, 1930s **22.00**
Political, 1924 Progressive Campaign, Robert A LaFollette, Burton K Wheeler, bronze **20.00**
Prohibition Pledge, darkened brass, eagle dec on hanger, red, white, and blue ribbon, aluminum token inscribed "Beautiful Water My Beverage Shall Be," reverse inscribed "Tis Here We Pledge Perpetual Hate, To All That Can Intoxicate," early 1900s **40.00**
Souvenir
  Columbian Expo, brass, 2" h, "New York" on hanger bar, pendant inscribed "Souvenir World's Columbian Exposition 1893" with central world globe design **30.00**
  Fire Parade, brass, 4" h, two bars, upper bar with "Hackettstown Fire Dept.," lower bar with "Elizabeth Oct. 11, 1906," hanging celluloid pendant with fireman portrait illus **20.00**
  Parade, 8" l, WW I, brass hanger bar with celluloid insert inscribed "First Regiment," red, white, and blue ribbon with gold lettering "Silk Industry of America and Allied Interests, Citizens Preparedness Parade, May 13th, 1916".................... **8.00**
Union, Chairman of Committee, 5" l, brass hanger with celluloid insert, red, white, and blue ribbon with gold lettering "Annual Ball Jan 27th, 1940," white metal medallion with celluloid insert inscribed "Bakery Workers Union, Local 50 AF of L" **25.00**

BAKELITE

This is a great example of a collecting category gone price-mad. Bakelite is a trademark used for a variety of synthetic resins and plastics used to manufacture colorful, inexpensive, utilitarian objects. The key word is inexpensive, which can also be interpreted as cheap.

There is nothing cheap about Bakelite collectibles in today's market. Collectors, especially those from large metropolitan areas who consider themselves design-conscious, want Bakelite in whatever form they can find it—from jewelry to radio cases.

Buy a Bakelite piece because you love it. The market has already started to collapse for commonly found material. Can the high-end pieces be far behind?

Radio, General Electric, 1941, $40.00.

Alarm Clock, electric, Telechron, 1930.	**25.00**
Bookends, pr, geometric Art Deco style, green and yellow	**65.00**
Cake Server, green handle	**5.00**
Cigarette Case, hand-shaped closure, France	**175.00**
Cocktail Set, Bakelite and chrome shaker, six cocktails, chrome tray	**45.00**
Dominoes	**25.00**
Flatware, service for six, red handles, 26 pcs	**85.00**
Food Chopper, red handle	**10.00**
Inkwell, black, streamlined	**24.00**
Jewelry	
Beads, amber, ovals, 14" l	**60.00**
Bracelet, bangle, bright yellow, red, black, and green enamel dec	**25.00**
Pendant, rose, yellow flower, green leaves	**25.00**
Pin, figural, cherries, cluster of three	**20.00**
Mortar and Pestle, yellow and orange swirl	**25.00**
Napkin Ring, figural	
Dog	**25.00**
Rabbit, orange	**40.00**
Pencil Sharpener, Scottie	**35.00**
Radio, General Electric	**45.00**
Razor, Packare Lifetime, leather case, orig box	**22.00**
Salt and Pepper Shakers, pr	
Cubes, maroon, handled tray	**15.00**
Half Moon, green and yellow, matching tray	**18.00**
Round domed top, red	**12.50**
Shotgun Bullets, green	**15.00**
Shaving Brush, green handle	**125.00**
Souvenir Pin, 1939 New York World's Fair, 1¼" h, trefoil, Trylon, inscribed	
"New York World's Fair/Bakelite," pink	**40.00**
Telephone, Kelloggs Series 1000, brown, Art Deco style, chrome dial	**90.00**
View-Master, Model B, black, 4" d, c1944, orig box	**65.00**

BANDANNAS

Women associate bandannas with keeping their hair in place. Men visualize stage coach holdups or rags to wipe the sweat from their brow. Neither approach recognizes the colorful and decorative role played by the bandanna.

Some of the earliest bandannas are political. By the turn of the century, bandannas joined pillow cases as the leading souvenir textile found at sites ranging from the beach to museums. Hillary Weiss's *The American Bandanna: Culture on Cloth from George Washington to Elvis* (Chronicle Books: 1990) provides a visual feast for this highly neglected collecting area.

The bandanna played an important role in the Scouting movement, serving as a neckerchief in Boy and Girl Scouts. Many special neckerchiefs were issued. There is also a close correlation between scarfs and the bandanna. Bandanna collectors tend to collect both.

Boy Scout, emblem in center, four scout activities in corners, semaphore border, brown and red, $45.00.

Davy Crockett, cotton, bright blue, yellow, red, and white Indian blankets, ranch symbols, spurs, boots, and cowboy hat design, center with Davy as bronc rider, 13½ × 14" **40.00**

Eisenhower, "Win with Ike for President" and portrait surrounded by bunting, blue and white, 27" sq **75.00**

Kennedy, rayon, full color portrait on white ground, red, white, and blue flag border, 31" sq, 1965 copyright tag **18.00**

Lone Ranger, printed white and blue design, bright red ground, portrait, rail fence, crossed guns, coiled lasso, and horseshoe design, Cheerios premium, 21 × 23", 1949–1950 .... **65.00**

Mickey Mouse, cotton, black, white, and red Mickey, Goofy, Minnie, and Donald figures, green border, 22" sq, c1960 .... **35.00**

Radio Orphan Annie, "Flying W" symbol surrounded by code letters, four corner portraits, black, white, and red, Ovaltine premium, 17 × 19", c1934 ... **75.00**

Roy Rogers, white Roy, Trigger, ranch brands, and rope designs on red ground, 17" sq, mid 1950s **35.00**

Straight Arrow, red, white, and blue Straight Arrow, Steve Adams, Packy, and Fury illus, red ground, 18 × 19", 1949 National Biscuit Co copyright ... **50.00**

Spanish-American War, "Remember the Maine," red, white, and blue slogan, ship, and flags dec, white ground, 17" sq, c1898 .... **25.00**

Tom Mix, Mix on Tony and facsimile signature, purple shirt, brown horse, red border, 16½ × 17" **60.00**

BANKS, STILL

Banks are classified into two types—mechanical (action) and still (nonaction). Chances are that any mechanical bank that you find at a flea market today is most likely a reproduction. If you find one that you think is real, check it out in one of the mechanical bank books before buying it.

The still, or nonaction, bank dominates the flea market scene. There is no limit to the way that you can collect still banks. Some favor type (e.g., advertising), others composition (cast iron, tin, plastic, etc.), figural (shaped like something), or theme (Western). Dad collects banks that were used to solicit money. Says something about him, doesn't it?

Beware of still bank reproductions, just as you are with mechanical banks, especially in the cast iron sector. Most banks

were used, so look for wear where you expect to find it. Save your money and do not buy if you are not certain that what you are buying is a period original.

Wolf's Head, Super Duty Motor Oil, tin top and base, paper label, 4" h, 2" d, $16.00.

Advertising
Amoco, 100th Anniversary L & MO, Model-T van, 1917 .... **25.00**
Bokar Coffee **35.00**
Briardale Food Stores, can **8.50**
Calumet Baking Powder, tin, 4" **75.00**
Charlie the Tuna, ceramic **25.00**
Coors Lite Beer Can, aluminum...... **5.00**
Donald Duck Orange Juice, can...... **20.00**
Electrolux, iron, refrigerator **28.00**
Exxon Tiger...................... **30.00**
Fidelity National Bank & Trust Co, bronze **15.00**
Frigidaire, metal **23.00**
Frito Lay, 1950 panel truck **30.00**
Fulton County Trust, Gloversville, NY, clock..................... **75.00**
Gulf Gas, cardboard, pump shape **15.00**
Koolmotor, oilcan.................. **9.00**
Mellow Cup Coffee................ **22.00**
Red Goose Shoes, celluloid.......... **45.00**
Rival Dog Food **10.00**
Sohio Premex Oil, tin **10.00**
Thompson Auto Products, Indian, teepee........................ **50.00**
Underwood Typewriter, 1½" h, white metal, dark gold paint........... **35.00**
Wolf's Head Oil, can shape **16.00**
World Book Encyclopedia, figural book, slide top **10.00**
Cast Iron
Car, Montgomery Ward, 1905....... **15.00**
Frog, 4⅛" l, Iron Art, 1973.......... **55.00**

Mail Box, blue and red, made in US, marked "Iron Art" **46.00**
Pig, sgd "Decker's" **85.00**
Character
  Baba Louie, Knickerbocker **30.00**
  Barney Rubble and Bam Bam, plastic **40.00**
  Batman, ceramic **40.00**
  Casper the Friendly Ghost, Renzi Co. **20.00**
  Davy Crockett, metal **35.00**
  Fred Flintstone, plastic, 1971 .... **20.00**
  Lucky Joe, glass **30.00**
  Miss Piggy, china, Sigma **45.00**
  Pinocchio, ceramic **75.00**
  Snoopy, glass **15.00**
Chalkware, buffalo **15.00**
China, cat, red sneakers, Kliban **40.00**
Glass, figural, pig **10.00**
Metal
  Jackpot Dime, 6 × 3½" **20.00**
  Mail Box, 9" h, olive green, schedule on front **35.00**
Papier Mache, Beatles, 8" h, rubber plug, Pride Creations **100.00**
Pottery
  Pig, spongeware **85.00**
  Uncle Sam, red, three coin, Western Stamping Co **25.00**
Tin, television, figural **10.00**

BARBED WIRE

Barbed wire is a farm, Western, and military collectible. It is usually collected in eighteen-inch lengths and displayed mounted on boards. While there are a few rare examples that sell in the hundreds of dollars for a piece, the vast majority of what is found are common types that sell between $2.00 to $5.00 for an example.

Club: International Barb Wire Collectors Historical Society, Sunset, TX 76270.

BARBERSHOP AND BEAUTY PARLOR COLLECTIBLES

Let's not discriminate. This is the age of the unisex hair salon. This category has been male-oriented for far too long. Haven't you wondered where a woman had her hair done in the nineteenth century?

Don't forget drug store products. Not everyone had the funds or luxury to spend time each day at the barbershop or beauty salon.

Blade Bank, life-like colors, gray hair, marked "Ceramic Arts Studio, Madison, Wis," 4" w base, 4¾" h, $75.00.

After Shave Talc, Palmolive **7.50**
Antiseptic Container, 8" h, plated brass **40.00**
Barber Bottle
  7" h, Witch Hazel, globular body, straight neck, milk glass, floral dec **60.00**
  7¾" h, KDX For Dandruff, label under glass **110.00**
  8" h, Rosewood Dandruff Cure, woman's head on label under glass **200.00**
  10¼" h, Hair Tonic, label under glass, milk glass **250.00**
Blade Bank
  J B Williams, tin litho **23.00**
  Yankee, tin, c1900 .... **55.00**
Bobby Pins, orig card
  Gayla Hold, woman illus on front **2.75**
  Sta-Rite **1.50**
Box, Fairies Bath Perfume, unopened, 1920s **6.00**
Brochure, Burma Shave, Vol X, 1942 ... **6.00**
Business Card, 6 × 3¼", man cutting hair, "The Newest and Most Sanitary Shop in Providence" **10.00**
Catalog, Human Hair Goods, 1896, 24 pgs, color lithos **65.00**
Chair, pedestal base, Theo Kochs Manufacturer **350.00**
Clippers, Andis, c1940 .... **20.00**
Cologne, stick
  Morning Glory **4.25**
  Zia **4.00**
Hair Groom, Brylcreem **6.00**
Hair Net
  Cameo, c1930 .... **3.00**
  Doloris **4.75**
  Gainsborough **4.25**
  Jal-Net **5.50**

Hair Tonic	
Lan-Tox	12.00
Nowland's Lanford Oil	7.50
Hair Treatment	
Marchand's Hair Rinse	4.25
Nestle	
Baby's	7.00
Curling Lotion	.75
Egyptian, hair tent	11.00
Hair Wax, Lucky Tiger, large jar	10.00
Post Card, Unsafe Safety Razor, c1910	12.00
Poster	
Bickmore Shave Cream, 30 × 21", man putting cream on brush, 1930	22.00
Satin Skin Powder, 42 × 26", 1903	35.00
Razor Blade	
Broadway Double Edge	5.00
Gold Tone	1.50
Pal Double Edge	1.50
Treet	1.50
Shaving Brush, aluminum handle, emb design, c1910	8.50
Shaving Cream	
Brisk, tin and display box	8.00
Krank's Brush Lather Shave	8.00
Palmolive	5.00
Prep Brushless Shave	8.00
Sign	
Beauty Shop, neon, pink, orig transformer	200.00
Hump Hairpins, 16 × 14", tin, die-cut	150.00
Parker's Cold Cream, 7½ × 11 ½", standup type, Victorian woman, 1905	90.00
Strop, Ingersoll, razor blade stropping kit, MIB	12.00
Thermometer, Schick adv, 1950s	75.00
Tin	
Ex-Cel-Siss Talcum	15.00
Gardenia Talcum	5.00
Lander's Lilacs and Roses, talc	18.00
Tuskeegee Belle Hair Cream, black girl wearing cap and gown	40.00
White Witch Talc	12.50
Trimmer, Saftrim, metal, fits on razor	4.00

BARBIE DOLLS

As a doll, Barbie is unique. She burst upon the scene in the late 1950s and remains a major factor in the doll market over forty years later. No other doll has enjoyed this longevity.

Every aspect of Barbie is collectible, from the doll to her clothing to her play accessories. Although collectors place the greatest emphasis on Barbie material from the 1950s and 1960s, there is some great stuff from the 1970s and 1980s that should

not be overlooked. Whenever possible, try to get original packaging. This is especially important for Barbie material from the 1980s forward.

Barbie #2, 11½" h, brown ponytail, pearl earrings, orig stand, 1960, $350.00.

Beauty Kit, 1961, MIB	25.00
Book	
Barbie Solves A Mystery, Random House	8.00
The World of Barbie, Random House	15.00
Clothing Accessories	
Barbie	
American Airlines Stewardess, #984, 1961	27.50
Ballerina, #989, 1961	20.00
Evening Gala, #1660, 1965	45.00
Orange Blossom, #987, 1962	25.00
Ken	
Baseball Cap, ball, mitt, plastic	3.00
Graduation gown and mortar board, black	12.50
Hunting Cap, red plastic	2.00
Rally Day, all weather coat and hat, #795	8.00
Roller Skates	2.50
Colorforms Set	7.50
Cookbook, Random House	45.00
Doll	
Barbie	
1926, Bubble Cut Fashion, MIB	90.00
1969, light auburn hair, MIB	250.00
1990, Happy Holidays, MIB	75.00
Julia, Twist 'n' Turn, 2 pc uniform, 1969	40.00

Ken, 12" h, molded hard plastic, movable head, arms, and legs, flocked blonde hair, orig "Sport Shorts" outfit #783, orig wire pedestal and box, 1961 . . . . **150.00**

Doll Carrying Case, vinyl cov cardboard Barbie and Midge, 14 × 18 × 4", light blue, metal snap closure, pink, tan, black and white illus, 1963 Mattel copyright, heavy play wear **25.00**

Ken, 11 × 13 × 4", olive-yellow, blue, yellow, white, and black illus of Ken, Barbie, and sports car, black plastic handle, 1962 copyright, heavy play wear **30.00**

Doll House
Barbie's Country Living House, #8662 . . . . **45.00**
Dream House, furnished, 1961 . . . . . . **55.00**
The World of Barbie House, #1048 . . . **40.00**

Game, Queen of the Prom **30.00**
Lunch Box, vinyl, 1960 . . . . **30.00**
Magazine, *Mattel Barbie Magazine*, Jan-Feb 1969, 22 pgs **15.00**
Manicure Set, Barbie Good Grooming Manicure Set, orig box **35.00**
Paper Doll Book, *Barbie and Her Friends*, Whitman #1981, unused, 1975 . . . . . . **14.00**
Record Case, 1961, MIB **20.00**
Soap, Barbie Doll Soap Circles, Jergens, MIB **30.00**
Sunglasses, child's, orig pkg, 1978 . . . . . . **15.00**
Telephone, Barbie Mattel-a-Phone, pink **50.00**
Thermos, 8½" h, litho metal, red plastic cap, full color illus, black ground, 1962 Mattel copyright **35.00**
Wallet, vinyl, 1961 . . . . **30.00**

BASEBALL CARDS

Collecting baseball cards is not for kids any longer. It is an adult game. Recent trends include buying and stashing away complete boxed sets of cards, placing special emphasis on rookie and other types of cards, and speculating on a few "rare" cards that have a funny habit of turning up in the market far more frequently than one would expect if they were so rare.

Baseball cards date from the late 19th century. The earliest series are tobacco company issues dating between 1909 and 1915. During the 1920s American Caramel, National Caramel, and York Caramel issued cards.

Goudey Gum Company (1933 to 1941) and Gum, Inc. (1939) carried on the tradition in the 1930s. When World War II ended, Bowman Gum of Philadelphia, the

successor to Gum, Inc., became the baseball giant. Topps, Inc., of Brooklyn, New York, followed. Topps purchased Bowman in 1956 and enjoyed almost a monopoly in card production until 1981 when Fleer of Philadelphia and Donruss of Memphis challenged its leadership.

In addition to sets produced by these major companies, there were hundreds of other sets issued by a variety of sources ranging from product manufacturers, such as Sunbeam Bread, to minor league teams. There are so many secondary sets now issued annually that it is virtually impossible for a collector to keep up with them.

The field is plagued with reissued sets and cards as well as outright forgeries. The color photocopier has been used to great advantage by unscrupulous dealers. Never buy cards from someone that you can't find six months later.

The listing below is simply designed to give you an idea of baseball card prices in good to very good condition and to show you how they change depending on the age of the cards that you wish to collect. For detailed information about card prices consult the following price guides: James Beckett, *Sports Americana Baseball Card Price Guide, No. 10*, Edgewater Book Co., 1988; Editors of Krause Publications, Sports, *Baseball Card Price Guide, Fourth Edition*, Krause Publications, 1990; Editors of Krause Publications, Sports, *Standard Catalog of Baseball Cards*, Krause Publications, 1990; and, Gene Florence, *The Standard Baseball Card Price Guide, Second Edition*, Collector Books, 1990. Although Beckett is the name most often mentioned in connection with price guides, I have found the Krause guides to be much more helpful.

Periodicals: *Baseball Card News*, 700 East State Street, Iola, WI 54990; *Beckett Baseball Monthly*, 3410 Mid Court, Suite 110, Carrolto, TX 75006; *Current Card Prices*, P. O. Box 480, East Islip, NY 11730; *Sports Collectors Digest*, 700 East State Street, Iola, WI 54990.

Bell Brand, 1958
Complete Set **250.00**
Common Player **10.00**
Bowman
Complete set
1949 . . . . **1,750.00**
1952 . . . . **2,000.00**
1954 . . . . **550.00**

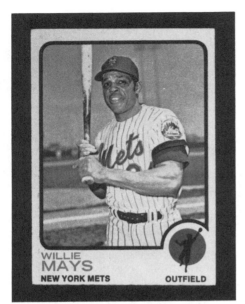

Topps, 1973, #305, Willie Mays, $3.50.

Common player	
1949, black and white	6.00
1951, color	5.00
1953, black and white	10.00
1955, color	4.50
Crown Orioles, 1991	
Complete Set	5.25
Common Player	.01
Donruss, 1981, complete set	9.00
Fleer, complete set	
1982	12.00
1984	33.00
Goudey, 1934, complete set	1,800.00
Hostess Twinkie, 1976	
Complete Set	16.50
Common Player	.10
Leaf Preview, 1991	
Complete Set	22.50
Common Player	.40
Score, 1991, complete set	3.25
Topps	
Complete set	
1953	2,000.00
1958	975.00
1966	750.00
1977	110.00
1981	60.00
Common player	
1951, blue back	12.00
1955	4.50
1957, cards 1–264 and 353–407	1.25
1959, cards 1–110	1.00
1961, cards 371–522	.75
1965, cards 199–446	.45
1973, cards 397–528	.25
1976, cards 1–660	.03

Upper Deck	
Complete Set	
1989	22.50
1991	4.00
Common Player, 1989	.01

BASEBALL MEMORABILIA

What a feast for the collector! Flea markets often contain caps, bats, gloves, autographed balls, and photos of your favorite all-stars, baseball statues, regular and world series game programs, and team manuals or rosters. Do not overlook secondary material such as magazine covers with a baseball theme. Condition and personal preference should always guide the eye.

Be careful of autograph forgeries. The general feeling among collectors is that over fifty percent of the autographed baseballs being offered for sale have faked signatures. But do not let this spoil your fun. There is plenty of great, good stuff out there.

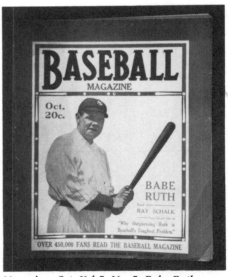

Magazine, Oct, Vol 5, No. 5, Babe Ruth cover, $35.00.

Annual, *Who's Who In Baseball*, 36th Edition, 1951	20.00
Bank, Cleveland Indians, ceramic, 1950s	185.00
Baseball, autographed	
Carl Hubbel, bold black marker signature	30.00
Jimmy Foxx	1,200.00

Lou Boudreau, bold blue ink signature 35.00
Ted Williams, blue ink signature "Best Wishes Ted Williams 1952" 125.00
Baseball Glove
Billy Martin, MIB 300.00
George Snuffy Stirnweiss, MIB 85.00
Phil Rizzuto, MIB 110.00
Ray Jablonski, MIB 85.00
Bedspread, chenille, baseball player, twin size 50.00
Beer Tray, Gil Hodges, round, four coasters, color picture 45.00
Book
Bob Feller, How To Pitch, A S Barnes Sports Library, 1948 copyright 18.00
Inside Baseball for Little Leaguers, Ted Kluszewski 42.50
The Willie Mays Story, 94 pgs, 1954 . . . . 20.00
Calendar, St Louis Cardinals, 1980 . . . . 15.00
Coin, Salada Tea, 1⅜" d, plastic, Mickey Mantle, black rim, 1962 . . . . 15.00
Dixie Lid, Joe Medwick/St Louis Cardinals, 2¼" d, brown photo, c1937 . . . . 50.00
Doll, Los Angeles Dodgers, 1960 . . . . 65.00
Game
All-Star Baseball Game, Cadaco-Ellis, 1962 . . . . 15.00
Big League Baseball Game, 3M Co, copyright 1966 . . . . 20.00
Los Angeles Dodgers Baseball Card Game, Educards Corp, 1964 . . . . 40.00
The Champion Game of Baseball, Proctor Amusement Co, Cambridge, MA, early 1890s 200.00
Glass, Rawlings Official League, 5¼" h, clear, weighted bottom, white and red design, 1960s 15.00
Guide, *1924 Spalding Baseball Guide* 65.00
Hartland Figure, Hank Aaron, 7" h, bat missing, late 1950s 80.00
Lapel Pin, Bert & Harry Fan Club 25.00
Magazine, *Weekly News*
Jackie Robinson, Oct 6, 1952 . . . . 15.00
Yogi Berra, Aug 4, 1952 . . . . 18.00
Mitt, Catfish Hunter 12.00
Mug, 1968 World Series, 6½" h, plastic, white 12.50
Napkin, World Series, Los Angeles, 1959, 7 × 5", "Dodgers Win It," Snider and Sherry pictured 10.00
Nodder
Los Angeles Dodger, 4½" h, composition, orig box, 1961–62 . . . . 150.00
Willie Mays, 7" h, composition, white round base, 1961–62 . . . . 200.00
Pennant
Cleveland Indians, felt, red, white lettering, c1950 . . . . 15.00
Pee Wee Reese, felt, white, red portrait illus and signature, 1950s 45.00
Philadelphia Athletics, 28" l, navy blue felt, white inscription 50.00
Photo Button, Indianapolis Champions 1897, 1½" d, sepia, 15 uniformed players 200.00
Pinback Button
⅞" d, Miller/Pittsburgh Pirates, Sweet Caporal Cigarettes 20.00
1¾" d, Brooklyn Dodgers, blue and white, c1945 . . . . 15.00
Postcard, Wrigley Field and Gabby Hartnett photo, linen, 1930s 15.00
Press Pin, World Series
1943, NY Yankees, ⅞" d, sterling silver, crossed bats beneath baseball, Dieges & Clust, threaded post fastener 300.00
1967, Chicago White Sox Phantom, 1⅛" d, enameled, gold batter, white stocking, deep red center, deep blue border, Balfour, needle post fastener 80.00
Program
Cubs-Detroit, 1935 World Series, score card and ticket 475.00
New York Yankees-Chicago White Sox, 20 pgs, 1956 . . . . 45.00
St Louis-Yankees, 1926 World Series 600.00
Record, Richie Ashburn, 7 × 7½", 1952 . . . . 20.00
Textile, tobacco silk, Phillies, 2 × 3", sepia portraits of John W Bates and John Titus, c1911 . . . . 25.00
Uniform, 2 pcs, flannel, Athletics, #36, gray, royal blue trim and logo 250.00
Yearbook, Cubs, 1949 . . . . 75.00

BASKETBALL

As the price of baseball cards and baseball memorabilia continues to rise, collectors are turning to other sports categories based on the affordability of their material. Basketball and football are new "hot" sport collecting fields.

Collecting generally centers on one team, as it does in most other sport collecting categories. Items have greater value in their "hometown" than they do "on the road." You know a category is becoming strong when its secondary material is starting to bring strong prices. Check the prices for the games in the list below.

Card
Bowman, 1948, complete set 550.00
Fleer, 1961–62, complete set 450.00
Hoops, 1989–90, complete set 5.00
Sky Box, 1990–91, complete set 2.80
Game
Bas-Ket, Cadaco, 1973 . . . . 25.00

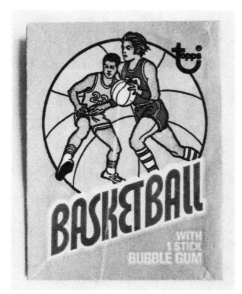

Gum Card Wrapper, Topps, 1975, $1.00.

NBA All-Star Basketball Game, Tudor
Metal Products, metal playing
board, plastic basketball figures, basketball net, and styrofoam ball,
1968. . . . . **45.00**
Mug, 3″ h, Milwaukee Bucks, china, car-
toon illus, black inscription, 1969–
1970 . . . . **15.00**
Nodder, 7″ h, composition, holding
brown basketball, gold base, inscribed
"Millersville," 1960s **30.00**
Palm Puzzle, 3″ d, styrene plastic case,
cardboard center with basketball de-
sign, metal ball, 1950s **12.00**
Pen, 6″ l, New York Knicks, plastic, or-
ange, clear cylinder with spectator im-
age **15.00**
Program, Harlem Globetrotters, 8½ ×
11″, 16 pgs, 1948–49 . . . . **25.00**

BATMAN

"Galloping globs of bat guano, Caped Crusader!" and similar cries may be heard as
the Dark Knight and his sidekick are sum-
moned to restore peace to Gotham City.

The saga of the search for Batman &
Robin-related items began with Batman's
appearance in 1939 in issue #27 of Detective Comics. Today, Boy Wonder and
Caped Crusader collectibles are found in
almost every medium imaginable. Local
flea markets offer a large variety of bat-
goodies capable of making any batcollector
go batty!

*The ideal flea market find: Comic Book, D. C.
Comics, No. 1, Spring 1940, fine condition,
$12,000 to $14,000.*

Action Figure, plastic
Batgirl, 8″ h, Super Hero, Mego, 1975,
orig box **450.00**
Batman
3″ h, Justice League, Ideal, 1966–
67. . . . . **50.00**
3¾″ h, Pocket Super Hero, Mego,
1979. . . . . **20.00**
4¼″ h, Wall Scaler, Dark Knight,
Kenner, #63130, 1990 . . . . **8.00**
5″ h, Super Powers, Kenner, 1984,
mini comic. **40.00**
8″ h, removable mask, Mego,
1974. . . . . **350.00**
12½″ h, Mego, 1976 . . . . **140.00**
Bruce Wayne, 8″ h, Mego, J C Penny
mail-in offer, brown box. **400.00**
Penguin
3¾″ h, Comic Action Hero,
Mego **75.00**
4¼″ h, missile firing umbrella, long
missile, Toy Biz #4409, 1989 . . . . **25.00**
Riddler
8″ h, World's Greatest Super He-
roes, Mego, orig box, 1974 . . . . . . **200.00**
Super Amigo, Pacipa, 1989. . . . . **50.00**
Robin
7″ h, fist fighting, Mego, 1975 . . . . . **400.00**
12½″ h, flyaway action, Mego,
1976. . . . . **140.00**
Alarm Clock, talking, Janex, 1975. . . . . **85.00**
Bank
Batman, glazed china, 7″ h, 2 × 3″
base, 1966 . . . . **60.00**
Robin, ceramic, M U, 1966. . . . . **65.00**

Batboat and Trailer, black plastic boat, gold trailer, Batman and Robin figures, Corgi #107, 1966. . . . . **150.00**

Batchute, Poynter, 1966 . . . . **65.00**

Batcopter, Batman at controls, AHI, 7½ × 1″ card, 1973. . . . . **50.00**

Batcycle, Batman and Robin figures, Taiwan, 1970 . . . . **45.00**

Batjet, Dark Knight, Kenner #63210, 1990. . . . . **20.00**

Batmobile

AHI, battery operated, radio controlled, 1977 . . . . **30.00**

ASC, litho tin, blue, battery operated, bump-and-go action, metal and plastic figures, 12″ l, 1966 . . . . **250.00**

Corgi #267, black diecast car, blue tinted cockpit dome, seated Batman and Robin figures, 1973 . . . . **80.00**

Ertl #2575, diecast, 1/43 scale **7.50**

Marx, litho tin, Batman driver, 4″ l, 1966. . . . . **90.00**

Matsushiro, radio controlled, 8″ l, 1989. . . . . **80.00**

Palitoy, talking, 1977 . . . . **150.00**

Batphone, hotline, talking, red plastic, Marx, 8″ w, 1966 . . . . **225.00**

Batplane, battery operated, AHI, 1977. . . . . **30.00**

Bat Ring, Samsons, 1966 . . . . **25.00**

Battery Tester, Batman, Nasta, 1975 . . . . **15.00**

Bike Reflector, Penguin, Charhill, 1978. . . . . **15.00**

Book

The Batman Murders, Craig Shaw Gardner, Warner, 1990, first edition **6.00**

Batman vs. Three Villains of Doom, Winston Lyon, Signet, first edition, 1966. . . . . **20.00**

Box, Batman Slam Bang Ice Cream, 1966. . . . . **20.00**

Cake Decoration, 4″ h figures, 1966 . . . . **30.00**

Carrying Case, Batcave, holds 3″ h figures, Ideal/Sears, 1966. . . . . **300.00**

Christmas Ornament, Batman, PVC, 3¾″ d. **9.00**

Clothing

Gloves, black vinyl, Batman emblem, Wells Lamont, 12″ l, 1966 . . . . **135.00**

Helmet and Cape, plastic and vinyl, Ideal, full color box, 1966 . . . . **125.00**

Utility Belt

Ideal, rope, hook, grenades, Batarang, handcuffs, flashlight, Bat pistol, radio belt buckle, 1966. . . . . **1,250.00**

Remco, Bat belt grappler, cuffs, clicker gun, walkie talkie, orig box, 1976. . . . . **120.00**

Code Card, 1966 . . . . **5.00**

Colorforms, 1966 . . . . **50.00**

Coloring Book, Whitman, #1140, 1967. . . . . **20.00**

Desk Set, executive set, Batsharpener, Joker stapler, and Batcalendar, Janex, 1977. . . . . **45.00**

Doll

Batman

17″ h, plush, 1960s **50.00**

24″ h, cloth, vinyl face, Commonwealth, 1966 . . . . **120.00**

28″ h, stuffed, Ace Novelty **25.00**

Escape Gun, plastic, Lincoln International, 1966 . . . . **75.00**

Figure

Joker, hanging figure on suction cup, Applause, 1989 . . . . **8.00**

Penguin, diecast, collector card, Ertl #718, 1990. **5.00**

Superhero, bendable, Mego, 5″ h, 1972–74

Batman **90.00**

Catwoman. **175.00**

Joker **150.00**

Robin **75.00**

Flasher Ring, plastic, silver, VariVue, 1966. . . . . **16.00**

Fork, Batman, stainless steel, Imperial, 1966. . . . . **20.00**

Game

Batman and Robin Marble Maze Game, pinball type, Hasbro, 1965, 12″ sq box **50.00**

Batman Game, Milton Bradley, 1966, 20 × 9″ box. **35.00**

Batman Road Race Game, Gordy International, 1989 . . . . **4.00**

Glass, Riddler, Pepsi promotion, 1976 . . . **15.00**

Gun, Batsignal, Gordy International, 1989. . . . . **4.00**

Handcuffs, Batman, Gordy International, 1989. . . . . **4.00**

Handpuppet

Joker, Ideal, 12″ h, 1966 . . . . **100.00**

Robin, vinyl, Ideal, 10″ h, 1966 . . . . . . **80.00**

Jigsaw Puzzle, Batman illus, Whitman, #4608, 150 pcs, 1966 . . . . **35.00**

Jokercycle, Toy Biz #4437, 1989 . . . . **10.00**

Jokermobile, Mego, 1975 . . . . **225.00**

Jokervan, diecast, Ertl #1532, 1/64 scale, 1989. . . . . **3.00**

Kite, Ski-Hi, 1979 . . . . **15.00**

License Plate, Batman Batmobile, Marx, 4″ l, 1966. . . . . **35.00**

Marionette, Batman, cloth and plastic, Hazelle, 15″ h, 1966 . . . . **250.00**

Magic Slate, wood stylus, Whitman, 8½ × 14″, 1966 . . . . **35.00**

Memo Pad, Robin, Alco, 1980 . . . . **9.00**

Mobile Bat-lab, Mego, 1975. . . . . **300.00**

Model Kit

Batman

Aurora #467, 1964 . . . . **350.00**

Horizon, 1989 . . . . **35.00**

Batplane, Aurora #487, 1966, 13″ box. **300.00**

Penguin, Aurora, 1967 . . . . **700.00**

Mug, Batman logo, 14 oz, 1990	2.50
Night Light, Riddler, Price Imports, 1978	75.00
Paint-By-Numbers Book, Whitman, 1966	45.00
Paint Set, Star Dust, Hasbro, 1966	125.00
Pen, ballpoint, Batman, Nite Writer, 1990	7.00
Pencil Sharpener, Robin Super Friends, 1980	12.50
Penguinmobile, Corgi	40.00
Periscope, Kelloggs, 14" l, 1966	45.00

Pez
Batman, hard head, cape, 1966	90.00
Penguin, soft head, 1970s	65.00
Pillow, Batman, 1966	45.00

Playset
Azrak-Hamway, Batman Road Racing, Batmobile, Jokermobile, and track, 1976	100.00
Ideal, Batman Shaker Maker, 11 × 9" box, 1974	65.00
Ideal/Sears, 23 pcs, plain box, 1966	500.00

Mego
Collapsible Bridge, ¾" h Batman, Robin, Joker, and Penguin figures, 1975	350.00
Wayne Foundation, 40" l, 1975	1,200.00
Toy Biz #4417, Batcave, 1989	40.00
Postcard, Dexter, 1966, set of eight	30.00
Poster, Batman movie serial, Columbia Pictures, 41 × 27", 1954	140.00
Projector, Batman Picture Pistol, plastic, four films, Marx, 15" l, 1966	300.00
Puppet, Batman, push-up, plastic, Kohner, 8" h, 1966	65.00
Raincoat, yellow, logo on front, Batman and Robin on back, Sears, 1975	60.00

Record
The Catwoman's Revenge, 33⅓ RPM, Peter Pan, 1975	10.00
There Goes Robin, 45 RPM, sleeve	60.00
Rifle, tin, 18" l, Japan	150.00
Robot, Batman, battery operated, vinyl head, cloth cape, Japan	500.00
Roller Skates, Laramie, 1970s	50.00
Rolykins, Batman and Robin, Marx, 1966, pr	450.00
Sliding Puzzle, Batman, American Publishing Corp, 1977	10.00
Soaky, Robin, Colgate/Palmolive, 1966	50.00
Stamp Set, Kelloggs, 1966	50.00
Towel, Batman bat, 1990	16.00
Valentines, Hallmark, set, 1966	15.00
Viewmaster Reel Set, GAF, 1966	60.00
Visor, black, logo, 1990	3.00
Walkie Talkies, Batman and Robin, figural, MU, 1974	80.00
Waste Paper Basket, Batman, 1966	40.00
Watch, Joker, Fossil Co, 1989	125.00
Yo-Yo, Duncan, 1978	15.00

BAUER POTTERY

J. A. Bauer established the Bauer Pottery in Los Angeles, CA, in 1909. Flowerpots were among the first items manufactured, followed by utilitarian items. Dinnerware was introduced in 1930. Artware came a decade later. The firm closed in 1962.

Mixing Bowls, Ring pattern, nesting, set of four, impresseed "Bauer" and "12, 18, 24," or "36," $115.00.

La Linda, 1939–1959
Chop Plate, 13" d	25.00
Creamer	8.00
Cup and Saucer	15.00
Plate, 9" d, dinner	8.00
Sugar	15.00
Teapot, olive green, glossy pastel, Aladdin	35.00
Vegetable, 10" l, oval	25.00

Monterey, 1936–45
Butter Dish	50.00
Casserole, cov, 2 qt, chartreuse, metal frame, crazed lid	35.00
Creamer	12.00
Cup, olive green	12.00
Gravy	35.00
Plate, 9½" d, chartreuse	9.00
Soup Bowl, 7" d	18.00
Sugar	20.00
Tumbler, 8 oz	15.00

Ring, c1931
Baking Dish, cov, orange-red, 4" d	25.00
Candlestick, spool	35.00
Coffee Server, wood handle, 6 cup	28.00
Creamer, jade green	10.00

Mixing Bowl
Olive Green, #12	28.00
Yellow, #24	15.00
Pie Baker, 9½" d, turquoise	16.00

Plate
6½" d, yellow	6.00
7½" d, orange	10.00
9½" d, yellow	12.00
10½" d, light blue	20.00
Ramekin, 4" d	7.50
Refrigerator Set, 4 pcs	80.00
Shaker, green	12.00
Souffle Dish	25.00

Vase, 10¼" h, orange **50.00**
Vegetable, oval, divided **50.00**

BEATLES

Ahhh! Look, it's the Fab Four! The collector will never need *Help* to find Beatle memorabilia at a flea market—place mats, dishes, records, posters, and much more. The list is a *Magical Mystery Tour.* John, Paul, George, and Ringo can be found in a variety of shapes and sizes. They are likely to be heavily played with, so their condition will vary from poor to good. Take a good look. You may see *Strawberry Fields Forever.*

Club: Beatles Fan Club of Great Britain, Superstore Publications, 123 Marina, St. Leonards on Sea, East Sussex, England TN 38 0BN.

Periodicals: *Beatlefan*, P. O. Box 33515, Decatur, GA 30033; *Good Day Sunshine*, Liverpool Productions, 397 Edgewood Avenue, New Haven, CT 06511.

Record Case, Disk-Go-Case, olive green ground, black figures, white handle, 1962 copyright by NEMS, plastic, black base, 8¼" h, $75.00.

Banner, 12" l, rayon, metal staff, photos, "Die Beatles," German **8.00**
Bath Towel, group illus with signatures, NEMS 1964 copyright **120.00**
Belt Buckle, 2 × 3", metal, gold, black, and white group picture **25.00**
Comb, 3¼ × 15", plastic, Beatles and signature label, Lido Toys, 1964 . . . . **90.00**

Doll, Paul McCartney, 4½" h, vinyl body, guitar, Remco, 1964 NEMS Enterprises, Ltd copyright **90.00**
Figure, set of 4, inflatable, rubber, 1960s **120.00**
Head Band, orig package **40.00**
Locket Set **35.00**
Lunch Box, Yellow Submarine, metal, color illus, King-Seeley Thermos Co, 1968 King Features Syndicate copyright **200.00**
Magazine, *Beatles 'Round The World*, #1, Acme News Co, Inc, 32 pgs, 1964 . . . . **45.00**
Magnet Set, set of four, three dimensional, Beatle's head, marked "Hong Kong" **75.00**
Pencil Case, 8" l, vinyl, blue, group picture and autographs, zipper top, Standard Plastic Products **35.00**
Photo Album, Sergeant Pepper **30.00**
Photograph
  John Lennon, Memory of a Rock Superstar, 1960s **12.00**
  Ringo, 1960s **10.00**
Pin, Fan Club **15.00**
Playing Cards, single deck, orig box **50.00**
Ring Set, flasher type **40.00**
Sheet Music
  She Loves You, red tone and white photo, 1963 copyright **18.00**
  Yesterday, 3 pgs, Paul photo on front cov with inset black and white band photo, copyright 1965 Northern Songs Ltd **10.00**
Tapestry, 19 × 29½", linen, black, white, and maroon Beatle illus, purple ground, black and white illus border, marked "Pure Irish Linen/Ulster/Fast Colours," 1960s **125.00**
Tie Tack, Ringo, orig card **35.00**

BEER CANS

Beer can collecting was very popular in the 1970s. Times have changed. The field is now dominated by the serious collector and most trading and selling goes on at specialized beer canventions.

The list below contains a number of highly sought-after cans. Do not assume these prices are typical. Most cans fall in the quarter to fifty–cent range. Do not pay more unless you are certain of the resale market.

There is no extra value to be gained by having a full beer can. In fact, selling a full can of beer without a license, even if only to a collector, violates the liquor law in a large number of states. Most collectors punch a hole in the bottom of the can and drain out the beer.

Finally, before you ask—Billy Beer, either in individual cans, six packs, or cases, is not worth hundreds or thousands of dollars. The going price for a can among collectors is between fifty cents and $1.00. Billy Beer has lost its fizz.

Club: Beer Can Collectors of America, 747 Merus Court, Fenton, MO 63026.

Left: Holihan Pilsner Beer, Diamond Spring Brewery, New Haven, CT, made by Hull, $4.00. Right: Hull's Export Beer, Hull Brewing Co, New Haven, CT, $3.00.

Adler Brau, Walter, Appleton, WI, 12 oz, flat top **12.00**
Altes, National, Detroit, MI, 12 oz, flat top **35.00**
Blackhawk, Premium, Cumberland, MD, 12 oz, flat top **35.00**
Blatz Old Heidelberg Castle, Blatz, Milwaukee, WI, 12 oz, cone top **35.00**
Budweiser, Anheuser-Busch, 7 cities, 10 oz, pull top **5.00**
Coors, Golden, CO, 7 oz, flat top **6.00**
Country Club, Pearl, 2 cities, 8 oz, pull top **5.00**
Dawson, Lager, Dawson, Hammonton, NJ, 11 oz, pull top **1.50**
Eastside Old Tap, Pabst, Los Angeles, CA, 12 oz, flat top **10.00**
Fehr's Draft, Fehr, Louisville, KY, 11 oz, pull top **15.00**
Great Falls Select, Great Falls, Great Falls, MT, 12 oz, flat top **15.00**
Hamm's, Hamm's, St Paul, MN, 12 oz, pull top **2.50**
Horlacher, Pilsner, Horlacher, Allentown, PA, 12 oz, flat top **8.00**
Krueger Ale, Krueger, Cranston, RI, 16 oz, pull top **12.00**
Lite, Miller, 3 cities, 10 oz, pull top **1.00**
Lucky Lager, Lucky Lager, San Francisco, CA, 7 oz, flat top **10.00**
Milwaukee's Best, Miller, Milwaukee, WI, 12 oz, pull top **5.00**

Mustang Malt Lager, Pittsburgh, PA, 16 oz, pull top **25.00**
North Star, Associated, 3 cities, 11 oz, pull top **2.00**
Ortlieb's Premium Lager, Philadelphia, PA, 12 oz, cone top **55.00**
Oyster House, Pittsburgh, PA, 12 oz, pull top . . . . **.50**
Progress, Oklahoma City, OK, 11 oz, flat top **75.00**
Rahr's, Rahr's Green Bay, Green Bay, WI, 12 oz, Crowntainer cone top **45.00**
Rheingold, Rheingold, 2 cities, 7 oz, pull top **1.50**
Stag Premium Dry, Griesedieck-Western, 2 cities, 12 oz, cone top **25.00**
Stoney's, Jones, Smithon, PA, 12 oz, pull top **1.00**
Storz-ette, Storz, Omaha, NE, 8 oz, flat top **40.00**
Tavern Pale, Atlantic, Chicago, IL, 12 oz, flat top **25.00**
University Club, Miller, Milwaukee, WI, 8 oz, flat top **15.00**
Weiss Bavarian, Maier, Los Angeles, CA, 15 oz, pull top **20.00**

BELLS

Bell collectors are fanatics. They tend to want every bell they can find. Admittedly, most confine themselves to bells that will fit on a shelf, but there are those who derive great pleasure from an old school bell sitting out in their front lawn.

Be alert for wine glasses that have been converted into bells. They are worth much less than bells that began life as bells. Also, collect limited edition bells because you like them, rather than with the hope they will rise in value. Many limited edition bells do not ring true on the resale market.

Club: American Bell Association, Rt. 1, Box 286, Natronia Heights, PA 15065.

Boxing, 10" d, trip hammer **75.00**
Brass
 4¼" h, emb figures and letters, head figural handle **125.00**
 7" h, emb designs and numbers, knight figural handle **135.00**
China, figural
 4" h, cow, pale blue, pink roses, gilded handle, Limoges **40.00**
 4½" h, lady, pink, yellow, and white dress, holding bouquet of flowers **65.00**
 6½" h, boy, dressed in white coat, blue trim, blue flowers, orange leaves, holding paper, gold trim **145.00**

Limited Edition Wedding Bell, Bing & Grondahl, porcelain, 4" h, rosewood handle, $25.00.

Commemorative, 4½" h, Queen Elizabeth II Silver Jubilee, marked "Aynsley" 25.00
Desk, bronze, white marble base, side tap, c1875 . . . . 45.00
Farm, cast iron, yoke 85.00
Fire, 12" d, brass 75.00
Glass
  Carnival, figural, Southern Belle, white imperial 38.00
  Cranberry, gold edge, acid leaves 30.00
  Milk, smocking, marked "Akeo, Made in USA" 22.00
Hand, brass, figural
  Lady, 3⅝" h, bust, quilted pattern on bell 35.00
  Turtle, bell bracket and striker on shell 30.00
Horse, 3" h, brass 15.00
School, 7½" h, brass, wood handle 45.00
Sleigh, four, graduated sizes, shaft type, iron strap 45.00
World War II, 6" h, metal, emb Roosevelt, Churchill, and Stalin heads 60.00
Yacht, 5¾" h, brass 40.00

BELT BUCKLES

This is a category loaded with reproductions and fakes. Beware of any cast buckle signed Tiffany. Surprisingly, many collectors do not mind the fakes. They like the designs and collect them for what they are.

A great specialized collection can be built around military buckles. These can be quite expensive. Once again, beware of recasts and fakes, especially Nazi buckles.

Buffalo Bill Jr 5.00
Bull's Head, lady's size 35.00
Coors Beer 10.00
Davy Crockett, silvered metal, raised border, inscription, Old Betsy rifle, 1½ × 3" 25.00
The Fonz 4.00
Hire's Rootbeer, Tiffany 30.00
Jefferson Starship 4.00
Mickey Mouse, Sun Rubber Co, 1937 . . . 45.00
Naval Officer, Indian War, brass, stamped "Horstman, Phila" 115.00
New York City Police, brass 75.00
Panama Red 25.00
Prussian, crown and motto, leather, gray 70.00
Red Ryder, silvered brass, cowboy on bronc, name spelled twice in rope script, 2" sq, 1940s 35.00
Stroh's Beer 5.00
Wells Butterfield 65.00

BIBLES

The general rule to follow is that any Bible less than two hundred years old has little or no value in the collectibles market. For a number of reasons, individuals are reluctant to buy religious items. Bibles are proof positive that nothing is worth anything without a buyer.

Many have trouble accepting this argument. They see a large late nineteenth century family Bible filled with engravings of religious scenes and several pages containing information about the family. It is old and impressive. It has to be worth money. Alas, it was mass-produced and survived in large quantities. The most valuable thing about it is the family data, and this can be saved simply by copying the few pages involved on a photocopier.

An average price for a large family Bible from the turn of the century is between $25.00 and $50.00. Of course, there are Bibles that sell for a lot more than this. I have listed a few of the heavy hitters from the seventeenth and eighteenth centuries. Bibles such as these tend to remain in private hands. Never speculate when buying a Bible, God would not like it.

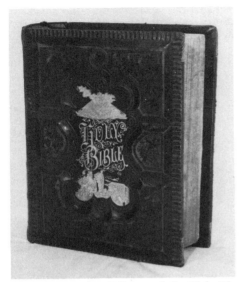

The Pronouncing Edition of the Holy Bible, *A. J. Holman & Co, Philadelphia, c1900, 10" w, 10¾" h, $35.00.*

1629, Latin, *Biblia Sacra,* Antwerp, six parts, five volumes, early morocco gilt, rubbed **175.00**
1668, English, *Holy Bible,* Cambridge, John Field, engraved title with fine architectural border by John Chantry, Van Hove copperplates, 8 × 10", 18th C mottled calf, neatly rebacked, gilt edges **350.00**
1702, German, *Bible,* Nuremberg, J L Buggel, two engraved titles, over 250 plates, 8 × 10", contemporary calf gilt over wooden boards, loose binding, lacking clasps. **350.00**
1798, English, *Bible,* Philadelphia, Thompson & Small, two volumes in one, 12 × 16", contemporary calf binding **65.00**
1805, German, *Biblia, Das 1st: Die Ganze Gottliche Heilige Schrift. . . Erst Auflage,* Reading, PA, Gottlob Jungmann, 1,235 pgs, 8 × 10", contemporary polished calf binding **125.00**
1810, English, *The Christian's New and Complete British Family Bible,* London, A Hogg, 12 × 5", morocco gilt. **195.00**
1846, English, *The Illuminated Bible,* New York, two engraved titles, 1,600 plates, 8 × 10", morocco gilt **250.00**
1908, English, *Bible,* London, Grolier Society, 14 vols, orig pigskin, soiled, fitted wooden book box **325.00**

BICENTENNIAL

America's 200th birthday in 1976 was PARTY TIME for the nation. Everyone and everything in the country had something stamped, painted, printed, molded, casted, and pressed with the commemortive dates 1776–1976. The American spirit of "overdo" and "outdo" always puts our nation in a great mood. We certainly overdid it during the Bicentennial.

The average flea market will have a wide variety of Bicentennial goodies. Prices have come down in recent years as the patriotic spirit waned and the only buyers left in the market were the collectors. Remember the Bicentennial was only sixteen years ago. This is one category where you only want to buy in fine or better condition.

Bank, American Can Co, Signers of Declaration of Independence, *2" d, 3½" h, $14.50.*

Commemorative Coin, U.S. mint, one dollar coin, 1976D copper-nickle clad variety I, representation of the Liberty Bell superimposed against the moon **14.00**
Drinking Glasses, set of four
   Burger King, 1776–1976 Have It Your Way Collector Series, 5½" h, American Revolution symbols **6.00**
   Coca-Cola, Heritage Collector Series, Revolutionary War heroes **4.00**
Pin, ¼ × ½" red, white, and blue enamel on brass flag, orig 1½" sq card inscribed "Official Pin, Quick Chek" **12.00**
Pinback Button, 2⅜" l oval, white Statue of Liberty, brown accents, yellow ground, red and white dates "1776"

and "1976," white lettered "Bicentennial"................................. **10.00**
U.S. Federal Reserves Two Dollar Bill, Series 1976 Neff-Simon, New York, signing of the Declaration of Independence scene printed on back **5.00**

BICYCLES

Bicycles are divided into two groups— antique and classic. Chances of finding an antique bicycle, e.g., a high wheeler, at a flea market are slim. Chances of spotting a great balloon tire classic are much greater.

Do not pay much for a bicycle that is incomplete, rusted, or repaired with non-original parts. Replacement of parts that deteriorate, e.g., leather seats, is acceptable. It is not uncommon to heavily restore a bicycle, i.e., to make it look like new. If the amount of original parts is less than fifty percent, question an extremely high price.

There is a great market in secondary material from accessories to paper ephemera in bicycle collectibles. Since most bicycle fanatics haunt the automobile flea markets, you might just get lucky and find a great bicycle item at a low cost at an antiques and collectibles flea market.

Club: Wheelmen, Henry Ford Museum, Dearborn, MI 48121.

Periodicals: *Antique/Classic Bicycle News*, P. O. Box 1049, Ann Arbor, MI 48106; *Bicycle Trader*, P. O. Box 5600, Pittsburgh, PA 15207.

Advertising Trade Card, two boys on high wheelers illus, $6.00.

Alarm
    Butcher......................... **25.00**
    Perfection **15.00**
Bicycle
    Bowden
        300................... **6,000.00**

Spacelander............... **7,000.00**
Colson
    Clipper, 1941............... **1,500.00**
    Firestone Cruiser, 1941 .... **1,500.00**
    Packard, 1936.............. **1,750.00**
Columbia
    3 Star 600.00
    Carnival, 1936.............. **2,500.00**
    Model 50, chainless pneumatic, 1898...................... 850.00
    Ranger, 1936................ **2,000.00**
    Super Deluxe, 1938 .... **2,500.00**
    Twinbar.................... **3,500.00**
    Victory, 1939............... **1,750.00**
Dayton
    Super Streamliner, 1936 ...... **3,250.00**
    Twin Flex, 1939 .... **2,000.00**
Elgin, Sears Roebuck
    Blackhawk **3,000.00**
    Dolly Bike, 1939............. **1,250.00**
    Skylark **1,750.00**
    Twin 30 .... 700.00
Firestone, Deluxe Speed Cruiser, 1959........................ 450.00
Gormully & Jeffery, Rambler, man's tandem, c1896 .... **1,325.00**
Hawthorne, Montgomery Ward, Comet Rollfast, 1936 .... **1,000.00**
Huffman (Huffy)
    Coca Cola Classic, 1987 .... 300.00
    Dial A Ride, 1952 .... **1,750.00**
    Radiobike, 1950s............. **2,500.00**
    Sportsman, 26", 1959............ 100.00
Huffman Dayton, Champion, 1940........................ **2,000.00**
Iroquois, Iroquois Cycleworks, 1898...................... **1,000.00**
Iver Johnson, drop handle racer, 1920s..................... **1,000.00**
J C Higgins, Sears Roebuck
    1949...................... **1,250.00**
    1953...................... 500.00
Kensington, tandem, c1900...... **1,000.00**
Marsh & Metz, tandem............ 200.00
Monark
    Coupe De Ville, 1954 .... 750.00
    Firestone Holiday, 1953 .... 750.00
    Firestone Super Cruiser, 1953 .. **1,000.00**
    Silver King
        L037.................... **2,000.00**
        M137................... **3,000.00**
        M237................... **1,000.00**
    Super Deluxe, 1953 .... **1,200.00**
Murray, Flatline, c1956 .... 800.00
Overman Victor Flyer, c1893..... **1,750.00**
Pacemaker, Cleveland Welding Co, 1941...................... **1,500.00**
Peerless Roadster, c1910 .... **1,000.00**
Pony-Byk **1,500.00**
Roadmaster, Cleveland Welding Co
    1941...................... **2,000.00**
    1947...................... **1,000.00**
    1952...................... **2,000.00**
    1965, Flying Falcon............ 100.00

Roamer, No. 36, ladies', 1941 .... **200.00**
Rollfast, D P Harris Co, Hopalong
    Cassidy, 20", 1951............ **2,500.00**
Rudge, light roadster, 58" high
    wheeler, British, 1880s........ **4,200.00**
Schwinn
    Autocycle **4,000.00**
    Corvette, 1955 .... **300.00**
    Deluxe Hornet................. **500.00**
    Flying Star.................... **225.00**
    Hollywood Special **500.00**
    Orange Krate.................. **400.00**
    Panther III, 1961............. **1,200.00**
    Pea Picker **350.00**
    Phantom Deluxe, 1950....... **1,500.00**
    Spitfire...................... **200.00**
    Stingray...................... **175.00**
    Straight Bar, 1949........... **1,000.00**
    Tiger, 1962................... **200.00**
    Typhoon Deluxe, 1968.......... **350.00**
    Wasp **200.00**
Shelby
    Flyer **1,000.00**
    Super Airflow, 1937 .... **800.00**
Star, 52" high-wheeler, 1886..... **2,225.00**
Western Flyer
    Jet Swept, 20", 1960s **75.00**
    Mercury, 1939 .... **1,500.00**
    Sonic Flyer, 1950s.............. **350.00**
Whizzer, Sportsman, motorized,
    1952..................... **2,500.00**
Winchester, Rollfast, 1936....... **1,250.00**
Calendar, New Departure Mfg Co, 1902,
    missing two months **80.00**
Catalog, Union Cycles, 1896, 8 × 5"..... **30.00**
Child Carrier, wicker, 1920s **120.00**
Clock, adv, "Columbia Built Bicycles
    Since 1877-America's First Bicycle,"
    electric, 15" d, 1950s **325.00**
Matchsafe, bisque, hp, figural woman on
    bike, 6" h, 19th C **150.00**
Medal, racing, brass, Pierce Cycle Co.... **145.00**
Photograph, man and bike illus........ **8.00**
Pinback Button
    Aetna Cycles, Mount Aetna illus **12.00**
    The P & F, bicycle seat illus **10.00**
Postcard, man on high-wheeler leading a
    stagecoach in a parade illus **18.00**
Poster
    Iver Johnson Bikes, bike illus, 42½ ×
        21½" **275.00**
    "Le Globe," France, c1890.......... **700.00**
    "Presto," cyclist and monoplane illus,
        half-sheet **775.00**
    Rambler Cycles, litho, lady riding bike
        illus, France, 48 × 35" **950.00**
Sign
    Columbia Bicycle, cardboard, litho,
        "MacDonald, Bald, Sims and
        their Columbias," racers on
        bikes illus, Gies & Co Litho, Buf-
        falo, NY **1,250.00**
    Monarch Bicycles, wood, gold letter-
        ing, 5" h, 43" l **250.00**

Whizzer Bike Motor, tin, emb, "Ride
    One-You'll Buy One," 23¾ ×
    15¾" **450.00**
Trade Card
    Columbia Bicycle, mechanical, bike
        illus, movable dials, 3 × 4"........ **60.00**
    Pope Mfg Co, Columbia Bicycle, men
        riding bikes at night illus.......... **10.00**
Tricycle
    Skyline, 1930s.................. **100.00**
    Tiller, 29" rear wheels, multicolored
        seat covering **200.00**
Trophy, vase shaped, cov, silver
    plated, inscribed "Presented by the
    Brooklyn Eagle to the League of
    American Wheelmen, Patchogue,
    Long Island, June 29-July 1,
    1899," Pairpoint Co, 21½" h **1,075.00**

BINOCULARS

Looking for field glasses or through them is an eye-opening experience. The binocular has been in use for more than two hundred years, continuing to improve our view of things. Though their greatest use has been by the military, civilian demand has given binocular production and versatility quite a push.

A flea market stand may not have that Bausch and Lomb super-deluxe, see-the-planet-like-it's-next-to-you model, but they might have an old pair of WWII spotter's glasses. Take care when going through a selection of binoculars. If they are still in the original case, they are more valuable than if they are just sitting on a seller's table. Look closely at the optics to check for cracks and loose lenses. Happy spotting.

Opera Glasses, brass frame, abalone shell dec,
$40.00.

Character
Hopalong Cassidy **50.00**
Roy Rogers, MIB **45.00**
Military
World War I, French officer's, leather carrying case, Hmed, Paris, 8
× 32 . . . . **30.00**
World War II, German
Trench, North Africa Corps, tan
camouflage, orig tripod and dual
sun shades, lenses swing to differ-
ent widths, 15″ h, base marked
"S.F.14z.Gi,H/6400", orig lens
covers. **350.00**
Tropical Canvas, neck strap, op-
tics, calibrated range finders on
the lenses, Hmed "EK, J.E.S., 6
× 9″ **30.00**
Opera Glasses, French, mother-of-pearl
exterior, dated 1902, Hmed "Lemaire
Fi., Paris". **35.00**
Premium, Kellogg's **60.00**
Voightlander, German, leather neck
strap and black leatherette carrying
case, 8 × 36 high power, Hmed
Braunschweig address, long range
glasses **150.00**

BIRD CAGES

Bird cages, what can be said? There are as
many different kinds of bird cages as there
are birds. With so many to choose from,
the buyer must ask himself "What am I
looking for?"

Bird cages are often designed with a particular species in mind and crafted with a
material that is sufficient to restrain that
species. Bamboo, wicker, and wood were
used in cages for smaller birds that did not
require a stronger construction. Larger
birds, such as cockatoos, parrots, and ma-
caws, often were housed in metal cages.
Bird cages are usually collected more for
their decorative nature than for their construction material.

14″ h, bent wire, spherical, heart-shaped
bent wire hanger and wood base, dec-
orative wire bird on trapeze **15.00**
16″ h, nickel plated brass, square,
hanging ring attached to flattened
ball finial, two horizontal braces, trapeze, dished tray, hanging stand, late
1940s. **200.00**
16½″ h, nickel plated brass, domed,
hanging ring attached to globular
finial, two horizontal braces, trapeze
and perch, dished tray, hanging stand,
mid 1940s **225.00**

24″ h, 18″ d, wicker, painted white,
conical roof, tapering sides, woven
gallery wall on circular tray, 74″ h woven crescent moon-shaped pedestal
stand **300.00**
28″ h, 20½″ d, brass plated, domed,
hanging ring, two horizontal braces,
trapeze and perch, circular dished tray,
62″ h brass plated arched stand with
circular stepped base. **175.00**
31″ h, bent wire, rectangular, turned
wood hanging finial, tin and wood
base, painted black and green **250.00**
32″ h, 18″ d, wrought iron, domed,
hanging ring **200.00**
34″ h, bent wire, square, peaked roof,
painted black. **175.00**
39″ h, 18½″ d, brass, domed, hanging
ring, two horizontal braces, circular
stepped base, c1950 . . . .**500.00**
41″ h, brass, domed, ball finial, three
horizontal braces, trapeze, brass food
and water cups attached to lower
perch, 39″ h circular Art Nouveau
style copper pedestal base. **750.00**
63″ h, wicker, bird cage/fernery combination, painted white, bird cage with
waisted cone-shaped roof with ornate
curlicue dec, tapering sides with
braided horizontal braces, and woven
gallery wall on circular tray, fernery
with openwork arch with stick and
ball dec, rect planter with braided
swags dec, and wrapped legs and
stretcher, late 19th C **700.00**

BISQUE

Every time I look at a bisque figure, I think
of grandmothers. I keep wondering why I
never see a flea market table labeled
"ONLY THINGS A GRANDMOTHER
WOULD LOVE."

Bisque is pottery ware that has only
been fired once and not glazed. It is a tech-
nique that is centuries old and is still being
practiced today. Unfortunately, some of
today's figures are exact copies of those
made hundreds of years ago. Be especially
aware of bisque piano babies.

Collectors differentiate between Continental (mostly German) and Japanese
bisque, with premiums generally paid for
Continental pieces. However, the Japanese made some great bisque. Do not confuse the cheap five-and-dime "Occupied
Japan" bisque with the better pieces.

Bank, Elmer The Elephant, movable
trunk, gray, yellow, and red. **275.00**

Match Holder, seated baby with chamber pot which reads "Scratch My Back," 4¾" h, $60.00.

Basket, 8" d, boy seated on rim, barefoot, wearing wide brim hat marked "Germany"........................ **50.00**
Candy Container, 5½" h, witch, holding vegetables...................... **35.00**
Cigarette Holder, 3½" d, youth on clothesline, marked "Japan"........ **15.00**
Creamer, figural, cow, Occupied Japan.......................... **20.00**
Figure
Bonnie Prince Charlie, 8" h, France...................... **30.00**
Cat, lying on green pillow with gold tassels, marked "Cappe, Italy"..... **30.00**
Chicken, 2" h, multicolored, marked "Japan"...................... **5.50**
Dog, 3¼" h, teaching two puppies how to read, tan book base............ **65.00**
Frog, 3½" h, Occupied Japan........ **15.00**
Lady and Man, 5" h, dressed as rooster and hen, embracing pose, Germany..................... **240.00**
Humidor, 8 × 8", baby's head....... **125.00**
Match Holder, figural, Dutch girl, copper and gold trim, includes striker....... **35.00**
Nodder
Hobo, holding walking stick, green coat, tan pants, bottle in pocket....**210.00**
Jester, seated, holding pipe, pastel peach and white, gold trim........ **75.00**
Pitcher, miniature, multicolored applied floral spray, pink ground, Occupied Japan.......................... **8.00**
Planter
Girl, sitting by well, holding water jug, coral and green................ **48.00**
Peasant Girl, 6", figural, standing beside leaf covered planter, Occupied Japan...................... **35.00**

Salt, 3" d, figural, wood, cream, branch base, matching spoon............. **70.00**
Tobacco Jar, figural, boy, hair forms cov, marked "Heubach"............... **150.00**
Toothpick Holder, lady with flower..... **35.00**
Vase, 7" h, ftd, emb floral dec, Occupied Japan.......................... **18.00**
Wall Pocket, 5" h, cuckoo clock, orange luster, pine cone weights, Occupied Japan.......................... **12.00**
Whimsy, 2¾ × 3¼", two frogs sitting in front of two eggs.................. **75.00**

BLACK GLASS

This glass gets its name from the fact that when it is sitting on a table, it looks black. When you hold it up to the light, sometimes it is actually a deep purple color. It was extremely popular in the period between World War I and II. Some forms were decorative, but most were meant for everyday use. As a result, you should expect to find signs of use on most pieces.

Ashtray, square, Hazel Atlas.......... **5.00**
Batter Set, batter jug and syrup pitcher, clear body, black cov and tray, Paden City, 1936...................... **60.00**
Berry Bowl, Ribbon pattern, Hazel Atlas, c1930.......................... **25.00**
Bookends, pr, Scottie Dog, 6½" h, Imperial Glass Co, frosted, made in 1979 for National Cambridge Collectors Inc... **50.00**
Candlesticks, pr, 3" h, Oak Leaf pattern, Fostoria...................... **85.00**
Candy Dish, cov, Ovide pattern, Hazel Atlas, 1930–35.................. **37.50**
Celery Tray, Lodestar pattern, Heisey... **50.00**
Cigarette Box, cov, Flower Garden with Butterflies pattern, US Glass, late 1920s......................... **125.00**
Creamer, Diamond Quilted pattern, Imperial, early 1930s.............. **15.00**
Cup and Saucer, Cloverleaf pattern, Hazel Atlas, 1930–36.............. **19.00**
Flowerpot, 3" h, L. E. Smith, c1930.... **15.00**
Place Card Holder, 2½" h, Fostoria..... **30.00**
Plate
6" d, Diamond Quilted pattern, Imperial...................... **5.00**
8" d, Mt Pleasant................. **14.00**
10" d, Flower Garden with Butterflies pattern, US Glass, late 1920s...... **100.00**
Salt and Pepper Shakers, pr, Ribbon pattern, Hazel Atlas, c1930............ **40.00**
Sherbet, Ovide pattern, Hazel Atlas, 1930–35...................... **7.50**
Sugar, cov, Orchid pattern, Paden City, early 1930s...................... **50.00**
Tumbler, Town & Country pattern, Heisey....................... **30.00**

Vase, 7¾" h, flared top, silver deposit dec, Diamond Glass Ware Co, c1939.......................... **45.00**

BLACK MEMORABILIA

Black memorabilia is enjoying its second renaissance. It is one of the "hot" areas in the present market. The category is viewed quite broadly, ranging from slavery era items to objects showing ethnic stereotypes. Prices range all over the place. It pays to shop around.

Because black memorabilia covers a wide variety of forms, the black memorabilia collector is constantly competing with collectors from other areas, e.g., cookie jar, kitchen, and salt and pepper shaker collectors. Surprisingly enough, it is the collectors of black memorabilia who realize the vast amount of material available and tend to resist high prices.

Reproductions, from advertising signs (Bull Durham Tobacco) to mechanical banks (Jolly Nigger), are an increasing problem. Remember—if it looks new, chances are it is new.

Periodical: *Black Ethnic Collectibles*, 1401 Asbury Court, Hyattsville, MD 20782.

Sheet Music, **Mammy Blossom's 'Possum Party,** *lyrics by Arthur Fields, music by Theodore Morse, 1917, multicolored cover, $10.00.*

Ashtray, cast iron
  Mammy and Chef, skillet shaped, pr........................... **65.00**
  Man playing banjo **160.00**
Bank
  Book of Knowledge, dentist with black boy in chair, cast iron, mechanical..................... **145.00**
  Girl, figural, nodding head.......... **45.00**
Blotter, golf scene with men and alligator, 1920s **10.00**
Book, hard cov
  Black Alice, 1968 .... **45.00**
  Color, 1925.....................**130.00**
  Epaminonda and His Auntie, 1938 ...**115.00**
  George Washington Carver, 1943....... **80.00**
  Heroes of the Dark Continent, 1890 .....**150.00**
  How Come Christmas, 1948...........**115.00**
  Little Black Quibba, 1964 .... **45.00**
  Little Black Sambo and the Monkey People, 1935...................... **90.00**
  Little Brown Koko, 1940 .... **85.00**
  Little Jeemes Henry, 1947 .... **95.00**
  Little Nemo in Slumberland, 1941...... **75.00**
  Little White Cotton, 1928............**125.00**
  Lyrics from Cottonland, 1922..........**145.00**
  The Negro Question, 1903 .... **80.00**
  Nigger Heaven, Carl Van Vechten, Grossett, 1928..................... **25.00**
  Old Folks at Home, 1890 ....**135.00**
  Old Mitt Laughs Last, 1944 .... **65.00**
  Petunia Be Keerful, 1934.............**120.00**
  Pinky Marie and Seven Bluebirds, 1939.......................**110.00**
  Ten Little Colored Boys, 1942.......... **80.00**
  Topsy Turvy and the Tin Clown, 1934 ... **75.00**
  Uncle Tom's Cabin, 1910 .... **45.00**
  Uncle Tom's Children, 1943 .... **50.00**
Bottle Opener, man's face **78.00**
Clock, Red Wing, mammy............**260.00**
Coffee Bag, Black Plantation Coffee **3.00**
Cookie Jar
  Abingdon, mammy, flowered apron........................**650.00**
  Brayton, mammy
    Light blue, hairline crack **950.00**
    Yellow **1,350.00**
  F & F, Aunt Jemima **395.00**
  McCoy, mammy..................**125.00**
  Mettlach
    Mammy, blue **295.00**
    Topsy Girl, yellow...............**350.00**
  Pearl China
    Chef........................**450.00**
    Mammy......................**675.00**
  Rockingham, mammy **240.00**
  Sears, little girl **475.00**
  Unknown Maker, mammy, gold tooth, gold trim, polka dot dress, hand dec, matching salt and pepper shakers, sgd **185.00**
Creamer, Mammy, full figure **135.00**
Creamer and Sugar, plastic, yellow, F & F **110.00**

Decanter, clown 39.00
Dish Towel 35.00
Doll, baby, bisque, jointed, 3½″ h 35.00
Drawing, black woman, color pencil on
   paper, artist Inza Walker 475.00
Dresser Jar, butler. 195.00
Figure
   Dancing Dan, jointed, man in front of
     lampost, Mystery Mike causes figure
     to dance, 9″ h, orig box. 225.00
   Lady sitting on chair knitting, German,
     8″ h 175.00
   Two boys kneeling on base, ceramic,
     Japan, Pioneer Mfg Co 30.00
Jigsaw Puzzle, Woozie 60.00
Lamp, Swami with turban sitting on
   pillow, holding shade 300.00
Letter Opener, man in alligator's
   mouth 48.00
Match Holder, adv, Coon Chicken Inn,
   metal 250.00
Memo Pad, mammy, orig pad 65.00
Mug
   Large mammy face 240.00
   Muscles Moe 65.00
Nodder
   Bahama Policeman, white uniform,
     minor paint flakes 85.00
   Children, pr 65.00
   Mammy, ceramic 175.00
Paper Towel Holder, mammy 125.00
Pencil Sharpener, man's face 125.00
Picture, Sambo, felt, framed. 40.00
Planter
   Banana boat and black man,
     McCoy 95.00
   Plaid mammy 95.00
Plaque, man 55.00
Pot Holder Hanger, boy 29.00
Puppet, Little Black Sambo, dated 1952,
   MIB 110.00
Recipe Box, plastic, red 150.00
Salt and Pepper Shakers, pair
   Boy and Girl
     Sitting in basket, china 95.00
     Sitting on peanut shell, china 110.00
   Boy sitting on alligator, china 68.00
   Boys, sitting on carrots, ceramic 68.00
   Chef, holding two barrels, wood 65.00
   Lady with child on back, native 68.00
   Mammies, chalk 45.00
   Mammy and Chef, 8″ h 150.00
   Porter, holding suitcases 195.00
   Suzanne Mammy, plastic, red,
     F & F 150.00
Scoop, mammy sitting on end, green,
   McCoy 110.00
Shaker, mammy, Pearl China
   Range size 100.00
   Small size 50.00
Soup Bowl, adv, Coon Chicken Inn 195.00
Spice Set, 5 pcs, jars with raised ceramic
   figures, wooden rack with wall
   hanger 350.00

Statue, Louis Armstrong 95.00
String Holder, Fredericksburg porter. . . . 275.00
Target Game, Black Sambo, tin, framed,
   Wyandotte Toys, 11 × 23½″ 325.00
Tea Bell, Aunt Jemima, MIB 90.00
Teapot, young chef 125.00
Thermometer, boy 26.00
Thermos, Sambos Restaurant, includes
   literature 60.00
Tin, Luzianne Coffee, white 80.00
Trade Card, Crescent Tobacco, black men
   and mules illus, poem, 4 × 4″ 5.00
Wristwatch, Buckwheat. 40.00

BLUE RIDGE

Southern Potteries of Erwin, TN, produced Blue Ridge dinnerware from the late 1930s until 1956. Four hundred patterns graced eight basic shapes.

Newsletter: *National Blue Ridge Newsletter*, P. O. Box 298, Blountville, IN 37617.

Periodical: *The Daze*, Box 57, Otisville, MI 48463.

Soup Plate, Apple, 7¾″ w, $4.00.

Arlington Apple, Skyline
   Cup, rope handle 3.00
   Plate, 9½″ d 5.00
Avon, plate, green transfer. 15.00
Brittany, demitasse cup and saucer 40.00
Cheers, plate, 6″ sq 28.00
Cherry Tree Glen
   Bowl
     5½″ d 5.00
     6¼″ d 6.00
     9½″ d 12.00
   Creamer 7.00

Plate

   6" d 3.00

   7½" sq 15.00

   9½" d 8.00

Vegetable Bowl, 9¼" l, oval 15.00

Chick, pitcher 135.00

Chintz

   Chocolate Pot 135.00

   Creamer, ftd 32.00

Christmas Tree

   Cup and Saucer 55.00

   Plate, 10" d 50.00

Corsage, soup bowl 16.00

County Fair, salad plate 15.00

Crab Apple

   Creamer, individual 20.00

   Demitasse Cup and Saucer 28.00

Grace, pitcher, pale yellow 55.00

Mardi Gras

   Creamer 2.50

   Cup 5.00

   Fruit Bowl 3.25

   Gravy Boat, underplate 18.00

   Plate

      6½" d, bread and butter 1.25

      7" d, luncheon 2.25

      9½" d, dinner 3.25

   Saucer 75

   Vegetable Bowl, 9" l 8.00

Mountain Ivy, vegetable bowl, oval 20.00

Nocturne, plate, 9" d 5.50

Nove Rose

   Bonbon, shell shape 65.00

   Candy Box 175.00

   Celery, leaf shape 35.00

Peasant, relish, leaf shape 95.00

Poinsettia

   Creamer 8.00

   Cup 6.00

   Plate

      6¼" d 3.00

      9¼" d 8.00

Rooster, cigarette set 135.00

Rustic Plaid

   Creamer 3.50

   Cup 2.00

   Plate

      6" d, bread and butter 1.50

      9" d, dinner 3.75

   Saucer 1.00

   Sugar 3.50

Serenade, relish, handle 60.00

Shell, relish 45.00

Sunflower, plate, 10" d 8.50

Sungold, vegetable, oval 13.00

BOND, JAMES

"The name is Bond—James Bond." Women swoon, men grin, and children clap as Agent 007 works his way through another dangerous assignment for Her Majesty's Secret Service. The collector only wishes that Mr. Bond wasn't so elusive at flea markets.

The character of James Bond was invented by Ian Fleming and made famous by MGM/UA movie studios. Over the years a number of different actors have portrayed the suave "under cover" agent—Sean Connery and Roger Moore being the most popular. The Bond adventures are also noted for the unique and descriptive names given to the sinister villains and voluptuous females in distress.

Collectors need only know that Her Majesty wishes them luck in the event of their being captured by Bond collectible fever.

Action Figure

   3" h

      Dr No, Gilbert, 1964 . . . . 15.00

      James Bond, wearing tuxedo, Gilbert, 1964 . . . . 18.00

   12" h

      Holly Goodhead, Mego, 1979 . . . . . 160.00

      James Bond

         Gilbert, 1965 . . . . 350.00

         Ideal, 1966 . . . . 150.00

         Mego, deluxe figure, Moonraker, 1979 . . . . 375.00

      Jaws, Mego, 1979 . . . . 550.00

      Odd Job, Gilbert, 1965 . . . . 425.00

Accessories, Gilbert

   For 3" h action figure, 1964

      Dr No's Dragon Tank/Largo's Yacht 30.00

      Secret Map Pool Table/Lazer Table 40.00

   For 12" h action figure, 1965

      Disguise Kit #1, boxed 125.00

      Scuba Outfit #2, scuba jacket, head piece, decoy duck, spring-action spear, three spears, dagger, boxed 120.00

      Tuxedo Set, boxed 150.00

Attache Case

   Multiple Toys, 1964 . . . . 400.00

   Tomy, Japan, 1965 . . . . 650.00

Badge, 1⅛" h, silvered tin, "Special Police 007," 1960s 12.00

Board Game

   Agent 007 Game, Milton Bradley, 1966 . . . . 50.00

   Goldfinger, Milton Bradley, 1966 . . . . 40.00

   Message from M, Ideal, 1966 . . . . 150.00

   Secret Agent Game, Milton Bradley, 1964 . . . . 25.00

   Thunderball, Milton Bradley, 1965 . . . 45.00

Book, Ian Fleming

   Diamonds Are Forever, Pocket Perma M3084, 1957 . . . . 24.00

Live and Let Die, Pocket Perma M3048,
    1955. . . . . **38.00**
Moonraker, Signet S1850, 1960 . . . . . . **8.00**
You Asked For It/Casino Royale, Popular
    660, 1956. **60.00**
Bookmark, LLS Ltd, 1987 . . . . **6.00**
Bottle, 007 Aftershave, Colgate-Palmo-
    live, 4½" h, black glass, orig silver box,
    1960s. **25.00**
Camera, Bond-X Automatic Shooting,
    Multiple Toymakers, 1966 . . . .**200.00**
Card Game, Somportex
    Exciting World of James Bond, 50
        cards, 1965 . . . .**275.00**
    Thunderball, 72 cards, 1965. . . . .**160.00**
    You Only Live Twice, 78 cards,
        1967. . . . .**300.00**
Code-O-Matic, Multiple Toymakers,
    1965. . . . . **60.00**
Display, Warner Home Video, *Never Say
    Never Again*, 8 ¼ × 10", cardboard, ea-
    sel back, Sean Connery flanked by two
    women illus, multicolored **20.00**
Dog Tags, Imperial, 1980s **5.00**
Doll, Jaws, 12" h, hard plastic, soft vinyl
    head, fabric clothing, marked "Copy-
    right 1979 Eon Productions Ltd" **115.00**
Electric Drawing Set, Lakeside, 1965. . . .**100.00**
Exploding Coin, Coibel, 1985 . . . . **5.00**
Gift Set, *License to Kill*, Matchbox,
    1989. . . . . **50.00**
Glass, drinking, *A View to a Kill*. **10.00**
Gum Cards
    Moonraker, Topps, 2½ × 3½", set of 99
        cards, 22 stickers, 1979. . . . . **30.00**
    Thunderball, Philadelphia Gum, set of
        66, 1965. . . . .**250.00**
Hand Puppet, Odd Job, Gilbert, 1965 . . .**200.00**
Lunch Box, Aladdin, metal, emb, multi-
    colored, 7 × 8 × 4", 1966 . . . . **85.00**
Magazine, *James Bond*, Dell, 8 × 11", 32
    pgs, glossy **45.00**
Model Kit
    Aston Martin, Airfix, 1965. . . . .**120.00**
    Autogyro, Airfix, 1967 . . . .**375.00**
    Dr No, with Bond and Honey, Imai,
        1984. . . . .**250.00**
    James Bond and Odd Job
        Airfix-12, Series 4, 1966. . . . .**225.00**
        Aurora, 1966. . . . .**400.00**
    Moonraker Shuttle, Revell, 1979. . . . . **30.00**
Pen, LLS Ltd, 1987 . . . . **10.00**
Press Kit, *From Russia with Love*, 1963 . . . **50.00**
Puzzle, jigsaw
    H G Toys, Bond kicking Jaws in mouth
        illus, orig box. **25.00**
    Milton Bradley, Goldfinger, 1965 . . . . **35.00**
Road Race Set, Gilbert, 1964 . . . .**650.00**
Sheet Music, *Thunderball*, 9 × 12", 3 pgs,
    Bond underwater in scuba outfit cov
    illus, 1965 . . . . **25.00**
Shoes, Hushpuppy, 1965 . . . .**175.00**
Spin Saw, *Octopussy*, Playcraft, 1980s. . . . **25.00**

Sticker Book, *A View to a Kill*, Dajaq, 100
    stickers, 1985 . . . . **45.00**
Vehicle
    Aston Martin
        Gamma, 1960s 500.00
        Gilbert, slot car, 1965 . . . . **35.00**
        Strombecker, slot car, 1968 . . . . . . .150.00
    Helicopter, Corgi, *The Spy Who Loved
        Me*, diecast metal replica, 3" l, black
        and yellow, 1976. . . . . **30.00**
    Moon Buggy, Corgi, 1972 . . . . .500.00
    Moonraker Jet Ranger, Corgi,
        1970. . . . . **75.00**
    Mustang Mach 1, Corgi, 1972 . . . . . . .350.00
    Set, four diecast metal replicas, 5" l As-
        ton Martin, 5" l Lotus Esprit, 6" l
        space shuttle, 2" l satellite, Corgi,
        1979. . . . . .200.00
    Toyota 2000, *You Only Live Twice*,
        Corgi, 4" l, 1967 . . . . .100.00
Video, James Bond 007 Trivia Game,
    MGM/UA, orig 10 × 13" envelope,
    1980s. **50.00**
Viewmaster Pack, *Live and Let Die*,
    1973. . . . . **25.00**
Walkie Talkie, Secret Service, Imperial,
    1984. . . . . **20.00**
Wristwatch
    Secret Wristwatch Radio, Vanity Fair,
        1970s. **75.00**
    Spy Watch, decoder, Gilbert, 1965 . . .400.00
Weapon
    Booby Trap, exploding code book,
        Multiple Toymakers, 1965 . . . . **45.00**
    Cap Gun, Lone Star, 100 shot repeater,
        1965. . . . . .200.00
    Gun, *For Your Eyes Only*, Automatic
        100, diecast, Crescent, 1982 . . . . . . .200.00
    Hideaway Pistol, Coibel, 1985 . . . . . . **25.00**
    Mayday Pistol, *A View to a Kill*,
        1980s. **30.00**
    Personal Attack Kit, Multiple Toys,
        1965. . . . . .250.00
    Rifle/Pistol Set, Secret Seven, Multiple
        Toymakers, 1965 . . . . .225.00
    SA Automatic Pistol, Multiple Toy-
        makers, 1965. . . . . .225.00
    Space Gun, *Moonraker*, Lone Star,
        1979. . . . . .150.00
    Sting Pistol, Coibel, 1985 . . . . **25.00**
    Submachine Gun, 9mm, Imperial,
        1984. . . . . **15.00**
    Thunderball Pistol, Coibel, 1985 . . . . . . **25.00**
    Walther PPK, *You Only Live Twice*, fires
        blanks, Japan. 325.00
    Water Pistol, Multiple Toys, 1965 . . . . **75.00**

BOOKENDS

Prices listed below are for pairs. Woe to the
dealer who splits pairs apart!

Anchor, bronze **35.00**
Cat, full figure, pottery, Rookwood, c1923 .... **200.00**
Cheshire Cat, brass, c1930 .... **135.00**
Cornucopia, 5¾" h, glass, New Martinsville **50.00**
Daddy Bear, 4½" h, glass, New Martinsville **100.00**
Donald Duck, 7" h, carrying school books, chalkware **20.00**
Elephants, ivory, teakwood base **165.00**
Fish, glass, Heisey **150.00**
Fleur-de-lis, 10 × 5", copper, Roycroft, orb mark **100.00**
Flower Basket, cast iron, painted **50.00**
Flower Urn, soapstone **85.00**
Lincoln Memorial, plaster, bronze finish, detailed **25.00**
Nudes, 5 × 7", cast iron, bronze finish, full figured, kneeling, Art Deco **70.00**
Race Horse and Jockey, white metal, bronze finish, Art Deco **75.00**
Sentry, 7½" h, brass, Bakelite trim, orb mounted base, Chase Chrome and Brass Co, impressed mark **165.00**
Setter, pointing, 4½ × 7½", cast iron, black, c1920 .... **95.00**
Terriers, 4¼" h, chrome plated, round back and base, c1920 .... **100.00**
Tooled Design, 6 × 6", leather, wood base, Roycroft, orb mark **150.00**

BOOKS

There are millions of books out there. Some are worth a fortune. Most are hardly worth the paper they are printed on. Listing specific titles serves little purpose in a price guide such as this. By following ten guidelines below, you can quickly determine if the books that you have uncovered have value potential.

1. Check your book titles in *American Book Prices Current*, which is published annually by Bancroft-Parkman, Inc., and is available at most libraries and *The Old Book Value Guide, Second Edition* (Collector Books: 1990). When listing your books in preparation for doing research include the full name of the author, expanded title, name of publisher, copyright date, and edition and/or printing number.

2. Examine the bindings. Decorators buy handsomely bound books by the foot at prices ranging from $40.00 to $75.00 per foot.

3. Carefully research any children's book. Illustration quality is an important

value key. Little Golden Books are one of the hottest book areas in the market today. In the late 1970s and early 1980s Big Little Books were hot.

4. Buy all hardcover books about antiques and collectibles that you find that are cheaply priced, i.e., less than five dollars. There is a growing demand for out-of-print antiques and collectibles books.

5. Check the edition number. Value, in most cases, rests with the first edition. However, not every first edition is valuable. Consult Blank's *Bibliography of American First Editions* or Tannen's *How to Identify and Collect American First Editions*.

6. Look at the multifaceted aspects of the book and the subject that it covers. Books tend to be collected by type, e.g., mysteries, Westerns, etc. Many collectors buy books as supplements to their main collection. A Hopalong Cassidy collector, although focusing primarily on the objects licensed by Bill Boyd, will want to own the Mulford novels in which Hopalong Cassidy originated.

7. Local histories and atlases always have a good market, particularly those printed between 1880 and 1930. Add to this centennial and other celebration volumes.

8. Check to see if the book was signed by the author. Generally an author's signature increases the value of the book. However, it was a common practice to put engraved signatures of authors in front of books during the last part of the nineteenth century. The Grant signature in the first volume of his two-volume memoir set is not original, but printed.

9. Book club editions have little or no value with the exception of books done by George and Helen Macy's Limited Editions Club.

10. Accept the fact that the value of most books falls in the 50¢ to $2.00 range and that after all the searching that you have done, this is probably what you have found.

BOOTJACKS

Unless you are into horseback riding, a bootjack is one of the most useless devices that you can have around the house. Why do so many individuals own one? The answer in our area is "just for nice." Actually, they are seen as a major accessory in trying to capture the country look.

Cast iron reproductions are a major problem, especially for "Naughty Nellie" and "Beetle" designs.

Cast Iron, "Boot Jack" emb on prongs, wrench socket end, 13½" l, $40.00.

Advertising, Musselmans Plug Tobacco, cast iron, ornate **150.00**
Brass, beetle, 10" l **90.00**
Cast Iron
  Beetle, 9¼" l, black **35.00**
  Closed Loop, painted **70.00**
  Cricket, 11¾" l, emb lacy design **25.00**
  Heart and Circle, open, 13" l, scalloped
    sides **225.00**
  Lyre shape, 10¼" l **48.00**
  Mule's head **40.00**
  Pheasants, pr, 19" l **225.00**
  Scissor Action, marked "Pat 1877" . . . **85.00**
  Vine design, 12" l **35.00**
  V-shaped, ornate **45.00**
Wood
  Fish, 19" l, relief carving, red stain **30.00**
  Oval Ends, 25" l, pine, sq nail con-
    struction **30.00**

BOTTLE OPENERS, FIGURAL

Although this listing focuses on cast iron figural bottle openers, the most sought-after type of bottle openers, do not forget the tin advertising openers, also known to some as church keys. The bulk still sell between $2.00 and $10.00, a very affordable price range.

All openers listed are cast iron unless otherwise specified.

Clubs: Figural Bottle Opener Collectors, 117 Basin Hill Road, Duncannon, PA 17020; Just For Openers, 63 October Lane, Trumbull, CT 06611.

Advertising, Harvard Brewing Co, Lowell, MA, red ground, white letters, 3½" l, $15.00.

Alligator **30.00**
Black Boy, hand in air, riding on green
  alligator, green base, John Wright
  Co **165.00**
Clown
  Brass, 4" h, wall mounted, white bow-
    tie, red polka dots, bald head, sgd
    "495" on back, John Wright Co **70.00**
  Cast Iron, moustache, four eyes **35.00**
Cowboy, 4⅞" h, marked "San Antonio,
  Texas" **225.00**
Dachshund
  Brass **50.00**
  Cast Iron, nickel plated, marked
    "Medford Lager Beer" **45.00**
Donkey **35.00**
Drunk
  With Palm Tree, 4" h, polychrome
    paint **65.00**
  With Signpost, polychrome paint,
    marked "Baltimore, MD" **10.00**
Girl, 3⅞" h, buck teeth, polychrome
  paint, marked "Wilton Prod" **50.00**
Hand, pointing, marked "Effinger Beer,
  Baraboo, Wisconsin" **15.00**
Horseshoe **25.00**
Nude, reclining, chromed metal **35.00**
Parrot **20.00**
Pelican, 3¾" h, cream colored, orange
  beak and feet, green base, John Wright
  Co **140.00**
Rooster, 3¼" h, polychrome paint **50.00**
Seagull, 3¼" h, on stump, polychrome
  paint **175.00**
Steel worker, 3¼" h, polychrome
  paint **175.00**
Swordfish **65.00**
Teeth, 3⅜" l, polychrome paint **95.00**
Toucan, on perch, 5" h, polychrome
  paint **55.00**

BOTTLES

Bottle collecting is such a broad topic that the only way one can hope to survive is by specialization. It is for this reason that several bottle topics are found elsewhere in this book.

Bottles have a bad habit of multiplying. Do not start collecting them until you have plenty of room. I know one person whose entire basement is filled with Coca-Cola bottles bearing the imprint of different cities.

There are many bottle categories that are still relatively inexpensive to collect. In many cases, you can find a free source of supply in old dumps. Before getting too deeply involved, it pays to talk with other bottle collectors and to visit one or more specialized bottle collector shows.

Club: Federation of Historical Bottle Collectors, 14521 Atlantic, Riverdale, IL 60627.

Periodical: *Antique Bottle And Glass Collector*, P. O. Box 187, East Greenville, PA 18041.

Adams Springs Mineral Water, Lake County, CA, Dr. W. R. Prather, Prop, light blue, c1895, 11½" h, $15.00.

BEVERAGES

Acme Soda Water, Pittsburgh, aqua	18.00
Alburgh A Springs, qt, yellow amber....	40.00
Bellmore Whiskey, qt, clear, labeled	25.00
Booths High & Dry Gin, 10¼" h, light blue	5.00
Bubble Up Pop	4.75
Buster Brown Rye, swirled, enameled	55.00

Cloverleaf Dairy, Quincy, Mass, qt emb	35.00
Double Line Soda, Kokomo, IN	6.00
Fruitbowl Grapefruit Wine	12.00
Glicquot Soda, paper label	5.00
Gordon Dry Gin, London, England, 9" h, light green	5.00
Grapette Pop	8.00
Klassy Tops In Taste Pop............	8.00
Knapp Root Beer, labeled............	15.00
Korker The OK Refresher Pop	5.50
Mountain Valley Mineral Water	13.00
Quality Beverages, Perryton, Texas, green, crown top.................	10.00
Royal Ruby Beer, 32 oz	35.00
Schlitz Beer, ruby red, label	15.00
Stroymers Grape Punch, 12" h, clear, metal cap.......................	140.00
Twitchell Superior Mineral Water, blue green	40.00

FLAVORINGS

A & S, lemon extract, c1905...........	24.00
Baker Flavoring Extract, 5" h, clear.....	10.00
Burnetts Standard Flavoring Extract, 5½" h, aqua.....................	4.00
Colgate, vanilla extract, c1910........	20.00
Dr Fenners Concentrated Flavors, 6" h, aqua..........................	3.00
Hanfords Flavoring Extracts, 5¼" h, clear..........................	2.00
Herberlings, banana flavoring, 8" h, paper label........................	8.00
HICO Imitation Lemon Flavoring, 8 oz, clear..........................	6.00
Highland Maple Sap Syrup	9.00
James Chaskel & Co Extract..........	35.00
Louis & Co, lemon extract	10.00
McCormick Imitation Pineapple	5.50
Newmans' Pure Cold Extracts, 5½" h, clear..........................	2.00
Sauers Extracts, 6" h, clear	4.00
Thompson & Taylor Root Beer Flavoring, 4" h, clear	3.00

FOOD

Bertin Brand Pure Olive Oil, 7½" h, dark green	12.00
Cathedral Peppersauce, 9" h, deep aqua..........................	110.00
Cross & Blackwell Mint Sauce	3.00
East Indian Pickles, qt, aqua..........	15.00
Frank's BBQ Sauce..................	6.50
Golden Tree Maple Syrup, 20 oz, clear, screw top......................	2.00
L & S Sweet Dill Strips	8.50
Marceau Spanish Olives, 7¾" h, barrel shape, clear.....................	14.00
Marvel Sweet Pickles	12.00
Old Style Mustard, pt, clear, label	5.00
Purity Oats, qt, clear, flower dec, screw cap.........................	12.00
Skilton Foote & Cos/Bunker Hill Pickles, 6¾" h, sq, yellow amber...........	50.00

Spears Vinegar	8.00
Warsaw Salt Co Choice Table Salt, 5¾" h, amber	60.00

HEALTH AND BEAUTY

Anticipitic [sic] Talcum Powder	5.00
Arnolds Vegetable Hair Balsam, 6⅛" h, clear	18.00
Athieus Cough Syrup	5.00
Bono Opto For The Eyes, 3¼" h, clear	4.00
B W Hair & Son Asthma Cure London, 5" h, aqua	25.00
Chattanooga Medicine Co, 8⅜" h, light green, screw top	5.00
Craigs Kidney & Liver Cure, 9½" h, amber	80.00
Dr C Grattans Diphtheria Remedy, 7" h, aqua	25.00
Dr Pettits Canker Balm, 3¼" h, flask shape, clear	8.00
Fletchers Castoria, 6" h, aqua	5.00
Genuine Old Fashioned Bitters, 5¾" h, clear, label and contents	20.00
Golden Eye Lotion, Leonardis, Tampa, Fla, 4½" h, aqua	8.00
Harter's Wild Cherry Bitters, Dayton, 8¼" h, rect, amber	75.00
Hoods Tooth Powder, CI Hood & Co, 3½" h, clear	5.00
Hostetter's Bitters	15.00
Leonardis Blood Elixir, 8¼" h, amber	15.00
Lufkin Eczema Remedy, 7" h, clear, label	8.00
Lydia E Pinkham's Vegetable Compound, green	8.00
Ponds Extract, 5½" h, amethyst	15.00
Rubifoam For The Teeth, 4" h, clear	5.00
Saint Jacobs Bitters, 8½" h, amber	40.00
Sparks Perfect Health For Kidney & Liver Diseases, 4" h, aqua	8.00
Thorns Hop & Burdock Tonic, 6⅜" h, yellow	30.00
US Marine Hospital Service	20.00
Warners Safe Diabetes Cure, Melbourne, 9½" h, amber	100.00
Willards, Golden Seal Bitters, 7⅝" h, aqua	45.00

HOUSEHOLD

Alma Polish, aqua, name emb on shoulder, 5" h, marked "M & Co" on base	5.00
Bengal Bluing, 5¾" h, aqua	3.00
Dutchers Dead Shot For Bed Bugs, 4⅞" h, aqua, label	60.00
Hercules Disinfectant, 6" h, amber	4.00
Liquid Stove Polish, 6¼" h, clear	2.00
Mexican Imperial Bluing, 10 oz, clear, gold cap	7.50
Poison, cobalt blue	28.00
Snow Bird Liquid Wax, 6 oz, brown bottle, red cap, blue and white label	7.50

Standardised Disinfectant Co, 4¼" h, light amber	2.00
Uptons Liquid Glue, 2⅞" h, aqua, twelve sided	40.00

BOXES

We have reached the point with some twentieth century collectibles where the original box may be more valuable than the object that came in it. If the box is colorful and contains a picture of the product, it has value.

Boxes have always been a favorite among advertising collectors. They are three-dimensional and often fairly large in size. The artwork reflects changing period tastes. Decorators like the pizazz that boxes offer. The wood box with a lithographed label is a fixture in the country household.

Advertising, Ideal, Not-A-Seed Raisins, American Seedless Raisin Co, white ground, green grapes, red and black letters, 6⅛" l, $10.00.

Advertising
Armour's Washing Powder, shipping	5.00
Baker's Chocolate, 12 lbs, wood, shipping	15.00
Bee Soap, wood, paper label	65.00
Blanar Banana	55.00
Bossie's Best Brand Butter, pound	2.00
Cupples Topseal Jar Rings, unused	4.00
Dr Johnson's Educator Crackers	35.00
Dwight Soda, wood, cow illus and adv on sides	25.00
Forbes Co, St Louis, allspice, Buster Brown illus	40.00
Gay Times Soft Drink, children illus	20.00
Jackson Fly Killer, display, wood	25.00
Pickney Spice, wood, store size	80.00
Reese Cigars, wood	20.00
Regal Underware, cardboard	15.00

Royal Baking Powder, wood, shipping,
  c1800 . . . . 125.00
Union Biscuit 20.00
Collar, gutta percha, 1876 Centen-
  nial. 125.00
Empty, original
Marx Toy, police siren motorcycle. . . . 170.00
Tootsietoy, furniture 85.00
Walt Disney, Mickey Mouse wrist-
  watch. 110.00
Pencil
Faber Castell 12.00
Lone Range 125.00
Sample, National Lead Co, paint chip
  samples 15.00

BOY SCOUTS

This is another collecting area in which
adults dominate where you would normally expect to find kids. When my dad
was a Boy Scout, emphasis was on swapping material with little concern for value.
One for one was the common rule.

Today old Scouting material is viewed in
monetary terms. Eagle badge books go for
seventy-five dollars or more. The key is to
find material that was officially licensed.
Unlicensed material is generally snubbed
by collectors.

Boy Scout collecting is so sophisticated
that it has its own shows or swap meets.
Strong retail value for Boy Scout material
occurs at these shows. Flea market prices
tend to be much lower.

*Signal Kit, Catalog No. 1098, battery operated,
$35.00.*

Award Plaque, 6½ × 9½", masonite, full
  color portrait picture, awarded by National Council of Boy Scouts for participation in Onward For God And My
  Country Program, 1958 . . . . 45.00
Bank, orig paint 95.00
Book, *Troop Committee*, 5½ × 8", 42 pgs,
  1931 Boy Scouts of America copy-
  right. 25.00

Canteen, aluminum, hip type, red can-
  vas cov 8.00
Certificate, Assistant Scout Master,
  Warren, PA, 1914, sgd by Theodore
  Roosevelt, framed 100.00
Handbook
Handbook for Scoutmasters, 1922, blue
  cov 15.00
Lone Scouts of America, 1915–20, 50 pgs,
  illus 25.00
Scouting For Boys, 1935 . . . . 17.50
Magazine, *Boy's Life*, Norman Rockwell
  cov 25.00
Membership Card, 2½ × 3¾", typed
  name and October 31, 1941, orig 2¾ ×
  4" brown manila envelope 12.00
Mirror 7.50
Neckerchief
Cub Scout Standard, 3rd issue, tender-
  foot emblem, band border 4.00
National Jamboree, 1973, blue cotton,
  emblem 5.00
National Order of the Arrow Confer-
  ence, 1967, tan cotton, emblem 18.00
World Scouting, purple, white design,
  white piping 8.50
Notepad, 2½ × 4", Boy Scout signaling
  illus on front, 1914 copyright 25.00
Paperweight, silver, Explorer symbol . . .   5.00
Pennant, 30" l, felt, blue, white inscrip-
  tion, c1940 . . . . 20.00
Pocket Watch, dollar type, Ingersol, pat-
  ented July 2, 1916. . . . . 350.00
Scarf Slide, plastic, white, raised red In-
  dian head, 1951 . . . .   8.00

BOYD CRYSTAL ART GLASS

The Boyds, Bernard and his son, purchased the Degenhart Glass Factory in
1978. Since that time they have reissued a
number of the Degenhart forms. Their
productions can be distinguished by the
color of the glass and the "D" in a diamond
mark. The Boyd family continues to make
contemporary collectible glass at its factory
in Cambridge, Ohio.

Animal
Bunny on Nest, White Opal 9.00
Butterfly, ruby, originally Cambridge
  mold. 30.00
Debbie Duck, English Yew 5.00
Ducklings
Crown Tuscan 2.75
Light Rose 2.50
Joey Pony
Candy Swirl. 15.00
Chocolate 30.00
Persimmon 25.00

Patrick, Balloon Bear, Golden Delight **7.50**
Rooster, Orange Calico **10.00**
Skippy, dog, sitting
    Light Rose **8.50**
    Pippin Green **7.50**
Suee Pig, Autumn Beige **7.50**
Willie, mouse, 2" h, Lime Carnival ... **10.00**
Basket, 4½" d, Milk White, hand painted dec **20.00**
Bell
    Owl, Violet Slate **15.00**
    Santa, Carnival **20.00**
Candleholder, sleigh, White **22.00**
Colonial Doll, Sunflower Yellow **20.00**
Hobo Clown, Freddie, Cobalt Blue **9.00**
Louise, doll
    Golden Delight **10.00**
    Lemon Ice **120.00**
Salt, lamb, Grape Parfait. **10.00**
Tractor, Spinnaker Blue, 2" h **10.00**

BRASS

Brass is a durable, malleable, and ductile metal alloy consisting mainly of copper and zinc. It appears in this guide because of the wide variety of objects made from it. I have never met a brass collector whose interest spans all forms, but I have met padlock and key collectors.

Candlestick, 9¼" h, $155.00.

Ashtray, 4½ × 5", figural, bull's head. ... **50.00**
Blotter, rocker shape, knob handle **10.00**
Bowl, handles, Dutch **50.00**
Box, 6¾" l, hanging, emb floral dec **25.00**

Call Bell, 6¼" h, red granite base **25.00**
Door Handles, pr, 16" l, sq elongated form, cast floral dec. **10.00**
Door Knocker, basket with flowers **78.00**
Fireplace Fan, 38" w, 25" h, folding, griffin detail. **65.00**
Hatpin, four kittens, 9" l. **85.00**
Jardiniere, 6" h, globular form, incised geometric and floral motif, 19th C **20.00**
Key
    Door, 5" l, standard bow and bit **8.00**
    Watch, 1" l, plain, swivel **2.00**
Knife, Golden Wedding Whiskey adv ... **20.00**
Letter Opener, Pittsburg Coal Co adv, Indian head on handle **15.00**
Matchsafe, International Tailoring adv, nickel plated, emb Indians and lion ... **55.00**
Mortar and Pestle, 2½" h **40.00**
Padlock
    Combination, 2½" h, Sesamee, dials on bottom **15.00**
    Lever Push Key, 2¼" d, Champion Six Lever, emb. **5.00**
Picture Frame, easel type, Art Nouveau style, gilded, four topaz colored jewels **175.00**
Plant Stand, gilded, white onyx shelf and top **50.00**
Suppository Mold **80.00**
Teapot, 8¼" h, Oriental dragons and trees dec. **40.00**

BREAD BOXES

Bread boxes are too much fun to be hidden in a Kitchen Collectibles category. There are plenty of great examples both in form and decoration. They have disappeared from the modern kitchen. I miss them.

Chrome, rect, black wood handle **10.00**
Graniteware
    Gray, sq, raised red handles and letters "Bread". **25.00**
    Green, c1880. .... **100.00**
    Green and White, 19" l, hinged lid, 1920s **95.00**
Metal
    Betsy Ross Moderne pattern, white, red trim, Roll-A-Way, E M Meder Co, 1930s **15.00**
    Fruit Decal, painted yellow **15.00**
    Red Poppy pattern **17.00**
    Stenciled "Bread," white enamel paint, c1900. .... **32.00**
Tin, 12" l, white, red enameled top **12.00**
Wood, 12½" h, carved "Give Us This Day" **80.00**

BREAD PLATES

Bread, the staff of life, has been served on ornate plates of all types, ranging from colored glass of the Victorian era to the handwrought aluminum of the 1950s. Some bread plates included mottos or commemorated historical events.

Avoid plain examples. A great bread plate should add class to the table.

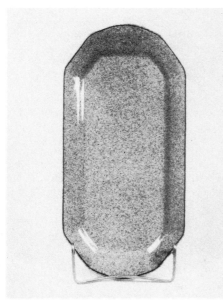

Porcelain, blue spongeware dec, marked "Midwinter Porcelon, Burslem, England," 6¼" w, 13¼" l, $30.00.

Aluminum, hand wrought, chrysanthe-
mum dec, ornate handles. 20.00
Cut Glass, 13½" l, brilliant cut, sgd "Lib-
bey". 175.00
Majolica, 12¼" l, Oak Leaf with Acorns
pattern. 120.00
Pattern Glass
  Actress, Miss Neilson center, 9 ×
  13". 80.00
  Aurora, ruby stained, 10" d, center
  star. 35.00
  Baltimore, 12½" d 70.00
  Butterfly and Fan 45.00
  California, emerald green. 45.00
  Cupid and Venus, amber 75.00
  Daisy and Button, apple green. 60.00
  Finecut and Panel, amber. 45.00
  Garden of Eden 75.00
  Kansas, emb "Our Daily Bread" 45.00
  New Jersey, ruby stained 100.00
  Palmette 30.00
  Royal Lady, vaseline. 135.00

Wheat and Barley. 25.00
Silver Plated, grape clusters on self han-
dles 65.00
Wooden, round, "Bread" emb on rim,
hand rubbed oil refinish 15.00

BREWERIANA

Beer is liquid bread, or so I was told growing up in Pennsylvania German country. It is hard to deny German linkage with the brewing industry when your home community contained the Horlacher, Neuweiler, and Uhl breweries.

Brewery signs and trays, especially from the late nineteenth and early twentieth century, contain some of the finest advertising lithography of the period. The three-dimensional advertising figures from the 1930s through the 1970s are no slouches either.

Brewery advertising has become expensive. Never fear. You can build a great breweriana collection concentrating on barroom accessories such as foam scrapers, coasters, and tap knobs.

Clubs: American Breweriana Association, P. O. Box 6082, Colorado Springs, CO 80934; National Association Breweriana Advertising, 2343 Mat-Tu-Wee Lane, Wauwatosa, WI 53226.

Beer Tray, Utica Club, 12" d, $22.00.

Ashtray
  Canadian Club 20.00
  Great Falls Select Beer, milk glass 12.00
Beer Can, Stroh's, miniature 4.00

Blotter, 7½ × 3", Bergdoll Brewing Co, black and white portrait of Louis Bergdoll, holly dec, 60th anniversary, 1909, unused **50.00**

Bottle
  Beckers Beer, Evanston, WY **10.00**
  Calgary Ale **10.00**
  Enterprise Brewing Co, qt **8.00**
  Fredericksburg Brewery, 11¼" h, red amber. **15.00**
  Schwarzenbach Brewing Co, 7¼" h, clear. **3.00**
Bottle Opener, Pabst, metal, figural bottle. **7.50**
Clock, Old Milwaukee, bar display, ship's bell time. **60.00**
Coaster, Simon Pure Beer, metal. **5.00**
Corkscrew, Anheuser-Busch, encased **75.00**
Fishing Lure, Schlitz, bottle shape **10.00**
Foam Scraper, Meister Brau, celluloid. **20.00**
Ice Pick, Empire Lager, Black Horse Ale **25.00**
Lamp, Budweiser, wall, pr **22.00**
Lapel Pin, Pabst Breweries, enameled 14K gold **25.00**
Matchbook, Stoeckle Beer, oversized, figural matches **20.00**
Matchsafe
  Genessee **65.00**
  Pabst Beer, pocket. **48.00**
  Schlitz **55.00**
Pinback Button
  Emil Sick's Select Beer, 1½" d, red number "6" logo, yellow ground, black letters, gold rim and accents, c1930. . . . . **20.00**
  Poth's Beer, 1" d, white letters, khaki ground, c1900. . . . . **12.00**
  Schlitz Beer, 1¼" d, white ground, red letters, crossed key center, early 1900s **20.00**
Poster, Budweiser, Spuds MacKenzie illus **6.00**
Sign, Piels Beer, Sammy Davis Jr, bust **100.00**
Stein
  Budweiser, ceramic, emb **11.00**
  Hamm's Beer, Octoberfest, 1973, McCoy. **25.00**
  Miller High Life, 1984. . . . . **25.00**
  Old Milwaukee **18.00**
  Schlitz **18.00**
Tap Knob, Hamm's Beer, metal. **15.00**
Thermometer, Rueter & Co, Highland Spring Brewery, Boston, patented 1885, brass **175.00**
Tip Tray, Budweiser **8.00**
Tray
  Hamm's Beer, bear illus **20.00**
  Miller Beer, girl sitting on moon **40.00**
Watch Fob, Anheuser-Busch, diecut, sil-

vered brass, enameled red, white, and blue trademark **50.00**

BRITISH ROYALTY COMMEMORATIVES

This is one of those categories where you can get in on the ground floor. Every king and queen, potential king and queen, and their spouses is collectible. Buy commemorative items when they are new. I have a few Prince Harry items. We may not have royal blood in common, but. . . .

Most individuals collect by monarch, prince, or princess. Take a different approach—collect by form, e.g., mugs, playing cards, etc. British royalty commemoratives were made at all quality levels. Stick to high-quality examples.

It is fun to find recent issues at flea markets for much less than their original selling price. Picking is competitive. There are a lot of British royalty commemorative collectors. The following list is in chronological order.

Mug, Prince William–3rd Birthday, Prince Henry–1st Birthday, black and white portraits on front, each child's age and information on either side of portrait, limited edition of 150, Dorincourt, 2⅝" h, each $45.00.

Queen Victoria
  Golden Jubilee, 1887, plate, pressed glass, clear, "1887, Year of Jubilee". **100.00**
  Diamond Jubilee, 1897, plate, white, color portrait center, raised design border, gold trim, Doulton **225.00**
Edward VII, coronation, June 28, 1902
  Beaker, transfer printed, portrait, date, and "The King's Coronation Dinner presented by His Majesty," Doulton **100.00**
  Candy Tin, 2¼ × 5", rect, Rowntree & Co. **35.00**
George V
  Coronation, June 22, 1911, program, issued by City of Lincoln **25.00**

Silver Jubilee, 1935, tin, 5½ × 4½",
McVitie & Price Biscuit Manufacturers, marked "Free Sample" on bottom 30.00
Edward VIII, coronation, May 12, 1937
Ashtray, round, scalloped edge 25.00
Glass, clear, etched portrait and inscriptions 35.00
Teapot, cov, portrait and shield, gold
trim 95.00
George VI, coronation, May 12, 1937
Cigarette Case, book type, emb medallion design on front cov, clasp,
1930s 38.00
Egg Cup, portrait illus.............. 35.00
Mug, tin, portrait illus.............. 35.00
Queen Elizabeth II
Coronation
Magazine, *The Illustrated London
News*...................... 20.00
Pocket Watch, 2" d, silvered metal,
back engraved with royal family
crest 250.00
Stamp Packet, 4 × 6" envelope, unseparated block of sixty different
stamps, 1953, pr 20.00
Silver Jubilee, 1977
Bell, 5½" h, applied roses, silver
trim, Crown Staffordshire....... 30.00
Pincushion, crown, silvered metal........................ 30.00
Playing Cards, portrait illus 10.00
Eightieth birthday, Aug 4, 1980, mug,
portrait in floral wreath, inscribed
"To Celebrate the 80th Birthday of
Her Majesty Queen Elizabeth the
Queen Mother, August 4, 1980,"
Spode....................... 75.00
Prince Charles
Investiture as Prince of Wales, July 1,
1969, dish, 5½" d, multicolored coat
of arms, ftd, Aynsley............ 50.00
Wedding to Lady Diana Spencer, July
29, 1981
Coca-Cola Bottle............... 40.00
Lace Panel, Nottingham lace,
twenty-point................ 25.00
Mug, 3½" h, sepia portraits, color
dec, Pall Mall Ware........... 35.00
Plate, 10½" d, black and white portraits, color and gold dec 40.00
Playing Cards, double deck, British
Monarchs, color portraits,
Grimaud 30.00
Tea Towel, Irish linen, color portraits....................... 15.00
Trinket Box, cov, 4" w, heart
shaped, portrait illus on cov, wedding information inside, Hammersley 35.00
Prince William of Wales, birth, June 21,
1982
Bowl, 6" d, color portraits and nursery

scenes 35.00
Post Card...................... 2.00
Spoon, silver plated, picture of Prince
and Princess of Wales holding William on handle 12.00
Thimbles, set of four, Queen Mother,
Queen Elizabeth, Princess Diana,
and crown illus, Caverswall 60.00

BROWNIES, PALMER COX

Palmer Cox created *The Brownies*, comical elf-like creatures, for *St. Nicholas* magazine. Each Brownie had a distinct personality and name. Thirteen books were published about them.

Beware of imitation Brownies. The Brownies' success led other illustrators to utilize elf figures in their cartoons. The only way to tell the copies from the originals is to carefully study and memorize the Cox illustrations.

Basket, 2 × 4", desk type, brass, Brownie
at base 75.00
Book
The Brownies Abroad, 18th printing, dj,
1941........................ 35.00
Palmer Cox Brownie Yearbook, McLoughlin Bros, 1895 .... 190.00
Box, Little Buster Popcorn 12.00
Charm, 1" d, white metal, black finish,
vest and cap, c1900............. 35.00
Creamer, 2½" h, china, Brownies smoking pipe, verse on back 60.00
Napkin Ring, figural, silver plated 80.00
Needle Book, Columbian Expo, Brownie
Policeman illus, 1893 .... 50.00
Paper Doll, Lion Coffee adv 20.00
Plate, marked "Cook & Hancock, Trenton"........................... 60.00
Ruler, Mrs Winslow's Soothing Syrup
adv............................ 25.00
Stickpin, Brownie Policeman.......... 20.00
Trade Card, American Machine Co, ice
cream freezers................... 18.00

BUBBLE GUM CARDS

Based on the publicity received by baseball cards, you would think that they were the only bubble gum cards sold. Wrong, wrong, wrong! There are a wealth of nonsport bubble gum cards.

Prices for many of these card sets are rather modest. Individual cards often sell for less than $1.00. The classic cards were issued in the 1950s, but I bought a pack of the recent Desert Storm cards just to be on the safe side.

Periodical: *The Wrapper*, 1903 Ronzheimer Avenue, St. Charles, IL 60174.

Topps, Davy Crockett, R712-1, from set of 80 cards, $.50.

Bowman
    1948, Movie Stars, 2¹/₁₆ × 1½", 36-card
      set. **75.00**
    1953, Antique Autos, 2½ × 3¾", 48-
      card set. **50.00**
    Buymore, 1962, Treasure Island, 66
      cards. **100.00**
Donruss
    1963, Idiot Cards, 66 cards **105.00**
    1966, Monkees, 44 cards **38.00**
    1973, Osmonds, 66 cards **30.00**
    1976, Bionic Woman, 44 cards **30.00**
    1980, Dukes of Hazzard, 66 cards. **3.50**
Fleer
    1963, Goofy Gags, 28 cards **60.00**
    1968, My Kookie Klassmates, 20 cards,
      9 autograph stamp sheets **15.00**
    1979, Gong Show, 66 cards, 10
      stickers. **5.00**
    1983, Mad, 128 stickers **15.00**
Leaf, 1967, Star Trek, 72 cards **550.00**
Philadelphia Chewing Gum Co
    1965, James Bond, 66 cards **55.00**
    1966, Tarzan, 66 cards **40.00**
    1969, Dark Shadows, Series II, 66
      cards, green **80.00**
Topps
    1965, Daniel Boone, 55 cards. **25.00**

1966, Batman, orange backs, 55
    cards. **145.00**
1970, Brady Bunch, 88 cards **150.00**
1980, Empire Strikes Back, Series I . . . **5.00**

BUSTER BROWN

R. F. Outcault could have rested on his Yellow Kid laurels. Fortunately, he did not and created a second great cartoon character—Buster Brown. The strip first appeared in the Sunday, May 4, 1902, *New York Herald.* Buster's fame was closely linked to Tige, his toothily grinning evil-looking bulldog.

Most of us remember Buster Brown and Tige because of Buster Brown Shoes. The shoe advertisements were popular on radio and television shows of the 1950s. "Look for me in there too."

Wiggle Picture, Froggie, $15.00.

Bandanna **50.00**
Bank, 5" h, Buster and Tige, cast iron,
    early 1900s **130.00**
Bike, merry-go-round horse, Buster and
    Tige advertisement, Hollywood Jr **295.00**
Book, *Book of Travels,* 1912 . . . . **45.00**
Box, stockings, graphics **39.00**
Calendar Plate, 7" d, Buster and Tige,
    1909. . . . . **48.00**
Cigar **10.00**
Clicker, Buster Brown Hosiery, red,
    white, and blue, 1930–1940 . . . . **22.00**
Coat Hook **28.00**
Compact, 2" d, brass, emb logo "Buster
    Brown Shoes, First Because Of The
    Last," Buster holding shoe beside Tige,
    reverse with hinged door and small
    mirror, c1930 . . . . **65.00**

Dictionary, *Buster Brown Webster Selected Dictionary*, Buster Brown shoe premium.......................... **32.00**
Dinnerware, 3 pcs, plate, cup, and saucer, white china, gold trim, Buster pouring tea for Tige illus, marked "3-Crown China, Germany".......... **95.00**
Fan, framed....................... **85.00**
Game, Pin the Tie on Buster Brown, 24 × 48" paper sheet, early 1900s........ **125.00**
Kite............................ **35.00**
Lapel Stud, 1¼" w, white metal, silver finish, Buster with hand on Tige's head, c1900.................. **40.00**
Mirror, pocket, 1946 .... **22.00**
Periscope, Secret Agent, unused **21.00**
Pinback Button
⅞" d
Buster Brown Gang, multicolored, litho, c1920.................. **20.00**
Buster Brown Hose Supporter, multicolored.................... **20.00**
1" d, Buster Brown Blue Ribbon Shoes, sepia, photo-like portrait of Buster and Tige, paper text on back, 1902–1910 .... **18.00**
Pitcher, 3¼" h, miniature **30.00**
Post Card, Buster and Tige, colorful, Tuck, 1906..................... **25.00**
Rug, runner, adv, 108" l, 26½" w, Buster and Tige illus, "For Boys, For Girls, Buster Brown, Brown bilt Shoes," design repeated three times **110.00**
Shoe Box, Buster Brown Shoes........ **15.00**
Shoehorn **40.00**
Sign, Buster Brown Shoes **45.00**
Spice Box, Forbes Co, St Louis, allspice.......................... **40.00**
Stickpin, diecut, emb, name on hat, c1900........................ **50.00**
Valentine, 8" h, diecut, mechanical, Buster standing behind large walnut shell, "All in a Nutshell, Valentine Greeting," eyes roll when nutshell is raised, c1900................... **20.00**
Wallet, 1946 .... **22.00**

BUTTONS, PINBACK

Around 1893 the Whitehead & Hoad Company filed the first patents for celluloid pinback buttons. By the turn of the century, the celluloid pinback button was used as a promotional tool covering a wide spectrum, ranging from presidential candidates to amusement parks, not that there is much difference between the two.

This category covers advertising pinback buttons. Presidential pinbacks can be found in the Political Items category. To discover the full range of non-political

pinbacks consult Ted Hake and Russ King's *Price Guide To Collectible Pin-back Buttons 1896–1986* (Hake's Americana & Collectibles Press: 1986).

Advertising, Maltex and Maypo Health Club, black letters, white ground, celluloid, ⅞" d, $5.00.

American Bottlers Protective Assn of the US, silvered brass, early 1900s **35.00**
American Express Money Orders, 1¼" d, red, white, and blue, global logo center, 1930–40 .... **18.00**
Aristos Flour, orange, yellow, and black, 1900–12 .... **15.00**
Boston Swift Club, red, white, and blue, dated July 17, 1926............... **15.00**
Comfort Soap, 1¼" d, multicolored, portrait of red headed child, toothy grin, blue ground, yellow letters, 1901–10 ....**300.00**
Diamond C Hams, 1½" d, multicolored, packaged ham from Cudahy Packing Co, dark green ground, white rim inscription, 1900–12 .... **35.00**
Frigidaire, 1¼" d, blue and white, Frigidaire delivery man, refrigeration unit on shoulder, c1930............... **15.00**
Golden Glow Butter, 1¼" d, multicolored, butter package on blue center, blue lettering on soft yellow border, early 1900s **40.00**
Golden Guernsey Products, gold and yellow, black inscriptions, 1930s **12.50**
Hats Off To The New Frigidaire, red, white, and blue, patriotic Uncle Sam design, 1930–40 .... **10.00**
Homeopathic Hospital, ⅞" d, black and white, homeopathic nurse, c1920 .... **15.00**
IGA Booster Club, 1" d, red, white, and blue, pink eagle logo, 1933.......... **15.00**
Iten's Quality Product, red rim, gold "Crackers-Biscuits-Wafers-Cake and Cookies," c1912 .... **12.00**
John Alden Flour, green rim, white lettering, early 1900s **25.00**

Kenton Baking Powder, canister on black ground, 1898–99 .... **30.00**

Lion Coffee, 1¼" d, multicolored, white rim with black lettering, 1903 Indianapolis celebration **20.00**

Mandan Brand Top Hat Turkey, brown turkey, red wattles, black top hat, white background, black lettering, 1930s **18.00**

Parrot Brand Biscuit, parrot eating cracker, white background, black lettering, c1896 .... **18.00**

Royal Typewriter Co, silvered metal, dark green enameled symbol, inscribed "Royal/Accuracy First," 1930s **10.00**

Sweet Clover Brand Condensed Milk, 1¼" d, multicolored, canned milk container with round clover design label, pale yellow and green sun rays, early 1900s **65.00**

Turkey From Henry Ballard's Flock, 1½" d, multicolored, Puritan hunter displaying large turkey to wife and daughter, yellow rim lettering, c1925 .... **50.00**

Westinghouse Electric & Manufacturing Company, service award, brass, blue enameled, logo and inscription, 1930s **12.50**

Yellow Label Syrup, yellow and blue can, blue and white background, 1930s ... **15.00**

CAKE

Dad's a pie man; I love cake, the more icing the better. At the moment cake collectors are concentrating on baking implements and wedding cake statues. It's a much broader category than that. Opportunity awaits.

Book
    Pattern Book, 1986, Wilton .... **.50**
    Yearbook, 1973, Wilton **5.00**
Cake Carrier, metal **12.50**
Cake Cutters, Jr Card Party, card shape, four suits, orig box **12.00**
Cake Decoration
    Bride and Groom, 6" h, bisque, sgd "Wilton," c1960 .... **15.00**
    Set, Howdy and Friends, seven figural candleholders, unopened on orig card **35.00**
Cake Decorator, aluminum, tube, six tips, MIB **10.00**
Cake Mold, Griswold
    Rabbit **225.00**
    Santa **525.00**
Cake Pan
    Angel Food Tube, small **12.00**

Round, metal **5.00**
Santa Shape-a-Cake, instructions, MIB **8.00**
Square, metal **6.00**
Upside Down, metal **7.00**
Cake Pan and Server Set, Swansdown **10.00**
Cake Plate, Wild Rose, Harker **18.00**
Cake Server, china, hp, tined, English registry marks **18.00**
Cake Tin, 11 × 12 × 6", multicolored litho scenes of Manhattan Island, c1915 ... **25.00**

CALCULATORS

The Texas Instruments TI-2500 Datamath entered the market in the early 1970s. This electronic calculator, the marvel of its era, performed four functions—addition, subtraction, multiplication, and division. This is all it did. It retailed for over $100.00. Within less than a decade, calculators selling for less than $20.00 were capable of doing five times as many functions.

Early electronic calculators are dinosaurs. They deserve to be preserved. When collecting them, make certain to buy examples that retain their power transformer, instruction booklet, and original box. Make certain any calculator that you buy works. There are few around who know how to repair one.

It is a little too early for a category on home computers. But a few smart collectors are starting to stash away the early Texas Instrument and Commodore models.

Calculator, four functions **10.00**
Calculator, five or more functions **5.00**
Calculator, thirty or more functions **20.00**
Calculator, solar-powered **3.00**
Calculator, not working **0.00**

CALENDAR PLATES

Calendar plates are one of the traditional, affordable collecting categories. A few years ago, they sold in the $10.00 to $20.00 range; now that has jumped to $35.00 to $50.00.

Value rests in the decorative motif and the place for which it was issued. A fun collection would be to collect the same plate and see how many different merchants and other advertisers utilized it.

1961, God Bless This House, zodiac signs, blue and white, marked "Alfred Meakin, Staffordshire, England," $10.00.

1908, harvesting scene, Lowel Fertilizer............................ **28.00**
1909, 8½" d, outdoor scenes, General
Merchandise, OR **36.00**
1910, Betsy Ross, Dresden **30.00**
1910, high school, bell border **32.00**
1911, deer in meadow, scenic panels between months................... **35.00**
1911, Moose Lake, MN **30.00**
1912, 8¼" d, fruits, months around rim,
Woodburn, OR **25.00**
1913, 9" d, roses and holly........... **25.00**
1915, 7" d, Panama Canal **25.00**
1916, 8¼" d, eagle with shield and
American flag **32.00**
1919, Betsy Ross sewing flag **28.00**
1922, dog watching rabbit **30.00**
1924, 9" d, flowers, holly, and berries,
San Francisco **35.00**
1928, 8¾" d, deer standing in field **30.00**
1929, 6¼" d, flowers, Valentine, NE **25.00**
1931, 8½" d, automobile **30.00**

CALENDARS

The primary reason calendars are collected is for the calendar art. Prices hinge on quality of printing and the pizazz of the subject. A strong advertising aspect adds to the value.

A highly overlooked calendar collecting area is the modern art and photographic calendar. For whatever reason, there is little interest in calendars dating after 1940. Collectors are making a major mistake. There are some great calendars from this later time period selling for less than $2.00.

"Gentlemen's" calendars did not grace the kitchen wall, but they are very collectible. Illustrations range from the pinup beauties of Elvgren and Moran and the *Esquire* Vargas ladies in the 1930s to the Playboy Playmates of the 1960s. Early Playboy calendars sell in the $50.00 plus range.

But, what's the fun of having something you cannot display openly? The following list will clear corporate censors with no problems.

Youth's Companion Magazine Calendar, 1898, foldout, company giveaway, 8 × 11" closed, $40.00.

1892, Sing Sing Prison **75.00**
1894, Hoyt's, lady's, perfumed **10.00**
1896, Singer Sewing Machines **37.50**
1900, Hood's, full pad, two girls........ **45.00**
1903, Franco American, miniature **15.00**
1906, Youth's Companion Minute-
men **65.00**
1909, Bank of Waupun, emb lady **30.00**
1913, Aunt Jemima Recipe Calendar ... **85.00**
1915, Cosgroves Detective Agency,
moose hunting scene **10.00**
1916, Putnam Dyes **37.50**
1919, Woodrow Wilson **10.00**
1927, Wrigley's Gum, desk style **40.00**
1929, Clothesline **60.00**
1931, Adelaide Hiebel **20.00**
1940, Columbian Rope **40.00**
1944, Sinclair Gasoline, twelve color
wildlife pictures **20.00**
1948, Squirt, pinup girls illus.......... **38.00**
1961, TWA, 16 × 24", six sheet **15.00**
1965, Jayne Mansfield, 9 × 14", full color
glossy photo **85.00**

CAMBRIDGE GLASS

The Cambridge Glass Company of Cambridge, Ohio, began operation in 1901. Its first products were clear tablewares. Later color, etched, and engraved pieces were added to the line. Production continued until 1954. The Imperial Glass Company of Bellaire, Ohio, bought some of the Cambridge molds and continued production of these pieces.

Club: National Cambridge Collectors, Inc., P. O. 416, Cambridge, OH 43725.

Dish, Crown Tuscan, hp rose motif center, 7³⁄₈" l, $28.00.

Ashtray, Caprice, blue, shell	8.00
Basket, Apple Blossom, pink	18.00
Bonbon, Chantilly	17.50
Bowl	
Diane, 11" d	35.00
Everglades, 12" d	50.00
Rosepoint, 5" d	25.00
Butter Dish, cov, Rosepoint	200.00
Cake Plate, Caprice	65.00
Candy Dish, cov, Crown Tuscan, gold trim, three parts	48.00
Champagne, Wild Flower	30.00
Cocktail, Nude Stem, amber	95.00
Cocktail Shaker, Chantilly, metal top	95.00
Compote, Elaine, gadroon etching	58.00
Console Bowl, Apple Blossom	19.00
Creamer, Caprice	7.00
Cruet, Deco, green	75.00
Cup and Saucer	
Rosepoint	45.00
Wild Flower	20.00
Decanter, Mosaic gold and ebony, orig handle and stopper	165.00
Flower Holder, Bashful Charlotte, 6½" h, figural, crystal	85.00
Goblet, water	
Chantilly	20.00
Mt Vernon	9.00
Rosepoint	25.00
Ice Bucket, Gloria, pink, chrome handle	65.00

Iced Tea, Portia	24.00
Mayonnaise, Caprice, blue, 2 pcs	60.00
Mustard, cov, Caprice, blue	40.00
Pitcher, Wild Flower	95.00
Plate	
Caprice, blue, 8½" d	38.00
Tally Ho, Carmen, 9½" d	28.00
Wild Flower, 10½" d	40.00
Platter, Decagon, light blue	40.00
Relish Tray, Everglades, three parts	45.00
Salt and Pepper Shakers, pr	
Apple Blossom	30.00
Diane	42.50
Sherbet	
Caprice, blue, 3¼" d	30.00
Diane, amber, tall	20.00
Elaine	17.50
Sugar	
Caprice, blue	17.50
Wild Flower	14.00
Swan, Crown Tuscan, 3½" h	35.00
Tumbler, Cascade, 3⁷⁄₈" h	8.50
Wine, Caprice, blue	59.00

CAMEOS

Cameos are one form of jewelry that has never lost its popularity. They have been made basically the same way for centuries. Most cameos are dated by their settings, although this is risky since historic settings can be duplicated very easily.

Normally one thinks of a cameo as carved from a piece of conch shell. However, the term cameo means a gem carved in relief. You can find cameos carved from gemstones and lava. Lava cameos are especially desirable.

Beware of plastic and other forms of copycat and fake cameos. Look carefully at the side. If you spot layers, shy away. A real cameo is carved from a single piece.

Your best defense when buying a cameo is to buy from a dealer that you can find later and then to have the authenticity of the cameo checked by a local retail jeweler. Do not use another antiques jewelry dealer. They have a bad habit of backing up other dealers even when they know the piece is bad.

Bracelet, carved lava, various color panels, Victorian 14K yg mounting	1,300.00
Brooch, woman, head and shoulders	
Flowers in hair, Victorian carved agate, gold knife edge and beadwork frame, 18K yg setting	800.00
Grapevine and leaves entwined in hair, 14K yg setting	300.00

Button, pearl, carved cameo and lily of
the valley dec 10.00
Compact, onyx cameo, marcasite ring,
yellow guilloche enamel 400.00
Earrings, hobe shell, rhinestones,
smoked crystals.................... 45.00
Hair Ribbon Holder, dated 1913 .... 12.50
Necklace, hard stone, silver filigree chain
with jet beads, marked "Czech" 65.00
Ring, lady's, 14K, yg................. 30.00
Stickpin, carved opal, gold frame, rubies
and diamonds highlights, 14K yg setting, marked "Tiffany & Co" 650.00

CAMERAS

Just because a camera is old does not mean
that it is valuable. Rather, assume that the
more examples of a camera that were
made the less likely it is to be valuable.
Collectors are after unusual cameras or
examples from companies that failed
quickly.

A portion of a camera's value rests on
how it works. Check all bellow cameras by
shining a strong light over the outside surface while looking at the inside. Check the
seating on removable lenses.

It is only recently that collectors have
begun to focus on the 35mm camera. You
can still build a collection of early models
at a modest cost per camera.

There is a growing market in camera
accessories and ephemera. A camera has
minimum value if you do not know how it
works. Whenever possible, insist on the
original instruction booklet as part of the
purchase.

Clubs: National Stereoscopic Association,
P. O. Box 14801, Columbus, OH 43214;
Photographic Historical Society, P. O. Box
9563, Rochester, NY 14606.

Argus, Argoflex EM, metal body,
1948.......................... 25.00
Blair Camera Company, Hawk-Eye Junior, box, 1895–1900............. 75.00
Canon, Dial 35, 35mm, 1963–1967 .... 50.00
Character
Dick Tracy, 3 × 5", plastic, black, Sey-
more Products, Chicago 45.00
Hopalong Cassidy................. 125.00
Mickey Mouse, 3 × 3 × 5", plastic,
black, red plastic straps, uses 127
film, early 1960s 50.00
Roy Rogers and Trigger, 3 × 3¼ × 3¼",
plastic, black, metal flash attachment, vinyl carrying strap, Herbert
George Company, Chicago, 1940–
1950......................... 100.00

*Eastman Kodak, Rochester, NY, #7 Weno
Hawk-Eye, box, successor to Blair Camera Co,
$25.00.*

Conley Camera Company, Kewpie No
2A, box 15.00
Eastman Kodak Company
Brownie, Flash IV, box, tan cov,
matching canvas case, 1957–
1959......................... 28.00
Buckeye Camera, folding, wood, lea-
ther cov, c1899 .... 125.00
Camp Fire Girls Kodak, folding, Camp
Fire Girls emblem on front door,
matching case, 1931–1934........ 375.00
Duex Camera, helical telescoping
front, doublet lens, 620 film, 1940–
1942......................... 15.00
Minox, EC, Point & Shoot, plastic,
black 90.00
Olympus, Flex A3.5, 1954–1956....... 85.00
Polaroid, Pathfinder 110A, 1957–
1960 .... 50.00
Ricoh, 35 Deluxe Rangefinder, c1956... 65.00
Sears, Marvel-flex, c1941 .... 25.00
Zeiss Ikon, Tenax I, East Germany,
1948–1953 .... 60.00

CANDLEWICK

Imperial Glass Corporation issued its No.
400 pattern, Candlewick, in 1936 and continued to produce it until 1982. In 1985
the Candlewick molds were dispersed to a
number of sources, e.g., Boyd Crystal Art
Glass, through sale.

Over 650 items and sets are known.
Shapes include round, oval, oblong, heart,

and square. The largest assortment of pieces and sets were made during the late 1940s and early 1950s.

For a list of reproduction Candlewick pieces, check the Candlewick category in *Warman's Americana and Collectibles*.

Newsletter: The National Candlewick Collector Newsletter, 275 Milledge Terrace, Athens, GA 30606.

Ashtray, oblong	5.00
Basket, 6½" h	25.00
Bowl	
5" d	12.00
6" sq	75.00
7" d, handle	12.00
8½" d, handle	24.50
11" d, float	35.00
Brandy Snifter	135.00
Butter Dish, cov, quarter pound	25.00
Cake Plate, 10" d	85.00
Canape Set	18.00
Candleholder, mushroom	25.00
Candy, cov, 7" d	95.00
Celery Tray, 11" l, oval	55.00
Champagne	15.00
Cheese and Cracker Set	45.00
Cigarette Set, 6 pcs	65.00
Coffee Cup	6.50
Compote, 5½" d	22.00
Cream Soup	40.00
Creamer, 3¼" d	8.00
Cup and Saucer, beaded handle cup, 5½" saucer	8.50
Demitasse Cup and Saucer	22.00
Deviled Egg Plate	110.00
Dish, 5" d, heart, handle	18.50
Fruit Bowl, 5" d	9.00
Juice Tumbler	10.00
Lemon Dish	35.00
Marmalade, 4 pc set, orig label	30.00
Mayonnaise, 2 pc set	25.00
Nappy, 4¾" d, two handles, orig label	8.50
Parfait, 6 oz	45.00
Pitcher, beaded handle, ice lip	75.00
Plate	
6" d	6.00
7" d, indent	15.00
8" d	12.50
9" d	15.00
10" d	40.00
Platter, 13" l, oval	70.00
Relish, 6½" d, 2 part	10.00
Salad Fork and Spoon	30.00
Salt and Pepper Shaker, pr, round, beaded foot, chrome tops	15.00
Sandwich Plate, 12½" d, center handle	18.00
Saucer	6.00
Sherbet, low	14.00
Sugar, cov, 3¼" d	8.00
Tea Cup	6.50
Tidbit, two tiers	60.00

Tray, 10" d, round	40.00
Tumbler	
10 oz	11.00
12 oz	14.00
Vase	
4" h, bud	35.00
7" h	45.00
Wafer Tray	22.00
Wine	27.50

CANDY COLLECTIBLES

Who doesn't love some form of candy? Forget the chocoholics. I'm a Juicy Fruit man.

Once you start looking for candy-related material, you are quickly overwhelmed by how much is available. Do not forget the boxes. They are usually discarded. Ask your local drugstore or candy shop to save the more decorative ones for you. What is free today may be worth money tomorrow.

Advertising Box, Payday, Hollywood Brands, Inc, Centralia, IL, yellow ground, black, red, and blue lettering, 24–bar box, 8 × 10 × 2", $5.00.

Bonbon Tongs, candy store, tin	4.00
Box	
Hershey Nougat-Almond	10.00
Milky Way, 24 5¢ bars	6.00
Candy Bar Mold, Clark Bar, multiple openings	15.00
Candy Bucket, green glass, hammered aluminum handle	12.00
Candy Container	
Chicken, round base	150.00

Clock, missing paper face dial. 300.00
Egg, tin, Dutch girl illus on front 15.00
George Washington, composition 95.00
Hat, milk glass, tin brim 60.00
Pelican, papier mache. 58.00
Rabbit, seated, white, carrot in mouth,
Germany 40.00
Suitcase, glass, tin closure, wire han-
dle 55.00
Change Receiver, Teaberry Gum. 75.00
Display Rack, Beech-Nut Beechies,
metal, two shelves 20.00
Eraser, Hershey's miniature candy wrap-
per, mint 10.00
Giveaway, Zatek Chocolate, Indian girl,
cutout, multicolored, 1918, uncut. . . . 20.00
Gum Wrapper, Wrigley's, yellow, pur-
ple, and gold 10.00
Hammer, 3½" l, Seeds Candies adv 20.00
Jar, Kiss Me Gum 85.00
Pinback Button
Baker's Chocolate, oval, pretty
lady 30.00
McDonald's Merry Widow Chocolates,
1¼" d, lady wearing exaggerated
feather hat, pr of well dressed
suitors, black and white, light blue
accents, 1900–1912 . . . . 30.00
Sommer-Richardson's Candies, 1" d,
red "Red Cross" logo, white ground,
blue letters, early 1900s 15.00
Zig Zag Modern Confection, 1¼" d,
multicolored, 1903–1905. . . . . 50.00
Ruler, Clark Bars, wood 6.00
Sign
Kibber's Candies, 9 × 8", brass 50.00
Ox Heart Chocolate, tin 75.00
Sweet Maris Gum, diecut 45.00
Tape Dispenser, Baby Ruth 25.00
Teddy Bear, Hershey's Chocolate, hold-
ing silver Kiss, dark brown 28.00
Tin
Bunte Candy, gold, 5 lb 25.00
Fireside Gems Candy, 8" d, round, girl
sitting on bench. 10.00
Orange Mellowmints 15.00
Sunny South Chocolate Peanut, black
face illus. .175.00
Trade Card
Monarch Teenie Weenie Toffies 15.00
Wilbur's Chocolate & Cocoa, diecut,
boy and girl, multicolored front and
back, c1890 . . . . 20.00
Wrapper, Home Run Candy, baseball
game illus, 1936 . . . . 45.00

CAP PISTOLS

Classic collectors collect the one-shot, cast iron pistols manufactured during the first third of the twentieth century. Kids of the 1950s collect roll cap pistols. Children of

the 1990s do not know what they are missing.

Prices for roll cap pistols are sky-rocketing. Buy them only if they are in working order. Ideally, acquire them with their appropriate accessories, e.g., holsters, fake bullets, etc.

Club: Toy Gun Purveyors, Box 243, Burke, VA 22015.

Actoy, Pony Boy. 65.00
Cowboys
Gold, 1947, pr 270.00
Nickel 110.00
Dent, Villa, cast iron, 4¾" l, 1934 . . . . . . 60.00
Gene Autry, cast iron 100.00
Hubley
Cap Firing Colt Detective Special, 4" l,
1958. . . . . 60.00
Cap Firing Flintlock, 9" l, 1950s. 45.00
Pirate, die cast zinc, 9⅜" l, 1941. . . . . . 50.00
Trooper, 5⅛" l, 1938. . . . . 50.00
Zip, cast iron, 5" l, 1930 . . . . 45.00
James Bond, 100 Shot Repeater, Lone
Star, 1965 . . . . .200.00
Kenton, Dixie, 6¼" l, 1935 . . . . 60.00
Kilgore
American, cast iron, 9⅝" l, 1940 . . . . . .120.00
Border Patrol, 4¼" l, 1935 . . . . 40.00
Hi-Ho, cast iron, 6½" l, 1940 . . . . 50.00
Kit Carson, pr 100.00
Rotor Fifty, 6⅛" l, 1930 . . . . 70.00
Mattel, Tommy Burb, 24" l, 1950s 45.00
National, Bunker Hill, 5¼" l, 1925 . . . . . 55.00
Stallion 45.00
Stevens, Bang-O Cast Iron Cap Pistol,
7" l, 1938. . . . . 40.00
Texan
Cast Iron, orig box. 135.00
Junior 30.00
Texas Ranger, includes holster 125.00
Top Gun, includes leather holster 30.00

CAPTAIN ACTION

This 12" tall fully poseable action figure was made by the Ideal Toy Company from 1966 to 1968. Captain Action had thirteen costume sets, numerous accessories, a youthful counterpart, Action Boy, and an evil villain, Dr. Evil.

A number of the Captain Action costume sets were used to transform Captain Action into a different super hero, such as DC Comics' Superman, Batman, or Aquaman and Marvel Comics' Spiderman, Captain America, or Sergeant Fury.

Action Figure, 12" h
Action Boy
First Issue, 3420, 1967 . . . . .600.00

Second Issue **475.00**
Captain Action
   Second Issue, 3400, 1967 .... **500.00**
   Third Issue.................... **650.00**
   Dr Evil, second issue, deluxe lab
     set **1,000.00**
Action Figure Accessories
   Action Cave Carrying Case.......... **400.00**
   Anti-Gravitational   Power   Pack,
     3455........................ **200.00**
   Dr Evil Sanctuary **850.00**
   Headquarters Carrying Case, vinyl ... **375.00**
   Inter-Galactic Jet Mortar, 3452 ..... **200.00**
   Inter-Spacial Directional Communica-
     tor **375.00**
   Parachute Set, 4' **200.00**
   Quick Change Chamber, Sears **550.00**
   Silver Streak Car **900.00**
   Silver Streak Garage, hide-out **550.00**
   Survival Kit, 20 pcs, 3450 .... **250.00**
   Weapons Arsenal, 10 pcs, 3451 ..... **250.00**
Action Figure Outfit
   Aqualad, Action Boy outfit, Octo the
     Octopus, 3423, 1967............ **400.00**
   Aquaman, videomatic ring, 3408,
     1967........................ **550.00**
   Buck Rogers, videomatic ring,
     3416, 1967 .... **1,200.00**
   Captain America, 1966............ **375.00**
   Flash Gordon, 1966 .... **475.00**
   Lone Ranger, red shirt, 1966 .... **550.00**
   Phantom, .45 automatic, 1967...... **650.00**
   Robin, Action Boy outfit, 3421,
     1967........................ **475.00**
   Steve Canyon, 1966 .... **475.00**
   Tonto, videomatic ring, 3415, 1967... **800.00**
Halloween Costume................. **150.00**
Model Kit, Aurora **150.00**

CAPTAIN AMERICA

Stars and stripes forever, as America's Super Hero helps preserve the American way from the onslaught of super villains.

Captain America was created in March, 1941, by Marvel Comics' artists Jack Kirby and Joe Simon. He became one of the leading manifestations of American patriotism during World War II. With his sidekick, Bucky, Captain America fought Nazis and "Japs" on all fronts.

This year I nominate Captain America as the American Hero collectible. A personal favorite, I enjoy searching for Captain America items at flea markets. They are readily available and collecting memorabilia of "The Sentinel of Liberty" can be very satisfying.

Captain America Toy, Spiderman, litho tin and plastic, Marx, orig box, $35.00.

Action Figure
   Just Toys, Marvel Super Heroes Bend-
     em, 12062, 1991 .... **6.00**
   Lakeside, bendie **120.00**
   Marx, 6" h, plastic, 1966 .... **15.00**
   Mego
     8" h, orig box, 1974 .... **175.00**
     12½" h, fly away action **125.00**
   Remco, 9" h, energized **60.00**
   Transogram, flying figure........... **70.00**
Badge, Sentinels of Liberty............ **325.00**
Coloring Book, Whitman, 1966........ **35.00**
Comic Book
   100, Avengers appearance, Jack Kirby,
     1968........................ **275.00**
   117, introduction of Falcon, Gene
     Colan and Joe Sinnott........... **12.00**
   138, Spider-Man appearance, John
     Romita...................... **10.00**
   241, Punisher appearance **65.00**
   264, X-Men, pencils by Mike Zeck.... **3.00**
   332, Rogers resignation, Bop Mc-
     Leod........................ **12.00**
   383, 50th anniversary, Jim Lee and
     Ron Lim, 64 pgs................ **4.00**
   384, Jack Frost appearance, Ron
     Lim......................... **1.00**
Hand Puppet, molded soft vinyl head,
   Imperial Toy Corp, 1978........... **20.00**
Pennant, vinyl sleeve over cardboard,
   6½" l, Marvel Comics, 1966........ **15.00**
Pez Dispenser, 4" h, plastic, blue body
   and helmet, white wings, marked
   "Made in Austria," 1978 .... **50.00**
Puzzle, jigsaw, Whitman, attacking
   Zombies illus, 14 × 18" orig box,
   1976........................ **20.00**
Transfer, iron-on, Kirby art, unused,
   1960s........................ **10.00**
Vehicle
   Captain Americar, fits 8" figure,
     Mego....................... **225.00**
   Jetmobile, Corgi **30.00**
   Rocket Racer, Buddy-L, Secret Wars,

remote controlled, battery operated,
1984. . . . . **40.00**
Turbo Car, Toy Biz, 1990 . . . . **15.00**

CARNIVAL CHALKWARE

Carnival chalkware is my candidate for the kitsch collectible of the 1980s. No one uses *quality* to describe these inexpensive prizes given out by games of chance at carnivals, amusement parks, and ocean boardwalks.

The best pieces are those depicting a specific individual or character. Since most were bootlegged (made without permission), they often appear with a fictitious name—e.g., ''Smile Doll'' is really supposed to be Shirley Temple. The other strong collecting subcategory is the animal figure. As long as the object comes close to capturing the appearance of a pet, people buy.

Jackass, braying, glitter trim, c1940, $18.00.

Betty Boop, 14½" h, c1935 . . . . **190.00**
Indian Head, 9" h, string holder, 1935–
1945 . . . . **60.00**
Kewpie, 12½" h, pink, marked ''Port-
land Miss,'' 1920s **120.00**
King Kong, 6¼" h, 1940s **18.00**
Kitten, 7" h, with ball of yarn, 1930–
1945 . . . . **8.00**
Lion, 8 × 9", 1940–1950 . . . . **20.00**
Mae West, 13" h, 1934 . . . . **65.00**
Majorette, 12" h, marked ''El Segundo
Novelty Co,'' 1949 . . . . **25.00**
Mickey Mouse, 8½" h, 1930–35 . . . . **75.00**
Parrot, 13½" h, 1935–1945 . . . . **35.00**

Paul Revere, 14½" h, 1935–1945 . . . . . . **25.00**
Pinocchio, 10" h, c1940 . . . . **20.00**
Popeye, 9¾" h, 1929–1950 . . . . **35.00**
Sailor Girl, 14" h, 1925–1935 . . . . **70.00**
Scotty Dog, 5½" h, 1935–1945 . . . . **10.00**
Snuffy Smith, 9¼" h, 1934–1945 . . . . . . **65.00**
Windmill, 10¾" h, 1935–1940 . . . . **20.00**

CARTOON COLLECTIBLES

This is a category with something for each generation. The characters represented here enjoyed a life in comic books and newspaper pages. Many also had a second career on movie screens and television.

Every collector has a favorite. Buy examples that bring back pleasant memories. ''That's All Folks.''

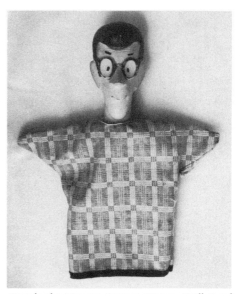

Dennis the Menace Puppet, Henry, Hall Synd Inc, 1959, 10" h, $5.00.

Alarm Clock
Betty Boop, animated, boxed. **45.00**
Woody Woodpecker, orig box **25.00**
Ashtray, Fred and Wilma Flintstone, por-
celain, 1961 . . . . **75.00**
Ball, juggler, Popeye, litho tin, 1929 . . . . **55.00**
Bank
Casper, glow in the dark, 1967 . . . . **75.00**
Krazy Kat, graduation outfit **55.00**
Barrette, Li'l Abner, 2⅛" l, oval, brass,
diecut, 1940s **18.00**
Book, *Woody Woodpecker's Peck of Trouble*,
Whitman, 1951 . . . . **5.00**
Bubble Gum Machine, figural, Fred
Flintstone head **40.00**

Candy Bar Wrapper, Dick Tracy, color picture, premium offer, 1950s 10.00

Card Game, Rummy, Flintstones illus on each card, tray, orig box, 1961 .... 45.00

Charm, Popeye, 1¼" w, celluloid, brass loop, orange, pink, black, and green, Japan, 1930s 20.00

Christmas Ornament, Garfield, round, 1981, orig box 9.00

Clicker, Felix the Cat, litho tin, Germany, 1929. .... 25.00

Colorform Set, Flintstones, 1972 .... 20.00

Coloring Book, 8½ × 11", Blondie, 1954, Dell Publishing, unused 20.00

Cookie Jar
    Fred Flintstone 135.00
    Popeye, Vandor. 450.00
    Yogi Bear, felt tongue 195.00

Dish, Pink Panther, plastic, three sections. 30.00

Doll
    Barney Google, Snuffy Smith, 17" h, stuffed, felt, movable head, amber and black eyes, 1930s 150.00
    Little Lulu, 15" h, stuffed cloth, black felt and yarn hair, western outfit, 1940s 80.00
    Mr Magoo, no shoes, 1962 .... 65.00

Figure
    Barney Google, syrocco, sailor suit ... 75.00
    Huckleberry Hound, ceramic 55.00
    Speedy Gonzales, 1970. .... 22.00
    Tweety Bird. 15.00

Game
    Flintstones Stone Age Game, Transogram, 1961 .... 35.00
    Harold Teen, spinner and orig tokens, boxed, 1930s 15.00
    Huckleberry Hound Bumps 38.00
    Quick Draw McGraw Private Eye, Milton Bradley, 1960 .... 40.00

Hand Puppet
    Barney Google 50.00
    Dick Tracy, 1961 .... 75.00
    Yosemite Sam, 1960s 25.00

Handkerchief, Foxy Grandpa, 1920 .... 40.00

Ice Cream Mold, Yellow Kid, 4¾" h, full figure, hinged 185.00

Key Chain, Winnie Winkle, characters on each side, 1940s 15.00

Lunch Box
    Bullwinkle and Rocky, steel, Jay Ward Productions copyright, Universal, c1962 .... 200.00
    Joe Palooka, litho tin, 1948 .... 45.00
    Underdog 300.00

Marionette, Fred Flintstone, 1960s 75.00

Mug, Fred Flintstone 4.00

Necktie, 10½" l, Bugs Bunny, clip-on, c1940. .... 50.00

Nodder
    Moon Mullins, 3⅞" h, bisque, Germany 60.00
    Smitty, bisque 85.00

Pen Holder, Snoopy 65.00

Pencil Sharpener, Popeye, tin, dated 1929. .... 95.00

Pinback Button
    Dan Dunn, 1¼" d, litho, Philadelphia Evening Ledger, "I'm Operative 48," orig back paper, 1930s 65.00
    Gasoline Alley, ¹³⁄₁₆" d, Uncle Walt, litho 12.00

Plaque, 7" h, Andy Panda, ceramic, figural, marked "Napco Ceramics," 1958. .... 55.00

Playsuit, Popeye 85.00

Salt and Pepper Shakers, pr
    Maggie and Jiggs, 2½" h, figural, marked "Made In Japan," 1930s ... 65.00
    Popeye and Olive Oyl, Vandor 35.00

Thermos, Casper the Friendly Ghost, metal 60.00

Toy
    Popeye, tin spinach can, pop-up head........................ 95.00
    Porky Pig, 5½" h, rubber, marked "Sun Rubber Co" 45.00

Tumbler, 5" h, glass, Li'l Abner running with two Shmoos, 1949 .... 8.50

Vase, 7½" h, Bugs Bunny, china, resting against tree stump, Warner Bros Copyright, c1940 .... 100.00

CASH REGISTERS

If you want to buy a cash register, you had better be prepared to put plenty of money in the till. Most are bought for decorative purposes. Serious collectors would go broke in a big hurry if they had to pay the prices listed below for every machine they buy.

Beware of modern reproductions. Cash registers were meant to be used. Signs of use should be present. There is also a tendency to restore machines to their original appearance through replating and rebuilding. Well and good. But when all is said and done, how do you tell the refurbished machine from a modern reproduction? When you cannot, it is hard to sustain long-term value.

A R Peek, Peek's Cash Register, No. 2651, oak box, brass hardware, NY, c1890. .... 275.00

McCaskey, oak, orig decal, metal account files, two drawers, refinished, 23 × 23 × 27" 150.00

Michigan #1, twenty-two keys 200.00

National
    Model 30, nickel over brass, painted green, 8½ × 22 × 15" ... 1,325.00

National, Model 442, orig bronze finish, mahogany base, $0.00 to $9.99, 1912, 20" w, 23" h, $675.00.

Model 317, marble change shelf,
  printer, 5¢ to $1.00, 16" h **1,200.00**
Model 321, brass, extended base, 17¼
  × 17 × 16", 1916 . . . . **650.00**
Model 342, brass, crank operated,
  drawer, 24" h **600.00**
Model 349, two drawers, 1910 . . . . . . **800.00**
Model 421, crank-operated, oak cash
  drawer, receipt machine on side,
  23" h **650.00**
Peninsula, Muren, nickel plated,
  c1912 . . . . **250.00**

CASSETTE TAPES

Flea markets thrive on two types of goods—those that are collectible and those that serve a second-hand function. Cassette tapes fall into the latter group. Buy them for the purpose of playing them.

The one exception is when the promotional pamphlet covering the tape shows a famous singer or group. In this case, you are really buying the piece of paper ephemera more than the tape, but you might as well have the whole shooting match.

Several times within recent years there have been a number of articles in the trade papers about collecting eight-tracks. When was the last time you saw an eight-track machine? They are going to be as popular in thirty years as the wire tape recorder is today. Interesting idea—too bad it bombed.

Average price . . . . **50¢ to $2.00**

CAST IRON

This is a category where you should be suspicious that virtually everything you see is a reproduction or copycat. More often than not, the object will not be original. They are even reproducing cast iron frying pans.

One of the keys to spotting the newer material is the rust. If it is orange in color and consists of small pinpoint flakes, forget it. Also check paint patina. It should have a mellow tone from years of exposure to air. Bright paint should be suspect.

Cast iron is a favorite of the country collector. It evokes memories of the great open kitchen fireplaces and wood/coal burning stoves of our ancestors. Unfortunately, few discover what a great cooking utensil cast iron can really be.

Skeleton Key, 5½" l, $15.00.

Bank, 6" h, black mammy, polychrome
  paint traces **55.00**
Bottle Opener, 3⅝" l, donkey, poly-
  chrome traces **65.00**
Cigarette Dispenser, 8½" l, elephant,
  bronze repaint **30.00**
Clothes Hook, 9" w, eagle shape, snake
  shape hooks, gold paint **40.00**
Door Knocker, 3¾" l, basket of flowers,
  orig polychrome paint **30.00**
Fence, 43" h, 70" l, four sections, old
  green paint **240.00**
Figure, parrot **12.00**
Garden Urn, 28½" h, removable ears,
  white repaint **290.00**
Hitching Post, 62½" h, tree form, branch
  stubs, marked "Patent" **100.00**
Lawn Ornament, jockey, polychrome re-
  paint **100.00**
Mortar and Pestle, 5½" h **20.00**
Nut Cracker, 11" l, figural, dog, nickel

finish, marked "The LA Althoff Mfg
Co, Chicago".................... **40.00**
Skillet, 9¾" d, three short feet, 9¼" l
handle......................... **35.00**
Tea Kettle, cov, Wagner No 0......... **125.00**

CAT COLLECTIBLES

It is hard to think of a collecting category
that does not have one or more cat-related
items in it. Chessie the Cat is railroad oriented; Felix is a cartoon, comic, and toy
collectible. There rests the problem. The
poor cat collector is always competing
with an outside collector for a favorite cat
item.

Cat collectors are apparently as stubborn
as their pets because I have never seen a
small cat collectibles collection. One additional thing that I have noticed is that,
unlike most dog collectibles collectors, cat
collectors are more willing to collect objects portraying other breeds of cats than
the one that they own.

Club: Cat Collectors, 31311 Blair Drive,
Warren, MI 48092.

*Napkin Ring, ceramic, marked "Japan," 3" h,
$20.00.*

Ashtray
4" d, black cat face, bow, #16 Shafford,
1953......................... **20.00**
5" l, ceramic, brown crouching cat,
front paws extended, marked
"Made in China".............. **20.00**
Bottle, glass, clear, blue bow, painted facial features, marked "Smiley" **48.00**

Calendar, wall, three parts, several peek-
ing cat faces, titled "Little Mischief,"
Tuck, 1903...................... **25.00**
Egg Cup, 3" h, black cat, Japan paper
label........................... **20.00**
Match Holder, cat scene, ftd, marked
"Wavecrest"..................... **225.00**
Mirror, pocket, White Cat Union Suits
adv, 2¾" l, black and white, celluloid,
cartoon illus, early 1900s **65.00**
Pinback Button
⅞" d, Cat's Paw Heels, yellow and
black, early 1900s **15.00**
1¼" d, tinted, multicolored, kitten in
high top shoe................... **12.00**
1⅜" d, groovy cat, red, white, and
blue, c1940 .... **10.00**
2¼" d, Morris For President, multicolored photo portrait, bright red,
white, and blue border, Nine Lives
Cat Food, 1988 .... **10.00**
Planter, 6¾" h, kitten with basket,
Hull **15.00**
Print, 14 × 11", two cats in hat, titled
"A Love Song," J Ottmann Litho,
1894........................... **25.00**
Puzzle, Felix the Cat, 1949............ **30.00**
Salt and Pepper Shakers, pr
3¾" h, teapot shape, black cat illus,
Japan label.................... **15.00**
4" h, comical Siamese, paper label
marked "Norcrest Japan"......... **10.00**
Toothpick Holder, kitten and boot...... **10.00**
Trade Card
Carter's Little Liver Pills, four striped
cats playing with yarn, Mayer, Mer-
kell & Ottmann Litho **5.00**
Choose Black Cat Reinforced Hosiery,
multicolored diecut.............. **15.00**
Clarks Mile End Spool Cotton, cat
walking over spool, calendar on
back, 1881.................... **10.00**

CAUSE COLLECTIBLES

Social cause collectibles are just now coming into their own as a collecting category.
Perhaps this is because the social activists
of the 1960s have mortgages, children,
and money in their pocket to buy back the
representations of their youth. In doing so,
they are looking back past their own pro-
test movements to all forms of social pro-
test that took place in the twentieth century.

Great collections can be built around a
single cause, e.g., women's suffrage or the
right to vote. Much of the surviving material tends to be two-dimensional. Stress
three-dimensional items the moment you

begin to collect. As years pass, these are the objects most likely to rise in value.

Autograph
  Pamphlet, 5 × 7", "The National First Aid Association of America," sgd Clara Barton photo **250.00**
  Quotation, 4 × 3", Anna E Dickinson, suffrage leader. **25.00**
  Medal, 1¼" d, Peace, emb brass, Angel of Peace waving palm branch, text on back with dates of opening and ending of World War I **15.00**
Pinback Button
  Laundry Workers Union No. 22, ⅞" d, black and white shirt, shaking hands, red ground, c1900. . . . . **15.00**
  Make Jobs, Return Musicians to Theaters, red, white, and blue, c1930 . . . **10.00**
  Peace and Freedom Party, 1¼" d, black and day glow red, 1968. . . . . **10.00**
  Scow Trimmers Union, red, white, blue, and black, flag center, c1910. . . . . **15.00**
  Supporting Labor's Cause, ¹³⁄₁₆" d, litho, gold letters, light purple ground, c1930. . . . . **12.00**
  Textile Workers/I Am For 8 Hours/Feb 3, 1919, red, white, and blue design **12.50**
  United We Shall Overcome, 1¾" d, black and white, early 1960s **18.00**
  Vote No On Woman Suffrage, ⅞" d, black, white, and dark reddish pink **15.00**
Post Card, prohibition, "I'm On The Water Wagon Now," 3½ × 5½", black, white, red, and yellow illus, 1906 . . . . **25.00**
Poster
  Give-Welfare Federation, 14 × 22", Jessie Wilcox Smith, little girl and two babies, green and yellow ground, c1920. . . . . **165.00**
  Lend Your Strength To The Red Triangle, 20 × 30", Gil Spear, man lifting YMCA stone **50.00**
  Vietnam, Anti-War, 23 × 27", anonymous, black and white montage, c1967. . . . . **85.00**
Sign, Bring Back Prosperity, tin, 4½ × 8", diecut and emb, beer glass shape, letter "B" shaped like twisted pretzel, made by De Vo Novelty Co, Asbury Park, NJ, c1932. . . . . **80.00**
Watch Fob, Transport Workers Union **10.00**

CELLULOID

Celluloid is the trade name for a thin, tough, flammable material made of cellulose nitrate and camphor. Originally used for toilet articles, it quickly found use as inexpensive jewelry, figurines, vases, and other household items. In the 1920s and 1930s, it was used heavily by the toy industry.

Be on the lookout for dealers who break apart sets and sell the pieces individually as a way of getting more money. Also check any ivory or tortoise shell piece that is offered to you. Both were well imitated by quality celluloid.

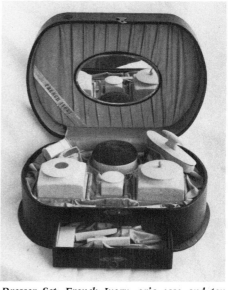

Dresser Set, French Ivory, orig case and ten items, $25.00.

Advertising
  Bookmark, Poole Piano **15.00**
  Flip-it, novelty, Golden Orangeade, mechanical, diecut, pin-on, orange, 1910s. **25.00**
  Matchbook Cover, Evansville Hat Works, celluloid on metal. **15.00**
  Sign, Coon Range Kentucky Whiskey. **95.00**
  Stamp Case, Tom Moore Cigar. **35.00**
Animal
  Camel, 1½" h **8.00**
  Pig, 2" l **6.00**
  Reindeer, Occupied Japan **22.00**
  Swan, white **5.00**
Bangle Bracelet, mottled brown, tortoise shell imitation, rhinestones **25.00**
Cigar Bowl, football player, Tampa, FL, Occupied Japan. **25.00**
Doll, cowboy, 7½" h, Japan, 1940–50. . . . . **24.00**
Dresser Set
  3 pcs, blue, rosebuds. **22.00**
  5 pcs, amberoid, Art Deco design **35.00**

Figure

Baseball Player, jointed, holds ball and glove, "#1" on back, Occupied Japan 125.00

Policeman, movable head and arms, Japan 22.00

Glove Box, light blue 25.00

Kewpies, bride and groom, 2½" h, pr ... 45.00

Manicure Set, leather roll-up-case, eight pcs 9.00

Pencil Clip, Diamond Edge, ⅞" d, black, white, and red, silvered tin clip, early 1900s 10.00

Pencil Sharpener, clock, amber, German 20.00

Place Card Holder, snowman, angels, and elves, set of eight, MIB 17.50

Rattle, 4½" l, cupid in wreath 15.00

Sewing Kit, red stripes 8.00

Tape Measure, fish 25.00

Toothbrush Holder, young girl, 1920s... 40.00

Toy

Boy, riding tricycle, Occupied Japan, MIB 95.00

Hawaiian Dancer, MIB 150.00

House of Fledglings, merry-go-round action, MIB 120.00

CEREAL BOXES

There is no better example of a collectible category gone mad than cereal boxes. Cereal boxes from the first half of the twentieth century sell in the $15.00 to $50.00 range. Cereal boxes from the 1950s through the 1970s sell in the $50.00 range and up. Where's the sense?

The answer rests in the fact that the post-World War II cereal box market is being manipulated by a shrewd speculator who is drawing upon his past experience with the lunch box market. Eventually, the bubble will burst. Don't get involved unless you have money to burn.

Cheerios, 1949, Hall of Fun Jack Oakie 64.00

Crystal Oats, Quaker, round 18.00

George Washington Corn Flakes, unopened 60.00

Highland Oats 30.00

Kellogg's Corn Flakes, sample size, c1920 .... 15.00

Mother Hubbard Wheat Cereal 22.00

Mother's Oats 20.00

Quaker Muffets Shredded Wheat, 3 × 6 × 7", side panel adv "Authentic Model Civil War Cannon," 1960s 37.50

Quaker Puffed Rice, 5 oz, 1919 .... 20.00

Puffed Wheat, Daniel Boone cutouts ... 48.00

Regal Brand Oats, 1 lb 12.00

Scotch Brand Oats 30.00

Sugar Pops, Andy Devine and Guy Madison 54.00

Superior Rolled Oats, Sioux City, IA 16.50

CEREAL PREMIUMS

Forget cereal boxes. The fun rests with the goodies inside the box that you got for buying the cereal in the first place. Cereal premiums have changed a great deal over the past decade. No self-respecting manufacturer in the 1950s would have included as their premium a tube of toothpaste. Yuck!

Collectors make a distinction between premiums that came with the box and those for which you had to send away. The latter group is valued more highly because the items are often more elaborate and better made. My dad keeps telling me about all the neat things he received through the mail as a kid. I think my generation has missed something.

Wheaties, Jogometer, metal, enameled center, belt clip, 2⅝" h, $18.00.

Booklet, *The Frolie Grasshopper Circus*, multicolored, grasshoppers and clowns, whimsical scenes, American Cereal Co, Quaker Oats, 1895 .... 65.00

Card, pop out, Dale Evans, Post Cereals, unused, mint 15.00

Comic Book, miniature, Cap'n Crunch, 1963 .... 20.00

Creamer, Kellogg's Correct Cereal...... 18.00

Doll, cloth, Snap, Krackle, and Pop, uncut, 1946, Rice Krispies, Kellogg's, set of 3 .... 180.00

Figure, 7" h, rubber, Snap, Crackle,

and Pop, Rice Krispies, Kelloggs's, set of 3 .... **50.00**
Flasher Card, Danny Thomas winks eye, Post Corn Flakes, 1950s **24.00**
Glass, cartoon, Toucan Sam, Fruit Loops, Kellogg's, 1977 .... **6.50**
Hike-o-meter, orig mailer, Wheaties.... **40.00**
Model, punch out, C-54 Skymaster war plane, Kellogg's Pep, WWII **24.00**
Plate, Kellogg's, 1985 .... **25.00**
Ring, Flash Gordon, Post Cereal **20.00**

CHILDREN'S COLLECTIBLES

Mothers of the world unite. This category is for you. The children who used it hardly remember it. It's the kind of stuff that keeps your children forever young in your mind.

There is virtually nothing written about this collecting category so what to collect is wide open. One collector I know has hundreds of baby planters!

Cooking Set, Like Mother's, tin, orig box marked "Set No. 08082, Made in USA," 14 pcs, $40.00.

Baby Record Book, C Burd illus on each page **32.00**
Baptism Set
　Dress and bonnet **65.00**
　Gown, slip, and matching cap, cotton, white, c1920 .... **85.00**
Bedspread, twin size, chenille, chicks coming out of eggs scene **35.00**
Bonnet, baby's, Victorian, white **38.00**
Book
　Adventures of Humpty Dumpty, 1877, baking soda giveaway **28.00**
　Little Red Riding Hood, litho, Star Soap giveaway **28.00**
　Little Tots ABC Book, c1900, linen **18.00**
　A Merry Coasting Party, Burgess, Cady **18.00**
　Mickey Mouse Alphabet Book, 1936..... **75.00**

The Three Bears, Platt & Munk **15.00**
Cape, Victorian, white cotton lace, 5 yr size **45.00**
Carriage, wicker, serpentine edges, natural finish, orig velvet upholstery, c1890 ....**450.00**
Catalog, Best & Co Lilliputian Bazaar, 1935, 48 pgs, children and infants speciality shop **20.00**
Christening Dress, 40" l **45.00**
Clock Radio, three mice, Fisher Price ... **20.00**
Coin Purse, beadwork, slightly rusted clasp......................... **35.00**
Creamer and Sugar, milk glass, Thumbelina............................ **25.00**
Desk, lift top **115.00**
Dish, 8" d, baby's, divided, three sections, Patriot China............... **50.00**
Mug
　Little Miss Muffet, colorful transfers and verse **45.00**
　Victorian, resilvered, engraved **75.00**
Pail, wood, metal bail handle, 4" h, 1890s **68.00**
Phonograph, General Electric Electronic Toys, metal, ruby red enamel, nursery rhymes, one speed switch, 1930s.....**185.00**
Rattle, sterling, includes birth record.... **20.00**
Record, Lullaby Time, Little Golden Record, 45 rpm, GL272, includes Twinkle Twinkle Little Star, Rock a Bye Baby, and Now I Lay Me Down To Sleep.... **4.00**
Rocking Horse, straw stuffed, red wheels **275.00**
Scale, baby, pink, 1940s **38.00**
Shoes, infant's
　Leather, ankle strap, white, pr **35.00**
　Side button, pair **30.00**
Spoon, baby, curved handle, kitten dec, Rogers **35.00**
Toy
　Busy Box, 14 × 20", twelve movable gadgets, Gabriel................ **15.00**
　Dippee Bug, pull, rubber, multicolor, MIB **40.00**
　Player Piano, eight muppets, Fisher Price......................... **45.00**
　Toot Toot Train, pull, Fisher Price **15.00**
　Wawky Tawky String Phone, 1940s....................... **10.00**
Toy Dishes
　Coffeepot, aluminum, red metal handle **7.50**
　Cookware Set, aluminum, 8 pcs, boxed.....................**110.00**
　Flour Sifter, aluminum, red metal handle, Bromwell............... **10.50**
　Tea Kettle, aluminum, red metal handle, whistle spout **6.00**
Tea Set
　Akro Agate, transparent green, 21 pcs **155.00**
　German, maroon luster, 13 pcs **210.00**
　Hazel Atlas Little Hostess, 16 pcs ...**140.00**

Mirro, 30 pcs, aluminum, orig box,
1930s **175.00**
Trunk, camel back **150.00**

CHRISTMAS

Of all the holiday collectibles, Christmas is the most popular. It has grown so large as a category that many collectors specialize in only one area, e.g., Santa Claus figures or tree ornaments.

Anything Victorian is "hot." The Victorians popularized Christmas. Many collectors love to recapture that spirit. However, prices for Victorian items, from feather trees to ornaments, are quickly moving out of sight.

This is a field where knowledgeable individuals can find bargains. Learn to tell a late nineteenth/early twentieth century ornament from a modern example. A surprising number of dealers cannot. If a dealer thinks a historic ornament is modern and prices it accordingly, she is actually playing Santa Claus by giving you a present. Ho, Ho, Ho!

Newsletters: *Golden Glow of Christmas Past,* P. O. Box 14808, Chicago, IL 60614; *Hearts of Holly, The Holiday Collectors Newsletter,* P. O. Box 105, Amherst, NH 03031; *Ornament Collector,* R. R. #1, Canton, IL 61520.

Bell, honeycomb, red, unused, set of
4 . . . . **19.00**
Book, *A Northern Christmas,* Kent Rockwell, American Artists Group Inc,
1941 . . . . **7.00**
Candy Container
Ball, silver foil with bow, West Germany **14.00**
Elf, cylinder type, wire neck, 8" **25.00**
House, cardboard, cotton Santa on
roof **75.00**
Santa
Cardboard, 13" h, spring head, West
Germany **60.00**
Fur beard, felt robe, holding
feather tree, separates at waist,
Germany **575.00**
Santa Face, hanging tree ornament,
3" d **35.00**
Snowman, 7½" h, papier mache, West
Germany, 1950s **22.00**
Card Book, flocked, 1950s **20.00**
Creche, paper, three-dimensional, USA,
1942 . . . . **15.00**
Doll, Santa Claus **32.00**

Ornament, Christmas tree, orange highlights, red capped mushrooms and Santa face at base, 3¼" h, $75.00.

Figure
Boot, 5½" h **24.00**
Santa
4¼" h, sitting on wood sleigh **95.00**
6¼" h, fur beard and hair, chime
hat **70.00**
7" h, papier mache, red coat, fur
beard, squeaks **55.00**
8½" h, felt, press me voice **95.00**
9½" h, Santa with tree, blue **85.00**
16" h, red coat, fur beard, Germany **185.00**
Snowman
Carrot nose, 7" h **28.00**
Papier Mache, set of 6, MIB **225.00**
Greeting Card
"Christmas Blessing," leather type, S
Hildersheimer & Co. **5.00**
"Merry Christmas From Our House,"
USA, 1930s **2.50**
"Wishing You A Happy Christmas,"
sepia tones, Raphael Tuck & Sons,
London **3.00**
Light Bulb
Chinese Lantern, milk glass, Japan . . . **10.00**
House, milk glass, pink and white, Japan **10.00**
Light Set, Noma Bubble Lite, boxed
set **27.00**
Nativity Scene, plastic, 3¾ × 4¾", Hong
Kong **12.00**
Ornament
Balls, miniature, boxed set of 12 . . . . . **12.00**
Barton Cross, Reed, 1974 . . . . **38.00**

Cat in Shoe, glass 38.00
Clown, glass, painted face, Germany 38.00
Flamingo, blue mercury glass. 40.00
French Hens, Towle, 1973 . . . . 34.00
Kugel, cobalt blue 55.00
Santa, figural, honeycomb 8.00
Snake. 32.00
Pinback Button, 1¼" d, Santa Claus, celluloid, multicolored, steering auto, c1911. . . . . 40.00
Planter, sleeping Santa sitting in chair, sgd, 5 × 6½ × 4¾" 18.00
Punch Bowl Set, Santa, includes eight cups 50.00
Postcard, hold to light type 35.00
Putz Items
    Animal
        Cow, 3" h, celluloid, brown, USA 7.00
        Dog, 1" h, celluloid, brown, marked "Japan" 5.00
        Horse, 3½" h, brown and tan, rubber, USA. 7.00
        Sheep, 1¼" h, composition, wool coat, wood legs 20.00
    Bank, 3" h, chalk, white, marked "Made in Japan". 10.00
    Church, 6" h, cardboard, litho, frosted roof 8.00
    Fence, 2½" h, eight 6" sections, wood, red and green 30.00
    House
        2½" h, cardboard, frosted roof, marked "Japan" 4.50
        3" h, log type, frosted roof, marked "Germany" 10.00
    Wagon, wood, driver and horses, Germany 38.00
Reflectors, copper foil, Germany, set of 10. . . . . 20.00
Snowdome, chimney, red brick, waterfilled fireplace, Santa, gifts, tree 20.00
Toy, squeaker, Santa, fur beard, 7½" h, Germany. 45.00
Tree
    5½" h, wire base, glass balls 18.00
    6" h, Japan 14.00
    9" h, brush, green, glass bead dec, red base 15.00
    15" h, cellophane 15.00
    18" h, feather, green, white base, Germany, 1920s 150.00
    60" h, feather, Germany 295.00
Tree Stand, revolving 18.00
Tree Topper, Angel, lighted, orig box . . . 18.00
Utensil Set, spoon and fork, A Michelsen, large tablespoon size, sterling silver, heavy gold plate, cloisonne handles
    1925, filigreed poinsettia 90.00
    1946, holly leaves and berries 85.00
    1949, Christmas wreath and candles. 85.00
    1953, white angels, blue and gold 85.00

1955, green and red spots. 75.00
1966, Madonna riding on donkey 75.00
1967, gold sunburst pattern 80.00
1968, modern Madonna and Child . . . 80.00

CHRISTMAS AND EASTER SEALS

Collecting Christmas and Easter Seals is one of the most inexpensive "stamp" hobbies. Sheets usually sell for between 50¢ and $1.00. Although most collectors do not buy single stamps, the very earliest Christmas seals have some appeal.

Club: Christmas Seal and Charity Stamp Society, 5825 Dorchester Avenue, Chicago, IL 60637.

CIGARETTE AND CIGAR

Cigarette products contain a warning that they might be hazardous to your health. Cigarette and cigar memorabilia should contain a warning that they may be hazardous to your pocketbook. With each passing year, the price for cigarette- and cigar-related material goes higher and higher. If it ever stabilizes and then drops, a number of collectors are going to see their collections go up in smoke.

The vast majority of cigarette and cigar material is two-dimensional, from advertising trade cards to posters. Seek out three-dimensional pieces. There are some great cigarette and cigar tins.

Clubs: Cigarette Pack Collectors Association, 61 Searle Street, Georgetown, MA 01833; International Seal, Label & Cigar Band Society, 8915 East Bellevue Street, Tuscon, AZ 85715.

Ashtray
    Fatima Cigarettes, matchbox holder, marked "Nippon" 100.00
    LaMinerva Cigars, goddess dec 12.00
    Winston Cigarettes, tin 5.00
Bookmark, Old Gold Cigarettes, plastic. 20.00
Chair, Piedmont Cigarettes, folding. 225.00
Cigar Holder, red, catalin, Germany 8.00
Cigar Lighter, Art Deco, porcelain, counter top style 40.00
Cigarette Box, Silver Crest, bronze 50.00
Cigarette Card
    Roses, Wills, c1912, set of 50 . . . . 95.00

115

Pinback Button, Hassan Cigarettes, white ground, black letters, red coat, orig label on back, ⅞" d, $10.00.

The King's Art Treasures, Wills, 1930s,
set of 40 . . . . **48.00**
Cigarette Lighter, 6" l, figural, knight, armor, chrome **16.00**
Pinback Button
Phillip Morris, 1" d, celluloid, Johnny,
c1930 . . . . **18.00**
Union Made Cigars, 1¼" d, red, white,
blue, and black, light green cigar label, c1890 . . . . **20.00**
Poster
Booster Cigars, 27 × 30", black
man and lady adjusting garter,
framed. **175.00**
Chesterfield Cigarettes, cardboard. . . . **18.00**
Kool Cigarettes, 12 × 18", smoking
penguin points to pack, c1933 . . . . . **35.00**
Raleigh Cigarette, 12 × 18", paper, full
color glossy portrait. **20.00**
Sign
Chesterfield Cigarettes, Lucille Norman illus, 20 × 43". **55.00**
Dark Horse Cigar, 12 × 23", paper, two
trotting race horses **65.00**
Denby Cigar, tin, man with cigar
illus **375.00**
El Wadora Cigars, 24 × 36", tin,
c1930. . . . . **45.00**
Hambone Cigar, 7" d, round, cardboard, two sided, hanging, caricature of black man wearing aviator
goggles in tiny airplane **48.50**
Nickel King Cigars, 16 × 18", cardboard **35.00**
Old Gold Cigarettes, 12 × 4", tin, emb
dancing box. **25.00**
Pollocks Cigar, riverboats unloading
and commercial buildings **175.00**
Red Dot Cigar, figural. **52.00**
Smoking Jacket, cigar ribbons **250.00**

Tee Shirt, adv, Camel Cigarettes, Camel
Joe **9.00**
Thermometer
Chesterfield Cigarettes, 13" l **40.00**
Salem Cigarettes **20.00**
Tin
Chesterfield's, cat under celluloid **38.00**
Good Cheer Cigar, handled **60.00**
Old Abe Cigars, round, paper label . . . **60.00**
Reichard's Cadet Cigar **65.00**
Tray, Tom Moore Cigars, change. **20.00**
Whisk Broom, Whiskbroom Cigars, cigar
shape. **30.00**

CIRCUS

The only circus that I ever saw was at a theme park in Florida. Dad keeps telling me about traveling tent circuses and how exciting they really were. Based on the memorabilia that they left behind, I think he might be right.

Dad keeps threatening to take me to see the great annual circus parade in Milwaukee featuring the equipment from the Circus World Museum in Baraboo, Wisconsin. The reason that I get to be his traveling companion is that Connie, his wife, wants nothing to do with his circus fantasies. She says living with him is all the circus that she needs.

Clubs: Circus Fans of America, Four Center Drive, Camp Hill, PA 17011; The Circus Historical Society, 743 Beverly Park Place, Jackson, MI 49203; The Circus Model Builders International, 347 Lonsdae Avenue, Dayton, OH 45419.

Calendar, Circus World Museum,
1974. . . . . **5.00**
Circus Wagon, horse-drawn, cast
iron **55.00**
Menu, Greatest Show on Earth, Nov 12,
1898, full color **100.00**
Pinback Button, 1½" d, Super Circus
Club, Canada Dry adv, pictures Mary
Hartline, c1950 . . . . **20.00**
Post Card, Ringling Brothers, Freak
Fisher Family **35.00**
Poster
Cole Bros, All The Marvels, animals in
cages, Erie Litho **210.00**
Ringling Bros and Barnum & Bailey,
The Greatest Wild Animal Display,
presents Terrell Jacobs, World's
Foremost Trainer, Strobridge Litho,
1938. . . . . **625.00**
Program, Barnum & Bailey, 1953 . . . . . . **10.00**

Cartes de Visite, Jo' Jo' The Russian Dog-Faced Boy, Chas Eisenham Photographer, NY, $15.00.

Stereograph, Windsor & Whipple, Olean, NY, people with elephant **35.00**
Ticket, Ringling Brothers, Railroad Dept complimentary ticket, 1956 . . . . **2.00**
Toy
  Mechanical, acrobat, celluloid, Banko **175.00**
  Windup, clown with cart and pony . . . **45.00**

CLICKERS

If you need a clicker, you would probably spend hours trying to locate a modern one. I am certain they exist. You can find a clicker at a flea market in a matter of minutes. As an experiment, I tried looking up the word in a dictionary. It was not there. Times change.

Clickers made noise, a slight sharp sound. I believe their principal purpose was to drive parents crazy. I understand they played a major role at parochial school, but I cannot attest to the fact since I attended public school.

Advertising
  Allen's Parlor Furnace, reddish-brown heating stove illus, yellow ground **20.00**

Frog, Life of the Party Products, Kirchof, Newark, NJ, 3" l, $7.50.

Benzo-Gas, red, blue, white, and lime green, "Does What Gasoline Can't" slogan **18.00**
Buster Brown **25.00**
Calvert Whiskey, red and white, 1950s **8.00**
Endicott Johnson Shoes, yellow and black **12.00**
Gridley Milk, baby face in milk bottle, red ground **25.00**
Humpty Dumpty Shoes, 2" l, litho tin, c1930 . . . . **25.00**
Mule-Hide Roofing and Shingles, yellow and black, logo symbol **22.00**
New and True Coffee, c1930 . . . . **15.00**
Peter's Weatherbird Shoes, ¾ × 1¾", litho tin, multicolored, 1930s **25.00**
Real-Kill Bug Killer **18.00**
Red Goose Shoes, ¾ × 1¾", litho tin, red goose, yellow lettering and ground, 1930s **22.50**
Studebaker/The Car With A Snap, blue and white, round, Whitehead & Hoag, 1904 copyright **45.00**
Twinkies Shoes For Boys and Girls, Twinkie character, blue ground **18.00**
Weatherbird Shoes, red, yellow, and black **15.00**
Cartoon Character
  Felix, 1¾" l, black and white, dark brown ground, caption "Fancy You Fancying Me Felix!", 1930s **50.00**
  Mickey Mouse, playing drum **35.00**
Clown, 1½ × 2¼", multicolored, Japan **3.00**
Cricket, yellow and black, insect design **10.00**
Halloween, witch and pumpkin, orange, black, and white **15.00**

CLOCKS

Look for clocks that are fun (have motion actions) or that are terrific in a decorating scheme (a school house clock in a country setting). Clocks are bought to be seen and used.

Avoid buying any clock that does not work. You do not know whether it is going to cost $5.00, $50.00, or $500.00 to repair. Are you prepared to risk the higher numbers? Likewise, avoid clocks that need extensive repair work to the case. There are plenty of clocks in fine condition awaiting purchase.

Club: National Association of Watch and Clock Collectors, Inc., P. O. Box 33, Columbia, PA 17512.

Alarm, Charlie the Tuna, Star-Kist Foods, Inc., Robertshaw Controls Company, Lux Time Division, Lebanon, TN, © 1969, $15.00.

Advertising
   Calumet Baking Powder, oak case.... **995.00**
   Jacob Lucks Clothier, Watkins, NY, figural, dog, black man holding sign above....................... **160.00**
   Purina Poultry Chows, electric, three dials, red, white, and blue checkerboard bag.................... **40.00**
Alarm
   Brass, double bells, Bradley, Germany....................... **35.00**
   Metal, 10¼" h, Seth Thomas, 1910–1920....................... **50.00**
   Banjo, 17⅝" h, inlaid mahogany case, eagle finial, New Haven Clock Co, c1920........................ **150.00**
   Beehive, 5¼" h, brass, porcelain dial, Chelsea, c1900 .... **50.00**
Character, alarm
   Cinderella, 2½ × 4½ × 4", windup, white metal case, orig box, Westclox **50.00**

Donald Duck, 2 × 4½ × 4½", metal case, light blue, orig box, Bayard ... **250.00**
Mickey Mouse, 2 × 4 × 4½", plastic case, Ingersoll, 1949 .... **250.00**
Popeye and Swee' Pea, ivory enameled steel case, color illus on dial, Smiths, c1968....................... **100.00**
Roy Rogers, windup, metal case, animated, Ingraham, c1951......... **300.00**
Strawberry Shortcake, orig box **25.00**
Cuckoo, 5 × 4 × 1¾", pressed log design, leaves, flowers, nest of birds, brass spring pendulum, Keebler Clock Co, Philadelphia, PA **90.00**
Electric, chrome, 5 × 5", General Electric, 1920s......................... **80.00**
Figural
   Refrigerator, 8½" h, white metal, GE label, Warren Telechron Co, Ashland, MA **185.00**
   Ship, walnut hull, chrome plated sails and rigs, lighted portholes, United Clock Co, 1955 .... **90.00**
Kitchen
   Oak, Ansonia, Belmont **265.00**
Walnut
   New Haven Clock Co, Clarita **250.00**
   Seth Thomas, Newark........... **295.00**
Mantel
   Fruitwood, Chelsea, c1910......... **80.00**
   Rosewood, 10½" h, veneered case, Seth Thomas, c1880 .... **75.00**
School House
   Mahogany, 24" h, veneered case, Waterbury Clock Co, c1890......... **200.00**
   Oak, 19½" h, orig label, Sessions Clock Co, 1915–1920 .... **300.00**

CLOTHING AND ACCESSORIES

Decide from the beginning whether you are buying clothing and accessories for use or display. If you are buying for use, apply very strict standards with respect to condition and long term survival prospects. If you only want the items for display, you can be a little less fussy about condition.

Vintage clothing was a hot collectible craze in the 1980s. Things seem to have cooled off a bit. Emphasis in the 1990s seems to be on accessories, with plastic purses from the 1950s leading the parade.

I love the wide ties from the late 1950s and early 1960s, but they have become so trendy and pricy that I find myself more often than not passing them by. Besides, Dad has a closet full at home that belonged to him as a young adult. He's come a long way in his tastes since then.

Club: The Costume Society of America, P. O. Box 761, Englishtown, NJ 08826.

Newsletter: *Vintage Clothing Newsletter*, P. O. Box 1422, Corvallis, OR 97339.

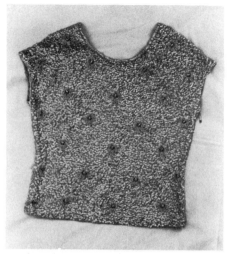

Evening Blouse, turquoise, sequins, $20.00.

Bathing Suit, black, stretchy fabric, flared skirt, c1930 .... 45.00
Bed Jacket, blue, satin, lace trim 20.00
Bloomers, crepe satin, peach, silk embroidery, lace 20.00
Blouse, white, cotton, Victorian cutwork 20.00
Change Purse
    Mesh
        Art Nouveau head 45.00
        Coins surrounding head 40.00
    Mother of Pearl 15.00
    Tin, small face opens mouth for change 35.00
Coat
    Cashmere, silver fox collar, c1940 .... 45.00
    Muskrat, bell shaped sleeves 95.00
Collar
    Beaded, white 15.00
    Linen, sq cutwork corners 25.00
Dress
    Chiffon, blue, braid edge trim, 1925 .... 40.00
    Crepe, brown, evening, matching velvet caplet, feather trim, c1930 ..... 45.00
    Silk, black, chiffon sleeves, embroidered, 1923 .... 50.00
    Victorian, teenager's, white, French lace insertions, tucks of embroidery 135.00
Dressing Gown, ruby red, satin, ruffled edges, 1930 .... 30.00
Gloves, pr
    Lady's, leather, France 15.00

Opera length, kid leather 20.00
Handbag
    Alligator, suede lining 20.00
    Beaded
        Blue and white checked, drawstring closure 48.00
        Fuchsia, silver frame, open work ... 95.00
        Pink and blue florals, gold frame ... 45.00
    Plastic, lucite, pearlized, round lid, twisted handle, seashell dec 18.00
    Silk, clutch, black, cut steel beads, marked "France," c1930 .... 40.00
Petticoat, Victorian, white 10.00
Prom Gown, pink, net and taffeta, layered skirt, bow trim, c1950 .... 35.00
Skirt
    Poodle dec, pink, felt 25.00
    Victorian, embroidered panels with French lace insert 60.00
Sleep Cap, lady's, silk, unused 60.00
Spats, gray, wool, c1900 .... 25.00
Sweater, cashmere, white pearl trim 35.00
Wedding Dress, two pcs, batiste and lace, high neck, early 1900s 90.00

COCA-COLA COLLECTIBLES

John Pemberton, a pharmacist from Atlanta, Georgia, is credited with creating the formula for Coca-Cola. Less than two years later, he sold out to Asa G. Chandler. Chandler improved the formula and began advertising. By the 1890s America was Coca-Cola conscious.

Coke, a term first used in 1941, is now recognized worldwide. American collectors still focus primarily on Coca-Cola material designed for the American market. Although it would take a little effort to obtain, a collection of foreign Coke advertising would make a terrific display. What a perfect excuse to fly to the Orient.

Club: The Coca-Cola Collectors Club International, P. O. Box 546, Holmdel, NJ 07733.

Blotter, 1944, 7³/₄" l, 3¹/₂" h, $2.50.

Ashtray, card suits dec, c1940 . . . . **40.00**
Blotter
 1903. . . . . **30.00**
 1951. . . . . **4.00**
Book, bottler's 50th anniversary **28.00**
Booklet, *The Truth About Coca-Cola*,
 1912. . . . . **30.00**
Bottle, aqua, straight sided. **25.00**
Bottle Opener, hand. **10.00**
Bridge Score Pad. **5.00**
Can, diamond with bottle center dec,
 c1960. . . . . **15.00**
Charm Bracelet, 6½" l, brass, NFL, four
 miniature charms, punter, football,
 NFL logo, Coke logo, enamel accents,
 c1970. . . . . **20.00**
Check, canceled **2.00**
Cigarette Lighter, 2½" h, plastic, bottle
 shape, c1950 . . . . **18.50**
Cribbage Game, MIB **55.00**
Dish, souvenir 1964 New York World's
 Fair **65.00**
Fan, cardboard, 1940s **22.00**
Fly Swatter **9.00**
Hat, beanie type, c1960 . . . . **7.00**
Key Chain, miniature bottle, c1950. . . . . **6.00**
Matchbook, c1930 . . . . **5.00**
Menu, girl serving tray, unused. **30.00**
Pencil, bullet shape. **4.00**
Pinback Button
 1⅛" d, red and white, "Drink Coca-
  Cola," c1950 . . . . **10.00**
 1¼" d, red and white, "Coca-Cola
  Big Wheels Club," *Cleveland Press*
  newspaper, ship's wheel center,
  c1930s **50.00**
Playing Cards, 52 card deck **90.00**
Post Card, showing c1940 Coke truck . . . **18.00**
Punch Board, small. **8.00**
Sign
 30" h, figural, bottle shaped. **250.00**
 45" d, round, porcelain, bottle illus . . . **200.00**
Thermometer, 17" l, bottle shape **90.00**
Toy
 Frisbee. **20.00**
 Pop Gun. **4.00**
 Truck, Buddy L, 1960s, MIB. **200.00**

COIN-OPERATED MACHINES

This category covers any machine operated by inserting a coin, from arcade
games to player pianos to vending machines. Since all these machines are mechanical, it is important to buy only machines in operating order. The techniques
to repair them rest in the hands of a few
enthusiasts. Many repair parts need to be
made by hand.
 Many museums, recognizing the long-
term collectibility of coin-operated games,

have already begun to acquire some of the
early video games. Imagine Pac-Man in a
museum. It doesn't seem so long ago that I
was playing it in an arcade.

Newsletters: *Coin-Op Newsletter*, 909 26th
Street, NW, Washington, DC 20037;
Jukebox Collector Newsletter, 2545 SE 60th
Street, Des Moines, IA 50317.

*Vending Machine, Deluxe Hot Nut Vendor, Ajax
Distributing Company, Newark, NJ, aluminum, $200.00.*

Cigarettes, Jennings Cigarolla, 5¢ and
 10¢, trade stimulator and vending machine, wood case, 20×60×22" **350.00**
Cigarettes and Ball Gum, Penny Smoke,
 1¢, trade stimulator and vending machine, pot metal, emb, three reels, 9½
 ×12×9", 1930 . . . . **375.00**
Cigars, Good Luck Poker, 1¢, trade stim-
 ulator and vending machine, oak and
 cast iron case, five reels, 10½ × 15 ×
 9". **350.00**
Dixie Cups, Dixie-Vortex Co, 1¢, iron
 and glass, 4×31". **250.00**
Game, Select-Em, dice game, Exhibit
 Supply Co, Chicago, IL **275.00**
Gum
 Chicago Club-House, 1¢, ball gum,
  emb pot metal case, Art Deco motif,
  five poker reels, 12×13½×9" **385.00**
 Chic-Mint, 1¢, ball gum, cast iron and
  pressed steel, labeled globe, coin
  trap in base, 6×12×8" **500.00**
 Pulver Chewing Gum, 1¢, yellow
  enameled case, mechanical clown

int., "One Cent Delivers A Tasty Chew," 9 × 20½ × 4½" **475.00**

Zeno Chewing Gum, 1¢, oak case, emb tin front, 10½ × 16½ × 9¼" **650.00**

Jukebox

Regina Hexaphone, 5¢, floor model, oak case, spring wound-mechanism, six selections, 27 × 64 × 18" **6,500.00**

Wurlitzer, Model 1650, 48 selections, light-up side columns, 55" h, 1954 . . . . **500.00**

Matches, Safety Matches, 1¢, glass dome, oak case, cigar cutter attachment, 11 × 18 × 10" **375.00**

Medicine and Gum, The Auto Doctor, Auto Doctor Company, Geneva, NY, 5¢, oak case, beveled mirror front, decaled sides and front, dispenses cough troches, cold tablets, dyspepsin tablets, headache tablets, breath perfume, and gum, 12¼ × 27 × 4¾" **11,000.00**

Peanuts

1¢, Advance, Simplex Variety, glass globe, emb cast metal base, 7 × 17 × 8", c1908 . . . . **1,050.00**

5¢, trade stimulator and vending machine, pressed steel, horserace gambling wheel, 7 × 11 × 6½" **150.00**

Pencils, Parker Pencil Service, 5¢, metal case, 10 × 9 × 5", c1930 . . . . **55.00**

Postage Stamps, Mills, 2¢ and 1¢ stamps, oak case, cast metal front, patriotic motif, two column vendor, 7 × 22 × 9", c1915 . . . . **2,375.00**

Scale

Mills, American Automatic Sales, NH, 1¢, platform scale, ornate cast iron, porcelain face, 16 × 69 × 24" **1,000.00**

The Washington Scale, Caille, Detroit, 1¢, platform scale, wood case, iron trim, 22 × 76 × 28" . . . **2,400.00**

Slot Machine, Mills

1¢, Q. T., diamond fronted, 12½ × 18½ × 13" **550.00**

5¢, F. O. K., cast white metal front, war eagle series, 16 × 26½ × 16¼", 1930s **1,050.00**

25¢, hightop, watermelon feature, two/five payout, 16 × 26 × 16", 1940s **1,425.00**

COINS, AMERICAN

Just because a coin is old does not mean that it is valuable. Value often depends more on condition than on age. This being the case, the first step in deciding if any of your coins are valuable is to grade them. Coins are graded on a scale of 70, with 70 being the best and 4 being good.

Start your research by acquiring Marc Hudgeons's *The Official 1993 Blackbook Price Guide To United States Coins, Thirty-First Edition* (House of Collectibles: 1992). Resist the temptation to look up your coins immediately. Read the hundred-page introduction, over half of which deals with the question of grading.

Do not overlook the melt (weight) value of silver content coins. In many cases, weight value will be far greater than collectible value. If only we'd have sold when the industry was paying twenty times face value in the midst of the 1980s silver craze!

Club: American Numismatic Association, 818 North Cascade Avenue, Colorado Springs, CO 80903.

COINS, FOREIGN

The foreign coins that you are most likely to find at a flea market are the leftover change that someone brought back with them from their travels. Since the coins were in circulation, they are common and of a low grade. In some countries, they have been withdrawn from circulation and cannot even be redeemed for face value.

If you are a dreamer and think you have uncovered hidden wealth, use Chester L. Krause and Clifford Mishler's *1993 Edition Standard Catalog of World Coins* (Krause Publications: 1992). This book covers world coinage from 1801 through 1991.

Avoid any ancient coinage. There are excellent fakes on the market. You need to be an expert to tell the good from the bad. Coins are one of those categories where it pays to walk away when the deal is too good. Honest coin dealers work on very small margins. They cannot afford to give away anything of value.

COLLEGE COLLECTIBLES

Rah, rah, sis-boom-bah! The Yuppies made a college education respectable again. They tout their old alma mater. They usually have a souvenir of their college days in their office at home or work.

You will not find a Harvard graduate with a room full of Yale memorabilia and vice versa. These items have value only to someone who attended the school. The exception is sport-related college memorabilia. This has a much broader appeal, either to a conference collector or a general sports collector.

Periodical: *Sports Collectors Digest*, 700 East State Street, Iola, WI 54990.

Lehigh University, Bethlehem, PA, cigarette silk, Richmond Straight Cut Cigarettes, 4" w, 5¼" h, $15.00.

Booklet, *The Freshman Herald, Princeton University, Class of 1941*, biographies, includes Malcolm Forbes **28.00**
Calendar, University of Wisconsin, Madison, Bascom Hall photo, 1916 . . . .**100.00**
Commemorative Glass, dinner **5.00**
Commemorative Spoon
   Cornell University, Art Nouveau woman **50.00**
   Iowa State College, Indian Chief, sterling silver. **28.00**
   Notre Dame. **100.00**
   State Normal School, Superior, Wisconsin **25.00**
   Wellesley College, woman in cap and gown handle **50.00**
Magazine, Phi Gamma Delta, 1955 . . . . . **10.00**
Nodder, 7" h, basketball player, composition, rounded gold base, sticker inscribed "Millersville," 1960s **22.00**
Plate, William and Mary College, 10" d, Wren building, Jonroth **10.00**
Program, Illinois-Notre Dame Football game, 8 × 11", 20 pgs, Oct 9, 1937 . . . . **25.00**

Sheet Music, *Everybody Loves A College Girl*, Kerry Mills, 1911 . . . . **3.00**
Tie Clip, Yale, 2" l, key shape, bright gold colored plating, inscribed "The Yale & Towne Mfg Co" and "First For Ike," issued by Yale Ike Club, 1952 . . . . **75.00**
Tobacco Silk, Lehigh University, Richmond Straight Cut Cigarettes. **15.00**
Yearbook
   Iowa State Teachers College, 1940. . . . **10.00**
   Princeton University
      1941. . . . . **10.00**
      1942. . . . . **28.00**

COLORING BOOKS

The key is to find these gems uncolored. Some collectors will accept a few pages colored, but the coloring had better be neat. If it is scribbled, forget it.

Most of the value rests in the outside cover. The closer the image is to the actual character or personality featured, the higher the value. The inside pages of most coloring books consist of cheap newsprint. It yellows and becomes brittle over time. However, resist buying only the cover. Collectors prefer to have the entire book.

Arden, Eve, 1953, unused **32.50**
Barney Google, 1968 . . . . **10.00**
Blondie, 8½ × 11", Dell Publishing, 1954, unused. **20.00**
Blyth, Ann, 1952, unused **35.00**
Buster Crabbe Foreign Legionaire **45.00**
Charlie Chaplin, 10 × 17", Donohue & Co, 1917 copyright **80.00**
Dennis The Menace, 1960, unused **12.50**
Dick Tracy, 8¼ × 11", Saalfield, #2536, 1946 copyright **25.00**
Donald Duck, 7½ × 8½", Whitman, 1946, unused **20.00**
Hopalong Cassidy, 5¼ × 5¼", "William Boyd/Star of Hopalong Cassidy/On The Range," 48 pgs, Samuel Lowe Co, 1951 copyright **25.00**
Li'l Abner, 8 × 11", Saalfield, #209, 80 pgs, copyright 1941 . . . . **30.00**
Lone Ranger, 8½ × 11", Whitman, 64 pgs, Cheerios premium, 1956 . . . . **75.00**
Mix, Tom, 11 × 14", Whitman, 96 pgs, 1935. . . . . **50.00**
Oakley, Annie, 11 × 14", Whitman, unused, 1955 . . . . **18.00**
Planet of the Apes, 8½ × 11", Saalfield, 1974 Apjac Productions copyright, unused. **15.00**
Rocky and Bullwinkle, "Bullwinkle's How To Have Fun Outdoors Without Getting Clobbered," unused **20.00**

Roy Rogers, 15 × 11″, Roy Rogers and
  Dale Evans, 1952 . . . . **20.00**
Shazam, 11 × 14″, Whitman, pin-up
  poster on back cov, National Periodical
  Publications copyright, 1975 . . . . **12.00**
Spiderman, large size **18.00**
Superman, 8 × 11″, Whitman, 1966 Na-
  tional Periodical Publications copy-
  right, unused. **25.00**

COMBS

The form is pretty basic. Value rests in how
and in what material the comb is presented. Some hair combs are fairly elaborate and actually should be considered as
jewelry accessories.

Beware of combs being sold separately
that were originally part of larger dresser
sets. Their value is less than combs that
were meant to stand alone.

You can build an interesting collection
inexpensively by collecting giveaway
combs. You will be amazed to see how
many individuals and businesses used this
advertising media, from politicians to funeral parlors.

*Bakelite, two layers, red on top, yellow on bot-
tom, lunette parrots in flight, tuck comb, 7 × 7″,
c1900, $75.00.*

Brass
  Embossed cracker barrel design, fold-
    ing purse comb **35.00**
  Rhinestone covered case, folding purse
    comb **50.00**
Celluloid
  Butterscotch colored, rhinestone
    band, side comb, c1900. . . . . **10.00**
  Imitation tortoise shell
    Amethyst-colored rhinestones, tuck
      comb **75.00**

Double arches shape, cobalt blue
  rhinestones around edges, tuck
  comb **80.00**
Peacock motif, rhinestone accents,
  tuck comb, early 1900s **40.00**
Pierced floral design, side comb **45.00**
Plain, side comb **20.00**
Spade shaped, rhinestones around
  edge, tuck comb, 1900–1915 . . . . **40.00**
Enameled, rhinestone champagne glass
  motif, folding purse comb **50.00**
Gutta Percha, black, chain link design,
  side comb **150.00**
Horn
  Black, white glass beaded band, side
    comb, early 20th C **45.00**
  Yellow, cut steel flower and rope dec,
    tuck comb **175.00**
Jet, faceted bead design, side comb, En-
  gland, c1890 . . . . **45.00**
Lucite, gold speckled case, folding purse
  comb, Curry Arts **25.00**
Metal, plastic comb, silver colored metal
  case with rhinestone and floral spray
  dec, folding purse comb **20.00**
Mother-of-Pearl, folding purse comb,
  Wiesner of Miami. **50.00**
Plastic
  Crown design, brilliant rhinestones,
    imitation tortoise shell, side comb,
    1940s **35.00**
  Domed top, three rows of eighteen
    rhinestones, side comb, 1940s **25.00**
  Eagle design, brilliant rhinestones set
    in brass frame, imitation tortoise
    shell, side comb, 5½″ w, 4″ l **45.00**
  Floral spray design, ornate, green
    and blue rhinestones, side comb,
    1960s. **20.00**
  Imitation mother-of-pearl, folding
    purse comb, Marhill, 1960s **25.00**
  Rhinestone band with pearl end, side
    comb **25.00**
  Tiara design, silver colored metal, bril-
    liant rhinestones, hinged, clear side
    comb **30.00**
Tortoise Shell, domed top, etched leaf
  design, nine rhinestones, tuck comb,
  1920s. **28.00**

COMEDIAN COLLECTIBLES

Laughter is said to be the best medicine. If
this is true, why does it hurt so much
when Abbott and Costello meet the
Mummy?

Comedians of all eras have gifted the
public with the pleasures of laughter. In
return the public has made them stars.

Comedian collectibles span mediums as
well as eras. Radio, vaudeville, television,

standup, and cinema are all represented. The plight of Charlie Chaplin is echoed in the antics of Whoopi Goldberg. So feel free to laugh out loud the next time you find a Groucho Marx eyeglass and mustache mask—I do.

Doll, Charlie McCarthy, composition face and hands, cloth body, pull string, $80.00.

Abbott & Costello, pinback button, 1939 New York World's Fair, 1¾″ d, "Lou 'I'm a Bad Boy' Costello for Mayor of World's Fair Midway/Abbott for Commissioner of Laffs," portrait illus, blue and white 65.00

Jackie Gleason
Bus, Wolverine, steel, wood wheels, 14″ l, 1955. . . . . 500.00
Climbing Toy, Poor Soul, c1955. . . . . 120.00
Cocktail Napkins, Honeymooners, set of 50, orig box, 1955 . . . . 45.00
Costume, bus driver, Empire Plastic, gray hat, money changer, 15 plastic coins, bus transfer sheet booklet, ticket punch, mid 1950s 350.00

Larry Semon, pinback button, "Larry Semon Comedies/Keep Smiling/ Laugh with Larry," portrait illus, 1930s. 7.00

Laurel & Hardy
Bank, figural Hardy, hard vinyl, multi-colored, Play Pal Plastics, 7½″ h, 1974. . . . . 30.00

Doll
Laurel & Hardy, pr, bisque head and shoulders, forearms, and lower legs, stuffed cloth body, 23″ h Laurel, 20″ h Hardy, 1970s 100.00
Oliver Hardy, Dakin, hard plastic, jointed arms, soft vinyl head, fabric outfit, orig display bag, 7″ h, 1960s 35.00

Mask Set, pr, Laurel & Hardy faces, molded plastic, 6½ × 10″, 1960s 35.00
Model Kit, 1925 T Roadster, AMT, plastic, 1970s. 60.00
Puzzle, frame tray, Whitman, Laurel, Hardy, and gorilla cartoon illus, 11½ × 14½″, 1967 . . . . 14.00
Sign, adv, Anco Wiper Blades, diecut and emb hard plastic, portrait illus, 18 × 31½″ 65.00

Lucille Ball
Coloring Book, Lucy, Desi, and Ricky Jr, Dell Publications, 80 pgs, 1955. . . . . 30.00
Doll, stuffed cloth, molded plastic face, yellow yarn hair, red and white fabric outfit, 27″ h, 1950s 150.00

Marx Brothers
Game, Groucho TV Quiz, Pressman. . . 75.00
Groucho Goggles and Cigar, plastic, carded, 1955 . . . . 40.00
Sheet Music, *Ev'ryone Says I Love You*, "Horse Feathers," 9 × 12″, 1932. . . . 25.00
Milton Berle, car, Marx, litho tin, windup, orig box, 5½″ l, 6½″ h, early 1950s. 300.00

Robin Williams
Board Game, Mork & Mindy, Parker Brothers, 1979 . . . . 15.00
Lunch Box, King-Seeley Thermos, steel box, plastic thermos, 1979 . . . . 30.00
T shirt, white, "Na Nu, Na Nu," size M 12.00

Rowan & Martin, Laugh-In
Board Game, Romart, 1969 . . . . 25.00
Paper Doll Book, Saalfield #1325, 8¼ × 11½″, 1969 . . . . 20.00
Waste Can, litho steel, photos, illustrations, and popular phrases from show, 13″ h. 25.00

Soupy Sales
Autograph, "Sincerely Soupy Sales," black and white glossy photo postcard 20.00
Board Game
Soupy Sales Go Go Go, Milton Bradley, 1961 . . . . 30.00
Soupy Sales Mini Board Card Game, Ideal, 1965. . . . . 25.00
Pencil Case, vinyl, light blue, zippered, 1960. . . . . 25.00
Pinback Button, Charter Member/ Soupy Sales Society, 3½″ d, 1960. . . . . 15.00

Three Stooges
  Bank, ceramic, figural, Stooges stand-
    ing back-to-back, glossy, 7" h, Ja-
    pan, 1960s **350.00**
  Board Game, Fun House, Lowell Toy
    Corp, 1959. **200.00**
  Flasher Ring, plastic, silver colored,
    "I'm Curly". 30.00
  Flying Cane, Empire Plastic Co, plastic,
    telescoping, 1959 . . . . **125.00**
  Pencil Coloring Set, Colorforms,
    1959. . . . . **250.00**
  Poster, "Three Stooges Meet Hercu-
    les," Columbia Pictures, 27 × 41",
    1961 . . . . 60.00
  Record, 33⅓ rpm, *Nonsense Songbook*,
    Coral Records, 12¼ × 12¼" album,
    1950s 50.00

COMIC BOOKS

Comic books come in all shapes and sizes.
The number that have survived is almost
endless. Although there were reprint
books of cartoon strips in the 1910s,
1920s, and 1930s, the modern comic book
had its origin in June 1938 when DC issued Action Comics No. 1, marking the
first appearance of Superman.

  Comics are divided into Golden Age, Silver Age, and Contemporary titles. Before
you begin buying, read John Hegenber-
ger's *Collector's Guide To Comic Books* (Wallace-Homestead: 1990) and D. W. Howard's *Investing In Comics* (The World of
Yesterday: 1988).

  The dominant price guide for comics is
Robert Overstreet's *The Official Overstreet
Comic Book Price Guide*. However, more and
more you see obsolete comics being offered in shops and at conventions for ten
to twenty-five percent less than Overstreet's prices. The comic book market
may be facing a revaluation crisis similar to
what happened in the stamp market several years ago when the editors of the Scott
catalog significantly lowered values for
many stamps.

Periodicals: *Comic Buyers Guide*, 700 State
Street, Iola, WI 54990; *Comics Values
Monthly*, Attic Books, P. O. Box 38, South
Salem, NY 10590.

Note: Most comics, due to condition, are
not worth more than 50¢ to a couple of
dollars. Very strict grading standards are
applied to comics less than ten years old.

The following list shows the potential in
the market. You need to check each comic
book separately.

Hanna-Barbera, **The Funky Phantom,** *white,
blue figures, orange ground, purple and red lettering, Gold Key Series 90274-409, $2.00.*

Avengers, Marvel, #62 . . . . 10.00
Bewitched, Dell, #7, Dec 1966, 7 ×
  10" 10.00
Buster Brown, #37, mint 12.50
Captain America, Marvel Comic, Vol 1,
  #100, April 1968 . . . . 10.00
Captain Marvel, "Captain Marvel Ad-
  venture," Wheaties adv and Bob Feller
  photo on back, 1964 copyright, 6½ ×
  8¼" 30.00
Cheyenne, Dell, #9, Nov–Jan 1959 . . . . . 12.00
Gene Autry Comics, Dell, Vol 1, #20, Oct
  1948 . . . . 18.00
GI Joe, Vol 2, #18, winter 1952, 7 ×
  10" 20.00
Gunsmoke, 1958 . . . . 14.00
Hawkman, Zatanna, #5 . . . . 6.00
Hopalong Cassidy, Fawcett, Vol 5, #29,
  March 1949. . . . . 55.00
Little Lulu, premium, 16 pgs, Marjorie
  Henderson Buell 1964 copyright, 5 ×
  7¼" 20.00
Rin Tin Tin and Rusty, Dell, #31, Aug-
  Oct 15.00
Roy Rogers Comics, Dell, Vol 1, #17, May
  1949. . . . . 80.00
The Danny Thomas Show, #1249, Nov-
  Jan 1962, 7½ × 10" 12.00

COMMEMORATIVE GLASSES

Before there were modern promotional drinking glasses (the kind you get from a fast food restaurant, gas station, or by eating the contents of a glass food container) people bought glasses as souvenirs. The earliest examples have acid-etched decorations. Although these are tough to find, they are not all that expensive. One collector I know specializes in advertising spirit glasses. Her collection numbers in the hundreds.

Tumbler, Rear Admiral William T Sampson, portrait in medallion, white ground, 3¾" h, $75.00.

Spirit Glasses, advertising
    Compliments of Jos. Spand, 589 Atlantic Avenue, Boston, MA, 2⅜" h, c1910 .... **18.00**
    Green Mill Whiskey, S. M. Denison, Wholesale Liquor Dealer, Chillicothe, OH, 2¼" h, c1910 .... **15.00**
    Seattle Liquor Co., 1123 First Avenue, Seattle, WA, 2⁵⁄₁₆" h, gold rim, c1908 .... **20.00**
Tumblers, commemorative
    End of Prohibition, 3⅝" h, clear, GOP elephant and DEM donkey on beer keg illus, "At Last! 1933" **30.00**
    Kentucky Derby, 1987, 5¼" h, frosted tan, horse wearing winner's roses, list of winners from 1875 through 1986 .... **5.00**
    McKinley and Teddy Roosevelt, 3¾" h, clear, frosted portraits and slogan "Integrity, Inspiration, Industry," gold rim **80.00**

    Minstrel Show, 5¼" h, clear, weighted bottom, black caricature performers, music and words from "Dixie's Land," 1930–1945 .... **15.00**
    New York World's Fair, 1939, 4½" h, clear, Theme Building and Court of Communications illus **25.00**
    Remember Pearl Harbor, 4¾" h, clear, red slogan, white date, red, white, and blue airplanes, warships, Hawaiian island, and Pearl Harbor Bay **75.00**
    Space Spectaculars of the United States, 5½" h, clear, Atlas D launch vehicle and Mercury 6 space capsule illus, red, white, and blue **12.00**
    Texas Centennial Exposition, 1936, 3½" h, clear, dark blue seal and cowboy on rearing horse illus **22.00**
    World Series, 5¾" h, clear, weighted bottom, white lettering, list of World Series winners from 1924 through 1951, gold batter illus **20.00**
    World War II, 4¾" h, clear, blue "Victory" over large "V" symbol. **25.00**
    Wright-Patterson Air Force Base, 5½" h, clear, weighted bottom, Wright Brothers plane, jets, and Air Force Museum insignia, late 1950s **8.00**

COMMEMORATIVE MEDALS

From the late nineteenth century through the 1930s, commemorative medals were highly prized possessions. The U. S. Mint and other mints still carry on the tradition today, but to a far lesser degree.

Distinguish between medals issued in mass and those struck for a limited purpose, in some cases in issues of one for presentation. An old medal should have a surface patina that has developed over the years causing it to have a very mellow appearance. Never, never clean a medal. Collectors like the patina.

In most medals, the metal content has little value. However, medals were struck in both silver and gold. If you are not certain, have the metal tested.

Club: Token and Medal Society, Inc., P. O. Box 951988, Lake Mary, FL 32795–1988.

Anti-Slavery, brass, kneeling black woman, slogan "Am I Not A Woman & Sister/1838," wreath design on back with motto **70.00**
Centennial, US, brass shell, New Mexico trading post, inscribed "J E Barrow & Co/Post Traders/Fort Union/New

Mexico," reverse with Miss Liberty and 1776 date, 1⅜" d **50.00**

Civil War, copper, Major General George McClellan, USA, eagle, shield, and flag design, slogan on back "I Am Born To Defend My Country," 1¼" d **35.00**

Exposition

Alaska Yukon Pacific, 1909, emb "Virgin Utah Copper," Utah exhibit on front, inscribed rim, reverse with state seal, 1½" d **20.00**

Cincinnati Industrial, 1883, Brewery Award, brass, six sided, "Complimentary Grand Medal" and George Washington profile on front, reverse with date, expo title, and "The Christian Moerlein Brewing Co, Cincinnati O," 1¼" d **60.00**

Columbian, 1893

Bronze, raised scene of Columbus, reverse with trumpeting angels, ship, and commemorative text, 1½" d **40.00**

White Metal, raised bust portrait of Columbus, rim inscribed "Souvenir World's Columbian Exposition, Chicago, USA, 1892–1893," worn silver flashing, 2" d **25.00**

Cotton States, 1895, white metal, dark finish, Phoenix bird, center inscribed "Resurgens/Atlanta, Ga," rim inscribed "Cotton States and International Exposition/Sept 18th to Dec 31st," 2" d **30.00**

Hudson-Fulton Celebration, aluminum, emb, Robert Fulton portrait above three seated goddesses on front, reverse with Hudson River discovery scene and text, 2" d **20.00**

Political

Andrew Johnson Inauguration, white metal, silver luster, portrait on front, reverse with "Andrew Johnson, 17 President U. S." **45.00**

Harrison Campaign, brass, name, birthdate, and portrait on front, reverse with log cabin and "The People's Choice In The Year 1840" **10.00**

Hoover Inauguration, metal, dark brass finish, name, portrait, and 1929 date on front, reverse with female figure and "Inaugurated March 4, 1929, Engineer, Scholar, Statesman, Humanist," 3" d **15.00**

Lincoln Campaign, eagle and "Success To Republican Principles" on front, reverse with Millions For Freedom Not One Cent For Slavery," 1860 .... **65.00**

Sesquicentennial, Hamden, CT, brass, emb "Eli Whitney Arms Plant" and details, 1936, 1¼" d **15.00**

Sports, bronze colored, baseball Hall of Fame induction, Carl Yastrzemski,

Boston Red Sox, July 23, 1989, and portrait on front, reverse with Kahn's Meats and Hillshire Farm sponsor logos, 1½" d **8.00**

World's Fair, Chicago, 1934, brass, emb, Travel and Transport building on front, reverse with Century of Progress symbol, 1¼" d **10.00**

COMMEMORATIVE (SOUVENIR) SPOONS

Collecting commemorative spoons was extremely popular from the last decade of the nineteenth century through 1940. Actually, it has never gone completely out of fashion. You can still buy commemorative spoons at many historical and city tourist sites.

The first thing that you want to check for is metal content. Sterling silver was a popular medium for commemorative spoons. Fine enamel work adds to value.

Club: American Spoon Collectors, 4922 State Line, Westwood Hills, KS 66205.

Newsletter: *Spoony Scoop Newsletter*, 84 Oak Avenue, Shelton, CT 06484.

Battle Monument, Trenton, New Jersey **25.00**
Ben Franklin, Philadelphia **40.00**
Canada, SS **25.00**
Chief Seattle, totem pole **22.00**
Columbian Exposition, 1893, inverted anchor handle, standing warrior goddess and "World's Fair 1893" in bowl, 4½" l, SP **15.00**
Columbus, bust, SP. **15.00**
Denver, Columbine handle **16.50**
Dionne Quintuplets, set of 5, standing figure and first name on handle, 6" h, SP.............................. **75.00**
Duba, Morro castle **40.00**
Fort Dearborn, SS **12.00**
Fredericton, New Brunswick, spiral handle, gold wash bowl **30.00**
GAR Encampment, 31st National Encampment of Grand Army of the Republic in Buffalo, NY, 1897, GAR symbol, war monument statue and buffalo head on handle, 4½" l, SP **18.00**
Golden Gate, San Francisco **30.00**
Indianapolis, Soldier's & Sailor's Monument **18.00**
Jamestown Exposition............... **35.00**
Lake Worth, Palm Beach, Florida **58.00**
Madison, Wisconsin................. **10.00**
Mt Vernon. **10.00**

William Penn, figure and date "1682" on handle, Liberty Bell and "Proclaim Liberty Throughout the Land" in bowl, sterling silver, $30.00.

New York Peace Monument, Lookout Mountain, Tennessee, picture bowl........................... **25.00**
Notre Dame....................... **110.00**
Old Hickory, Jackson Monument **55.00**
Palm Springs Aerial Tramway, SP, John Brown, marked "Antico"........... **100.00**
Pan-American Expo, 1901, "Pan-American Candy Co" on handle, standing buffalo in bowl, 4" l, silvered brass ... **15.00**
Pittsburgh, Ft Pitt **38.00**
Quebec, openwork handle........... **15.00**
Queen Elizabeth, 1953 Coronation..... **15.00**
Rochester, New York **35.00**
San Francisco, Mission Dolores 1776, bear on dec handle, gold bowl **35.00**
Settle Memorial Church, Owensboro, Kentucky....................... **25.00**
Statue of Liberty, Tiffany **60.00**
St Louis World's Fair, 1904, Thomas Jefferson portrait above crossed US and Louisiana Purchase flags on handle, Agriculture building in bowl, Cascade Gardens and Louisiana Purchase Monument on reverse, US Silver Co, 4½" l........................ **20.00**
Teddy Roosevelt, riding horse, full figure handle....................... **85.00**
Washington DC, capitol **28.00**
William Penn, Independence Hall...... **58.00**

COMPACTS

The jewelry market is now so sophisticated that you have to look to its components to find out what is hot and what is not. Compacts are hot. They increased significantly in price in the 1980s. They are still rising in value.

Look for compacts that are major design statements or have gadget mechanisms. Many compacts came with elaborate boxes and pouches. These must be present if the compact is going to be viewed as complete.

Club: The Compact Collectors Club, P. O. Box Letter S, Lynbrook, NY 11563.

Vanity Case and Matching Cigarette Lighter, Weltzunder, blue marbleized enamel, silvered metal cut out of US Zone map, Kamra-Pak style, orig presentation box, German, $175.00.

Ansico, sq, high relief-carved rose surrounded by mother-of-pearl border............................ **125.00**
Austria, round, enameled, SS openwork flower basket dec, hand engraved **175.00**
Coty, sq, chromium plated, scenic Rio center design made from butterfly wing........................... **55.00**
Curry Arts, oval, pink speckled lucite ... **50.00**
Elgin American, rect, engraved script "Mother" **80.00**
Estee Lauder, round, mother-of-pearl, goldtone medallion center **50.00**
Evans Case Company, rect, goldtone, watchcase, plaid design, 1940s....... **160.00**
Finberg Manufacturing Company, round, SS, enameled, pink flowers on yellow ground................... **100.00**
John Wanamaker, round, plastic, pink,

flower basket design on foil paper insert, 1930s 50.00
Kotler and Kopit, rect, goldtone, rhinestone encrusted lid 85.00
Lin-Bren, oval, goldtone, multicolored rhinestones on grid design 65.00
Marhill, round
    Bakelite, green, gold plated band with engraved floral design. 80.00
    Imitation mother-of-pearl 75.00
Revlon, round, goldtone, paisley design, case designed by Van Cleef & Arpels 90.00
Rex Fifth Avenue, round, celluloid, floral transfer on lid, 1939–1940 . . . . 65.00
Richard Hudnut, rect, gold plated, DuBarry, emb leaf design 75.00
Schildkraut, sq, tortoise shell 95.00
Souvenir
    Empire State Building, enamel, painted green 40.00
    New York World's Fair 1939, wood, tapestry design 80.00
    Pennsylvania Turnpike scene 35.00
Wadsworth, round, gold plated, enameled playing card motif on lid 60.00
Yardley, round, brass, scenic transfer on celluloid lid, London 80.00

CONSTRUCTION SETS

Children love to build things. Building block sets originated in the nineteenth century. They exist in modern form as Legos and Lego imitators.

Construction toys also were popular, especially with young boys who aspired to be engineers. The best known is the Erector Set, but it also had plenty of imitators. Alfred Carlton Gilbert, Jr., began his business by producing magic sets as the Mysto Manufacturing Company. With the help of his father, he bought out his partner and created the A. C. Gilbert Company, located on Erector Square in New Haven, Connecticut.

A. C. Gilbert, Erector Set
    No. 2, Junior, 1949 . . . . 40.00
    No. 4, 1930 . . . . 250.00
    No. 6½, 1954 . . . . 40.00
    No. 7, steam shovel 350.00
    No. 8½ 70.00
    No. 10, deluxe, Zeppelin, Hudson and Tender 2,000.00
    No. 10½, 1949 . . . . 140.00
    No. 77, Trumodel Set, Sears, 1929 . . . . 125.00
    No. 10021 . . . . 30.00
    No. 10032 . . . . 30.00
    No. 10042, Radar Scope Set 35.00
    No. 10053, Rocket Launcher Set 90.00
    No. 10062, Steam Engine Set 35.00
    No. 10093, Master Builder Set 300.00
    No. 10181, Action Helicopter 100.00
    No. 10621, 5 in 1 . . . . 50.00
    Mysto Erector Set
        No. 1 . . . . 150.00
        No. 2A 120.00
    Remote Control Senior Power Line, 1971 . . . . 80.00
American Logs, 1940s 40.00
Auburn
    Flexi-Blocks, No. 949 . . . . 45.00
    Plexi Bricks 60.00
Chautauqua Architectural Building Blocks, No. 510, 1920s 150.00
Crandall's Building Blocks, No. 3, patented 1867 . . . . 75.00
Elgo, American Plastic Bricks, No. 715, 1950s 30.00
Hai-San, Hewn American Logs, No. 815 . . . . 30.00
Halsam
    American Plastic Bricks
        No. 60, 1939 . . . . 75.00
        No. 705 . . . . 40.00
    Logs, Senior Size, No. 815 . . . . 30.00
    New American Bricks, No. 725 . . . . . . 50.00
Hasbro, Astrolite 70.00
Ideal, Super City, No. 3361–3 . . . . 30.00
Kenner
    Girder and Panel
        No. 2, 1950s 55.00
        No. 72000 . . . . 30.00
    Girder and Panel Airport Set 40.00
    Girder and Panel Bridge and Turnpike Motorized Set, 1960 . . . . 120.00
    Girder and Power, Build A Home and Subdivision 200.00
    Girder Bridge and Highway Set, No. 6 . . . . 90.00
Lincoln Logs
    No. 1A, 1920 . . . . 20.00
    No. 1C 70.00
    No. 29 . . . . 125.00
Marx, Riverside Construction Set, 1960s 120.00
Meccano
    No. 1, 1914 . . . . 50.00
    Engineering Erector Set 20.00
M-I Toys, Building Bricks, No. 955 . . . . 40.00
Pressman, Crystal Climbers 30.00
Remco, Jumbo Construction Set, 1968 . . . . 125.00
Richter & Co, Richter's Anchor Blocks, No. 7 . . . . 125.00
Scott Manufacturing, Bilt-E-Z Skyscraper Building Blocks, c1925 . . . . . . 175.00
Structo, No. 3 . . . . 150.00
Tinkertoy
    No. 104 . . . . 30.00
    Wonder Builder 40.00
Union Building Blocks, No. 7 . . . . 150.00

COOKBOOKS

There are eighteenth and nineteenth century cookbooks. But, they are expensive, very expensive. It pays to look through old piles of books in hopes that a dealer has overlooked one of these gems. But, in truth, you are going to go unrewarded ninety-nine percent or more of the time.

The cookbooks that you are most likely to find date from the twentieth century. Most were promotional giveaways. A fair number came with appliances. Some were associated with famous authors.

A few years ago, you could buy them in the 50¢ to $1.00 range and had a large selection from which to choose. No longer. These later cookbooks have been discovered. Now you are going to pay between $2.00 and $10.00 for most of them.

Cover art does affect price. Most are bought for display purposes. Seek out the ones that feature a recognizable personality on the cover.

Club: Cookbook Collectors Club of America, Inc., P. O. Box 56, St. James, MO 65559.

Chiquita Banana's Recipe Book, © *1947 United Fruit Co, $6.00.*

ABC Casserole, Peter Pauper Press, 1954, 61 pgs.	**3.50**
American Home Cookbook by Ladies of Detroit, 1878	**45.00**

Anyone Can Bake, Royal Baking Powder, 1929, 100 pgs	**6.50**
Ball Blue Book, Russel, 1930, 56 pgs	**15.00**
Better Homes and Gardens, 1953	**16.00**
Blondie's, 5½ × 8½", hard cov, recipes selected and illus by Chic Young, 142 pgs, 1947 copyright	**35.00**
Budget Watchers	**8.00**
Campbell's Main Dishes	**8.00**
Cook It Right	**8.00**
Desserts of the World, Jell-O	**5.00**
Dishes For All Year Round, S Rorer, 1903, 62 pgs	**6.00**
Duncan Hines Food Odyssey, 1955, 274 pgs	**5.00**
Economy Administration Cookbook, 1913, 696 pgs	**45.00**
Electric Cooking with Your Kenmore, 1941	**2.00**
A Few Hints About Cooking, S Grier, 1887, 319 pgs	**30.00**
Food Favorites, Kraft, 1951, 32 pgs	**1.50**
Gold Medal Flour Cookbook, 1910	**15.00**
Handy Cook Book, Kerosine Soap, 1897	**15.00**
Housekeeping in Old Virginia, slave recipes by Mozis Addams, 1965 reprint	**35.00**
Joys of Jell-O	**5.00**
Knox Gelatin, black child cov illus, 1915	**5.00**
Maytag Dutch Oven Cookbook, 49 pgs	**5.50**
Norge Recipe Book, 1930	**2.00**
Old Shaker Recipes, Bear Wallow, 1982, 30 pgs	**3.00**
Pillsbury Family Cookbook, 1963	**10.00**
Prudential, little girl giving tea party with two teddy bears on cov, 1910	**39.00**
Royal Baking Powder, 1922	**15.00**
Rumford Southern Recipes, M Wilson, 1894, 65 pgs	**7.00**
Simply Elegant Desserts, American Dairy Association, 23 pgs	**1.00**
Sourdough Jack's	**8.00**
Sunset Cookbook for Entertaining, 1968, 210 pgs	**4.50**
Treasure of Great Recipes, Price	**30.00**
Universal Cookbooks, Jeanie L Taylor, 1888m 185 pgs	**15.00**
Vermont Maple Recipes, 1952, 87 pgs	**5.00**
Williamsburg Art of Cookery, H Bullock, 1942	**12.00**

COOKIE CUTTERS

When most individuals think of cookie cutters, they envision the metal cutters, often mass produced, that were popular during the nineteenth century and first third of the twentieth century. This is too narrow a view. Do not overlook the plastic cutter of recent years. Not only are they colorful, but they come in a variety of shapes quite different from their metal counterparts.

If you want to build a great specialized collection, look for cutters that were give-away premiums by flour and baking-related business. Most of these cutters are in the $10.00 to $40.00 range.

Club: Cookie Cutters Club, 1167 Teal Road, W. W., Dellroy, OH 44620.

Metal, duck, hand made in Nazareth, PA, piece of depression glass for eye, handle on back, $125.00.

Advertising
Bisquick, round, plastic, yellow	.50
Egg Baking Powder Co, 1½" d, 1902	40.00
Pioneer Seed Company, plastic, white	1.00
Swans Down Cake Flour, premium, aluminum	22.00
Arrow, plastic, hot pink, Wilton	1.00
Bear, 2½ × 3", handcrafted, tin, irregular back, missing handle	10.00
Bird, 4½" l, spread wings, tin	15.00
Camel	8.50
Dog, 4½" l, tin	20.00
Dutchman, 5¼" h, tin	115.00
Goblet, 4" h, tin	100.00
Leprechaun, plastic, green and tan, Hallmark, 1979	2.00
Man, 3 × 5½", handcrafted, tin, hat and coat, handle removed	85.00
Penn State University Mascot, lion, plastic, white and blue, Monogram Plastics	3.00
Pitcher, 4¼" h, tin	110.00
Pretzel, metal, handle	3.00
Question Mark, plastic, white, Wilton	.50

Reindeer, 5 × 6", handcrafted, tin, irregular back, four legs, grouped antlers	115.00
Scissors, 5¼" l, tin	100.00
Sprinkling Can, metal, Wilton	2.50
Whale, 3¾" l, tin	20.00
Wreath, plastic, red, handle, Educational Products	.50

COOKIE JARS

Talk about categories that have gone nuts over the past years. Thanks to the Andy Warhol sale, cookie jars became the talk of the town. Unfortunately, the prices reported for the Warhol cookie jars were so far removed from reality that many individuals were deceived into believing their cookie jars are far more valuable than they really are.

The market seems to be having trouble finding the right pricing structure. A recent cookie jar price guide lowballed a large number of jar prices. Big city dealers are trying to sell cookie jars as art objects at high prices instead of the kitcsh they really are. You have to be the judge. Remember, all you are buying is a place to store your cookies.

Morton Pottery Co, poodle, white ground, red dec, $25.00.

Aunt Jemima, soft plastic	325.00
Bandit Raccoon, Metlox	75.00
Bartender, tan, Napco	80.00
Bear and Beehive, McCoy	55.00
Beer Stein	60.00
Bluebonnet Sue	30.00
Brown Bear, Brush	65.00
Bulldog Cafe, Treasure Craft	60.00

Cat Head, wearing hat, Metlox 85.00
Chef's head 40.00
Churn, American Bisque 25.00
Cinderella, Napco 300.00
Clown on Alphabet Block, American
    Bisque 80.00
Coffee Grinder 9.00
Collegiate Owl, American Bisque 80.00
Cookie Cabin, McCoy. 60.00
Cookie Kettle, American Bisque 45.00
Cookie Truck, American Bisque 80.00
Cow, tan, Brush-McCoy 110.00
Dalmatian. 50.00
Donkey, Twin Winton 40.00
Dutch Girl, Pottery Guild 65.00
Elephant
    McCoy. 125.00
    Twin Winton. 40.00
Elf, wearing green hat 40.00
Emmett Kelly, Japan 135.00
Farm Yard Follie Chicken, Doranne 45.00
Flasher Clown, ABC, painted face, miss-
    ing flasher 120.00
Frontier Family, McCoy. 50.00
Granny, red skirt, McCoy. 90.00
Granny Ann, lavender, Shawnee 85.00
Gumball Machine, yellow 60.00
Hippopotamus, white, Abingdon 165.00
Honey Bear, McCoy 70.00
Indian Tepee. 45.00
Jack Frost, Red Wing 250.00
Kissing Penguins, McCoy. 45.00
Kitten Head, Lefton 60.00
Kraft Bear, Regal. 175.00
Lantern, Brush-McCoy 185.00
Little Red Riding Hood, Hull, closed bas-
    ket 180.00
Magic Bunny 40.00
Maurice Shoe House 50.00
Monk, Twin Winton. 40.00
Mr Rabbit, standing, ABC 60.00
Mrs Fields 35.00
Noah's Ark 40.00
Owl, Shawnee 95.00
Peter Rabbit, Sigma 150.00
Poodle Head, white. 75.00
Popeye, McCoy. 85.00
Porky Pig, sitting in chair 75.00
Pot Belly Stove, McCoy 25.00
Puss 'N Boots, Shawnee 135.00
Quaker Oats, Regal. 130.00
Raggedy Ann
    California Originals. 30.00
    McCoy. 85.00
Ranger Bear, Twin Winton 40.00
R2-D2 . . . . .100.00
Rocking Chair Dalmatian. 300.00
Rooster, American Bisque 80.00
School Bus, yellow 40.00
Sir Frances Drake, Metlox 70.00
Smiley Pig, Shawnee
    Pink flowers 250.00
    Shamrocks 200.00
Snail, worm in hat 75.00

Stanfordware Corn, RRP 75.00
Three Little Kittens, McCoy. 65.00
Timmy Tortoise, McCoy. 35.00
Toy Soldier, standing in guard house . . .100.00
Wagon Train, McCoy 95.00
Winking Owl, gold 235.00
Winnie the Pooh, with shamrocks,
    Shawnee 210.00

COPPER PAINTINGS

Copper paintings, actually pictures stamped out of copper or copper foil, deserve a prize as one of the finest "ticky-tacky" collectibles ever created. My dad remembers getting a four-picture set from a bank as a premium in the late 1950s or early 1960s. He takes great pride in noting that this is one of the few things that he has no regrets about throwing out.

However, to each his own—somewhere out there are individuals who like this unique form of mass-produced art. Their treasures generally cost them in the $15.00 to $50.00 range, depending on subject.

COSTUMES

Remember how much fun it was to play dress-up as a kid? Seems silly to only do it once a year around Halloween. Down South and in Europe, Mardis Gras provides an excuse; but, in my area, we eat doughnuts instead.

Collectors are beginning to discover children's Halloween costumes. I'll bet you are staggered by some of the prices listed below. Yet, I see costumes traded at these prices all the time.

There doesn't seem to be much market in adult costumes—those used in the theater and for theme parties. Costume rental shops are used to picking them up for a few dollars each.

Ace Frehley, KISS, Aucion, 1978. . . . . . . 90.00
Astronaut, Collegeville, 1962 . . . . 40.00
Beatnik, Collegeville, 1961 . . . . 50.00
Bambi, Ben Cooper, 1950s. 40.00
Betsy Ross, Ben Cooper 30.00
Blondie, Collegeville, 1960s. 75.00
Boba Fett, Collegeville, 1980 . . . . 30.00
Brady Bunch, Collegeville, 1969 . . . . . . .125.00
Bugs Bunny, Collegeville, 1965. . . . . 60.00
Bunny, Collegeville 85.00
Caveman, Ben Cooper, 1963. . . . . 45.00

Chaps, child's, gabardine and fake fur, c1930, 31" l, $30.00.

King Kong, Ben Cooper, 1976	**30.00**
Klinger, MASH, Ben Cooper, 1981	**75.00**
Koko the Clown, 1960s	**65.00**
Lamb Chop, 1958	**50.00**
Little Audry, Collegeville, 1959	**75.00**
Lost in Space, Ben Cooper, 1966	**250.00**
Luke Duke, Ben Cooper	**6.00**
Man From Mars, Halco, 1950s	**60.00**
Man On the Moon, 1970	**25.00**
Meadowlark Lemon, Ben Cooper, 1971	**25.00**
Mickey Dolenz, 1960s	**150.00**
Mork, Mork & Mindy, Ben Cooper, 1978	**20.00**
Mouseketeer Sheriff, Ben Cooper, 1950s	**90.00**
Mummy, Ben Cooper, 1973	**30.00**
Mutant, Universal Studios, 1980	**25.00**
Peter Potamus, Ben Cooper, 1965	**50.00**
Phantom, Collegeville, 1956	**250.00**
Pink Panther, Kusan, 1969	**75.00**
Popeye, Collegeville, 1958	**60.00**
Roger Rabbit, Ben Cooper, 1980s	**40.00**
Rosie the Robot, The Jetsons, Ben Cooper, 1963	**225.00**
Scooby Doo, Ben Cooper, 1973	**25.00**
Secret Squirrel, 1965	**125.00**
Six Million Dollar Man, Ben Cooper, 1978	**35.00**
Steve Canyon, Halco, 1959	**50.00**
Strawberry Shortcake	**15.00**
Suzy Super Spy, Ben Cooper, 1965	**30.00**
Tarzan, Collegeville, 1967	**50.00**
Tom the Cat, Halco, 1952	**40.00**
Uncle Fester, Addams Family, Ben Cooper, 1965	**150.00**
Uncle Sam, Ben Cooper	**30.00**
Underdog, Collegeville, 1975	**75.00**
Vampira, Collegeville, 1972	**30.00**
Wile E Coyote, 1974	**25.00**
Witchie Poo, Collegeville, 1971	**65.00**
Woody Woodpecker, Collegeville, 1950	**50.00**
Yogi Bear, 1974	**20.00**
Zebra, Ben Cooper, 1960s	**30.00**

Centurion Ace McCloud, Ben Cooper, 1982	**15.00**
Daniel Boone, Ben Cooper, 1960s	**80.00**
Deputy Dawg, Ben Cooper, 1961	**75.00**
Devil, Masquerade, 1960	**40.00**
Donald Duck, Ben Cooper, 1962	**75.00**
Donny Osmond, Collegeville, 1977	**35.00**
Drac, Groovie Ghoulies, Ben Cooper, 1971	**90.00**
Farmer Alfalfa, 1950s	**45.00**
Flipper, Ben Cooper, 1964	**50.00**
Fonzie, Ben Cooper	**30.00**
Frankenstein, Universal, 1980	**30.00**
Ghastly Gertie, Ben Cooper, 1962	**50.00**
Girl From UNCLE, MGM, 1967	**275.00**
Grandpa Munster, Ben Cooper, 1964	**225.00**
Green Hornet, Ben Cooper, 1966	**425.00**
Green Lantern, 1960s	**60.00**
Hee Haw, 1976	**20.00**
Herman Munster, Ben Cooper, 1964	**225.00**
Hong Kong Fooey, 1974	**35.00**
H R Pufnstuf, Collegeville, 1971	**75.00**
Huckleberry Hound, Ben Cooper, 1960	**50.00**
Illya Kuryakin, Halco, 1965	**150.00**
Indiana Jones, Ben Cooper, 1982	**35.00**
Inspector, Pink Panther, 1970	**35.00**
Jane Jetson, Austin Art, 1972	**150.00**
Jeannie, I Dream of Jeannie, 1974	**30.00**
Jet Man, Ben Cooper, 1950s	**45.00**
Jughead, Halco	**60.00**

COUNTRY STORE

There is something special about country stores. My favorite is Bergstresser's in Wassergass, Pennsylvania. There is probably one near you that you feel as strongly about. Perhaps the appeal is that they continue to deny the present. I am always amazed at what a country store owner can dig out of the backroom, basement, or barn.

Country store collectibles focus heavily on front counter and back counter material from the last quarter of the nineteenth century and first quarter of the twentieth century. The look is tied in closely with Country. It also has a strong small town, rural emphasis.

Drop in and prop your feet up on the potbelly stove. Don't visit a country store if you are in a hurry.

Cigar Cutter, Cressman's Counsellor, The Brunhoff Mfg Co, $90.00.

Barrel, Davis Baking Powder, wood, paper label, 16½" d, 23½" h **165.00**
Box, American Biscuit & Mfg Co, wood, paper label, parrot illus, 18 × 12 × 10½" **65.00**
Calendar, 1903, A & P Tea Company, cardboard, shopkeeper, customers, and products illus, full pad, 10 × 13¾" **110.00**
Canister, cov, Blue-Jay Corn Plasters, tin, woman applying plaster illus, 7" d, 6" h **50.00**
Catalog, Farquahar's Garden Annual Seed Catalog, 1908–1909. .... **20.00**
Cigar Store Figure, 28" h, Indian maiden, pine, carved and painted, c1870. .... **3,575.00**
Clock, Liberty Flour, wood case, tin face, electric, center Statue of Liberty illus, 15¼" sq **350.00**
Coffee Grinder, Golden Rule Coffee, wall mounted, iron and wood, glass insert, 5½ × 4 × 17". **115.00**
Display Box
 Boston Garters, tin, man wearing garter illus, 14½ × 13" **170.00**
 Brownie Laundry Wax, cardboard, glass front, slant top, paper label, Palmer Cox Brownies illus, 9½ × 5¾" **30.00**
 Feen-A-Mint Laxatives, tin, woman holding laxative and open package illus, top with inset oval mirror, 7½ × 16¼". **175.00**
 Hartwell Handles, tin, holds wooden tool handles, 14½" l, 8" h. **50.00**

Poster
 Damschinsky's Liquid Hair Dye, strands of dyed and natural hair, 13¾ × 18½" **65.00**
 Satin Skin Cream, woman's head illus, 28 × 41", 1903 .... **150.00**
Receipt Holder, metal. **3.00**
Scale, iron, emb shield design beneath window, 9½ × 10½" **250.00**
Seed Box, Lake Shore Seed Co, wood, paper label, vegetables illus, 24 × 10 × 5". **95.00**
Sign
 American Stock Food, paper, Uncle Sam at barnyard, feeding horse **425.00**
 Cow Brand Baking Soda, cardboard, three tigers, 14½ × 11¼", 1915..... **85.00**
 Gold Dust Washing Powder, cardboard, Gold Dust twins sitting on pile of gold coins, 7½ × 10½" **50.00**
 Kellogg's Cereals, canvas, woman holding quart of milk, reaching for box of cereal, "Morning Noon and Night for every taste," 18½ × 29"... **450.00**
Spool Cabinet, Clark's ONT Spool Cotton, oak, two drawers, cased glass drawer inserts, 22 × 7½". **250.00**
String Holder, Higgins German Laundry Soap, cast iron, black, wall mount, "Use Higgins German Laundry Soap/It is the Best," 6" h. **150.00**
Thermometer, Arbuckle's Coffee, tin, yellow top, white center, red bottom, yellow coffee package, red, white, and black lettering, 19" l, 1915 .... **175.00**

COUNTRY WESTERN COLLECTIBLES

You don't have to be a *rhinestone cowboy* to enjoy Country Western music, and you don't have to travel to Nashville to find its memorabilia. With a large assortment of items available such as sheet music, signed photographs, and record albums, Country Western collectibles won't bring ya' back home empty handed. So go ahead and enjoy yourselves, and "Ya'll come back now, ya' here?"

Autograph
 Britt, Elton, 78 rpm record sleeve, sgd and dated 1951 .... **15.00**
 Davis, Jimmie, sgd calling card. **5.00**
 Snow, Hank, sgd LP record album cov. **35.00**
 Tubb, Ernest, sgd 45 rpm record sleeve. **3.00**
 Williams, Hank, sgd 78 rpm record album cov, c1952. .... **150.00**

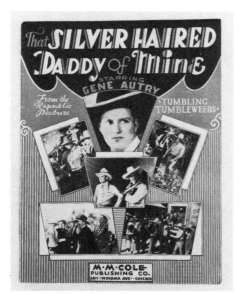

Sheet Music, **That Silvered Haired Daddy of Mine,** *lyrics and music by Jimmy Long and Gene Autry, M. M. Cole, Chicago publisher, $15.00.*

Lobby Card, Tex Ritter, 27 × 41" 100.00
Magazine, *TV Guide,* sgd by Grandpa
   Jones, "Hee Haw" feature 6.50
Map, Nashville, TN, sgd by Roy Acuff and
   others, c1948. . . . . 125.00
Necktie, Ernest Tubb likeness and name
   illus 15.00
Paper Dolls
   Hee Haw, punch-out, Saalfield, #5139,
     Gunilla, Lulu, Kathy, and Jeannie
     dolls, uncut, 1971 . . . . 12.00
   Hootenanny, punch-out, Saalfield,
     #4440, four dolls, uncut, 1964 . . . . . 18.00
Photograph
   Atkins, Chet, 6 × 7", sgd and dated
     1956. . . . . 20.00
   Gayle, Crystal, 8 × 10", sgd, framed . . . 8.00
   Parton, Dolly, 8 × 10", sgd 24.00
   Rodgers, Jimmie, holding banjo, 8 ×
     10", sgd, c1932 . . . . 300.00
   Tanner, Gid, playing fiddle, sgd 60.00
Record, 78 rpm
   Acuff, Roy, Columbia label, "Are You
     Thinking of Me Darling/I Called and
     Nobody Answered" 5.00
   Allen, Rosalie, Bluebird label, "Never
     Trust a Man/Take it Back and
     Change it for a Boy" 10.00
   Arnold, Eddy, Bluebird label,
     "Mommy, Please Stay Home With
     Me/Many Tears Ago" 30.00
   Britt, Elton, Bluebird label, "I'm a
     Convict with Old Glory in My Heart/
     The Best of Travel" 10.00

Carson, Fiddlin' John, Bluebird label,
   "The Honest Farmer/Taxes on the
   Farmer Feeds Them All". 85.00
Carter, Wilf, Bluebird label, "I'm Only
   a Dude in Cowboy Clothes/My Hon-
   eymoon Bridge Broke Down" 35.00
Delmore Brothers, Bluebird label, "I
   Believe It for My Mother Told Me
   So/Hey! Hey! I'm Memphis
   Bound" 40.00
Gid Tanner and His Skillet Lickers,
   Bluebird label, "Skillet Licker
   Breakdown/Hawkin's Rag" 50.00
Guthrie, Jack, Captiol label, "You
   Laughed and I Cried/It's Too Late to
   Change Your Mind" 12.00
Kincaid, Bradley, Decca label, "Ain't
   We Crazy/The Little Shirt That
   Mother Made For Me" 8.00
Macon, Uncle Dave, Bluebird label,
   "Cumberland Mountain Deer Race/
   Country Ham and Red Gravy". 80.00
Stanley Brothers, King label, "I'm a
   Man of Constant Sorrow/How
   Mountain Girls Can Love" 10.00
Williams, Hank, Sterling label, "My
   Son Calls Another Man Daddy/Long
   Ago Lonesome Blues" 15.00
Sheet Music
Acuff, Roy, *Wabash Cannonball,* sgd . . . 115.00
Copas, Cowboy, *Filipino Baby,* sgd 30.00
Dalhart, Vernon, *John T. Scopes Trial,*
   sgd, framed, 1920s 100.00
Dexter, Al, *Pistol Packin' Mama,* sgd . . . 18.00
Ritter, Tex, *Old Chisum Trail,* sgd 30.00
Tubb, Ernest, *Walking the Floor Over
   You,* sgd 25.00
Tyler, T Texas, *Deck of Cards,* sgd 28.00

COW COLLECTIBLES

Holy cow! This is a moovelous category, as entrenched collectors already know.

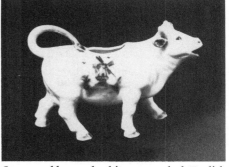

Creamer, blue and white, unmarked English pottery, $70.00.

Advertising

Pin, Dominion Washing Sodas, enameled cow symbol, dark cherry red background, early 1900s **15.00**
Pinback Button, 1¾" d, Aberdeen Angus, cow's head with ring in nose, c1900 . . . . **25.00**
Standup, 6" l, Holstein, tin, cow shape, black and white **75.00**
Tray, 3½ × 5½", Carnation Milk, oval, cows in pasture **20.00**
Butter Stamp, 4¼" d, cow, turned handle **150.00**
Cookie Cutter, 4½" l, tin, missing handle **5.00**
Cookie Jar, cow jumping over moon, gold, RRP Co **80.00**
Creamer, figural, Occupied Japan **25.00**
Doll, 12" h, Elsie the Cow, plush and vinyl, orig stitched tag, My-Toy Co, 1950–1960 . . . . **75.00**
Figure, 3" h, metal **15.00**
Footstool, cow horn legs, needlepoint top **60.00**
Milk Bottle, ½ pint, Hillcrest Farm, cow illus **15.00**
Mug, 3" h, white china, Elsie dancing through meadow of daisies, Continental Kilns signature, Borden Co copyright, late 1930s **50.00**
Pitcher, ceramic, white, cow shape **15.00**
Print, 20 × 16", cattle scene, ornate gold frame, ES Porter, 1908 . . . . **195.00**
Puppet, 10" h, Ferdinand the Bull, composition head, black and white fabric body, marked "Crown Toy Co," Walt Disney Enterprises copyright **50.00**
Stereograph, cows and sheep, Kilburn #739, 1870s **4.00**
Stuffed Animal, 5½" h, felt, brown and white, glass eyes, wood wheels **65.00**
Tee Shirt, blue, black and white cow on front, rear view on back, vertical lettering front and back: Vermont **4.00**
Toy, cow, Fisher Price, #132 . . . . **20.00**
Weathervane, 27½" l, 24" h, zinc, full figure, old paint traces, wood base **800.00**

COWAN

R. Guy Cowan founded the Cowan Pottery in 1913 in Cleveland, Ohio. It remained in almost continuous operation until financial difficulties forced it to close in 1931. Initially utilitarian redware was produced. Cowan began experimenting with glazes, resulting in a unique lusterware glaze.

Bowl, 6 × 7½", mottled tan glaze **60.00**
Console Bowl, 16" l, canoe shaped,

molded seahorse dec, mottled blue glaze **110.00**
Flower Frog, deer **175.00**
Lamp, table, 14" h, relief-molded flowers on blue lustre glazed base, dragon handles **750.00**
Paperweight, elephant, blue-green glaze **325.00**
Soap Dish, 4" d, seahorse, blue **35.00**
Teapot, 7¼", white glaze **75.00**
Vase, 6½" h, ovoid, underwater seascape silhouette, dark and light blue glazes, imp "Cowan," c1925 . . . . **600.00**

COWBOY HEROES

The cowboy heroes in this category rode the range in movies and on television. In a way, they were larger than their real-life counterparts, shaping the image of how the west was won in the minds of several generations. Contemporary westerns may be historically correct, but they do not measure up in sense of rightness.

The movie and television cowboy heroes were pioneers in merchandise licensing. If you were a child in the 1949 to 1951 period and did not own a Hopalong Cassidy item, you were deprived.

Collectors tend to favor one cowboy hero. My dad owns a few Roy Rogers and Gene Autry items, but he would never admit it publicly. As far as the world knows, he's a Hoppy man.

Gene Autry
Boots, rubber, orig box, pr **125.00**
Comic Book, 1955 . . . . **16.00**
Guitar, Emenee, MIB **175.00**
Holster and Texan Jr Cap Gun **75.00**
Movie Poster, "Silver Canyon" **60.00**
Pinback Button, photo, 1930s-early1940s **25.00**
Post Card, Mile City, MT roundup **18.00**
Song Folio **20.00**
Hopalong Cassidy
Badge, teller's, Hopalong Cassidy Saving Club **30.00**
Bedspread, chenille, Hoppy scenes . . . **225.00**
Binoculars, decals **65.00**
Bread Loaf Wrapper, Butter-Nut Bread **65.00**
Bread Plate, milk glass **60.00**
Calendar, 1952 . . . . **225.00**
Crayon and Stencil Set, orig box **95.00**
Figure, lead **45.00**
Folder, Hoppy and Topper on cov, includes writing paper and envelopes, Hoppy bust on stationery **95.00**
Marble, black, Hoopy illus **15.00**

*Book, **Gunsmoke,** Authorized Edition Featuring Matt Dillion, Robert Turner author, Robert L. Jenney, illustrator, Whitman, 1958, $10.00.*

Pin, gun and holster 50.00
Pinback Button, Hopalong Cassidy
   Daily News 9.00
Post Card, Chrysler adv, 1942 . . . . 8.00
Radio, red 390.00
Ring, club, metal 45.00
Scrapbook, 12 × 15", leather, cov with
   engraved color Hoppy on Topper . . . 150.00
Sign, tin, radio adv 55.00
Wristwatch, US Time, 1950 . . . . 350.00
Cisco Kid, puzzle, picture, Cisco Kid and
   Pancho, framed 25.00
Davy Crockett
   Badge, frontier, orig card 25.00
   Bowl 15.00
   Game
      Target, tin, hand held, rubber darts,
         orig box, pr 55.00
      Walt Disney Fess Parker Indian
        Scouting Game, board, orig
        box 75.00
   Lamp, composition, Davy sitting, hold-
      ing long rifle 125.00
   Shirt, child's 28.00
   Tool Box, tin, Fess Parker 75.00
   Wristwatch 110.00
Wyatt Earp
   Coloring Book, Hugh O'Brien cov,
      unused 35.00
   Mug, milk glass 22.00
   Puzzle, photo 15.00
Lone Ranger
   Belt, glow-in-the-dark, orig box and
      instructions 185.00
   Guitar, Tonto and Silver, MIB 145.00

Merita Bread Cut-Outs 225.00
Ring, filmstrip, saddle shape, includes
   filmstrip 175.00
Snowdome, Lone Ranger lassoing calf,
   orig decal 95.00
Target Game, tin, Marx, 1938 . . . . 75.00
Tom Mix
   Arrow, lucite 85.00
   Belt Buckle, decoder, secret compart-
      ment 95.00
   Good Luck Spinner 30.00
   Periscope, mailer 75.00
   Ring, branded "TM" 125.00
   Telegraph, mailer 75.00
Annie Oakley
   Board Game 25.00
   Shirt and Vest 45.00
Ranger Joe, bowl and mug, milk glass,
   red lettering and figures, set 27.00
Red Ryder
   Mittens, unopened, orig pkg, pr 75.00
   Target Game, orig box, complete 39.00
Rifleman
   Comic Book, 1962 . . . . 14.00
   Game, complete 40.00
   Puzzle, photo 15.00
Roy Rogers
   Belt, leather, buckle 35.00
   Binoculars, Roy and Trigger, three
      power, MIB 150.00
   Camera 50.00
   Cigarette Lighter, Dale Evans, horse
      head 15.00
   Guitar, red, orig box 145.00
   Lunch Box, Roy Rogers and Dale Ev-
      ans, thermos 120.00
   Microscope Ring 125.00
   Paint Set 150.00
   Ranch Lantern, orig box 200.00
   Ring, branding iron 45.00
   Telephone, wall, crank type 95.00
   Toy, Trigger and Trigger Jr, tin horse
      trailer truck, back and side doors,
      Marx 195.00
John Wayne
   Belt Buckle, brass, portrait from "True
      Grit" 45.00
   Knife, pearl finish 16.00
   Playing Cards, 1956 . . . . 20.00
Wild Bill Hickock
   Bunkhouse Kit, orig pkg 20.00
   Lunch Box 45.00

CRACKER JACK COLLECTIBLES

You can still buy Cracker Jack with a prize in every box. The only problem is that when you compare today's prizes with those from decades ago, you feel cheated. Modern prizes simply do not measure up.

For this reason, collectors tend to focus on prizes put in the box prior to 1960.

Most Cracker Jack prizes were not marked. As a result, many dealers have Cracker Jack prizes without even knowing it. This allows an experienced collector to get some terrific bargains at flea markets. Alex Jaramillo's *Cracker Jack Prizes* (Abbeville Press: 1989) provides a wonderful survey of what prizes were available.

Whistle, tin, 1930s, $10.00.

Bookmark, 2¾" l, diecut litho tin, c1930 .... **15.00**
Bubble Gum Card, Cracker Jack in baseball uniform, 1915 .... **17.50**
Cereal Bowl and Cup Set **25.00**
Clicker, aluminum **15.00**
Cookbook, 4 × 6", "Angelus Recipes," black and white, 14 pgs **15.00**
Doll, stuffed cloth body, vinyl head, Vogue Dolls, 1980 copyright, unopened display card **25.00**
Hat, paper, "Me For Cracker Jack," red, white, and blue design, early 1900s... **65.00**
Lunch Box......................... **35.00**
Mask, 8½ × 10", "Cracker Jack" on front, c1960........................... **15.00**
Pencil, wood **15.00**
Prize
   Plate, 1¾" d, tin, silver, "Cracker Jack" in center **30.00**
   Top, 1½" d, tin, silver, wood peg **25.00**
Puzzle Book, 2½ × 4", 4 pgs, Series One, 1917 copyright **75.00**
Radio, orig box **38.00**
Whistle, tin **30.00**

CUPIDS

Be suspicious of naked infants bearing bows and arrows. It is not clear if their arrows are tipped with passion or poison.

Booklet, Diamond Dyes, two rabbits watching cupid blowing bubbles, 6 × 8", 1901........................ **18.00**
Christmas Ornament, white cupid, gold trim, gold hanger, plastic, 4" h....... **5.00**
Diecut, emb, cupids with flowers, K & B No. 1830, 6 × 3", set of four **12.00**

Figure, Cupid and Psyche, pastel colors, Meissen, $995.00.

Dresser Scarf, linen, embroidered dec ... **45.00**
Fan, cardboard, cupids in center, "Diamond Candy Store, manufacturers of Ice Cream, Springfield, Mass," gilded edge........................... **30.00**
Garden Statuette, sitting, legs crossed, wings folded around body, stone, antique finish, 12" h................. **28.00**
Napkin Ring, figural, sitting, legs crossed, combination candleholder and napkin ring, silver plated **175.00**
Post Card, Happy New Year, sgd "Rosie O'Neill"........................ **26.00**
Print
   Cupid Awake and Cupid Asleep, oval, framed
      Photograph, medium size......... **25.00**
      Stone lithographed, small size **35.00**
   Woman in gauze dress with cupid on rock, 8 × 10".................... **30.00**
Toothpick Holder, cupid holding flower basket, bisque **35.00**
Trade Card, Hoods Sarsaparilla, cupid with trumpet.................... **6.00**
Valentine, heart, diecut
   6" h, iron cross shape, emb, center cupid lifts up **20.00**
   7" h, three layer fold down, cupid, swan, boat, and flower heart **8.00**

8" h, easel back, diecut cupid on parchment.................... 15.00

9" h, 14" l, easel back, emb, cupid driving car, two children and flowers....................... 20.00

CUSPIDORS

After examining the interiors of some of the cuspidors for sale at flea markets, I am glad I have never been in a bar where people "spit." Most collectors are enamored by the brass cuspidor. The form came in many other varieties as well. You could build a marvelous collection focusing on pottery cuspidors.

Within the past year a large number of fake cuspidors have entered the market. I have seen them at flea markets across the United States. Double-check any cuspidor with a railroad marking and totally discount any with a Wells Fargo marking.

Bennington Pottery Type, yellow ground, brown glaze, 7¼" d, $85.00.

Advertising, Redskin Cut Plug Chewing Tobacco, brass....................110.00

China

Floral dec, 6½" h, marked "IOGA" ... 70.00

Lady's hand, violets, turquoise beading, Nippon, green M in wreath mark 150.00

Graniteware, blue................... 55.00

Pewter, 8" d, Gleason, Roswell, Dorchester, MA, c1850 ....200.00

Pottery, 4½" h, pansies, marked "Loy-Nel Art"........................100.00

Redware, 8 × 4¼", tooled bands, brown and green running glaze with brown dashes 250.00

Roseville, Donatello 110.00

Salt Glazed, blue and white 55.00

Spatterware, 5 × 7½", blue stripes 65.00

Spongeware

Blue sponging, white ground, molded basketweave dec...............150.00

Yellow and brown dec 65.00

Stoneware

Cobalt blue leaf and floral motif, 8" d........................175.00

Emb sponged blue earthworm pattern 120.00

CZECHOSLOVAKIAN

Czechoslovakia was created at the end of World War I out of the area of Bohemia, Moravia, and Austrian Silesia. Although best known for glass products, Czechoslovakia also produced a large number of pottery and porcelain wares for export.

Czechoslovakia objects do not enjoy a great reputation for quality, but I think they deserve a second look. They certainly reflect what was found in the average American's home from the 1920s through the 1950s.

Shaving Mug, courting couple, iridescent background, marked "Gloria, Karlovarsky, Kvalitni, Porculan," $25.00.

Bowl, yellow int., black ext., polished pontil........................ 45.00

Box, cov, 4" d, 3" h, cut glass, engraved 45.00

Card Holder, 2¾" h, ornate gold metal frame and base, green ground, glass cameo 40.00

Cologne Bottle, 4" h, blue, glossy, bow front......................... 12.00

Container, head, fisherman, hat lid..... 75.00

Creamer and Sugar, orange luster, pink
roses. **55.00**
Cup and Saucer, pheasant **32.50**
Dish, frosted, cameo inset, filigree,
ftd **45.00**
Perfume Bottle, 5" h, engraved design,
amber frosted flowers, stopper, 5" **25.00**
Pitcher
4" h, red, black handle **15.00**
10", sheep and shepherdess dec **55.00**
Plate, 10" d, Art Deco, maiden, black and
yellow, 1920s **50.00**
Salt and Pepper Shakers, pr, 2" h, figural,
duck, clear glass body, orange porce-
lain tops **42.00**
Vase, 6" h, cased, blue ground, white lin-
ing, red ruffled top, marked **145.00**

DAIRY ITEMS

The dairy industry has been doing a good
job for decades of encouraging us to drink
our milk and eat only real butter. The
objects used to get this message across as
well as the packaging for dairy products
have long been favorites with collectors.

Concentrate on the material associated
with a single dairy, region, or national
firm. If you tried to collect one example of
every milk bottle used, you simply would
not succeed. The amount of dairy collectibles is enormous.

Periodical: *The Milk Route*, 4 Ox Bow
Road, Westport, CT 06880.

*Milk Bottle Caps, right: Norman Dairy Inc, New
Canaan, CT, orange, green letters, 1⅝" d, $.10;
left: Dutch Mill Dairy, black letters, blue windmill, 1⅝" d, $.15.*

Bank, Rutter Bros Dairy Products,
dairy truck, plastic, white, red decal,
c1960. . . . . **40.00**
Booklet, Jones Milk Co, color lithos,
giveaway, 1935. . . . . **18.00**
Box, Bing Crosby Ice Cream. **5.00**
Brochure, Eskimo Pie, premium,
c1952. . . . . **15.00**

Bucket, Sunny Field Lard, 4 lbs **28.00**
Clicker, Gridley Milk Did It!, color milk
bottle with baby face, red ground **25.00**
Clock
Foremost Ice Cream, light up **170.00**
Garst Bros Dairy, double globe. **125.00**
Sealtest Milk **75.00**
Cookbook, Carnation Milk, 32 pgs,
1915. . . . . **10.00**
Creamer
Anthony's Cream **13.00**
Rosebud Dairy. **9.00**
Doilies, Carver Ice Cream, linen-like,
emb, Christmas, 1920s, pkg of 12 . . . . **10.00**
Doll, Elsie, 12" h, plush **40.00**
Figure, cow, De Laval, glued on legs **125.00**
Flashlight, miniature, Eagle Brand Ice
Cream carton shape **4.00**
Letter Opener, De Laval, brass, 1878–
1928 . . . . **38.00**
Match Holder, De Laval **50.00**
Milk Bottle
Borden Weiland, emb, round, qt **20.00**
Borden's, Elsie illus. **8.00**
Dairylea. **6.00**
Forresters, round, red print and illus,
½ gal **15.00**
Gail Borden, amber, 1½ gal **22.00**
Hood, qt. **4.00**
VM&I Co, emb, amber, qt. **50.00**
Milk Bottle Cap, Deerfoot Farms, South-
borough, MA. **5.00**
Milk Can, plain **10.00**
Mug, Elsie in daisy on outside, Elsie head
on inside bottom. **35.00**
Pinback Button
Acadia Butter, oval, yellow, brown,
and white package dec, red ground,
1900–12 . . . . **25.00**
Drink Aristrocrat Milk, red and white,
1930s **10.00**
Land O' Lakes, oval, Indian princess
serving turkey on platter dec,
1930s **50.00**
Punch-Out Train, Borden, 1950s. **80.00**
Ruler, Breyer Ice Cream, colorful **15.00**
Sign
Borden, tin, red. **55.00**
De Laval, blue and yellow **40.00**
Meiers Ice Cream, porcelain. **65.00**
Thermometer
Primrose Dairy Products. **60.00**
Sealtest Milk, carton **75.00**
Tie Clasp, Elsie medallion, c1930. . . . . . **35.00**
Tip Tray, De Laval **85.00**

DAKIN FIGURES

The term "Dakin" refers to a type of hollow vinyl figure produced by the R. Dakin

Company. These figures are found with a number of variations—molded or cloth costumed, jointed or nonjointed—and range in size from 5 to 10″ high.

As with any popular and profitable product, Dakin figures were copied. There are a number of Dakin-like figures found on the market. Produced by Sutton & Son Inc., Knickerbocker Toy Company, and a production company for Hanna-Barbera, these figures are also collectible and are often mistaken for the original Dakin products. Be careful when purchasing.

Bozo, figure, hard plastic and vinyl, movable head and arms, orange hair, blue body, white gloves, 7½″ h, 1974 . . . . . **12.00**

Bugs Bunny, gray and white body, yellow gloves

    Bank, standing on yellow basket filled with carrots, holding carrot, hard plastic and vinyl, movable head and arms, 10″ h, 1971 . . . . **35.00**

    Figure

        7″ h, vinyl **15.00**

        10″ h, holding carrot, hard plastic and vinyl, movable head, arms, and legs, 1971 . . . . **18.00**

Bullwinkle, figure, TV Cartoon Theater series, holding megaphone, hard plastic and vinyl, movable head, arms, and legs, tan and brown body, ivory gloves, red "B" on green sweater, "What's-A-Matta U" on green megaphone, 7½″ h, 1976, orig box **35.00**

Cool Cat, figure, hard plastic and vinyl, movable head, arms, and legs, green beret and tie, orange and white body, black markings, 9″ h, 1968 . . . . **25.00**

Deputy Dawg, figure, Fun Farm series, hard plastic and vinyl, movable head, arms, and upper torso, white body, glossy black plastic hat and vest, blue trousers, yellow badge, orange belt and holster, 6″ h, 1977, orig pkg **30.00**

Elmer Fudd, figure, vinyl, Fun Farm series, movable head, arms, and legs, red top hat, tie, and shoes, white shirt and gloves, black jacket, yellow pants, 6½″ h, 1978, orig pkg **30.00**

Hokey Wolf, figure, vinyl, movable head, arms, feet, and tail, brown body, tan and black markings, 8″ h, 1971 . . . . . . **20.00**

Mickey Mouse, figure, hard plastic and vinyl, movable head, arms, and legs, black body, yellow shirt, red pants, white gloves, orange shoes, 5½″ h **20.00**

Mouse, figure, standing on pedestal, holding champagne glass, Goofy Grams series, vinyl, movable head, arms, and upper torso, W C Fields like-ness, gray body, red nose, black and gray top hat, maroon and white fabric jacket, "I'll drink to that!" on marbleized base, 8″ h, 1971 . . . . **35.00**

Oliver Hardy, figure, hard plastic and vinyl, movable head and arms, brown hat, black hair, lavender fabric jacket, white fabric shirt, blue fabric tie, blue trousers, black shoes, 7½″ h, 1960s . . . **35.00**

Pebbles Flintstone, figure, vinyl, movable head, arms, and legs, orange hair, purple and black fabric outfit, 8″ h, 1970 . . . . **28.00**

Porky Pig, figure, vinyl, pink cap and shirt, black jacket, white gloves, blue and white polka dot bow tie, 5″ h **15.00**

Road Runner, figure, hard plastic and vinyl, movable head, light and dark blue body, yellow beak, orange legs, 10″ h, 1968 . . . . **20.00**

Rocky Squirrel, figure, TV Cartoon Theater series, hard plastic and vinyl, movable head, arms, legs, and tail, gray body, blue aviator's cap, 6½″ h, 1976, orig box **35.00**

Smokey Bear, figure, hard plastic and vinyl, movable head and arms, yellow hat, brown body and belt, blue denim fabric jeans, 8″ h, 1960s **28.00**

Speedy Gonzales, brown body, yellow sombrero, green shirt, white trousers, red neckerchief

    Bank, standing on cheese wedge, hard plastic and vinyl, movable head, arms, and tail, fabric outfit, 9¾″ h, 1970 . . . . **20.00**

    Figure

        5″ h, vinyl **15.00**

        7″ h, standing on pedestal, hard plastic and vinyl, Goofy Gram series, "Have A Speedy Recovery" on white pedestal, 1971 . . . . **28.00**

Sylvester, black and white body

    Bank, standing on sea chest, hard plastic and vinyl, movable head, arms, tail, and upper torso, blue sea chest, 11″ h, 1969, orig pkg **25.00**

    Figure, vinyl, red nose

        5½″ h **15.00**

        8″ h, movable head, arms, legs, and tail, 1969, orig pkg **20.00**

Tweety Bird, movable head, yellow body, orange beak and feet, blue eyes, 6″ h

    Bank, hard plastic, 1976 . . . . **10.00**

    Figure, vinyl, 1969, orig pkg **25.00**

Wile E Coyote

    Bank, standing on explosives crate, holding bomb, hard plastic and vinyl, movable head, arms, and upper torso, dark brown and tan, "Acme Explosives" and "Handle With Care" on base, 10″ h, 1971 . . . . **35.00**

Figure, standing on pedestal, holding black bomb, Goofy Grams series, movable head, arms, torso, and tail, brown and gray body, "Some Days Nothing Seems To Go Right!" on base, 10" h, 1971 . . . . 28.00

Yosemite Sam, blue hat and trousers, yellow shirt, orange hair, black gun belt and boots

Bank, standing on brown trunk, hard plastic and vinyl, movable arms, yellow painted hair, orange "cotton" beard, fabric outfit, 7" h, 1970 . . . . . 30.00

Figure, vinyl, red neckerchief 5" h 15.00

6½" h, Fun Farm series, movable arms and upper torso, silver gun, 1977–1978, orig pkg 28.00

DAN PATCH COLLECTIBLES

Dan Patch, the legendary harness racing horse, was born in Oxford, IN, in 1896. In 1905 he set a record by running a mile in 1:55 (1 minute, 55 seconds). This time has never been beaten. This sleek race horse was purchased by W. Savage of Minneapolis, whose International Stock Food Co. sold everything from tobacco products to washing machines, all with the Dan Patch logo. Dan Patch died in 1916 at twenty years of age.

Belt Buckle, silver and turquoise, image of Dan Patch in center. 180.00
Book, *Racing Life of Dan Patch* 250.00
Bottle, horse shoe shape, emb: Dan Patch 400.00
Cigar Box, Dan Patch logo on lid 230.00
Lantern, railroad type, red and green globes 1,500.00
Pinback Button, Dan Patch Days, multicolored litho 25.00
Plate, 8" d, Dan Patch in center with inscription: Dan–1:55 . . . . 60.00
Pocket Watch, name on front, engraved likeness on case. 600.00
Sheet Music, *Dan Patch Match*. 25.00
Sled, child's, red 500.00
Tobacco Tin. 60.00
Wagon, child's, wooden, sides lettered: Dan Patch 425.00

DEARLY DEPARTED

I know this category is a little morbid, but the stuff is collected. Several museums have staged special exhibitions devoted to mourning art and jewelry. Funeral parlors need to advertise for business.

I did not put one in the listing, but do you know what makes a great coffee table? A coffin carrier or coffin stand. Just put a piece of glass over the top. It's the right size, has leg room underneath, and makes one heck of a conversation piece.

Case, coffin shaped, brass top, wood sides, int. fitted with erotica-type mummy, 2⅛" l, $95.00.

Blotter, Magical 999 Embalmer Formula 1898, c1900. 5.00
Book, *Champion Expanding Encyclopedia of Embalming*, Champion Chemical Co, Springfield, OH, added to monthly, 9 × 12", approx 30 pgs each month, 1923–1928 . . . . 32.00
Booklet, *Incineration*, John B Beugless, United States Cremation Company, Ltd, 9¾ × 6", Portland vase pictured on front, 14 pgs, wraps. 18.00
Bottle
Coffin Poison, 4½" h, cobalt blue, diamond design, emb "Poison". 40.00
Dr George Lenninger's Formaldehyde Generator, 5½" h, sq. 125.00
Warner Co Poison, 3" h, triangle, skull, and crossbones, blue, paper label 35.00
Casket Plate, brass, "Rest in Peace," mounted 27.00
Catalog
A B Haskell Co, Bangor, ME, 1906, funeral goods, 110 pgs, illus, 6 × 10". 45.00
F H Hill Co, Chicago, IL, 1886, "Illus Catalogue of Wood Finished, Cloth Covered and Metallic Caskets," 108 pgs, illus, cloth cover, 8 × 10" 50.00
Jenkins Brothers & Co, Boston, MA, "Illustrated Catalogue of Coffins and Caskets," 1887, 102 pgs, 46 black and white plates, cloth binding, 5 × 7" 85.00
Keystone Coffin Works, Allegheny,

PA, 1875, coffins and caskets, color
illus **45.00**
Fan, cardboard, advertising on reverse
Sisler Bros, Inc, Fine Monuments, 8½
× 7½", multicolored, garden and
mountain scene, 11" l wooden handle **25.00**
Swallow Funeral Home, four
panel, folding, floral bouquet
illustration.................... **30.00**
Jewelry, mourning
Ring, 18K gold, seed pearls, one diamond, locket on inside of shank,
enamel "In Memory Of" on shank,
English........................ **300.00**
Stickpin, gold, round, black enamel
"In Memory Of," lock of hair under
glass, 19th C **165.00**
Memorial, 3⅜ × 4¼", abalone shell, watercolor, applied straw, paper willow,
tomb, German inscription, black lac-
quered frame................... **55.00**
Mortician's Basket, woven, adult size ... **125.00**
Mourning Picture, 8⅜ × 10⅜", waterco-
lor, paper memorial, tomb, inscription,
matted, gilt frame, dated 1810 ...... **65.00**
Pinback Button, adv
1¼" d, "Pan-American, Pass Bearer
One Way, Rock Falls Mfg Co, Sterling, IL," funeral wagon, 1901–
1910......................... **12.50**
1¼" d, "Tag Day, Ninette Sanato-
rium," multicolored, angel at ceme-
tery plot, 1910s **8.00**
1¼" d, "This Man Died From Over-
work, Trying To Beat The Parsons
Feeder," multicolored, man lying in
coffin, two tall candlesticks, wheat,
1896–1900 .... **85.00**
Post-Mortem Set, saws, scalpels, and
hooks, mahogany case **485.00**
Remembrance Card, 4⅛ × 6⅜", cardboard, diecut, gold lettering and illus
on black ground, 1888 .... **6.00**
Umbrella, black, "Beck & Fisher Funeral
Home" on handle **35.00**

DEEDS AND DOCUMENTS

All certificates, awards, deeds, and official
forms can be considered documents, since
a document is any printed paper that
shows evidence or proof of something.
Flea markets are loaded with old deeds
and stock certificates. These generally
have little value and are usually copies of
the original. It makes good sense, however, to check before discarding any manner of document. The document might still
be of value to its owner or to a collector.

Many eighteenth and early nineteenth
century deeds are on parchment. In most
cases, value is minimal, ranging from a few
dollars to a high of $10.00.

First, most of the deeds are copies. The
actual document is often on file in the
courthouse. Second, check the signatures.
Benjamin Franklin signed a number of
Pennsylvania deeds. These are worth a
great deal more than $10.00. Third, check
the location of the deed. If it is a city deed,
the current property owner may like to
acquire it. If it is for a country farm, forget
it.

Finally, a number of early deeds have an
elaborate wax seal at the bottom. Framed,
these make wonderful display pieces in attorneys' offices. When a deed is to be used
for this purpose, the price charged has
little to do with the intrinsic worth of the
deed. Sock it to the attorney—charge decorator prices.

*Birth and Baptism Certificate, 14 × 10", marked
"Lith. & Pub. by Currier & Ives, 152 Nassau St.
New York," 1873, $15.00.*

Baptismal Certificate, 6" sq, hand-
colored, Germany, 1830........... **10.00**
Confirmation Certificate, 11½ × 16",
Abingdon Press, NY and Cincinnati,
No. 80, 1926 .... **8.00**
Marriage Certificate, 13 × 17", Ernst
Kaufmann, NY, No. 105, 1898 ...... **15.00**
Stock Certificate
B & O Railroad Co, Dutch revenue,
Tom Thumb engine and train illus,
blue, 1914 .... **18.00**
Highway Bond, State of Arkansas,
$10,000, state house vignette, green
border, 1831 .... **12.00**
Lump Gulch Silver Mines Co, ornate
multicolored border with eagle illus
at top, unissued................ **20.00**
PA Canal Co Bond, $1,000, canal boat
and train illus, sgd, 1870.......... **150.00**

DEGENHART GLASS

Degenhart pressed glass novelties are collected by mold, by individual color, or by group of colors. Hundreds of colors, some almost identical, were produced between 1947 and 1978. Prior to 1972 most pieces were unmarked. After that date a "D" or "D" in a heart was used.

Do not confuse Kanawha's bird salt and bow slipper or L. G. Wright's mini-slipper, daisy and button salt, and 5" robin covered dish with Degenhart pieces. They are similar, but there are differences. See Gene Florence's *Degenhart Glass and Paperweights: A Collector's Guide To Colors And Values* (Degenhart Paperweight and Glass Museum: 1982) for a detailed list of Degenhart patterns.

Club: The Friends of Degenhart, Degenhart Paperweight and Glass Museum, Inc., P. O. Box 186, Cambridge, OH 43725.

Owl, Old Lavendar, $50.00.

Animal Dishes, covered
    Hen, 3" h, pigeon blood 48.00
    Lamb, cobalt 40.00
    Robin, taffeta. 50.00
    Turkey, amethyst 50.00
Bicentennial Bell
    Heatherbloom.................... 4.00
    Peach.......................... 8.50
Boot, Daisy and Button 25.00

Candy Dish, cov, wildflower, crystal 15.00
Creamer and Sugar, Texas, pink 45.00
Cup Plate
    Heart and Lyre, mulberry........... 15.00
    Seal of Ohio, amethyst 15.00
Hand
    Blue and White.................. 20.00
    Persimmon 8.00
Hat, Daisy and Button, opalescent...... 12.00
Jewelry Box, heart
    Blue Jay....................... 25.00
    Fawn 18.00
Owl
    Bluebell....................... 30.00
    Frosty Jade 45.00
    Sunset 25.00
    Willow Blue 48.00
Pooch
    Canary........................ 15.00
    Ivory Slag 20.00
Salt
    Daisy and Button, bittersweet 15.00
    Star and Dew Drop, forest green 12.00
Salt and Pepper Shakers, pr, birds, antique blue 20.00
Skate 30.00
Slipper
    Bow, caramel 30.00
    Kat, sapphire................... 15.00
Toothpick Holder
    Basket, sparrow slag.............. 15.00
    Colonial Drape and Heart, ruby 20.00
    Daisy and Button, dichromatic 24.00
    Forget-Me-Not, heatherbloom 20.00
    Gypsy Pot, blue fire.............. 15.00

DEPRESSION GLASS

Depression Glass refers to glassware made between 1920 and 1940. It was mass produced by a number of different companies. It was sold cheaply and often given away as a purchasing premium.

Specialize in one pattern or color. Once again, there is no way that you can own every piece made. Also, because Depression Glass was produced in vast quantities, buy only pieces in excellent or better condition.

A number of patterns have been reproduced. See Gene Florence's *The Collector's Encyclopedia of Depression Glass* (Collector Books, revised annually) for a complete list of reproductions.

Club: National Depression Glass Association, Inc., P. O. Box 1128, Springfield, MO 65808.

Newspaper: *The Daze*, Box 57, Otisville, MI 48463.

AMERICAN SWEETHEART

Made by MacBeth-Evans Glass Co, 1930–1936. Made in pink, monax, red, blue, cremax, color-trimmed monax, and smoke.

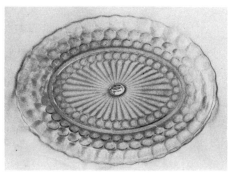

Bubble, platter, blue, 12" l, $14.00.

Floral, butter dish, cov, pink, $70.00.

Bowl
  3¾" d, berry, pink............... 25.00
  6" d, cereal
    Cremax 8.00
    Monax....................... 12.00
    Pink 10.00
  11" l, oval, vegetable
    Monax....................... 45.00
    Pink 32.00
Creamer
  Monax......................... 8.00
  Pink 7.00
Cup and Saucer
  Blue 90.00
  Monax......................... 9.50
  Pink 12.00
  Red 130.00
Plate
  8" d, salad
    Monax....................... 6.00
    Pink 15.00
  9¾" d, dinner
    Monax....................... 13.00

Pink 15.00
  Smoke, black rim trim 50.00
Platter
  Monax......................... 40.00
  Pink 31.00
  Smoke, black rim trim 95.00
Salt and Pepper Shakers, pr
  Monax........................210.00
  Pink 275.00
Sherbet, 4¼", ftd
  Monax......................... 13.00
  Pink 10.00
  Smoke, black rim trim 30.00
Sugar, open, ftd
  Blue 70.00
  Monax......................... 5.00
  Pink 5.00
  Smoke, black rim trim 60.00

ANNIVERSARY

Made by Jeannette Glass Co, 1947–1949, late 1960s, and mid 1970s. Made in crystal, iridescent carnival-type, and pink.

Berry Bowl, 4⅞" d
  Crystal........................ 2.50
  Iridescent..................... 4.50
Butter, cov
  Crystal........................ 22.50
  Pink 45.00
Cake Plate, crystal................. 6.00
Candlesticks, pr, 4⅞" h, crystal 17.50
Candy, cov, crystal 18.50
Compote, 3 toes, iridescent 6.00
Creamer, ftd, crystal................ 5.00
Cup and Saucer
  Crystal........................ 5.50
  Pink 5.25
Plate
  6¼" d, sherbet
    Crystal...................... 2.00
    Iridescent................... 1.00
    Pink 2.00
  9" d, dinner
    Crystal...................... 5.50
    Iridescent................... 5.00
    Pink 5.50
Soup, flat
  Crystal........................ 4.75
  Iridescent..................... 6.00
  Pink 7.50
Sugar, cov, crystal................. 10.00
Vase, 6½" h, crystal 14.00
Wine
  Crystal........................ 6.00
  Pink 15.00

BLOCK OPTIC

Hocking Glass Co, 1929–1933. Made in green, pink, yellow, crystal, and blue.

Bowl
  5¼" d, cereal
    Green...................... 10.00

Pink	6.00
7" d, salad, green	17.00
Butter Dish, cov, green..............	40.00

Creamer
Green.....................	10.00
Pink	9.00
Yellow	10.00

Cup and Saucer
Green.....................	12.00
Pink	10.00

Goblet, 4½" h
Green.....................	28.00
Pink	25.00

Pitcher, 8½" h, 54 oz
Green.....................	25.00
Pink	27.50

Plate

8" d, luncheon
Green.....................	3.00
Pink	2.50
Yellow	3.75

9" d, dinner
Green.....................	13.00
Pink	20.00
Yellow	30.00

9" d, grill
Green.....................	9.00
Pink	12.00
Yellow	30.00

Salt and Pepper Shakers, pr, ftd
Green.....................	25.00
Pink	55.00
Yellow	60.00

Sherbet, 3¼" d
Green.....................	4.50
Pink	6.00
Yellow	7.00

Tumbler, 9 oz, ftd
Green.....................	12.00
Pink	11.00
Yellow	18.00

BUBBLE (Bullseye, Provincial)

Made by Anchor Hocking Glass Co, 1935–1965. Made in blue, crystal, forest green, pink, and ruby.

Bowl

4½" d
Blue	10.00
Crystal	3.50

8⅜" d
Blue	14.00
Crystal	9.50

Candlesticks, pr, crystal	14.00

Cereal Bowl, 5¼" d
Blue	11.00
Crystal	8.50

Creamer and Sugar
Blue	45.00
Crystal	12.00
Green.....................	20.00

Cup and Saucer
Blue	4.50
Crystal	4.50
Green.....................	10.00
Pitcher, 64 oz, ice lip, ruby	55.00

Plate

6¾" d, bread and butter
Blue	3.50
Crystal	2.50
Green.....................	5.50

9⅜" d, dinner
Blue	6.00
Green.....................	15.00
9⅜" d, grill, blue	17.00
Platter, 12" l, blue................	14.00
Soup, 7¾" d, blue................	12.50

Tumbler, 9 oz
Crystal	11.50
Ruby	9.00

CHERRY BLOSSOM

Jeannette Glass Co, 1930–1939. Made in pink, green, delphite, crystal, jadite, and red. Heavily reproduced.

Bowl

4¾" d, berry
Delphite.....................	10.00
Green.....................	12.50
Pink	13.00

9" d, vegetable
Delphite.....................	38.00
Green.....................	22.00
Pink	20.00

Butter Dish, cov
Green.....................	75.00
Pink	65.00

Cake Plate, 10¼" d
Green.....................	16.00
Pink	15.00

Creamer
Delphite.....................	16.50
Green.....................	18.00
Pink	15.00

Cup and Saucer
Delphite.....................	15.50
Green.....................	20.00
Pink	16.50

Plate

7" d, salad
Green.....................	16.00
Pink	14.50

9" d, dinner
Delphite.....................	13.00
Green.....................	17.50
Pink	15.00

Sherbet
Delphite.....................	11.00
Green.....................	13.50
Pink	14.00

Sugar
Delphite.....................	15.00

Green.......................... **14.00**
Pink.......................... **10.00**
Tumbler, 9 oz, round foot, all over pattern
Delphite....................... **15.00**
Green.......................... **27.00**
Pink.......................... **26.00**

DAISY

Indiana Glass Co. Made in crystal, 1933; fired-on red, 1935; amber, 1940; and dark green and milk glass, 1960s and 1970s.

Bowl
4½" d, berry
Amber or red.................. **7.00**
Crystal or green................ **4.00**
6" d, cereal
Amber or red.................. **22.50**
Crystal or green................ **10.00**
10" l, oval, vegetable
Amber or red.................. **12.00**
Crystal or green................ **8.00**
Creamer, ftd
Amber or red.................. **7.00**
Crystal or green................ **5.00**
Cup and Saucer
Amber or red.................. **6.00**
Crystal or green................ **3.50**
Plate
6" d, sherbet
Amber or red.................. **2.00**
Crystal or green................ **1.00**
8⅜" d, luncheon
Amber or red.................. **5.00**
Crystal or green................ **2.00**
9⅜" d, dinner
Amber or red.................. **7.00**
Crystal or green................ **3.50**
Relish Dish, three part
Amber or red.................. **20.00**
Crystal or green................ **10.00**
Sherbet
Amber or red.................. **8.50**
Crystal or green................ **3.50**
Sugar, ftd
Amber or red.................. **6.50**
Crystal or green................ **3.00**

FLORAL

Jeannette Glass Co, 1931–1935. Made in pink, green, delphite, jadite, crystal, amber, red, and yellow.

Bowl
4" d, berry
Delphite....................... **25.00**
Green.......................... **12.00**
Pink.......................... **11.00**
9" d, vegetable
Green.......................... **12.00**
Pink.......................... **10.00**

Butter Dish, cov
Green.......................... **75.00**
Pink.......................... **70.00**
Candy Jar, cov
Green.......................... **34.00**
Pink.......................... **27.50**
Creamer
Delphite....................... **65.00**
Green.......................... **10.00**
Pink.......................... **9.00**
Cup and Saucer
Green.......................... **15.00**
Pink.......................... **12.50**
Pitcher, 8" h, 32 oz, ftd, cone
Green.......................... **25.00**
Pink.......................... **20.00**
Plate
8" d, salad
Green.......................... **8.00**
Pink.......................... **7.50**
9" d, dinner
Delphite.......................**110.00**
Green.......................... **13.50**
Pink.......................... **11.00**
Relish Dish, 2 part, oval
Green.......................... **11.00**
Pink.......................... **10.00**
Sherbet
Delphite....................... **75.00**
Green.......................... **13.00**
Pink.......................... **11.00**
Sugar
Delphite....................... **55.00**
Green.......................... **8.50**
Pink.......................... **7.50**
Tumbler, 9 oz, ftd
Green.......................... **35.00**
Pink.......................... **32.50**

FOREST GREEN

Made by Anchor Hocking Glass Co, 1950–1957. Made only in forest green.

Ashtray, 5¾" w, hexagonal........... **7.50**
Berry Bowl **5.00**
Bowl
4¾" w, sq **5.00**
5¼" d, round................... **9.00**
Cup, sq **4.50**
Iced Tea Tumbler **6.50**
Juice Pitcher **20.00**
Mixing Bowl, nested set of four **45.00**
Plate
6¾" d, salad................... **3.00**
8⅜" d, luncheon................. **5.00**
10" d, dinner................... **25.00**
Platter, 11 × 8".................. **25.00**
Punch Bowl Set, bowl, 14 cups **60.00**
Saucer.......................... **4.00**
Sherbet **5.75**
Soup **15.00**
Sugar, sq **5.50**

Tumbler, 4" h 18.00
Water Pitcher, ice lip 30.00

IRIS

Jeannette Glass Co, 1928–1932, 1950s, 1970s. Made in crystal, iridescent, and pink. Recently made in bi-colored red/yellow and blue/green, as well as white.

Bowl
  5" d, sauce, ruffled
    Crystal 6.00
    Iridescent 15.00
  7½" d, soup
    Crystal 80.00
    Iridescent 35.00
  11½" d, fruit, ruffled
    Crystal 8.50
    Iridescent 6.00
Butter Dish, cov
  Crystal or iridescent 27.50
Coaster, crystal 40.00
Creamer, ftd
  Crystal 7.00
  Iridescent 8.00
Cup and Saucer
  Crystal 15.00
  Iridescent 14.00
Plate
  5½" d, sherbet
    Crystal 8.00
    Iridescent 7.00
  8" d, luncheon, crystal 37.50
  9" d, dinner
    Crystal 35.00
    Iridescent 30.00
Sherbet, 2½"
  Crystal 15.00
  Iridescent 10.00
Sugar
  Crystal 6.00
  Iridescent 6.50
Tumbler, 6" h, ftd
  Crystal 12.00
  Iridescent 12.50

MAYFAIR

Hocking Glass Co, 1931–1937. Made in ice blue, pink, green, yellow, and crystal.

Bowl
  5½" d, cereal
    Blue 37.50
    Green 60.00
    Pink 17.50
    Yellow 60.00
  7" l, vegetable
    Blue 38.00
    Green 100.00
    Pink 17.50
    Yellow 100.00
Butter Dish, cov
  Blue 225.00
  Pink 45.00

Celery Dish
  Blue 32.00
  Green 90.00
  Pink 25.00
  Yellow 90.00
Creamer, ftd
  Blue 50.00
  Green 175.00
  Pink 18.00
  Yellow 150.00
Cup
  Blue 37.00
  Green 125.00
  Pink 15.00
  Yellow 125.00
Plate
  6½" d, round, off-center indent
    Blue 20.00
    Green 100.00
    Pink 20.00
  8½" d, luncheon
    Blue 27.50
    Green 60.00
    Pink 17.50
    Yellow 60.00
  9½" d, dinner
    Blue 48.00
    Green 100.00
    Pink 37.50
    Yellow 100.00
  9½" d, grill
    Blue 27.50
    Green 60.00
    Pink 27.50
    Yellow 60.00
Salt and Pepper Shakers, flat, pr
  Blue 200.00
  Pink 45.00
  Yellow 750.00
Sugar, ftd
  Blue 50.00
  Green 165.00
  Pink 17.50
  Yellow 165.00
Tumbler
  3½" h, 5 oz, juice
    Blue 80.00
    Pink 32.00
  4¾" h, 11 oz, water
    Blue 85.00
    Green 150.00
    Pink 115.00
    Yellow 160.00
  5¼" h, 13½ oz, iced tea
    Blue 135.00
    Pink 35.00

MISS AMERICA (Diamond Pattern)

Made by Hocking Glass Co, 1935–1937. Made in crystal, pink, some green, ice blue, jadite, and red.

Bowl
  6¼", berry
    Crystal 6.00

Green	10.00
Pink	14.00

10", oval, vegetable
Crystal	10.00
Pink	17.50

Butter Dish, cov
Crystal	190.00
Pink	435.00

Cake Plate, 12", ftd
Crystal	17.50
Pink	29.00

Celery Dish, 10½", oblong
Crystal	8.00
Pink	16.00

Creamer, ftd
Crystal	6.50
Pink	13.00
Red	145.00

Cup
Crystal	7.50
Green	8.00
Pink	16.00

Pitcher, 8" h
Crystal	40.00
Pink	90.00

Plate

8½" d, salad
Crystal	5.00
Green	8.00
Pink	15.00
Red	65.00

10¼" d, dinner
Crystal	10.00
Pink	18.00

Platter, 12¼" l, oval
Crystal	10.00
Pink	18.00

Salt and Pepper Shaker, pr
Crystal	22.50
Green	275.00
Pink	42.50

Saucer
Crystal	2.50
Pink	4.00

Sugar
Crystal	6.00
Pink	12.50

OLD CAFE

Made by Hocking Glass Co, 1936–1938, 1940. Made in pink, crystal, and Royal Ruby.

Bowl

3¾" d, berry
Crystal	2.00
Pink	2.00
Royal Ruby	4.00

5½" d, cereal
Crystal	4.00
Pink	4.00
Royal Ruby	8.50

9" d, closed handles
Crystal	7.50

Pink	7.50
Royal Ruby	11.50

Cup
Crystal	3.00
Pink	3.00
Royal Ruby	6.00

Pitcher, 6" h
Crystal	50.00
Pink	50.00

Plate

6" d, sherbet
Crystal	1.50
Pink	1.50

10" d, dinner
Crystal	20.00
Pink	20.00

Saucer
Crystal	1.50
Pink	1.50

Tumbler, 3" h, juice
Crystal	8.00
Pink	8.00
Royal Ruby	7.50

Vase, 7¼" h
Crystal	9.50
Pink	9.50
Royal Ruby	14.00

PATRICIAN (Spoke)

Made by Federal Glass Co, 1933–1937. Made in amber, crystal, green, and pink.

Berry Bowl, amber	10.00

Bowl, 8½" d
Amber	40.00
Green	30.00

Butter Dish, cov
Amber	80.00
Green	80.00
Pink	225.00

Cereal Bowl, 6" d
Amber	22.50
Green	20.00

Cookie Jar, cov, amber	80.00

Cream Soup
Amber	15.00
Pink	15.00

Creamer
Amber	9.50
Pink	10.00

Cup
Amber	7.00
Green	10.00

Jam Dish
Amber	27.50
Pink	27.50

Juice Tumbler, amber	27.50
Pitcher, 8" h, amber	100.00

Plate

6" d, bread and butter
Amber	8.50
Green	6.00

7½" d, salad, amber	13.00

9" d, luncheon
Amber	10.00

Pink	10.00
10½" d, dinner	
Amber	5.00
Pink	35.00
10½" d, grill	
Amber	12.00
Green.	20.00
Platter, oval	
Amber	27.00
Green.	22.50
Salt and Pepper Shakers, pr, amber	50.00
Saucer	
Amber	7.00
Green.	5.00
Sherbet, amber	11.00
Tumbler, 5¼" h, ftd	
Amber	40.00
Green.	42.00
Vegetable Bowl, oval	
Amber	27.00
Green.	24.00

PETALWARE

Made by MacBeth-Evans Glass Co, 1930–1940. Made in Monax, Cremax, pink, crystal, and cobalt, as well as in fired-on red, blue, green, and yellow. Cremax, Monax, Florette, and Fired-on decorations have the same value as do pink and crystal.

Bowl	
4½" d, cream soup	
Cremax	8.50
Pink	4.00
Plain.	7.50
5¾" d, cereal	
Cremax	6.50
Pink	3.50
Plain.	4.50
7" d, soup, plain	40.00
9" d, large berry	
Cobalt	40.00
Cremax	15.00
Pink	7.50
Plain.	12.50
Red Trim Floral	45.00
Creamer, ftd	
Cobalt	25.00
Cremax	8.00
Pink	2.50
Plain.	4.50
Red Trim Floral	15.00
Cup	
Cremax	6.00
Pink	2.50
Plain.	4.50
Red Trim Floral	12.00
Mustard, metal cov, cobalt blue	8.00
Pitcher, pink, crystal dec bands	22.00
Plate	
6" d, sherbet	
Cremax	4.00

Pink	1.50
Plain.	2.00
8" d, salad	
Cremax	6.00
Pink	1.75
Plain.	3.00
Red Trim Floral	10.00
9" d, dinner	
Cremax	8.00
Pink	3.50
Plain.	5.00
12" d, salver	
Cremax	15.00
Plain.	6.50
Red Trim Floral	22.50
Platter, 13" l, oval	
Cremax	15.00
Pink	7.50
Plain.	12.00
Saucer	
Cremax	2.50
Pink	1.00
Plain.	1.50
Red Trim Floral	3.00
Sugar, ftd	
Cobalt	25.00
Cremax	7.50
Pink	2.50
Plain.	4.50
Red Trim Floral	15.00

ROYAL LACE

Made by Hazel Atlas Co, 1934–1941. Made in amethyst, cobalt blue, crystal, green, and pink.

Berry Bowl, green.	22.00
Candlesticks, pr, ruffled, cobalt blue	185.00
Candy Dish, cov, cobalt blue	40.00
Console Bowl, ruffled, pink	55.00
Cream Soup	
Cobalt Blue	37.00
Pink	22.50
Creamer	
Crystal.	18.00
Pink	15.00
Cup and Saucer	
Cobalt Blue	38.50
Pink	18.50
Jug, 64 oz, cobalt blue	235.00
Juice Tumbler, 5 oz	
Cobalt Blue	42.50
Green.	25.00
Pitcher, pink	135.00
Plate	
8½" d, luncheon	
Cobalt Blue	45.00
Green.	22.50
Pink	12.00
9⅞" d, dinner	
Cobalt Blue	40.00
Crystal	12.00
Sherbet, metal holder	
Amethyst.	32.00

Crystal **3.50**
Sugar, cov
  Cobalt Blue **185.00**
  Crystal **22.00**
Tumbler
  Cobalt Blue **37.50**
  Pink **17.50**
Vegetable, oval
  Cobalt Blue **70.00**
  Green. **25.00**
  Pink **20.00**

SANDWICH

Made by Hocking Glass Co, 1939–1964, 1977. Made in crystal, forest green, and white/ivory (opaque), 1950–1960; amber, 1960s; pink, 1939–1940; and royal ruby, 1939–1940.

Bowl
  4⁵⁄₁₆" d
    Crystal **4.00**
    Forest Green **2.00**
  4⁷⁄₈" d, ruffled, crystal **9.50**
  5¼" d, scalloped
    Crystal **6.00**
    Ruby Red **15.00**
  6½" d, cereal, crystal **20.00**
  7" d, salad
    Crystal **6.50**
    Forest Green **45.00**
  8" d, scalloped
    Crystal **6.50**
    Forest Green **50.00**
    Pink **13.00**
    Ruby Red **30.00**
  8¼" l, oval, crystal **6.00**
  9" d, salad, crystal **20.00**
Butter Dish, crystal **32.50**
Cookie Jar
  Crystal **30.00**
  Forest Green **16.00**
Creamer
  Crystal **4.00**
  Forest Green **20.00**
Cup
  Crystal **1.50**
  Forest Green **13.00**
Custard Cup
  Crystal **3.50**
  Forest Green **1.50**
Pitcher, 6" h, juice
  Crystal **45.00**
  Forest Green **95.00**
Plate
  7" d, dessert, crystal **8.00**
  8" d, crystal **3.00**
  9" d, dinner
    Crystal **12.00**
    Forest Green **52.50**
  12" d, sandwich
    Amber **10.00**
    Crystal **9.00**
Punch Bowl, 9¾" d, crystal **15.00**

Saucer
  Amber **3.00**
  Crystal **1.00**
  Forest Green **6.00**
Sugar
  Crystal **12.50**
  Forest Green **17.00**
Tumbler
  Juice, crystal **10.00**
Water
  Crystal **6.50**
  Forest Green **3.25**

SHARON (Cabbage Rose)

Made by Federal Glass Co, 1935–1939. Made in amber, crystal, green, and pink.

Berry Bowl, 5" d
  Amber **7.00**
  Pink **9.00**
Bowl, 10½" d, pink **28.00**
Butter, cov
  Amber **45.00**
  Pink **40.00**
Cake Plate
  Amber **22.00**
  Pink **30.00**
Candy, cov, amber **40.00**
Cereal Bowl
  Green. **20.00**
  Pink **18.00**
Cream Soup
  Green. **36.00**
  Pink **35.00**
Creamer
  Amber **11.50**
  Pink **15.00**
Cup and Saucer
  Amber **12.00**
  Green. **20.00**
  Pink **18.00**
Pitcher, ice lip, amber **115.00**
Plate
  6" d, bread and butter
    Amber **4.00**
    Green. **6.00**
    Pink **5.00**
  7½" d, salad
    Amber **12.00**
    Green. **18.00**
    Pink **22.50**
  9½" d, dinner
    Amber **10.00**
    Green. **15.00**
    Pink **14.00**
Platter, oval
  Amber **12.00**
  Pink **18.00**
Salt and Pepper Shakers, pr
  Amber **36.00**
  Pink **47.50**
Sherbet
  Amber **10.00**
  Pink **12.00**

Item	Price
Soup, 7½" d, pink	**37.50**
Sugar, cov, pink	**30.00**
Tumbler, 4⅛" h, pink	**27.00**
Vegetable Bowl, 9½" l, oval	
Green	**24.00**
Pink	**18.00**

WINDSOR (Windsor Diamond)

Made by Jeannette Glass Co, 1936–1946. Made in pink, green, crystal, some Delphite, amberina red, and ice blue.

Item	Price
Bowl	
4¾" d, berry	
Crystal	**2.50**
Green	**7.00**
Pink	**5.00**
5" d	
Crystal	**4.50**
Green	**20.00**
Pink	**15.00**
5⅛" d	
Crystal	**7.00**
Green	**15.00**
Pink	**12.00**
8" d, pointed edge	
Crystal	**8.00**
Pink	**25.00**
8½" d, large berry	
Crystal	**4.50**
Green	**12.00**
Pink	**10.00**
9½" d, oval	
Crystal	**5.00**
Green	**17.50**
Pink	**12.00**
10½" d, salad, crystal	**6.00**
12½" d, fruit console	
Crystal	**20.00**
Pink	**75.00**
Butter Dish	
Crystal	**22.50**
Green	**70.00**
Pink	**37.50**
Candlesticks, 3" h, pr	
Crystal	**15.00**
Pink	**65.00**
Creamer	
Blue	**55.00**
Crystal	**3.00**
Green	**8.00**
Pink	**7.50**
Cup	
Blue	**55.00**
Crystal	**2.50**
Green	**7.00**
Pink	**6.00**
Pitcher, 6¾" h	
Crystal	**11.00**
Green	**40.00**
Pink	**18.50**
Red	**400.00**
Plate	
6" d, sherbet	
Crystal	**1.50**
Green	**3.50**
Pink	**2.50**
7" d, salad	
Crystal	**3.00**
Green	**13.50**
Pink	**9.50**
9" d, dinner	
Blue	**55.00**
Crystal	**3.50**
Green	**13.50**
Pink	**9.50**
10¼" d, sandwich, handle	
Crystal	**4.00**
Green	**10.00**
Pink	**9.00**
13⅝" d, chop	
Crystal	**7.50**
Green	**30.00**
Pink	**30.00**
Platter, 11½" l, oval	
Crystal	**4.50**
Green	**12.00**
Pink	**10.00**
Relish Platter, 11½" l, divided	
Crystal	**9.50**
Pink	**175.00**
Salt and Pepper Shakers, pr	
Crystal	**12.50**
Green	**40.00**
Pink	**30.00**
Saucer	
Crystal	**1.50**
Green	**3.00**
Pink	**2.50**
Sugar	
Crystal	**4.50**
Green	**22.00**
Pink	**17.50**
Tray	
4" sq, handles	
Crystal	**2.50**
Green	**8.00**
Pink	**6.00**
8½ × 9¾"	
Crystal	**12.50**
Green	**35.00**
Pink	**75.00**
Tumbler	
3¼" h	
Blue	**55.00**
Crystal	**6.00**
Green	**25.00**
Pink	**15.00**
5" h	
Crystal	**7.50**
Green	**37.50**
Pink	**20.00**
7¼" h, ftd, crystal	**10.00**

DIONNE QUINTUPLETS

On May 28, 1934, on a small farm in Callander, Ontario, Canada, five baby girls weighing a total of 10 pounds 1¼ ounces were delivered into this world with the help of Dr. DaFoe and two midwives: the Dionne Quintuplets.

Due to their parents' poor circumstances and the public's curiosity, the quintuplets were put on display. For a small fee, the world was invited to come and see the quints at play in their custom-built home or to buy a souvenir to mark their birth.

The field of collectibles for Dionne Quintuplets memorabilia is a very fertile one!

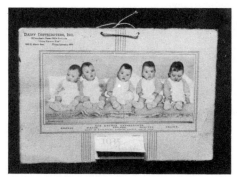

Calendar, 1935 and 1936, Dairy Distributors, Inc, Milwaukee, WI, multicolored picture, 11¼" w, 8" h, $18.00.

Blotter, celluloid cov, quints on toy, 1935......................... **20.00**
Book
  The Dionne Quintuplets Growing Up, 8½ × 11", brown and white cov, 1935......................... **40.00**
  Dionne Quintuplets Picture Album, The Complete Story of Their First Two Years, Dell, 1936 .... **28.00**
  Dionne Quintuplets Play Mother Goose, Dell, 1938 .... **25.00**
  Now We're Two Years Old, Whitman, 1936......................... **30.00**
  Soon We'll Be Three Years Old: The Five Dionne Quintuplets Book, Whitman, 1936......................... **22.00**
Booklet, adv, "Lysol vs. Germs," Dionne photos inside, Lehn & Fink Products Corp, 4½ × 5½", 30 pgs, 1938........ **15.00**
Box
  Baby Ruth, cardboard, 2 × 8 × 11", "Baby Ruth—First and Only Candy Served the Dionne Quints" **75.00**
  Dionne Pops, 4 × 10½ × 1", Vitamin Candy Co, Providence, RI, 1936.... **125.00**
Cake Plate, china, 11½" d, white, gold maple leaf at top, red rim, center color portraits titled "Dionne Quintuplets, Born May 28, 1934, Callander, Ontario, Canada"................... **135.00**

Calendar
  1936, Watch Us Grow, photos and stories......................... **20.00**
  1937, Robotman & Sons Dairy, quints wearing pink dresses............. **15.00**
  1943, Sunny Day, beach illus........ **25.00**
Cereal Bowl, china, 5½" d, Marie in highchair, 1935................... **20.00**
Coloring Book, *The Dionne Quintuplets Pictures to Paint,* Merrill, 10 × 15", 1940......................... **40.00**
Doll, Madame Alexander, 7½" h, mohair wig, painted brown eyes, 1936 ......**250.00**
Fan, 8¼ × 8¾", diecut cardboard, tinted color photo portraits, light blue ground, funeral parlor adv reverse, 1936......................... **18.00**
Handkerchief, linen weave cotton, 8 × 8", three quints playing, two with birthday cakes, sgd "Tom Lamb," 1936–37 .... **25.00**
Hanger Adv, Quintuplet Bread, 5 × 7", stiff paper, silhouette quints illus..... **65.00**
Keychain, celluloid, 3" l, dark green, gold lettering, "Souvenir of Quint Land, Callander, Canada" **30.00**
Lobby Card, 11 × 14", "Five Of A Kind," color, girls playing piano, 1938 ...... **70.00**
Magazine, *Woman's World,* Feb, 1937 ... **10.00**
Paper Doll Book
  Palmolive Soap, premium, 9¼ × 9¾", four pgs of uncut clothing, punch out dolls back cov, orig mailing envelope, 1937 .... **100.00**
  Whitman, Annette, 9½ × 10½", 1936......................... **100.00**
Photograph, 10 × 14", parents' signature on reverse, framed, 1935 .... **65.00**
Playing Cards, quints gathering flowers illus, pink and white checkered box **40.00**
Poster, adv, "Today the Dionne Quints Had Quaker Oats," 14 × 32", 1935.... **65.00**
Program, theater, promotion for "The Country Doctor," 1936 .... **20.00**
Puzzle, palm, steel balls, glass cov, place quints in buggy **35.00**
Sheet Music, *Quintuplets' Lullaby,* tinted photo front cov, 6 pgs **10.00**
Spoons, set of five.................. **125.00**
Thermometer, adv, Cupp's Dairy, cardboard, 4 × 6", multicolored.......... **25.00**

DISNEYANA

"Steamboat Willie" introduced Mickey Mouse to the world in 1928. Walt and Roy Disney, brothers, worked together to create an entertainment empire filled with a myriad of memorable characters ranging from Donald Duck to Zorro.

Early Disney is getting very expensive.

No problem. Disney continues to license material. In thirty years the stuff from the 1960s and 1970s is going to be scarce and eagerly sought after. Now is the time to buy it.

Club: Mouse Club, 2056 Cirone Way, San Jose, CA 95124.

Stuffed Toy, Mickey Mouse, red pants, yellow shoes, 17" l, $30.00.

Advent Calendar, Mickey Mouse, early
  1970s........................... 30.00
Bank
  Dopey, dime register, tin, dated
    1939...........................145.00
  Pinocchio........................ 30.00
Book, *Winnie the Pooh*, scratch and
  sniff............................ 10.00
Box, Mickey Mouse Straws, 1960s..... 15.00
Butterfly Net, Mickey Mouse.......... 85.00
Button, Seven Dwarfs, bakelite, red.... 9.50
Ceiling Fixture, 11" d, round globe,
  Donald Duck and Pluto chasing but-
  terflies.........................295.00
Cookie Jar
  Alice In Wonderland, Japan........195.00
  Donald Duck and Nephews......... 95.00
  Dumbo, mouse finial.............. 95.00
  Mickey Mouse on Drum............195.00
  Pinocchio, Mettlach.............. 65.00
  Winnie the Pooh, Walt Disney Produc-
    tions.......................... 85.00
Drawing Set, Walt Disney Electric Draw-
  ing Set, carrying case, dated 1961....115.00

Figure
  Donald Duck, bisque, strutting...... 68.00
  Dopey, 5½" h, bisque............. 65.00
  Mickey Mouse, jointed, decal, early
    1920s.........................275.00
  Snow White and Seven Dwarfs,
    bisque, 1938..................325.00
  Three Little Pigs, musicians, bisque...145.00
Lantern, Pluto, tin, Line Mar, 1950s....325.00
Map
  Mickey Mouse and Donald Duck,
    Race to Treasure Island, no stamps,
    1939.......................... 60.00
  Mickey Mouse Travel Club Star Bak-
    ery, 1938...................... 95.00
Napkin, linen
  Happy, bathing, name on soap dish... 25.00
  Snow White with Dopey, Disney la-
    bel............................ 25.00
Nodder
  Mickey Mouse.................... 65.00
  Pluto, orig tag.................. 55.00
Paint Box, Alice In Wonderland, tin, orig
  paints........................... 30.00
Pattern, Cinderella, apron, paper...... 8.00
Phonograph, Alice In Wonderland,
  1951...........................150.00
Plate, 7" d, Mickey Mouse, tin enamel,
  red and blue....................110.00
Press Box, Alice In Wonderland, uncut,
  1974............................ 15.00
Puppet, Ferdinand the Bull, composition
  head, flower in hand.............120.00
Purse, Snow White, 1938........... 60.00
Puzzle, jigsaw, orig box, set of 4.......125.00
Salt and Pepper Shakers, pr Pinocchio,
  1940s........................... 45.00
Sheet Music
  Cinderella...................... 7.00
  Snow White..................... 7.00
Song Album, Alice in Wonderland, 20
  pgs, 1951....................... 95.00
Tea Set, Alice in Wonderland, china, orig
  box............................ 45.00
Tie Bar, Mickey Mouse............. 15.00
Transfer, color, Davy Crockett, unused,
  1955............................ 30.00
Toy
  Stuffed
    Dopey, Knickerbocker, 1930s.....175.00
    Pluto, 14" h, velvet, black leather
      collar, orig label.............110.00
  Watering Can, Snow White and Seven
    Dwarfs, Ohio Art Co, 1938.......145.00
  Windup
    Mickey Mouse, climbing fireman,
      orig box..................... 95.00
    Nautilus, 20,000 Leagues Under the
      Sea, tin, orig box, 1930s........295.00
    Pinocchio, tin, walking figure, Line
      Mar.........................395.00
Wristwatch
  Alice in Wonderland, 1958.........225.00
  Mickey Mouse, Bradley...........350.00

DOG COLLECTIBLES

The easiest way to curb your collection is to concentrate on the representations for a single breed. Many collectors focus only on three-dimensional figures. Whatever approach you take, buy pieces because you love them. Try to develop some restraint and taste and not buy every piece you see. Easy to say, hard to do!

Club: Canine Collectibles Club of America, 736 N. Western Ave., Suite 314, Lake Forest, IL 60045.

Figurine, Bulldog, china, white, black highlights, marked "Made in Japan," 6" l, 3" h, $4.00.

Advertising
   Sign, 23 × 23", Old Boston Beer, cardboard, dog illus **25.00**
   Tape Measure, Armco Steel, red and white, collie and company slogan on one side, logo on other, inscribed "Lyle Culvert and Road Equipment Co, Minneapolis" **18.00**
Bank, cast iron
   German Shepherd **38.00**
   Retriever, 3⅜" h, with pack, traces of black paint.................... **50.00**
   Scottie, 5" h, white **60.00**
Candy Container, figural, glass **10.00**
Doorstop
   Boston Terrier, full figure.......... **50.00**
   German Shepherd, standing **40.00**
   Russian Wolfhound **155.00**
   Wire Haired Terrier, orig paint, c1929....................... **115.00**
Figure
   Boxer, 3½" h, bone china **5.00**
   Chihuahua, 3¼" h **4.00**
   Collie, 5½ × 8¼", porcelain, "Made in Japan"....................... **10.00**
   English Bulldog, 3⅛" h, porcelain **7.00**
   Poodle, 9½ × 9½", porcelain, "Made in Austria"...................... **75.00**
   Rin Tin Tin, 19" h, chalkware **50.00**
   Scottie, 8½ × 10½", composition **30.00**

   Springer Spaniel, 3¾ × 5¾", earthenware, hp nose and eyes, airbrushed **6.00**
Napkin Ring, dog pulling sled, silver plated........................ **250.00**
Pin, Scottie, Bakelite, black **75.00**
Planter, Scottie, 5 × 6", chalkware **9.00**
Record, *Train Your Dog*, Lee Duncan, 12¼" sq cardboard album, 33⅓ rpm, 1961, produced by Carlton Record Corp.......................... **15.00**
Tobacco Jar, Pug.................... **75.00**
Toy, stuffed, 4½" h, Cocker Spaniel **30.00**

DOLLS

People buy dolls primarily on the basis of sentiment and condition. Most begin by buying the dolls with which they remember playing as a child.

Speculating in dolls is risky business. The doll market is subject to crazes. The doll that is in today may be out tomorrow.

Place great emphasis on originality. Make certain that every doll you buy has the complete original costume. Ideally, the box or packing also should be present. Remember, you are not buying these dolls to play with. You are buying them for display.

Magazines: *Doll Reader*, P. O. Box 467, Mount Morris, IL 61054; *The Collector's Magazine*, P. O. Box 1972, Marion, OH 43305.

Clubs: Madame Alexander Fan Club, P. O. Box 146, New Lenox, IL 60451; Ginny Doll Club, 305 West Beacon Road, Lakeland, FL 33803; United Federation of Doll Clubs, P. O. Box 14146, Parkville, MO 64152.

Note: The dolls listed date from the 1930s through the present. For information about antique dolls, see Jan Foulke's *10th Blue Book Dolls and Values* (Hobby House Press: 1991) and R. Lane Herron's *Herron's Price Guide To Dolls* (Wallace-Homestead: 1990).

Advertising
   6" h, Pillsbury Poppie Fresh, molded soft vinyl **10.00**
   8" h, Blue Bonnet Sue, hard plastic, orig dress **8.00**
   12" h, Simplicity, complete with pattern book, measuring tape **70.00**
   15" h, Vermont Maid Syrup, vinyl ... **30.00**
   17" h, Swiss Miss, cloth **15.00**

Horsman, Cindy, #82, orig clothes, 1959, 18" h, $110.00.

American Character
9" h, Toddler, soft vinyl, baby style
  hair and clothes **30.00**
12" h, Tiny Tears, vinyl **160.00**
Arranbee
8" h, Baby Marie, vinyl head, arms,
  and legs, plastic body, 1963 . . . . **18.00**
12" h, My Dream Baby, bisque solid
  head, cloth body **400.00**
19" h, Rosie, composition swivel head
  on shoulder plate, cloth body **80.00**
Cameo
12" h, Kewpie, composition, flowered
  sun dress and bonnet, c1940 . . . . . . **125.00**
19" h, Miss Peeps, vinyl, brown skin,
  1973 . . . . **35.00**
Coleco, Cabbage Patch
16" h, cowgirl, vinyl head, cowgirl
  outfit **85.00**
Deluxe Toys
6" h, Dawn, blonde hair, vinyl
  body **15.00**
18" h, Baby Catch A Ball, vinyl head,
  plastic body, battery operated,
  throws ball, 1969 . . . . **30.00**
Eegee
11" h, Tina, vinyl head, hard plastic
  body, walker, 1959 . . . . **15.00**
16" h, Newborn Baby, vinyl head and
  limbs, cloth body, 1963 . . . . **20.00**

Effanbee
9" h, Patsyette, composition, molded
  hair, painted features **125.00**
11" h, Miss Black America, vinyl,
  1975, MIB **75.00**
15" h, Peaches, vinyl head and limbs,
  cloth body, 1965 . . . . **40.00**
19" h, Patsy-Ann, composition,
  molded and painted hair, blue eyes,
  c1928 . . . . **85.00**
Horsman
12" h, Billiken, plush jointed body . . . **350.00**
16" h, Baby Dimples, composition
  head and limbs, soft cloth body, re-
  dressed, 1930 . . . . **150.00**
Ideal
12" h, Betsy Wetsy, composition head,
  rubber body **75.00**
13" h, Shirley Temple, composition
  head, orig dress, c1935 . . . . **350.00**
14" h, Miss Curity, orig nurse's uni-
  form and play nurse kit **75.00**
17" h, Saucy Walker, hard plastic
  head, walker, c1951, MIB **150.00**
Knickerbocker, 24" h, Holly Hobbie **15.00**
Madame Alexander
7½" h, Alexander-Kin, hard plastic . . . **110.00**
8" h, International Series, Japan,
  1972 . . . . **175.00**
14" h, Caroline Kennedy, vinyl head,
  hard plastic body **300.00**
18" h, Cinderalla, hard plastic, orig
  dress and tags **725.00**
19" h, Marlo Thomas, orig clothes and
  tags **550.00**
Mattel, Inc
10" h, Barbie, Sweet 16, vinyl, 1975,
  MIB **75.00**
11½" h
Barbie, #1, 1959, vinyl, blonde hair,
  MIB **950.00**
Barbie, #3, 1960, vinyl, blonde hair,
  MIB **375.00**
Ken, 1961, flocked hair **85.00**
Roberts, Xavier, 16" h, Georgia Dee,
  Cabbage Patch, porcelain head, limited
  edition, 1985 . . . . **350.00**
Sun Rubber
10" h, Peter Pan, 1953 . . . . **35.00**
11" h, Gerber Baby, molded rubber . . . **45.00**
17" h, Sun-Dee, vinyl, dark skin,
  1956 . . . . **48.00**
Terri Lee
8" h, Girl Scout, MIB **65.00**
15½" h, Terri Lee, vinyl **100.00**
16" h, Gene Autry, hard plastic **225.00**
17" h, Cowgirl, plastic, orig cowgirl
  outfit, 1950 . . . . **225.00**
Vogue
8" h, Ginny, hard plastic, moving eyes,
  orig outfit, 1950 . . . . **125.00**
10" h, Jill, bride outfit, 1958 . . . . **50.00**

DOORSTOPS

Cast iron doorstops have gone through a number of collecting crazes over the past twenty years. The last craze occurred just a few years ago and drove prices up to a level that made doorstops more likely to appear at an antiques show than at a flea market.

Reproductions abound. A few helpful clues are: (1) check size (many reproductions are slightly smaller than the period piece); (2) check detail (the less detail, the more suspicious you need to be); and (3) check rust (a bright orange rust indicates a new piece).

Sunbonnet Baby, cast iron, marked "72," 6" h, $40.00.

Advertising, John Deere, 13" h 45.00
Black Cat, lying on pillow, red ribbon
  and bow. 125.00
Cinderella's Carriage, 9¾ × 19" 175.00
Conestoga Wagon, 8 × 11". 95.00
Cornucopia and Roses, 10¼" h, orig
  paint 85.00
Dog
  Boston Terrier, 8¼" h. 75.00
  Cocker Spaniel, bronze, relief detail,
    worn green patina. 150.00
  St Bernard, wearing keg. 145.00
  Whippet, 6¾" h 110.00

Wire Haired Terrier, bushes, orig paint,
  c1929. . . . . 115.00
Doll on Base, 4½ × 4⅞". 100.00
Flower Basket, 5⅞ × 5⅝", National
  Foundry. 75.00
Frog, 3 × 5¼". 45.00
High Heel Shoe 75.00
House, Cape Cod, 5¾ × 8¾", Albany
  Foundry. 125.00
Pansy Bowl, 7 × 6½", Hubley 125.00
Parrot, sitting on ring, 8 × 7" 100.00
Peacock, 6¼ × 6¼" 150.00
Pineapple, 13" h, cast brass 115.00
Poppies and Cornflowers, 7¼ × 6½",
  Hubley. 115.00
Rabbit, 12" h, black repaint, pink and
  white trim 125.00
Rooster, 10½" h, painted 150.00
Ship. 50.00
Victorian Woman, holding muff,
  10" h. 170.00

DRESSER SETS

I remember visiting my grandmother while growing up and wondering about all those bottles and little containers on her dresser. They seemed to contain such exotic things and were always arranged neatly. A small tray held her comb and brush and sometimes even a piece of jewelry or two.

Now that I'm older and wiser, I have learned to recognize these things as dresser sets and accessories, a fast-growing collectible category. Her powder jar with the Scottie on top always held a big fluffy powder puff that was just perfect for bombing my little sister when she least expected it. Sure beats trying to peel the childproof protective tops off of today's powder containers.

Atomizer, Devilbiss, Magic-Mist, bottle
  marked: Made in West Germany 6.75
Bath Set, scented, original package reads:
  "Starts the Day on a Fresh and Joyful
  Path". 18.00
Brush and Comb
  Celluloid, pink, hand painted flowers,
    1920s. 40.00
  Silver Plated, emb florals and scrolls,
    monogram, worn bristles 35.00
Cologne Bottle, orig stopper
  Fenton, Aquacrest, melon rib 60.00
  Heisey, Horizontal Rib, crystal 70.00
Cream, Desert Flower Beauty Clean For
  Deep Skin Cleansing, 5 oz bottle 8.75

Hair Receiver
  Ceramic
    Limoges, small blue flowers and but-
      terflies, gold trim **75.00**
    Nippon, yellow and red roses, black
      ground, blue maple leaf mark. . . . **60.00**
    RS Prussia, pink roses, white
      ground, green border, red
      mark. **65.00**
  Glass, Fostoria, American pattern **85.00**
Nail File, celluloid, figural, lady's leg,
  painted high heel and garter, folds in
  center **35.00**
Perfume, original contents
  Aimant Mist, Coty, 8 oz bottle **11.00**
  Chanel No. 5, 1½ oz bottle **12.00**
  Tussy Midnight Cologne, 2 oz bot-
    tle. **8.50**
Powder Jar, cov, glass, figural
  Bambi, iridescent **25.00**
  Bulldog, pink, frosted **65.00**
  Dancing Girls, transparent blue **250.00**
  Elephant, crystal **16.00**
  Lady, Akro Agate
    Blue, medium **95.00**
    Pink **75.00**
    Turquoise **95.00**
  Lovebirds, pink, frosted **65.00**
  Melon Base, blue overlay, Fenton **45.00**
  Sailboat
    Crystal **30.00**
    Pink **65.00**
  Scottie
    Akro Agate, white **65.00**
    Pink **45.00**
Puff Box, cov, round, glass
  Duncan & Miller, 4" d, pink opales-
    cent **85.00**
  New Martinsville, amethyst, gold
    dec **50.00**
Sachet, powder, original Avon enve-
  lopes, 1908 . . . . **35.00**
Set
  Bakelite, yellow and orange, enameled
    Art Deco dec, brush, comb, ma-
    nicure accessories, and mirror **75.00**
  Celluloid, ivory, orig case, 11 pcs **85.00**
  Glass
    New Martinsville, #18, crystal and
      black, 3 pcs. **85.00**
    Westmoreland, Paneled Grape, milk
      glass, 7 pcs **282.50**
Tray
  Ceramic, hand painted, forget-me-
    nots and pink ribbon dec **45.00**
  Mirror, round, pierced metal frame,
    four small feet **15.00**
Trinket Box, glass, Sandwich pattern,
  Duncan & Miller, 3¾" × 5" **85.00**
Vanity Box, cov, glass, Fostoria
  Blue **100.00**
  Vaseline **125.00**

DRINKING GLASSES, PROMOTIONAL

It is time to start dealing seriously with promotional glasses given away by fast food restaurants, garages, and other merchants. This category also includes drinking glasses that start out life as product containers.

Most glasses are issued in a series. If you collect one, you better plan on keeping at it until you have the complete series. Also, many of the promotions are regional. A collector in Denver is not likely to find a Philadelphia Eagles glass at her favorite restaurant.

Just a few washings in a dishwasher can seriously change the color on promotional drinking glasses. Collectors insist on unused, unwashed glasses whenever possible. Get the glass, drink your drink out of a paper cup.

Arby's, name in stain glass look, 5" h . . . **3.50**
Big Boy, 50th anniversary **3.00**
Borden's, Elsie The Cow, dutch cos-
  tume **10.00**
Burger Chef, Burger Chef and Jeff Go
  Trail Riding, 1976 . . . . **8.00**
Burger King
  1978, See These Burgers. **11.00**
  1979, Sir Shake A Lot **5.00**
Chuck E Cheese, Pizza Time Theater **5.00**
Country Time Lemonade, Norman Rock-
  well, Saturday Evening Post scene,
  Grandpa's Girl. **5.00**
Domino's Pizza, Noid at the Beach **3.00**
Kentucky Fried Chicken, bucket and bal-
  loon **6.50**
McDonald's
  Adventureland Series, Grimace climbs
    a mountain, 1980 . . . . **6.50**
  Camp Snoopy, 1983 . . . . **3.00**
  Capt Cook, 12 oz, thick base **10.00**
  McDonaldland Series, Big Mac on
    roller skates, 5⅝" h, 1977 . . . . **3.50**
Pizza Hut, ET Collector Series, Be Good,
  1982. . . . . **2.50**
Popeye's Fried Chicken, Swee' Pea,
  1979. . . . . **10.00**
Taco Bell, Star Trek, four different de-
  signs. **5.00**
Welch's Jelly, Mr Magoo, 1962 . . . . **7.00**
Wendy's, Cleveland Browns, Brian Sipe,
  1981. . . . . **5.00**

DRUGSTORE COLLECTIBLES

The corner drugstore, especially one with a soda fountain, was a major hangout center in almost every small town in the United States. Almost all of them dispensed much more than drugs. They were the 7–11s of their era.

This category documents the wide variety of material that you could acquire in a drugstore. It barely scratches the surface. This is a new collecting approach that has real promise.

W. H. Bull's Vegetable Worm Syrup, cardboard box, 1920s boy on front, orig contents, $20.00.

Bath Set, Spring Morning Shower Mitt
  Set, 3 pcs **14.00**
Book, *Hand Book of Pharmacy & Therapeutics*, Eli Lilley & Co **85.00**
Booklet, Royal Tooth Powder, 1890s ... **23.00**
Bottle
  Eli Lilley & Co, gentian, 1 pt **16.00**
  Wallace Laboratories, Brunswick, NJ,
    soma carisoprodol **6.50**
Box
  Cutex Deluxe, wood, Art Deco, gift
    set **85.00**
  Feen-A-Mint Chewing Gum Laxative **20.00**
  Smith Brothers Cough Drops, 39 × 18
    × 10", wood **75.00**
Calendar, Colgate, miniature, flower,
  1901 .... **15.00**
Clock, Rexall, double face, electric **155.00**

Display, Peter Rabbit Safety Pins, colorful
  cartoon **25.00**
Fan
  666 Laxative **17.50**
  Tums, 1920s **18.50**
Glass, Bromo Seltzer **25.00**
Hair Care Products
  Capri Automatic Hair Curler, 5¼ × 4¾"
    orig box **12.00**
  Richard Hudnut Home Permanent
    Plastic Curling Rods, orig box containing 50 standard and 10 extra
    long rods **12.00**
Liniment, Banalag Mild Non-Greasy, ½
  oz bottle **6.00**
Mirror
  People's Drug, birthstones, pocket.... **20.00**
  Star Soap, pocket **20.00**
Needle Case, Bromo Seltzer **10.00**
Playing Cards, Speedy Alka Seltzer **30.00**
Post Card, Speedy Alka Seltzer **15.00**
Sign
  Dolly Madison Cigar, 6 × 20", tin **20.00**
  Nature's Remedy, porcelain **265.00**
  Professional Pharmacists, brass **18.00**
Thermometer
  Ex-Lax, 8 × 36", porcelain **135.00**
  Ramon's Kidney & Laxative Pills, 8½ ×
    21", wood, c1930 .... **175.00**
Tin
  Bayer Aspirin, 7" d **100.00**
  Century Tobacco, factory graphics,
    flat, pocket **110.00**
  Golden Pheasant Condom **88.00**
  Ramses Condoms, 1929 .... **60.00**
  Rexall Foot Powder, blue **15.00**
  Three Merry Widows, condoms...... **25.00**
  Velvet Night Talc **26.00**
Vitamins
  Beta-Concemin Ferrated Vitamins,
    Wm S Merrill Co, 100 capsules..... **8.75**
  Gelatric Vitamin-Mineral Supplement,
    Premo Pharm Lab, 100 capsules.... **8.75**
  Kelpamalt Vitamins, Kelpamalt Co ... **4.50**

EASTER COLLECTIBLES

Now that Christmas and Halloween collectibles have been collected to death, holiday collectors are finally turning their attention to Easter Collectibles. The old Easter bonnet still hangs in the Clothing Collectibles closet, but chicken and rabbit collectors now have to contend with Easter enthusiasts for their favorite animal collectible.

Newsletter: *Hearts to Holly: The Holiday Collectors Newsletter*, P. O. Box 105, Amherst, NH 03031.

Toy, celluloid, pink, black, and yellow, 3½" l, $25.00.

Basket
    6" h, reeded, pink, handle, Germany **20.00**
    8" d, yellow metal, metal handle, rabbits and chicks painted on outside, Chein Toy Co. **15.00**
Candy Container
    Basket, cardboard, rect, two chicks on each end, marked "Ertel Bros Wmspt, PA" **18.00**
    Duck, 4" h, yellow composition, ribbon around neck, standing on 3" d round cardboard box, opens at base, Germany **35.00**
    Egg, 6" l, litho tin, rabbits and chicks dec, marked "Colmar, USA" **22.00**
    Rabbit, 8" h, pot belly, white, head and ears on wire spring, white glass beaded trim, separates at belt line, marked "US Zone, Germany" **15.00**
Egg
    Bisque, 2 pc, cupid, dove with letter, Germany **150.00**
    China, daisies, gold dec, Dresden **35.00**
    Glass, 5" l, white, opaque, painted spring scene, "Happy Easter" painted in gold trim **25.00**
Post Card
    "Bright and Happy Easter for You," Gibson Girl kissing chick in garden **1.25**
    "Easter Greetings," children watching two rabbits kissing, 1910 . . . . **2.00**
Rabbit
    1½" h, diecut, multicolored, marked "Germany" **1.25**
    5" h, plastic, hard, mother rabbit dressed in yellow, brown glasses . . . **7.00**

EGG CUPS

Where modern Americans would be hard-pressed to recognize, let alone know how to use, an egg cup, their European counterparts still utilize the form as an everyday breakfast utensil. Their greatest period of popularity in America was between 1875 and 1950—long before cholesterol became a four-letter word.

A plain white porcelain egg cup works just as well as a fancifully decorated one. The fact that so many different and highly decorative egg cups exist show our unwillingness to accept the mundane at the breakfast table.

Collectors place a premium on character egg cups. You can make a great collection consisting of egg cups from breakfast services of hotels, railroads, steamships, or restaurants. As tourists, many of our ancestors had a bad case of sticky fingers.

Finally, do not forget the various scissor-like devices designed to decapitate the egg. Would you even recognize one if you saw one? I saw one once at a flea market marked as a circumcision device. *Ouch!*

Porcelain, French, blue florals, white ground, marked "Made In France," 3½" h, price for pair, $35.00.

Belleek, Irish, basketweave, pink rim, first black mark **150.00**
Character, ceramic
    Lone Ranger, 2½" h, raised portrait, Lone Ranger Inc. copyright on base, c1950 . . . . **35.00**
    Supercar, 2¼" h, white, raised Supercar, marked "Keele St. Pty. Co. Ltd., England," 1962 AP Film Ltd copyright **80.00**
French Porcelain, blue floral dec, white ground, marked "Made In France," pr **30.00**
Homer Laughlin, Yellowstone pattern, Southwestern motif decal **20.00**
John Maddock & Sons, Ltd, Indian Tree pattern, 4" h **25.00**
Limoges, France, multicolored florals, 2½" h **12.00**

Meissen, Blue Onion pattern **20.00**
Quimper, peasant man, yellow
    ground, marked "Henriot Quimper,
    France" **35.00**
Southern Potteries, Blue Ridge, green
    and red floral design, white ground . . . **25.00**
Taylor, Smith & Taylor, Lu Ray pattern,
    Sharon Pink **18.00**
Universal Pottery, Ballerina pattern, Jade
    Green **12.00**
Watcombe Pottery, Torquay pattern, cot-
    tage dec, motto "Straight From the
    Nest," 1¾" h **12.00**
Wedgwood, Caneware, brown scrolling
    vine dec, c1820 . . . . **275.00**
Willow Ware, blue, marked "Wood and
    Sons" **15.00**
W S George Co, Petalware, light blue . . . **14.00**

ELEPHANT COLLECTIBLES

Public television's unending series of doc-
umentaries on African wildlife has destroyed the fascination associated with
wild animals. By the time parents take
their children to the zoo or circus, elephants are old hat, blasé. Boo, hiss to public television—those pompous pachy-
derms. We want the mystery and
excitement of wildlife returned to us.

Things were different for the pre-televi-
sion generations. The elephant held a fascination that is difficult for us to compre-
hend. When Barnum brought Jumbo from
England to America, English children (and
a fair amount of adults) wept.

There are a few elephant-related political collectibles listed. It is hard to escape
the G.O.P. standard bearer. However, real
elephant collectors focus on the mag-
nificent beasts themselves or cartoon representations ranging from Dumbo to Colonel Hathi.

Club: The National Elephant Collector's
Society, 380 Medford Street, Somerville,
MA 02145.

Advertising Trade Card, Clark's O N T
    Spool Cotton, Jumbo Aesthetic, ele-
    phant walking on hind legs **5.00**
Book, *Walt Disney's Dumbo of The Circus,*
    Garden City, 1941, 10 × 11", 52 pgs . . . **50.00**
Bookmark, 7½" l, cardboard, triangular
    shape, text "Here's Walt Disney's
    Dumbo Of The Circus And His Little
    Pal Timothy," c1940 . . . . **25.00**

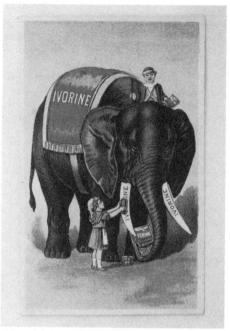

*Advertising Trade Card, Ivorine, adv on back,
5" h, $5.00.*

Cheese Cutting Board, 8 × 13", elephant
    shape, cherry hardwood **85.00**
Child's Tea Set, 11 pcs, elephant dec **35.00**
Chocolate Mold, tin, three cavities **75.00**
Doorstop, 10" h, cast iron **25.00**
Figure
    Dumbo, 5½" h, china, Shaw Pottery,
        mid 1940s **100.00**
    Fantasia Elephant, 5½" h, ceramic,
        wearing pink dress, American Pot-
        tery **150.00**
Ink Blotter, 6⅛ × 3⅜", Hummel Ware-
    house Co, elephant and monkey illus
    and 1941 calendar on cov **4.00**
Pin, 1" d, elephant shape, inscribed
    "Carlsberg Beer," diecut, silvered
    brass **15.00**
Pinback Button, 1½" d, elephant shape,
    inscribed "Willkie," silvered brass **10.00**
Pitcher, Dumbo, ceramic, white, pink
    and blue dec, Leeds China, marked
    "Walt Disney Dumbo 2 Qt Jug,"
    1947 . . . . **85.00**
Toy
    Pull, litho tin, marked "Made In Ger-
        many" **30.00**
    Squeaker, 6½" h, Dumbo, rubber,
        movable head, Walt Disney Produc-
        tions copyright, 1950s **20.00**
Vase, 12½" h, Satsuma, elephant head
    handles, Japanese **85.00**

ELVIS

Dad grew up with Elvis and ignored him. Always knew he was a bit of a prude. Fortunately, millions of others did not. Elvis was hot, is hot, and promises to be hot well into the future. Elvis is a collectible that is bought from the heart, not the head. A great deal of totally tacky material has been forgiven by his devoted fans.

Elvis material breaks down into two groups: (1) items licensed while Elvis was alive and (2) items licensed after his death. The latter are known as "fantasy" items. Fantasy Elvis is collectible, but real value rests with the material licensed during his lifetime.

Beware of any limited edition Elvis. It was manufactured in such large numbers that its long-term prospects are very poor. If you love it, fine. If you expect it to pay for your retirement, forget it.

Whiskey Bottle, McCormick, second in series, $90.00.

Autograph, photo, sgd "To Liz, love Elvis".......................**185.00**
Book, *The Elvis Presley Story*, Hillman Books, 1960, 160 pgs **35.00**
Bust, 8" h, plaster, copyright symbol "TR Pottery 63" **50.00**

Calendar, 11" sq, full color glossy, RCA, 1963.......................... **30.00**
Catalog, RCA Victor Records, Elvis pictorial, 1964....................... **48.00**
Cup, souvenir, "Elvis," Memphis, TN ... **45.00**
Decanter, musical, 1955............. **55.00**
Jewelry
  Dog Tag Bracelet, 2 × 6½", orig insert card and plastic bag, 1956........ **40.00**
  Necklace, *Love Me Tender* heart, orig pkg........................**175.00**
Lobby Card, 11 × 14", *Flaming Star*, color illus, 20th Century Fox, 1960........ **12.50**
Magazine, *Rock 'N Roll Jamboree*, 8 × 11", issue #1, six-page article and black and white photos, 1956.............. **25.00**
Photo, 8 × 10", color glossy, signature, Speedway record album insert, 1968........................ **18.00**
Photo Album, souvenir, 8½ × 11", 12 pgs, copyright 1956 Elvis Presley Enterprises....................... **50.00**
Poster, 21 × 27", *Girls! Girls! Girls!*, color, Paramount, 1960 .... **5.00**
Purse, clutch, 1956................. **35.00**
Record
  King Creole, RCA Victor, black label, long play **15.00**
  Love Me Tender/Any Way You Want Me, RCA Victor label, 1956 .... **50.00**
Scarf, concert souvenir.............. **10.00**
Sheet Music, *Love Me Tender*, pink tone photo cov, 2 pgs, copyright 1956 Elvis Presley Music Inc **25.00**
Tab, 2" d, litho tin, orange and blue "I Love Elvis" lettering, white ground, 1970s........................ **20.00**

EYEGLASSES

Look around. Eyeglasses come in all shapes and sizes. There are even designer models. Form and shape changes to correspond with subsequent fashion shifts. Yet, given all this, the number of eyeglass collectors is relatively small. Existing collectors love this; it keeps prices very low.

Do not forget those cool shades. I am constantly amazed at what people are willing to wear in order to protect their eyes from the sun. You could create a pizazz collection if you simply concentrated on 1950s sunglasses.

Eyeglasses
  Driving, white leather side pieces **25.00**
  Opera, orig case................... **50.00**
  Plastic tortoise shell rims, near round lenses, 1950s.................. **75.00**
  Safety, round lenses, mesh protection pieces on side, orig box **20.00**

Wire rims, oval lenses, c1900 . . . . **5.00**
Sunglasses, plastic
    Purple frames, round lenses, c1965 . . . **2.00**
    White frames, oval lenses, wing-like
    flaired upper edge on each side,
    1950s **3.00**

FAIRY TALE COLLECTIBLES

Thank goodness for fairies. They keep the line between myth and reality blurred. Where would children be without the tooth fairy or Cinderella without her fairy godmother? I have told some fairy tales in my time that I hoped the listener would believe were true.

This category is a celebration of the characters and the tales. It also celebrates the spirit of fairy tales—the hopes and dreams. There is a pot of gold at the end of the rainbow, isn't there?

Puzzle, Mother Goose Scroll Puzzle, McLoughlin Brothers, NY, $65.00.

Book
  Alice's Adventures in Wonderland, Lewis
    Carroll, Garden City, 216 pgs **12.00**
  Beautiful Stories for Children, Charles
    Dickens, 1908 . . . . **5.00**
  Favorite Fairy Tales Told in Italy, Vir-
    ginia Haviland, Little Brown, 1965,
    90 pgs. **15.00**
  Hansel & Gretel, 1908 . . . . **7.00**
  The Happy Prunie and Other Fairy Tales,
    Oscar Wilde, 1913, 204 pgs. **225.00**

The Land of Oz, Rand McNally, 1939
    copyright, 64 pgs **40.00**
Once Upon A Monday, Dixie Willson,
    Volland, 1931 . . . . **16.00**
Rumpelstiltskin, Edith Tarcov, Four
    Winds, 1974, 46 pgs **45.00**
Bracelet, "Who's Afraid of the Big Bad
  Wolf," silvered brass, black, green, and
  yellow accents, early 1930s **125.00**
Butter Dish, Little Red Riding Hood,
  Hull **290.00**
Carrying Case, Alice In Wonderland, 4 ×
  11 × 8½", heavy cardboard, white plas-
  tic handle, Neevel, Disney copyright
  1951 . . . . **40.00**
Child's Dinnerware Set, Alice in Won-
  derland, 17 pcs, service for four, beige,
  Plasco **40.00**
Christmas Card, Peter Pan, 4 × 5", diecut,
  orig envelope, c1953 . . . . **10.00**
Cookie Jar
  Goldilocks **195.00**
  Old King Cole **395.00**
Doll
  Limited Edition, Edwin M. Knowles,
    Heroines from the Fairy Tale Forests
    of the Brother's Grimm
    Goldilocks, 1989 . . . . **65.00**
    Little Red Riding Hood **70.00**
  Madame Alexander, Snow White,
    14" h, plastic, green plastic sleep
    eyes, real lashes, painted features,
    closed mouth, orig tagged ivory
    satin gown, marked "Walt Disney
    Snow White Madame Alexander
    USA," c1952 . . . . **500.00**
Figure, Snow White, 5" h, china, Japan,
  c1960 . . . . **20.00**
Game, The Wonderful Game of Oz, Par-
  ker Brothers, 1921 . . . . **300.00**
Plaque, 13 × 16", figural, Cinderella, die-
  cut laminated cardboard, 1951 copy-
  right **20.00**
Puppet, hand, Pinocchio, 10" h, velvet
  body, molded cardboard head with
  flocking, c1940 . . . . **125.00**
Sheet Music
  Over The Rainbow, 9¼ × 12¼", brown
    tone photo **30.00**
  So This Is Love, Cinderella, 9 × 12",
    white and pink cov, 1949 . . . . **20.00**
Snowdome, souvenir, Story Land, plas-
  tic, fairy tale characters, 1960s **8.00**
Tea Set
  Aluminum, nursery rhyme dec, 15
    pcs **22.00**
  Tin, Snow White, 8 pcs, orig box, Ohio
    Art **125.00**

FARM COLLECTIBLES

The agrarian myth of the rugged individual pitting his or her mental and physical

talents against the elements remains a strong part of the American character in the 1990s. There is something pure about returning to the soil.

The Country look heavily utilizes the objects of rural life, from cast iron seats to wooden rakes. This is one collectible where collectors want an aged, i.e., well worn, appearance. Although most of the items were factory-made, they have a handcrafted look. The key is to find objects that have character, a look that gives them a sense of individuality.

Club: Cast Iron Seat Collectors Association, RFD #2, Box 40, Le Center, MN 56057.

multicolored, woman wearing Western outfit, feeding chickens, c1930 . . .	8.00
Sap Spout, wood, carved	5.00
Sheep Shears, 13¾" l, steel, marked "Cast Steel, W P Ward"	20.00
Shovel, cast iron, wooden handle	25.00
Sign, Goodyear Farm Tires, porcelain, two-sided, diecut	225.00
Stickpin, P & O Canton, plow shape	20.00
Thermometer, John Deere, commemorating 150th Anniversary	45.00

Watch Fob
Allis Chalmers	
Grader	28.00
Tractor	28.00
Caterpiller, tractor	20.00
Gardner Denver Jackhammer	25.00
Lima Shovels, Draglines	22.00
Unit Crane Shovels	25.00

Advertising Brochure, **The Adventures of Ceresota,** *©1912 Northwestern Consolidated Milling Co, written by Marshall Whitlach, illustrated by Alice Sargent Johnson, 8" l, 6" h, $20.00.*

Calendar, John Deere, 1920s	35.00
Catalog, Kraus Farm Cultivators, 1911, 62 pgs.	20.00
Chick Feeder, tin.	15.00
Corn Dryer, wrought iron	15.00
Corn Sheller	
F F Company	800.00
Gray Brothers	350.00
Egg Candler, 8" h, tin, kerosene burner, mica window	20.00
Feed Bag, cotton, black illus of sheep . . .	7.50
Hay Rake, varnished, 48½" l	50.00
Hinge, barn, wrought iron, strap, 27" l	60.00
Implement Seat, cast iron, Hoover & Co	65.00
Medallion	
John Deere Centennial, 1937	10.00
Syracuse Chilled Plow, plow and Admiral Dewey illus	12.00
Milking Stool, wooden, three short legs.	50.00
Pinback Button, Brinkler Ranch, 1" d,	

FARM TOYS

The average age of those who play with farm toys is probably well over thirty. Farm toys are adult toys. Collectors number in the tens of thousands. The annual farm toy show in Dyersville, Ohio, draws a crowd in excess of 15,000.

Beware of recent limited and special edition farm toys. The number of each toy being produced hardly qualifies them as limited. If you buy them other than for enjoyment, you are speculating. No strong resale market has been established. Collectors who are not careful are going to be plowed under.

Magazines: *Miniature Tractor and Implement,* R. D. #1, Box 90, East Springfield, PA 16411; *The Toy Farmer,* R. R. #2, Box 5, LaMoure, ND 58458; *The Toy Tractor Times,* P. O. Box 156, Osage, IA 50461.

Club: Ertl Replica Collectors' Club, Highways 136 and 10, Dyersville, IA 52040.

Baler, International Harvester, diecast, 1/16 scale, four bales, Ertl, 1967	18.00
Bulldozer, Caterpillar, driver, yellow, Matchbox, 1963	20.00
Combine Harvester, Corgi, #1111-A, 1959–1963	85.00
Corn Picker, Tru-Scale, pressed steel, 1/16 scale, Carter, 1971	70.00
Dairy Farm Set, Buddy L, No. 5050, includes blue No. 5210 Milkman Truck, red and gray No. 5260 Milk Tanker, and orange No. 5270 Farm Tractor, boxed set, 1961	65.00
Disc, International Harvester, diecast,	

Tractor, litho tin wind-up, rubber treads, green, red, and white, marked "Marx, Made in USA," $95.00.

1/16 scale, sure-lock hitch blades, Ertl, 1965 . . . . **20.00**
Disc Harrow, Dinky, #27-H, 1951 . . . . . . **25.00**
Elevator, John Deere, pressed steel, 1/16 scale, Carter, 1960 . . . . **85.00**
Farm Machinery Hauler, trailer and truck, Buddy L, No. 5586, 31½" l, 1956–1958 . . . . **95.00**
Farmyard Animals, Dinky, No. 2, pre– 1933 . . . . **35.00**
Furrow Plow, Corgi, #56-A1, four furrows, 1961–1963 . . . . **20.00**
Hay Rake, Dinky, #27-K, 1953 . . . . **20.00**
Horse-Drawn Farm Wagon, pull-n-ride, Buddy L, No. 1809, paper litho horse, steel wagon and seat, black rubber wheels, "Buddy L Farms" decals on wagon sides, 10" h, 23¾" l, 1952 . . . **75.00**
Horse Transporter, Corgi, #1105-B, 1976–1980 . . . . **50.00**
Industrial Crawler, Lionel, plastic, 1/43 scale, 1950 . . . . **35.00**
Livestock Trailer Truck
    Dodge, Corgi, #484-A, 1967–1972 . . . **50.00**
    Indian Head Trademark, Japan, friction, litho tin, black rubber tires, rear door opens, 9½" l, 1960s **90.00**
Manure Spreader, Dinky, #27-C, 1949 . . . . **45.00**
Milk Truck and Trailer, Corgi, #21-A, 1962–1966 . . . . **85.00**
Planter, White **15.00**
Tandem Disc Harrow, Corgi, #71-A, 1967–1972 . . . . **18.00**
Tipping Trailer, Corgi, #62-A, 1965– 1972 . . . . **22.00**
Tractor
    Ackerschlepper, Marklin, Germany, diecast, painted red, black rubber tires, orig driver and box, 3" l, 1950s **150.00**
    Allis Chalmers, Yoder, plastic, 1/25 scale, Beaver Falls Show insert **75.00**
    Ford, Tootsietoy, red, rubber tires **25.00**
    Fordson Halftrack, Corgi, #54-A, 1962–1964 . . . . **75.00**

K55 Electric, TM, Japan, battery operated, litho tin, multicolored, white rubber treads, forward and reverse gears, driver, orig box, 7" l, 1950s **275.00**
Massey-Harris, Dinky, #27-A, 1948 . . . . **75.00**
Tractor and Trailer
    Marx, litho tin, multicolored, self-reversing, orig box, 1936 . . . . **85.00**
    Matchbox, TP108-2, yellow **5.00**
Tractor Set, American Tractor, Marx, litho tin, multicolored tractor with driver, wagon, rake, and harrow, 1926 . . . .**200.00**
Triple Gang Mower, Dinky, #27-J, 1952 . . . . **60.00**
Truck
    Campbell Kids Farm Truck, Fisher Price, #845, pull toy, paper litho driver and side panels, orig box and booklet, 9" l **625.00**
    Dodge, Dinky, #30-N, green body, yellow stakes, 1950 . . . . **50.00**
Wagon, Minneapolis Moline, Slik, pressed steel, 1/32 scale, rubber wheels, 1950 . . . . **20.00**

FAST FOOD COLLECTIBLES

If you haunt fast food restaurants for the food, you are a true fast food junkie. Most collectors haunt them for the giveaways. If you stop and think about it, fast food collectibles are the radio and cereal premiums of the second half of the twentieth century. Look at what you have to eat to get them.

Whenever possible, try to preserve the original packaging of the premiums. Also, save those things which are most likely to be thrown out. I see a great many Happy Meals toys and few Happy Meals boxes. Dad saves fast food company bags. There is no accounting for taste.

Club: For Here or To Go, 2773 Curtis Way Sacramento, CA 95818.

A & W
    Decals, sheet, iron-on, Root Beer Bear and A & W logo, 1977 . . . . **2.50**
    Puppet, hand, Root Beer Bear, cloth **6.50**
Big Boy, figure, soft rubber **10.00**
Burger King
    Crown, cardboard, jewel-like design, "Have It Your Way" slogan **7.00**
    Doll, 16" h, cloth, red, yellow, peach, black, and white **7.50**

Burger King, doll, printed cloth, red, yellow, peach, black, and white, 16" h, $7.50.

Frisbee, 3¼" d, plastic, emb with
   Burger King character. 6.50
Pinback Button, ¾" d, metal, "Happy
   Face," eyes made of the Burger King
   Corporate logo 3.50
Carl's Jr
   Meal Box, Star Flyer, flying saucer,
     cardboard, 1985 . . . . 2.50
   Ring, plastic, Happy Star character in
     center of circle. 2.75
Dairy Queen, Glass, 5⅝" h, Little Miss
   Dairy Queen and red and white
   logo 2.00
Domino's Pizza
   Glass, 4⅛" h, frosted design and
     logo 2.00
   Toy, 5" h, Noid, plastic, poseable and
     bendable, 1987 . . . . 5.00
Kentucky Fried Chicken
   Meal Box, "Colonel's Kids," features
     Foghorn Leghorn, 1987 . . . . 2.00
   Nodder, Colonel Sanders 135.00
McDonald's
   Bank, plastic, McDonaldland, waste-
     basket, 1975 . . . . 7.50
   Colorforms   Playset,   premium,
     1986. . . . . 2.00
   Comb, Ronald McDonald, plastic,
     1980. 75
   Figure, Ronald McDonald, 12" h, ce-
     ramic, 1980s 12.00
   Glass, 5⅝" h, Collector Series, Big
     Mac, Captain Crook, Grimace, Ham-
     burglar, Mayor McCheese, and
     Ronald McDonald, mid 1970s, set of
     6 . . . . 25.00
   Mug, 4¹⁵⁄₁₆" h, ceramic, white, golden
     arches and red lettering 7.00
   Radio, french fry, 1st version, AM,
     1977. . . . . 25.00

Wendy's
   Doll, 11½" h, cloth 5.00
   Glass, 5⅞" h, white, black, and
     pink "Where's The Beef?" design,
     1984. . . . . 6.00
   Mug, 3¹³⁄₁₆" h, ceramic, white ground,
     red, white, and black design 4.00
   Ring, 3½" d, Fun Flyer, plastic. 1.00

FENTON ART GLASS

Frank L. Fenton founded the Fenton Art
Glass Company as a glass-cutting operation in Martins Ferry, Ohio, in 1905. In
1906 construction began on a plant in Williamstown, West Virginia. Production began in 1907 and has been continuing ever
since.

The list of Fenton glass products is endless. Early production included carnival,
chocolate, custard, pressed, and opalescent glass. In the 1920s stretch glass, Fenton dolphins, and art glass were added.
Hobnail, opalescent, and two-color overlay pieces were popular in the 1940s. In
the 1950s Fenton began reproducing Bur-
mese and other early glass types.

Throughout its production period, Fenton has made reproductions and copycats
of famous glass types and patterns. Today
these reproductions and copycats are
collectible in their own right. Check out
Dorothy Hammond's *Confusing Collectibles:
A Guide to the Identification of Contemporary
Objects* (Wallace-Homestead: 1979, revised
edition) for clues to spotting the reproductions and copycats of Fenton and other
glass manufacturers of the 1950s and
1960s.

Club: Fenton Art Glass Collectors of
America, Inc., P. O. Box 384, Williamstown, WV 26187.

Banana Boat, Silver Crest. 30.00
Basket,   Opalescent   Hobnail,   blue,
   4" h. 40.00
Bonbon, Violets In Snow, dec 12.00
Candlestick, Opalescent Hobnail, cran-
   berry, handle. 55.00
Console Set, Jadite, 8" d bowl and pr
   candlesticks. 50.00
Cornucopia, Ivory Crest 40.00
Cruet, orig stopper
   Aqua Crest. 75.00
   Opalescent Hobnail, blue 32.00
Cup and Saucer
   Aqua Crest. 45.00
   Jadite 15.00

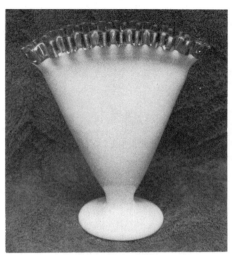

Gold Crest, vase, fan shape, frosted white body, ruffled amber rim, 6" w, 7" h, $20.00.

Fairy Lamp, Burmese, hp rose dec	55.00
Ginger Jar, cov, French Opalescent Hobnail, 4½" h	55.00
Hat, Opalescent Hobnail, blue, 4" h	25.00
Ivy Ball, Ruby Overlay	50.00
Juice Tumbler, Opalescent Hobnail, blue	12.00
Mayonnaise Set, Opalescent Hobnail, blue, 3 pcs	60.00
Plate	
Aqua Crest, 6½" d	13.50
Emerald Crest, 6½" d	18.00
Jadite, 10" d	25.00
Sherbet	
Georgian, low, flared	12.50
Silver Crest	15.00
Stretch, green	18.00
Tidbit Tray, Silver Crest, three tiers	30.00
Tumbler	
Opalescent Hobnail	
Blue, 4¼" h	14.00
Lime green, 4¼" h, set of six	27.00
Silver Crest, 5¾" h, ftd	50.00
Salt and Pepper Shakers, pr, Opalescent Hobnail, cranberry	66.00
Vase	
Diamond Optic, opalescent blue, 8" h	40.00
Emerald Crest, 4½" h	35.00
Hand, milk glass	25.00
Opalescent Hobnail, blue, fan, 6" h	30.00
Sheffield, blue, 8" h	25.00
Silver Crest, 12" h, fan	95.00

FIESTA WARE

Fiesta was the Melmac ware of the mid 1930s. The Homer Laughlin China Company introduced Fiesta dinnerware in January 1936 at the Pottery and Glass Show in Pittsburgh, Pennsylvania. It was a huge success.

The original five colors were red, dark blue, light green (with a trace of blue), brilliant yellow, and ivory. Other colors were added later. Fiesta was redesigned in 1960, discontinued in 1972–1973, and reintroduced in 1986. It appears destined to go on forever.

Value rests in form and color. Forget the rumors about the uranium content of early red-colored Fiesta. No one died of radiation poisoning from using Fiesta. However, rumor has it that they glowed in the dark when they went to bed at night.

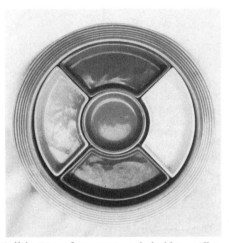

Relish Tray, four parts, cobalt blue, yellow, white, and orange, turquoise base, $75.00.

Ashtray	
Green	25.00
Red	35.00
Bowl	
4¾" d, fruit, dark green	16.00
6" d, dessert, red	38.00
8½" d, rose	30.00
Bud Vase, ivory	48.00
Cake Plate, yellow, Kitchen Kraft	30.00
Candlesticks, pr	
Bulbous, cobalt blue	65.00
Tripod, pink	85.00
Carafe, turquoise	140.00
Casserole, cov, 8½" d, ivory	90.00
Chop Plate, 13" d	
Gray	30.00
Light green	20.00
Coffeepot, cov, chartreuse	235.00
Compote, 12" d, cobalt blue	135.00
Cream Soup, yellow	30.00

Creamer
 Medium Green **60.00**
 Red, individual **120.00**
Cup
 Cobalt Blue **18.00**
 Light Green **12.00**
Cup and Saucer, rose **30.00**
Deep Plate
 Ivory **18.00**
 Yellow **20.00**
Egg Cup, chartreuse **70.00**
Gravy Boat, light blue. **32.00**
Jar, cov, large, cobalt blue, Kitchen
 Kraft **260.00**
Jug, 2 pint, ivory. **35.00**
Juicer, cobalt blue. **20.00**
Marmalade, turquoise **160.00**
Mixing Bowl
 #1, red **90.00**
 #2, green **70.00**
 #3, ivory **65.00**
 #4, turquoise. **60.00**
 #5, cobalt blue. **85.00**
 #6, turquoise. **80.00**
 #7, green **150.00**
Mug
 Cobalt Blue **60.00**
 Yellow **45.00**
Mustard, cov, light green **50.00**
Nappy, 8½" d, forest green **32.00**
Pitcher, disc
 Juice, yellow **27.00**
 Water, ivory **70.00**
Plate
 6" d, dessert, gray **7.00**
 7½" d, bread and butter, cobalt
 blue **8.00**
 9" d, luncheon, red. **13.00**
 10" d, dinner, cobalt blue **28.00**
 10" d, grill, light green **22.00**
 12" d, grill, yellow **30.00**
 13" d, grill, cobalt blue **25.00**
Platter, 12" l, oval, dark green **20.00**
Refrigerator Dish, cov, round, blue,
 Kitchen Kraft **75.00**
Relish Tray, light blue. **18.00**
Salad Bowl
 Green, footed **190.00**
 Red, individual **60.00**
Salt and Pepper Shakers, pr, red-or-
 ange. **15.00**
Saucer, green **3.00**
Soup, cov, cobalt and cream. **35.00**
Stack Set, green **22.00**
Sugar, cov, turquoise **18.00**
Syrup, yellow **125.00**
Tea Cup, red **20.00**
Tea Cup and Saucer, gray. **35.00**
Teapot
 Large, green **125.00**
 Medium, turquoise. **85.00**
Tidbit Tray, medium green, three
 tiered. **175.00**
Tray, cobalt blue, figure eight shape **55.00**

Tumbler
 Juice, rose **35.00**
 Water, yellow **38.00**
Utility Tray, light green **25.00**
Vase, 6½" h, red **25.00**
Vegetable Bowl, medium green. **65.00**

FIGURINES

Looking for a "small" with character? Try collecting ceramic figurines. Collecting interest in the colorful figurines produced by firms such as Ceramic Arts Studio, Florence Ceramics, Vernon Kilns, and others has grown considerably during the past ten years. Pieces are starting to become pricy. However, there are still bargains to be found. A surprising number of these figurines are found at garage sales and flea markets at prices below $10.00.

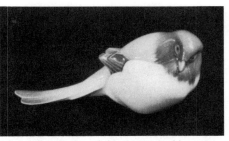

Bird, Bing & Grondahl, #1635-R, blue, gray, and white, 4½" l, $68.00.

Alice in Wonderland, 6" h, 1960 Disney
 copyright. **18.00**
Archibald the Dragon, Ceramic Arts Stu-
 dio **70.00**
Arthur, boy with chicken, Brayton Pot-
 tery **35.00**
Bear, brown spray glaze, 10" h, Midwest
 Potteries, 1940–1944 . . . . **30.00**
Bernhardt, Sarah, 13¼" h, Florence Ce-
 ramics **375.00**
Boy, fishing, Weller Pottery. **215.00**
Bugs Bunny, light gray, white, and
 pink, brown base, name inscribed on
 front, 7¼" h, Warner Bros copyright,
 c1940. . . . . **110.00**
Cat, Persian, white, Royal Doulton,
 #2539 . . . . **150.00**
Collie, gray, 9" l, Gonder Pottery. **15.00**
Cowboy on Bronco, black, gold dec,
 7½" h, Midwest Potteries, 1940–
 1944 . . . . **25.00**
Donkey, miniature, 2" h, Hagen Rena-
 ker, 1986. . . . . **10.00**
Dumbo, seated, wearing yellow bonnet,
 5½" h, Shaw **60.00**

Dutch Shoe, pig sitting inside 35.00
Elephant, standing on log, ginger jar on
  back, chocolate drip glaze, 6½" h,
  Cliftwood Art Potteries 60.00
Frog, Niloak Pottery 20.00
Fruit Girl, 10" h, Abingdon Pottery 90.00
Goose, long neck, white, yellow dec,
  5¾" h, Midwest Potteries, 1940–
  1944 . . . . 8.00
Hen, cream body, brown trim, 11" h,
  Pennsbury Pottery 225.00
Horse's Head, bluish-green, 13" h, Gon-
  der Pottery 35.00
Kangaroo, burgundy, 2½" h, Morton
  Pottery 6.50
Kitten, white, on brown shoe, 3" l, Ja-
  pan 9.00
Native Girl, hand on hip, blue and white
  slit skirt, bikini top, Brayton Laguna-
  type Pottery, 12" h 40.00
Nude, kneeling, 7" h, Abingdon Pot-
  tery 160.00
Oriental Coolie, pink and green glaze,
  8" h, Gonder Pottery 18.00
Panther, jade green, Gonder Pottery,
  18¼" l 90.00
Parrot, perched on stump, blue, yellow,
  and white, brown spray glaze on
  white, 4½" h, Midwest Potteries,
  1940–1944 . . . . 12.00
Polar Bear, white matte, Niloak Pot-
  tery 35.00
Pony, miniature, Wade, England, Tom
  Smith artist 15.00
Sprite, Vernon Kilns 135.00
Stallion, rearing, gold, 10¾" h, Midwest
  Potteries, 1940–1944 . . . . 25.00
Swordfish, yellow, 5" h, Morton Pot-
  tery 8.00
Unicorn, black, Disney movie
  "Fantasia," Vernon Kilns 200.00
Whippet, Morton Studios, c1940 . . . . 80.00

FIREARMS

A majority of Americans own firearms.
However, many have them and do not use
them. Neglecting to properly care for a
firearm can seriously damage its value.
Avoid any weapons that show excessive
use or heavy signs of rust.

Before selling or buying a handgun,
check federal, state, and local laws. (A dis-
crete call to your local state police or a local
gun dealer will provide you with much
needed information). Modern handguns
must be sold only by a licensed federal
firearms dealer. Do not take a chance by
selling outside the law.

Gun collectors are a world unto their
own. They buy and sell through specialized gun shows. Check your local paper for
the one closest to you.

A surprising number of firearms have
low value. Do not be deceived by age. Age
alone does not make a gun valuable. The
key is collectibility.

The following sampling barely scratches
the surface. For antique firearms consult
Norman Flayderman's *Flayderman's Guide
To Antique American Firearms. . . . And Their
Values, 4th Edition* (DBI Books: 1987). For
modern weapons, see Russell and Steve
Quetermous's *Modern Guns: Identification &
Values, Revised 8th Edition* (Collector Books:
1991).

Newspaper: *Gun List*, 700 East State
Street, Iola, WI 54990.

*Pistol, E. Whitney, New Haven, CT, Navy Re-
volver, 6 cylinder, $45.00.*

Handgun
  Beretta Model 1923, .9mm Luger,
    semi-automatic, exposed hammer,
    9-shot magazine, 4" barrel, blued,
    wood grips .250.00
  Charter Arms Bulldog, .44 Special, sin-
    gle action, 5-shot swing out cylin-
    der, 4" barrel, blued, checkered wal-
    nut bulldog grips 135.00
  Cobray Mac-11 .9mm, semi-automatic
    pistol, 5¼" barrel with machined
    threads for barrel extension or
    surpressor, 12 and 32 shot staggered
    magazines, O. D. green cotton web
    sling with mounting clips 250.00
  Colt Peacemaker, .22 caliber, single ac-
    tion, 6-shot cylinder, side load, 7½"
    barrel, case-hardened grips 175.00
  C. V. A. Colt Walter, .44 caliber percus-
    sion black powder pistol, blued steel
    frame, engraved cylinder, walnut
    grips, brass trigger guard, 9" barrel, 4
    lbs 11 oz, 15½" l overall 165.00
  High Standard Sentinel Mark II, .357
    Magnum, single action, 6-shot
    swing out, 4" barrel, blued, check-
    ered walnut grips 150.00
  Ruger Mark I Target, .22 caliber
    long rifle, semi-automatic, con-
    cealed hammer thumb safety, 9-

shot magazine, 6" tapered round barrel, blued, checkered hard rubber grips **125.00**

Sterling, Model 283, .22 caliber long rifle, semi-automatic, exposed hammer, adjustable trigger, rear safety lock, 10-shot magazine, 8" heavy bull barrel, blued, checkered plastic grips **120.00**

Rifle

Colt Coltsman, Sako-Medium, .308 Winchester, medium stroke, Sako-type bolt action, repeating, 5-shot box, 24" blued barrel, checkered walnut Monte Carlo one piece pistol grip stock **275.00**

Military, British, Lee-Enfield, No. 1 SMLE MK1, .303 caliber, bolt action, curved bolt handle, 10-shot detachable box magazine, cut-off 25¼" barrel, plain wood military stock . . . **140.00**

Military, United States, U.S. M1 Carbine, .30 caliber, semi-automatic, 30 shot staggered row detachable box magazine, 18" barrel, one piece wood stock and forearm **350.00**

Remington Nylon 11, .22 caliber, bolt action, repeating, 10 shot magazine, 19½" round barrel, polished brown nylon one piece stock **75.00**

Shotgun

Bretta Model A-301, 12 gauge, semi-automatic, hammerless, 3-shot tubular, 30" full barrel, checkered walnut pistol grip stock and forearm . . . **300.00**

High Standard Supermatic Field, 20 gauge, semi-automatic, hammerless, 3-shot tube magazine, 26" barrel, plain walnut semi-pistol grip stock and fluted forearm **150.00**

Remington Model 27, 20 gauge, pump action, hammerless, bottom ejection, repeating, 3-shot tube magazine, 32" steel barrel, checkered walnut pistol grip and forearm **225.00**

Savage, 12 guage, regular, pump action, hammerless, 4-shot tube magazine, 28" modified barrel, hardwood semi-pistol grip stock and grooved side handle **150.00**

Winchester, Model 23 Pigeon Grade, lightweight, 20 gauge, magnum, box lock, break open top lever, hammerless, selective automatic ejectors, double, 26" modified barrel, Winchoke, checkered walnut semi-pistol grip stock and forearm **900.00**

FIRE-KING

Remember those great coffee mugs you used to find at diners? Those nice big

warm cups filled to the brim by a smiling waitress, not the styrofoam of this decade. Chances are they were Fire-King mugs. Fire-King dinnerware and ovenware were sold in sets in the 1940s through the 1970s. The company guaranteed to replace broken pieces, which made these colorful wares quite popular with housewives. While Fire-King has been around for many years, collectors are only now discovering quantities of it at flea markets and deciding to enjoy this new collecting area.

Restaurant Ware, jadite, mug, 7 oz, $5.00.

Dinnerware

Bowl, 4⅞" d, Jane Ray, jadite **4.00**

Creamer and Sugar

Game bird decal **20.00**

Jane Ray, jadite, orig label **14.00**

Swirl, white, brushed gold trim **5.00**

Cup and Saucer

Alice, white, blue trim **8.00**

Jane Ray, jadite **3.00**

Egg Plate, Turquoise Blue, 1950, orig label **10.00**

Iced Tea Tumbler, 11 oz, game bird decal **14.00**

Mug, game bird decal **12.50**

Plate

6⅛" d, game bird decal **6.50**

9" d, game bird decal **12.50**

9⅛" d, Jane Ray, jadite **6.00**

Salad Bowl, Turquoise Blue **10.00**

Salad Plate, 7¾" d, Jane Ray, jadite . . . **4.75**

Set, Jane Ray, jadite, 24 pc starter set, orig box **110.00**

Snack Plate, Plain Jane, turquoise, gold trim **4.00**

Soup Bowl, Jane Ray, jadite **9.00**

Vegetable Bowl, Turquoise Blue, 8" d **9.50**

Restaurant Ware, jadite

Bowl, 15 oz	**9.25**
Cereal Bowl, flange	**9.00**
Coffee Mug	**5.00**
Cup and Saucer, St Denis type	**9.50**
Pie Plate, 6¾" d	**3.00**
Plate, 9" d	**5.00**
Platter	**13.00**

Oven Glass, blue

Casserole, cov, 1 pint	**15.00**
Cereal Bowl, 5⅜" d	**12.50**
Coffee Mug, 7 oz	**24.50**
Cup and Saucer	**6.00**
Custard Cup, orig paper label	**3.00**
Loaf Pan	**20.00**
Mixing Bowl, 2 qt	**11.00**
Mug	**23.00**
Nurser, 4 oz	**14.00**
Percolator Top	**4.50**
Pie Plate, 8⅛" d	**8.50**

Plate

7" d	**10.00**
9" d	**8.50**
Roaster, cov, 10⅜" l	**70.00**
Utility Bowl, 10⅛" d	**17.00**
Vegetable Bowl, 8" d	**14.00**

FISH SETS

The Victorians had special china and silver serving pieces for every type of fruit, vegtable, and meat. There is no reason to expect fish to be treated any differently. Victorian and early twentieth century fish serving sets are desirable and elegant.

Some dealers break up sets feeling there is more profit in the individual piece than in the set. Do not buy from them. A minimum set consists of a serving platter and four to six plates. A sauce boat and other accessory pieces are a bonus.

5 pcs, platter, four plates, milk glass, Atterbury **225.00**
8 pcs, 24" l platter, four plates, sauce boat with attached underplate, and cov tureen, Rosenthal.................**350.00**
9 pcs, 24" l platter and eight 9" d plates, different fish with seaweed and floral dec, gold scalloped and emb borders, Limoges........................**495.00**
12 pcs, 23" l platter, ten 8¼" sq plates, and sauceboat, different fish, pale brown fish on ivory ground, heavy gold trim, Martial Redon, Limoges, 1880s.........................**895.00**
13 pcs, twelve sq plates and rect sauce boat, six different fishing scenes, cobalt blue border, gilt dec, underglaze green Limoges mark **275.00**
14 pcs, 24" l tray, twelve 9¼" d

plates, and sauceboat, fish swimming underwater with flying seagulls dec, wide gilt border, Imperial Limoges, France **1,540.00**
16 pcs, 24" l platter, twelve 9" plates, sauce boat with attached underplate, and cov tureen, hp, raised gold dec edge, artist sgd, Limoges...........**750.00**

FISHER PRICE TOYS

In 1930 Herman Guy Fisher, Helen Schelle, and Irving R. Price founded the Fisher Price Toy Company in Birmingham, New York. From that year forward Fisher Price Toys were built with a five-point creed. Each toy was built with intrinsic play value, ingenuity, strong construction, good value for the money, and action. With these principles and manufacturing contributions, the Fisher Price Toy Company has successfully produced quality and creativity in the toy market.

The collectibility of Fisher Price toys is a direct reflection of their desirability, which is due to their unique characteristics and subject matter.

Squeaky the Clown, 1958, $35.00.

Amusement Park, vinyl playmat, includes rides, train, swing, cars, boats, and seven figures, #932, 1963–65.... **65.00**
Bunny with Cart, wood, #456, 1939....**110.00**
Buzzy Bee, wood, spring antennas, #325, 1950..........................**20.00**
Cash Register, plastic keys, wood coins, #972, 1960 ....**40.00**
Change-A-Tune Piano, plastic keyboard, knob on one side, #910, 1969–72 .... **20.00**
Clown Jalopy, #724 ....**14.00**

Concrete-Mixer Truck, rotating corn popper mixer drum, tandem wheels, plastic grille, #926, 1959. . . . . **100.00**
Corn Popper, plastic dome, 17½" l, handle, #788 . . . . **35.00**
Duck, #190 . . . . **375.00**
Ducky Cart, wood, #470, 1946 . . . . **75.00**
Dump Truckers, #979, 1965–70 . . . . **35.00**
Elsie's Dairy Truck, wood, two milk bottles, orig box, #745, 1948 . . . . **225.00**
Ferris Wheel, plastic and wood, #969, 1966–81 . . . . **25.00**
Fisher Price Choo-Choo, engine, three wood and plastic cars, four wood little people, #719, 1963 . . . . **25.00**
Gabby Duck, opens and closes bill, #767, 1952–53 . . . . **20.00**
Giant Rock-A-Stack, plastic, screw-on top, 1961–80. **8.00**
Happy Helicopter, #498, 1953 . . . . **110.00**
Katy Kackler the Red Hen, wings and feet move up and down, plastic comb, orig box, #140, 1954. . . . . **85.00**
Looky Fire Truck, three round-headed fireman, two with bobbing heads, #7, 1950. . . . . **95.00**
Molly Moo Moo, orig box. **125.00**
Music Box Radio, plastic, #792, 1979–80. . . . . **8.00**
Music Box Record Player, plastic, windup knob, five numbered records play two songs each, #995, 1970s **25.00**
Musical Carousel, #969 . . . . **16.00**
Musical Push Chime, plastic, red handle with yellow knob, #722, 1950 . . . . . . **45.00**
Musical Sweeper, steel cov with two honey bears, 18½" l red handle with yellow knob, #225, 1953 . . . . **50.00**
Musical Teaching Clock **12.00**
Nifty Station Wagon, wood body and wheels, removable top, fold-down rear gate, four removable little people, #234, 1960 . . . . **120.00**
Peter Bunny Engine, wood, nickel plated bell, #721, 1949 . . . . **110.00**
Play Family A-Frame, plastic cabin, five family figures, #990, 1975–76 . . . . **45.00**
Play Family Airport, plastic, #996, 1972–76. . . . . **45.00**
Play Family Camper, plastic truck, lift-off cab, fishing boat, five little people, #994, 1972–76 . . . . **40.00**
Pop 'N Ring, three colored wood balls, nickel plated bell, 20" l handle, #808, 1956. . . . . **65.00**
Pop Up Kritter. **95.00**
Pull-A-Tune Xylophone, #870, 1957 . . . **45.00**
Quacko Duck, wood, #300, 1939. . . . . . . **70.00**
Safety School Bus, wood bottom and wheels, plastic top with removable wood center section, six removable little people, stationary driver, #938, 14" l, 1959. . . . . **100.00**

Strutter Donald Duck, wood, swinging arms, #510, 11" l, 1941 . . . . **110.00**
Sunny Fish, spring mounted wood tail, vinyl fin, #420, 6¾" l, 1955 . . . . **95.00**
Super Jet, pilot's head pivots around, acetate tail, wood wheels, #415, 1952. . . . . **85.00**
Tabby Ding Dong, wood, kitten engineer, jointed arm, #730, 1939 . . . . **200.00**
Teddy Tooter, wood, litho bear sits on rolling bandstand, 14" h, 1940 . . . . . . **125.00**
Timmy Turtle, legs swing back and forth, wood tail, acetate shell, orig box, #150, 1953. . . . . **75.00**
Tool Box Workbench, wood bench, molded plastic hinged lid holds tools, #935, 1969–70 . . . . **25.00**
Winky-Blinky Fire Truck, wood horn, orig box, #200, 1954. . . . . **75.00**
Woofy Wagger, wood, #447, 1947 . . . . . **65.00**

FISHING COLLECTIBLES

There has been a lot written recently about the increasing value of fishing tackle of all types. What has not been said is that high ticket items are very limited in number. The vast majority of items sell below $5.00.

Fishing collectors place strong emphasis on condition. If a rod, reel, lure, or accessory shows heavy use, chances are that its value is minimal. The original box and packaging are also important, often doubling value.

You will make a good catch if you find early wooden plugs made before 1920 (most that survive were made long after that date), split bamboo fly rods made by master craftsmen (not much value for commercial rods), or reels constructed of German silver with special detail and unique mechanical action. Fishing collectors also like to supplement their collection with advertising and other paper ephemera. Find a pile of this material and you have a lucky strike.

Club: National Fishing Lure Collectors Club, P. O. Box 01841, Chicago, IL 60690.

Advertising
Calendar, 14 × 18", Bristol Steel Rod Co, 1935 . . . . **55.00**
Catalog, Heddon Co, color illus, 1934. . . . . **45.00**
Sign, South Bend Co, boy holding stringer of fish **65.00**

Casting Reel, Pernell Reel Co, Philadelphia, 40-yard line capacity, all brass, 1½" d, $15.00.

Bobber, 5" l, panfish float, hp, black, red, and white stripes................. **10.00**
Book, *Fishing For Fun and To Wash Your Soul*, Random House, copyright 1963, 86 pgs, hard cov, dj............... **12.00**
Creel, 14 × 9 × 7", crushed willow, leather bound, form fit............... **24.00**
Decoy
  Oliver Reigstad, 1960............. **17.00**
  Sletten, cast aluminum, unopened, 1950s...................... **22.00**
Fly Rod, Horrocks & Ibbotson, 9' l, 3 pc, split bamboo, two tips, maroon wraps......................... **40.00**
Lure, wood
  Creek Chub Co, baby beetle, yellow and green wings............... **35.00**
  Heddon, Frog pattern, crazy crawler, wood........................ **35.00**
  Paw Paw, underwater minnow, green and black, tack eyes, three hooks... **15.00**
  Shakespeare Co, Mouse, 3⅝" l, white and red, thin body, glass eyes...... **27.00**
Minnow Trap, Orvis, clear glass, emb name, metal hardware, 1 gal....... **65.00**
Reel
  Hendryx, raised pillar type, multiplying, nickel plated brass, fancy handle, horn knob, two buttons on back plate drag/click................ **25.00**
  Takapart, No 480, A F Meisselbach Mfg, patent 1904–09........... **40.00**
  Winchester, Model #1135, fly, black finish....................... **60.00**

FLAGS AND FLAG COLLECTIBLES

There certainly has been a great deal of flag waving as a result of Operations Desert Shield and Desert Storm. Collectors have already stashed away "yellow ribbon" flags. They have forgotten a basic rule of collecting—the more made, the less likely to have value in the future. Ask anyone who owns a forty-eight star flag.

Flags themselves are difficult to display. Old flags are quite fragile. Hanging them often leads to deterioration. If you own flags, you should be aware of flag etiquette as outlined in Public Law 829, 7th Congress, approved December 22, 1942.

Many collectors do not collect flags themselves but items that display the flag as a decorative motif. A flag-related sheet-music collection is one example.

Club: North American Vexilological Association, 3 Egdehill Road, Winchester, MA 01890.

Plate, china, shield and flags in center, flag border, marked on back "Old Glory and Her Allies" and "KT & KS, V-China VDA," 9" d, $8.00.

Advertising Trade Card, Merick's Thread, two infant children, one beating Civil War type drum, other waving flag, titled "Young America," 2¼ × 4½".... **10.00**
Button, 1½" d, glass dome, flag printed inside, set of six mounted on card.... **18.00**
Calendar Plate, Betsy Ross sewing flag, 1919......................... **28.00**
Catalog, Detra Flag Company, #24, New York and Los Angeles, 6½ × 9", 1941..........................**100.00**
Certificate, 12 × 16", Betsy Ross Flag Association, serial #38181, Series N, C H Weisgerber painting, 1917.......... **45.00**
Fan, 9 × 14", Admiral Dewey, flags, admirals, and ships, lace trim.........**125.00**
Flag
  37 stars, 16 × 24", parade flag, printed muslin, 1867–1877.............. **95.00**

44 stars, 3½ × 2¼", child's parade flag, 8,7,7,7,7,8 star pattern and five point star **40.00**

48 stars, 9¼ × 6", "This Flag Enthusiastically Waved To Greet President Hoover Nov 2, 1928" printed on stripes **20.00**

Magic Lantern Slide, 42 star flag, hand tinted, wood frame, c1889 .... **30.00**

Mustache Cup and Saucer, red, white, and blue, "The Union Forever," Civil War period **150.00**

Pinback Button, ⅞" d, flag on white ground, black rim lettering "Win the War Day, April 6, 1918" **8.00**

Plate, 10" d, "Washington's Headquarters, Newburg, NY, 1783–1883," crossed flags under house, cream, brown printing **25.00**

Poster, 14 × 29", lithograph, "History of Old Glory". **145.00**

Receipt, 6¼ × 9", 1908 presidential election contribution, Byron, eagle holding four crossed flags dec **18.00**

Sheet Music, *America Forever March*, E T Paul Music Co, Columbia draped in flag, shield, and eagle **45.00**

Stickpin, 2¼" l, diecut celluloid flag, brass stickpin, George Washington portrait on flag, early 1900s **15.00**

FLUE COVERS

When someone hears "flu" in the 1990s, they immediately think of a cold. There aren't many individuals left who remember wood- and coal-burning kitchen and parlor stoves. When the stovepipe was removed for the summer for cleaning or repair, the exhaust flue in the wall needed to be covered. The answer was a flue cover.

A flue cover is generally round with a small section of chain attached to the back so that the cover can be hung from a nail in the wall. They were made from a variety of materials. Covers that sport a pretty woman or advertising have the most value.

Brass, rural winter landscape.......... **15.00**

Glass

Girl Holding Flowers............... **30.00**

Mountain Landscape **38.00**

Victorian Parlor Scene, 9" d **40.00**

Tin

Cottage and Flowers, stamped, emb yellow border **8.00**

Four Seasons, multicolored, stamped....................... **15.00**

"Hoover For President," 8" d, litho, c1928....................... **40.00**

FOOD MOLDS

Commercial ice cream and chocolate molds appear to be the collectors' favorites. Buying them is now a bit risky because of the large number of reproductions. Beware of all Santa and rabbit molds.

Country collectors have long touted the vast array of kitchen food molds, ranging from butter prints to Turk's head cake molds. Look for molds with signs of use and patina.

Do not forget the Jell-o molds. If you grew up in the 1950s or 1960s, you ate Jell-o and plenty of it. The aluminum Jell-o molds came in a tremendous variety of shapes and sizes. Most sell between ten cents and one dollar, cheap by any stretch of the imagination.

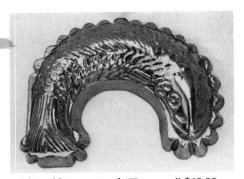

Fish Mold, copper, sgd "Kreamer," $60.00.

Butter, round, wheat design **75.00**

Cheese, 5 × 13", wood, carved design, branded "Los," carved date 1893..... **45.00**

Chocolate

Basket, single cavity **45.00**

Hen on basket, clamp type, 2 pcs, marked "E & Co/Toy" **45.00**

Rabbit, 12 × 10", four cavities....... **48.00**

Cookie, pewter, wood back, six classical heads........................ **45.00**

Ice Cream

Black child killing turkey, marked "E & Co"...................... **75.00**

Castle, chess game piece, marked "S & Co" **60.00**

Pudding, 6" d, tin, fluted sides........ **10.00**

Turk's Head, redware, 7" d, brown sponged rim **40.00**

FOOTBALL CARDS

Football cards are "hot." It was bound to happen. The price of baseball cards has reached the point where even some of the common cards are outside the price range of the average collector. If you cannot afford baseball, why not try football?

Football card collecting is not as sophisticated as baseball card collecting. However, it will be. Smart collectors who see a similarity between the two collecting areas are beginning to stress Pro-Bowlers and NFL All-Stars. Stay away from World Football material. The league is a loser among collectors, just as it was in real life.

Newspapers: *Current Card prices,* P. O. Box 480, East Islip, NY 11730; *Sports Collectors Digest,* 700 East State Street, Iola, WI 54990.

Bowman Gum Company
1948
    Complete Set................550.00
    Common Card.................**2.25**
    99 Harry Gilmer **15.00**
1951
    Complete Set.................300.00
    Common Card.................**1.00**
    20 Tom Landry **42.00**
1953
    Complete Set.................250.00
    Common Card.................**1.25**
    43 Frank Gifford **30.00**
1955
    Complete Set.................150.00
    Common Card....................**.40**
    32 Norm VanBrocklin...........**2.10**
Fleer Gum Company
1960
    Complete Set.................**55.00**
    Common Card....................**.15**
    20 Sammy Baugh **2.70**
1962
    Complete Set.................**55.00**
    Common Card....................**.35**
    46 George Blanda **3.75**
Philadelphia Gum Company
1964
    Complete Set.................**75.00**
    Common Card....................**.10**
    30 Jim Brown **6.50**
1966
    Complete Set.................**70.00**
    Common Card....................**.10**
    114 Fran Tarkenton **2.40**
1967
    Complete Set.................**50.00**
    Common Card....................**.10**
    57 Don Meredith...............**1.60**
Topps Chewing Gum Inc
1955
    Complete Set.................300.00
    Common Card.................**1.00**
    16 Knute Rockne **20.00**

1958
    Complete Set.................**125.00**
    Common Card....................**.20**
    22 John Unitas **15.00**
1961
    Complete Set.................**95.00**
    Common Card....................**.20**
    166 Jack Kemp **11.00**
1964
    Complete Set.................**150.00**
    Common Card....................**.25**
    96 Len Dawson **6.00**
1967
    Complete Set.................**55.00**
    Common Card....................**.15**
    98 Joe Namath **11.00**
1970
    Complete Set.................**45.00**
    Common Card....................**.05**
    30 Bart Starr **1.40**
1974
    Complete Set.................**30.00**
    Common Card....................**.05**
    129 Fran Tarkenton **1.50**
1978
    Complete Set.................**15.00**
    Common Card....................**.02**
    315 Tony Dorsett...............**5.00**
1987
    Complete Set.................**5.00**
    Common Card....................**.00**
    296 Randall Cunningham **1.80**

FOOTBALL COLLECTIBLES

At the moment, this category is heavily weighted toward professional football. Do not overlook some great college memorabilia.

Local pride dominates most collecting. Taking an item back to its "hometown" often doubles its value. Because of their limited production and the tendency of most individuals to discard them within a short time, some of the hardest things to find are game promotional giveaways. Also check the breweriana collectors. A surprising number of beer companies sponsor football broadcasts. Go Bud Light!

Newspaper: *Sports Collectors Digest,* 700 East State Street, Iola, WI 54990.

Bank, 6" h, Pittsburgh Steelers, helmet shape, plastic, 1970s..............**24.00**
Beer Can, 5" h, 1975 Steelers Commemorative, aluminum, Iron City Beer, 12 oz...................................**15.00**
Bubble Gum Card, Joe Namath, #96, Topps Chewing Gum, 1966 ....**12.00**

Big Little Book, **Coach Bernie Bierman's Brick Barton And The Winning Eleven,** *#1480, Whitman, illustrator R. W. Williamson, $20.00.*

Game, Vince Lombardi's Game, Research Games Inc, 1960s 40.00
Nodder, 5½" h, composition
    Baltimore Colts, 1961–62 NFL series........................... **75.00**
    Green Bay Packers, inked "1961 Champions" **50.00**
Pennant
    Los Angeles Rams, 29½" l, blue and white felt, National Football League logo and 1967 date **20.00**
    St Louis Cardinals, red and white felt, c1967........................ **15.00**
Program, Notre Dame vs Navy, 1940s–1950s......................... **12.00**
Stadium Cushion, 11 × 16", vinyl, stuffed, red, NFL team names and mascot illus, orig tag, unused, 1950s........................ **18.00**

FOSTORIA GLASS

The Fostoria Glass Company began in Fostoria, Ohio, and moved to Moundsville, West Virginia, in 1891. In 1983 Lancaster Colony purchased the company and produced glass under the Fostoria trademark.

Fostoria is collected by pattern, with the American pattern being the most common and sought after. Other patterns include Baroque, Georgian, Holly, Midnight Rose, Navarre, Rhapsody, and Wister. Hazel Weatherman's *Fostoria, Its First Fifty Years,* published by the author in about 1972, helps identify patterns.

Club: Fostoria Glass Society of America, P. O. Box 826, Moundsville, WV 26041.

Ashtray, Coin, red **25.00**
Bonbon
    Navarre, crystal, 7" d **28.50**
    Versailles, green **27.00**
Bookends, pr, Lyre, crystal........... **110.00**
Bouillon, saucer, Fairfax, yellow....... **9.00**
Bowl
    American, crystal, 10" d, flared, three toes **40.00**
    Camellia, crystal, 4½" d, handle **18.00**
    Navarre, crystal, 4⅝" d **20.00**
Butter, cov
    Bouquet, crystal **50.00**
    Fairfax, amber................... **65.00**
Cake Plate, 10" d
    Chintz, crystal, two handles **30.00**
    Colony, crystal **28.00**
Candlestick
    Chintz, crystal, 4" h **28.00**
    Mayflower, crystal, 4½" h **22.00**
    Romance, crystal, 4" h **18.00**
Celery Tray
    Beverly, green, 11" l.............. **23.00**
    Colony, crystal, 11½" l, oval **28.50**
Champagne
    Fairfax, azure **18.00**
    June, topaz **25.00**
    Meadow Rose, crystal............. **20.00**
    Navarre, crystal................. **23.00**
Cheese Dish, Navarre, crystal......... **30.00**
Cocktail
    Chintz, crystal **17.00**
    June, topaz **30.00**
    Navarre, crystal................. **25.00**
Compote
    Baroque, crystal **20.00**
    Grape, 7" h, orchid **60.00**
    Heather, crystal.................. **15.00**
Cordial
    Holly, crystal **30.00**
    Navarre, crystal................. **38.00**
Cream Soup, Versailles, green **40.00**
Creamer
    Baroque, crystal, 3¾" h **10.00**
    Coin, emerald green **30.00**
    Navarre, crystal................. **16.00**
Cruet, orig stopper, Chintz, crystal **110.00**
Cup and Saucer
    American, crystal **9.00**
    Baroque, crystal **14.00**
    Chintz, crystal.................. **24.00**
    Navarre, crystal................. **23.00**
Demitasse Cup, Beverly, green **24.00**
Goblet
    Baroque, blue **32.00**
    Chintz, crystal.................. **24.50**
    Jamestown, cinnamon............. **11.00**
    June, topaz **27.00**
    Meadow Rose, crystal............. **23.00**

Grapefruit, liner, Versailles, green...... **85.00**
Ice Bucket
   Meadow Rose, crystal.............. **80.00**
   Trojan, topaz..................... **95.00**
Iced Tea Tumbler, ftd
   Colony, crystal **18.00**
   Jamestown, red................... **15.00**
Juice Tumbler
   American, crystal **11.00**
   Colony, crystal **14.00**
   Meadow Rose, crystal............. **20.00**
Lemon Dish, Fairfax, blue **17.50**
Mayonnaise Bowl, orig ladle
   June, blue **140.00**
   Midnight Rose, crystal **36.00**
Muffin Tray, Colony, crystal **28.00**
Nappy, Baroque, crystal............. **19.00**
Nut Cup, Fairfax, yellow, rolled edge ... **19.00**
Oyster Cocktail
   Holly, crystal.................... **15.00**
   Navarre, crystal................. **16.00**
   Versailles, yellow **20.00**
Parfait, Heather, crystal **32.00**
Pickle Dish, Colony, crystal, 9½" l, oval **22.50**
Pitcher
   Midnight Rose, crystal **350.00**
   Mystic, crystal...................**140.00**
Plate
   Colony, crystal, 8" d, lunch **9.00**
   Fairfax, blue, 6" d, bread and butter........................ **3.50**
   Jamestown, red, 8" d, lunch **15.00**
   June, yellow, 9" d, dinner **55.00**
   Mayfair, crystal, 7" d **10.00**
   Navarre, crystal, 7½" d, salad....... **13.50**
   Romance, topaz, 8¾" d **9.00**
Relish
   June, yellow, 8½" l, two parts **30.00**
   Mayfair, crystal, 10" l, three parts **35.00**
Salt and Pepper Shakers, pr
   American, crystal, individual size, matching tray **25.00**
   June, crystal, ftd **220.00**
Sandwich Server, center handle
   Camellia, crystal **40.00**
   Colony, crystal **24.00**
   Holly, crystal.................... **30.00**
Sauce Bowl, June, blue **345.00**
Sherbet
   Baroque, crystal **9.50**
   Chintz, crystal................... **13.50**
   Meadow Rose, crystal............. **18.00**
Sugar, cov, Chintz, crystal **18.00**
Sundae, American, crystal **10.00**
Sweetmeat, Versailles, blue **38.00**
Tidbit, Chintz, crystal, 8" d, three toes **30.00**
Torte Plate, Meadow Rose, crystal, 14" d...................... **48.00**
Tumbler
   Fairfax, wisteria **35.00**
   Navarre, crystal................. **15.00**
   Versailles, azure **45.00**

Vase
   American, crystal, 8" h............ **38.00**
   Baroque, crystal, 7¾" h **55.00**
   Grape, green, 8" h, ftd **85.00**
   Midnight Rose, crystal, 10" h........ **65.00**
   Starflower, crystal, 6" h **30.00**
Vegetable, Trojan, yellow, 9" l, oval **55.00**
Whipped Cream Bowl, Versailles, blue **35.00**
Wine
   Chintz, crystal................... **35.00**
   Jamestown, red.................. **27.50**
   Meadow Rose, crystal............. **35.00**
   Rogene, crystal **30.00**

FRANKART

Every time there is an Art Deco revival, Frankart gets rediscovered. Frankart was founded by Arthur Von Frankenberg, a sculptor and artist, in the mid 1920s. The key is to remember that his pieces were mass-produced.

Frankart figures are identified through form and style, not specific features. Do I have to tell you that the nudes are the most collectible? Probably not. Nudes are always collectible. Do not overlook other animal and human figures.

Vase, seated figure, mounted on wrought iron stand, removable green Steuben glass vase, 12" h, $495.00.

Almost every Frankart piece is marked with the company name followed by a patent number of "pat. appl. for." Avoid unmarked pieces that dealers are trying to pass as Frankart. Frankenberg experienced plenty of reproductions during the late 1920s and early 1930s.

Ashtray
  Duck, stylized, outstretched wings support green glass ash receiver.... **90.00**
  Monkey, caricature, tail supports 3" d glass ash receiver............... **85.00**
Bookends, pr
  Angel Fish, 5½" h, stylized, exaggerated fins...................... **90.00**
  Bear, 6" h, seated................. **70.00**
  Horse Head, 5" h, flowing manes..... **45.00**
Figurine, 6¼" h, elk, bronze patina finish.........................**120.00**
Incense Burner, cov, 10" h, draped figure holds burner...............**250.00**
Lamp, 11" h, standing nude, embracing orig 8" candlelight bulb.........**310.00**
Night Light, 11" h, sailor leaning against lamppost, bronze patina, orig shade........................**250.00**
Wall Pocket, 12" h, seated nude supported by wrought iron metal framework, metal flower pan **285.00**

FRANKOMA

This is one of those pottery groups, such as Gonder and Hull, that runs hot and cold. Last edition, I suggested it was freezing. There has been a mild thaw, especially in the Midwest. Frankoma has great potential as 1950s-style ware. It's just that collectors and dealers have not yet discovered it as such.

In 1933 John N. Frank, a ceramic art instructor at Oklahoma University, founded Frankoma, Oklahoma's first commercial pottery. Originally located in Norman, it eventually moved to Sapulpa, Oklahoma, in 1938. A series of disastrous fires, the last in 1983, struck the plant. Look for pieces bearing a pacing leopard mark. These pieces are earlier than pieces marked "FRANKOMA."

Bookends, boots, #433, pr **24.00**
Bottle, 11½" h, morning glory blue, white int., 1979................... **28.00**
Bowl, 10" d, cactus, carved **40.00**
Christmas Card
  1952, Donna Frank................ **45.00**
  1975, Grace Lee & Milton Smith **85.00**
Dish, leaf shape, Gracetone **15.00**

Cider Set, pitcher and six matching mugs, green and brown, $48.00.

Figure
  5" h, English Setter................ **48.00**
  9" h, swan, open tail, brown glaze.... **20.00**
Mask, Tragedy **5.00**
Match Holder, 1¾" h, #89-A.......... **15.00**
Mug, Donkey, red and white, 1976..... **18.00**
Plate, Christmas, 1986 .... **12.00**
Salt and Pepper Shakers, pr, wagon wheels......................... **10.00**
Toby Mug, 4½" h, cowboy............ **8.00**
Trivet, Lazybones **30.00**
Vase
  Bottle Shape, V-2, sgd "John Frank," 1970........................ **50.00**
  Fireside, 17" h.................... **30.00**
  Wagon Wheel, 6¾" h, mottled green **18.00**
Wall Pocket, ram's head............. **50.00**
Water Pitcher, 6½" h, 7" w, circular, spiral motif, stepped at handle, metallic blue and black................... **65.00**

FRATERNAL ORDER COLLECTIBLES

In the 1990s few individuals understand the dominant societal role played by fraternal orders and benevolent societies between 1850 and 1950. Because many had membership qualifications that were prejudicial, these "secret" societies often were targets for the social activists of the 1960s.

As the twentieth century ends, America's identity as a nation of joiners also seems to be ending. Many fraternal and benevolent organizations have disbanded. A surprising amount of their material has worked its way into the market. Lodge hall material is often given a "folk art" label and correspondingly high price.

The symbolism is fun. Some of the convention souvenir objects are downright funky. Costumes are great for dress-up. Do not pay big money for them. Same goes for ornamental swords.

Loving Cup, three handles, blue, gold rim, St Albans Lodge, 1865–1915, 50th Anniversary, marked "Thomas Maddock & Sons Co, Trenton, NJ," 7¼" h, $85.00.

Benevolent & Protective Order of Elks (BPOE)
  Badge, Omaha Elks Fair, 1902 . . . . **20.00**
  Book, *National Memorial*, 1931 . . . . **30.00**
  Bookmark, emb, elk's head, SS **18.00**
  Plate, 10" d, elk's head, BPOE & 463, Johnson Bros, England **45.00**
  Shaving Mug, elk, gold letters **30.00**
  Tie Tack, SS, jeweled dec **28.00**
Fraternal Order of Eagles (FOE)
  Ashtray **12.00**
  Shaving Mug, eagle standing on rock, "Liberty, Truth, Justice, Equality" **15.00**
  Watch Fob, bronze, FOE, Liberty, Truth, Justice, Equality, 1918 . . . . . **8.00**
Independent Order of Odd Fellows (IOOF)
  Dish, 5¾" d, pink luster, c1840 . . . . . . **65.00**
  Teaspoon, IOOF, SS, 1915 . . . . **25.00**
  Trivet, 8¼" l, insignia and heart in hand in laurel wreath **30.00**
Knights of Columbus
  Plate, Vienna Art, 1905 . . . . **38.00**
  Shaving Mug, gold trim, black and gold lettering, red, white, blue, and gold shield **50.00**
Loyal Order of Moose, watch fob, double tooth **75.00**
Masonic
  Belt Buckle, SP **22.00**
  Cup and Saucer, Concordia Lodge #67, 1911 . . . . **35.00**
  Mug, enamel, three handles, Syria, 1905 . . . . **60.00**
  Ring, man's, gold, 19th C **145.00**
  Shot Glass, 3" h, cut glass, enclosed bottom holds three dice **150.00**
Order of Eastern Star (OES)
  Cup and Saucer, emblem **15.00**

Pencil, mechanical **10.00**
Shrine
  Fez Hat, brass scarab **22.00**
  Letter Opener, 32nd emblem, c1920 . . . . **20.00**
  Pin, lapel, 32nd emblem, SS **12.00**
  Tie Tack, gold, jeweled dec **28.00**

FROG COLLECTIBLES

A frog collector I know keeps her collection in the guest bathroom. All the fixtures are green also. How long do you think it took me to find the toilet? Thank goodness I have good bladder control.

In fairy tales frogs usually received good press. Not true for their cousin, the toad. Television introduced us to Kermit the Frog, thus putting to rest the villainous frog image of Froggy the Gremlin. I am willing to bet Froggy's "magic twanger" would not get past today's TV censors.

Newsletter: *Flower Frog Gazette*, P. O. Box 106, Trumbull, CT 06611. (Okay, I admit I'm stretching it a bit.)

Club: The Frog Pond, P. O. Box 193, Beech Grove, IN 46107.

Diecut Frog, $1.50.

Advertising
  Paperweight, celluloid and iron **35.00**
Trade Card
  French Laundry Soap, diecut frog **4.50**

Semon Ice Cream, 14" l, diecut, printed on both sides **25.00**
Ashtray, 4½" d, porcelain, sitting frog with wide mouth, Japan **20.00**
Avon Bottle, bubble bath, Freddy the Frog, mug shape, white, red top, 1970 . . . . **6.50**
Bank, 4" h, figural, pottery **40.00**
Basket, figural **30.00**
Clicker, yellow, green, and red **2.00**
Doorstop, 3" h, full figure, sitting, yellow and green **50.00**
Figure, glass, blue satin, #5166, Fenton **28.00**
Flower Frog, figural, white, green, and yellow spray glaze, American Art Potteries **12.00**
Game, Frog Pond, 1895–97 . . . . **45.00**
Key Chain, 1" d, metal, frog riding bicycle, c1940 . . . . **8.00**
Salt and Pepper Shaker Set, 3 pcs, figural shakers and tray, Occupied Japan **12.50**
Stuffed Animal
5" h, velvet, glass eyes **85.00**
8" h, smoking pipe **45.00**
9" h, green, velvet top, white satin bottom, c1960 . . . . **12.00**
Toothpick Holder
Porcelain, singing frog **24.00**
Silverplated, frog pulling snail shell . . . **55.00**
Toy, windup, cloth over tin, glass eyes, Germany **50.00**

Mason, Drey, square, clear, zinc lid, ½ pt, $4.00.

Reverse Ball, aqua, qt **5.00**
Smalley's Royal Trademark Nu-Seal, pt **10.00**
Texas Mason, clear, qt **15.00**
Victory, clear, glass lid, top emb "Victory Reg'd 1925," pt **5.00**

FRUIT JARS

Most fruit jars that you find are worth less than $1.00. Their value rests in reuse through canning, rather than in the collectors' market. Do not be fooled by patent dates that appear on the jar. Over fifty different types of jars bear a patent date of 1858, and many were made as much as fifty years later.

However, there are some expensive fruit jars. A good pricing guide is Alice M. Creswick's *Red Book No. 6: The Collector's Guide To Old Fruit Jars* published privately by the author in 1990.

Newsletter: *Fruit Jar Newsletter*, 364 Gregory Avenue, West Orange, NJ 07052.

Ball, Masons' Patent 1858, green, qt **5.00**
Bulach, green, glass lid, wire clip, qt **3.00**
Clark's Peerless, aqua, glass lid, qt **10.00**
Double Safety, pt **5.00**
Faxon, blue, qt **8.00**
Garden Queen, qt **4.00**
Mason's, Improved, light green, qt **15.00**
Pearl, aqua, handmade, emb "The Pearl," qt **25.00**

FURNITURE

I am not going to compete with my father. If you want to learn about antique or collectible furniture, consult his *Warman's Furniture*, one of the many great volumes in the Warman's Encyclopedia of Antiques and Collectibles. (Psst! Pop, now do I get my raise?)

Much of the furniture found at flea markets is of the secondhand variety. Just remember, all the furniture in my Dad's book was once at this level, too.

Bed, mahogany, pineapple post, 61" h **200.00**
Blanket Chest
Mahogany stained, dovetailed, iron bail handles on sides, casters, 36" w **100.00**
Walnut veneer, cedar lined, diamond shaped molding on front, Lane, 1930s **150.00**
Bookcase, oak, stacking, five sections, glass sliding doors, 48" h **525.00**
Bucket Bench, pine, bootjack feet, painted gray, 62" l **80.00**

Rocker, banister back, arm, rush seat, $125.00.

Chair
    Child's, ladderback, rabbit ears, two
    slats, paper rush seat, dark finish,
    25" h **45.00**
    Ladderback, armchair, maple, acorn
    finials, four slats, woven splint seat,
    44" h **75.00**
    T-back, dining, oak, black vinyl uphol-
    stered slip seat, square stretchers, set
    of four **250.00**
Chest of Drawers, mahogany, line inlaid
    drawers, two short drawers and two
    long drawers, 42" w, 38" h, 1920s. . . . **275.00**
China Cabinet, oak, bow front, convex
    glass side panels, four shelves, mir-
    rored back, 38" w, 60" h, 1920s. **575.00**
Coffee Table, kidney shaped, blue glass
    top, walnut frame **175.00**
    Striped Walnut Veneer, turtle shaped
    top, holly inlaid border, four red
    dyed flower accents, cabriole legs,
    34" w **180.00**
Curio Cabinet, oak, hanging, glass door,
    six shelves, 38" h **150.00**
Desk, child's, oak, roll top, three draw-
    ers, matching chair **125.00**
Dining Table
    Duncan Phyfe style, mahogany, drop
    leaves, brass caps and castors, 42" w,
    1940s **225.00**
    Extension, walnut veneer, molded
    apron, six legs, U-shaped stretchers,
    60" w, 1925. . . . . **175.00**
    Pedestal, oak veneer, circular top,
    scroll feet, two leaves, 1920s **300.00**

Dry Sink, pine, shallow well, two pan-
    eled doors, feet missing, 36" w **350.00**
Fernery, wicker, rectangular well,
    painted white **75.00**
File Cabinet, steel, four drawers, olive
    drab **45.00**
Garden Bench, cast iron, grape design,
    painted white, 42" l **300.00**
High Chair, oak, pressed back, cane seat,
    40" h **175.00**
Hoosier Style Cabinet, Sellers, pine pan-
    els, oak frame, tambour door, flour
    bin, sliding porcelain work surface,
    bread drawer, sliding cutting board,
    painted white **350.00**
Jelly Cupboard, pine, shaped crest,
    long drawer over two paneled doors,
    interior shelf, wood pulls, painted
    green **400.00**
Kitchen Set, rect oak table with porcelain
    top, four chairs, painted white **250.00**
Library Table, Empire style, oak, pillar
    base, scroll feet, 48" w, 28" h,
    1920s **400.00**
Parlor Suite, sofa and two chairs,
    overstuffed, ball feet, floral upholstery,
    1930s **250.00**
Parlor Table, oak, square top, spiral
    turned legs, base shelf, claw and ball
    feet **175.00**
Piano Bench, oak, rect top, square legs,
    40" w **125.00**
Plant Stand, oak, 12" square top, cutout
    keyhole design in legs **90.00**
Porch Rocker, woven splint back and
    seat, painted dark green **35.00**
Potty Chair, child's, rocking, pine, cutout
    carrying handle in back, arms **125.00**
Rocker, Windsor style, birch, comb back,
    28" h **175.00**
Sewing Stand
    Martha Washington type, mahogany,
    three drawers, 29" h, 1920s **100.00**
    Priscilla type, painted red, dark trim,
    floral decal, rod carrying handle,
    25" h, 1930s **28.00**
Smoking Stand, walnut veneer, brass
    gallery on top, figured veneer on door,
    base shelf, zinc lined **85.00**
Washstand, oak, harp shaped towel bar,
    serpentine top, single drawer over two
    paneled doors, casters, refinished **275.00**

GAMBLING COLLECTIBLES

Casino gambling and many other types of
gambling are spreading across the country,
just as they did over a century ago. Gaming devices, gaming accessories, and souvenirs of gambling establishments from
hotels to riverboats are all collectible.

Gambling collectors compete with Western collectors for the same material. Sometimes the gunfight gets bloody. With the price of old (i.e., late nineteenth and early twentieth century) gambling material skyrocketing, many new collectors are focusing on more modern material, dating from the speakeasies of the 1920s to the glitz of Las Vegas in the 1950s and 1960s.

You might as well pick up modern examples when you can. Some places last only slightly longer than a throw of the dice. Atlantic City has already seen the Atlantis and Playboy disappear. Is Trump's Taj Mahal next?

Roulette Table Card, Sarony Cigarettes, 12³/₈" l, yellow, black, and red letters, green ground, England, $65.00.

Bingo Cage, 9" h, metal, red celluloid handle, eleven wood balls, nine cards, 1941 copyright 15.00
Book, *Gambler's Don't Gamble,* Michael MacDougall & JC Furnas, 1939, 167 pgs 30.00
Card Counter, plated, imitation ivory face, black lettering 18.00
Card Press, 9¼ × 4¼ × 3", dovetailed, holds ten decks, handle 140.00
Catalog, KC Card Co, Blue Book No. 520, Gambling Equipment, 68 pgs 40.00
Dice
  Poker, celluloid, set of 5 . . . . 24.00
  Weighted, always total 12, set of 3 . . . . 35.00
Faro Cards, sq corners, Samuel Hart & Co, New York, complete 110.00
Poker Chip
  Inlaid, four crosses 4.00
  Ivory, scrimshawed, eagle 30.00
  Molded Rubber, dollar 4.00
Poker Chip Rack, 11¼ × 4", revolving, wood, holds four decks of cards and 400 chips 35.00
Roulette Ball, set of three, one metal, two composition 15.00
Shot Glass, ribbed dec, porcelain dice in bottom 24.00
Slot Machine
  Liberty Bell, 5¢, 3 reel, orig red, white, and blue decal 160.00

The Puritan Ball, 5¢, 10¼" h 135.00
Trade Stimulator, 3 × 10 × 8½", wood and metal case, glass top, silver and black scenes, side lever spin dice 350.00

GAMES

Many game collectors distinguish between classic games, those made between 1840 and 1940, and modern games, those dating after 1940. This is the type of snobbiness that gives collecting a bad name. In time 1990s games will be one hundred years old. I can just imagine a collector in 2090 asking dealers at a toy show for a copy of the Morton Downey "Loudmouth" game. I am one of the few who have one put aside in mint condition.

Condition is everything. Games that have been taped or have price tags stickered to the face of their covers should be avoided. Beware of games at flea markets where exposure to sunlight and dirt causes fading, warping, and decay.

Avoid common games, e.g., "Go to the Head of the Class," "Monopoly," and "Rook." They were produced in such vast quantities that they hold little attraction for collectors.

Most boxed board games are found in heavily used condition. Box lids have excessive wear, tears, and are warped. Pieces are missing. In this condition, most games are in the $2.00 to $10.00 range. However, the minute a game is available in fine condition or better, value jumps considerably.

Club: American Game Collectors Association, 4628 Barlow Drive, Bartlesville, OK 74006.

Barbie Keys To Fame Career Game, Mattel, 1963 . . . . 40.00
Bobbsey Twins on the Farm Game, Milton Bradley, 1957 . . . . 20.00
Charlie's Angels, Milton Bradley, 1977 . . . .   4.00
Captain Gallant, Transogram, 1955 . . . . . 40.00
Comic Card, Milton Bradley, 1972 . . . . . 25.00
Dark Shadows, Whitman, 1968 . . . . 50.00
Derby Bingo, 1939 . . . . 100.00
Dr. Kildare, Ideal, 1962 . . . . 35.00
Dukes of Hazzard, Ideal, 1981 . . . .   2.50
Fall Guy, Milton Bradley, 1982 . . . .   3.00
Felix The Cat, Milton Bradley, 1968 . . . . 20.00
Flintstones Stone Age, Transogram, 1961 . . . . 20.00
Go To The Head Of The Class, Milton Bradley, 1955 . . . . 15.00
Gunsmoke, Lowell, 1958 . . . . 50.00

182

Game, Bargain Day, Parker Brothers, Inc, $25.00.

Happy Days, Parker Bros **25.00**
I-Spy, Ideal, 1965 . . . . **45.00**
Land of the Giants, Ideal, 1968 . . . . **50.00**
Laverne & Shirley, Parker Brothers,
   1977. . . . . **4.00**
Magilla Gorilla, Ideal, 1964 . . . . **75.00**
Mr. Ree Murder Mystery, Selchow &
   Righter, 1948 . . . . **55.00**
Nancy Drew, Parker Brothers, 1959 . . . . **22.50**
Napoleon Solo, Milton Bradley, 1964 . . . **20.00**
Park & Shop, Milton Bradley, 1960 . . . . . **37.50**
Pirates & Traveller, Milton Bradley,
   1936. . . . . **25.00**
Popeye the Juggler Ball & Pipe Game,
   1929. . . . . **60.00**
Rat Patrol, Transogram, 1967 . . . . **65.00**
Restless Gun, Milton Bradley, 1959,
   unused. **135.00**
Road Runner, Whitman, 1969 . . . . **25.00**
Sambo Five Pin Bowling Game, Parker
   Bros, 1921. . . . .**350.00**
Strawberry Shortcake, Parker Bros **7.50**
Turkey Doodle, radio premium, orig
   mailing envelope, 1936 . . . .**125.00**
Twelve O'Clock High, Ideal, 1965 . . . . . . **30.00**
Twilight Zone, Ideal, 1964 . . . .**150.00**
Video Village TV Quiz Game, Milton
   Bradley, 1960 . . . . **25.00**
Voyage to the Bottom of the Sea, Milton
   Bradley, 1964 . . . . **45.00**
Wagon Train Game, unused **25.00**

GAS STATION COLLECTIBLES

Approach this from two perspectives—
items associated with gas stations and gasoline company giveaways. Competition for this material is fierce. Advertising collectors want the advertising; automobile collectors want material to supplement their collections.

Beware of reproductions ranging from advertising signs to pump globes. Do not accept too much restoration and repair. There were hundreds of thousands of gasoline stations across America. Not all their back rooms have been exhausted.

Newspaper/Magazine: *Hemmings Motor News*, Box 100, Bennington, VT 05201.

Clubs: Automobile License Plate Collectors Association, Box 712, Weston, WV 26452; International Petrolina Collectors Association, 2151 East Dublin-Granville Road, Suite G292, Columbus, OH 43229.

Gas Globe, 16″ d, glass, $200.00.

Bank, pump, Sinclair **22.50**
Coin Set, Shell Oil Co, fifty states, com-
   plete, 1969. . . . . **35.00**
Credit Card Machine, Texaco, metal,
   green and red, logo **85.00**
Flag, Texaco, 44 × 72″. **30.00**
Gas Globe
   Glass, Texaco, black border, T Hull
     body. **300.00**
   Plastic, Pemco **110.00**
Hat, western style, Phillips 66, felt,
   black **18.00**
Key Holder, Dezol. **5.00**
Lubricant Can, Badger **85.00**
Map, Texaco **5.00**
Oil Can, Marble's Nitro Solvent **45.00**
Padlock, Gas Pump, Standard Oil,
   brass. **40.00**
Sign
   Champlin Motor Oil **75.00**
   Complete Greasing Service Every Cup
     Every Time, 40 × 28″. **795.00**

Conoco Radiator Alcohol, tin, thermometer on other side, hand with check list, "Let Us Check Your Car Before Your Holiday Trip," 38 × 24"........................875.00
Husky, fiberglass, graphics, pump **85.00**
Mobil Gas Special, porcelain, pump... **95.00**
Pan-Am Gas, porcelain............. **65.00**
Texaco, letters with stars, plastic, 18" h.......................275.00
Texaco Marine Lubricants, tin, 21 × 11".........................765.00
Soap, Sinclair Gasoline, dinosaur shape, orig box........................ **30.00**
Stamp Album, Sinclair, 1930s......... **6.00**
Thermometer, Lube King Motor Oil **125.00**

GEISHA GIRL

Geisha Girl porcelain is a Japanese export ware whose production began in the last quarter of the 19th century and continues today. Manufacturing came to a standstill during World War II.

Collectors have identified over 150 different patterns from over one hundred manufacturers. When buying a set, check the pattern of the pieces carefully. Dealers will mix and match in an effort to achieve a complete set.

Beware of reproductions that have a very white porcelain, minimal background washes, sparse detail coloring, no gold, or very bright gold enameling. Some of the reproductions came from Czechoslovakia.

Bowl, 4½" d, 2" h, underplate, mkd "Made in Japan," $18.00.

Bowl, 9½" d, Geisha In Sampan E, octagon shape, red-orange, gold buds, Nippon **43.00**
Child's Dishes
 Celery Set, 6 pcs, master and five salts,

Flower Gathering A, pine green, Made in Japan.................. **40.00**
Pitcher, 3⅝ × 1¼", Parasol B, cylindrical slenderizing towards top, almost indistinguishable pouring lip, red, Japan........................ **15.00**
Chocolate Pot, Parasol & Lesson, blue and gold, floral and butterfly ground........................100.00
Creamer, 4" h, Feeding The Carp, red, hourglass shape, ribbed **18.00**
Cup and Saucer, Kite A, brown and gold **12.00**
Dish, 7" d, oval, Mother and Son C, red-orange........................ **25.00**
Hair Receiver, Geisha In Sampan, sq, red, marked "t't' Japan" **18.00**
Olive Dish, 7" l, oval, Mother and Son C, red-orange, Kutani................ **25.00**
Plate, 8½" d, Geisha In Sampan A, brown and gold................... **25.00**
Sake Cup, Garden Bench B, red rim **6.00**
Salt and Pepper Shakers, pr, sq, pine green........................... **18.00**
Salt, Temple A, floral and turquoise border, pedestal, marked **25.00**
Teapot, Butterfly, apple green and gold, ftd **30.00**

G.I. JOE

The first G.I. Joe 12" poseable action figures were produced in 1964 by the Hasbro Manufacturing Company. The original line was made up of one male action figure for each branch of military service. Their outfits were styled after military uniforms from World War II, the Korean Conflict, and the Vietnam Conflict.

In 1965 the first black figure was introduced. The year 1967 saw two additions to the line—a female nurse and Talking G.I. Joe. To stay abreast of the changing times, Joe was given flocked hair and a beard in 1970.

The creation of the G.I. Joe Adventure Team made Joe the marveled explorer, hunter, deep sea diver, and astronaut, rather than just an American serviceman. Due to the Arab oil embargo in 1976, the figure was reduced in size to 8" tall and was renamed the Super Joe. In 1977 production stopped.

It wasn't until 1982 that G.I. Joe made his comeback, with a few changes made to the character line and to the way in which the Joe team was viewed. "The Great American Hero" line now consists of 3¾" poseable plastic figures with code names corresponding to their various costumes. The new Joe must deal with both current and futuristic villains and issues.

Action Figure
  3¾" h, Real American Hero
    Series One, straight arm, 1982
      Cobra Officer **80.00**
      Grunt **60.00**
      Scarlet **90.00**
    Series Two, swivel arm, 1983
      Breaker **60.00**
      Snake Eyes. **75.00**
      Tripwire **65.00**
    Series Three, 1983–84
      Baroness **45.00**
      Mutt with Junkyard **45.00**
    Series Four, 1984
      Bazooka. **35.00**
      Footloose. **30.00**
      Lady Jaye **48.00**
    Series Five, 1985
      Dial-Tone. **10.00**
      Iceberg **15.00**
      Sergeant Slaughter, mail-in offer **45.00**
    Series Six, 1986–87
      Chuckles **10.00**
      Law and Order. **12.00**
      Sneak Peek **8.00**
    Series Seven, 1988
      Astro Viper. **7.00**
      Blocker and Maverick **25.00**
      Dodger **15.00**
      Road Pig. **9.00**
      Tripwire, Tiger Force outfit **9.00**
    Series Eight, 1988–89
      Annihilator **5.00**
      Barbecue, Slaughter's Marauders **9.00**
      Trooper, Python Patrol **9.00**
    Series Nine, 1990
      Night Creeper **5.00**
      Tunnel Rat, Sonic Fighters **7.00**
    Series Ten, 1991
      Cloudburst, Air Commandos **12.00**
      General Hawk **4.00**
      Life-Line, Rice Krispies premium **8.00**
      Overkill, Talking Battle Commanders. **10.00**
      Rapid Fire, videotape **10.00**
      Red Star, Cobra **15.00**
      Sludge Viper, Eco-Warriors **7.00**
    Series Eleven, Storm Shadow, Ninja Force, 1992 . . . . **4.00**
  11½" h, 1964–76
    Marine, 7700, fatigues, boots, green cap, dog tags, insignia, training manual, 1964 . . . . **400.00**
    Pilot, 7890, talking, 1967 . . . . **900.00**
    Soldier
      7500, regulation fatigues, jump

boots, cap, dog tags, insignia, manual, 1964. . . . . **200.00**
      7900, Negro, regulation fatigues, jump boots, cap, dog tags, insignia, manual, 1965. . . . . **2,000.00**
  12" h, Duke, Hall of Fame, series ten, 1991. . . . . **80.00**
  Adventure Team Series
    Adventure Team Commander, talking, black, bearded **400.00**
    Adventurer, Kung Fu grip, sea **200.00**
    Mike Powers, Atomic Man **75.00**
Boxed Set with Figure, Action Soldiers of the World
  British Commando, 8104, 1966. . . . . . **900.00**
  Japanese Imperial Soldier, 8101, 1966. . . . . **1,200.00**
Outfits and Accessories
  Air Police Accessories, 7813, field phone, carbine, bayonet, white helmet, 1964–65 . . . . **60.00**
  Atomic Man Secret Mountain Outpost, Adventure Team Series . . . **150.00**
  Beachhead Assault Field Pack Set, 7712, rifle, grenades, cartridge belt, field pack, entrenching tool, canteen, manual, orig box, 1964 . . . **200.00**
  Bivouac Deluxe Pup Tent Set, 7513, tent, netting foliage, machine gun, ammo box, entrenching tool, manual, orig box, 1964–65 . . . . **225.00**
  Black Widow Rendevous, Adventure Team Series **150.00**
  Combat Camouflage Netting, 7511, foliage and posts, 1964–65 . . . . **45.00**
  Combat Field Jacket Set, 7501, jacket, M-1 rifle, bayonet, cartridge belt, hand grenades, manual, orig box, 1964–65 . . . . **75.00**
  Combat Sandbags, 7508, three bags, 1964–65 . . . . **50.00**
  Command Post Poncho Set, 7517, field telephone and case, wire roll, field radio, pistol and holster, map and case, manual, orig box, 1964–65 . . . **165.00**
  Communications Flag Set, 7704, Army, Air Corps, Marines, Navy, and American Flags, 1964–65 . . . . . **250.00**
  Deep Sea Diver Equipment Set, 7620, diving suit, helmet, weighted belts and shoes, air pump, hose, tools, signal floats, orig box, 1964–65 . . . . . . **400.00**
  Desert Explorer, Adventure Team Series **75.00**
  Equipment Tester, Adventure Team Series **30.00**
  Fantastic Freefall, Adventure Team Series **250.00**
  First-Aid Set, 7721, first-aid pouch, arm band, helmet, 1964–65 . . . . **100.00**
  Footlocker, 8000, wood tray, 1964 . . . **75.00**
  Frogman Accessories, 7605, face mask,

swim fins, depth gauge, knife, scabbard, 1964–65 . . . . **70.00**
Frogman Underwater Demolition Set, rubber suit, headpiece, face mask, swim fins, scuba tank, knife, depth gauge, dynamite, manual, orig box, 1964–65 . . . . **450.00**
High Voltage Escape, Adventure Team Series, 1971 . . . . **75.00**
Lifeline Catapult, Adventure Team Series **60.00**
Marine Medic Set, 7719, stretcher, first-aid shoulder pouch, stethoscope, plasma bottle, bandages, Red Cross flag, arm bands, manual, orig box, 1964–65 . . . . **225.00**
Mine Shaft Breakout, Adventure Team Series **80.00**
Mountain Troops Set, 7530, camouflage pack, web belt, snow shoes, ice axe, ropes, grenades, manual, orig box, 1964–65 . . . . **180.00**
Navy Attack Deluxe Set, 7607, life jacket, field glasses, blinker light, signal flags, manual, orig box, 1964–65 . . . . **200.00**
Paratrooper Camouflage Set, 7708, netting and foliage, 1964–65 . . . . . . **60.00**
Scramble Crash Helmet, 7810, face mask, hose, tinted visor, 1964–65 . . . . **120.00**
Shore Patrol Helmet Set, 7616, .45 pistol, white belt, billy stick, white helmet, 1964–65 . . . . **100.00**
Ski Patrol Deluxe Set, 7531, white parka, boots, goggles, mittens, skis, poles, manual, orig box 1964–65 . . . **300.00**
Sky Dive to Danger, Adventure Team Series **150.00**
Survival Life Raft Set, 7801, raft, oar, flare gun, knife, air vest, first-aid kit, sea anchor, manual, orig box, 1964–65 . . . . **240.00**
Thermal Terrain Scanner, Adventure Team Series **30.00**
Underwater Explorer, Adventure Team Series **70.00**

GOLD

Twenty-four karat gold is pure gold. Twelve karat gold is fifty percent gold and fifty percent other elements. Many gold items have more weight value than antique or collectible value. The gold weight scale is different from our regular English pounds scale. Learn the proper conversion procedure. Review the value of an ounce of gold once a week and practice keeping that figure in your mind.

Pieces with gold wash, gold gilding, and gold bands have no weight value. Value rests in other areas. In many cases the gold is applied on the surface. Washing and handling leads to its removal.

Take time to research and learn the difference between gold and gold plating before starting your collection. This is not an area in which to speculate. How many times have you heard that an old pocket watch has to be worth a lot of money because it has a gold case? Many people cannot tell the difference between gold and gold plating. In most cases, the gold value is much less than you think.

Gold coinage is a whole other story. Every coin suspected of being gold should first be checked by a jeweler and then in coin price guides.

GOLF COLLECTIBLES

Golf was first played in Scotland in the 15th century. The game achieved popularity in the late 1840s when the "gutty" ball was introduced. Although golf was played in America before the Revolution, it gained a strong foothold in the recreational area only after 1890.

The problem with most golf collectibles is that they are common while their owners think they are rare. This is an area where homework pays, especially when trying to determine the value of clubs.

Do not limit yourself only to items used on the course. Books about golf, decorative accessories with a golf motif, and clubhouse collectibles are eagerly sought by collectors. This is a great sports collectible to tee off on.

Club (no pun intended): Golf Collectors' Society, 235 East Helena Street, Dayton, OH 45404.

Annual
   Golf Digest, 1984 . . . . **4.00**
   60th PGA, 1978 . . . . **15.00**
Ashtray, metal, trophy, figural golfer . . . **45.00**
Book
   Anderson, John, *The American Annual Golf Guide*, 1924 . . . . **40.00**
   Nelson, Byron, *Winning Golf*, 1947 . . . . **7.50**
   Ray, Edward, *Driving, Approaching and Putting*, 1922 . . . . **30.00**
Bag, leather, Tony Lema, 1964 British Open Champion **50.00**
Ball
   Bramble Ball, The Crown **15.00**
   Chemico Bob, yellow dot **35.00**

Ashtray, white metal, pewter finish, figural caddy, 4" h, $80.00.

Gutty, Mitchell, Manchester	35.00
Bookends, pr, 4 × 6", golfer in relief	55.00
Cigarette Box, bronze, Art Deco, Silver Crest	130.00
Cigarette Lighter, Craftsman, golfer on front	50.00

Club
Iron, Burke juvenile mashie, wood shaft	22.00
Putter, Spalding Cash-in, steel shaft	45.00
Wood, set of 4	50.00
Decanter, golf ball on green grass	95.00
Flask, pocket, 5¼ × 4", three dimensional, golfer on green with two ladies, nickel silver	195.00
Game, Golf-o-matics, Royal London	18.00
Golf Ball Pail, Billy Casper	15.00
Paperweight, glass, US Open, 1980	25.00
Pipe Stand, bronze golf bag with chrome clubs, wooden rack	125.00

Plate
Morgantown Glass Co, 7½" d, cobalt blue	18.00
Royal Doulton Bunnykins, golfing rabbits	40.00

Print
"The First Tee," Dendy Sadler, etching, colored	30.00
"In the Sand, St Andrews," after Michael Brown	35.00
Radiator Cap, 6" d, Art Deco, figural, male golfer, Weidlich	150.00
Score Card, celluloid, leather case	125.00
Souvenir Spoon, SS, golfer, Milford, PA	80.00

Stemware, stem with golf ball in center
Morgantown Glass Co
Champagne, red	27.50
Juice Tumbler, green	22.50
Sherbet, cobalt blue	35.00
Tie Bar and Cuff Links Set, golfers	20.00

Toy, wind-up, bear golfer, Japan, MIB, 1950s	395.00
Utensils, bar type, silver and chrome, Art Deco	125.00
Whiskey Bottle, putter	20.00

GONDER POTTERY

In 1941 Lawton Gonder established Gonder Ceramic Arts, Inc., at Zanesville, Ohio. The company is known for its glazes, such as Chinese crackle, gold crackle, and flambe. Pieces are clearly marked. Gonder manufactured lamp bases at a second plant and marketed them under the trademark "Eglee." Gonder Ceramic Arts, Inc. ceased production in 1957.

Ewer, 9" h, light green, matte, mkd "Gonder U.S.A. H-34," $25.00.

Ashtray, 9" sq, charcoal and white crackle design, #805	40.00
Bank, 8" h, figural, sheriff, glossy green, marked "Gonder Original"	325.00
Basket, 9" h, 13" l, mottled brown, L-19	60.00
Bookends, pr, horse heads, burgundy, #582	100.00

Candle Holder, pr
Crescent Moons, 6½" h, gold, J-56	45.00
Lotus Flowers, E-14	20.00
Cookie Jar, 12" h, pirate, blue hat and shoes, yellow clothes, marked "Gonder Original"	700.00
Cornucopia, white and brown speckled dec, #521	65.00

Ewer
13" h, ribbed, green and brown, M-9	65.00
14" h, inverted conch shell, white, #508	110.00

Figure

Bali Girl, 14" h, carrying basket on head, glossy yellow, marked "1950 Gonder Ceramic Art" **50.00**

Chinese Coolie, 9" h, glossy yellow ... **25.00**

Deer, 11" h, stylized, pair leaping, glossy brown, #690 .... **30.00**

Panther, 15" l, stalking, glossy black, unmarked **35.00**

Ginger Jar, cov, 10" h, crackle type design, green and brown, #530 .... **115.00**

Lamp Base, 18" h, giraffe head, green and brown **275.00**

Pitcher, 8" h, volcanic glaze, #917 ...... **45.00**

Planter, 8" h, swan, light green, J-31 ... **85.00**

Salt and Pepper Shakers, pr, figural "S" and "P", glossy green **12.00**

Television Lamp

Seagull, 12" h, stylized, black seagull over yellow waves. **80.00**

Ship, 14" h, green and brown **40.00**

Vase, 9" h

Fish, green and brown, #522 .... **175.00**

Hat, inverted, flared brim, light green, H-34. .... **40.00**

Lyre, white, J-57. .... **75.00**

Wall Tile, white, hunting dog decal **20.00**

GOOFUS GLASS

Goofus glass is a patterned glass where the reverse of the principal portion of the pattern is colored in red or green and covered with a metallic gold ground. It was distributed at carnivals between 1890 and 1920. There are no records of it being manufactured after that date. Among the companies that made Goofus glass are: Cresent Glass Company, Imperial Glass Corporation, LaBelle Glass Works, and Northwood Glass Company.

Value rests with pieces that have both the main color and ground color still intact. The reverse painting often wore off. It is not uncommon to find the clear pattern glass with no painting on it whatsoever.

Goofus glass can be known as Mexican Ware, Hooligan Glass, and Pickle Glass. Says a lot, doesn't it?

Bowl

5½" d, La Belle Rose pattern, sq. **30.00**

7" d, thistle and scrolling leaves, red dec, gold ground, ruffled rim **20.00**

9" d, Cherries pattern, red dec, gold ground. **20.00**

10" d, Dahlias, scalloped **50.00**

10½" d, Roses pattern, relief molded, red roses, gold ground. **35.00**

Cake Plate, 12" d, Roses pattern, red dec, gold ground. **15.00**

Plate, 7¾" d, red carnation dec, gold ground, $15.00.

Compote

6½" d, Poppy pattern, red flowers, gold foliage, green ground, sgd "Northwood" **32.00**

9½" d, Strawberry pattern, red and green strawberries, gold ground, ruffled **45.00**

Dish, 7¼" l, floral dec, green, fluted **12.00**

Jar, cov, red butterflies dec, gold ground. **20.00**

Mug, Cabbage Rose pattern, gold ground. **30.00**

Pickle Jar, relief molded, gold, blue, and red flowers, aqua ground **25.00**

Plate

7½" d, red apple dec, gold ground **18.00**

11" d, Dahlia pattern, red dec, gold ground. **35.00**

Powder Jar, cov, 4½" d, Cabbage Rose pattern, relief molded, white dec **20.00**

Salt and Pepper Shakers, pr, Poppy pattern **35.00**

Syrup, Strawberry pattern, relief molded **32.50**

Vase

6½" h, Grape and Rose pattern, crackle glass, red dec, gold ground **10.00**

7¼" h, grape dec. **25.00**

10½" h, Peacock pattern **75.00**

GRANITEWARE

Graniteware, also know as agateware, is the name commonly given to iron or steel kitchenware covered with an enamel coating. American production began in the 1860s and is still going on today.

White and gray are the most common colors. However, wares can be found in shades of blue, brown, cream, green, red, and violet. Mottled pieces, those combining swirls of color, are especially desirable.

For the past few years a deliberate attempt to drive prices upward has been taking place. The dealers behind it were quite successful until the 1990 recession. Never lose sight of the fact that graniteware was inexpensive utilitarian kitchen and household ware. Modern prices should reflect this humble origin.

Club: National Graniteware Society, P. O. Box 10013, Center Rapids, IA 52410-0013.

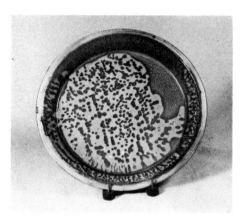

Pie Pan, 9" d, mottled gray, $10.00.

Berry Bucket, black and white speckled,
  tin lid, bail handle 40.00
Bundt Pan, gray 15.00
Chamber Pot
  Child's, gray, paper label 20.00
  Covered, gray, labeled 12.00
Coffeepot, child's, blue, missing lid 50.00
Colander, 10½" d 45.00
Cup, child's, green, cat on side 22.00
Dipper
  Gray and White. 20.00
  Red and White 15.00
Double Boiler, red, blue trim 45.00
Dry Measure, light blue and white 35.00
Funnel, gray mottled 20.00
Lunch Pail, gray, with cup 90.00
Measure, gray, 8" h 40.00
Milk Pan, blue and white swirl 45.00
Muffin Tin, gray 20.00
Pie Pan, gray 20.00
Pitcher and Bowl Set
  Blue, large 195.00
  White, black trim 45.00
Plate
  Blue and white swirl. 15.00
  Gray mottled. 9.00
Potty, child's, light blue 12.50
Pudding Pan, emerald green, white
  specks, 10⅝ × 7¾". 35.00

Roaster, cream and red, large. 30.00
Skimmer, gray 28.00
Soap Dish, blue and white swirl. 25.00
Soup Ladle, red and white 22.00
Spittoon, blue 35.00
Strainer Insert, 8½" d, wire bail, brown and white, large mottle, straight sides. 55.00

GREETING CARDS

Greeting cards still fall largely within the domain of post card collectors and dealers. They deserve to be a collector group of their own.

At the moment, high ticket greeting cards are character-related. But, someday collectors will discover Hallmark and other greeting cards as social barometers of their era. Meanwhile, enjoy picking them up for 25¢ or less.

Book, **Make Your Own Christmas Cards,** *designed by Eve Rockwell, $5.00.*

Christmas
  "Hail, Day of Joy," L Prang and Co,
    kneeling angel holding dove,
    1870s 15.00
  "Merry Christmas and Happy New
    Year," flowers and birds, four
    pgs 12.00
  "My Lips May Give a Message," Kate
    Greenaway, girl holding letter,
    c1880. . . . . 50.00

"With Best Christmas Wishes," Raphael Tuck and Sons, girl holding flowers, c1890................. **15.00**

Easter
  Angels, Whitney, NY, 19th C....... **5.00**
  Floral Cross, Germany, 19th C...... **5.50**
  Religious, floral, Tuck............. **12.00**

Get Well, Amos 'n' Andy, 4¼ × 5½", black and white photo, Hall Bros, 1951.......................... **30.00**

Greetings, children's heads in flowerpot, 19th C....................... **3.00**

Happy Birthday
  Amos 'n' Andy, brown portraits, message includes song title "Check and Double Check," inked birthday note, Rust Craft................ **20.00**
  Dagwood, 5 × 6", Hallmark, 1939 .... **15.00**
  Snow White and the Seven Dwarfs, c1938....................... **40.00**
  Space Patrol Man, 5" sq, full color, diecut, small green transparent helmet, orig envelope.................. **20.00**

Mother's Day, Cracker Jack, diecut, full color, puppy, c1940 .... **40.00**

New Year, girl holding bird, palm tree, 19th C **4.50**

GUNDERSON GLASS

Peachblow-type art glass was manufactured by the Gunderson Glass Company beginning around 1950. This special order glass resembled peachblow in color, shading from an opaque white with a hint of pink to a deep rose. Many pieces of Gunderson Glass are sold as "old peachblow" by dealers who cannot identify the copies from the period pieces. Gunderson Peachblow is collectible in its own right.

Basket, 7½" d **285.00**
Box, cov, 5¼ × 7", hinged puff lid, large finial, emb brass bindings, satin finish **250.00**
Compote, 6" d, 5⅛" h, white, pink accents, flared rim, baluster shaped standard, c1953 ....**435.00**
Creamer and Sugar.................**420.00**
Cruet, 6½" h.....................**175.00**
Cup and Saucer....................**175.00**
Goblet **140.00**
Mug, orig paper label, c1970 ....**125.00**
Sugar, open, ftd **75.00**
Toothpick Holder **50.00**
Tumbler, 4" h **125.00**
Vase
  4½" h, 3" d, satin finish **90.00**
  6½" h, crimped rim **135.00**
  9" h, lily shape **485.00**

HALL CHINA

In 1903 Robert Hall founded the Hall China Company in East Liverpool, Ohio. Upon his death in 1904, Robert T. Hall, his son, succeeded him. Hall produced a large selection of kitchenware and dinnerware in a wide variety of patterns, as well as refrigerator sets. The company was a major supplier of institutional (hotel and restaurant) ware.

Hall also manufactured some patterns on an exclusive basis: Autumn Leaf for Jewel Tea, Blue Bouquet for the Standard Coffee Company of New Orleans, and Red Poppy for the Grand Union Tea Company. Hall teapots are a favorite among teapot collectors.

For the past several years, Hall has been reissuing a number of its solid color pieces as an "Americana" line. Items featuring a decal or gold decoration have not been reproduced. Because of the difficulty in distinguishing old from new solid color pieces, prices on many older pieces have dropped.

Pretzel Jar, cov, Orange Poppy, pretzel handles, $45.00.

Blue Blossom
  Casserole, oval, handle............. **45.00**
  Custard Cup **17.50**
  Salt and Pepper Shakers, pr **40.00**
Blue Bouquet
  Bowl, 5½" d **7.50**
  Pie Baker....................... **24.00**
  Platter, 11¼" l................... **14.00**
Cameo Rose
  Creamer and Sugar............... **15.00**
  Cup and Saucer.................. **6.50**

Fruit Bowl, 5¼" d	3.50

Plate
7¼" d	7.00
10" d	8.00
Platter, 11¼" l	16.50
Salt and Pepper Shakers, pr	17.50
Soup, flat, 8" d	10.00
Teapot, cov	50.00
Vegetable, 9" d	15.00

Heather Rose
Cup and Saucer	6.50
Fruit Bowl, 5¼" d	3.50
Plate, 10" d	7.50

Liberty Blue
Butter, cov	40.00
Creamer	12.50
Mug	10.00
Platter, 12" l	30.00
Salt and Pepper Shakers, pr	16.50
Teapot, cov	50.00

Orange Poppy
Casserole, cov	32.00
Custard Cup	5.50
French Baker	15.00
Salad Bowl	12.00
Salt and Pepper Shakers, pr, loop	30.00

Red Poppy
Cake Plate	17.50
Casserole, cov, 7" l	20.00
Cereal Bowl, 6" d	15.00
Cup, interior pattern	9.00
Pie Baker	38.00

Plate
7¼" d	16.50
9" d	11.50
Teapot, Aladdin	50.00

Rose Parade
Bean Pot	35.00
Casserole	25.00
Pepper Shaker	11.00
Salad Bowl	17.50

Springtime
Bowl, 9¼" d	14.00
Custard Cup	5.00
Gravy Boat	18.00
Platter, oval, 13¼" l	14.00
Soup Plate	9.00

Taverne
Coffeepot, china drop	115.00
Leftover, rect	20.00
Mug	30.00
Salt, Colonial shape	22.00
Tea Tile, 6" d	90.00
Westinghouse, casserole, cov, yellow	20.00
Wildfire, platter, 13½" l	14.00

we're talking about architectural and carpentry hardware. Any self-respecting flea market will have an abundance of assorted items capable of pleasing any collector.

Drawer Pulls, turned wood drops, brass hardware, c1850, set of four, $30.00.

Door Bell, brass, spheres hanging from metal netting, mounting bracket	85.00
Door Knob, faceted crystal, 2½" d, brass hardware	2.00

Door Knocker
Dog's Head, figural, 7" h, brass	65.00
Eagle, figural, brass	55.00
Fox Head, figural, 5½" h, cast iron, ring hanging from mouth	85.00
Lion's Head, figural, bronze, ring hanging from mouth	50.00
Ram's Head, cast iron, England	65.00
Door Latch, butterfly shaped, iron	75.00
Flagpole Finial, 7" w, spreadwinged eagle, brass	25.00
Garden Stake, 30" h, sunburst and scrolls, wrought iron	250.00

Hinges, pr, iron
Barn Door, 32" l	50.00
Ram's horn, 12" l	175.00
Lock, 4 × 6", iron, turn handle with key, c1840	100.00
Padlock, wrought iron, key and fastening spikes	75.00
Shelf Brackets, pr, 5½" h, iron, swivel	18.00
Shutter Dogs, 8½" l, cast iron, mkd "Brevete SGDG" with anchor, set of four	150.00
Snowbirds, pr, 5¼" h, eagles, figural, cast iron	125.00

HARDWARE

The first thing one should realize about computer systems ... Wait! ... Stop! Sorry, wrong kind of hardware. Here

HARKER POTTERY

In 1840 Benjamin Harker of East Liverpool, Ohio, built a kiln and produced yellow ware products. During the Civil War,

David Boyce managed the firm. Harker and Boyce played important roles in the management of the firm through much of its history. In 1931 the company moved to Chester, West Virginia. Eventually Jeannette Glass Company purchased Harker, closing the plant in March 1972.

Much of Harker's wares were utilitarian. The company introduced Cameo ware in 1945 and a Rockingham ware line in 1960. A wide range of backstamps and names were used.

Newspaper: *The Daze,* P. O. Box 57, Otisville, MI 48463.

HATPIN HOLDERS AND HATPINS

Hatpins were used by women to hold on their hats. Since a woman was likely to own many and they were rather large, special holders were developed for them. Hatpins became a fashion accessory in themselves. The ends were decorated in a wide variety of materials ranging from gemstones to china.

Club: International Club for Collectors of Hatpins and Hatpin Holders, 15237 Chanera Avenue, Gardena, CA 90249.

Plate, gray border, 8¼" d, $3.00.

Left: pear shape, amber glass, brass filigree base, $7.50; right: flower, bronze metal, red stones surrounding faux diamond center, $8.00.

Batter Jug, Deco, Ohio, 5½" h	15.00
Bean Pot, Ameth.	6.00
Bowl, Cameo, pink	10.00
Cake Server, Modern Tulip, brown	15.00
Casserole, cov, Petit Point	18.00
Child's Feeding Dish, Cameo	35.00
Creamer and Sugar, Amy	7.50
Custard Cup, Ameth.	5.00
Fork, Red Apple II	30.00
Mixing Bowl, Red Apple	15.00
Pie Baker, 9" d, Deco	7.00
Pie Server, Rose II	15.00
Plate	
7½" d, Amy	4.00
9" d, Amy	6.00
10" d, Cameo, blue and white	7.50
Platter, Modern Tulip	8.00
Rolling Pin	
Amy	85.00
Flower Basket	85.00
Salt and Pepper Shakers, pr, Pate Sur Pate, gray	7.00
Spoon, Red Apple II	15.00
Teapot, Amy	35.00
Utility Plate, 12" d, Deco, Dahlia	15.00

HOLDERS

Bavarian China	
Bluebirds	55.00
Hand painted dec, 7" h	95.00
Floral	
Cobalt and pink, Japan	28.00
Cobalt and white	55.00
Kewpie	160.00
Porcelain	
Schafer & Vater, Jasperware medallion, woman's profile, 5" h	125.00
Schlegelmilch, RS Germany, white, gold dec	42.00

PINS

Art Nouveau, lady's head, 10K yg	235.00
Crystal stones, large ball	15.00
Enamel	
Bow shape, pearl center	45.00
St Louis World's Fair, 1904	30.00
Kewpie	50.00
Mother-of-Pearl, snake motif, ruby head, gold top, USA	175.00
Porcelain, scenic design, ornate mounting	35.00
Rhinestone, figural, butterfly, blue body	30.00

Silver Filigree, lotus blossom, 12" l **23.00**
Sterling Silver, maple leaf **20.00**
Tortoise Shell, pear shape, ribboned pi-
que work, 1¼" l **120.00**

HATS AND CAPS

No clothing accessory, except jewelry,
mirrors changing fashion tastes better
than a hat. Hats also express our individuality. How else do you explain some of the
hats that grace peoples' heads? Hang
twenty on a wall as decoration for a sure-
fire conversation piece.

Formal hats are fine. Want some real
fun? Start a collection of advertising base-
ball-style caps. The sources are endless—
from truck stops to farm equipment dealers. Why, you can even collect baseball
team hats. New, they cost between $5.00
and $20.00. At flea markets you can ac-
quire them for a couple of dollars each.

Straw, man's, red stripe on navy band, size 7,
1911, $35.00.

Beanie, 9" w, Kellogg's Pep, felt, blue
and white, 1940s.................. **75.00**
Bonnet
Baby's, cotton, tatted, ribbon ro-
settes **15.00**
Lady's, straw, finely woven, worn silk
lining...................... **135.00**
Boudoir Cap, crocheted, pink ro-
settes **12.00**
Cap, Hopalong Cassidy, fabric, small bill,
blue, white center panel with red,
blue, and yellow Hoppy illus, white
top button and piping, lined........ **60.00**
Cloche
Straw, lavender, Milan, 1920s....... **8.00**
Velvet, brown **15.00**
Crew Cap, canvas, white, blue, and orange panels, front panel with Trylon,

ship's tiller wheel, and seagull illus
above "New York World's Fair 1939"
inscription, adult size **40.00**
Derby, black **18.00**
Pillbox
Leopard Skin, matching purse **100.00**
Satin, black, netting **18.00**
Railroad, agent, Boston & Maine, gold
finish, curved top **38.00**
Sombrero, Cisco Kid, 15" d, 5" h, felt,
green, white piping, wood slide on
green and white cord, large **45.00**
Straw Hat, wide brim, multicolored chif-
fon flowers, c1940 .... **20.00**
Top Hat, beaver, child's **37.50**

HEISEY GLASS

A. H. Heisey Company of Newark, Ohio,
began operations in 1896. Within a short
period of time, it was one of the major
suppliers of glass to middle America. Its
many blown and molded patterns were
produced in crystal, colored, milk (opalescent), and Ivorina Verde (custard). Pieces
also featured cutting, etching, and silver
deposit decoration. Glass figurines were
made between 1933 and 1957.

Not all Heisey glass is marked. Marked
pieces have an "H" within a diamond.
However, I have seen some non-Heisey
pieces with this same marking at several
flea markets.

The key to Heisey glass is to identify the
pattern. Neila Brederhoft's *The Collector's
Encyclopedia of Heisey Glass, 1925–1938*
(Collector Books: 1986) is helpful for early
material. The best help for post-World War
II patterns are old Heisey catalogs.

Club: Heisey Collectors of America, P. O.
Box 4367, Newark, OH 43055.

Creamer and Sugar, banded and fluted, crystal,
sgd, $40.00.

Ashtray, Orchid, sq. **30.00**
Basket, Crystolite **170.00**
Bookends, pr, fish. **165.00**
Bowl, Provincial, crystal, 12" d, rolled
   edge **35.00**
Candlesticks, pr, Crystolite, crystal, sq
   base **50.00**
Champagne, Colonial, crystal **10.00**
Cheese Compote, Crystolite, crystal **24.00**
Coaster, Colonial, crystal **10.00**
Cocktail, Arcadia, crystal **16.00**
Cocktail Shaker, Rooster, 3 pcs **130.00**
Compote, Old Sandwich, green, 6" d. . . . **80.00**
Creamer, individual, Crystolite, crys-
   tal. **10.00**
Creamer and Sugar, Lariat, crystal. **18.00**
Cruet, orig stopper
   Pleat and Panel, green **75.00**
   Ridgeleigh, crystal. **50.00**
Custard, Colonial, crystal. **5.00**
Finger Bowl, Colonial, crystal **12.00**
Goblet, Arcadia, crystal **18.00**
Iced Tea Tumbler, Orchid Etch, crys-
   tal. **50.00**
Juice Tumbler, Provincial, crystal **12.00**
Mayonnaise, Waverly, crystal, orchid
   foot **85.00**
Mustard, cov, Colonial, crystal **40.00**
Nappy, Provincial, crystal. **15.00**
Plate
   Colonial, crystal, 4½" d **8.00**
   Old Colony, Sahara, 8½" sq **25.00**
   Provincial, crystal, 7" d. **9.00**
Relish, Crystolite, crystal, round, 5
   parts. **40.00**
Sherbet
   Arcadia, crystal **12.00**
   Orchid Etch, crystal **30.00**
Sherry, Colonial, crystal. **10.00**
Sugar, cov, individual, Crystolite, crys-
   tal. **12.00**
Torte Plate
   Crystolite, crystal, 13½" d. **30.00**
   Waverly, crystal **24.00**
Tumbler, New Era, crystal **24.00**

HEISEY GLASS ANIMALS

Heisey produced glass animals between 1937 and 1957. It is difficult to date an animal because many remained in production for decades.

Although the animal line was introduced in 1937, some forms made in the 1920s featured animal motifs, e.g., dolphin-footed and dolphin finial articles and a lion head bowl with paw feet marketed under the pattern name Empress, later Queen Anne. Other examples are the kingfisher and duck flower frogs. Collectors believe the dolphin candlestick was

made from molds obtained from the Sandwich Glass Company.

Royal Hickman and Horace King were two of the Heisey employees who were involved in the design of the animal figures. Many of King's designs resulted in animal head stoppers.

The most commonly found color is crystal. The price listings here are all for crystal. Many other colors were used, including Tangerine, Vaseline, Cobalt, Alexandrite, Amber, Limelight, Dawn, Marigold, Moongleam, Sahara, and Flamingo.

One final note: Collecting Heisey animal figures is not for those with a limited pocketbook. As you can see from the prices below, they are on the expensive side.

Club: Heisey Collectors of America, P. O. Box 4367, Newark, OH 43055.

Chick, head down. **70.00**
Cygnet. **150.00**
Donkey **250.00**
Duckling, floating. **150.00**
Elephant **350.00**
Giraffe **200.00**
Goose, wings up **90.00**
Hen **350.00**
Horse
   Clydesdale. **350.00**
   Colt
      Balking **175.00**
      Kicking **175.00**
      Standing **80.00**
   Filly
      Head backward **1,200.00**
      Head forward **900.00**
Piglet, walking **90.00**
Rabbit, head down **175.00**
Rooster **350.00**
Sparrow. **80.00**

HOLIDAY COLLECTIBLES

Holidays play an important part in American life. Besides providing a break from work, they allow time for patriotism, religious renewal, and fun. Because of America's size and ethnic diversity, there are many holiday events of a regional nature. Attend some of them and pick up their collectibles. I have started a Fastnacht Day collection.

This listing is confined to national holidays. If I included special days, from Secretary's Day to Public Speaker's Day, I would fill this book with holiday collectibles alone. Besides, in fifty years is anyone going to care about Public Speaker's Day? No one does now.

Newsletters: *Hearts to Holly: The Holiday Collectors Newsletter,* P. O. Box 105, Amherst, NH 03031; *Trick or Treat Trader,* P. O. Box 1058, Derry, NH 03038.

Halloween Clicker, litho tin, $7.00.

FOURTH OF JULY

Candy Box, 2¼ × 2½", shield shape, red, white, and blue 10.00
Flag, 10" h, 48 stars, wood stick 2.00
Post Card, "4th of July Greeting," red, white, and blue, gold ground, Germany, 1910 . . . . 2.00

GEORGE WASHINGTON'S BIRTHDAY

Candy Container, stump, 3" h, papier mache, surrounded by cherries, marked "Germany" 45.00
Diecut, 2½" h, George Washington, three different scenes, set of 3 . . . . 8.00
Post Card
  "Three Cheers for George Washington," children waving flag beneath Washington's portrait, 1909 . . . . . . 1.75
  "Washington The Father of His Country," 1912 . . . . 2.00

HALLOWEEN

Candy Container, papier mache, cone shaped, West Germany
  Devil, 7" h 28.00
  Witch, 7½" h 26.00
Centerpiece, cat, 12" h 15.00

Costume
  Clown, home made, baggy, yellow and black, trimmed in bells, matching pointed clown hat with bells, 1940s 8.00
  Porky Pig, child's, large, plastic mask, cloth suit and cap, Warner Bros, orig box, 1950s 10.00
  Star Trek, Mr Spock, 1967 . . . . 30.00
  Diecut, 14" h, copyright H E Lehrs, cat on moon 35.00
Jack-O-Lantern
  Glass Globe, battery operated, tin base, bail handle 45.00
  Papier Mache, bail handle, orig paper insert 62.00
  Tissue Face, green seams, Germany . . . 75.00
  Lantern, 7" h, papier mache, devil head, two tone red, paper insert behind cutout eyes and mouth, wire bail handle, Germany 100.00
Mask
  Katzenjammer Kids, Fritz, molded . . . 24.00
  Pirate, papier mache, string ties, marked "Germany" 10.00
Noisemaker, 3" d, rattle, round, tin, wooden handle, orange, white, and green, pumpkin and cats litho, USA 7.50

ST PATRICK'S DAY

Candy Container, 4½" h, Irish girl holding harp, standing on box, marked "Germany" 32.00
Diecut, 3" h, gold harp entwined with shamrocks and green ribbon, marked "Germany" 1.50
Pin, "Erin Go Bragh" across face, Irish and American flags, shamrock, harp, green satin ribbon attached to pin, paper on back of pin marked "12th St Badge and Novelty House, Phila, PA" 6.50
Post Card
  "Ireland Forever," shamrock with view of Ireland in each leaf, marked "Germany" 1.00
  "To My Little Colleen," girl dressed in green, large shamrock for hair bow, marked "London" 1.50
Sheet Music, "Sing Me A Song of Ireland," New York Publishing House, 1905 . . . . 10.00

THANKSGIVING

Candy Container, papier mache, Germany
  Hen Turkey
    4½" h 12.00
    6¾" h 35.00
  Tom Turkey
    2¾" h 12.00
    7¼" h 40.00

Turkey on Toothpick, papier mache,
Germany 10.00
Figurine, 4" h
Pilgrim Couple, composition, man and
woman, marked "Germany" 45.00
Turkey, celluloid, white, pink, and
blue, weighted bottom, marked
"Irwin, USA" 25.00
Post Card
"A Thanksgiving Greeting," large harvest pumpkin in background, three
turkeys eating from dish outside a
home, 1910 .... 1.00
"Thanksgiving Greetings," children
playing with with turkeys, 1909 ... 2.50

VALENTINE'S DAY

Greeting Card
Folding,
"Best Wishes," shades of blue,
picture of bird in center, poem
beneath, no greeting inside,
4½" h 5.00
"To My Sweetheart," small girl in
green dress and hat, red wild rose
border, verse inside, 6½" h 10.00
Mechanical, steamroller filled with
children holding hearts, wheels turn
and children move up and down,
tab operated, 6 × 10", marked "Germany" 18.00
Stand-up, "To My Sweetheart," white
dog, envelope in mouth, 6" h,
marked "Germany" 3.50
Post Card
Cupid on swing of roses, bordered by
red hearts and gold scroll work,
small verse, marked "E Nash" 1.25
"February 14th," trimmed in green
ivy, cupids shooting hearts and
arrows at two lovers, enclosed in
heart, marked "Germany, 1910"... 1.50
"To My Valentine with Love," portrait
of a young girl, emb background ... 2.00

HORSE COLLECTIBLES

This is one of those collectible categories
where you can collect the real thing, riding
equipment ranging from bridles to
wagons, and/or representational items. It
is also a category where the predominant
number of collectors are women.

The figurine is the most favored collectible. However, horse-related items can be
found in almost every collectible category
from Western movie posters to souvenir
spoons. As long as there is a horse on it, it
is collectible.

A neglected area among collectors is the
rodeo. I am amazed at how much rodeo
material I find at East Coast flea markets. I
never realized how big the eastern rodeo
circuit was.

*Ashtray, glass, black Art Deco-style horse, pink
ash receiver, $35.00.*

EQUIPMENT AND RELATED ITEMS

Bridle, braided leather strips, 1930s 45.00
Brush, leather back, stamped "US," patent date 1860s, Herbert Brush Mfg ... 60.00
Comb, mane and tail, marked "Oliver
Slant Tooth," 1940s 15.00
Saddle, Rocky Mountain crosstree type,
pack saddle, weathered wood supports. 75.00
Saddle Ring, SS 35.00
Stirrup, wood, rounded bottom, worn
leather cover 15.00
Wagon Seat, leather cov, springs and
steel frame 150.00

THEME ITEMS

Ashtray, figural, horse head, White
Horse Whiskey adv, white china,
painted 10.00
Belt Buckle, Roy Rogers and Trigger 35.00
Bookends, pr, aluminum, square, emb
horse head, sgd "Bruce Cox" 100.00
Calendar, Iroquois Brewing Co, Indian
on painted pony, 1897 .... 75.00
Christmas Ornament, hobby horse, Dresden. 80.00
Cigarette Lighter, Dale Evans, horse
head. 15.00
Decanter, Appaloosa, Jim Beam, Regal
China, 1974. .... 25.00
Doorstop, 5" l, cast iron, horse figure,
Hubley. 175.00
Figure
Chestnut Mare and Foal, Royal Doulton, HN2522 .... 450.00
Horse Jumping Fence, Breyer 45.00
Game, Derby Day, board folds out to 72",
six wooden horses and hurdles, Parker
Brothers, copyright 1959 .... 40.00
Horseshoe, Hopalong Cassidy, "Good
Luck," orig insert card, 1950 .... 20.00
Lunch Box, Trigger 45.00

Lunch Pail, Gene Autry and Champion,
1950s......................... **50.00**
Medal, Ohio horseshoer's, ribbon,
1917.......................... **57.50**
Photo, rancher on horse, mountain
scene **15.00**
Pin Cushion, metal, horseshoe shape ... **10.00**
Souvenir Spoon, Cheyenne, WY, buck-
ing horse, SS **22.00**
Toy
  Pull, 16" h, horsehair mane and tail,
  glass eyes, wood base, red wood
  wheels, late 19th C **600.00**
  Stuffed, mule, collar inscription "One
  of the Twenty Mule Team," Boraxo
  promotion, 1980s **15.00**
  Windup, tin, Lone Ranger on rearing
  horse **95.00**
Tray, horseback riders and roadster
scene, Coca Cola adv.............. **35.00**

HOT WHEELS

In 1968 Mattel introduced a line of 2"-long
plastic and diecast metal cars. Dubbed
"Hot Wheels," the line originally consisted
of sixteen cars, eight playsets, and two collector sets.

Hot Wheels are identified by the name
of the model and its year casted on the
bottom of each vehicle. The most desirable
Hot Wheels cars have red striping on the
tires. These early vehicles are the toughest
to find and were produced from 1968 to
1978. In 1979 black tires became standard
on all models. The most valuable Hot
Wheel vehicles are usually those with production runs limited to a single year or
those of a rare color.

So hop in your own set of wheels and
race off to your nearest flea market to find
your own hot collectibles.

1127, Greyhound MC8 Bus, three axles,
silver and white, 1980s............ **15.00**
1129, Super Scraper, Chevy pickup with
snow plow, orange, 1980s **10.00**
1169, Cement Mixer, Peterbilt, three
axles, red and white, 1980s **12.00**
1172, Bulldozer, yellow, 1980s **10.00**
2014, Hot Bird, brown **60.00**
2017, Lickety-Six, six wheels, blue,
1980........................... **15.00**
3004, Superfine Turbine, 1973 .... **45.00**
5699, Rear Engine Mongoose, 1972 .... **100.00**
5880, Double Header, 1973 .... **60.00**
6007, Sweet "16", 1973.............. **60.00**
6020, Cherry Picker/Snorkel, red and
white, 1970s **25.00**
6192, Waste Wagon, sanitation truck, orange, 1970s.................... **20.00**

6402, Paddy Wagon, T Van, windshield,
black, 1972 .... **50.00**
6403, Sand Crab Dunebuggy, clear roof,
1972......................... **30.00**
6436, Sky Show, playset, 1970 ....**350.00**
6450, Tow Truck, yellow, 1970s **20.00**
6459, Power Pad, Dunebuggy camper,
red and yellow, 1974 .... **35.00**
6461, Jeep Grasshopper, two engines,
roof, green, 1973................ **40.00**
6469, Sedan Fire Chief Cruiser, red,
1974......................... **30.00**
6472, Classic Ford, 1971............. **100.00**
6963, Police Cruiser, 1969 .... **40.00**
6965, Prowler, 1973................ **42.00**
6968, Alive '55, blue, 1973 .... **40.00**
6969, Snake, funny car, 1973 ....**200.00**
6971, Street Snorter, 1973............ **40.00**
6976, Buzz Off, 1974 .... **45.00**
6979, Hiway Robber, 1973............ **40.00**
6981, Odd Job, 1973................ **35.00**
6982, Show-Off **40.00**
7615, Peterbilt Road King Gravel Semi,
three axles, yellow, 1970s **25.00**
7619, Heavy Chevy, yellow, 1974...... **40.00**
7650, Emergency Squad Rescue Unit,
red, 1980s **10.00**
7659, Ramblin' Wrecker, "Larry's 24
Hr.," blue and white, 1980s **8.00**
7670, Backwoods Bomb, Chevy camper
pickup, 1971 .... **40.00**
8258, Ford Baja Bruiser, rollcage, orange, 1970s **25.00**
8260, Steam Roller Racer, white,
1970s........................ **20.00**
8262, Breakaway Bucket, Trans Am
pickup, blue, 1974 .... **65.00**
8273, El Rey Special, blue, 1974 .... **85.00**
9119, Formula 5000 Racer, white,
1970s........................ **25.00**
9120, Cool One Dragster, green,
1970s........................ **20.00**
9203, Mustang Stocker, yellow, 1975... **65.00**
9504, Military Machines, playset, with
staff car, 1976 ....**350.00**
9521, Army Staff Car, Oldsmobile, olive
drab, 1978.................... **20.00**
9641, Spoiler Sport Van, rear spoiler,
green, 1980s **10.00**
9643, Letter Getter, U. S. Mail van,
1977.......................... **65.00**
9645, GMC Motor Home, green,
1977......................... **60.00**
9649, '31 Doozie, orange, green fenders,
1977......................... **65.00**

HOWDY DOODY

The Howdy Doody show is the most famous of early television's children's programs. Created by "Buffalo" Bob Smith,
the show ran for 2,343 performances be-

tween December 27, 1947, and September 30, 1960. Among the puppet characters were Howdy Doody, Mr. Bluster, Flub-A-Dub, and Dilly-Dally. Princess Summerfall-Winterspring and Clarabelle, the clown, were played by humans.

There is a whole generation out there who knows there is only one answer to the question: "What time is it?"

Mug, plastic, red, decal, $25.00.

Activity Book
   Dot-To-Dot **20.00**
   Sticker Book **22.00**
Alarm Clock, figural, Howdy sitting on Clarabelle, Bob Smith wake up voice, MIB **135.00**
Bank, Howdy, sitting on pig..........**200.00**
Belt Buckle, 1950s **8.00**
Bubble Pipe Set, Howdy and Clarabell **95.00**
Catalog, products and illus, 22 pgs, reprint, 1955. .... **10.00**
Cookie Jar, tin, merry-go-round, marked "Cookie-Go-Round, Krispy".........**145.00**
Detective Disguises, Poll Parrot Shoes, cutout premium, mint, uncut **70.00**
Dinner Set, 3 pcs, plate, mug, and bowl, porcelain, mint **155.00**
Figure
   Mechanical
      Acrobat **225.00**
      Standing behind NBC microphone, wood, jointed **120.00**
      Push-up, wood, jointed, Howdy in front of NBC microphone, orig box.........................**195.00**
Football, white **75.00**
Game
   Bean Bag........................**125.00**
   Bowling, flip over, Howdy and four characters **145.00**
   Flub-A-Dub Flip A Ring, orig pkg **95.00**

Hand Puppet...................... **45.00**
Jigsaw Puzzle, ABC................. **95.00**
Little Golden Book **15.00**
Marionette, orig box.................**275.00**
Mug, Shake-Up, Ovaltine, orig top, decal **120.00**
Night Lamp, figural................**145.00**
Plaque, 14" d, Howdy with Santa, orig box, 1950 .... **95.00**
Plate, child's **35.00**
Pocket Watch, toy.................. **15.00**
Record Album, Howdy and Bob, The Air-O Doodle **75.00**
Shoe Polish, orig box **45.00**
Toy
   Squeeze, 13" h, wearing cowboy outfit **125.00**
   Wall Walker **35.00**
Transfer, unused................... **30.00**

HULL POTTERY

Hull Pottery traces its beginnings to the 1905 purchase of the Acme Pottery Company of Crooksville, Ohio, by Addis E. Hull. By 1917 a line of art pottery designed specifically for flower and gift shops was added to Hull's standard fare of novelties, kitchenware, and stoneware. A flood and fire destroyed the plant in 1950. When the plant reopened in 1952, Hull products had a newer glossy finish.

Hull is collected by pattern. A favorite with collectors is the Little Red Riding Hood kitchenware line, made between 1943 and 1957. Most Hull pieces are marked. Pre-1950 pieces have a numbering system to identify pattern and height. Post-1950 pieces have "hull" or "Hull" in large script writing.

Blossom Flite, console bowl, T10...... **50.00**
Bow Knot
   Basket, 10½" d, B-21 ....**350.00**
   Cornucopia, 5" l, pink and blue, B-2............................ **55.00**
   Jardiniere, 5¾" h, B-18 .... **65.00**
   Planter...........................**110.00**
Butterfly, cornucopia, 6½" l, B-2 ...... **40.00**
Camelia, (Open Rose)
   Candleholder, 6½" h, doves, 117, pr........................... **90.00**
   Console Bowl, 12" d, bird handles, 116.........................**125.00**
   Pitcher, 4¾" h, 128............... **35.00**
Ebbtide, basket **65.00**
Iris
   Basket, 4" d, hanging, 412.......... **50.00**
   Bowl, 12" d, oval, 409 .... **95.00**
   Vase, 16" h, tan.................**325.00**

Vase, 10⅞" h, pink, white interior, ftd, mkd "Hull, USA," $35.00.

Little Red Riding Hood, string
  holder **1,850.00**
Magnolia
  Basket, 10½" d **175.00**
  Ewer, 7" d, 5 . . . . **50.00**
  Teapot, 6½" h, orig paper label, 23 . . . **55.00**
  Vase, 6¼" h, matte, pink and blue,
    11 . . . . **35.00**
Poppy
  Bowl, 8" d, boat shape, 604 . . . . **75.00**
  Jardiniere, 4¾" h, 603 . . . . **50.00**
Rosella
  Ewer **40.00**
  Pitcher, 6½" h, R. **45.00**
Sunglow
  Basket, 6¼" d, pink, 84 . . . . **25.00**
  Wall Pocket **35.00**
Tokay
  Ewer, pink, tall **150.00**
  Planter, 6" h **20.00**
Tulip
  Flowerpot, 6" h, 116-33 . . . . **75.00**
  Vase, 6½" h, handles **32.00**
Water Lily
  Candleholder, L-22, pr **50.00**
  Console Bowl, 13½" d, L-21 . . . . **85.00**
  Vase
    6½" h, L-1-6 . . . . **35.00**
    10½" h, 12. . . . . **50.00**
Wildflower
  Candleholder, 4" h, double, 69 . . . . . . **75.00**
  Ewer, 13½" d, W-19. . . . . **250.00**
  Vase, 10½" h, W-15 . . . . **75.00**

Woodland
  Bud Vase, 8½" h, double, W-15. . . . . . **50.00**
  Planter, 10" h, W-14. . . . . **55.00**
  Wall Pocket, pink, glossy **55.00**

HUMMELS

Hummel items are the original creations of Beta Hummel, a German artist. At the age of 18, she enrolled in the Academy of Fine Arts in Munich. In 1934 Beta Hummel entered the Convent of Siessen and became Sister Maria Innocentia. She continued to draw.

In 1935, W. Goebel Co. of Rodental, Germany, used some of her sketches as the basis for three-dimensional figures. American distribution was handled by the Schmid Brothers of Randolph, Massachusetts. In 1967 a controversy developed between the two companies involving the Hummel family and the convent. The German courts decided the convent had the rights to Beta Hummel's sketches made between 1934 and her death in 1964. Schmid Bros could deal directly with the family for reproduction rights to any sketches made before 1934.

All authentic Hummels bear both the M. I. Hummel signature and a Goebel trademark. Various trademarks were used to identify the year of production. The Crown Mark (CM) was used in 1935, Full Bee (FB) 1940–1959; Small Stylized Bee (SSB) 1960–1972; Large Stylized Bee (LSB) 1960–1963; Three Line Mark (3L) 1964–1972; Last Bee Mark (LB), 1972–1980, and Missing Bee Mark (MBM) 1979–1990. In 1991 the trademark was changed. The W. (West) was dropped and the original crown mark was added.

Hummel lovers are emotional collectors. They do not like to read or hear anything negative about their treasure. At the moment, they are very unhappy campers. The Hummel market for ordinary pieces is flat, with little signs of recovery in the years ahead.

Hummel material was copied widely. These copycats also are attracting interest among collectors. For more information about them, see Lawrence L. Wonsch's *Hummel Copycats: A Guide to Those Other "Hummels"* (Wallace-Homestead: 1987).

Ashtray, Joyful, #33, CM **325.00**
Bookends, pr, Apple Tree Boy and Apple
  Tree Girl, #252 A&B, SSB **250.00**

Figurine, Singing Lesson, #63, stylized bee mark, 2⅞″ h, $80.00.

Candleholder, Happy Pastime, #111/69,
  3L. **125.00**
Figure
  Hello, FB **155.00**
  Little Goat Herder, #200, FB. **175.00**
  March Winds, #43, LB **75.00**
  Prayer Before Battle, FB **155.00**
  Village Boy, #51/3/0, CM. **115.00**
Figurine
  Accordion Boy,#185, FB **120.00**
  Baker, #128, SSB **85.00**
  Bird Duet, #169, 3L. **90.00**
  Chick Girl, #57/0, FB **100.00**
  Chimney Sweep, #122/0, LB **70.00**
  Heavenly Lullaby, #262, LB **110.00**
Font
  Angel Cloud, #206, LB **40.00**
  Seated Angel, #167, FB **75.00**
Lamp, Just Resting, #225/II, 3L **275.00**
Plaque, Mail Coach, #140, LB **135.00**

ICE BOXES

You know the play ''The Ice Man Cometh.'' Well, this listing is the legitimate reason why the ice man came. Never offer to help an ice box collector move!

Acme, ash, extra high, brass locks **750.00**
Economy, elm, golden finish, galvanized
  steel lining, brass hinges, 45 pound ice
  capacity, 41¼″ h **500.00**
Lapland Monitor, Ramey Refrigerator
  Co, Greenville, MI, oak, three paneled
  doors, paneled ends, square feet, metal
  name plate, 35″ w, 20″ d, 48″ h **575.00**
North Pole, oak, applied dec on two paneled doors, paneled ends, bracket feet,
  zinc lined, orig hardware, metal name
  plate, 25″ w, 19″ d, 55″ h. **475.00**

Victor, Challenge Refrigerator Co, Grand
  Haven, MI, oak, single raised panel
  door, paneled ends, zinc lined, orig
  hardware, metal name plate, 22″ w,
  15″ d, 40″ h **500.00**

INK BOTTLES

In the eighteenth and early nineteenth centuries, individuals mixed their own ink. With the development of the untippable bottle in the middle of the nineteenth century, the small individual ink bottles were introduced. Ink bottles are found in a variety of shapes, ranging from umbrella style to turtles. When the fountain pen arrived on the scene, ink bottles became increasingly plain.

Magazine: *Antique Bottle and Glass Collector*, P. O. Box 187, East Greenville, PA 18041.

Green, emb ''Staffords Ink,'' 3 × 2¼″, $20.00.

Allings Pat Apl 25 1871, medium blue
  green **50.00**
Billings, J T & Son, aqua **7.00**
Carter's Ink, amethyst, mold blown, ap-
  plied lip **4.00**
Drapers Improved Patent, cleear, 3 ×
  4″ **100.00**
Eells Writing Fluid, Mansfield, pottery,
  4⅜″ h. **55.00**
Greenwood's, clear, sheared top **8.00**
Higgins Inks, Brooklyn, NY, amethyst. . .**4.00**
Moses Brickett, olive green **12.00**
Paul's, aqua. **12.00**

Sanford, clear, round, crown top **2.00**
Signet Ink, cobalt blue **18.00**
Todd, W B, green **6.00**
Umbrella Ink, blue green, eight sided, 2¼" h. **40.00**
Wades Unchangeable Blue Writing Fluid, amber, twelve sided, 2½" h **60.00**

INKWELLS

Inkwells enjoyed a "golden age" between 1870 and 1920. They were a sign of wealth and office. The common man dipped his ink directly from the bottle. The arrival of the fountain pen and ball point pen led to their demise.

Inkwells were made from a wide variety of materials. Collectors seem to have the most fun collecting figural inkwells—but beware, there are some modern reproductions.

Club: Society For Inkwell Collectors, 5136 Thomas Avenue, Minneapolis, MN 55410.

Cast Iron Frame, pressed glass well, hinged lid, c1900, $85.00.

Brass, glass insert, hinged lid
   Art Nouveau **80.00**
   Egyptian Bust **60.00**
Cast Iron, double well, storks on sides. . . **50.00**
Glass, two screw-in hexagonal inkwells, attached cast metal George Washington statuette standing beside horse, wood stand, 6 × 7". **125.00**
Metal, cat's head on tray, glass insert . . . **70.00**

Pewter, pen rest with cherub dec, glass insert, floral dec on cov. **65.00**
Porcelain
   Domed, multicolored floral dec, white glaze, metal cap. **30.00**
   Figural, two children playing, Germany **85.00**
Traveling, cov, 2" d, round, leather, Russia. **75.00**
Wood, maple, cobalt blue glass liner **15.00**

INSULATORS

This trendy collectible of the 1960s has rested primarily in the collectors' realm since the early 1970s. As a result, prices have been stable.

Insulators are sold by "CD" numbers and color. Check N. R. Woodward's *The Glass Insulator In America* (privately printed, 1973) to determine the correct "CD" number. Beware of "rare" colors. Unfortunately, some collectors and dealers have altered the color by using heat and chemicals to increase the rarity value. The National Insulators Association is leading the movement to identify and stop this practice. They are one of the few clubs in the field that take their "policing" role seriously.

Club: National Insulators Association, 5 Brownstone Road, East Grandby, CT 06026.

CD 152, Aqua, Hemingray No. 40, $4.00.

Threaded

CD 102, Brookfield, NY, smooth base, aqua **4.00**
CD 102, Diamond, smooth base, root beer amber **5.00**
CD 102, Hawley, PA, smooth base, jade blue milk **85.00**
CD 104, New England Tel & Tel Co, smooth base, aqua **12.00**
CD 106, Ayala, round drip points, light green **35.00**
CD 106.3, Duquesne Glass Co, smooth base, cornflower blue **35.00**
CD 112.4, Hemingray, smooth base, light blue **25.00**
CD 121, AT & T Co, smooth base, dark aqua **2.00**
CD 131, Tillotson & Co, NY, smooth base, light aqua **225.00**
CD 134, California, smooth base, light rose **185.00**
CD 149, unmarked, smooth base, blue aqua **18.00**
CD 154, Lynchburg, round drip points, green **8.00**
CD 162, Fort Wayne, smooth base, aqua **25.00**
CD 163, Whitall Tatum, smooth base, light pink **4.00**
CD 167, Armstrong, corrugated base, root beer amber **4.00**
CD 170, unmarked, smooth base, aqua **12.00**
CD 190/191, Prism, smooth base, ice blue **65.00**
CD 200, Star, smooth base, yellow-green **275.00**
CD 239, Kimble, corrugated base, clear **4.00**
CD 248/311, Pyrex, smooth base, straw **35.00**
CD 252, Cable, smooth base, light steel blue **8.00**
CD 252, Knowles, smooth base, light green **20.00**
CD 263, Columbia, smooth base, light aqua **75.00**
CD 293.1, Locke, smooth base, blue aqua **45.00**
CD 317, Chambers, smooth base, dark aqua **150.00**
CD 320, Pyrex, smooth base, carnival **35.00**

Threadless

CD 701.6, unmarked, smooth base, olive black glass **225.00**
CD 723, unmarked, smooth base, celery green **350.00**
CD 735, Chester, NY, smooth base, ice aqua **450.00**
CD 735, Mulford & Biddle, smooth base, light blue **200.00**

IRONS

Country and kitchen collectors have kept nonelectric iron collecting alive. The form changed little for centuries. Some types were produced for decades. Age is not as important as appearance—the more unusual or decorated the iron, the more likely its value will be high.

There are still bargains to be found, but cast iron and brass irons are becoming expensive. The iron collectible of the future is the electric.

Clubs: Friends of Ancient Smoothing Irons, Box 215 Carlsbad, CA 92008; Midwest Sad Iron Collectors Club, 3915 Lay Street, Des Moines, IA 50317.

Natural Gas, Sunshine, Household Gas Iron Co, Philadelphia & New York, $30.00.

Alcohol
Comfort, Hawkes Flat-Iron Co, Chicago, cast aluminum cylinder tank, single row of vent holes, turned wood handle, patent 1903 . . . . **35.00**
Sun Gas Machine Co, cylinder tank on side **140.00**
Charcoal
Colebrookdale Iron Co, Boyertown, PA, #4, 7" l, tall spout with face damper **125.00**
Eclipse, single damper, two-tier top with handle, patent 1903 . . . . **35.00**
Electric, Wolverine **10.00**
Flat Iron and Sad Irons
Carver, Racine, WI, combination flat and reversible fluter, pointed ends, patent 1898 . . . . **50.00**
Mahoney, Troy, NY, wavy bottom **80.00**

Fluter

Crown, Philadelphia, PA, crank type,
brass rollers, table clamp, c1880.... **75.00**

Hewitt Revolving Iron, fluter attachment **170.00**

New Geneva, rocker style.......... **50.00**

The Best, rocker style **65.00**

Gasoline

American Gas Machine Co, Inc, #66,
7" l, light green porcelain base..... **90.00**

Coleman, round rear tank, pressure
pump, plastic handle............. **25.00**

Montgomery Ward, pump in handle,
triangular tank in rear............ **70.00**

Hat, brim, cast iron **150.00**

Natural Gas

Imperial, hose coupling at rear, five
holes on each side of base **55.00**

The Rhythm 3754 Radiation, 7" l,
green porcelain body, black plastic
handle **120.00**

Sleeve, Grand Union Tea Co, 8" l, charcoal, detachable bentwood handle ... **45.00**

Slug

Bless and Drake, combination fluter
and flat iron................... **55.00**

Star, American Machine Co, fluter,
cast iron base, crank type **75.00**

IRONSTONE POTTERY

This was the common household china of
the last half of the nineteenth century and
first two decades of the twentieth century.
Its name came because the ceramic ware
was supposed to wear like iron. Many different manufacturers used "ironstone"
when marking their pieces. However, the
vast majority of pieces do not bear the
"ironstone" mark.

When a piece is plain white and has a
pattern, it is known as "White Patterned
Ironstone." A decorative appearance was
achieved by using the transfer process.

Cake Plate, 12" d, Cable and Ring pattern, reticulated handles, Anthony
Shaw and Son, England **10.00**

Chamber Pot, cov, white, Corn and Oats
pattern, marked "Ironstone China,
Wedgwood," 1863 .... **130.00**

Creamer, white, Wheat and Clover pattern, Turner & Tomkinson **60.00**

Cup and Saucer

Oriental transfer, polychrome
enamel...................... **25.00**

White, Acorn and Tiny Oak pattern,
Pankhurst **25.00**

*Plate, transfer design, Vintage, J & G Alcock,
Cobridge, 10½" d, $15.00.*

Gravy Boat, 5" h, white, Wheat and
Blackberry pattern, 1860s **40.00**

Pitcher, white

8½" h, Wheat pattern, ribbed **30.00**

11" h, Ceres shape, marked "Elsmore
& Forster, Tunstall," 1859 .... **250.00**

Plate, white

7" d, Wheat and Clover pattern,
Turner & Tomkinson **15.00**

9¼" d, purple transfer, polychrome
enamel, Maastricht.............. **20.00**

10½" d, Corn pattern, Davenport **20.00**

Platter, 14½" l, white, Lily of the Valley
pattern, Alfred Meakin............. **40.00**

Relish Dish, 8¼" l, white, Wheat pattern,
1860s......................... **20.00**

Sauce Tureen, 6⅝" h, oval, white,
Ribbed Bud pattern, 1860s........ **220.00**

Soup Plate, 9" d, blue transfer, marked
"Adams"...................... **20.00**

Tea Set, child's, red Punch and Judy
transfer, three plates, four cups and
saucers, teapot, waste bowl, sugar.... **165.00**

Toothbrush Holder, cov, 8⅛" l, 2⅝" d,
white, Wheat and Blackberry pattern,
1860s......................... **70.00**

IVORY

Ivory is a yellowish-white organic material
that comes from the teeth and tusks of
animals. In many cases, it is now protected
under the Endangered Species Act of
1973, amended in 1978, which limits the
importation and sale of antique ivory and
tortoise shell items. Make certain that any
ivory that you buy is being sold within the
provisions of this law.

Vegetable ivory, bone, stag horn, and plastic are ivory substitutes. Do not be fooled. Most plastic substitutes do not approach the density of ivory nor do they have crosshatched patterns. Learn the grain patterns of ivory, tusk, teeth, and bone. Once you have, a good magnifying glass will quickly tell you if you have the real thing.

Box, 3" h, carved, round, fishermen and
waterscape dec, ftd, c1910 . . . . **400.00**
Button, ¾" sq, stylized bird **8.00**
Cameo, carved, five hunting dogs in for-
est, gold rope twist frame, c1830 . . . . . **475.00**
Crochet Hook, carved. **12.50**
Darning Egg, 1¼" l, miniature, mush-
room shape **12.00**
Figure
Apple, 3" h, carved scene inside **120.00**
Buddha, 3" h, sitting. **95.00**
King and Queen, pr, 3" h, sitting on
dragon and phoenix thrones **200.00**
Monkeys, 2½" h, three evils **200.00**
Hat Pin, carved, bird motif, steel pin, En-
gland, c1830 . . . . **300.00**
Knitting Needles, pr, 14" l, black
heads **25.00**
Needle Case
Cylinder, carved basketweave pat-
tern **85.00**
Fish shape **95.00**
Netsuke, 1¼" h, musician with
stringed instrument, sgd, Japan, early
20th C **175.00**
Pen Holder, 4" h, three carved monkeys
and tree **180.00**
Pendant, 2¼" l, hand shape, gold chain,
19th C **850.00**
Pincushion
Basket, 3 × 2", handle **85.00**
Pedestal base, 2" h, red velvet cush-
ion **40.00**
Ruler, carved demarcations **150.00**
Sewing Box, holds thread, thimble, and
punch holder. **65.00**
Stickpin, carved dog, gold pin, 19th C . . . **275.00**
Stiletto, 3" l, turned top **32.00**
Tape Measure
Cylinder, Stanhope finial, painted. . . . **45.00**
Top, spinning **50.00**
Teapot, 5½" h, carved panels. **325.00**
Thimble Case, 1½" h, barrel shape,
carved lines **55.00**
Tatting Shuttle, carved geometric
lines **40.00**
Thread Holder, acorn shape, holds one
spool **75.00**
Thread Winder, snowflake shape **45.00**

JEWELRY

All jewelry is collectible. Check the prices on costume jewelry from as late as the 1980s. You will be amazed. In the current market, "antique" jewelry refers to pieces that are one hundred years old or older, although an awful lot of jewelry from the 1920s and 1930s is passed as "antique." "Heirloom/estate" jewelry normally refers to pieces between twenty-five and one hundred years old. "Costume" refers to quality and type, not age. Costume jewelry exists for every historical period.

The first step to determining value is to identify the classification of jewelry. Have stones and settings checked by a jeweler or gemologist. If a piece is unmarked, do not create hope where none deserves to be.

Finally, never buy from an individual that you will not be able to find six months later. The market is flooded with reproductions, copycats, fakes, and newly made pieces. Get a receipt that clearly spells out what you believe you bought. Do not hesitate to have it checked. If it is not what it is supposed to be, insist that the seller refund your money.

Necklace Set, Art Nouveau, sterling silver, putti motif, matching necklace, clasp, and belt buckle, mkd "Kerr," $950.00.

Bar Pin
Gold, 15K, set with three cabochon
garnets. **200.00**
Sterling Silver, "MIZPAH" and ribbon
motif, English hallmarks. **45.00**
Bracelet
Art Nouveau, 18K yg, enameled blue
and green dec, Tiffany. **285.00**
Bangle, gold filled, etched band dec. . . **75.00**
Brooch, porcelain, hp portrait, gold filled
frame. **250.00**

Brooch/Pendant, tri-color 14K yg,
filigree mounting, Wedgwood **185.00**
Cuff Links, pr
Ball motif, 14K yg **90.00**
Shamrock motif, SS **80.00**
Earrings, small hoop, 14K yg **130.00**
Locket
Gold, yellow, oval painted miniature,
half pearl floral frame **225.00**
Silver, black onyx shield centered by
turquoise and half pearl floral bas-
ket **200.00**
Necklace, Art Deco, enamel dec, SS links,
set with lapis color glass **165.00**
Pendant, figural, carved lava, gold
fittings **250.00**
Pin
Art Deco, antelope motif, SS **55.00**
Arts and Crafts, SS, round orange
petaled flowers, star points, hall-
marked and stamped "JF," 1½" d,
pr **140.00**
Victorian, ivory, carved floral de-
sign **35.00**
Pocket Watch, lady's, 14K tri-color gold,
hunting case, emb background, ap-
plied birds, Elgin **650.00**
Ring
Platinum, .45 pt dark blue sapphire,
filigree spokes radiating to eight
sided mounting with sixteen 2 pt cut
diamonds **450.00**
Yellow Gold, 10K, rose cut garnet
stones **140.00**
Scarf Pin, gold, Etruscan bead work,
pietra dura center **175.00**
Stick Pin, 14K yg, gargoyle motif, set
with ruby **125.00**

JEWELRY, COSTUME

Diamonds might be a girl's best friend, but
costume jewelry is what most women
own. Costume jewelry is design and form
gone mad. There is a piece for everyone's
taste—good, bad, or indifferent.

Collect it by period or design—high-
brow or lowbrow. Remember that it is
mass-produced. If you do not like the price
the first time you see a piece, shop around.
Most sellers put a high price on the pieces
that appeal to them and a lower price on
those that do not. Since people's tastes
differ, so do the prices on identical pieces.

Costume jewelry often was sold in sets.
A piece from a broken set has much less
value than the entire unit. Collectors have
not placed a strong emphasis on original
packaging. I think they are making a mistake. In many cases, the packaging provides the only identification of a maker.

*Scatter Pins, thread motif, gold plated, 1½" h,
$200.00.*

Bracelet
Abalone **40.00**
Bakelite, black, carved **25.00**
Faux Pearls, three rows, sterling
filigree medallion **46.00**
Bracelet and Earring Set
Bakelite, hinged, cream color, rhine-
stones **45.00**
Rhinestones, green, Occupied Ja-
pan **32.00**
Brooch, figural
Dragonfly, sgd "BSK" **35.00**
Floral, Coro Duette **35.00**
Poodle **35.00**
Brooch and Earrings Set, coral, gold
overlay **20.00**
Choker, faux pearls, center drop **12.00**
Charm, Santa, metal, red enamel **28.00**
Earrings, pr
Copper, enameled, Matisse **25.00**
Lavender and Rhinestones, Lisner **25.00**
Rhinestone, drop **15.00**
Sterling, swordfish, Taxco **20.00**
Lapel Pin, Donald Duck, rhinestones, red
stones **35.00**
Necklace
Agate, 15" l, large gold beads, green
and black enamel over brass trim . . . **35.00**
Amethyst, 31" l **26.00**
Art Deco, three enameled brass discs,
four alternating blue glass drops . . . **48.00**
Coral, 16" l, three strands **45.00**
Crystal, facet cut, sterling clasp **65.00**
Faux Cultured Pearls, double strand,
Ciner **45.00**
Hawaiian Seed **4.00**
Jet Black **65.00**
Lucite **50.00**
Oyster Shell, three blue Venetian trade
beads **40.00**
Plastic, pastel fruit **6.00**
Rope Twist, 16" l, pearls and amethyst
carnival beads **30.00**
Turquoise, gold enameled, two mer-
maids kissing **30.00**
Necklace and Earring Set
Rhinestone, center drop, 15" l
chain **35.00**

Satin Glass, purple, 1930s **60.00**
Pendant
  Bakelite, 2 × 2½", black cameo, clear
    base, 26" l chain **28.00**
  Cornucopia, 3" d, hanging pearls, Kra-
    mer **40.00**
  Faux Topaz, Emmons **25.00**
  Marcasite, mother-of-pearl, chain **24.00**
Pin
  Arts & Crafts, copper, sterling silver
    dec **45.00**
  Bakelite and Ivory, 3" d, flower,
    carved, France **40.00**
  Brass, fly, amethyst stones **37.00**
  Lucite, rooster **27.00**
  Marcasite, "Mother" **22.00**
  Rhinestones, Weiss
    Colored **28.00**
    Pink **30.00**
  Sterling Silver
    Floral and leaf **30.00**
    Openwork, faceted amethysts **27.00**
Ring
  Bakelite, red, white, and blue **20.00**
  Garnet, Bohemian, lady's **75.00**
  Sterling Silver, filigree, large jelly
    opal **55.00**

Bowl, gray glaze, cobalt trim, orange peel tex-
ture, imp signature, 4½" d, 3" h, $25.00.

Pie Plate, 9½" d, orange ground, black
  concentric circles dec **70.00**
Rose Jar, cov, 4½" h, blended olive green
  glaze **50.00**
Sugar, cov, 3¾" h, Tobacco Spit glaze,
  marked **35.00**
Vase
  3¾" h, brown glaze, two handles **35.00**
  7" h, 4½" d, bulbous ovoid body, nar-
    row flat mouth, green glaze,
    marked **145.00**

JUGTOWN

Jugtown is the pottery that refused to die. Founded in 1920 in Moore County, North Carolina, by Jacques and Julianna Busbee, the pottery continued under Julianna and Ben Owens when Jacques died in 1947. It closed in 1958 only to reopen in 1960. It is now run by Country Roads, Inc., a non-profit organization.

The principal difficulty is that the pottery continues to produce the same type of wares using the same glazes as it did decades ago. Even the mark is the same. Since it takes an expert to tell the newer pieces from the older pieces, this is a category that novices should avoid until they have done a fair amount of study.

Carolina pottery is developing a dedicated core group of collectors. For more information read Charle G. Zug III's *Turners and Burners: The Folk Potters of North Carolina* (University of North Carolina Press: 1986).

Bowl, 4¾" d, 1¼" h, Chinese blue
  glaze **85.00**
Cookie Jar, cov, 12" h, ovoid, strap han-
  dles **75.00**
Creamer, cov, 4¾" h, yellow, marked . . . **45.00**
Jar, cov, 6" h, green glaze **95.00**
Mug, brown glaze **25.00**

JUICERS

Dad lists them as "Reamers" in *Warman's Americana and Collectibles*. Here I call them "Juicers." Finding them in mint condition is next to impossible. The variety of material in which they are found is staggering, ranging from wood to sterling silver. As in many other categories, the fun examples are figural. Scholarly collectors might enjoy focusing on mechanical examples, although I am not certain that I would mention on the cocktail circuit or at the church social hall that I collect "mechanical reamers."

Reamers are identified by a number system developed by Ken and Linda Ricketts in 1974. This cataloging system was continued by Mary Walker in her two books on reamers.

Edna Barnes has reproduced a number of reamers in limited editions. These are marked with a "B" in a circle.

Club: National Reamer Collectors Association, Rt. #1, Box 200, Grantsburg, WI 54840.

China
  Clown, figural, 4½" h, pastel yellow,
    Rising Sun Mark, Japan **35.00**

Delft-type dec, blue and white, Germany 42.00

Happy Face, 2 pcs, lemon rind textured surface, yellow spots, green leaves and handle, painted face, white ground, Japan, c1950 . . . . 50.00

Orange Shape, figural, 3¼" h, 2 pcs, orange body, green leaves, England 24.00

Glass

Amber, ribbed, loop handle, Federal 20.00

Black, fired on, ribbed, tab handle, Anchor Hocking 12.00

Clambroth, ribbed, curved tab handle, marked "Orange Juice Extractor" 95.00

Clear

Easley Mfg Co, baby, 1 pc, four blades, basket pattern, rope border, c1902 . . . . 35.00

Fenton, baby, 2 pcs, red and white elephant and "Orange" inscription on base 75.00

Ideal, baby, patent 1888 . . . . 25.00

Westmoreland, baby, 2 pcs, painted flowers and "Baby's Orange" inscription on base, c1900 . . . . 30.00

Delphite, Jeannette, loop handle, small 60.00

Frosted crystal, baby, 2 pcs, painted "Baby" inscription on base 90.00

Green

Fry, 1 pc, tab handle 25.00

Jenkins, baby, 2 pcs 100.00

Light Jadite, Jeannette, loop handle, large 20.00

Milk Glass

Hazel Atlas, 2 pcs, blue dots dec 35.00

McKee, "Sunkist" in block letters 20.00

Pink, Indiana, ribbed, loop handle 45.00

Sun-colored amber, Westmoreland, baby, 2 pcs 85.00

Metal

Aluminum

Handy Andy, 10½" h, 6⅞" d, table type, crank, red base 20.00

Knapp's, crank at top, hand held, patent 1930 . . . . 10.00

Mason's Sealed Sweet Juicer, wall mounted, 1930s 10.00

Rival Mfg Co, Kansas City, MO, lever action, c1935 . . . . 40.00

Wearever E-12-1, Ebaloy Inc, Rockford, IL, 6" h, 20th C 6.00

Stainless Steel, 2½" h, 2 pcs, flat, Hong Kong 8.50

Steel and Aluminum, Kwikway Products, Inc, St Louis, Mo, hand held, wire reamer, domed lid with crank, hinged handles, patent 1929 . . . . . . 18.00

Plastic, figural chef, combination reamer/lemon slicer, red, c1950 . . . . . 5.00

Pottery, grapefruit size, yellow, sgd Red Wing 150.00

KEWPIES

Kewpies are the creation of Rose Cecil O'Neill (1876–1944), artist, novelist, illustrator, poet, and sculptor. The Kewpie first appeared in the December 1909 issue of *Ladies Home Journal*. The first Kewpie doll followed in 1913.

Many early Kewpie items were made in Germany. An attached label enhances value. Kewpie items also were made in the United States and Japan. The generations that grew up with Kewpie dolls are dying off. O'Neill's memory and products are being kept alive by a small but dedicated group of collectors.

Club: International Rose O'Neill Club, P. O. Box 688, Branson, MO 65616.

Doll, celluloid, Japan, 5½" h, $15.00.

Blanket, 15 × 28", flannel, center with five Kewpies, Kewpie border, "C" and "Rose O'Neill" marks 50.00

Candy Container 40.00

Christmas Plate, 1973, orig package 8.00

Crumb Tray, brass.................. **30.00**
Cup and Saucer, Royal Rudolstadt **225.00**
Doll, 11" h, vinyl, glass eyes, orig clothes
and tag, Cameo Dolls Products....... **85.00**
Door Knocker, brass................ **65.00**
Figure, 5" h, bisque, O'Neill.......... **60.00**
Handkerchief **28.00**
Paper Dolls, Kewpies in Kewpieland,
uncut book **20.00**
Pin, 2" d, cameo Kewpie **50.00**
Post Card, 3½ × 5½", Valentine, Kewpie
pair snuggled on chair, Gibson Art Co,
c1920......................... **30.00**
Recipe Book, Jell-O **30.00**

KEY CHAINS

Talk about an inexpensive collecting category. Most examples sell under $10.00. If you are really cheap, you can pick up plenty of modern examples for free. Why not? They are going to be collectible in thirty years and antiques in a hundred. Who knows, maybe you will live that long!

One of the favorite charity fundraising gimmicks in the 1940s and 1950s was the license plate key chain tag. There is a collectors' club devoted to this single topic.

Club: Key Chain Tag Collectors Club, 888 8th Avenue, New York, NY 10019.

Newsletter: *The Chain Gang*, P. O. Box 9397, Phoenix, AZ 85068.

Advertising
Atlas Powder Co, 1½" l, rect, brass,
commemorates office building dedi-
cation in Wilmington, DE, 1955.... **18.00**
Camel Cigarettes, 1¼" d silvered brass
pendant with trademark camel and
Spanish inscription, silvered brass
chain, 1930s **24.00**
Hercules Powder Co, 1¼" l, rect, brass,
logo and company name, reverse
with "Fiftieth Anniversary 1912–
1962" **12.00**
Indian Bicycles, 1¼" l, brass, detailed
Indian in canoe, tree lined river
scene, c1900 .... **60.00**
Oilzum, 1½" l, brass, diecut trade-
mark **30.00**
Swift Premium Hams, enamel **12.00**
Automobile, inscription on back to re-
turn to owner
Chrysler, ⅞ × 1¾", emb copper,
Airflow model, 1934............ **20.00**
Studebaker, ⅞ × 1¾", silvered brass,
c1930........................ **25.00**

Advertising, Duquesne Brewing Co, aluminum, penny center, brass chain, $2.00.

Good Luck, rabbit's foot, pink fur **5.00**
Identification, US Social Security, 1½" l,
SS, raised wings design, engraved se-
rial number on front, owner's name
and address on back **18.00**
Political
John F Kennedy, metal, brass finish,
diecut initials, brass chain........ **15.00**
Robert F Kennedy, plastic, red, gold
portrait and "He Cared," brass chain
and ring **8.00**
Willkey/McNary, plastic, elephant
shape, amber, brass chain........ **25.00**
Premium
Ked's, 1½" l, blue plastic, combination signaling device/magnifying
glass, brass chain, 1960s **20.00**
P F Sneakers, 3" l, ivory plastic, large
animal tooth shape, logo and antelope head dec, built-in siren
whistle, sun dial, and alphabet
code, 1960s **25.00**
Souvenir
Chicago World's Fair, 1 × 1¾", brass,
emb city seal, 1893 .... **20.00**
Franklin Institute, horseshoe, aluminum, penny center **2.50**
New York World's Fair, 3" l, miniature
flashlight, orange plastic, silver and
blue stripes, 1939 .... **50.00**

KEYS

There are millions of keys. Focus on a special type of key, e.g., automobile, railroad switch, etc. Few keys are rare; prices above $10.00 are unusual.

Collect keys with a strong decorative motif. These range from keys with advertising logos to cast keys with animal or interlocking scroll decorations. Be suspicious if someone offers you a key to King Tut's Tomb, Newgate Prison, or the Tower of London.

Club: Key Collectors International, P. O. Box 9397, Phoenix, AZ 85068.

Railroad Switch Keys

Cabinet, barrel type
  Brass
    Decorative bow, 1½" l **3.00**
    Standard bow and bit, 3" l **3.50**
  Bronze, dolphin design, 2½" l **12.00**
  Iron, painted, Art Deco plastic bow, 3" l **9.50**
  Nickel plated, Art Deco bow, 2½" l . . .   **5.00**
  Steel
    Art Deco, 2" l **6.00**
    Standard bow and bit, 3" l . . . .   **.75**
Car
  Basco, steel, flat, early **1.50**
  Edsel, any maker. **2.50**
  Ford, Model "T," brass, crown mark **8.00**
  Studebaker, Eagle Lock Co, logo key **1.50**
Car, special
  Auto Dealer Presentation Keys, gold plated. **1.50**
  Crest Key, common cars. **1.50**
Casting Plate, bronze, 4" l **22.00**

Door
  Brass, standard bow and bit, 6" l **12.00**
  Bronze, special logo bow, 6" l. **15.00**
  Steel, Keen Kutter bow **3.50**
Folding, jackknife
  Bronze and Steel, bit cuts, maker's name, 5" l **18.00**
  Steel, bit cuts, Graham, 5½" l. **6.50**
Gate, iron, bit type, 6" l **4.00**
Hotel
  White Metal, bit type, silhouette of hotel, 4" l **10.00**
  Steel, bit type, bronze tag, 4" l **3.50**
Jail
  Nickel-Silver, pin tumbler, Yale Mogul, uncut blank **12.00**
  Spike Key, steel plated bow, serial number, Yale, 5½" l **40.00**
  Steel, flat, lever tumbler, Folger-Adams, cut. **18.00**
Keys to the City, presentation, antique bronze, 6" l **14.00**
Pocket Door, bow folds sideways, nickel plated, Art Nouveau, oval bow **15.00**
Railroad
  B&M RR, Boston & Maine **20.00**
  DT RR, Detroit Terminal. **18.50**
  IC RR, Illinois Central **10.00**
Ship
  Bit Type, bronze, foreign ship tag. **6.00**
  Pin Tumbler Type, US Coast Guard tag **3.00**
Watch
  Brass, plain, swivel **2.00**
  Gold Plated, advertising **12.00**

KITCHEN COLLECTIBLES

Kitchen collectibles are closely linked to Country, where the concentration is on the 1860–1900 period. This approach is far too narrow. There are a lot of great kitchen utensils and gadgets from the 1900 to 1940 period. Do not overlook them.

Kitchen collectibles were used. While collectors appreciate the used look, they also want an item in very good or better condition. It is a difficult balancing act in many cases. The field is broad, so it pays to specialize. Tomato slicers are not for me; I am more of a chopping knife person.

Basting Spoon, granite, cobalt handle . . . **12.00**
Brochure, Queen Kitchen Cabinets, 1890s. **15.00**
Butter Churn, table top type, stave construction, handle. **110.00**
Can Opener, cast iron, Universal Dazey, pat pend. **87.00**

Tea Strainer, porcelain, Germany, 4" h, $125.00.

Catalog, Republican Kitchen Ware, 1911, 394 pgs, tin, enameled, and granite wares. 85.00
Cheese Spreader, sterling. 25.00
Coffee Grinder
   Lap type, wood 20.00
   Wall mount, Landers #24. . . . . 60.00
Coffeepot Stand, Griswold, 7" d 125.00
Corn Stick Pan, Griswold #273, 13" l . . . 115.00
Cream Can, cov, aluminum, wood bail handle 10.00
Cutlery Tray, tin, center handle. 25.00
Dish Towels, embroidered days of week, set of 6 . . . . 15.00
Dutch Oven, Wagnerware, No. 9. . . . . . . 40.00
Egg Basket, wire, collapsible 20.00
Egg Whip, red handle, dated 1906. . . . . . 12.00
Eggbeater, red Bakelite trim, Androck 22.00
Food Chopper, Universal 6.00
Funnel/Measure/Strainer, tin, red handle 10.00
Juicer, aluminum, crank handle 10.00
Kettle, light blue swirl, marked "Wrought Iron Range" 235.00
Meat Fork, marked "Vintage". 18.00
Onion Chopper, glass jar, paper label . . . 10.00
Pea Sheller, iron, crank handle 27.50
Pie Server, sterling 25.00
Popover Pan, Griswold #10 . . . . 75.00
Pot Scrubber, wire rings 39.00
Recipe Box, metal, blue, includes recipes 10.00
Refrigerator Dish, cov, rect, glass, green. 12.00
Skillet, Griswold
   No. 3 . . . . 16.00
   No. 6 . . . . 18.00
   No. 12 . . . . 95.00
Stove, table top type, Armstrong 85.00

Toaster, swing out type
   Estate, No. 117, four slice 55.00
   Gold Seal Electric Co, No. 12780 . . . . . 38.00

KNOWLES CHINA

There are two Knowles companies that made china. The Edwin M. Knowles China Company, Newell and Chester, West Virginia, made dinnerware from 1900 until 1963. Knowles, Taylor, Knowles, East Liverpool, Ohio, operated from 1854 until 1931. Edwin was the son of Isaac Knowles of Knowles, Taylor, Knowles.

The Edwin M. Knowles Company opened in the 1970s when it entered into a special relationship with the Bradford Exchange to produce limited edition collector plates, such as Gone with the Wind and the Wizard of Oz. The company also produces Rockwell items.

Collector's Plate, Gone With the Wind Series, Scarlett, Raymond Kursar artist, 1978, $100.00.

Coaster, Yorktown shape, white 8.00
Collector's Plate
   Annie and the Orphans, 1984, Little Orphan Annie series. 20.00
   Easter, 1980, Americana Holiday series. 30.00
   Over The Rainbow, 1977, first edition, Wizard of Oz series 65.00
   Scarlett's Green Dress, 1984. . . . . 50.00
Coffee Server, Deanna shape
   Green. 35.00
   Stripes 37.00
Cookie Jar, Tulip, Utility Ware. 35.00
Creamer, Pink Pastel 3.00
Gravy Boat, Penthouse, Yorktown shape. 10.00

Lug Soup, Deanna shape, yellow. **5.00**
Mixing Bowl, Tia Juana **30.00**
Pie Plate, Tulip, Utility Ware **15.00**
Pitcher, cov, Fruits, Utility Ware **25.00**
Plate
  10″ d, dinner, Picket Fence, Yorktown
    shape **10.00**
  10¾″ d, chop burgundy, Yorktown
    shape **18.00**
Platter
  Daisies, Deanna shape **8.00**
  Tuliptime, eight sided **10.00**
Refrigerator Dish, Tia Juana, Utility
  Ware, stacking, set of 3 . . . .   **15.00**
Saucer, Wildflower. **3.00**
Serving Tray, Tia Juana, Utility Ware . . .   **20.00**
Shaker
  Fruits **12.00**
  Shaker Plaid, Deanna shape **8.00**
Soup, flat, 8″ d, Tia Juana **15.00**
Teapot, cov, Yorktown shape, Mango
  red **45.00**
Vegetable Bowl
  Bench, 9″ d, round **15.00**
  Tuliptime, eight sided **12.00**

LABELS

The first fruit crate art was created by California fruit growers in about 1880. The labels became very colorful and covered many subjects. Most depict the type of fruit held in the box. With the advent of cardboard boxes in the 1940s, fruit crate art ended and the labels became collectible.

When collecting fruit crate labels or any other paper label, condition is extremely important. Damaged, trimmed, or torn labels are significantly less valuable than labels in mint condition.

Club: Citrus Label Society, 16633 Ventura Blvd, No. 1011, Encino, CA 91436.

Beverages, Pete Nichaus Wines & Liquors, 3″ l, hand shaped, "Get Your Money's Worth," red and white, gummed **8.00**
Carpet, Bibb Manufacturing Co, 5 × 15″, "carpet warp, 20 cuts, long reel," Beatty & Co Lith, NY. **20.00**
Clothing
  Baiers Shoes, St Louis, oval sunburst shaped, gummed. **6.00**
  Fruit of the Loom, 7 × 9″, fruit illus, mkd "copyright secured by BB & R Knight" **20.00**
  Jersey Outing Shirt, printed and gilded, rect **10.00**

Food
  H J Heinz Co, 3¾″ l, pickle shaped, gummed **15.00**
  Shredded Wheat Biscuits, four leaf clover shaped, gummed **6.00**
  Verhampshire Pure Peanut Butter, rect. **5.00**
Fruit Crate
  Better 'N Ever, half sliced grapefruit, blue ground. . . . .   **.50**
  Caledonia, thistle spray, tartan plaid ground, Placential **1.00**
  Desert Bloom, grapefruit, desert scene, white blooming yucca, blue sky, Redlands **2.00**
  Don't Worry, little boy holding apple, black ground **1.00**
  Eat One, arrow pointing to juicy orange, aqua ground, Lindsay **2.00**
  Forever First, red holly berries, greens, and plump juicy pears, blue ground **2.00**
  Great Valley, scenic, orange orchard, Orange Cove **1.00**
  L-Z, smiling boy holding green grapes . . . .   **.50**
  Littlerock, bunch of pears, orchard . . .   **1.00**
  Morning Smile, lemon on opened Sunkist wrapper, blue ground **1.00**
  Red Diamond, red and yellow apples, red diamond, blue ground **1.00**
  Sea Coast, two lemons, blue triangle, brown ground, Ventura **2.00**
  Sunkist California lemons, lemon, yellow letters, black ground **1.00**
  Tell, red apple pierced by arrow, gray ground. **1.00**
  Wilko, red apple, red border, yellow ground. **1.00**
Household Goods, Winshine Window Cleaner, rect **6.00**
Toiletries, "Try Gemiletum Antiseptic Tooth Paste," leaf shaped, gummed **8.00**

LACE

While there are collectors of lace, most old lace is still bought for use. Those buying lace for reuse are not willing to pay high prices. A general rule is the larger the amount or piece in a single pattern, the higher the price is likely to be. In this instance, price is directly related to supply and demand.

On the other hand, items decorated with lace that can be used in their existing form, e.g., costumes and tablecloths, have value that transcends the lace itself. Learn to differentiate between handmade and machine-made lace. Value for these pieces rests in the item as a whole, not the lace.

Ask yourself one basic question: When was the last time you used any lace or anything with lace on it? Enough said.

Club: International Old Lacers, Box 1029, West Minster, CO 80030.

LADY HEAD VASES

Heart-shaped lips and dark eyelashes mark the charm of the typical lady head vase. Manufactured in the early 1950s, these semi-porcelain, glazed, or matte-finished vases were produced in Japan and the United States. The sizes of lady head vases range from 4½" to 7" high. The decoration is thoughtfully done with a flair for the modeled feminine form. Many of the vases show the character from the shoulders up with elaborate jewelry, delicate gloves, and a stylized hair-do or decorated hat. A majority of the head vases are marked on the base with the company and place of manufacture.

Dickson, Japan, 7½" h, Madonna, downcast eyes, crossed arms, pastel blue and pink robes **25.00**

Inarco, Cleveland, OH

C-2322, 7" h, lady, brown hair, downcast eyes, raised right hand, black hat with white and gold ribbon, black dress, white glove with gold accents, pearl drop earrings and necklace **18.00**

E-1852, 6" h, Jacqueline Kennedy, in mourning, brown eyes, raised left hand, white scarf over hair, black dress and glove, 1964 . . . . **42.00**

Irice, Japan, 4½" h, Geisha girl, short black hair, white skin, downcast eyes, gold eyebrows and eyelashes, holding white and gold fan in raised left hand white and gold hairpiece with yellow tassel, pink kimono, painted fingernails **25.00**

Japan, 5" h, young black lady, downcast eyes, yellow turban, red sarong, large gold hoop earrings, three-strand pearl necklace **30.00**

Lefton's, Japan, PY641, 5¾" h, lady, white hair with gold accents, upswept hairdo, white skin, downcast eyes, gold arched eyebrows and eyelashes, pink flounced hat with yellow rose dec, matching dress **15.00**

Napco, Japan, CX5409, 5" h, young lady

wearing Christmas outfit, hp, blond wavy hair, downcast eyes, red stocking cap with white ribbed band and tassel, poinsettia on band, red neckerchief with white polka dots, white dress with raised collar, gold accents **17.50**

Norleans, Japan, 7½" h, young lady, blond hair, downcast eyes, white bonnet with blue ribbons, white ruffled dress, gold accents **25.00**

Parma by AAI, Japan, A-222, 5¼" h, young girl, long blond hair, straight bangs, blue flowers at ponytail on top of head, eyes looking right, raised hand, slender neck, blue dress **12.50**

Reliable Glassware and Pottery, 3088, 6" h, young girl, blond hair, blue eyes looking right, open-mouth smile, rosy cheeks, large red hat tied with red bow under chin, holly leaves dec, red and white candy-striped mittens, red coat with white fur cuffs and gold button, 1956 . . . . **22.00**

Relpo, Sampson Import Co, Chicago, IL, Japan

2004, 7" h, girl, long blond hair, large blue eyes, purple bows in hair, purple and white dress, pearl drop earrings **18.00**

2031, 5½" h, young lady, black hat with white and gold ribbon tied in large bow under chin, black and white dress, bare shoulders **15.00**

Royal Sealy, Japan, 5¾" h, Malaysian princess, gold skin, closed eyes, arms crossed in front of chest, white headdress with gold dec, pearl drop earrings **30.00**

Rubens Originals Los Angeles, Japan

495, 5¾" h, lady, blond hair, downcast eyes, raised arms, chin resting on intertwined fingers, white hat with gold trim, brown dress with white raised collar, white gloves, pearl drop earrings and necklace, white and gold flower brooch **15.00**

530, 6" h, equestrian lady, blond hair pinned up, open eyes, smile with teeth, gray and black riding habit with top hat and high collar, gold and white brooch with horse head dec **32.00**

Shawnee, U. S. A., 896, 6" h, Island girl, wearing hibiscus in black hair, downcast eyes, green sarong, carrying basket on head **25.00**

Stanfordware, Sterling, OH, 6½" h, Spanish Dona, black hair, white skin, blue eyes, tilted head, white and gold dress, tiara, and mantilla, gold necklace **28.00**

Unmarked

4¾" h, teenager, long brown hair,

eyes looking left, smiling, holding blue telephone receiver in raised left hand, white bow in hair, white dress......................... 20.00

5" h, girl graduate, blond shoulder-length straight hair, open eyes, pink cap and tassel, pink and white gown with gold accents............... 25.00

5¼" h, nurse, short blond hair, down-cast eyes, raised right hand, white cap with Red Cross insignia, white uniform with gold accents, painted fingernails.................... 25.00

5½" h, girl, brown hair, short bangs, looped pigtails held by green bows, open eyes, white and gold spectacles, holding vase with flowers in raised right hand, striped hat with black ribbon and bow, matching dress......................... 25.00

5¾" h, baby, blond hair, open eyes, pink cheeks, open mouth, pink ruffled bonnet tied under chin, pink dress......................... 15.00

6" h

Cowboy, brown hat, blue eyes, yellow hat and neckerchief, white shirt, yellow star badge......... 30.00

Lady, gray hair with ringlets, white and gold flowers and bows in hair, black ribbon at throat, orange dress, raised right hand with pointed finger, rect planter behind 20.00

Vcagco Ceramics, Japan, 8¼" h, young lady, white hair, downcast eyes, holding umbrella in right hand, matching black and white plaid umbrella, hat, and dress, black bow on umbrella, gold earrings and brooch, gold accents 20.00

LAMPS

Collecting lamps can be considered an illuminating hobby. Not only is the collection practical, versatile, and decorative, but it keeps you out of the dark. Whether you prefer a particular lamp style, color, or theme, you will find a wonderful and enlightening assortment at any flea market.

Boudoir

Art Deco Style, ribbed cone-shaped green depression glass shade flanked by pair of metal stylized rearing horses, stepped black glass base, 1930s........................125.00

Art Nouveau Style, tall tubular octagon-shaped pink depression glass shade with emb nudes on four sides, square black metal base.......... 85.00

Boudoir, Pairpoint, blossom dec, medium blue ground, wood base, sgd, 12" h, $750.00.

Figural

Calypso Dancer, plaster, dark skin, red costume, circular red shade, 1950s........................ 20.00

Draped Maiden, leaning against lamppost, bronzed white metal, white glass globe, rectangular stepped base 95.00

Fish, ceramic, brown, leaping out of waves, brown and ivory circular paper shade 25.00

Flower Basket, wire basket, plastic flowers with miniature bulb centers, 1950s........................ 15.00

Flowers, stylized, three flaring wrought iron stems with curlicue leaves, plastic globular shades, circular brass base, 1930s 45.00

French Poodle, ceramic, pink, circular base, matching circular pink paper shade 22.00

Gypsy, ceramic, playing tambourine, wearing flowered dress, gold accents, ivory colored fringed fabric shade, 1940s 40.00

Hula Girl, white metal, wearing grass skirt, motorized hip movement, circular base, late 1940s 75.00

Light Bulb, black socket-shaped base 25.00

Oriental Man, ceramic, holding sword, wicker shade 18.00

Rooster, ceramic, red, black, and white, crowing, circular paper shade with hex sign dec, 1950s.......... 12.00

Saturn, blue depression glass, circular stepped base, 1930s............. 60.00

Telephone, plaster, turquoise, black and white speckled, desk-type phone with clock face replacing dial, removable receiver with built-in cigarette lighter, matching rectangular venetian blind shade............ **35.00**

Western Theme, ceramic, cowboy and cowgirl flanking inverted horseshoe surrounding clock face, white, gold trim, rect white plastic venetian blind shade, 1950s **25.00**

Novelty

Artillery Shell, brass, metal dome shade........................ **40.00**

Deer Trophy, tripod base made from three deer legs, photo transfer shade with grazing animals dec **30.00**

Fish Bowl Stand, ceramic, green double tree stump base, black cat sitting on one stump, glass fish bowl on other **35.00**

Lava, bottle-shaped, Lava Simplex Corp, Chicago, IL............... **50.00**

Motion, illustrated plastic cylinder, Econolite, 11" h

Antique Cars, 1957.............. **35.00**

Niagara Falls, 1957 .... **30.00**

Waterskiers, 1958.............. **55.00**

Silhouette

Harem Girl, plaster, green, red and gold accents, circular frame with central harem girl carrying lantern, blue glass panel, PGH Statuary Co **50.00**

Nude, figural, pot metal, painted green, standing before shield-shaped frosted glass panel, 1930s...**110.00**

Table

Candlestick Type, brass, ribbed and fluted column, circular dished base, orange paper shade............. **15.00**

Reverse Painted, glass dome-shaped shade with sailing ships dec, gilded white metal vasiform column with painted and emb leaves, flowers, and swags, circular base **300.00**

Tiffany Type, six green and yellow slag glass panels in dome-shaped shade, reeded vasiform column on fluted circular base, two bulbs with pull chains **225.00**

LAW ENFORCEMENT

Do not sell this category short. Collecting is largely confined to the law enforcement community, but within that group, collecting badges, patches, and other police paraphernalia is big. Most collections are based upon items from a specific locality. As a result, prices are regionalized.

There are some crooks afoot. Reproduction and fake badges, especially railroad police badges, are prevalent. Blow the whistle on them when you see them.

Badge

Deputy Sheriff, Juneau County, 2½" h, shield shape, metal, gold finish, blue inscription, raised seal design, c1940................... **40.00**

Special Police, 2½ h, sunburst shape, silvered brass, black inscription, 1930s...................... **25.00**

Trenton Police, 2¼ × 2½", star shape, silvered brass, black inscription, raised "70" in center, 1930s....... **25.00**

Billy Club, wooden.................. **20.00**

Bottle, Grenadier, Texas Ranger, 1977..................... **25.00**

Buckle, New York City, c1900 .... **75.00**

Bumper Shield, "Anti-Automobile Thief Association, Headquarters. Denver, Colo." inscription, 2¼ × 3", silvered metal, emb, attaches to car's bumper, police officer pointing gun at driver's head illus, reverse with threaded rod and wing nut, pre-1920s **25.00**

Cracker Jack Prize, 1½" l, ½" h, litho tin paddy wagon, blue, white, and yellow **12.00**

Helmet, New York City, riot type, leather **200.00**

Magazine Cover, *Collier's*, cov illus by Jay Irving, c1939.................... **15.00**

Patch

Maricopa County Deputy Sheriff, star center........................ **2.00**

San Francisco, eagle **3.00**

Sheet Music, *Police Parade March*, c1917........................... **25.00**

Token, 3" d, round, celluloid, center policeman and fireman illus, "The Boys in Blue Give Their All For You! You Can Give Them a Living Wage! Vote Yes on Proposition #3," blue and red lettering, white ground **10.00**

Toy, windup, litho tin, policeman on motorcycle, Unique Art **150.00**

LENOX

Johnathan Cox and Walter Scott Lenox founded the Ceramic Art Company, Trenton, New Jersey, in 1889. In 1906 Lenox established his own company. Much of Lenox's products resemble Belleek, not unexpectedly since Lenox lured several Belleek potters to New Jersey.

Lenox has an upscale reputation. China service sets sell, but within a narrow price range, e.g., $600 to $1,200 for an ordinary service of eight. The key is Lenox gift and accessory items. Prices are still reasonable. The category has not yet been truly "discovered."

Lenox produces limited edition items. Potential for long-term value is limited.

Honey Pot, ivory colored, gold bee and trim, mkd "894–86," 3 pcs, 5" h, $75.00.

Bowl, ftd, Art Deco, sterling silver overlay, blue glazed ground. **115.00**
Chocolate Set, cov chocolate pot, six cups and saucers, Golden Wheat pattern, cobalt ground, 13 pcs **275.00**
Cup and Saucer, Golden Wreath pattern **20.00**
Jug, 4" h, hp, grapes and leaves, shaded brown ground, sgd "G Morley" **240.00**
Mug, 6¼" h, monk, smiling, holding up glass of wine, shaded brown ground, sterling silver rim **150.00**
Nappy, 4½ × 7", ftd, shell shape, pink tinged beige **35.00**
Perfume Lamp, 9" h, figural, Marie Antoinette, bisque finish, dated 1929. . . .**650.00**
Plate, salad, Tuxedo pattern, gold mark **10.00**
Platter, 13" d, Temple Blossom pattern **90.00**
Shoe, white, bow trim **185.00**
Tea Set, teapot, creamer, and sugar, Hawthorne pattern, silver overlay. . . .**215.00**
Toby Mug, William Penn, pink handle **150.00**
Vase
  6" h, roses dec, sgd "W Morley" **165.00**
  8" h, tree stump, robin, white **125.00**

LETTER OPENERS

Isn't it amazing what can be done to a basic form? I have seen letter openers that are so large that one does not have a ghost's chance in hell of slipping them under the flap of a No. 10 envelope. As they say in eastern Pennsylvania, these letter openers are "just for nice."

Advertising letter openers are the crowd pleaser in this category. However, you can build an equally great collection based on material (brass, plastic, wood, etc.) or theme (animal shapes, swords, etc.).

Advertising, Welsback Company, Philadelphia, litho tin, 10½" l, $35.00.

Advertising
  Donegal & Conoy Mutual Fire Insurance Co, brass, 9" l, c1920 . . . . **35.00**
  Fuller Brushman. **6.50**
  Pacific Mutual. **25.00**
  Victor J Evans & Co Patent Attorneys, Main Office, Victor Bldg, Washington DC, bronze, lists branch offices **65.00**
Art Deco, rooster. **25.00**
Dragon, brass **40.00**
Elephant, ivory **30.00**
Horse, rearing, brass, cutout floral blade, 7¼" l **18.00**
Indian, beige, black accents **60.00**
Israel, Terra Cotta Guild, 1969. . . . . **7.50**
Ivory, three layer handle, mother-of-pearl insets, ornate **125.00**
Owl, celluloid **65.00**
Seagull, bronze **24.00**

LICENSE PLATES

With license plates mounted row after row on walls in their garage, den, and even living room, license plate collectors are truly among the possessed.

Collectors specialize. The most obvious approach is by state. But this just scratches the surface. Government plates, vanity plates, law enforcement plates, and special issue plates are just a few of the other potential collecting categories.

License plates are found most frequently at automobile flea markets. When they are found at general flea markets, they are usually encountered in large groups. Be prepared to buy the lot. Most sellers do not want them picked over. They know they can never sell the junk.

Club: Automobile License Plate Collectors Association, Inc., Box 712, Weston, WV 26452.

Novelty
 Boy Scout, 1957 National Jamboree, Michigan, No 30, Valley Forge, Water Wonderland................. 28.00
 District of Columbia, Inauguration 1977, metal, beige background, red and dark blue design............. 20.00
 Eisenhower, In 1954 Give Ike A Republican Congress, metal, dark blue, white lettering, 6 × 12".......... 55.00
 Harrisburg Republican Club with Dewey-Bricker, fiberboard, dark blue background, yellow inscription, 1944 .... 25.00
 Jimmy Carter/A New Beginning, plastic, red, white, blue, and green design, 6 × 12", c1976.............. 15.00
 John F Kennedy, black, yellow California and JFK 464, 2 × 4" 35.00
 Napoleon Solo, The Man from UNCLE, red, emb name and logo, Marx, 1967 Metro-Goldwyn-Mayer, Inc..................... 25.00
State
 California
  1939, New York World's Fair 20.00
  1956......................... 8.00
 Chicago, 1924, round, raised letters.......................... 30.00
 Illinois, 1950 .... 20.00
 Michigan, 1923................... 15.00
 Nebraska, 1930, enamel........... 15.00
 New York, 1912, porcelain......... 100.00
 North Dakota, 1933, pr............. 7.50
 South Dakota, 1926 .... 10.00

LIMITED EDITION COLLECTIBLES

Collect limited edition collectibles because you love them, not because you want to invest in them. While a few items sell well above their initial retail price, the vast majority sell between twenty-five and fifty cents on original retail dollar. The one consistent winner is the first issue in any series.

 Whenever possible, buy items with their original box and inserts. The box adds another ten to twenty percent to the value of the item. Also, buy only items in excellent or better condition. Very good is not good enough. So many of each issue survive that market price holds only for the top condition grades.

Clubs: Foxfire Farm (Lowell Davis) Club, 55 Pacella Park Drive, Randolph, MA 02368; Gorham Collectors Club, P. O. Box 6472, Providence, RI 02940; Precious Moments Collectors' Club, 1 Enesco Plaza, Elk Grove Village, IL 60009.

Magazines: *Collector Editions*, 170 Fifth Avenue, New York, NY 10010; *Collectors Mart*, 15100 West Kellogg, Wichita, KS 67235; *Plate World*, 9200 North Maryland Avenue, Niles, IL 60648; *Precious Moments Collector*, P. O. Box 410707, Kansas City, MO 64141.

Plate, Reco International, John McClelland artist, Mother Goose Series, Little Boy Blue, 8½" d, 1980, $80.00.

BELLS

Anri, J Ferrandiz, artist, wooden
 Christmas, 1977 .... 40.00
 Indian Brave, 1990............... 25.00
Bing & Grondahl, Christmas
 1981......................... 15.00
 1987......................... 48.00
Danbury Mint, Norman Rockwell art,
 Grandpa's Girl, 1979.............. 28.00
Enesco Corp, Precious Moments, Mother
 Sew Dear, 1982.................. 25.00
Franklin Mint, Unicorn, porcelain,
 1979......................... 35.00
Gorham
 Tavern Sign Painter, 1976 .... 30.00
 Young Love, 1984................ 28.00
Pickard, O Little Town of Bethlehem,
 1978......................... 70.00
Reco International, Charity, 1988...... 15.00
Reed and Barton
 Caroller, 1985................... 17.50
 Little Shepherd, 1982............. 14.00
Schmid, Peanuts, Perfect Performance,
 1982......................... 18.00

Towle Silversmiths, silver plated, musical, 1984 .... **25.00**
Wedgwood, Fur Seals, 1983. .... **32.00**

DOLLS

Enesco Imports, Precious Moments, Wishing You Cloudless Skies, 1989 ... **115.00**
Gorham
    Melinda, 14" h, 1981 .... **285.00**
    Mr. Anton, 12" h, 1982 .... **165.00**
    Valentine Lady, Jane, 1987 .... **145.00**
Hamilton Collection, Nicole, 1986. ..... **50.00**
Royal Doulton by Nisbet, Pink Sash. **145.00**

EGGS

Anri, Beatrix Potter, 1979 .... **5.00**
Goebel, Easter, 1979. .... **8.00**
Gorham, bone china, pink rose, 4¼" l. ... **18.00**
Noritake, Easter, 1978 .... **14.00**
Royal Bayreuth, 1980 .... **15.00**
Veneto Flair, 1979 .... **18.00**
Wedgwood, 1977 .... **35.00**

FIGURINES

Anri, Sarah Kay artist, Our Puppy, 1½" h, 1986 .... **75.00**
Burgues, Joy, 1981 .... **85.00**
Cybis
    Rebecca, 1964 .... **345.00**
    Nativity Lamb, 1985 .... **125.00**
Enesco Corp, Precious Moments, Cameo, 1982. .... **30.00**
Goebel, The Garden Fancier, 1982 ..... **40.00**
Lladro, California Poppy, 1983 .... **100.00**
River Shore, Lamb, 1980 .... **48.00**
Royal Doulton
    Dickens Series, Mrs Bardell **24.00**
    Lord of the Rings Series, Gandalf **50.00**
    Sweet and Twenties, Monte Carlo, 1982. .... **175.00**
Schmid, Lowell Davis artist, Right Church, Wrong Pew, 1982 .... **80.00**

MUGS

Bing & Grondahl, 1978, FE **50.00**
Gorham, Tom & Jerry, 4" h, 1981 ...... **9.00**
Lynell Studios, FE, Gnome Series, Gnome Sweet Gnome, 1983 .... **6.50**
Royal Copenhagen
    Large, 1976 .... **25.00**
    Small, 1981 .... **35.00**
Wedgwood
    Christmas, 1974 .... **30.00**
    Father's Day, 1978 .... **25.00**

MUSIC BOXES

Anri, Peter Rabbit **100.00**
Gorham, Happy Birthday, animals **35.00**
Schmid, Paddington Bear, 1982 .... **22.00**
Walt Disney, Christmas, 1981 .... **30.00**

ORNAMENTS

Anri, Beatrix Potter Series, Pigling Bland. **12.00**
Davis, Lowell, R.F.D. Series, FE **15.00**
Ferrandiz, 1980. .... **15.00**
Goebel, Santa, white, FE, 1978 .... **10.00**
Gorham, Tiny Tim, FE, 1979 .... **8.00**
Hallmark, Betsy Clark, 1975 .... **7.50**
Haviland, 1977 .... **8.00**
Internation Silver, Twelve Days of Christmas, sterling silver **25.00**
Lunt, Medallion, 1980 .... **18.00**
Reed & Barton, Bringing Home the Tree, silver plated, 1981. .... **15.00**
Schmid, Raggedy Ann Series, 1980 ..... **3.00**
Wallace Silversmiths, Sleigh Bell, 1985. .... **45.00**

PLATES

Anri, J Ferrandiz artist
    Christmas, 12" d, Flight into Egypt, 1975. .... **80.00**
    Mother's Day, Alpine Stroll, 1977 .... **125.00**
Bareuther, Christmas, Hans Mueller artist
    Toys for Sale, 1971 .... **20.00**
    Zeil on the Fiver Main, 1984 .... **42.50**
Berlin, Christmas, 7¾" d, Christmas in Bremen, 1974 .... **25.00**
Bing and Grondahl, Denmark
    Christmas
        Arrival of Christmas Guests, 1937. .... **75.00**
        The Fir Tree and Hare, 1964 .... **50.00**
        Royal Castle of Amalienborg, Copenhagen, 1914. .... **65.00**
        Sleighing to Church on Christmas Eve, 1906. .... **95.00**
        White Christmas, 1979. .... **30.00**
    Mother's Day, Henry Thelander artist, 6" d
        Doe and Fawns, 1975 .... **20.00**
        Fox and Cubs, 1979 .... **30.00**
Franklin Mint, United States
    Audubon Society, Goldfinch, 1972 ... **115.00**
    Christmas, Hanging the Wreath, 1974. .... **100.00**
Gorham, United States, Christmas, Norman Rockwell artist, Letter to Santa, 1980. .... **38.00**
Haviland, France
    Mother's Day, The French Collection, In the Park, 1975. .... **25.00**
    The Twelve Day of Christmas, Remy Hetreau artist, 8⅜" d, Seven Swans A'Swimming, 1976 .... **30.00**
Haviland and Parlon, France
    Christmas, Madonna and Child, Murillo artist, 1975. .... **45.00**
    Lady and the Unicorn, 10" d, Sound, 1979. .... **50.00**
Reco International Corp, United States, Childrens Circus Series, John McClel-

land artist, 9" d, Johnny the Strong-
man, 1983 . . . . **31.00**
Reed & Barton, United States, Christmas,
Damascene silver, 11" d, Adoration of
the Kings, 1973 . . . . **75.00**
Rosenthal, Germany, Christmas Celebra-
tion in Franconia, 1972 . . . . **90.00**
Royal Bayreuth, Germany, Mother's
Day, Leo Jansen artist, Young Ameri-
cans IX, 1982 . . . . **66.00**
Royal Copenhagen, Denmark
Christmas, 6" d
    Blackbird   at   Christmastime,
    1966 . . . . **55.00**
    Shepherd in the Field on Christmas
    Night, 1916 . . . . **85.00**
    Mother's Day, 6¼" d, Mother and
    Child, 1978 . . . . **25.00**
Royal Doulton, Great Britain
    Mother and Child Series, Edna Hibel
    artist, 8¼" d, Kathleen and Child,
    1978 . . . . **95.00**
    Valentine's Day Series, Accept These
    Flowers, 1985 . . . . **40.00**
Schmid, Japan
    Christmas, J Malfertheiner artist, A
    Groeden Christmas, 1986 . . . . **75.00**
    Disney Christmas, 7½" d, Fantasia Re-
    lief, 1990 . . . . **25.00**
    Raggedy Ann Annual, 7½" d, Flying
    High, 1982 . . . . **20.00**
U S Historical Society, United States,
Stained Glass Cathedral, Good Tidings
of Great Joy, Boston, 1985 . . . . **125.00**
Wedgwood, Great Britain
    Calendar Series, Bountiful Butterfly,
    1973 . . . . **14.00**
    Christmas, jasper stoneware, 8" d,
    Christmas in Trafalgar Square,
    1970 . . . . **30.00**
    Mothers Series, jasper stoneware,
    6½" d, Leisure Time, 1977 . . . . **30.00**
    Queen's Christmas, A Price artist, Pic-
    cadilly Circus, 1982 . . . . **35.00**

LINENS

Carefully examine linens for signs of wear,
patching, and stains. Be cautious of estate
linens that are unwashed and unironed.
Question why the dealer has not prepared
them for sale. Remember, you have no
knowledge that the stains will come out.
Also check all sets to make certain the
pieces match.

Caring for Linens: If you are not planning
to use your linens, store them unpressed,
rolled, covered with an old pillow case,
and stored out of bright sunlight. Rinse
linens and the storage pillow case several

times to make certain all detergent residue
is removed.

If you are going to use your linens on a
regular basis, wrap them in acid-free white
tissue or muslin folders. Whenever possible, store linens on rollers to prevent
creasing. You can get acid-free storage materials from Talas, 104 Fifth Avenue, New
York, NY 10011.

Club: International Old Lacers, Box 1029
West Minster, CO 80030.

Pot Holders, crocheted, red and white, pr, $9.00.

Antimacassar, filet crochet, ivory, reclin-
ing cat design, 3 pcs **35.00**
Bread Tray Cover, 12½" l, filet crochet,
white, "Staff of Life," c1925 . . . . **5.00**
Bridge Cloth, cross-stitch dec, Quimper
pattern, green, blue, rose, and yellow,
c1920 . . . . **100.00**
Dish Towel
    Embroidered, 38 × 18", white textile
    bag, designs and days of week, 7 pc
    set **25.00**
    Printed cotton, strawberries design,
    blue border **8.00**
Doily, 18" d, crocheted twine cotton
thread, pineapple pattern **12.00**
Dresser Set, cotton, white, embroidered
ladies and flowers, blue, pink, yellow,
and green, crocheted edge **35.00**
Mattress Cover, 60 × 104", homespun,
blue and white, one seam, white
homespun backing, minor wear and
age stains **115.00**
Pillow Case, 17 × 28", white 25 lb flour
bag, pr **15.00**
Sheet, 54 × 40", crib size, cotton textile
bag, white **10.00**
Tablecloth, 52" sq, blue, green, and white
snowflake pattern **12.00**
Towel, 14 × 39", linen, red embroidered
initials, hand hemmed **7.50**

LITTLE GOLDEN BOOKS

Read me a story! For millions of children
that story came from a Little Golden Book.
Colorful, inexpensive, and readily avail-

able, these wonderful books are a hot collectible. You see them everywhere.

Be careful, you may be subject to a nostalgia attack because sooner or later you are going to spot your favorite. Relive your childhood. Buy the book. You won't be sorry.

Walt Disney's **Zorro and the Secret Plan,** *D77, 1958, $10.00.*

A Day At The Playground, Miriam Schlein, illus by Eloise Wilkin, c1951	10.00
Buffalo Bill Jr, Gladys Wyatt, c1956	5.50
Doctor Dan at the Circus, Pauline Wilkins, c1960	17.50
Grandpa Bunny, Jane Werner, illus by Walt Disney Studios, c1951	15.00
Howdy Doody and Santa Claus, Simon & Schuster, 155 first edition	10.00
Huckleberry Hound Safety Signs, Ann McGovern, c1961	7.00
It's Howdy Doody Time, Edward Kean, c1955	12.00
Little Red Riding Hood, illus Sharon Koester, with paper dolls	25.00
Maverick, Carl Memling	7.50
Mickey Mouse Club Stamp Book, Kathleen N Daily, c1956, orig stamps	20.00
Our Puppy, Elsa Ruth Nast, c1948	10.00
Rootie Kazootie Joins The Circus, Steve Carlin, c1955	12.00
Roy Rogers and the Mountain Lion, Ann McGovern, c1955	10.00
Rusty Goes to School, Pierre Probst, c1962	5.00
Tales of Wells Fargo, Simon & Schuster, 158	10.00
Tiger's Adventure, William P Gottlieb, c1954	5.50
Top Cat, Golden Press, 1962	15.00

LITTLE ORPHAN ANNIE

Little Orphan Annie is one of those characters that pops up everywhere—radio, newspapers, movies, etc. In the early 1930s "Radio Orphan Annie" was syndicated regionally. It went network in 1933. The show's only sponsor was Ovaltine. Many Little Orphan Annie collectibles were Ovaltine premiums.

Actually, Little Orphan Annie resulted from a sex-change operation. Harold Gray, an assistant on the "Gumps" strip, changed the sex of the leading character and submitted the same basic strip concept as a proposal to the *New York News*. The 1924 operation was a success.

Annie's early companions were Sandy, her dog, and Emily Marie, her doll. "Daddy" Warbucks replaced the doll, and the strip went big time. Gray died in 1968. The strip was farmed out to a succession of artists and writers. The result was disastrous.

Radio and cartoon strip Little Orphan Annie material is becoming expensive. Try the more recent movie- and stage-related items if you are looking for something a bit more affordable.

Mug, Beetleware, Ovaltine premium, Wander Co, Chicago, 3" h, $50.00.

Big Little Book, *Little Orphan Annie in the Thieves' Den,* Helen Berke, Harold Gray artist, 1948	20.00
Book, *The Little Orphan Annie Book,* James Whitcomb Riley, color illus by Ethel Betts, 1908	25.00
Bracelet, identification disc, 1934	20.00
Clicker, red, white, and black, Mysto members, 1941	35.00

Gravy Boat, lusterware, white, orange, yellow, and black **175.00**

Handbook, *Secret Guard,* paper sheet, decoder, and clicker, orig mailing envelope, Quaker Puffed Wheat Sparkies and Rice Sparkies premium, 1941 .... **90.00**

Manual, Radio Orphan Annie's Secret Society, 1937.................... **30.00**

Mask, Annie, 1933.................. **30.00**

Mug, ceramic, 1932 .... **20.00**

Nodder, 3½" h, painted bisque, stamped on back "Orphan Annie," 1930s **150.00**

Pastry Set, miniature baking utensils, Transogram "Gold Medal" Toy, 1930s...................... **75.00**

Photo, 8 × 10", black and white, glossy, Shirley Bell, sgd "To My Friend/Radio's Little Orphan Annie/Shirley Bell," 1932 .... **40.00**

Salt and Pepper Shakers, pr, 3" h, Annie and Sandy, plaster, 1940s........... **25.00**

Sheet Music, *Little Orphan Annie* **15.00**

Snowdome, 3⅝" × 2⅞" × 2¾", plastic, Annie and Sandy, 1970s........... **10.00**

Talking Stationery, 12 sheets and envelopes, 4 pg folder, orig mailing envelope, Ovaltine premium, 1937....... **100.00**

Whistle, tin, signal, three tones **30.00**

LLADRO PORCELAINS

Lladro porcelains are Spain's contribution to the world of collectible figures. Some figures are released on a limited edition basis; others remain in production for an extended period of time. Learn what kinds of production numbers are involved.

Lladro porcelains are sold through jewelry and "upscale" gift shops. However, they are the type of item you either love or hate. As a result, Lladro porcelains from estates or from individuals tired of dusting

Figure, pastel colors, 4½" l, $100.00.

that thing that Aunt Millie gave for Christmas in 1985 do show up at flea markets.

Beagle Puppy, L-1071-G/M........... **125.00**
Bride's Maid, L-5598 .... **160.00**
Curiosity, L-5393 .... **40.00**
Ducklings, L-1307 .... **130.00**
Girl with Calla Lillies, L-4650....... **120.00**
Heavenly Sounds, L-2195-M....... **170.00**
Japanese Camelia, L-5181 .... **90.00**
Picture Perfect.................... **350.00**
Rag Doll, L-1501.................. **195.00**
Sharpening the Cutlery, L-5204 ...... **450.00**
Spring Flowers, L-1509 .... **175.00**

LOCKS

Padlocks are the most desirable lock collectible. While examples date back to the 1600s, the mass production of identifiable padlocks was pioneered in America in the mid-1800s.

Padlocks are categorized primarily according to tradition or use: Combination, Pin Tumber, Scandinavian, etc. Cast, brass, and iron are among the more sought-after types.

Reproductions, copycats, and fakes are a big problem. Among the trouble spots are screw key, trick, iron lever, and brass lever locks from the Middle East; railroad switch locks from Taiwan; and switch lock keys from the U.S. Midwest. All components of an old lock must have exactly the same color and finish. Authentic railroad, express, and logo locks will have only one user name or set of initials.

Club: American Lock Collectors Association, 36076 Grennada, Livonia, MI 48154.

Eight Lever, iron, Samson, Corbin, 2½" h.......................... **15.00**
Four Lever, iron, Ajax, Corbin, 2" h **12.00**
Gate Lock
    Iron, handmade, large **28.00**
    Iron and Brass, manufacturer's name, 10" h **70.00**
Lever
    Brass
        Corbin, 2" h.................. **18.00**
        Yale, 2⅝" h **30.00**
    Iron
        #333, 2" h **12.00**
        Emb Indian head, 2³⁄₁₆" h **30.00**
        Jupiter, Corbin, 2¼" h **12.00**
        Master, No. 41, 2" h **15.00**
        Sargent, 2" h **12.00**
Money Bag Lock, brass, 3" l........... **35.00**

Trunk Latch Lock, Eagle Lock Co, $20.00.

Pin Tumbler
  Brass
    Best, Phil Fuels Co, logo lock, key-
      hole cov, 1½" h **18.00**
    Fraim, 2¹⁵⁄₁₆" h **15.00**
    Reese US, 1¾" h **5.00**
    USA Ordinance Dept, Corbin, logo
      lock, 2" h **18.00**
    Yale, push key, 2" h **15.00**
  Iron
    Eagle, push key, brass hasp, 2" h . . . **30.00**
    Pritzlaff, push key, brass hasp and
      chain, 2¹⁄₁₆" h **35.00**
    Yale, push key, brass hasp, 2" h **10.00**
Railroad
    C & El RR, signal, brass, XLCR, Corbin,
      2" h **28.00**
    C & NW RY, steel, Eagle, 2½" h **25.00**
    CMSTP & P, iron, brass hasp, Adlake,
      3⅛" h **32.00**
    CSTPM & O, iron, Fraim, 2¼" h **20.00**
    L & N RR, switch, steel, Slaymaker,
      2½" h **40.00**
    Milwaukee, brass, Leoffelhotz & Prier,
      2½" h **100.00**
    MSTP & SSM RY, switch, brass,
      Adlake, 2¾" h **125.00**
    P RR, switch, steel, Slaymaker,
      2¼" h **25.00**
    Shackle, rotating, iron, Sterling,
      2⅞" h **28.00**

Six Lever
  Brass
    Harvard, push key, 2¼" h **24.00**
    Yale, 2" h **15.00**
  Iron
    Fraim, brass levers, 2" h **12.00**
    Ironclad, Corbin, brass hasp,
      2" h **8.00**
    O M Edwards Company, 2" h **12.00**
    Reese, bronze plated, 2" h **10.00**
    Secure, Excelsior, 2" h **5.00**
    Steinke, 2" h **38.00**
    Winchester, brass plated, 2" h **85.00**
Trunk Latch Lock, Eagle Lock Co **20.00**
Warded
  Brass
    Corbin, long hasp, 1⁹⁄₁₆" h **10.00**
    Miller, 2⅛" h **8.00**
    Yale, 2" h **15.00**
    Yale & Towne, 2" h **18.00**
    Iron, Tital, Yale, 2¼" h **10.00**

LUGGAGE

Until recently luggage collectors focused primarily on old steamship and railroad trunks. Unrestored they sell in the $50 to $150 range. Dealers have the exterior refinished and the interior relined with new paper and then promptly sell them to decorators who charge up to $400. A restored trunk works well in both a Country or Victorian bedroom. This is why decorators love them so much.

Within the past three years, there has been a growing collector interest in old leather luggage. It is not uncommon to find early twentieth century leather overnight bags in good condition priced at $150 to $300. Leather suitcases sell in the $75 to $150 range.

LUNCH KITS

Lunch kits, consisting of a lunch box and matching thermos, were the most price-manipulated collectibles category of the 1980s. Prices in excess of $2,500 were achieved for some of the early Disney examples. What everyone seemed to forget is that lunch boxes were mass-produced.

The lunch kit bubble is in the process of bursting. Price are dropping for the commonly found examples. A few dealers and collectors are attempting to prop up the market, but their efforts are failing. If you are buying, it will pay to shop around for the best price.

Buy lunch kits. Resist the temptation to buy the lunch box and thermos separately.

I know this is a flea market price guide, but lunch kits can get pricy by the time they arrive at a flea market. The best buys remain at garage sales where the kits first hit the market and sellers are glad to get rid of them at any price.

Newsletter: *Hot Boxing,* P. O. Box 87, Somerville, MA 02143.

Adam-12, Aladdin, 1972, $20.00.

Adam-12, plastic thermos, Aladdin, 1973–74 .... **30.00**
A-Team, steel, plastic thermos, King-Seeley, 1985 .... **25.00**
Auto Race, steel, King-Seeley, 1969 .... **35.00**
Banana Splits, vinyl, 1970 .... **130.00**
Battlestar Galactica, plastic thermos, Aladdin, 1963–65 .... **75.00**
Bobby Sherman, steel, King-Seeley, 1972 .... **50.00**
Captain Kangaroo, vinyl, thermos, King-Seeley, 1964–66 .... **95.00**
Charlie's Angels, steel, Aladdin, 1978 ... **35.00**
Dawn, vinyl, plastic thermos, Aladdin, 1971 .... **50.00**
Deputy Dawg, vinyl, thermos, Aladdin, 1979–80 .... **30.00**
Dick Tracy, 1967 .... **95.00**
Disco, steel, plastic thermos, Aladdin, 1979–80 .... **30.00**
Disney School Bus, steel dome type, Aladdin, 1961–73 .... **35.00**
Dr Seuss, steel, plastic thermos, Aladdin, 1970 .... **50.00**
Ellie Mae Clampett **15.00**
E. T., steel, plastic thermos, Aladdin, 1983 .... **25.00**
Flintstones, steel, Aladdin, 1962–63 .... **145.00**
Glamour Girl, vinyl, Aladdin, 1960 ..... **20.00**

Gone With The Wind, 1940 .... **450.00**
Have Gun Will Travel, steel, Aladdin, 1960 .... **125.00**
Holly Hobbie, steel, Aladdin, 1973–74 .... **16.00**
Joe Palooka, 1948 .... **120.00**
Julia, steel, thermos, King-Seeley, 1969 .... **110.00**
Jungle Book, steel, plastic thermos, Aladdin, 1968–69 .... **65.00**
Knight Rider, steel, plastic thermos, King-Seeley, 1984–85 .... **25.00**
Laugh-In, steel, plastic thermos, Aladdin, 1970 .... **70.00**
Lawman, steel, 1961 .... **50.00**
Little House on the Prairie, steel, plastic thermos, 1976 .... **55.00**
Masters of the Universe, steel, plastic thermos, Aladdin, 1983–84 .... **35.00**
Nancy Drew, steel, plastic thermos, King-Seeley, 1978 .... **35.00**
New Zoo Review, vinyl, plastic thermos, Aladdin, 1975 .... **65.00**
Peter Pan, steel, plastic thermos, Aladdin, 1969 .... **65.00**
Pigs In Space, steel, plastic thermos, King-Seeley, 1979–80 .... **35.00**
Pink Panther, steel, 1984 .... **30.00**
Pony Express, steel, plastic thermos, Ohio Art, 1982–84 .... **22.00**
Rat Patrol, steel, Aladdin, 1967 .... **120.00**
Scotch Plaid, steel, Ohio Art, 1957–59 .... **12.00**
Sesame Street, steel, Aladdin, 1980–82 .... **16.00**
Space Cadet, 1952 .... **120.00**
Star Trek I, steel, 1979 .... **30.00**
Superman, steel, thermos, King-Seeley, 1967 .... **125.00**
The Osmonds, steel, Aladdin, 1973 ..... **60.00**
Thundercats, steel, plastic thermos, Aladdin, 1985–86 .... **25.00**
Twiggy, vinyl, thermos, King-Seeley, 1967–68 .... **190.00**
Universal Hi-Way Markers, steel, Ohio Art, 1972–75 .... **40.00**
Wagon Train, steel, thermos, King-Seeley, 1964 .... **140.00**
Welcome Back Kotter, steel, plastic thermos, Aladdin, 1977 .... **30.00**
Yogi Bear and Friends, steel, Aladdin, 1963 .... **85.00**
Yosemite Sam, vinyl, thermos, King-Seeley, 1971–72 .... **100.00**
Ziggy's Brunch Bag, vinyl, plastic thermos, Aladdin, 1979 .... **40.00**

MAGAZINES

The vast majority of magazines, especially if they are less than thirty years old, are worth between 10¢ and 25¢. A fair number of pre-1960 magazines fall within this price range as well.

There are three ways in which a magazine can have value: (1) the cover artist, (2) the cover personality, and (3) framable interior advertising. In these three instances, value rests not with the magazine collector, but with the speciality collectors.

At almost any flea market, you will find a seller of matted magazine advertisements. Remember that the value being asked almost always rests in the matting and not the individual magazine page.

Newspaper: *PCM (Paper Collector's Marketplace)*, P. O. Box 127, Scandinavia, WI 54977.

Saturday Evening Post, *March 21, 1959, Alajalov cov illus, $5.00.*

American Home	2.00
Art and Beauty, 1926	4.00
Atlantic Monthly, 1914	1.00
Boy's Life, August 1957	15.00
Cosmopolitan, 1942	1.00
Country Home	.75
Democrat Press, The Great Flood Disaster of 1955, pictorial, black and white, 60 pgs	20.00
Esquire, Sept 1934	12.00
Field and Stream	3.00
Harper's Bazaar, illus cov	10.00
Harper's Monthly, Nov 1886	30.00
Harper's Weekly, Dec 1900	15.00
House Beautiful, illustrator cov	8.00
Ladies' Home Journal, 1925	5.00
Life, artist sgd cov	20.00
Look, celebrity	5.00
Mattel Barbie Magazine, Nov-Dec 1963	5.00
Movie & Theatre News, 1933	7.00

Newsweek, after 1950	.25
Outdoor Life	1.00
Pictorial Review, March 1915	12.50
Playboy, 1958	2.00
Saturday Evening Post, Pearl Harbor	10.00
The Theater Magazine, 1908	5.00
Time, 1941–1960	1.00
TV Guide, NYC-TeleVision Guide, 1948–1953	40.00
Woman's Home Companion, 1916	20.00

MAGIC

Presto, chango—the world of magic has fascinated collectors for centuries. The category is broad; it pays to specialize. Possible approaches include children's magic sets, posters about magicians, or sleight-of-hand tricks.

When buying a trick, make certain to get instructions—if possible, the original set. Without them, you need to be a mystic rather than a magician to figure out how the trick works.

Magic catalogs are treasure chests of information. Look for company names such as Abbott's, Brema, Douglas Magicland, Felsman, U. F. Grant, Magic Inc., Martinka, National Magic, Nelson Enterprises, Owen Magic Supreme, Petrie-Lewis, D. Robbins, Tannen, Thayer, and Willmann. Petrie-Lewis is a favorite among collectors. Look for the interwoven ''P & L'' on magic props.

Magicians of note include: Alexander, Blackstone, Carter The Great, Germain The Wizard, Houdini, Kar—I, Kellar, Stock, and Thornston. Anything associated with these magicians has potentially strong market value.

Club: Magic Collectors Association, 19 Logan Street, New Britain, CT 06051.

Book

Fred Keating/Magic's Greatest Entertainer, 16 pgs, c1950	25.00
Gilbert Knots & Splices, rope tying tricks, 66 pgs, 1909	40.00
Magic Made Easy, 28 pgs, 1930 copyright	20.00
Magicdotes, Robert Orben, 44 pgs, 1948 copyright	15.00
Transcendental Magic, Eliphas Levi	85.00

Catalog

Heaney Company, 1924	20.00
Learn to Entertain with Super Magic Tricks & Puzzles	20.00

Magazine, *Linking Ring, Magicians of the World*, 1939 | 15.00

Magic Kit

PF Fliers Blackstone Magic Wedge Kit, sealed bag with Balance Magic, Disappearing Coin Trick, and Defy Gravity, box with Blackstone Jr illus, 1970s. **15.00**

Scarecrow Magic Kit, Ralston Purina Co premium, 1960s. **25.00**

Pinback Button

14th Annual International Brotherhood of Magicians Convention, Battle Creek, Michigan, blue and white, 1939. . . . . **6.00**

Houdini Convention Club of Wisconsin, blue and white, 1930s **8.00**

The International Brotherhood of Magicians, orange, 1930s. **12.00**

MAGNIFYING GLASSES

The vast majority of magnifying glasses that are offered for sale at flea markets are made-up examples. Their handles come from old umbrellas, dresser sets, and even knives. They look old and are highly decorative—a deadly combination for someone who thinks they are getting a one-hundred-year-old-plus example.

There are few collectors of magnifying glasses. Therefore, prices are low, often a few dollars or less, even for some unusual examples. The most collectible magnifying glasses are the Sherlock Holmes type and examples from upscale desk accessory sets. These often exceed $25.00.

MARBLES

Marbles can be divided into handmade glass marbles and machine-made glass, clay, and mineral marbles. Marble identification is serious business. Read and re-read these books before buying your first marble: Paul Baumann, *Collecting Antique Marbles, Second Edition* (Wallace-Homestead, 1991) and Mark E. Randall and Dennis Webb, *Greenberg's Guide to Marbles* (Greenberg Publishing, 1988.)

Children played with marbles. A large number are found in a damaged state. Avoid these. There are plenty of examples in excellent condition.

Beware of reproductions and modern copycats and fakes. Comic marbles are just one of the types that is currently being reproduced.

Clubs: Marble Collectors' Unlimited, 503 West Pine, Marengo, IA 52301; Marble Collectors Society of America, P. O. Box 222, Trumbull, CT 06611; National Marble Club of America, 440 Easton Road, Drexel Hill, PA 19026.

Akro Agate
⅝" d, contemporary **3.00**
½" d, bull's eye **20.00**
Bennington Type
⅝" d, mottled blue **25.00**
⅞" d, mottled brown **30.00**
Cat's Eyes, Vitro-Agate, bag of 100, c1950. . . . . **35.00**
Comic Strip, glass
Emma **60.00**
Koko **30.00**
Skeezix **45.00**
Tom Mix **55.00**
Onionskin
½" d, blue and white swirls **25.00**
2" d, red and yellow swirls **275.00**
Opaque Swirl, ⅝" d **35.00**
Sulphide
1¼" d, pig **60.00**
1⅝" d, woman **150.00**
1¾" d, Chow dog **75.00**
Swirl, 1" d, blue, orange, and green **55.00**
Transparent Swirl, ⅝" d
Divided Core Swirl **15.00**
Latticino Core Swirl **10.00**
Solid Core Swirl **20.00**

MARILYN MONROE

In the 1940s a blonde bombshell exploded across the American movie screen. Born Norma Jean Mortonson in 1926, she made her debut in several magazines in the mid-1940s and appeared in the Twentieth Century Fox movie "Scudda Hoo! Scudda Hey!" in 1948.

Now known as Marilyn Monroe, she captured the public eye with her flamboyant nature and hourglass figure. Her roles in such films as "The Dangerous Years" in 1948, "Bus Stop" in 1956, "Some Like It Hot" in 1959, and "The Misfits" in 1961 brought much attention to this glamour queen.

Her marriages to baseball hero Joe DiMaggio and famous playright Arthur Miller, not to mention her assorted illicit affairs with other famous gentlemen, served to keep Marilyn's personal life on the front burner. It is commonly believed that the pressures of her personal life contributed to her untimely death on August 5, 1962.

Autograph, on white paper **150.00**
Book, *Marilyn*, Norman Mailer, hard cov,
  dj, 270 glossy pgs, black and white and
  color photos, library copy **10.00**
Calendar
  1954, "Golden Dreams," nude on red
    background portrait, glossy, full pad,
    11 × 24" **175.00**
  1954, spiral bound, October Monroe
    portrait, nude on red background,
    added lace overprint, various
    models other months, 8 × 11" **65.00**
Lobby Card, "The Seven Year Itch," No.
  8, 11 × 14", 1955 . . . . **35.00**
Magazine
  Life, April 7, 1952, issue, cover article,
    172 pgs, 10½ × 14" **25.00**
  Marilyn Monroe Pin-Ups, 32 pgs, black
    and white and color photos, 8½ ×
    11", 1953 . . . . **70.00**
  That Girl Marilyn!, 56 pgs, black and
    white photos, 4 × 6", c1955 . . . . **18.00**
  TV Guide, volume 6, #4, January 23–
    29, 1953 . . . . **35.00**
Paper Dolls, Saalfield, No. 158610,
  uncut, 10¾ × 12½", 1953 . . . . **145.00**
Playing Cards, Photo Art, nude on red
  background portrait illus on card backs
  and box, c1955 . . . . **75.00**
Script, *Bus Stop*, 123 pgs, 1956 . . . . **120.00**
Snowdome, red plastic, marked
  "Koziol" **35.00**
Tip Tray, litho metal, round, color por-
  trait on red ground, mahogany frame,
  4⅛" d, 1950s **40.00**
Title Card, *We're Not Married*, Twentieth
  Century Fox, Marilyn with Ginger
  Rogers, Fred Allen, and Victor Moore,
  1952. . . . . **35.00**

MARX TOY COLLECTIBLES

My favorite days as a child were filled with
the adventures of cowboys and Indians in
their constant struggle for control of Fort
Apache. I have only Louis Marx to thank
for those hours of imagination and adventure, for I was a proud owner of a Marx
playset.

The Marx Toy Company was founded
after World War I when Louis and David
Marx purchased a series of dies and molds
from the bankrupt Strauss Toy Company.
In the following years the Marx Toy Company produced a huge assortment of tin
and plastic toys, including 60 to 80 playsets with hundreds of variations. These
playsets, some with lithographed tin struc-
tures, are very collectible if complete.
Marx also manufactured a number of

windup and action toys like Rock-em
Sock-em Robots and the very popular Big
Wheel tricycle.

The Marx Toy Company was bought
and sold a number of times before finally
filing for bankruptcy in 1980. The Quaker
Oats Company owned Marx from the late
1950s until 1978, at which time it was sold
to its final owner, the British toy company,
Dunbee-Combex.

Car, tin, windup, $90.00.

Airmail Biplane, 13½" l, 18" wingspan,
  litho tin, windup, red body, yellow
  wings, four red engines with blue
  celluloid propellers, green, yellow,
  and black trim, open front window,
  1936. . . . . **375.00**
Ambulance, 13½" l, litho tin, windup,
  brake, siren, red and black trim on
  ivory ground, 1937 . . . . **450.00**
American Trucking Co Moving Van, 5" l,
  tin, friction, green lettering on blue
  ground, rear door opens **175.00**
Army Truck, 12" l, plastic, steel frame,
  rubber tires, tailgate opens, olive drab,
  c1950. . . . . **75.00**
Auto Transport, 30½" l, tin, carries
  coupe, roadster, and dump truck, eight
  wheels and spare, 1938 . . . . **500.00**
Cadillac Coupe, 11" l, litho tin, windup,
  orange body, black trim, trunk rack,
  1931. . . . . **375.00**
City Airport, 17 × 11" red steel base, bat-
  tery operated lights, two monoplanes,
  litho tin control tower and two han-
  gars, c1935 . . . . **125.00**
City Delivery Van, 11" l, steel, yellow,
  red fenders, tin grille **200.00**
City Hospital Ambulance, litho tin,
  windup, red trim on blue ground, rear
  opens, c1930 . . . . **350.00**
Climbing Tractor, 8¼" l, litho tin,
  windup, 1930 . . . . **175.00**
Convertible, 11" l, steel, blue top, red
  body, white tires, 1930s **325.00**
Coo Coo Car, crazy car, 8" l, litho tin,
  windup, 1931 . . . . **750.00**
Dial Typewriter, 11" l, 5¾" w, black, red,
  and gold, flat keyboard, 1930s **125.00**
Dick Tracy Squad Car, 11¼" l, litho tin,
  windup, siren, flashing red spotlight,

two rubber and two wooden wheels, 1949............................**300.00**

Dippy Dumper, crazy car, 8¾" l, litho tin, windup, celluloid Popeye and Brutus figures, movable dump cart, 1940 .... **650.00**

Doughboy Tank, 10" l, litho tin, windup, tan ground, 1942 ....**250.00**

Dump Truck, #1013, 18" l, plastic, c1950............................**150.00**

Eagle Air Scout, 26" l, 26½" wingspan, litho tin, windup, silver body, blue trim, revolving propeller, 1929 ......**350.00**

Fighter Plane, 5" wingspan, litho tin, windup, two engines, wooden wheels, stars and bars decal on wings and fuselage, 1940s.......................**75.00**

Fire Chief Car, 8" l, steel, friction, red body, black fenders and bumper, black and white wheels, siren, 1936 ....**250.00**

Fire Truck, 14½" l, steel, windup, baked enamel finish, two ladders, two fire extinguishers, cranking fire tower, tin fireman, 1948 ....**225.00**

Flash Gordon Signal Pistol, 6¾" l, steel, enameled, green, sparking mechanism, siren, 1936.................**95.00**

Flying Fortress, 13½" l, 18" wingspan, litho tin, windup, red and silver, four engines, silver propellers, white balloon wheels, sparking machine guns...........................**325.00**

G-Man Pursuit Car, #7000, 14½" l, litho tin, windup, sparking mechanism, red and navy blue body, cream trim, aluminum rear bumper, 1935..........**500.00**

Greyhound Bus Terminal, 16" l, 11" w, litho tin, two pumps, two sign boards, two garage entrances, drug store, waiting room, c1938 ....**300.00**

Hey Hey the Chicken Snatcher, 8½" h, litho tin, windup, 1926.............**250.00**

Hill Climbing Dump Truck, 13½" l, litho tin, windup, rubber treads, 1932 .....**150.00**

Honeymoon Special, 6" d, litho tin, windup, train with engine and three cars, 1927 ....**150.00**

Joy Rider, crazy car, 8" l, litho tin, windup, 1928 ....**650.00**

Liberty Bus, 5" l, litho tin, windup, 1931..............................**125.00**

Mammy's Boy, 11" h, litho tin, windup, walking, changeable expression, holding cane, 1929....................**200.00**

Meadow Brook Dairy Truck, 10" l, tin, carries milk bottles, 1940 ....**300.00**

Midget Tractor, 5¼" l, litho tin, red, green, yellow, and black, curved radiator, 1940 ....**65.00**

Mortimer Snerd's Tricky Auto, 7½" l, litho tin, windup, crazy car, 1939 .....**800.00**

Mystery Car, 9" l, steel, tin radiator, red, 1936............................**175.00**

Mystic Motorcycle, 4¼" l, litho tin,

windup, blue, yellow, and white, 1936........................**175.00**

New Sky Bird Flyer, litho tin, 9½" h control tower, 24" l crossbar, two planes, one motor, 1947 ....**450.00**

North American Van Lines Tractor Trailer, 13" l, litho tin, windup **200.00**

Old Jalopy, 5¾" l, litho tin, windup, crazy car, driver wearing glasses, 1950............................**250.00**

Peter Rabbit, 5½" l, plastic, windup, crazy car, 1950s...................**450.00**

Pinocchio the Acrobat, 16" h, 11" w, litho tin, windup, composition, jointed, cardboard legs, 1939..............**250.00**

Popeye Pirate Click Pistol, 10" l, litho tin, 1930s.........................**115.00**

Roadside Rest Service Station, 13½" l, 10" w, battery operated, 1935 ....**500.00**

Rocket Racer, 16" l, litho tin, windup, litho tin driver, red body, blue backrest, green, yellow, blue, and black trim, green and black wheels, 1935 ...**500.00**

School Bus, 11½" l, steel, wood wheels, pull toy, 1930s....................**225.00**

Smoky Sam, 6½" l, plastic hat, body, and car, litho tin head and wheels, windup, crazy car, 1950 ....**200.00**

Sparks Racer, 8¼" l, litho tin, windup, yellow body, red and black trim, sparking mechanism, 1928 ....**300.00**

Trans-Atlantic Zeppelin, 10" l, litho tin, windup, striped rudder, c1930.......**400.00**

Tricky Taxi, 4½" l, litho steel, clockwork motor, 1935 ....**75.00**

Tumbling Monkey, 4½" h, litho tin, windup, 1942 ....**110.00**

Turnover Tank, 9" l, litho tin, windup, 1930.............................**250.00**

Uncle Wiggily Car, 7½" l, litho tin, windup, crazy car, 1935 ....**850.00**

Walking Porter, 8" h, litho tin, movable head, 1930s....................**150.00**

MARY GREGORY GLASS

Who was Mary Gregory anyway? Her stuff certainly is expensive. Beware of objects that seem like too much of a bargain. They may have been painted by Mary Gregory's great-great granddaughter in the 1950s rather than in the 1880s. Also, watch the eyes. The original Mary Gregory did not paint children with slanted eyes. Guess who did?

Box, cov, 3⅛" d, round, cranberry, girl and floral sprays, hinged lid **265.00**

Cruet, green, young girl carrying flowers, applied clear handle and stopper **90.00**

Tumblers, pr, honey amber, cobalt blue base,
6¾" h, $160.00.

Liqueur Glass, 3⅜" h, lime green, little
girl 50.00
Match Holder, 2¼" h, cranberry, young
boy 90.00
Mug, 4½" h, amber, ribbed, girl pray-
ing 55.00
Perfume Bottle, 4⅝" h, cranberry, little
girl, clear ball stopper 165.00
Pitcher, ruffled top
10½" h, clear, man in sailboat 125.00
11" h, royal blue, woman playing
trumpet 325.00
Plate
6¼" d, cobalt blue, white enamel girl
with butterfly net 125.00
11" d, black amethyst, stag run-
ning 285.00
Toothpick Holder, cranberry, girl and
floral sprays 55.00
Tumbler, 5¾" h, blue, white enameled
boy, gold bands, pedestal foot 140.00
Vase
4" h, cranberry, boy and girl reading
books, pr 110.00
9" h, emerald green, frosted, girl hold-
ing flowers in apron and hand 150.00
10" h, lime green, man holding
gun, woman holding basket of
fruit, pr 265.00

MATCHBOOKS

Don't play with matches. Save their covers
instead. A great collection can be built for a
relatively small sum of money. Matchcover collectors gain a fair amount of their
new material through swapping.

A few collectors specialize in covers that
include figural-shaped or decorated
matches. If you get into this, make certain
you keep them stored in a covered tin container and in a cool location. If you don't,
your collection may catch fire and go up in
smoke.

Club: Rathkamp Matchcover Society,
1359 Surrey Road, Vandalia, OH 43577.
Note: There are over thirty regional clubs
throughout the United States and Canada.

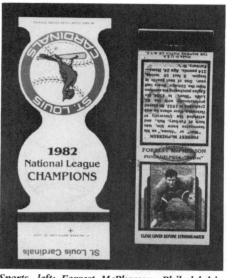

Sports, left: Forrest McPherson, Philadelphia
"Eagles," Diamond Match Co, NYC, $.50; right:
St Louis Cardinals, 1982 National League
Champions, Universal Match Co, $.10.

American Ace, boxes	.12
Banks	.02
Billiards	.05
Casinos	.05
Diamond Quality	.50
Fairs	.15
Foreign	.05
Girlies, non stock	.40
Holiday Inns, stock design	.10
Joe Louis & Max Schmeling Champion-
ship Fight, Giant	18.00
Matchtones, Universal trademark	.10
Patriotic	.05
Political	1.00
Presidential Yacht, "Patricia"	10.00
Pull for Willkie, Pullquick Match	28.00
Pull Quick	1.00
Remember Pearl Harbor, red, white, and
blue, anti-Japan slogan on cover, Un-
cle Sam on back, early 1940s	10.00
Ship Lines	.10
Stoeckle Select Beer, Stoeckle Brew-
ery	6.00
Transportation	.15
Washington Redskins, set of 20	40.00

MATCHBOX TOYS

Leslie Smith and Rodney Smith founded Lesney Products, an English company, in 1947. They produced the first Matchbox toys. In 1953 the trade name "Matchbox" was registered and the first diecast cars were made on a 1:75 scale. In 1979 Lesney produced over 5.5 million cars per week. In 1982 Universal International bought Lesney.

Clubs: American-International Matchbox, 522 Chestnut Street, Lynn, MA 01904; Matchbox Collectors Club, 141 West Commercial Avenue, Moonachie, NJ 07075.

Morris Cowley, #8, light tan body, brown fender, 1926, $65.00.

Alfa Carabo, 1975	10.00
Baja Dune Buggy, 1971	10.00
BMW, sport coupe, orange, 1980	2.00
Boss Mustang, 1972	12.00
Cadillac, 1965	6.00
Cement Truck, 1977	7.50
Dodge Challenger, 1976	10.00
Ferrari, green, 1970	5.00
Ford, Capri, red and silver, 1975	3.00
Ford Mustang, 1970	20.00
GT 350, 1970	8.00
Hot Rocker, 1973	10.00
Hot Rod, 1971	5.00
Jeep Hot Rod, 1971	20.00
Lamborghini Miura, 1970	15.00
Lincoln Continental, 1970	15.00
Lotus, roadster, orange, 1961	5.00
Mack Dump Truck, 1968	30.00
Mercedes, convertible, 1982	3.00
Midnight Magic, 1972	6.00
Orange Peel, 1971	8.00
Pepsi Truck	8.00
Police Patrol, 1975	15.00
Pontiac, Trans Am, black, 1980	2.50
Renault 5TL	9.00
Rolls Royce, Yesteryears 2nd Series	20.00
Steam Roller, MIB	40.00
Sun Burner, 1972	8.00
Swamp Rat, 1976	8.00

Weazel, 1974	10.00
Zoo Truck, 1981	12.00

MCCOY POTTERY

Like Abingdon Pottery, this attractive pottery is sought by those no longer able to afford Roseville and Weller pottery. Commemorative cookie jars and planters seem to be rapidly increasing in price, e.g., the Apollo Spaceship cookie jar at $45.00. These specialty items bring more from secondary collectors than from McCoy collectors who realize the vast quantity of material available in the market.

Beware of reproductions. The Nelson McCoy Pottery Company is making modern copies of their period pieces. New collectors are often confused by them.

Vase, urn shape, pink flowers, green leaves, brown twigs, white ground, 6¼" h, $18.00.

Bank	
Hobo, 6" h	75.00
Sailor, duffel bag over shoulder	20.00
Batter Jug, 4½" h, Nurock	75.00
Bookends, pr, jumping horses, marked "Nu-Art"	18.50
Bowl, 6" d, matte green	25.00
Bud Vase, 8" h, matte green	5.00
Centerpiece Bowl, 8¾" d, blue, tulip dec	7.50
Chamber Pot, cov, Lucile	75.00
Cookie Jar	
Apple, red	20.00
Coffee Grinder	25.00
Mammy	45.00
Picnic Basket	35.00

Smiley Face 25.00
Stove, black 20.00
Timmy Tortoise 35.00
Yosemite Sam 40.00
Cuspidor, frog dec. 125.00
Flower Frog, 2½″ d, heart shape, blue
  onyx 30.00
Mug, Suburbia pattern, yellow 7.50
Planter
  Dog, light green and white 12.00
  Frog, green 8.50
  Sprinkling Can, white, rose decal 6.50
Salt and Pepper Shakers, pr, cabbage . . .   10.00
Soap Dish, Lucile 100.00
Teapot, Grecian pattern 25.00
Vase
  7½″ h, mottled green, marked "Brush,
    #709" 18.00
  9″ h, sq, light green, stylized floral
    dec 8.00

MEDICAL ITEMS

Anything medical is collectible. Doctors often discard instruments, never realizing that the minute an object becomes obsolete, it also becomes collectible. Many a flea market treasure begins life in a garbage can behind the doctor's office.

Stress condition and completeness. Specialize in one area. Remember some instruments do not display well. Dad's wife will not let him keep his collection of rectal examiners in the living room.

Apothecary
  Book, *Four Thousand Years of Pharmacy*,
    Charles H LaWall, 1927 . . . .   12.50
  Bottle, 5⅞″ h, pressed glass, amber,
    tole lid 25.00
  Calendar, 1916, Bromo-Seltzer, note-
    pad 4.00
  Calendar Plate, 1908, Compliments of
    Bell's Pharmacy, Walhalla, SC 25.00
  Capsule Holder, pressed pasteboard
    box, six graduated levels, Parke,
    Davis & Co 5.00
  Mortar and Pestle, 9″ h, turned, ash
    burl, wide foot, plain birch pestle . . .125.00
  Pill Roller, 2 pcs, 7 × 14″, walnut and
    brass, makes 24 pills 100.00
  Scale, oak, glass top lid, two pans,
    weights, Griffin & Tatlock 100.00
Dental
  Book, *Principles of Crowning Teeth*,
    Goslee, 1903 . . . .   5.00
  Catalog, William Dixon Dental Goods,
    New York, 136 pgs, c1912 . . . .   40.00
  Cheek Retractor, carved, MOP han-
    dle 75.00
  Drill, Electro Dental Mfg Co, foot con-
    trol 50.00

Extracting Forceps, Jno B Daniel, At-
  lanta, No. 64 . . . .   6.00
Mirror, 3½″ d, celluloid, Crocker-Fels
  Dental Supplies 15.00
Pliers, nerve canal 15.00
Sterilizer, formaldehyde, wall
  mounted 50.00
Trade Card, C R Scholl, DDS 3.00
Medical
Anesthesia Mask, brass, folding,
  c1870 . . . .   75.00
Blood Cell Calculator, Dr M M
  Marbell, dated 1922 . . . .   35.00
Book
  Bone Graft Surgery, Albee, 1915 . . . . .   6.00
  Textbook of Dermatology, Darier,
    1920 . . . .   8.00
Bottle, glass
  6½″ h, Chlorate Potassique, clear,
    pontil, painted brown 20.00
  8″ h, Granular Citrate of Magnesia,
    cobalt, kite with letter inside, ring
    top 30.00
Catalog, General Catalogue of Physi-
  cians, Druggists, Dentists & Veteri-
  nary Specialties, Becton, Dickinson
  & Co, Rutherford, NJ, 1918, 160
  pgs 28.00
Doctor's Bag, leather, late 19th C. 55.00
Ear Syringe, bakelite, 3 pcs, case,
  Charles Lentz and Sons, Philadel-
  phia, c1890 . . . .   75.00
Ether Mask, brass, England, c1900 . . .   50.00
Hearing Aid, silk tubing 85.00
Journal, *Annuals of Medical History*,
  c1930 . . . .   4.00
Mirror, Frank Mollema, Chiroprac-
  tor 20.00
Nasal Speculum, steel, etched handles,
  England, c1890 . . . .   18.00
Saw, amputation, bow blade, ebony
  handle 120.00
Specimen Bottle, glass, clear 2.00
Stethoscope, monaural, metal 100.00
Surgical Knife, sterling silver, marked
  "Gorham" 45.00
Optical
Book
  Diseases of the Eye and Ear, C H Vilas,
    1890 . . . .   5.00
  Optical Dictionary and Encyclopedia,
    1908 . . . .   25.00
Cabinet, 20″ h, oak, roll top, drawers
  and compartments hold test lenses
  and frames .325.00
Eye Cup
  Ceramic, white 12.00
  Glass, clear, emb "M" 8.00
Eyelid Retractor, ivory handle, marked
  "Hills King St," c1853 . . . . .125.00
Lens Set, Fits-U-Eyeglasses Kit, velvet
  lined case 12.00
Ophthalmic Instrument Set, retracting
  forceps with ivory handle, four ster-

ling silver lachrymal probes, Genou,
Paris....................................**200.00**
Retinascope, ivory handle, England,
c1880............................. **25.00**
Ophthalmoscope, Morton, cased.....**100.00**
Trial Lens and Frame Set, 5¼" sq min-
iature mahogany case...........**210.00**

MEGO ACTION FIGURES

Mego action figures were made from 1972 to 1982. Ranging in size from 3¾" to 12½" tall, they were characterizations of Marvel and DC comic book heroes. Later runs were characters from popular TV shows and movies.

There can be a number of variations on the individual figures, as well as on the packaging techniques—e.g., boxes or blister packs. Mego action series include: The Mad Monster Series, 1974; The Official Greatest Super Heroes, 1972–78; The Wizard of Oz, 1974; Star Trek (television) 1974–76; and Star Trek: The Motion Picture, 1979.

Amazing Spiderman
  8" h, orig box **100.00**
  12½" h
    Fly Away Action **125.00**
    Poseable....................... **70.00**
    Web Spinning **150.00**
The Black Hole, 1979
  3¾" h
    Dr Durant **10.00**
    Kate McCrae **20.00**
    Humanoid.................... **30.00**
    Maximillian................... **20.00**
    Old Bob **35.00**
    Pizer........................ **10.00**
  12" h
    Captain Hollard................ **40.00**
    Dr Reinhardt **40.00**
Buck Rogers
  3¾" h
    Ardella....................... **8.00**
    Buck......................... **15.00**
    Draconian Guard **15.00**
    Draconian Marauder **35.00**
    Twiki **10.00**
  12" h
    Dr Huer **40.00**
    Killer Kane **40.00**
    Wilma **30.00**
CHiPs, Jimmy Squeeks, 3¾" h........ **5.00**
Comic Action Heroes, 3¾" h, 1975–78
  Aquaman **50.00**
  Green Goblin.................... **45.00**
  Hulk......................... **35.00**
  Spiderman..................... **40.00**

Conan, 8" h, orig box, mid 1970s **425.00**
Dukes of Hazzard
  3¾" h
    Boss Hogg **6.00**
    Cletus...................... **30.00**
    Daisy **6.00**
    Uncle Jessie **25.00**
  8" h
    Bo.......................... **20.00**
    Boss Hogg **20.00**
Fantastic Four, 8" h
  Human Torch, blister pack **40.00**
  Invisible Girl, orig box **90.00**
  Thing, blister pack................. **40.00**
Flash Gordon
  Dr Zarkov **50.00**
  Ming **70.00**
Green Arrow, 8", orig box **175.00**
Green Goblin, 8" h, carded **375.00**
Happy Days
  Chachi......................... **30.00**
  Potsie......................... **30.00**
Incredible Hulk, fly away action **90.00**
Iron Man, 8" h, orig box............**150.00**
Kiss, Gene, 12" h **75.00**
Knights
  King Arthur....................**250.00**
  Sir Galahad...................**200.00**
Laverne and Shirley................. **50.00**
Love Boat, Gopher **8.00**
Mad Monster Series, 8" h
  Dracula **175.00**
  Mummy **95.00**
  Wolfman **150.00**
Micronauts
  Acroyear II **15.00**
  Baron Karza **20.00**
  Biotherm....................... **30.00**
  Galactic Defender **10.00**
  Rhodim Orbitor **15.00**
Moonraker, 12" h, 1979
  Drax..........................**150.00**
  Holly Goodhead **150.00**
  James Bond....................**100.00**
  Jaws..........................**500.00**
One Million Years B.C., Trog **35.00**
Our Gang, Buckwheat **60.00**
Planet of the Apes, 8" h
  Astronaut **25.00**
  Burke......................... **50.00**
  Cornelius...................... **25.00**
  Dr Zaius, Bend 'n' Flex **20.00**
  Soldier Ape **25.00**
Pocket Super Heroes, 3¾" h, 1979
  Aquaman **50.00**
  Captain Marvel................. **20.00**
  General Zod.................... **15.00**
  Jor-El......................... **15.00**
  Wonder Woman................ **20.00**
Robin Hood
  Friar Tuck **75.00**
  Maid Marian **100.00**
  Robin.........................**100.00**
  Sheriff of Nottingham............. **75.00**

Sonny and Cher
  Cher.......................... 45.00
  Sonny Bono 40.00
Star Trek, 8" h, 1974
  Andorian........................150.00
  Cheron..........................100.00
  Kirk............................ 30.00
  McCoy........................... 30.00
  Mugato 175.00
  Romulan.........................150.00
  The Gorn........................120.00
  The Keeper 120.00
  Uhura 35.00
Star Trek: The Motion Picture, 1979
3¾" h
  Betelgeusian 25.00
  Decker 15.00
  Megarite 25.00
  Scotty.......................... 15.00
12" h
  Arcturian....................... 50.00
  Illia........................... 30.00
  Klingon 50.00
  Spock........................... 30.00
Superhero Bendables, 5" h, 1972–74
  Batgirl 120.00
  Catwoman........................175.00
  Mr Mxyzptik.....................125.00
  Robin........................... 75.00
  Shazam 125.00
  Tarzan 75.00
  Wonder Woman....................100.00
Superman, 12" h, 1967 ....100.00
Superman the Movie, 12" h
  Luthor.......................... 40.00
  Superman 50.00
Tarzan
  5" h, bendie.................... 60.00
  8" h, mid 1970s................. 60.00
Teen Titans, 7" h, 1977
  Kid Flash, carded...............300.00
  Speedy, carded 350.00
Thor, 8" h, orig box 400.00
Western Heroes
  Buffalo Bill Cody...............150.00
  Cochise.........................150.00
  Davy Crockett...................200.00
Wizard of Oz, Munchkin Flower Girl ... 40.00
Wonder Woman
  Nubia, 1976..................... 90.00
  Queen Hippolite, 1976 .... 90.00
  Steve Trevor, 12" h, 1976....... 75.00
Wonder Woman
  8" h, orig box, 1974 ....300.00
  12" h
    Diana Prince outfit, Linda Carter
      photo box, 1976 ....100.00
    Evening gown, second issue box,
      1977...................... 40.00
World's Greatest Super Heroes, 8" h,
1972–78
  Aqualad, carded 325.00
  Batman, removable cowl, orig box ...350.00
  Conan, carded...................350.00

Falcon, carded...................200.00
Green Arrow, orig box 175.00
Human Torch, carded............. 40.00
Invisible Girl, orig box 90.00
Iron Man, carded 200.00
Joker, fist fighting, orig box 450.00
Kid Flash, carded................350.00
Mr Fantastic, carded............. 40.00
Robin, removable mask, orig box 350.00
Supergirl, orig box 420.00
Thing, carded 40.00
Wonder Girl, carded 300.00

MILITARIA

Soldiers have returned home with the spoils of war as long as there have been soldiers and wars. Look at the Desert Storm material that is starting to arrive on the market. Many collectors tend to collect material relating to wars taking place in their young adulthood or related to re-enactment groups to which they belong.

It pays to specialize. The two obvious choices are a specific war or piece of equipment. Never underestimate the enemy. Nazi material remains the strongest segment of the market.

Reproductions abound. Be especially careful of any Civil War and Nazi material.

Magazines: *Military Collectors' News*, P. O. Box 702073, Tulsa, OK 74170; *North South Trader*, 724 Caroline Street, Fredericksburg, VA 22401.

Clubs: American Society of Military Insignia Collectors, 1331 Bradley Avenue, Hummelstown, PA 17036; Association of American Military Uniform Collectors, 446 Berkshire Rd, Elyria, OH 44035; Company of Military Historians, North Main Street, Westbrook, CT 06498; Imperial German Military Collectors Association, Box 38, Keyport, NJ 07735.

CIVIL WAR
Autograph, 4 × 3" card, Confederate, A H
  Garland, dated 60.00
Belt, Union infantry soldier, 1863......150.00
Bullet Mold, picket pattern bullet 45.00
Cartridge Box, Weston...............300.00
Field Glasses, 7½" l, brass, Lemaire Fabt,
  Paris..........................125.00
Helmet Badge, brass shield and eagle,
  company number in center 45.00
Insignia, brass, lieutenant 25.00
Mess Kit, bone handles, orig leather
  case 175.00

Civil War, pistol box, R Dingee New York manufacturer, $150.00.

Muster Roll, 20th Regt Illinois, August to
   October 1863, folds out to 20 × 30",
   document entries 100.00
Ribbon, blue-gray, Lincoln's head surrounded by "With Malice Toward
   None, With Charity For All," 1861–
   65............................... 90.00
Shell Jacket, Union cavalry, buttons, lining, and inspector's marks 425.00
Tintype, full length, unidentified Confederate Cavalry man, gear, sword,
   and carbine 450.00

WORLD WAR I

Badge, Tank Corps, British cap, 8th
   Churka 20.00
Belt, web 15.00
Document, 16⅛ × 20⅛", US Army, pho-
   tograph and discharge paper, Warren
   Bennethum, reverse painted flag,
   framed, 1919.................... 65.00
Gas Mask, carrying can, shoulder
   strap, canister attached to bottom,
   German........................ 75.00
Helmet, Army..................... 50.00
Medal, Iron Cross 35.00
Periscope, wood, used in trench war-
   fare 75.00
Pinback Button
   ⅞" d, Western Electric Soldier's Com-
      fort Club, black and white 8.00
   1¼" d, Welcome Home Soldiers of
      York County, PA................ 20.00
Poster, "Lend the Way They Fight, Buy
   Bonds to Your Utmost," full color ac-
   tion scene, red and black lettering,
   green border 50.00
Uniform, US Army, engineer, coat, belt,
   pants, cap, canvas leggings, wood put-
   tees, leather gaiters, canteen 300.00
Watch Fob, brass, US soldier and
   sailor 20.00

WORLD WAR II

Arm Band, 4" w, Civilian Defense Air
   Raid Warden, white, blue circle, red
   and white diagonal stripes within triangle 12.00
Badge, Nazi, General Assault, silver,
   c1940......................... 30.00
Binoculars, Army, M-17, field type,
   7½" l, olive drab, 7 × 50 power, fixed
   optics......................... 100.00
Book, A. Hitler, *Mein Kampf*, 1933, 407
   pgs, dust jacket 15.00
Cap, AAF Officer's, 50-Mission, gabar-
   dine, gilded eagle, marked "Flighter by
   Bancroft, O D" 120.00
Envelope, Iwo Jima flag raising, 8/29/45,
   artist G F Hadley 15.00
Hat, Nazi SS, rabbit fur, quilted int., black
   ties at ear flaps, olive green wool body,
   RZM/SS, skull and eagle devices 325.00
Knife, black finish blade, "USN" and
   "Mark S Sheath" marked on guard,
   gray web belt, gray fiber scabbard 50.00
Manual, *Recognition Pictorial Manual*, Bureau of Aeronautics, Navy Department, Washington, DC, June 1943,
   contains silhouettes and technical information on Allied and Axis aircraft, 6
   × 10", 80 pgs, black and white 45.00
Patch, pilot's wings, leather, AAF, emb,
   standard design, flying jacket attachment type 30.00
Pencil Holder, 3½" h, plastic, red, white,
   and blue, marked "Victory"........ 10.00
Pin, Maritime Commission Award of
   Merit, sterling, raised eagle with inscribed chest "Ships For Victory" in
   front of red enamel "M," blue enamel
   ground........................ 18.00
Poster, 22 × 28", "Fill It! Harvest War
   Crops," full color................ 45.00
Ring, Nazi, silver, crossed swords, helmet, and swastika 50.00
Shirt, Nazi, brown, S.A., black collar tabs
   and piping, eagle buttons, c1933 ..... 150.00
Sweater, sleeveless, olive drab, "V"
   neck.......................... 25.00
Victory Pin, 1" d, diecut, plastic, gold,
   white and red British lion and US eagle, blue letter "V" behind figures 22.00

VIETNAM

Book, *Frontline-The Commands of Wm
   Chase*, 1975, autographed 1st edition,
   228 pgs 38.00
Helmet, US tanker, Fiberglas, dark green,
   intercom system on side............ 50.00
Medal
   Air Force Commendation, parade rib-
      bon and lapel bar, orig case........ 20.00
   Vietnam Service 15.00

Uniform Tunic, US Army, sergeant, 5th
Division, green, red diamonds insignia,
gold stripes **40.00**

MILK BOTTLES

There is an entire generation of young
adults to whom the concept of milk in a
bottle is a foreign idea. In another fifteen
years a book like this will have to contain a
chapter on plastic milk cartons. I hope you
are saving some.

When buying a bottle, make certain the
glass is clear of defects from manufacture
and wear and the label and/or wording is
in fine or better condition. Buy odd-sized
bottles and bottles with special features.
Don't forget the caps. They are collectible
too.

Newsletter: *The Milk Route*, 4 Ox Bow
Road, Westport, CT 06880.

Alden Bros, round, emb	**25.00**
Andersons Creamery, emb, 7 oz	**4.00**
Beech Grove Dairy, Utica, NY, pyro-glazed, qt	**48.00**
Borden's Golden Crest, amber	**18.00**
Cloverleaf Dairy, Quincy, MA, emb, qt	**35.00**
The Croney Dairy, Clymer, NY, baby reaching for bottle	**4.00**
Dunmyer Dairy	**20.00**
Erdman & Sons, Lykens, PA, pyroglazed, pt	**34.00**
Fairview Dairy Co, Lockhaven, PA, emb, 1/2 pt	**30.00**
Gold Spot, green	**40.00**
Grasslands Dairy	**10.00**
Greenleaf Dairy, Petersburg, VA, sq, green, qt	**40.00**
Murphy's Dairy, Neenah	**30.00**
Nelson's Dairy, sq, qt	**30.00**
Palmer Dairy, dripless	**25.00**
Price's Dairy Co, clear	**5.00**
Sanitary Dairy, sq, orange	**8.00**
Shelton Bros Dairy, clear, pt	**4.00**
Victory Bottle, Birmingham, AL, round, emb, qt	**12.00**
Wells Dairy Cooperative, Columbus, GA, round, emb, qt	**3.00**

MILK GLASS

Milk glass is an opaque white glass that
became popular during the Victorian era.
A scientist will tell you that it is made by
adding oxide of tin to a batch of clear glass.
Most collect it because it's pretty.

Companies like Atterbury, McKee, and
Westmoreland have all produced fine examples in novelties, often of the souvenir
variety, as well as household items. Old
timers focus heavily on milk glass made
before 1920. However, there are some
great pieces from the post-1920 period
that you would be wise not to overlook.

Milk glass has remained in continuous
production since it was first invented.
Many firms reproduce old patterns. Be
careful. Old timers will tell you that if a
piece has straw marks, it is probably correct. Some modern manufacturers who
want to fool you might have also added
them in the mold. Watch out for a "K" in a
diamond. This is the mark on milk glass
reproductions from the 1960s made by the
Kemple Glass Company.

Milk glass is practical. A glass sitting beside a plate of cookies gives others in the
room the impression that you are drinking
milk. Hint, hint!

Club: National Milk Glass Collectors Society, P. O. Box 402, Northfield, MN 55057.

Animal Dish, cov	
Deer, fallen tree base, sgd "E. C. Flaccus Co, Wheeling, WV"	**175.00**
Hen, 7 1/2" l, lacy base, head turned to left, marbleized white and deep blue, Atterbury	**150.00**
Squirrel, acorn base	**125.00**
Turkey, nest base	**85.00**
Ashtray, 5 1/4" sq, English Hobnail pattern, Westmoreland	**22.50**
Bottle, 10 3/4" h, figural, bear, sitting, forelegs folded across chest	**120.00**
Bowl	
8" d, Ball and Chain pattern, openwork rim	**45.00**
9" d, Old Quilt pattern, ftd, Westmoreland	**40.00**
9 1/2" d, Rock Crystal, orig label, McKee	**55.00**
Butter Dish, cov, 4 7/8" l, Roman Cross pattern, sq ftd base, cube shape finial	**50.00**
Candlestick	
Paneled Grape pattern, Westmoreland, pr	**25.00**
Swirled, 7 3/4" h, ribbing twists counterclockwise from base, wax guard	**35.00**
Compote, 8 1/2" d, Lattice Edge pattern, floral dec, Daisy and Button-type pattern pedestal base, Challinor, Taylor	**75.00**

Creamer
    Beaded Grape, Westmoreland **15.00**
    Forget-Me-Not pattern **35.00**
Figure, 5½″ h, owl, glass eyes, Hot
    Springs, SD, souvenir **100.00**
Match Holder, 4½″ h, Jolly Jester, patent
    date on bottom **85.00**
Mug, 3″ h, Ivy in Snow pattern **32.00**
Mustard, 5″ h, owl, glass insert, orig
    threaded top, Atterbury **150.00**
Pitcher, 8″ h, Dart and Bar pattern, blue,
    rect handle, ftd **95.00**
Plate
    6″ d, three owl heads, fluted open-
      work rim, gold paint **50.00**
    7½″ d, Blackberries pattern, beaded
      rim, Westmoreland **12.00**
    8″ d, Eagle pattern, star rim, Fen-
      ton **40.00**
Platter, 13¼″ l, retriever swimming
    through cattails, lily pad border **70.00**
Salt and Pepper Shakers, pr, Paneled
    Grape pattern, Westmoreland **20.00**
Salt Shaker, 2¾″ h, Diamond Point and
    Leaf pattern, blue **40.00**
Spooner, 5⅝″ h, Beaded Circle pattern,
    scalloped, ftd, Sandwich **50.00**
Sugar, cov, Sunflower pattern **50.00**
Vase, 9½″ h, Paneled Grape pattern,
    Westmoreland **28.00**

MINIATURES

If you want to find miniatures at flea markets, look in the cases. The size that you are most likely to find there is "doll house." The other two sizes are child's and salesman's sample; these rarely show up at flea markets.

Beware. Miniatures have been sold for years. Modern crafts people continue to make great examples. Alas, their handiwork can be easily aged so that it will fool most buyers. Also Cracker Jack giveaways, charms, and the like should not be confused with miniatures.

Magazines: *Miniature Collectors*, Collector Communications Corp., 170 Fifth Ave., New York, NY 10010; *Nutshell News*, Clifton House, Clifton, VA 22024.

Clubs: International Guild of Miniature Artisans, P. O. Box 842, Summit, NJ 07901; National Association of Miniature Enthusiasts, 123 N. Lemon Street, Fullerton, CA 92632.

Child's
    Bed, brass, 21¾″ h, 28¾″ l, 18″ w,
      early 20th C **195.00**

Mantel Clock, china, purple numerals, gold highlights, white ground, European, 2¾″ h, $20.00.

    Carriage, 34″ l, wicker, open, parasol,
      brocade upholstery, early 20th C . . . **385.00**
    Measuring Cup, Pyrex **10.00**
    Rocker, 9¼″ h, arms, painted blue . . . **165.00**
Doll House
    Cradle, wood **25.00**
    Floor Lamp, 4″ h, metal, black, gilded
      frame, glass beaded shade **100.00**
    Ironing Board, cast iron, folding, Kil-
      gore, c1930 . . . . **20.00**
    Desk, 5½″ h, lady's, chair, c1875 . . . . . **90.00**
    Patio Set, litho tin, round table, four
      chairs, floral design **35.00**
    Piano, matching bench, Renwal **30.00**
    Stool, metal, Tootsietoy **12.00**
    Tea Set, porcelain, cov teapot,
      creamer, cov sugar, and tray **50.00**
Salesman's Samples
    Cash Register, R C Allen, dated
      1958 . . . . **25.00**
    Food Grinder, 3″ h, J P Co **35.00**
    Harrow, 7½″ l, iron and wood, horse-
      drawn **95.00**
    Porch Swing, 16″ l, wood **125.00**

MODEL KITS

A plastic model kit is a world of fun and fantasy for people of all ages. Model kit manufacturers such as Revell/Monogram, Aurora, and Horizon create and produce detailed kits that let the builder's imagination run wild. Creative kits give movie monsters a creepy stare, F16 fighter planes a sense of movement, and hot rod roadsters the ability to race on a dragstrip across a table top.

Most model kits were packed in a decorated cardboard box with an image of the model on the surface. The box contained the requisite pieces and a set of assembly instructions. Model kits are snapped together or glued together. Painting and decoration is left up to the assembler. Model kits are produced from plastic, resin, or vinyl, and they require a bit of dexterity and patience to assemble.

Buying model kits at flea markets should be done with a degree of caution. An open box spells trouble. Look for missing pieces or loss of the instructions. Sealed boxes are your best bet, but even these should be questioned because of the availablity of home shrink-wrap kits. Don't be afraid—inquire about a model's completeness before purchasing it.

1914 Suttz Bearcat, Bearcats, MPC, 1971. . . . . 55.00
A-Team Van, AMT, 1983 . . . . 20.00
Addams Family House, Aurora, 1965 . . . 850.00
Alfred E Neuman, Aurora, 1965 . . . . 325.00
Archie's Car, Aurora, 1969 . . . . 120.00
Armored Dinosaur, Prehistoric Scenes, Aurora, 1972. . . . . 40.00
Attack Trak, Masters of the Universe, Monogram, 1984 . . . . 15.00
Autogyro, James Bond, Airfix, 1969 . . . . 300.00
Banana Splits Banana Buggy, Aurora, 1969. . . . . 325.00
Barnabas Collins, Dark Shadows, MPC, 1968. . . . . 275.00
Batmobile, Imai, 1983 . . . . 45.00
The Black Knight of Nürnberg, Aurora, 1956. . . . . 120.00
Bonanza, Revell, 1965 . . . . 150.00
The Bride of Frankenstein, Horizon, 1988. . . . . 45.00
Captain Kidd, Bloodthirsty Pirates, Aurora, 1965 . . . . 120.00
Charlie's Angels Van, Revell, 1977 . . . . . 30.00
Compact Pussycat, Wacky Racers, MPC, 1969. . . . . 175.00
Cornfield Roundup Diarama, Planet of the Apes, Addar, 1975 . . . . 45.00
Creature From the Black Lagoon, Glow Kit, Aurora, 1972 . . . . 140.00
Cyclops and Robinson Family, Lost in Space, Aurora, 1965. . . . . 1,200.00
Daddy the Surburbanite, Weird-Ohs, Hawk, 1963. 75.00
Dempsey vs Firpo, Great Moments in Sports, Aurora, 1965 . . . . 100.00
Draconian Marauder, Buck Rogers, Monogram, 1979 . . . . 20.00
Dragnut, Ed "Big Daddy" Roth, Revell, 1963. . . . . 60.00
Dragula, Blueprinters series, AMT/ERTL, 1991. . . . . 20.00
Dr Deadly's Daughter, Monster Scenes, Aurora, 1971. . . . . 120.00

Dr Jekyll as Mr Hyde, Monsters of the Movies, Aurora, 1974. . . . . 90.00
Duke's Digger, Dukes of Hazzard, MPC, 1980. . . . . 25.00
Escape From the Crypt, Haunted Mansion, Disney, MPC, 1974 . . . . 45.00
Esmerelda Whoozis, Aurora, 1968 . . . . . 120.00
Evil Kneivel's Sky Cycle X2, Addar, 1974. . . . . 25.00
Flag Raising at Iwo Jima, Aurora, 1968. . . . . 150.00
Flipper and Sandy, Revell, 1968 . . . . 100.00
The Fonz Dream Rod, Happy Days, AMT, 1976. . . . . 35.00
The Frog, Castle Creatures, Aurora, 1966. . . . . 90.00
Galaxy Runner, Message from Space, Entex, 1978. 20.00
George Harrison, Revell, 1965. . . . . 140.00
George Washington, Aurora, 1967 . . . . . 125.00
Ghost of the Treasure Guard, Pirates of the Caribbean, Disney, MPC, 1972 . . . 45.00
Giant Wasp, Gigantics, MPC, 1975 . . . . . 50.00
Godzilla's Go-Kart, Aurora, 1966 . . . 1,500.00
Good Ship Flounder, Dr Doolittle, Aurora, 1967 . . . . 140.00
Gowdy the Dowdy Grackle, Dr Seuss, Revell, 1960 . . . . 120.00
Guillotine, Aurora, 1964 . . . . 225.00
H M S Bounty, Mutiny on the Bounty, Revell, 1961 . . . . 100.00
Hercules and the Lion, Aurora, 1966. . . . 425.00
Hitler, Born Losers, Parks, 1965. . . . . . . 150.00
Hot Dogger Hangin' Ten, Silly Surfers, Hawk, 1964. 45.00
Indian Warrior, Pyro, 1960 . . . . 60.00
Invaders Flying Saucer, Monogram 45.00
Invisible Man, Horizon, 1988. . . . . 45.00
Jaguar XJS, Return of the Saint, Revell, 1979. . . . . 45.00
Jaws of Doom, Six Million Dollar Man, MPC, 1975. . . . . 30.00
Joker's Goon Car/Gotham City Police Car, AMT/ERTL, 1990 . . . . 15.00
John F Kennedy, Aurora, 1965 . . . . 125.00
King Arthur, Camelot Scenes, Aurora, 1968. . . . . 150.00
Ma Barker's Getaway Car, Bloody Mama, MPC, 1970 . . . . 65.00
Mars Probe Landing Module, Lindberg, 1969. . . . . 90.00
Mazinga, Shogun Warriors, Monogram, 1977. . . . . 30.00
Metaluna Mutant, Jumbo Kit, Tskuda, 1986. . . . . 80.00
Mexican Senorita, Aurora, 1957 . . . . 45.00
Mod Squad Woody Surf Wagon, Aurora, 1969. . . . . 150.00
Monkeemobile, Airfix, 1967 . . . . 375.00
Moonbus, 2001, Aurora, 1969. . . . . 350.00
The Mummy, Luminators Series, Monogram, 1991 . . . . 7.00
Munster's Koach, AMT, 1964 . . . . 275.00
My Mother the Car, AMT, 1965 . . . . 75.00

Nutty Nose Nipper, Aurora, 1965 . . . . . . **165.00**
The Phantom and the Voodoo Witch
  Doctor, Revell, 1965 . . . . **175.00**
Phantom of the Opera, Horizon,
  1988. . . . . **45.00**
Pink Panther Custom Car, Eldon,
  1969. . . . . **90.00**
Rawhide, Gil Favor, Pyro, 1958 . . . . **60.00**
Road Hog, Lindy Loonys, Lindberg,
  1964. . . . . **145.00**
Roadster, Mannix, MPC, 1968 . . . . **75.00**
Robin, Comic Scenes, Aurora, 1974 . . . . **35.00**
Roman Gladiator with Trident, Aurora,
  1959. . . . . **325.00**
Roto the Assault Vehicle, Masters of the
  Universe, Monogram, 1984 . . . . **15.00**
Sand Worm, Dune, Revell, 1985 . . . . **20.00**
Seaview, Voyage to the Bottom of the
  Sea, Aurora, 1966 . . . . **250.00**
Signaling Device for Shipwrecked
  Sailors, Multiple Toymakers, 1965 . . . **50.00**
Simple Simon Pie Wagon, Revell,
  1966. . . . . **75.00**
Snoopy and His Motorcycle, Monogram,
  1971. . . . . **40.00**
Speed Shift Fred Flypogger, Monogram,
  1965. . . . . **250.00**
Spindrift, Land of the Giants, Aurora,
  1968. . . . . **200.00**
Sta-Puft Marshmallow Man, Jumbo Kit,
  Tskuda, 1986. **45.00**
Steel Plunkers, Frantics, Hawk, 1965 . . . **45.00**
Strange Change Time Machine, MPC,
  1974. . . . . **65.00**
Stroker McGurk and His Surf/Rod, MPC,
  1964. . . . . **125.00**
SWAT Command Van, Revell, 1976 . . . . **25.00**
Sweathogs Car, Welcome Back Kotter,
  MPC, 1976. . . . . **40.00**
Tarpit, Prehistoric Scenes, Aurora,
  1972. . . . . **45.00**
Three Musketeers, Athos, Porthos, and
  Aramis, Aurora, 1959 . . . . **375.00**
T J Hooker Police Car, MPC, 1982 . . . . . . **15.00**
Totally Fab, Frantics, Hawk, 1965 . . . . . . **45.00**
Tree House Diarama, Planet of the Apes,
  Addar, 1975 . . . . **45.00**
Twenty Mule Team, Death Valley Days,
  Borax premium. **45.00**
United States Infantryman, Aurora,
  1956. . . . . **90.00**
Vampire Glow Heads, MPC, 1975 . . . . . . **35.00**
Va-Va-Vette, Krazy Kar Kustom Kit,
  AMT, 1968 . . . . **90.00**
Vincent, Black Hole, MPC, 1982 . . . . **25.00**
Voyager, Fantastic Voyage, Aurora,
  1969. . . . . **325.00**
Wacky Back Whacker, Aurora, 1965 . . . **165.00**
Witch, Glow in the Dark, Aurora,
  1972. . . . . **100.00**
Wyatt Earp, Pyro, 1958 . . . . **60.00**
Yellow Submarine, MPC, 1968 . . . . **200.00**
Zorro, Aurora, 1965 . . . . **275.00**

MORTON POTTERIES

Morton is an example of a regional pottery that has a national collecting base. Actually, there were several potteries in Morton, Illinois: Morton Pottery Works and Morton Earthenware Company, 1897–1917; Cliftwood Art Potteries, 1920–1940; Midwest Potteries, 1940–1944; and, Morton Pottery Company, 1922–1976.

Prior to 1940 local clay was used and fired to a golden ecru. After 1940 clay was imported and fired white. Few pieces are marked. The key to identifying Morton pieces is through the company's catalogs and Doris and Burdell Hall's book, *Morton's Potteries: 99 Years*, (published by the authors, 1982).

Morton Pottery Company, wall pockets, gardeners, one with hoe, other with watering can, ringed pot in front, each $10.00.

Morton Pottery Works and Morton
  Earthenware Co, 1877–1917
  Coffeepot, 5 part, brown Rockingham
    glaze, ornate emb dec **90.00**
  Pitcher, 1¼" h, miniature, bulbous
    body, green glaze **25.00**
  Spittoon, 15" d, scalloped design, mottled brown Rockingham glaze **55.00**
Cliftwood Art Potteries, Inc, 1920–1940
  Candlesticks, pr, 11" h, sq base, chocolate drip glaze **50.00**
  Compote, 6" h, 8½" d, four dolphins
    support bowl, old rose glaze **75.00**
  Lamp, 7½" h, owl on log, yellow **35.00**
Midwest Potteries, Inc, 1940–1944
  Figurine, 8½" h, female dancer, stylized, white, gold dec **25.00**
  Flower Bowl, 10" d, 5½" h, circular,
    brown, yellow drip glaze, 2 pcs **16.00**
  Wall Mask, 5 × 3¼", smiling, curly
    hair **16.00**
Morton Pottery Company, 1922–1976
  Bank, 5½ × 7", pig, black **25.00**
  Pie Bird, 5" h, white, multicolored
    wings and back **22.00**

Planter, 7" h, cowboy and cactus, natural colors **12.00**
Vase, 8½" h, cornucopia, shell base, blue **14.00**
American Art Potteries, 1947–1961
Creamer and Sugar, 3" h, stylized flowers, blue, peach spray glaze **18.00**
Television Lamp, 7 × 10", conch shell, purple, pink spray glaze **18.00**
Wall Pocket, 5" h, tree stump, applied woodpecker, brown spray glaze **12.00**

MOTHER'S DAY COLLECTIBLES

It's not fair. The amount of Mother's Day memorabilia is about ten times that of Father's Day memorabilia. It has something to do with apple pie.

A great deal of the Mother's Day memorabilia seen at flea markets is "limited edition." The fact that you see so much is an indication that few of these issues were truly limited. Insist on excellent or better condition and the original box when buying.

Since so many collectors are focusing on limited edition material, why not direct your efforts in another direction—for example, greeting cards or pinback buttons. Your costs will be lower, and your collection will be out of the ordinary, just like your mother.

Plate, limited edition, Bing & Grondahl, 1983, $40.00.

Bell, limited edition, S
1976, Mother's Day Se
for Mothers . . . .
1977, *Peanuts* Mother's Day,
Mom . . . .
Doll, limited edition, Reco, 1990, Precious Memories of Motherhood series, Loving Steps **125.00**
Figurine
1983–84, Avon, Little Things, 3¾" h, porcelain boy, hp, MIB **18.00**
1987, Artaffects, limited edition, musical, Motherhood **65.00**
1988, Byers' Choice Ltd, Mother's Day, daughter **175.00**
Pinback Button, 1920s
¾" d
Bust of woman in center, carnation on either side, "Mothers Day" on banner below, multicolored **3.50**
Carnation, "Anna Jarvis Founder Philadelphia, Mother's Day," multicolored **3.00**
1¼" d, carnation behind heart inscribed "Mother," "May, 2nd Sunday, Mothers Day," red and white **5.00**
Plate
1973, Anri, Mother's Day Series, Alpine Mother and Children **55.00**
1981
Avon, Cherished Moments, 5" d, porcelain, MIB. **10.00**
Kaiser, Mother's Day Series, Safe Near Mother **40.00**
1970
Bareuther **20.00**
Svend Jensen, Mother's Day Series, Bouquet for Mother **75.00**

MOTORCYCLES

Some of these beauties are getting as expensive as classic and antique cars. This category is personal. I owned motorcycles, until an elderly lady ran a red light and my dad put a stop to my motorcycling career.

Motorcycles are generational. My grandfather would identify with an Indian, my dad with a BMW or Harley Davidson, and I with the Japanese imports. I suspect that most users of this book are not likely to buy an older motorcyle. However, just in case you see a 1916 Indian Power Plus with sidecar for a thousand or less, pick it up. Its book value is $15,000.00.

Magazine: *Hemmings Motor News*, P. O. Box 100, Bennington, VT 05201.

...en have fasci-
...ree-quarters of
this fascination
...heir private lives
...rmances.

...ere individuals fo-
...here are super stars
...1. Two examples are
Cha...   Marilyn Monroe.

Posters a...   ...sive. However, there
are plenty of other categories where a major collection can be built for under $25.00 per object. Also, do not overlook the present-day material. If it's cheap, pick it up. Movie material will always be collectible.

Newspaper: *Big Reel*, P. O. Box 83, Madison, NC 27025; *Classic Images*, P. O. Box 4077, Davenport, IA 52808; *Movie Collectors' World*, P. O. Box 309, Fraser, MI 48026; *Nostalgia World*, P. O. Box 231, New Haven, CT 06473.

Club: Studio Collectors Club, P. O. Box 1566, Apple Valley, CA 92307.

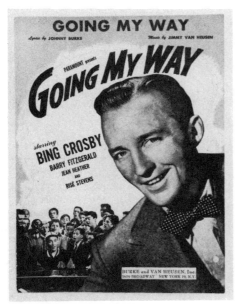

Sheet Music, Bing Crosby, **Going My Way,** *Burke and Van Heusen, NY, 1944, $18.00.*

Activity Book
  Paint, *Ziegfeld*, 10¼ × 15", Merrill, 1941 . . . . **25.00**
  Sticker, *My Fair Lady*, 8½ × 11", Ottenheimer Inc 1965 . . . . **5.00**

Almanac, *International Motion Picture Almanac*, 6½ × 9¼", 1026 pgs, Quigley Publishing Co, 1946–1947 . . . . **25.00**
Book, *Screen Personalities*, Grosset & Dunlap, biography picture book, 1933 copyright **40.00**
Handbill, *Spellbound*, Gregory Peck and Ingrid Bergman, 8 × 11", 4 pgs **20.00**
Lobby Card, *M*A*S*H*, Donald Sutherland **5.00**
Memorial Album, Rudolph Valentino, sepia photo illus, c1926 . . . . **55.00**
Movie Poster
  Horrors of the Black Museum, 27 × 41", black and white illus, England, 1959 . . . . **50.00**
  Jungle Drums of Africa, 27 × 41", features Clayton Moore, 1952 . . . . **30.00**
  Sands of Iwo Jima, 14 × 36", paper, John Wayne, John Agar, and Adela Mara **50.00**
Photograph, Rock Hudson, color, brass frame, 1950s **15.00**
Photograph, Rudolph Valentino with Shiek, framed **45.00**
Portrait, movie giveaway, Rudolph Valentino, *Blood & Sand* adv on back **15.00**
Poster
  American Graffiti **50.00**
  Fistful of Dollars **150.00**
  Midnight Cowboy **200.00**
Program
  Gone With The Wind, 6¼ × 9½", buff paper, brown illus, 1939 . . . . **50.00**
  MacBeth, 9 × 12", 16 pgs, film scenes, photos, biography pages of Orson Welles and stage production, 1948 . . . **25.00**
  Scaramouche, Ramon Navarro **35.00**
Sheet Music, As Time Goes By, *Casablanca*, 9 × 12", 8 pgs, 1931 copyright **50.00**
Window Card, 14 × 22"
  The Errand Boy, Paramount, 1961 copyright **30.00**
  For Me And My Gal, MGM, 1942 . . . . . . **100.00**

MUGS

The problem with every general price guide is that they do not cover the broad sweeping form categories, e.g., wash pitchers and bowls, any longer. A surprising number of individuals still collect this way.

If you stay away from beer mugs, you can find a lot of examples in this category for under $10.00. Look for the unusual, either in form or labeling. Don't forget to fill one now and then and toast your cleverness in collecting these treasures.

Hobo Joe, "Hold the Onions," Norman Rockwell Museum, 3¾" h, 1985, $3.00.

Advertising

A & W Root Beer, clear glass, logo	**5.00**
Big Boy Restaurant, clear glass	**3.00**
Carter Carburetor, stoneware	**15.00**
Choo Choo Cherry, 3" h, plastic, red, blue and white accents, orig mailing box, copyright 1969 The Pillsbury Co	**25.00**
Frosty Root Beer, clear glass, set of 6	**30.00**
Lefty Lemon, 3½" h, plastic, yellow, black, white, and red accents, baseball bat handle, orig mailing box, copyright 1969 The Pillsbury Co . . .	**22.00**
Nestle's Quik, 4" h, plastic, figural, bunny head, ear handles, back with raised "Quik," marked "The Nestle Co Inc," 1970s	**20.00**
Whitetower Restaurant	**22.00**
Carebear, days of week, American Greeting Corp	**2.00**
Grog, BC Comics	**3.00**
Hopalong Cassidy, 3" h, milk glass, red Hoppy illus and name on front, western scene on back	**25.00**
Mickey Through The Year	
Brave Little Tailor, 1937	**2.00**
Mickey Mouse Club, 1955	**3.00**
Minnie Mouse, 3" h, china, color transfer, Bavaria China	**175.00**
Pogo Possum and Beauregard Hound, pr, 4¼" h, plastic, blue, full color decals, Walt Kelly copyright, 1960s	**25.00**

MUSICAL INSTRUMENTS

Didn't you just love music lessons? Still play your clarinet or trumpet? Probably not! Yet, I bet you still have the instrument. Why is it that you can never seem to throw it out?

The number of antique and classic musical instrument collectors is small, but growing. Actually, most instruments are sold for reuse. As a result, the key is playability. Check out the cost of renting an instrument or purchasing one new. Now you know why prices on "used" instruments are so high. Fifty dollars for a playable instrument of any quality is a bargain price. Of course, it's a bargain only if someone needs and wants to play it. Otherwise, it is fifty dollars ill-spent.

Harmonica, Hohner, the 64 Chromonica, orig box, 8¼" l, $50.00.

Accordion, Concertone, two stops, two sets of reeds, 10 keys, gilt valves, ebonized panels and frames, 12 × 6"	**125.00**
Banjo, Wondertone, S S Steward, walnut, marquetry inlay, 1920s	**185.00**
Bugle, officer's, c1900	**100.00**
Castinets, pr, early 20th C	**38.00**
Cello, Sears Roebuck, inlaid edges, c1900	**475.00**
Clarinet, Laube, thirteen keys, two rings, Grenadilla wood, C, low pitch	**350.00**
Cornet, Concertone, brass, one water key, pearl buttons nickle silver mouthpiece, 16½" l, 1920s	**150.00**
Cymbals, pr, leather handles, 13" d, c1900	**140.00**
Drum, snare, Acme Professional, 14" d, c1900	**175.00**
Flute, eight-keyed, 1920s	**125.00**
Guitar, The Marlowe, c1900	**160.00**
Harmonica, Hohner Marine Band, ten single holes, twenty reeds, brass plates, nickel covers, gilt lettering on red hinged case, c1903	**30.00**
Jews' Harp, 2½" w frame, c1900	**15.00**
Kazoo, saxophone shape, brass finish, eight plungers, 20" l	**12.00**
Ocarina, F, soprano, European, c1900	**25.00**
Saxophone, Marceau, B-flat, tenor, brass, polished	**150.00**
Tambourine, Mexican, c1900	**80.00**

Trumpet, Holton, B-flat, red brass
bell **400.00**
Ukulele, mahogany, brass peds, in-
laid **60.00**
Violin, Otto Hoyer, round stick with
ivory face, silver and ebony frog, plain
sides, silver-sheathed adjuster **300.00**

Sterling Silver
Art Nouveau, girl with flowing hair . . . **25.00**
Eagle, figural **85.00**
Knight, standing alongside ring, round
base, Babcock & Co **40.00**
Scottie Dog **35.00**

NAPKIN RINGS

If you get lucky, you may find a great
Victorian silver-plated figural napkin ring
at a flea market. Chances are that you are
going to find napkins rings used by the
common man. But do not look down your
nose at them. Some are pretty spectacular.

If you do not specialize from the beginning, you are going to find yourself going
around in circles. Animal-shaped rings are
a favorite. Avoid Bakelite. Bakelite rings
carry an extremely high value because of
the Bakelite jewelry craze of a few years
ago. The craze is now over, but prices seem
to remain high. They will come down
when no one buys.

NAUTICAL

There is magic in the sea, whether one is
reading the novels of Melville, watching
Popeye cartoons, or standing on a beach
staring at the vast expanse of ocean. Anyone who loves water has something nautical around the house.

This is one case where the weathered
look is a plus. No one wants a piece of
nautical material that appears to have
never left the dock.

Magazine: *Nautical Brass*, P. O. Box 3966,
North Ft. Myers, FL 33918.

Price Annual: *Conklin's Guide: Maritime
Auction Annual*, Leeward Shore Press, P. O.
Box 838-20, Brisbane, CA 94005.

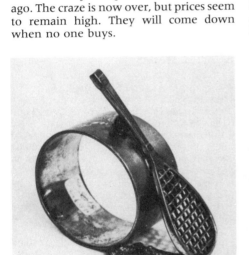

Tennis Racquet, figural, $145.00.

Bisque, cat, marked "Japan" **20.00**
Celluloid, figural, bear **6.00**
China, flowers and butterfly, Nori-
take **15.00**
Cloisonne, dragon, white ground **25.00**
Cut Glass, Harvard pattern **75.00**
Metal, lady holding stick, c1942 . . . . **15.00**
Milk Glass, triangular shape **30.00**
Pattern Glass, Hobstar and Fan **35.00**
Silver Plated
Fox, chasing bird **75.00**
Parrot, rect base, Rogers Mfg Co **50.00**
Ring, etched dogwood branch **20.00**

Book, **List of Merchant Vessels of the
United States, 1891,** *Bureau of Navigation,
History Dept., Washington, DC, $125.00.*

Book
*Masting, Mast-making and Rigging of
Ships*, Robert Kipping, 1877, orig
cov **90.00**
Whaling Masters, Old Dartmouth His-
torical Society, New Bedford, MA,
1938 . . . . **225.00**
Crew List, whale ship *Montpelier*, Sept 6,

1853, names, positions, number of shares in voyages to be received **125.00**
Deck Spade, 56¼" l, pike extension, pitted 110.00
Fog Horn, 30" l, brass, 19th C **85.00**
Harpoon Head, 3⅛" l, whale ivory, incised designs 100.00
Log Book, bark *Manchester*, voyage between Boston and New Orleans, c1884 . . . . .125.00
Navigation Scale, 24" l, boxwood, B Dodd, 19th C .210.00
Promotional Ad, movie, *Pirates of the High Seas*, Buster Crabbe 10.00
Quarterboard, *Edith Nute*, traces of black paint, orig gold lettering 200.00
Rudder, 59" l, orig white paint traces, 19th C 50.00
Signal Horn, 15" l, foot operated, "E A Gill, Gloucester, MA" 110.00
Station Pointer, brass, cased, sgd "Coxe & Coombes/Davenport & Plymouth" 150.00
Weathervane, 44" l, wood, seaman blowing foghorn, 19th C **2,500.00**

December 8, 1941, The Post Standard, *Syracuse, NY, $35.00.*

NEWSPAPERS

"Read all about it" is the cry of corner newspaper vendors across the country. Maybe these vendors should be collected. They appear to be a vanishing breed.

Some newspapers are collected for their headlines, others because they represent a special day, birthday, or anniversary. Everybody saved the newspaper announcing that JFK was shot. Did you save a paper from the day war was declared against Iraq? I did.

Magazine: *PCM—Paper Collectors' Marketplace*, P. O. Box 127, Scandinavia, WI 54977.

Club: Newspaper Collectors' Society of American, Box 19134, Lansing, MI 48901.

1813, October 27, Harrison's victory **22.00**
1845, June 21, Andrew Jackson death **55.00**
1885, July 23, Ulysses S Grant death **70.00**
1898, February 15, sinking of the *Maine* **40.00**
1901, September 14, McKinley death . . . **35.00**
1906, April 18, San Francisco earthquake **40.00**
1917, October 6, White Sox win opener **55.00**
1926, September 23, Tunney defeats Jack Dempsey **25.00**
1927, May 21, Lindberg crosses Atlantic **35.00**

1929, October 28, stock market crash . . . **65.00**
1934, May 23, Bonnie and Clyde killed **70.00**
1937, May 7, Hindenburg crash **56.00**
1941, December 7, Pearl Harbor attacked **45.00**
1944, November 8, Roosevelt elected . . . **20.00**
1945, February 20, marines on Iwo Jima **14.00**
1954, May 17, school segregation decision **10.00**
1962, February 20, John Glenn's space flight **15.00**
1963, November 22, Kennedy assassination **30.00**
1973, October 11, Agnew resignation . . . **10.00**
1974, August 9, Nixon resignation **25.00**
1986, January 29, Challenger Space Shuttle explodes **25.00**

NILOAK POTTERY

When you mention Niloak, most people immediately think of swirled brown, red, and tan pottery, formally known as Mission Ware. However, Niloak also made items in a host of other designs through 1946. These included utilitarian wares and ceramics used by florists that can be bought for a reasonable price. If Niloak prices follow the trend established by Roseville prices, now is the time to stash some of these later pieces away.

Planter, parrot, blue, paper label, $18.00.

Ashtray, hat shape, blue, glossy finish. . . **7.50**
Bowl, 7½" d, marbleized swirls, Mission
   Ware **65.00**
Bud Vase, 4" h, blue and pink, matte
   finish **22.00**
Candlestick
   2" h, brown, blue, and cream, Mission
     Ware **24.00**
   8½" h, blue, brown, and cream mar-
     bleized swirls, Mission Ware **125.00**
Cornucopia, light pink **5.00**
Ewer, 11" h, turquoise shading to pink,
   matte finish, relief floral dec **65.00**
Match Holder, figural, duck, brown and
   white swirls **15.00**
Pitcher, 7" h, pink, glossy finish **25.00**
Planter, Hywood Line
   Camel **20.00**
   Frog, rose glaze **27.50**
   Polar Bear **20.00**
   Squirrel, brown, glossy finish **21.00**
Urn, 4½" h, brown and blue marbleized
   swirls, Mission Ware **35.00**
Vase
   3" h, 5" d, blue and brown marbleized
     swirls, Mission Ware **55.00**
   3⅞" h, brown, green, blue, and cream
     marbleized swirls, wide neck, paper
     label, Mission Ware **65.00**
   6" h, green, wing handles **25.00**
   6½" h, wing handles
     Blue, glossy finish **25.00**
     Green and Orange, matte finish **25.00**
   7½" h, green, matte finish, ribbed, full
     length handles, orig paper label **35.00**
   8" h, marbleized swirls, corset top,
     bulbous bottom, Mission Ware **125.00**

NIPPON

Nippon is handpainted Japanese porcelain
made between 1891 and 1921. The Mc-
Kinley tariff of 1891 required goods im-

ported into the United States to be marked
with their country of origin. Until 1921,
goods from Japan were marked "Made in
Nippon."

Over two hundred different manufacturer's marks have been discovered for
Nippon. The three most popular are the
wreath, maple leaf, and rising sun. While
marks are important, the key is the theme
and quality of the decoration.

Nippon has become quite expensive.
Rumors in the field indicate that Japanese
buyers are now actively competing with
American buyers.

Club: International Nippon Collectors
Club, P. O. 230, Peotone, IL 60468.

*Salt and Pepper Shakers, pr, hand painted, gold
tops, $35.00; Toothpick Holder, hand painted,
$15.00.*

Ashtray, 3" h, blue on cream, reverse
   Wedgwood, green "M" in Wreath
   mark **400.00**
Basket Vase, 5¼" h, Moriage, Royal
   Moriye mark **350.00**
Bowl
   7" d, molded peanuts, two handles,
     green mark **150.00**
   8½" l, relief molded vintage dec, two
     handles, green "M" in Wreath
     mark **200.00**
   8¾" d, gold leaves, blue mark **90.00**
Cake Plate, 10½" l handle to handle,
   handpainted floral dec, gold and cobalt
   border, green Maple Leaf mark **275.00**
Cake Set, 10½" d cake platter, six 6¼" d
   plates, pink roses, green mark **200.00**
Calling Card Tray, 7½" l, floral dec, co-
   balt, green "M" in Wreath mark **200.00**
Candlesticks, pr, 7½" h, lavender, Wedgwood, green "M" in Wreath mark. . . .**650.00**
Chocolate Set, 10 pcs, 11" h cov pot, four
   cups and saucers, handpainted roses,
   gold leaves, blue Maple Leaf mark. . . .**800.00**
Cigar Holder, oval tray, sailboat design,
   green mark **135.00**

Cinnamon Stick Holder, 4½" h, cylinder
shape, ftd, blue mark 200.00
Coaster, 3¾" d, floral, blue mark. 28.00
Cracker Jar, cov, 4¼" h, Moriage, red
and orange floral dec, handled, blue
Maple Leaf mark. 300.00
Demitasse Set, 10 pcs, 6" h cov pot, four
cups and saucers, silver overlay, white
ground, RC Noritake Nippon mark . . . 275.00
Dish, 7½" w, divided, three sections,
green mark 90.00
Doll, 4¾" h, girl, pink bow in hair,
incised mark 110.00
Dresser Set, 6 pcs, cov ftd hair receiver,
cov ftd bowl, pedestal dish, 11¼" l octagonal tray, cobalt and gold, blue "M"
in Wreath mark. 450.00
Feeding Dish, child's, 8" d, girl and dog
illus, blue mark 75.00
Ferner, 8¼" h, handpainted landscape,
gold and cobalt borders, two handles,
ftd, green "M" in Wreath mark 350.00
Hatpin Holder, 4½" h, WW I airplane
illus, green mark. 175.00
Incense Burner, 3¼" h, blue, red
mark 125.00
Ink Blotter, 4¼" h, gold sticker, red
mark 140.00
Inkwell, 3" sq, int. well, horse and rider,
green mark 165.00
Lemonade Set, 5 pcs, pitcher and four
tumblers, handpainted purple grapes,
Art Deco border dec, Apple Blossom
mark 175.00
Milk Pitcher, 10½" h, stylized flowers,
yellow and brown. 150.00
Mug, 5½" h, Moriage, sailboat scene . . . 100.00
Napkin Ring, 2" d, green mark 60.00
Nappy, 6" w, white floral dec, Wedg-
wood blue, eight sided, two handles,
green "M" in Wreath mark 125.00
Nut Set, 7 pcs, 7½" d master bowl and six
individual bowls, round, ruffled, nut
and leaf cluster dec int., ftd. 55.00
Pancake Server, cov, floral dec, gold
and cobalt borders, blue Maple Leaf
mark 300.00
Plaque, pierced to hang
8" d, handpainted sunset with sailboat
scene, blue Maple Leaf mark 95.00
9⅝" sq, handpainted landscape,
houses, mountains, water, boats,
geese, and man carrying water ves-
sel, gold rim 135.00
10" d, handpainted house on hillside,
green "M" in Wreath mark 235.00
Plate, 10½" d, floral dec, heavy gold
beading and designs, scalloped rim,
green "M" in Wreath mark 80.00
Relish Dish, 8½" l, landscape scene,
green mark 125.00
Rose Bowl, 5¾" h, handpainted floral
dec, lavender, Wedgwood, green "M"
in Wreath mark. 500.00

Shaving Mug, 3¾" h, yellow flowers,
gold trim, green mark. 120.00
Spoon Holder, 7¾" l, blue mark 85.00
Sugar Shaker, 4½" h, cobalt and floral,
blue Maple Leaf mark. 175.00
Syrup, underplate, 3½" h, handpainted
floral dec, Wedgwood, green "M" in
Wreath mark. 225.00
Tankard
12" h, handpainted iris dec, Royal Nip-
pon mark. 295.00
16" h, handpainted roses dec, gold
trim, cobalt ground 450.00
Tea Set
13 pcs, 6¼" h cov teapot, creamer, cov
sugar, four cups and saucers, cobalt
and gold, green and red Paulownia
mark 350.00
17 pcs, 9" h cov teapot, six cups, five
saucers, four tall cups, paneled hexagonal form, white chrysanthemum
blossoms and colored leaves, white
ground. 75.00
Tea Strainer, 6" l, floral dec, cobalt
ground, lug handle, blue Maple Leaf
mark 125.00
Urn, 9¼" h, 2 pcs, bolted, floral dec, co-
balt ground, blue Maple Leaf mark . . . 450.00
Vase, handpainted
5½" h, white flowers, Wedgwood blue
ground, ring handles. 200.00
6" h, pink thorny roses, hexagonal
body, handled, six legs 65.00
8" h, floral dec, trumpet shape, green
"M" in Wreath mark 90.00
9" h, Egyptian scene, gold trim, hexagonal body, wide shoulder, green
"M" in Wreath mark 210.00
Vegetable Tureen, cov, 11½" l, medal-
lions in flowers, butterfly dec, heavy
gold beading 145.00

NORITAKE

Noritake is quality Japanese china imported to the United States by the Noritake
China Company. The company, founded
by the Morimura Brothers in Nagoya in
1904, is best known for its dinnerware
lines. Over one hundred different marks
were used, which are helpful in dating
pieces.

The Larkin Company of Buffalo, New
York, issued several patterns as premiums,
including the Azalea, Briarcliff, Linden,
Savory, Sheridan, and Tree in the Meadow
patterns, which are found in quantity.

Be careful. Not all Noritake china is
what it seems. The company also sold
blanks to home decorators. Check the art-

work before deciding that a piece is genuine.

Ashtray, 4¾" w, triangular, figural pipe in center, shades of brown and tan, green mark **75.00**

Bowl, 8" d

Figural bird inside, red blossom and pointed green leaves on tan and russet lustre int., white ext., black rim **70.00**

Handpainted pink, yellow, and white roses int., gilt dec ext., scalloped edge, artist sgd. **145.00**

Bread Plate, 14" l, 6¼" w, white, pale green and gold floral border, open handles **24.00**

Calling Card Tray, adv, Morimura Brothers, NY, Geisha artists painting ceramics dec, dated 1907 .... **335.00**

Candy Dish, cov, 6½" d, cov with Art Deco style girl in black and white checkered skirt on red ground and gold knob finial, black sides **165.00**

Children's Dishes, six plates, cups, and saucers, teapot, creamer and sugar, cookie plate, platter, and cov casserole, white, gold trim, orig box, 1922 ...... **250.00**

Coffeepot, cov, Scheherazade pattern... **48.00**

Condiment Tray, 7" l, rect, gilt dec, white ground. **25.00**

Creamer and Sugar, cov, Scheherazade pattern. **30.00**

Demitasse Cup and Saucer, orange and blue flowers. **18.00**

Dinner Service, 85 pcs, autumn floral dec, c1950 .... **325.00**

Dresser Doll, figural, gold lustre. **185.00**

Humidor, cov

6" h, stylized floral and dotted panels

Cup and Saucer, white ground, pink and blue flowers, gold trim, 3" h cup, 5" d saucer, $28.00.

and white bands, compressed ball finial. **225.00**

7" h, figural, owl, red head and wings, yellow around eyes, tan chest, luster finish **300.00**

Nut Set, 7 pcs, figural, peanut, 7¼" d master bowl, six 3" d individual bowls. **175.00**

Plaque, 8½" d, silhouette of girl in bouffant dress, looking into hand mirror, green "M" in Wreath mark **100.00**

Powder Box, desert scene, Arab on camel, cobalt blue ground, ornate gold beading **300.00**

Punch Bowl Set, 9 pcs, banquet size bowl, eight cups, swans, cottage, island, and trees landscape, heavy raised gold dec, green "M" in Wreath mark **675.00**

Shaving Mug, 3¾" h, handpainted stalking tiger scene, green "M" in Wreath mark **200.00**

Tobacco Jar, 6½" h, handpainted golfer wearing red jacket and cap and black and white checkerboard knickers, green "M" in Wreath mark **190.00**

Vase

5½" h, relief molded, squirrel on berried leafy branch, shaded brown ground. **150.00**

10" h, handpainted, two bluebirds, apple blossoms, handled. **275.00**

Wall Pocket, 6¾" l, bulbous, exotic bird dec, blue luster **60.00**

NORITAKE AZALEA

Noritake china in the azalea pattern was first produced in the early 1900s. Several backstamps were used. You will find them listed in *Warman's Americana and Collectibles* (Wallace-Homestead). They will help date your piece.

Azalea pattern wares were distributed as a premium by the Larkin Company of Buffalo and sold by Sears, Roebuck and Company. As a result, it is the most commonly found pattern of Noritake china.

Each piece is handpainted, adding individuality to the piece. Hard-to-find examples include children's tea sets and salesmen's samples. Do not ignore the handpainted glassware in the azalea pattern that was manufactured to accompany the china service.

Basket, #193 .... **120.00**

Bowl

Divided, #439 .... **225.00**

Plate, 7½" d, $8.50.

NORITAKE TREE IN THE MEADOW

If you ever want to see variation in a pattern, collect Tree in the Meadow. You will go nuts trying to match pieces. In the end you will do what everyone else does. Learn to live with the differences. Is there a lesson here?

Tree in the Meadow was distributed by the Larkin Company of Buffalo, New York. Importation began in the 1920s, almost twenty years after the arrival of azalea pattern wares. Check the backstamp to identify the date of the piece.

Bowl, handled, 9" d, $35.00.

Fruit, #9	10.00
Grapefruit, 4½" d, #185	110.00
Bread Tray, 12" l, #99	40.00
Butter Dish, cov, 6¼" d, #314	78.00
Butter Tub, insert, #54	30.00
Cake Plate, 9¾" d, #10	40.00
Casserole, cov, gold finial, #372	400.00
Celery Dish, 10" l, #444	250.00
Coffeepot, #182	450.00
Compote, #170	65.00
Condiment Set, 5 pcs, #14	38.00
Creamer and Sugar, pr	
Covered, gold finial, #401	425.00
Open, demitasse, #123	70.00
Demitasse Cup and Saucer, #183	120.00
Gravy Boat, attached underplate, #40	40.00
Jam Jar Set, 3 pcs, #125	120.00
Mayonnaise Set, 3 pcs, scalloped, #453	400.00
Milk Jug, #100	150.00
Plate	
7½" d, tea, #4	8.50
7⅝" sq, #315	45.00
9¾" d, dinner, #13	20.00
10¼" d, grill, #338	125.00
Platter	
10¼" l, #311	150.00
14" l, #17	42.00
16" l, #186	300.00
Refreshment Set, 2 pcs, #39	38.00
Relish Dish, oval	
7¼" l, #194	50.00
8½" l, #18	15.00
Relish Set, 10" l, four sections, #119	100.00
Salt and Pepper Shakers, pr, 2½" h, #126	12.00
Spoon Holder, 8" h, #189	70.00
Syrup Pitcher, underplate, #97	75.00
Teapot, regular, #15	80.00
Tobacco Jar, cov, #313	500.00
Vase, bulbous, #452	900.00
Vegetable Bowl, oval, 10½" l, #101	35.00

Ashtray, 5¼" d, green mark	35.00
Basket, 4⅜" l, 4" h	110.00
Butter Tub	58.00
Cake Plate	32.00
Celery Tray	40.00
Compote, 6½" d, 2¾" h	185.00
Condiment Set, 5 pcs, mustard pot, ladle, salt and pepper shakers, and tray	40.00
Cup and Saucer	12.00
Dinner Service, six tea plates, bread and butter plates, breakfast plates, dinner plates, and fruit bowls, four cups and saucers, cake plate, compote, divided relish, 12" l platter, 14" l platter, pr salt and pepper shakers, cov butter dish with drain insert, double cruet set, gravy boat with underplate, cov vegetable bowl, creamer, and sugar bowl	650.00
Fruit Bowl, 7¾" l, shell shaped	230.00
Gravy Boat, attached underplate	70.00
Jam Jar, underplate, spoon	65.00
Plate	
6½" d	10.00
8½" d	15.00
Platter, 14" l	35.00
Salad Bowl, 8½" d	55.00

Sauce Dish, underplate, spoon, green
mark **50.00**
Shaving Mug, 3¾″ h, green mark **85.00**
Tea Set, teapot, creamer, and cov sugar,
six cups and saucers **135.00**
Vase, 7″ h, fan shape **120.00**
Vegetable Dish, 9¾″ l, oval, Noritake
mark **30.00**
Wall Plaque, 8½″ l, green mark **75.00**

Playing Cards, Royal Flushes, nudes,
king size, boxed.................. **14.00**
Print, woman, orig frame and matting,
Earl Moran **150.00**
Rose Bowl, full figure nude sitting on
edge, sgd "Clio Huneker"........... **195.00**
Statue, 7″ h, ivory, three women em-
bracing each other, sgd "G R" **85.00**
Vase, 3″ h, cameo white relief nude,
brown handles **15.00**

NUDES

Mom, Dad made me put this category in.
Honest, Mom! He really did!

Ashtray, pot metal, painted brown, 26½″ h,
$200.00.

Ashtray, 10″ d, nude holding tray over
head, marked "Rembrandt" **185.00**
Bookends, pr, figural, cast iron, woman
kneeling, leg extended forward,
bronze finish.................... **70.00**
Figure, female, 9½ × 10½″, Sanzio **25.00**
Knife, 3¼″ l, silvered metal, black and
white female portrait, dark red glitter
accents, c1920................... **25.00**
Lamp, 9″ h, nude sitting atop ribbed
column, arms support crackle glass
globe **370.00**
Magazine, *Playgirl*, 1976.............. **10.00**
Pin, ⅞″ d, female standing, brass frame,
early 1900s **20.00**

NUTCRACKERS

Fast food and time did in the nut-cracking
community. From the mid-nineteenth
through the mid-twentieth century it was
not uncommon to find a bowl of nuts
awaiting cracking in the kitchen, living
room, or dining room.

Just as there is a never-ending search for
a better mousetrap, so was man never content with his nutcracker design. The variety is endless, from cast iron dogs of the
turn-of-the-century to brass legs from the
Art Deco period.

Many modern collectors like the
wooden military and civilian figures that
come from Germany. Have you ever tried
cracking a nut in them? Useless, utterly
useless.

Nickel-Plated Iron Nutcracker, L. A. Althoff
Corp., $70.00.

Bear, wood, glass eyes **100.00**
Bird, wood, curved neck, long tail, worn
finish......................... **100.00**
Dog, cast iron
Bronze finish.................... **45.00**
Nickel finish, 11″ l, marked "The LA
Althoff Mfg Co, Chicago"........ **45.00**
Eagle, brass **25.00**
Elephant, cast iron, painted **145.00**
Jester, brass..................... **75.00**
Lady's Legs, brass **35.00**
Man's Head, wood, carved mustache ... **115.00**
Monkey, wood, painted eyes.......... **80.00**
Parrot, cast iron, painted green, red, and
gold, 10″ l **30.00**

Rooster, brass	40.00
Squirrel, cast iron	48.00
St Bernard, brass, 8¾" l	60.00
Toy Soldier, wood, red, black, and white paint, furry beard, Germany	75.00

OCCUPIED JAPAN

America occupied Japan from 1945 to 1952. Not all objects made during this period are marked "Occupied Japan." Some were simply marked "Japan" and "Made in Japan." Occupied Japan collectors ignore these two groups. They want to see their two favorite little words.

Beware of falsely labeled pieces. Rubber-stamp-marked pieces have appeared on the market. Apply a little fingernail polish remover. Fake marks will disappear. True marks are under glaze. Of course, if the piece is unglazed to begin with, ignore this test.

Clubs: Occupied Japan Collectors Club, 18309 Faysmith Avenue, Torrance, CA 90504; O. J. Club, 29 Freeborn Street, Newport, RI 02840.

Toby Creamer, black hat, yellow coat, green vest, brown pants, 3" h, $12.00.

Ashtray	
4" d, sq, porcelain, green floral	12.00
6¾" d, chrome plated, pierced floral rim	10.00
Cigarette Box, 3¾ × 4 × 5", multicolored, gold floral and scroll	10.00

Cigarette Lighter, metal, cornucopia	15.00
Demitasse Cup and Saucer, floral, pink and lavender	8.00
Figure	
2½ × 2¼", three monkeys, see no evil, hear no evil, speak no evil	18.00
3½" h, couple, man wearing red coat, yellow pants, holding hat, woman wearing blue, green, and purple dress, pedestal base	17.00
3¾" h, swan, wings spread	10.00
4" h, boy playing violin, seated, white shirt, brown shorts, green hat	12.50
4" l, dog, brown	15.00
4½ × 4¾", bird, pink body, gray wings, yellow beak	20.00
6¼" h, colonial girl holding skirt, orange and blue dress, pink bow, gold trim	18.00
10" h, Oriental girl, blue and green outfit, gold trim	28.00
Jewelry Box, 1" h, metal, twelve drawers	12.00
Pin, bird, celluloid	8.50
Pin Cushion, tin, red velvet top, mirror inside lid	20.00
Pitcher, 4½" h, windmill scene	17.50
Planter	
2½" h, dog	8.00
4¾" l, donkey, pulling wagon	10.00
Reamer, 3¾" h, 2 pcs, strawberry shape, red, green leaves and handle	65.00
Teapot, 6½" h, floral dec on brown ground	22.00
Toby Mug, 2½" h, black hat, blue collar	15.00
Toy, 3½ × 4½ × 8½", windup, dancer, litho tin and celluloid, man standing by black and white tin street sign "Hollywood" and "Vine"	165.00
Tray, 5 × 3", metal, souvenir, Chicago	6.00
Vase	
3¾" h, bud vase, cherub playing tuba	14.00
4½" h, landscape scene	12.00

OCEAN LINER COLLECTIBLES

Although the age of the clipper ships technically fits into this category, the period that you are most likely to uncover at flea markets is that of the ocean liner. Don't focus solely on American ships. England, Germany, France, and many other foreign countries had transoceanic liners that competed with and bested American vessels.

Today is the age of the cruise ship. This aspect of the category is being largely ignored. Climb aboard and sail into the sunset.

Ashtray, S. S. Argentina, Moore-McCormark lines, brass plated, made in Switzerland, 5½" d, $35.00.

Advertising Tin, Bremen Coffee, *Bremen* at sea on front panel, litho tin, 1930s 50.00
Ashtray, *Princess*, glass, Sweden 8.00
Booklet, White Star Line Sailing List, 1933. . . . . 38.00
Cabinet Card, 1890s steamboat 36.00
Candy Container, litho tin, full color *Queen Mary* illus on lid, 1930s. 40.00
Creamer, *Cunard White Star*, 3" h, white, tan and light gray striping, logo on bottom, 1930s. 50.00
Cup, *Lattorff Ocean Liner* 20.00
Log, Lykes Bros 1938 *Ripley SS*, New Orleans to Calcutta 8.00
Menu
   Johnson Line. 10.00
   Matson Line 7.00
   SS *City of Omaha*, Christmas 1940 . . . . 5.00
   SS *Oakwood*, American Export Lines, Christmas 1939 . . . . 5.00
   Sun Line cruise ship, titled *Stella Solaris*, 1930s, set of 7 . . . . 18.00
Passenger List
   SS *Leviathan*, 1924. . . . . 15.00
   Transylvania II, Anchor Line, June 22, 1938. . . . . 18.00
Pocket Mirror, Steamship *Augustus*, emb 52.00
Stock Certificate, Cunard Steam Ship Co, Ltd 7.50
Ticket Folio, Cunard Line, c1928 . . . . 50.00

OLD SLEEPY EYE

The Old Sleepy Eye Flour Company of Sleepy Eye, Minnesota, offered Sleepy Eye premiums in the early 1900s. Many of the early stoneware products were made by the Weir Pottery Company, which eventually became the Monmouth Pottery Company.

The company's advertising is just as popular as its giveaway premiums. Beware of fantasy items, e.g., pocket mirrors, glass plates, and toothpick holders, as well as reproduction stoneware pitchers (marked "Ironstone" on the bottom) being imported from Taiwan.

Mug, Indian head on handle, one side with Indian, other side Indian village, 7½" h, $325.00.

Bread Board Scraper. 625.00
Calendar, 1904 . . . . 200.00
Cookbook, bread loaf shape. 125.00
Demitasse Spoon 130.00
Mug, 4¼" h, cobalt blue dec, gray ground, small Indian head on handle, Western Stoneware Co, 1914–1918 . . . . 325.00
Pillow Cover, Before The Great Father, unused. 350.00
Pitcher, cobalt blue dec, white ground, small Indian head on handle, Western Stoneware Co, 1906–1937
   4" h, half pint 165.00

248

6¼" h, quart **200.00**
Post Card, mill scene **18.00**
Salt Bowl, 6½" d, 4" h, Flemish blue dec,
gray ground, stoneware, Weir Pottery
Co, 1903 . . . . **450.00**
Stein
Chestnut Brown, 40 oz, 1952 . . . . **450.00**
Flemish Blue dec, gray ground, stone-
ware, Weir Pottery Co, 1903 . . . . . . **675.00**
Teaspoon, silver plated **90.00**
Vase
8½" h, stoneware, cylindrical **185.00**
9" h
Brown dec, yellow ground, molded
cattails and dragonflies, Western
Stoneware Co **850.00**
Flemish Blue dec, gray ground,
stoneware, dragonfly, frog, and
bulrushes, Indian head sgd, Weir
Pottery Co, 1903 . . . . **300.00**

OLYMPIC COLLECTIBLES

Gallantly marching behind their flags, the best athletes from nations around the world enter the Olympic Colosseum. Whether the first modern olympic games in 1896 or the recent 1992 games, the spirit of competition remains the same. The olympic collector shares this feeling.

It's a contest to see who can garner the most and have the rarest items. Olympic collectors are adept at leaping hurdles and running miles in pursuit of their oft elusive gold-medal collectibles.

A few select collectors focus on objects picturing the games of ancient Greece. Bronze and ceramic figures, decorated pottery, and jewelry with an Olympic motif do surface occasionally.

Olympic collectibles run hot and cold. They are more popular in Olympic years than in years when there are no games. American collectors concentrate on the Olympic games held in the United States. The one exception is the 1936 Olympics, which are popular with collectors world-wide.

XI, Berlin, Germany, 1936
Book, *1936 Olympic Games*, photos of
Sonja Henie and other world ath-
letes **450.00**
Figurine, 11" h, porcelain, nude male
shotputter, white, holding gold ball,
Hutschenreuther **275.00**
Judge's Badge, bronze, Olympic rings
above Brandenburg Gate, "XI
Olympiade Berlin 1936" **75.00**

XXII Olympiad, Moscow, USSR, 1980, stickpin, $12.00.

Souvenir Pin, white, gold outline and
lettering, Nazi swastika above cutout columns and Olympic rings,
"1936 XI Olympiade Berlin" **50.00**
XIV, London, Great Britain, 1948
Official's Badge, Big Ben above multicolored Olympic rings, "XIV Olympiad London 1948," hanging multicolored ribbon with "Official" tag,
white ribbon with gold "Interna-
tional Federation" **100.00**
Pin, Olympic rings **35.00**
XV, Helsinki, Finland, 1952
Competitor's Badge, bronze colored,
Helsinki skyline, multicolored
Olympic rings, yellow ribbon, gold
lettering, "Yoeosurheilu Ath-
letisme" **75.00**
Pin, Russian team, Soviet flag, red
enamel, gold mast **125.00**
XVI, Melbourne, Australia, 1956
Guest of Honor Badge, gold, white
outline, map of Australia, white rib-
bon, red lettering, "Guest of
Honor" **85.00**
Pin, Romanian, gold, torch shape,
multicolored Olympic rings on
white enamel flame, "Romania" on
torch **30.00**
XVII, Rome, Italy, 1960
Ewer, 12" h, ceramic, nude athlete
stringing bow, Olympic logo, and
"1960" **33.00**

Official's Badge, gold laurel leaf edge on green rim, gold center, Trojan horse above Olympic rings, "Roma MCMLX," gold "Ufficiale" on red hanging tag **85.00**

Pin, Great Britain, shield shape, gold enameled, Union Jack above Olympic rings, "Great Britain Rome 1960". **85.00**

XVIII, Tokyo, Japan, 1964

Mascot Pin, white figure standing behind sign with Rising Sun, Olympic rings, and "Tokyo" **100.00**

Press Pin, white, gold outline, radio tower with Rising Sun at apex, emitting radio waves, Olympic rings, black lettering, "UER-EBU Tokyo 1964". **150.00**

XIX, Mexico City, Mexico, 1968

Pin, Soviet Union, silver, enameled, basketball and hoop, "CCCP" on basketball, "Mexiko-65 XIX" and Olympic rings on hoop **30.00**

Security Badge, white metal, rect, enameled. **100.00**

XX, Munich, Germany, 1972

Coaster, paper, "Munscher Bier," double sided **25.00**

Guest Badge, sunburst, gold, white lettering, "Gast" **90.00**

Pin, oval, gold, enameled, Olympic rings on white ground, "Munich 1972". **20.00**

Plate, porcelain, Bing & Grondahl **45.00**

Stickpin, Poland, gold, enameled, white eagle on red ground **25.00**

XXI, Montreal, Canada, 1976

Team Pin

Netherlands, Olympic rings over rampant lion, "1976" **10.00**

Spain, "Espana" over Montreal's Olympic logo **65.00**

Tie Tack, diecut, Montreal's Olympic logo, gold plated **15.00**

XXII, Moscow, USSR, 1980

Medallion, participant's medal, bronze, Red Square on obverse, Olympic rings and logo, Cyrillic lettering, "XXII Mockba 1980" on reverse **225.00**

Souvenir Pin, Misha the bear standing on winner's block **10.00**

Tickets, pr, unused **8.00**

XXIII, Los Angeles, USA, 1984

Media Pin, cloisonne, "ABC" and stars **55.00**

Sponsor Pin, Olympic rings and snowflake, Campbell's Soup adv . . . **10.00**

Staff Pin, stars in motion logo over Olympic rings, "Staff" **25.00**

XXIV, Seoul, South Korea, 1988

Media Pin, *Sports Illustrated*, cloisonne, rect, white ground, "Seoul 88" **25.00**

National Olympic Committee Pin

Bangladesh, domed, gold ground, "XXIV Olympiad" **28.00**

Ivory Coast, domed, green ground, elephant. **32.00**

Netherlands Antilles, round, white circle, red, white, and blue shield **45.00**

Romania, red, yellow, and blue flag **15.00**

Tonga, domed, red flag with cross **50.00**

Zimbabwe, map shape, white ground, "Seoul 88". **35.00**

XXV, Barcelona, Spain, 1992

Media Pin, NBC, domed, gold colored, multicolored peacock, Olympic rings, "Barcelona 92" **10.00**

Sponsor Pin, multicolored Barcelona logo above red Coca-Cola logo **5.00**

OWL COLLECTIBLES

Most people do not give a hoot about this category, but those who do are serious birds. Like all animal collectors, the only thing owl collectors care about is that their bird is represented.

Newsletter: *The Owl's Nest*, Howard Alphanumeric, P. O. Box 5491, Fresno, CA 93755.

Club: Russell's Owl Collector's Club, P. O. Box 1292, Bandon, OR 97411.

Jar, yellow-brown glaze, black base, black int., 7" h, $12.50.

Bank, brass, glass eyes **65.00**
Cookie Jar, Woodsey Owl **95.00**
Creamer, Sugar, and Shaker Set, gold,
   green trim **20.00**
Doll, 6½" h, Woodsey Owl, plush, "Give
   A Hoot, Don't Pollute" **10.00**
Figurine, ceramic, glass eyes **15.00**
Letter Opener, bronze **30.00**
Pin, blue, green, and gold enamel, amber
   eyes, pearl tail feathers **15.00**
Salt and Pepper Shakers, pr
   China, brown and white, scholarly ex-
      pression, horn rim glasses. **6.50**
   Shawnee Pottery, 3" h, #23/3/2 . . . . . **20.00**
Toothpick Holder **22.00**
Toy
   Stuffed, Wittie, Steiff **165.00**
   Windup, Musician The Owl, 6" h,
      brown plush body, litho tin eyes,
      beak, and sheet music, rubber feet,
      built-in key, orig box, TN, Japan,
      1960s **65.00**

PADEN CITY

The Paden City Glass Manufacturing Company, Paden City, West Virginia, was founded in 1916. The plant closed in 1951, two years after acquiring the American Glass Company.

Paden City glass was handmade in molds. There are no known free-blown examples. Most pieces were unmarked. The key is color. Among the most popular are opal (opaque white), dark green (forest), and red. The company did not produce opalescent glass.

Bowl, pink
   8½" l, oval, Cupid, ftd. **150.00**
   9" d, Peacock and Rose, ftd **50.00**
Cake Saver, Peacock and Rose, green . . . **60.00**
Cake Stand, Black Forest, low foot **60.00**
Candlesticks, pr, Crow's Foot, red **35.00**
Candy Dish, Mrs B, three sections, ruby,
   gold trim **50.00**
Cheese and Cracker Server, Glades, co-
   balt blue. **45.00**
Compote
   6" d, cov, Peacock and Rose, clear **38.00**
   7" d, open, Gothic Garden, yellow. . . . **35.00**
   8" d, Gazebo, clear **40.00**
Console Bowl, 11" sq, Peacock and Rose,
   green **55.00**
Cream Soup Bowl, liner, Crow's Foot,
   red **17.00**
Creamer and Sugar, cov, Cupid,
   green **24.00**
Cruet, Inna, clear, orig stopper **145.00**
Cup and Saucer, Crow's Foot
   Amber **7.00**

Red **13.00**
Figure
   Cottontail Rabbit, clear. **60.00**
   Rooster **70.00**
Goblet
   Georgian, 10 oz, red, set of four **45.00**
Penny
   Green. **12.00**
   Red, 6" h, low foot **15.00**
Mayonnaise Dish, Nora Bird, pink,
   ftd **38.00**
Mayonnaise Set, 3 pcs, dish, underplate,
   and ladle, Gazebo, clear **48.00**
Pitcher, cov, Party, green **60.00**
Plate
   Cupid, 10" d, dinner. **15.00**
   Largo, blue, ftd **18.00**
   Popeye and Olive, 10" d, dinner,
      ruby **18.50**
Salt and Pepper Shakers, pr, Party Line,
   orig tops, red **45.00**
Server, center handle
   Gothic Garden, 9½" sq, yellow. **40.00**
   Mrs B, amber. **20.00**
Tray, 11" l, oval, Cupid, pink, ftd. **150.00**
Tumbler, 5" h, Penny, green **12.00**
Vase
   10" h, Crow's Foot, red **125.00**
   12" h, California Poppy **125.00**
Water Set, 9 pcs, pitcher and eight gob-
   lets, Penny, amber **125.00**

PAPER DOLLS

Paper dolls have already been through one craze cycle and appear to be in the midst of another. The recent publication of Mary Young's *A Collector's Guide To Magazine Paper Dolls: An Identification & Value Guide* (Collector Books, 1990) is one indication of the craze. It also introduces a slightly different approach to the subject than the traditional paper doll book.

The best way to collect paper dolls is in uncut books, sheets, and boxed sets. Dolls that have been cut out, but still have all their clothing and accessories, sell for fifty percent or less of their uncut value.

Paper doll collectors have no desire to play with their dolls. They just want to admire them and enjoy the satisfaction of owning them.

Magazine: *Doll Reader*, P. O. Box 467, Mount Morris, IL 61054.

Newsletter: *Paper Doll News*, P. O. Box 807, Vivian, LA 71082.

Club: The Original Paper Doll Artists Guild, P. O. Box 176, Skandia, MI 49885.

Ballet Dancers, Merrill Company, #3447, 1947, $18.00.

Books
    A Day with Diane, Saalfield **30.00**
    Arlene Dahl, five dolls, eight pgs,
       Saalfield Publishing Co **50.00**
    Barbie's Boutique, Whitman, 1973 ... **7.50**
    Betsy McCall, Biggest Paper Doll, Ga-
       briel & Sons, 1955 .... **20.00**
    Buffy, six pgs, Whitman, 1969 .... **18.50**
    Carol & Her Dresses, Gabriel &
       Sons **18.00**
    Cinderella, four dolls, four pgs,
       Saalfield Publishing Co **15.00**
    Deanna Durbin, Merrill Publishing Co,
       1940 ....**170.00**
    Janet Leigh Cutouts & Coloring, two
       dolls, Merrill Publishing Co **45.00**
    June Allyson, eight pgs, Whitman,
       1953 .... **60.00**
    Let's Play Paper Dolls, McLoughlin,
       1938 .... **20.00**
    Miss America Magic Doll, Parker Bros,
       1953 .... **18.00**
    My Twin Babies, Whitman, #970,
       1940 .... **45.00**
    Nanny & the Professor, six dolls, four
       pgs, Artcraft, 1971 .... **20.00**
    Patty's Party, Stephens Publishing Co,
       c1950 .... **8.00**
    Sally Dimple, Burton Playthings,
       1935 .... **25.00**
    Shari Lewis, five pgs, Treasure
       Books **32.00**
    Folder, Dolly's Wardrobe, chromo litho,
       Dean & Son, c1910 .... **75.00**
    Uncut Sheets
    Betsy McCall, Dress n' Play, McCall's
       Magazine, 1963 .... **12.00**
    Enameline Flower Girls, adv, set of
       three **25.00**
    Dolly Dingle **28.00**

Lucille Ball and Desi Arnaz, Whitman,
    1953 .... **75.00**

PAPER MONEY

People hid money in the strangest places. Occasionally it turns up at flea markets. Likewise early paper money came in a variety of forms and sizes quite different from modern paper currency.

Essentially, paper money breaks down into three groups—money issued by the federal government, by individual states, and by private banks, businesses, or individuals. Money from the last group is designated as obsolete bank notes.

As with coins, condition is everything. Paper money that has been heavily circulated has only a small fraction of the value of a bill in excellent condition. Proper grading rests in the hands of coin dealers.

Krause Publications (700 East State Street, Iola, WI 54990) is a leading publisher in the area of coinage and currency. Among Krause's books are *Standard Catalog of World Paper Money* 2 vol, *Standard Catalog of United States Obsolete Bank Notes, 1782–1866* 4 vol, *Standard Catalog of United States Paper Money* ninth edition, *Standard Catalog of National Bank Notes* second edition, and *Early Paper Money of America*. Recently Krause published the *Standard Catalog of Depression Scrip of the United States*. As you can see, there is a wealth of information available to identify and price any bill that you find. *Bank Note Reporter*, a Krause newspaper, keeps collectors up-to-date on current developments in the currency field.

Before you sell or turn in that old bill for face value, do your homework. It may be worth more than a Continental, which, by the way, continues to be a real "dog" in the paper money field.

PAPERBACK BOOKS

This is a category with millions of titles and billions of copies. Keep this in mind before paying a high price for anything.

A great deal of the value of paperbacks rests in the cover art. A risqué lady can raise prices as well as blood pressure. Great art can make up for a lousy story by an insignificant author. However, nothing can make up for a book's being in poor condition, a fate which has befallen a large number of paperbacks.

For a detailed listing, I recommend that you consult Kevin Hancer's *Hancer's Price Guide To Paperback Books, Third Edition* (Wallace-Homestead, 1990) and Jon Warren's *The Official Price Guide to Paperbacks, First Edition,* (House of Collectibles, 1991). Both are organized by company first and then issue number. Hence, when trying to locate a book, publisher and code number are more important than author and title.

The vast majority of paperbacks sell in the 50¢ to $2.50 range.

PAPERWEIGHTS

This is a tough category. Learning to tell the difference between modern and antique paperweights takes years. Your best approach at a flea market is to treat each weight as modern. If you get lucky and pay modern paperweight prices for an antique weight, you are ahead. If you pay antique prices for a modern paperweight, you lose and lose big.

Paperweights can be divided into antique (prior to 1945) and modern. Modern breaks down into early modern (1945 to 1980) and contemporary (1980 and later). There is a great deal of speculation going on in the area of contemporary paperweights. It is not a place for amateurs or those with money they can ill afford to lose. If you are not certain, do not buy.

Newsletters: *Paperweight Gaffer,* 35 Williamstown Circule, York, PA 17404; *Paperweight News,* 761 Chestnut Street, Santa Cruz, CA 95060.

Club: Paperweight Collectors, 150 Fulton Ave., Garden City Park, NY 11040.

Advertising
Bell System, glass, bell shape, blue. . . . **95.00**
Best Pig Forceps, compliments J Reimers, Davenport, IA, glass, pig shape, 6" d. **100.00**
Chelton Trust Co, 2½" d, celluloid over metal, bright green, red, and white design, diecut celluloid perpetual calendar disk wheel on bottom, orig box, early 1900s **40.00**
Columbia National Bank, glass **10.00**
Consolidated Ice Co, 3 × 5½ × 3½" h,

Glass, advertising, Hotel Griswold Barber Shop, 4 × 2½ × ¾", $20.00.

white metal, figural, polar bear sitting on block of ice, inscribed "Pure Ice" and "Distilled Water," company name on sides of base, early 1900s **65.00**
Eagle Electric, 2½" d, celluloid over metal, revolving celluloid disk wheel mounted on top, diecut opening reveals fuse adv, 1920s **35.00**
El Roco Gas, iron, figural **25.00**
Hoover Ball & Bearing Co, 1¾" d, 2" h, chromed steel, eight ball bearings in channel around one large bearing. **35.00**
Laco Drawn Wire Quality, ceramic, white ground, black letters, half-lightbulb shape, backstamped "Rosenthal". **60.00**
Lehigh Sewer Pipe & Tile Co, Ft Dodge, IA, glass **12.00**
National Surety Co, bronze, eagle on world globe **45.00**
Parke-Davis, pewter, baby in womb. **25.00**
Pike Sharpening Stones, ½ × 2 × 3", glass, whetstone block, fused glass cov on oilstone base, multicolored paper label pictures pike and sharpening tools, c1900s **65.00**
Purdue Foundry, cast iron, Kewpie . . . **35.00**
The Ransbottom Bros Pottery Co, Roseville, OH, glass, dome type, illus of brothers **70.00**
Speyer Building, 2¾" d, celluloid, black and white, tin band, detailed drawing of building. **30.00**

St John Mill, ½ × 1½ × 3½", brass, figural, inscribed "Extra," issued by Furber, Stockford & Co, Boston, MA, early 1900s 30.00
Star Line Goods, 1¾ × 2¼ × ½" h, cast iron, brass colored, figural, turtle, 1" oval celluloid shell, inscription in center of shell, 1904 copyright 80.00
Personality
Col Albert A Pope, 1 × 2½ × 4", glass, rect, dated '87 . . . . 50.00
John F Kennedy, 2⅞" d, sulfide, bust, black amethyst ground, Baccarat . . . 90.00
McKinley, 1 × 2½ × 4", glass, rect, sepia photo, inscribed "Pres McKinley, Wife and Home, Canton, O," marked "Cent Glass & Nov Co" on reverse, 1900s 50.00
Souvenir & Commemorative
Chicago World's Fair, Hall of Science, 1 × 2½ × 4", glass, rect, full color image 30.00
Crane Co, Chicago, 75th Anniversary, brass, 2⅜" d, round 30.00
Factory Scene, NY office, 7 Cedar St, 1 × 2½ × 4", glass, rect 50.00
Independent Press Room, Los Angeles, 1 × 2½ × 4", glass, rect 15.00
Mt St Helens, iridized, dated 1988 . . . . 25.00
New Deal, 2 × 3", metal, high relief portrait on front, flat back, copyright 1932 . . . . 45.00
Pan-American Expo, Temple of Music, 1 × 2½ × 4", glass, rect, small caption, 1901 . . . . 35.00

PARKING METERS

I have seen them for sale. I have even been tempted to buy one. The meter was a lamp base, complete with new lamp wiring and an attractive shade. To make the light work, you put a coin in the meter. Can you imagine my date's face when I ran out of quarters? I'm not sure why, but they are rather pricey, usually in the $50 to $100 range. Maybe it has something to do with the fine that you will pay if you obtain one illegally.

Might be a good idea to stash a few coin-operated meters away. Have you experienced one of the new electronic meters? Isn't progress wonderful?

PATRIOTIC COLLECTIBLES

Americans love symbols. We express our patriotism through eagles, flags and shield, the Liberty Bell, Statue of Liberty, and Un-

cle Sam. We even throw in a few patriots, such as Benjamin Franklin. It was great to see the American symbols proudly displayed across the country due to the success of Operation Desert Storm.

Sheet Music, **Father of the Land We Love,** *words and lyrics by George M. Cohen, copyright 1931 by Sol Bloom, James Montgomery Flagg cover artist, $6.00.*

Advertising Trade Card, 3½ × 6¼", "Hub Gore Makers of Elastic For Shoes, It Was Honored at the World's Fair of 1893," Uncle Sam holding shoe 15.00
Bank, Dime Register, Uncle Sam, 1941 . . . . 38.00
Clock, mantel, God Bless America, American flag second hand waves back and forth, Howard Miller Mfg . . . 125.00
Cookie Cutter, 6½" w, tin, Eagle 85.00
Figure, 16" h, Uncle Sam rolling up sleeves, plaster 30.00
Hat, paper, "Liberty," red, white, and blue, picture of Statue, c1918 . . . . 20.00
Needle Case, Statue of Liberty 12.00
Pin, diecut silvered metal eagle with shield symbol on chest, holding miniature replica brass alarm clock, c1890 . . . . 30.00
Pinback Button, 1¼" d
Columbus Day, Columbus illus, white ground, black lettering, 1920s 15.00
On the Way To Cuba, Uncle Sam marching past sign to Cuba, c1898 . . . . 50.00
The Yanko Spanko War, Uncle Sam with Spaniard over knee, holding paddle, c1898 . . . . 40.00

Plate, bread and butter, clear glass, Constitution signer's names, emb 1776–1876 .... **80.00**

Reverse Painting on Glass, Statue of Liberty, oval **100.00**

Seal, "Patriotic Decorations," diecut gummed seals, red, white, and blue, ten of orig 25, Dennison, c1925 ...... **15.00**

Sheet Music

America Forever March, John Phillip Sousa **30.00**

Liberty Bell Time to Ring Again, 1918. .... **3.50**

Tray

Flag, trademark on star center, 12" d, American Brewing Co adv, Indianapolis, IN **150.00**

Uncle Sam and five ethnic people illus, Cascade Beer adv, San Francisco ...**650.00**

PEANUTS

Peanuts is a newspaper cartoon strip written and illustrated by Charles M. Schulz. The strip started about 1950 and starred a boy named Charlie Brown and his dog, Snoopy. Its popularity grew slowly. In 1955, merchandising was begun with the hope of expanding the strip's popularity. By the 1970s Charlie Brown and the gang were more than just cartoon strip characters. They greeted every holiday with T.V. specials; their images adorned lunch boxes, pencils, pins, T-shirts, and stuffed toys. Macy's Thanksgiving Day Parade wouldn't be complete without a huge Snoopy floating down Seventh Avenue.

Bank

Linus, figural, ceramic, hp, Determined, 8½" h, 1969 .... **50.00**

Peppermint Patty, baseball series, papier mache, Determined, 1973. .... **45.00**

Snoopy

Ceramic, lying on flowered egg, Determined, #1551, late 1970s **25.00**

Papier Mache Composition, "Joe Cool" on orange shirt, Ideal, #5255-5, orig box, 1977 .... **35.00**

Plastic, clear, cylindrical, holds dimes, threaded lid, Snoopy illus and "Snoopy Dime Bank" on side, Rival Dog Food premium, 1970s **15.00**

Woodstock, standing, papier mache, Determined, #1503, 1970s **12.00**

Banner, Lucy in psychiatrist booth, "For a Nickel I Can Cure Anything," Determined, 1971 .... **8.00**

Bell

Schroeder, Schmid, #278-419, 6" h, 1974. .... **50.00**

Snoopy and the Beaglescouts, Schmid, orig box, 1984 .... **25.00**

Bib Apron, Snoopy on doghouse design, "Home is where the supper dish is!" **12.50**

Board Game, Peanuts, Selchow & Righter, 1959 .... **45.00**

Book

Happiness Is a Warm Puppy, Charles M Schulz, Determined, hard cov, Lucy hugging Snoopy cov illus, 1962 .... **3.00**

Peanuts Treasury, Charles M Schulz, Holt, Rinehart & Winston, first edition, cartoon anthology, 1968 ..... **15.00**

Bookends, pr, figural, one with Charlie Brown leaning against door, other with Snoopy holding food dish in mouth and kicking door, Butterfly, 1970s **75.00**

Bookmark, Ruler, and Stencil, Snoopy, clear plastic, Dolly Madison premium, "Snoopy for President/Dolly Madison for Cakes," 1972 .... **25.00**

Comic Book, Peanuts, Dell, #878, Charlie Brown and Snoopy watching TV cov illus, 1958 .... **20.00**

Doll

Belle, Dolly Madison style, rubber, red and white outfit, Collector Dolls, Determined, 8" h, 1982 .... **25.00**

Lucy, plastic, jointed, red dress, saddle shoes, Determined, #378, orig box, 1970s **35.00**

Peppermint Patty, rag, removable outfit, green and white shirt, black pants, Ideal, #1413-4, 1976 ...... **15.00**

Pigpen, blue overalls, Hungerford, 8½" h, orig pkg **100.00**

Snoopy, sitting, plush, felt eyes, eyebrows, and nose, red paper tag, Determined, #835, 12" h, 1971 ...... **15.00**

Earring Tree, Snoopy **12.50**

Figure, Snoopy, musical, wood, UFS, 1968. .... **35.00**

Hand Puppet, Peanuts Magic Catch Puppets, Lucy, blue dress, Synergistics, 1978. .... **15.00**

Ice Bucket, vinyl, white, dancing Snoopy and Woodstock on rainbow illus, Shelton Ware, #9002, 1979 .... **50.00**

Lunch Box, vinyl, white, Schroeder playing piano surrounded by Peanuts gang one side, baseball illus other side, Charlie Brown swinging bat illus on plastic thermos, King Seeley, #6168/3, 1973. .... **30.00**

Mirror, Snoopy in hot air balloon surrounded by flying Woodstocks illus, Determined, 8×10½", 1970s **20.00**

Mug, milk glass, yellow metal lid, Lucy holding balloon illus, Avon Shampoo, orig box, 1969 .... **12.00**

Music Box, Schmid, 1980 .... **40.00**

Night Light, Snoopy, WWI flying ace ... **10.00**

Nodder

Charlie Brown, 5½" h, Japan, 1960s **50.00**

Lucy, wearing red dress **90.00**

Paper Dolls, Snoopy, ten outfits, Determined, #274, 1976 .... **25.00**

Paperweight, Woodstock, glass, stippled, Determined, #8576, 2½ × 3", late 1970s **15.00**

Patch, fabric, Frieda, "I'm in Love," Butternut premium, 1970s **4.00**

Pinback Button, Lucy, dressed as Halloween witch, carrying broom, cloth front, metal back, 2¼" d, 1980s **8.00**

Plate

Mother's Day, Linus holding rose, Schmid, orig box, 1972 .... **20.00**

Woodstock's Christmas, Schmid, orig box, 1976 .... **25.00**

Playing Cards, Linus holding security blanket, "Security," Hallmark, #125BC98-1, 1975 .... **15.00**

Pop-Up Book, *It's Good to Have a Friend*, Charles M Schulz, Hallmark, #400HEC 36, dancing Snoopy and Woodstock cov illus, 1972 .... **35.00**

Poster, Pigpen, "If You're Going to Be an Ecologist, You've Got to Stir Things Up a Little," Springbok, #PTR 302-3, 1971 .... **12.00**

Pull Toy, Snoopy **12.00**

Punching Bag, inflatable, Charlie Brown, "I Need All the Friends I Can Get," Determined, 1970s **35.00**

Radio, Snoopy, figural, plastic, Determined, #351, 1975 .... **15.00**

Record, *Oh Good Grief*, Vince Guaraldi, Warner Bros, #1747, 1968 .... **10.00**

Rug, latch hook, "Buddies," Snoopy hugging Woodstock illus, Malina, #26/13, 20 × 27", 1970s **35.00**

Scissors, plastic, red, Joe Cool figure on front **9.50**

Snowdome, Snoopy kissing Lucy, floating red hearts, Butterfly, #4601, orig box, 1981 .... **18.00**

Tea Set, Snoopy Tea Set, metal, J Chein & Co, #276, orig box, 1970s **100.00**

Toothbrush, plastic, battery operated, Snoopy on doghouse stand, Kenner, #30301, 1972 .... **40.00**

Toy

Rowing Snoopy, battery operated, orig box, 1965 .... **35.00**

Snoopy Chef, windup, flips food, orig box, 1958 .... **45.00**

Snoopy's Beagle Bugle, plastic, Child Guidance, #1730, 1970s **65.00**

Transfer, Snoopy, fabric, iron-on, Interstate Brands premium, 1972 presidential election themes, set of six **15.00**

Wallet, Snoopy dressed as cowboy design **15.00**

Waste Basket, metal, Charlie Brown and Snoopy illus, Chein Co, 13" h, 1970s **20.00**

Windchimes, plastic, figural Woodstock and Snoopy on doghouse, metal chimes, Aviva, orig box, 1973 .... **30.00**

Wristwatch, Lucy's Watch Wardrobe, blue, white, and pink interchangeable bands, Determined, ⅞" d dial, 1970s **75.00**

PENCIL CLIPS AND PAPER CLIPS

Paper clips clip pieces of paper together. Pencil clips hold pencils in one's pocket. Both were popular; both were used to advertise products. Neither form is used much today. After seeing several hundred examples, I think they should be missed.

The listings below are for paper clips with celluloid buttons and metal spring clips, all dating from the early 1900s. Pencil clips have celluloid buttons with metal pencil holders.

PAPER CLIP

Bickmore's Gall Cure, ⅞" l, black and white **20.00**

Bissel Company, 1" l, multicolored, red inscription **30.00**

Boston Varnish Co, 1¼" l, multicolored, gold inscription **30.00**

Edison Portland Cement Co, 1¾" d, celluloid, yellow and black design, Thomas A Edison Trademark, 1920s **25.00**

Eureka Jewelry Co, 1¼" l, sepia photo portrait of woman wearing pearl necklace, sheer off-the-shoulder white gown, light green and white inscription on dark brown border **40.00**

Farm & Home, ⅞" l, black and white.... **18.50**

Lane Mfg Co, Montpelier, VT, 2½" l, black and white sawmill illus, c1900 .... **25.00**

McKibbin Hat, 1¼" l, brown portrait of gentleman, tinted fleshtone face, light blue-green ground **45.00**

Peacock Condoms, 2 × 2", litho metal, yellow, green and red design, c1940 .... **35.00**

Star Egg Carriers and Trays, 1¼" l, multicolored, dark olive green ground, red, yellow, and white inscription **60.00**

PENCIL CLIP

Advertising

Butternut Chips, ⅞" d, yellow, red, and black **12.00**

Cliquot Club Beverages, maroon lettering, white ground **10.00**

Diamond Crystal Salt **8.00**
Dr Pepper, ⅞" d, orange, black, and white **8.50**
The Edwin Clapp Shoes/East Weymouth, MA, silvered brass, early 1900s **15.00**
Fletcher, "It's The Better Glass Cutter," gold and green **15.00**
Grapette Soda, blue, white, and orange **12.00**
Habbersett's Pork Products, ⅞" d, red, white, and blue logo, "There Is No Substitute For Quality" slogan **18.00**
Keller's Butter/Eggs, ⅞" d, red, white, and blue, celluloid, silvered tin clip, c1940 . . . . **15.00**
Meyer's Ice Cream, ⅝" d, red and white **18.00**
Morton's Salt. **6.00**
Nesbitt's California Orange, ⅞" d, blue, white, and orange **10.00**
Peppard's Funk-G Hybrid, ear of corn logo, red lettering, white ground . . . **12.00**
Ritz Crackers, ⅞" d, litho tin, yellow, blue, and red, Nabisco logo, c1930 . . . . **8.50**
Seven-Up, ⅞" d, red, green, black, and white logo **10.00**
Shapleigh's Hardware, ⅞" d, red, black, and white, Diamond Edge logo, c1930 . . . . **12.50**
Squirt, ⅞" d, lemon half with bottle center, red lettering. **6.00**
Staf-O-Life Dog Food, yellow and black, two dogs illus **15.00**
Viking Snuff, blue and white, silvered tin clip, c1930 . . . . **20.00**
White House Coffee, ¾" d, White House illus, white lettering, dark blue ground, c1920 . . . . **10.00**
Baseball, ¾" d, black and white, photo portrait, silvered metal clip, 1948–1951
Al Rosen, Cleveland Indians **20.00**
Thurman Tucker, Cleveland Indians **18.50**
Patriotic, ½" d, "God Bless America," red, white, and blue, white ground, blue inscription **12.00**

PENS AND PENCILS

Forget the ordinary and look for the unusual. The more special the object or set is, the more likely that it will have a high value. Defects of any kind diminish value dramatically.

When buying a set, try to get the original box along with any instruction sheets and guarantee cards (you will be amazed at how many people actually save them).

Clubs: American Pencil Collectors Society, 2222 S. Millwood, Wichita, KS 67213; Pen Fancier's Club, 1169 Overcash Drive, Dunedin, FL 34698.

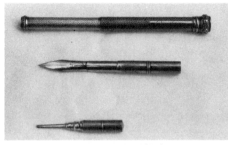

B. T. Benton, #1851, New York, three-part combination pen and pencil set, gold-plated case, faceted stone in top, $85.00.

Pen
Advertising
Arvin Glaesman, Ready Mix Concrete, Leoloa, SD, concrete truck in top **95.00**
Gerber General Merchandise, 8½" l, Hong Kong. **75.00**
Character
Hopalong Cassidy, 6" l, black plastic and silvered metal, 3-D plastic portrait, Parker Pen Co, c1950 . . . **50.00**
Tom Mix, 4¾", marbleized, rope script, 14K, gold plated, Southern Pen Co, c1920 . . . . **75.00**
Epenco, black case, gold-plated trim **20.00**
Mother-of-pearl, Victorian, lady's **26.00**
Novelty, bracelet. **65.00**
Parker, maroon, stainless steel cap, chrome-plated trim, 1950 . . . . **30.00**
Sheaffer, Lifetime, black, brown stripe **50.00**
Pen and Pencil Set
Advertising, Parbeaco Best Nibs, Japan, orig box **95.00**
Lone Ranger, standing figures with gun. **350.00**
Pencil
Advertising, Elsie, 5" l, mechanical, Secretary Pen Co, Borden Co copyright, 1930–1940 . . . . **60.00**
Baseball, mechanical
Chicago Cubs, wood, baseball bat shape, red "Atlantic" premium sponsor, 1940–50 . . . . **15.00**
Joe DiMaggio, 6" l, wood, baseball bat shape, black signature, 1940–1950. . . . . **50.00**
Character
Disneyland, 11" l, wood, white, red, yellow, and blue figures of Mickey, Donald, and Pluto **12.00**

Popeye, 10½" l, metal, mechanical, silver-gray, black and dark red illus and text, Eagle Pencil Co, 1930–40 .... **25.00**
Fire Chief, mechanical **20.00**
Political, Adlai Stevenson, plastic, mechanical, red, white, and blue, "Win With Adlai Stevenson/Stevenson For President"................. **15.00**
Souvenir, Pearl Harbor, mechanical........................... **18.00**
Wahl-Eversharp, lady's **14.00**

PERFUME BOTTLES

Perfume bottles come in all shapes and sizes. In addition to perfume bottles, there are atomizers (a bottle with a spray mechanism), colognes (large bottles whose stoppers often have an application device), scents (small bottles used to hold a scent or smelling salts), and vinaigrettes (an ornamental box or bottle with a perforated top). The stopper of a perfume is used for application and is elongated.

Perfume bottles were one of the hottest collectibles of the 1980s. As a result of market manipulation and speculative buying, prices soared. The wind started to blow in the wrong direction. The field began to stink. Many prices collapsed.

Club: Perfume and Scent Bottle Collectors, 2022 East Charleston Blvd, Las Vegas, NV 89104.

Atomizer, octagonal dark amethyst base, rubber bulb, silver-plated neck, amethyst cone finial, 3½" h, $38.00.

Atomizer, 4" h, 2½" sq, cut glass, Harvard pattern, gold washed top **125.00**
Avon, 3¼" h, California Perfume Co,

glass, violet sachet, half full, violet paper label, 1912. .... **125.00**
Baccarat, 4½" h, glass, Rose Teinte, swirl...................... **65.00**
Blown Three Mold, glass, pale aqua, Gothic Arch, cork stopper, c1825..... **110.00**
Cranberry Glass
  3¾" h, bulbous, enameled blue and gray flowers, blue, orange, and white leaves, clear flattened ball stopper...................... **90.00**
  5¼" h, gold bands, blue and white florals, gold ball stopper **120.00**
  5½" h, beveled, clear cut faceted bubble stopper.................... **110.00**
Cut Glass, 6½" h, Button and Star pattern, rayed base, faceted stopper, Brilliant period **100.00**
Czechoslovakian, glass
  3½" h, clear and frosted **100.00**
  3⅝" h, opaque black, clear stopper ... **85.00**
Figural
  Child, 4¼" h, china, seated in yellow bag, purple collar and black hat, metal and cork stopper, marked "Germany".................... **40.00**
  Dog, glass, clown collar, gray, c1890...................... **40.00**
  Heart Shape, 5½" h, glass, cut flowers on front and back, clear cut faceted stopper....................... **75.00**
  Lady and Parrot, 3⅜" h, china, blue, white, black, yellow, green, and orange, metal and cork stopper **70.00**
Moser Glass, blue, white enamel and gold trim, gilded metal rose shaker stopper, c1900................... **110.00**
Pairpoint, 5½" h, heavy crystal, controlled bubbles **60.00**
Porcelain, floral dec, marked "Germany"......................... **40.00**
Sandwich Glass, 2⅞" h, dark green..... **30.00**
Venetian Glass, blue, green, and gold stripe **50.00**

PEZ DISPENSERS

The Pez dispenser originated in Germany and was invented by Edvard Haas in 1927. The name "Pez" is an abreviation of the German word for peppermint—"pfefferminz." The peppermint candy was touted as an alternative to smoking.

The first Pez container was shaped like a disposable cigarette lighter and is referred to by collectors as the non-headed or regular dispenser.

By 1952 Pez arrived in the United States. New fruit flavored candy and novelty dispensers were also introduced. Early containers were designed to commemorate holidays or favorite children's characters including Bozo the Clown, Mickey Mouse, and other popular Disney, Warner Brothers, and Universal personalities.

Collecting Pez containers at flea markets must be done with care. Inspect each dispenser to guarantee it is intact and free from cracks and chips. Also, familiarize yourself with proper color and marking characteristics.

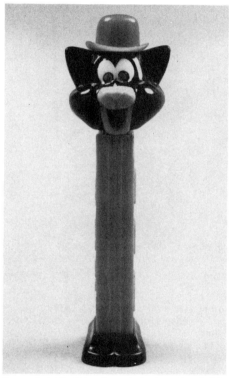

Puzzy Cat, black head, made in Austria, 4½" h, $10.00.

Angel, Christmas, 1960s	5.00
Annie, licensed character, 1970s	20.00
Baloo, Disney, 1980s	10.00
Barney Bear, MGM cartoon characters, 1980s	10.00
Baseball Glove, 1960s	100.00
Batman, Super Friends, soft head, 1970s	40.00
Betsy Ross, bicentennial, 1976	35.00
Blob Octopus, Halloween, 1960s	70.00
Boy with Hat, Pez pal, 1960–79	10.00
Bozo, diecut, 1960s	100.00
Bride, Pez pal, 1960–79	250.00
Bugs Bunny, Warner Brothers cartoon characters, 1970–89	2.00
Bullwinkle, licensed character, 1960s	150.00

Bunny, fat ears, Easter, 1960s	1.00
Captain America, Super Heroes, 1970s	15.00
Captain Hook, Disney, 1960s	20.00
Casper, diecut, 1960s	100.00
Cockatoo, Kooky Zoo, 1970s	10.00
Cocoa Marsh, premium, 1960s	100.00
Cool Cat, Warner Brothers cartoon characters, 1970–89	20.00
Creature from the Black Lagoon, movie monster, 1960s	150.00
Creature, Halloween, 1960s	75.00
Crocodile, Kooky Zoo, 1970s	30.00
Daniel Boone, bicentennial, 1976	100.00
Dead Head Dr Skull, Halloween, 1960s	1.00
Diabolic, Eerie Spectres, 1960s	50.00
Donkey, Merry Music Makers, 1980s	10.00
Donkey Kong, Jr, premium, 1980s	200.00
Dumbo, Disney, 1960s	5.00
Easter Bunny, diecut, 1960s	150.00
Engineer, Pez pal, 1960–79	30.00
Foghorn Leghorn, Warner Brothers cartoon characters, 1970–89	20.00
Football Player, 1960s	50.00
Fozzie Bear, licensed character, Sesame Street, 1991	1.00
Frog, Merry Music Makers, 1980s	10.00
Goofy, Disney, 1970s	1.00
Gorilla, circus, 1970s	10.00
Green Hornet, licensed character, 1960s	300.00
Happy Bear, circus, 1970s	10.00
Incredible Hulk, Super Heroes, 1970s	5.00
Jiminy Cricket, Disney, 1960s	15.00
Koala, Merry Music Makers, 1980s	25.00
Lamb, Easter, 1960s	1.00
Li'l Bad Wolf, Disney, 1960s	5.00
Maharaja, Pez pal, 1960–79	60.00
Mama Giraffe, circus, 1970s	20.00
Mary Poppins, Disney, 1960s	200.00
Mickey Mouse, diecut, 1960s	90.00
Mimic the Monkey, circus, 1970s	40.00
Moo Moo Cow, Kooky Zoo, 1960s	20.00
Mopsy, Beatrix Potter, Eden, 1972	30.00
Mr Ugly Scrooge, Halloween, 1960s	1.00
Olive Oyl, licensed character, 1960s	125.00
Orange, crazy fruit, 1970s	40.00
Panther, Kooky Zoo, 1970s	40.00
Papa Smurf, licensed character, 1980s	2.00
Penguin, Super Friends, soft head, 1970s	35.00
Peter Pez, licensed character, 1960s	40.00
Pilgrim, bicentennial, 1976	60.00
Pineapple, crazy fruit, 1970s	200.00
Pinocchio, Disney, 1950s	10.00
Pirate, Pez pal, 1960–79	25.00
Policeman, Pez pal, 1960–79	15.00
Pony-Go-Round, circus, 1970s	10.00
Practical Pig, Disney, 1960s	10.00
Psychedelic Eye, 1960s	200.00
Pumpkin, Halloween, 1960s	1.00
Raven, Kooky Zoo, 1970s	10.00

Rhino, Merry Music Makers, 1980s **25.00**
Ringmaster, circus, 1970s **25.00**
Rooster, Easter, 1960s **8.00**
Rudolph the Red-Nosed Reindeer,
    Christmas, 1960s **5.00**
Santa Claus, 1950s **1.00**
Sheik, Pez pal, 1960–79 .... **75.00**
Silly Clown, 1970s **25.00**
Snow White, Disney, 1960s **60.00**
Space Gun, premium, 1950s **100.00**
Spaceman, full body, 1950s **90.00**
Speedy Gonzales, Warner Brothers car-
    toon characters, 1970–89 .... **10.00**
Spike, MGM cartoon characters,
    1980s **10.00**
Stewardess, Pez pal, 1960–79 .... **40.00**
Thor, Super Heroes, 1970s **60.00**
Truck
    Cab #1, single rear axle, 1960s **10.00**
    Cab #16, dual rear axle, no fender in-
    dentation, 1970s **5.00**
Uncle Sam, bicentennial, 1976 .... **25.00**
Whistle, 1980s **2.00**
Wile E Coyote, Warner Brothers cartoon
    characters, 1970–89 .... **5.00**
Wonder Woman, Super Friends, hard
    head, 1970s **5.00**
Woodstock, licensed character, 1991 ... **1.00**
Wounded Soldier, bicentennial, 1976... **75.00**
Yappy Dog, Kooky Zoo, 1970s **80.00**
Zorro, Disney, 1960s **75.00**

PIANO STOOLS

They are around. How's that for a grade "D" pun? All kidding aside, there are some great piano stool forms, especially from the Victorian era. Most individuals focus on the wooden stools. Do not over-look the metal examples.

Metal, circular seat, adjustable height,
    claw and glass ball feet, 1880–1915
    Ornate **125.00**
    Plain........................ **65.00**
Wood, circular seat, adjustable height,
    1880–1915
    Ornate **150.00**
    Plain........................ **75.00**

PICKLE CASTORS

Imagine a matched table setting elaborate enough to include a pickle castor. When was the last time that you were served pickles with your evening meal? What's wrong with the pickle lobbyists?

Almost all the emphasis is on the Victo-rian pieces, i.e., castors from the 1870 to 1915 period.

Deduct 25 percent if the pickle fork is missing. Even more if the lid is missing. People don't want a fly in their pickles any more than they do in their soup.

Pattern Glass, Cane, blue, #286, 10" h, $265.00.

Amber, Inverted Thumbprint pattern,
    silver-plated frame **265.00**
Blue
    Currier and Ives pattern, silver-plated
    frame **165.00**
    Sprig pattern, ornate Reed and Barton
    frame, orig fork and fancy lid **175.00**
Cranberry, 12" h, Inverted Thumbprint
    pattern, gold leaves and plums on one
    side, green leaves and pear on other
    side, ornate frame, marked "Wilcox
    4648" **800.00**
Crystal
    10" h, Swirl pattern insert, begging
    dog finial, orig tongs, marked "Hart-
    ford Quadplate" **200.00**
    11¾" h, acid etched octagonal insert
    with floral and bird medallion, orig
    tongs, frame marked "Meriden Co.
    182".......................... **245.00**
Emerald Green, paneled insert with
    enameled florals, ornate silver-plated
    frame........................ **225.00**
Opalescent, 14⅜" h, Coinspot pattern,
    cranberry ground, polychrome enam-
    eled flowers, opalescent spots, silver-

plated frame with lion and shield
finial **215.00**
Pigeon Blood, Beaded Drape pattern insert, Consolidated Glass Co **425.00**
Satin, pink, swirled insert, ornate ftd Pairpoint frame **235.00**
Vaseline, white opalescent design, polished pontil, emb flower shaped ruffled cov with stem finial, ornate ftd frame **450.00**

12½ × 15", deep well, black inner edge, pr **80.00**
Rosewood Veneer, 7⅝ × 8¾", beveled **50.00**
Silver Plated, 9¾ × 17½", 2" wide border with raised peasant figures, houses, trees, village scene, rough textured finish **100.00**
Tramp Art, 19½ × 17¼", Philadelphia area, 1915 . . . . **48.00**
Walnut, 16 × 19½", chip carved edge, applied hearts **50.00**

PICTURE FRAMES

We have reached the point where the frame is often worth more than the picture in it. Decorators have fallen in love with old frames. If you find one with character and pizazz at a flea market for a few dollars, pick it up. It will not be hard to resell it.

Who said picture frames have to be used for pictures? They make great frames for mirrors. Use your imagination.

PIEBIRDS

They were never meant to whistle, although they look like they could. Piebirds were inserted in the middle of pies when baking them to stop the contents from overflowing.

They come in a variety of shapes and are usually made of porcelain. Many are collected as secondary objects by collectors from other categories.

Glass, Art-Deco style, tinted light blue, tin-plated corner mounts, 4 × 5", $20.00.

Brass
    2¾ × 3½", plain **10.00**
    7 × 12", Art Nouveau style, two oval openings, easel back **125.00**
Curly Maple, 16¾ × 20½", refinished . . . **90.00**
Gesso, pine framework, oval, acorns and leaves dec, gilded inner edge, beaded outer edge, mahogany stained **48.00**
Golden Oak, 14¼ × 17½", molded **20.00**
Mahogany
    9 × 12¾", laminated, folk art pyramid dec, old varnish finish **45.00**

Bird, white, green eyes and wings, pink beak and base, glossy finish, Shawnee, unmarked, 5" h, $35.00.

Bird
    Black, Royal Worcester **38.00**
    Blackbird, white base **22.00**
    Blue Willow **18.00**
    White, big mouth **30.00**

Black Chef, holding rolling pin	**55.00**
Black Man, holding pie, blackbird flying out of pie depicted on shirt	**55.00**
Chicken	**48.00**
Chinaman	**50.00**
Crow, black	**40.00**
Dog, baying, white with black spots	**50.00**
Duck	
Pink	**23.00**
Wearing blue striped beret	**50.00**
Elephant, standing on hind legs, white, England	**50.00**
English Bobby, blue uniform, English ...	**54.00**
Funnel, white	
Inscribed "Nut Brown Pie Funnel" ...	**50.00**
Yellow top, pie man followed by three children and dog	**50.00**
Mermaid, black face and arms, white hair, green tail	**52.00**
Merman, yellow hair, green tail	**35.00**
Minstrel, wearing black suit and hat, white face with black features	**52.00**
Owl, stylized	**45.00**
Penguin, wearing green scarf and hat ...	**54.00**
Rooster, Pearl China Co, instruction leaflet	**18.00**
Woman, holding pie	**50.00**

PIG COLLECTIBLES

This is one animal that does better as a collectible than in real life. Pig collectibles have never been oinkers.

Established pig collectors focus on the bisque and porcelain pigs of the late nineteenth and early twentieth centuries. This is a limited view. Try banks in the shape of a pig as a specialized collecting area. If that's not appealing, look at the use of pigs in advertising. If neither pleases you, there is always Porky. "That's all, folks!"

Planter, pigs and sled, Germany, 6" l, $200.00.

Ashtray, 4½" w, two pigs looking into old-fashioned camera	**75.00**
Baggage Tag, 2⅛" d, celluloid, black and white, farmer riding large ear of corn pulled by two hogs, inscribed "Canaan Land For Grapes" and "Wine, Iowa Land For Corn and Swine," unused, 1913	**22.00**
Bank, white clay, seated, clear glaze	**30.00**
Bottle, 6½" h, figural, ceramic, tan glaze, blue eyes	**150.00**
Chocolate Mold, figural, tin, two parts	**65.00**
Comic Book, Porky Pig, Whitman, #1408, 1942	**25.00**
Figure	
Mama bathing baby at pump, pink ...	**75.00**
Pig in washtub	**54.00**
Gravy Boat, porcelain, two pink pigs swinging	**45.00**
Matchsafe, pink pig poking head through fence	**60.00**
Pail, 6½" d, 3" h, litho tin, Three Little Pigs illus, 1930s	**75.00**
Paperweight, figural, glass, Best Pig Forceps, compliments J Reimers, Davenport, IA	**100.00**
Pillow, figural	**15.00**
Pinback Button, 1¼" d, Weilands/The Finest Pork Products, dancing yellow pig named Willie, light blue ground, 1930s	**25.00**
Playing Cards, Three Little Pigs, complete deck, orig box marked "By Special Permission Walt Disney Enterprises," 1930s	**50.00**
Salt and Pepper Shakers, pr, 4" h, figural, one playing accordion, other playing saxophone, glazed and painted, marked "Japan," c1930	**45.00**
Statue, 7" h, Porky Pig, plaster, painted, 1940–1950	**50.00**
Stickpin, brass	**5.50**
Tape Measure, figural, celluloid.	**25.00**
Toy	
Stuffed, velvet, Steiff	**60.00**
Windup, 7½" h, Porky Pig, litho tin, wearing cowboy outfit, orig box, 1949 Leon Schesinger copyright ...	**350.00**

PIN-UP ART

The stuff looks so innocent, one has to wonder what all the fuss was about when it first arrived on the scene. Personally, I like it when a little is left to the imagination.

George Petty and Alberto Vargas (the "s" was later dropped at *Esquire's* request) have received far more attention than they deserve. You would be smart to focus on artwork by Gillete Elvgren, Billy DeVorss, Joyce Ballantyne, and Earl Moran. While Charles Dana Gibson's girls are also pinups, they are far too respectable to be considered here.

Playing Cards, 53 Vargas Girls, plastic coated, $75.00.

Calendar
  Rolf Armstrong, 1947, See You Soon, 11 × 23", salesman's sample, Sept pad 45.00
  Chippendale Revue, 1988 .... 8.00
  Gillete Elvgren
    1952, 8½ × 13", glossy, spiral bound, full color art, Brown & Bigelow 90.00
    1955, Stepping Out, 16 × 33", December pad 85.00
  Earl Moran, 1946, Evening Star, 16 × 33", unused 175.00
  George Petty, 1949, Come On Along, 7½ × 16", full color art, unused 65.00
  Alberto Vargas, 1946, pocket folder, 3 × 4½" closed, opens to 4½ × 21½" strip, Vargas and Esquire copyrights 60.00
Christmas Card, 5½ × 8", multicolored, MacPherson 22.00
Cigarette Lighter, 3" d, 6½" h, Torchee, figural aluminum can, lighter wheel under removable cap, pin-up in red dress and two Scottie dogs around outside, inscribed "The Light of Your Life," attached card reads "For Dad as Advertised in *Esquire*," 1950s 30.00
Date Book, 1945 *Esquire*, 5 × 7", spiral bound, subtitled "G I Edition," pinup art by Vargas," movie star photos 60.00
Folder, Sally of Hollywood & Vine, cardboard, sliding insert changes dress to underwear to nude 22.00
Hairpin, George Petty, orig 4 × 5½" yellow, red, black, and white card, artist sgd, 1948 .... 20.00

Illusion Glass, 5" h, full color decal of pin-up wearing sheer clothing, clothing disappears when glass sweats, set of 5, c1938 .... 100.00
Keychain, souvenir, 2¼" h, plastic, painted, figural, female bather drying herself with towel, attached to cardboard tag, 1940s 14.00
Letter Opener, 8½" h, plastic, figural, flat back, standing nude holding adv disk overhead, designed by Gillete Elvgren, 1940–1950 .... 18.00
Magazine, *Hollywood Tales*, Vol 1, #36, full color art, 24 pgs, 1930s 30.00
Matchbook Cover, Petty girl, "Snug As A Bug," Martins Tavern, Chicago, late 1940s 3.00
Note Pad, 3 × 4½", pastel, 1944 calendar on back 6.00
Playing Cards
  Elvgren Cuties, full color art, titled "Having a Bang-Up Time," orig box and flyleaf, 1940s 50.00
  Petty Pippins, complete deck, orig box with cowgirl leaning against fence, c1940 .... 62.50
  Vargas, Gorgeous Girls, full color art, orig box, Creative Playing Card Co, c1950 .... 75.00
Post Card, nude woman shown waist up, arms folded over chest, divided back 10.00
Poster, 17 × 33", full color, woman in shorts walking wire-haired terrier, Walt Otto, c1951 .... 50.00
Print, woman sitting on red bench, marked "Copr C Moss 1947 Litho in USA" 50.00

PLANTERS

No, I am not talking about Planter's Peanuts. I am chronicling those strange and decorative containers that people seem intent to force vegetation to grow from. If I had a "You Have To Be Nuts To Own It" category in this book, I might have been tempted to include planters in it. Don't you find it just a bit strange to see English ivy growing out of the top of a ceramic pig's head?

A planter is any container suitable for growing vegetation. It may be constructed of any number of materials, ranging from wooden fruit crates and painted tires found on suburban front lawns to ceramic panthers stalking 1950s television sets. If you thought all those planters you got from the florist were junk, read on. Too bad you threw them out or sold them for a dime each at your last garage sale.

This category deals with the figural ceramic variety found in abundance at all flea markets.

Kitten in Basket, pastel colors, glossy finish, Copley, unmarked, 8" h, 8½" w, 1950s, $35.00.

Alligator, hiding in weeds, green, glossy, mkd "McCoy USA" 12.00
Anvil, black, applied gray chain and hammer, matte, mkd "McCoy USA" 10.00
Basket, black and white, mkd "McCoy USA" 12.00
Bear, brown, glossy, Brush-McCoy, 5" h 18.00
Birds on Perch, four white, yellow, and black birds on brown tree branch, glossy, mkd "Shawnee 502" 30.00
Bucket, green, emb wood grain and bands, bail handle, glossy, Hull, #B94 .... 20.00
Butterfly on Log, brown and white, glossy, mkd "Shawnee USA 524" 3.00
Canoe, white ext., brown int., matte, mkd "Red Wing U.S.A. #735" 20.00
Cart, blue ext., yellow int., glossy, Shawnee, mkd "USA 775" 6.00
Cat, pink, green eyes and bow, glossy, McCoy, unmarked 12.00
Conch Shell, yellow and green, glossy, Hull 35.00
Conestoga Wagon, green, glossy, mkd "Shawnee 733" 20.00
Cowboy and Cactus, natural colors, Morton, 7" h 12.00
Cowboy Boot, blue, pink spray glaze, American Art Potteries, 6" h 12.00
Cradle, blue, semi gloss, emb basketweave design with flowers and swags dec, mkd "McCoy" 8.00
Cucumber, natural color, Mother Earth Line, Morton, #395 .... 3.00

Dachshund, brown, glossy, Hull, #119, 15" l 70.00
Dog in Boat, white with pastel accents, glossy, mkd "Shawnee 736" 12.00
Duck, swimming, white, orange beak and feet, Brush-McCoy, #133 .... 45.00
Dutch Children, blue, yellow, and white girl and boy flanking green well, gold trim, glossy, emb "Wishing Well" on base, mkd "Shawnee 710" 18.00
Elf, sitting on large elf shoe, multicolored, glossy, mkd "Shawnee 765" 6.00
Fish, pink, green fins, glossy, mkd "McCoy USA" 35.00
Flower Box, rect, emb grape clusters at corners, white, semi gloss, Red Wing, mkd "Rum Rill #623" 8.00
Frog on Lily Pad, green and brown, glossy, mkd "Shawnee 726" 18.00
Giraffe, green, glossy, Hull, #115, 9" h 30.00
Globe, blue and green globe on yellow stand, glossy, mkd "Shawnee USA" 12.00
Gondolier, black, glossy, mkd "Royal Haeger by Royal Hickman 657," 19½" l 20.00
Gourd, red, Abingdon, #667, 5½" h 25.00
Gristmill, white with gold trim, glossy, movable paddle wheel, mkd "Shawnee 769" 24.00
Guitar, black, semi gloss, mkd "Red Wing U.S.A. #M-1484" 15.00
Hat, inverted, flared brim, pink, matte, Red Wing, mkd "Rum Rill #H-36 U.S.A." 10.00
Knight on Horse, black and white knight, pink horse, glossy, Hull, #55 .... 50.00
Lamb, white, pink ears, blue ribbon, matte, Hull, #965 .... 45.00
Llama Pulling Cart, coral colored, matte, Capri, Hull, #C80 .... 65.00
Log, applied squirrel figure, gray spray glaze, American Art Potteries, 7" h ... 15.00
Monkey, sitting, holding coconut shell, brown, Brush-McCoy, #23, 5" h 25.00
Mouse, leaning on cheese wedge, multicolored, glossy, Shawnee, mkd "USA 705" 12.00
Oak Leaf, white ext., green int., matte, mkd "Red Wing U.S.A. #428" 10.00
Panther, stalking, black, glossy, McCoy, unmarked, 1950s 18.00
Pear, yellow, lying on green leaf, glossy, mkd "McCoy USA" 12.00
Pelican, turquoise, matte, McCoy, mkd "NM USA" 10.00
Piano, upright, green, glossy, Shawnee, mkd "USA 528" 15.00
Pigeon, turquoise, black spatter and shading, Royal, Hull, #91 .... 20.00
Pirate's Head, white, semi gloss, Brush-McCoy 20.00

Poodle Head, wearing hat and bow, white, matte, Hull, #114. . . . . **40.00**

Quail, natural color spray glaze, American Art Potteries, 9½" h **22.00**

Rocking Horse, pink, glossy, Shawnee, mkd "USA 526" **12.00**

Rolling Pin, mkd "Camark N1-51" **8.00**

Rooster, gray feathers, red comb, green grassy base, glossy, mkd "McCoy USA" **15.00**

Santa Claus, natural colors, Morton **25.00**

Scroll, green and brown, glossy, Parchment & Pine pattern, Hull, #S-5. . . . . . **40.00**

Skunk, black and white, pastel pink and blue basket, airbrushed, Brush-Mc-Coy, #249, 6½" h **30.00**

Spinning Wheel, kitten hiding underneath, brown and yellow, glossy, mkd "McCoy USA" **8.00**

Swan, pink, matte, mkd "Red Wing U.S.A. #259". **12.00**

Turkey, brown, red wattle, Morton. **10.00**

Turtle, white, matte, McCoy, mkd "NM" **5.00**

Watering Can, emb flowers on basketweave design, yellow, glossy, Shawnee, mkd "USA". **6.00**

Whisk Broom, yellow, glossy, Sun Glow pattern, Hull, #82 . . . . **45.00**

PLANTERS PEANUTS

Amedeo Obici and Mario Peruzzi organized the Planter's Nut and Chocolate Company in Wilkes-Barre, Pennsylvania, in 1906. The monocled Mr. Peanut resulted from a trademark contest in 1916. Standard Brands bought Planters only to be bought themselves by Nabisco.

Planter's developed a wide range of premiums and promotional items. Beware of reproductions.

Club: Peanut Pals, P. O. Box 4465, Huntsville, AL 35815.

Bank, 8½" h, figural, Mr Peanut, plastic, dark red, removable hat **35.00**

Book, *Presidents Paint Book,* 1953 . . . . **45.00**

Bookmark, diecut, cardboard, 1920–1930 . . . . **20.00**

Bracelet, charm, three beige and blue Mr Peanut figures, c1930 . . . . **12.00**

Counter Container, 12" h, figural, Mr Peanut, plastic, hollow, amber base, raised facial features, blue hat, blue and yellow Mr Peanut paper sticker label, dated 1979 . . . . **20.00**

Doll, 20" h, Mr Peanut, cloth, stuffed, orig clear plastic mailer, unopened, 1960s. **20.00**

Mug, plastic, blue, $5.00.

Figure, 10" h, cardboard **6.00**

Jar, streamlined **85.00**

Keychain, 2¼" h, figural, Mr Peanut, plastic, day-glow, molded keychain loop, 1940s **25.00**

Mug, pewter **20.00**

Nut Tray, 5½" d, 1¼" h, plastic, green, divided, 3" Mr Peanut in center, matching 3" l serving spoon with figural handle **40.00**

Paint Book, 7½ × 10½", "Colorful Story of Peanuts as Told by Mr Peanut," soft cov, 28 pgs, copyright 1957 . . . . **30.00**

Pinback Button, 1⅛" d, black and white illus and "Mr Peanut" on white ground, "Vote for the Peoples Choice" in white lettering on red rim, 1930s. **12.50**

Ring, Mr Peanut, metal, adjustable, yellow and black enamel figure, 1960s **30.00**

Salt and Pepper Shakers, pr, 3" h, plastic, figural Mr Peanut, silver flashing, removable top hats, made in USA, 1940s. **18.00**

Serving Set, 1939 New York World's Fair souvenir, one large bowl and four small peanut serving dishes, litho tin, Mr Peanut, Trylon, Perisphere, and inscription in center of each dish. **70.00**

Serving Spoon, 5¼" l, SP, Carlton, c1930. . . . . **12.00**

Swizzle Stick, figural **3.50**

Tab, 1½" d, metal, litho, diecut, yellow, black, and white Mr Peanut, 1920–30. . . . . **12.00**

Whistle, plastic, red and white, chain loop, "Mr Peanut" on hat brim, 1940–50. . . . . **10.00**

PLAYBOY

The Playboy empire of the 1960s and 1970s is dead. The clubs and casino are closed. Hugh got married. Is there no God?

Playboy was promotion-minded. Anything associated with it is collectible. Most *Playboy* magazines sell in the $1.00 to $3.00 range except for very early (1953 to 1960) issues. The key magazine to own is Volume One, Number One, but isn't this always the case?

Book
   Playboy Jazz Festival, hard cover, 1959 . . . . **12.00**
   Twelfth Anniversary Playboy Reader, 874 pgs, hard cover, 1966 . . . . **25.00**
Cake Pan, bunny logo shape, Wilton Enterprises **10.00**
Calendar
   1961, 5½ × 6½", desk, MIB **45.00**
   1964, 8½ × 12½", spiral bound, photo for each month **25.00**
   1969, 6 × 8", desk, easel back, Playmate photos for each month, unused, orig envelope **22.00**
   1973, 8¼ × 12½", spiral bound, glossy full color Playmate photos **18.00**
Car Freshener, Playboy logo, black and white **2.00**
Magazine
   1955, September, includes black and white Marilyn Monroe photos **30.00**
   1957 . . . . **4.00**
   1961, Jan–Dec, set of 12 . . . . **75.00**
   1966 . . . . **3.00**
Mug, black, white Playboy logo **4.00**
Puzzle
   1967, Miss October, Majken Haugedal, carboard canister **40.00**
   1970, blonde Playmate centerfold on white airbag cushion, red carpeting, carboard canister **25.00**
Swizzle Stick, bunny head top **4.00**

PLAYING CARDS

The key is not the deck, but the design on the deck surface. Souvenir decks are especially desirable. Look for special decks such as Tarot and other fortune-telling items.

Always buy complete decks. There are individuals who just collect Jokers and have a bad habit of removing them from a deck and then reselling it. Also, if you are buying a playing card game, make certain that the instruction card is included.

Magazine: *Playing Card World,* 188 Sheen Lane, East Sheen, London SW1 48LF, England.

Clubs: Chicago Playing Card Collectors, Inc., 1559 West Platt Boulevard, Chicago, IL 60626; Playing Card Collectors Association, Inc., 3621 Douglas Avenue, Racine, WI 53404.

Century of Progress Exposition, Chicago, 1934, Belgian Village, gilt edges, $25.00.

Advertising
   Coca-Cola, 1943 . . . . **65.00**
   Sylvania, 1940s, orig box **30.00**
Airline, complete deck **2.50**
Charlie Chan Card Game, 35 playing cards and instruction card, boxed, Whitman, 1939 . . . . **50.00**
Eastern/Ryder, MIB **5.00**
Great Northern Railway, pictures Buckskin Pinto Woman and Chief Middle Rider with logo, complete deck **350.00**
Holland/America, orig box **25.00**
Nile Fortune Cards, boxed, c1900 . . . . . . **45.00**
Ozark Airlines, 1984 World's Fair, sealed deck **2.00**
Poker Taurino, Mexican, complete deck, Spanish inscription on box, c1950 . . . . **12.00**
Squadron Insignia Card Game, 17 pairs of duplicated cards and single "Enemy" titled card, orig box, All-Fair, mid-1940s **75.00**
Tee-Up, golf cartoon on each card, complete deck, orig box, c1950 . . . . **10.00**
The Vista Dome, complete deck, 1950–60 . . . . **15.00**
Whirlaway, race horse, two complete decks and joker cards, orig box, Fanfare, early 1940s **30.00**
World War II **4.00**
World's Fair, 1933 Chicago World's Fair, Wallgreen building, two complete decks, unopened box **25.00**

POLITICAL ITEMS

Collect the winners. For whatever reason, time has not treated the losers well, with the exception of the famous Cox-Roosevelt pinback button.

This is a good category to apply my Dad's Thirty Year Rule—"For the first thirty years of anything's life, all its value is speculative." Do not pay much for items less than thirty years old. But, do remember that time flies. The Nixon-JFK election was over thirty years ago.

Also concentrate on the non-traditional categories. Everyone collects pinbacks and posters. Try something unusual. How about political ties, mugs, or license plates?

Newspaper: *The Political Collector*, P. O. Box 5171, York, PA 17405.

Club: American Political Items Collectors, P. O. Box 340339, San Antonio, TX 78234.

Pinback Button, Eisenhower and Nixon, red, white, and blue, 3" d, $7.50.

Bandanna, 31" sq, JFK, rayon type fabric, full color portrait, white ground, red, white, and blue flag border, 1965 copyright tag 18.00
Bell, brass, Ring for Coolidge 15.00
Coloring Book, 8 × 11", 1973, titled "Watergate Coloring Book/Join The Fun/Color The Facts," 48 pgs 25.00
Comb, McGovern, plastic, blue, smiling face 4.00
Convention Badge, National
   1948, Democrat, Philadelphia, 1½ × 5½", brass hanger with Betsy Ross house, fob with City Hall and Wm Penn statue, blue enameled "Press" bar, white fabric ribbons 18.00
   1968, Republican, Miami, brass, state-shaped top hanger, PA/Press, lower hanger keystone shaped, raised state seal, white fabric ribbon 20.00

Glass, Eisenhower campaign 10.00
Hand Puppet, Nixon, grotesque caricature, marked "Western Germany" . . . 36.00
Lapel Stud, ⅞" l, McKinley-Protection '96, brass, diecut, Napoleon's hat shape 25.00
License Plate, 4 × 13½", Willkie, orange, gold letters outlined in dark blue, blue edge 20.00
Necktie, 47" l, Wilson/Marshall, black, white embroidered names, red, white, and blue flag 50.00
Nodder, papier mache, Nixon for President, Japanese features 125.00
Pen, 5" l, Eisenhower, brass, black and white plastic, slogan "For The Love Of Ike-Vote Republican" 25.00
Pennant, 11 × 30", Dewey, olive green felt, white portrait and inscription 20.00
Pin, 2 × 3½", Willkie, red, white, and blue enameled white metal, ribbon-like design, ten inset rhinestones and center Willkie button 35.00
Pinback Button
   Eisenhower/Nixon, 3½" d, Ike and Dick, Sure To Click, black and white slogan, 1952 . . . . 27.50
   Johnson, 6" d, inauguration, full color portrait, red, white, and blue rim . . . 10.00
   Reagan/Bush, '84, flashing red lights, musical, 2¼" d red, white and blue button, 3½ × 6" colorful orig card, clear plastic cov, battery operated, pr 20.00
Plate, 12" d, FDR, cobalt border 30.00
Pocket Mirror, Teddy Roosevelt, sepia portrait 65.00
Post Card, 3½ × 5½", Taft, black, white, gray, and dark brown, "Our Presidents/Past/Present/Future," portraits of McKinley, Roosevelt, and Taft, Sept 1908 postmark 15.00
Poster, 14 × 21", Goldwater, "A Choice . . . Not An Echo," red, white, and blue 15.00
Ribbon, 3 × 5¾", For President Gen. W. S. Hancock, dark pink ribbon, gold design, 1" sepia paper photo of Hancock 81.00
Sheet Music, 7 × 11", *Dedicated To The GOP/A Victory Is Ours/A Rousing Republican Campaign Song*, 1904 copyright, blue and white 15.00
Sticker, 3½ × 6", diecut foil, silver, blue, and red, inscribed "Willkie/The Hope of America" 15.00
Tab, 2" d, Humphrey, blue, green, red, white, and black, "Labor for Humphrey" 4.50
Tray, 3 × 5", McKinley, aluminum, center jugate photos of McKinley and Teddy Roosevelt, red and blue shield 18.00

Watch Fob
  Bryan and Kern, enameled, eagles and
    flags center, orig strap **35.00**
  Roosevelt and Fairbanks, 1¾ × 2″,
    brass **20.00**

POST CARDS

This is a category where the average golden age card has gone from 50¢ to several dollars in the last decade. Post cards' golden age is between 1898 and 1918. As the cards have become expensive, new collectors are discovering the white border cards of the 1920s and 1930s, the linens of the 1940s, and the early glossy photograph cards of the 1950s and 1960s.

It pays to specialize. This is the only way that you can build a meaningful collection. The literature is extensive. It is worth reviewing before buying. Jack Smith's *Postcard Companion: The Collector's Reference* (Wallace-Homestead, 1989), while not a favorite among serious collectors and dealers, can be used for a quick overview before moving on to more specialized books.

Newspapers: *Barr's Postcard News*, 70 S. 6th Street, Lansing, IA 52151; *Postcard Collector*, Joe Jones Publishing, P. O. Box 337, Iola, WI 54945.

Clubs: *Barr's* and *Postcard Collector* list over fifty regional clubs scattered across the United States.

Post Card, P. Ebner, artist signed, $8.00.

Advertising
  Bulova Watch, government postal
    back **6.00**
  Moxie, two children with cutouts and
    sign **25.00**
  The Animals Picnic, dressed bears riding
    bicycles, Nister, unused **18.00**
  Burlington Zephyr, stationed at 1934

Century of Progress Exposition, in-
    scription, unused **12.00**
Dreadnoughts, three baby bears **12.00**
Holiday
  Christmas, Santa, red suit **8.00**
  Fourth of July, red, white, and blue,
    gold ground, Germany, 1910 . . . . . .   **2.00**
  Halloween, orange pumpkin, artist sgd
    "Ellen Clapsaddle" **8.00**
  Valentine, children and women **4.00**
Political
  George Washington, multicolored **3.75**
  Hitler, glossy black and white cartoon
    picture, penciled note, May 15, 1943
    postmark **15.00**
  McKinley's death **6.00**
  Truman, campaign card **25.00**
Roy Rogers, "Apple Valley Inn," full
  color photo, unused, c1970 . . . .   **15.00**
State
  Alabama **1.00**
  Idaho . . . .   **.50**
  South Carolina . . . .   **.75**

POSTERS

Want a great way to decorate? Use posters. Buy ones you like. This can get a bit expensive if your tastes run to old movie or advertising posters. Prices in the hundreds of dollars are not uncommon. When you get to the great lithography posters of the late nineteenth and early twentieth century, prices in the thousands are possible.

Concentrate on one subject, manufacturer, illustrator, or period. Remember that print runs of two million copies and more are not unheard of. Many collectors have struck deals with their local video store and movie theater to get their posters when they are ready to throw them out. Not a bad idea. But why not carry it a step further? Talk with your local merchants about their advertising posters. These are going to be far harder to find in the future than movie posters.

Because so many people save modern posters, never pay more than a few dollars for any copy below fine condition. A modern poster in very good condition is unlikely to have long-term value. Its condition will simply not be acceptable to the serious collector of the future.

Club: Poster Society, 138 West 18th St., New York, NY 10011.

Advertising
  Buckwheat Flour, 19 × 10″, flour bag
    shape **25.00**

Buy A Poppy, American Legion Auxiliary, 14 × 20", silk screen **40.00**

Coca-Cola-Yes, 11 × 27", 1946 bathing beauty, Harold Sundblum **150.00**

Hilton-The Starched Collar For Fall-Tooke Brothers Ltd, 11 × 21", c1915 . . . . **50.00**

San-Tox Pine Balsam, 35 × 19", stone litho, linen back, early 20th C **50.00**

Use Virginia Dare Double Strength Extracts, 21 × 28", smiling 1925 housewife making cookies **175.00**

Welch's Wine Coolers-Wouldn't This Hit The Spot Right Now? Taste It...You'll Love It, Says Eddie Cantor, 11 × 21", 1952 . . . . **100.00**

Movie and Theater

Carter Beats The Devil, 14 × 22", Otis Litho, 1920 . . . . **75.00**

Dangerous When Wet, MGM, 41 × 81", Esther Williams, Fernando Lamas, Jack Carson, 1953 . . . . **65.00**

King Kong, RKO, 27 × 41", Fay Wray, Robert Armstrong, Bruce Cabot, 1936 . . . . **800.00**

Threepenny Opera, 41 × 81", Paul Davis, two panels, 1976 . . . . **275.00**

Tim McCoy Two Gun Justice, Monogram, 27 × 41", 1938 . . . . **65.00**

Sports

Fidass Sporting Goods, 29 × 52", F Romoli, Italian soccer player, 1962 . . . . **300.00**

Munich Olympics 1972-Fencing, 33 × 46", Gaebele, posted at Olympics . . . **125.00**

York Streamlined Barbell and Body Building System, 14 × 22", red and blue, 1950s **15.00**

PUZZLES

The keys to jigsaw puzzle value in order of importance are: (1) completeness (once three or more pieces are missing, forget value); (2) picture (no one is turned on by old mills and mountain scenery); (3) surface condition (missing tabs or paper or silver fish damage causes value to drop dramatically); (4) age (1940 is a major cutting off point); (5) number of pieces (the more the better for wood); and (6) original box and label (especially important for wooden puzzles). Because of the limitless number of themes, jigsaw puzzle collectors find themselves competing with collectors from virtually every other category.

Jigsaw puzzle collectors want an assurance of completeness, either a photograph or a statement by the seller that they actu-

ally put the puzzle together. "I bought it as complete" carries no weight whatsoever. Unassembled cardboard puzzles with no guarantees sell for $1.00 or less, wooden puzzles for $3.00 or less. One missing piece lowers price by 20 percent, two missing pieces by 35 percent, and three missing pieces by 50 percent or more. Missing packaging (a box or envelope) deducts 25 percent from the price.

Clubs: American Game Collectors Association, 4628 Barlow Drive, Bartlesville, OK 74006.

Note: The following retail prices are for puzzles that are complete, in very good condition, and have their original box.

Adult, litho on wood, Christmas Eve, Arthur G. Grinnell, c1906, 6¼ × 13¾", $30.00.

ADULT PUZZLES

Cardboard

Depression Era, late 1920s through 1940

Milton Bradley, Movieland, four puzzle set	**30.00**
Movie stars and movie-related	**12.00**
Nonweeklies	**2.00**
Perfect Picture Puzzles	**3.00**
Tuco	**3.00**
Weeklies	**8.00**
World War II theme	**6.00**

Post World War II

Up to 500 pieces	**.50**
500 to 1,000 pieces	**1.00**
Over 1,000 pieces	**1.50**
Springbok, circular box	**2.50**
Springbok, square box	**1.50**

Wood

1908–1910 craze

Up to 200 pieces	**25.00**
200 to 500 pieces	**30.00**
Over 500 pieces	**35.00**

Mid-1920s to mid-1930s craze

Up to 200 pieces	**15.00**
200 to 500 pieces	**20.00**
500 to 1,000 pieces	**30.00**
Over 1,000 pieces	**50.00**

Post-1945

Up to 500 pieces	**15.00**

Over 500 pieces................	**20.00**
Par	
Up to 500 pieces	**50.00**
Over 500 pieces................	**100.00**

CHILDREN'S PUZZLES
Cardboard
Pre-1945

Less than 20 pieces	**2.00**
Over 20 pieces.................	**3.00**
Puzzle set, three to four puzzles	**10.00**

Post-1945

Less than 20 pieces	**1.00**
20 to 200 pieces................	**1.50**
Over 200 pieces.................	**2.00**
Frame Tray, cartoon	**6.00**
Frame Tray, cowboy	**12.00**
Frame Tray, general	**3.00**

Composition, 1880s to 1920s
McLoughlin Brothers

General scene	**75.00**
Transportation theme............	**150.00**

Others

Fairy tale	**25.00**
General scene	**50.00**
Transportation scene	**100.00**

Wood
Madmar

General scene	**15.00**
Patriotic scene	**20.00**

Map

Pre-1880	**75.00**
1880 to 1915	**50.00**
1915 to 1940	**20.00**

Others

General scene	**12.50**
Transportation scene	**17.50**

Parker Brothers

Dolly Danty series..............	**35.00**
General scene	**20.00**

ADVERTISING & NOVELTY PUZZLES
Cardboard

1930s........................	**10.00**
Post-1945	**5.00**

Wood

Pre-1945	**35.00**
Pseudo.......................	**25.00**

RADIO CHARACTERS AND PERSONALITIES

Radio dominated American life between the 1920s and the early 1950s. Radio characters and personalities enjoyed the same star status as their movie counterparts. Phrases such as "The shadow knows" or "Welcome breakfast clubbers" quickly date an individual.

Many collectors focus on radio premiums, objects offered during the course of a radio show and usually received by sending in proof of purchase of the sponsor's product. Make certain an object is a premium before paying extra for it as part of this classification.

Many radio characters also found their way into movies and television. Trying to separate the products related to each medium is time consuming. Why bother? If you enjoyed the character or personality, collect everything that is related to him or her.

Lum and Abner, envelope, issued by Horlick's Malted Milk Corp., Racine, WI, postmarked January 28, 1936, NBC Blue Network radio program schedule on front, 6½ × 3⅝", $4.50.

Jimmie Allen
Model, 19" l, 24" wingspan, Thunderbolt, orig box, unused, 1930s **100.00**
Pocketknife, 3¼" l, plastic simulated wood grips, pair raised wings marked "Jimmie Allen" on one side, two blades, 1930s **285.00**
Amos 'n' Andy
Ashtray, 5 × 5 × 8", plaster, Amos and Andy standing on either side of barrel, "Ise Regusted" incised on front edge, c1930s **90.00**
Book, *Amos & Andy*, hard cov, 1929 ... **75.00**
Pinback Button, ⅞" d, black and white, photo, "Amos 'n' Andy Pantages" on rim, 1930s............ **35.00**
Jack Armstrong
Hike O Meter.................... **20.00**
Ring, Egyptian siren, brass, siren on top, Egyptian symbols on side, 1938......................... **75.00**
Captain Midnight, record, "The Years to Remember," 7" d, flexible vinyl, punch out decoder, Longines Symphonette Society, #6 from "The Silver Dagger Strikes" series, 1960s **35.00**
Chandu the Magician, Svengali Mind-Reading Trick, Beech-Nut premium, orig mailing box, 1932–1935 .... **60.00**
Mitzi Green, pinback button, 1¼" d, photo and "I'm on the Air, Mitzi Green, in Happy Landings" in center, "Ward's Soft Bun Bread, WKAN, Tues

& Thurs, 6:00 pm" in white lettering on rim, 1930s 5.00

The Gumps, book, *The Gumps in Radio Land*, 3½ × 5½", soft cov, Pebeco Toothpaste premium, 96 pgs, 1937 copyright 35.00

Little Orphan Annie

Bandanna, 17 × 19", black, white, and red, Ovaltine premium, c1934 ..... 65.00

Book, *Book About Dogs*, 1936 .... 35.00

Bottle, bubble bath, 10½" h, vinyl, figural, Annie holding bouquet, removable molded hair cap, paper sticker on base, 1977 copyright 20.00

Doll Pattern, 5 × 10", fabric, printed design, Harold Gray copyright, J Pressman & Co of New York City, 1930s 60.00

Manual, Secret Society, 6 × 8½", 8 pgs, 1937 .... 55.00

Lone Ranger

Badge

Horseshoe shaped, brass, 1930s 20.00

Safety Scout 15.00

Bolo Tie, gold colored six-point star slide 12.00

Compass, 1¼" d, Silver Bullet Compass, silvered brass, hollow, compass in removable end cap, orig card and mailer, c1948 .... 58.00

Figure, 1½" h, Lone Ranger riding Silver, TLR Inc, 1941 .... 25.00

Tent, Wigwam Tent, Lone Ranger and Tonto 90.00

Charlie McCarthy

Dummy, 8 × 18½", cardboard, diecut, multicolored, movable lever controls mouth and eyes, 1930–40 .... 58.00

Game, Put and Take Bingo, Whitman, #2931, orig box, 1938 copyright ... 35.00

Perfume Bottle, 3½" h, clear glass, removable black plastic hat, late 1930s 40.00

Statue, 15½" h, carnival chalkware, multicolored, glitter accents, 1930–1940 .... 85.00

Fibber McGee and Molly

Game, The Amazing Adventures of Fibber McGee, Milton Bradley, 1936 .... 35.00

Photo, 8¼ × 12", black and white, glossy, cast members, Fibber and Molly pictured at top, late 1930s ... 25.00

Joe Penner, pinback button, ⅞" d, "I'm a Joe Penner Quacker," black duck illus and rim lettering, yellow ground, 1930s 6.00

Sergeant Preston

Distance Finder, 2½ × 3½", diecut, silver, Quaker Cereal premium, 1955 .... 35.00

Dog Whistle, gold colored 45.00

Map, 7½ × 9½", Yukon Territory, c1955 .... 40.00

The Shadow

Lapel Stud, ¾" d, impressed image of Shadow in cape and hat, silvered, 1930s 275.00

Pinback Button, 1¼" d, celluloid, yellow and green, "The Shadow of Fu Manchu," 1930s 75.00

Red Skelton, post card, 3½ × 5½", radio show cast photo, matte finish, postmarked 1948 .... 20.00

RADIOS

If a radio does not work, do not buy it unless you need it for parts. If you do, do not pay more than $10.00. A radio that does not work and is expensive to repair is a useless radio.

The radio market has gone through a number of collecting crazes in the 1980s and 1990s. It began with Bakelite radios, moved on to figural and novelty radios, and now is centered on early transistors and 1940s plastic case radios. These crazes are often created by manipulative dealers. Be suspicious of the prices in any specialized price guide focusing on these limited topics. There are several general guides that do a good job of keeping prices in perspective.

Magazine: *Radio Age,* 636 Cambridge Road, Augusta, GA 30909.

Newspaper: *Antique Radio Classified,* 9511 Sunrise Blvd., Cleveland, OH 44133.

Clubs: Antique Radio Club of America, 81 Steeplechase Road, Devon, PA 19333; Antique Wireless Association, #4 Main St., Holcomb, NY 14469.

RCA, Model 96-X-1, table, white plastic, Art Deco style, curved wraparound louvers, raised top, AC, 1939, $185.00.

271

Adler, Model 201-A Royal, table, rect wood case, three front dials, five tubes, battery, 1924 . . . . **125.00**

Admiral

Model 4W19, portable, plastic, raised front dial, lattice grill, flex handle, right button, broadcast, AC/DC, battery, 1951 . . . . **40.00**

Model 7T10E-N, table, plastic, right front square dial, left horizontal louvers, two knobs, broadcast, AC/DC, 1947 . . . . **35.00**

Air Castle

Model 606-400WB, table, wood, right rect dial, left cloth grill with fretwork, two knobs, broadcast, battery, 1951 . . . . **35.00**

Model 9904, tombstone, wood, lower round dial, upper grill with fretwork, seven tubes, four knobs, broadcast, short wave, AC, 1934 . . . **140.00**

Airline, Model 14BR-514B, table, plastic, ivory painted, Art Deco style, right slide rule dial, push-button, left horizontal louvers, two knobs, 1946 . . . . . **100.00**

Atwater Kent, Model 165Q, cathedral, wood, right window dial, cloth grill with scrolled fretwork, three knobs, broadcast, short wave, battery, 1933 . . . . **225.00**

Balkeit, Model 44, portable, two-tone case, Art Deco style, center front grill with vertical fretwork, carrying case, 1933 . . . . **65.00**

Bendix, Model 55P2, table, plastic, imitation walnut, slide rule dial, vertical grill bars, rear handle, two knobs, broadcast, AC/DC, 1949 . . . . **40.00**

Bulova, Model 270, portable, transistor, leatherette, right round dial knob, plastic grill with crest, broadcast, battery, 1957 . . . . **35.00**

Continental, Model TR-208, portable, transistor, diagonally divided front, window dial, checkered grill, AM, battery, 1959 . . . . **25.00**

Crosley

Model 22CB, console, wood, upper front slanted "Giant Circle" dial, push-button, broadcast, short wave, FM, AC, 1941 . . . . **200.00**

Model E15TN, table, plastic, upper front dial, perforated grill with horizontal bar, two knobs, broadcast, AC/DC, 1953 . . . . **75.00**

Emerson

Model 69, console, walnut, round dial, lower cloth grill with three vertical bars, step-down top, AC, 1934 . . . . . **120.00**

Model 343, table, plastic, right dial, left horizontal grill bars, center veritcal bars, broadcast, short wave, AC, 1940 . . . . **50.00**

Model 656, portable, plastic, slide rule dial, half-moon grill, two thumbwheel knobs, handle, AC/DC, battery, 1950 . . . . **35.00**

Model CX-284, portable, cloth covered, inner right dial, left louvers, slide-in door, handle, two knobs, battery, 1939 . . . . **30.00**

Fada, Model 260B, table, black Bakelite and chrome, right front dial, left cloth grill with Art Deco style bars, two knobs, broadcast, AC/DC, 1936 . . . . . . **85.00**

Farnsworth, Model ET-061, table, plastic, upper front slide rule dial, lower checkered grill, two knobs, broadcast, short wave, AC/DC,m 1946 . . . . **60.00**

Firestone, Model 4-A-78, table, plastic, oblong panel, right semi-circular dial, left grill, two knobs, broadcast, AC/DC, 1950 . . . . **45.00**

General Electric

Model 62, table, clock, plastic, ivory, upper thumbwheel dial, left clock, horizontal grill bars, broadcast, AC, 1948 . . . . **45.00**

Model 221, table, wood, large lower slide rule dial, crosshatched grill, two knobs, broadcast, short wave, AC/DC, 1946 . . . . **50.00**

Model P776A, portable, transistor, leather case, right round dial, horizontal grill bars, handle, AM, battery, 1959 . . . . **25.00**

Howard, Model 307, table, wood, two-tone, lower front rect slide rule dial, upper grill, broadcast, short wave, AC, 1940 . . . . **55.00**

Majestic, Model 5T, table, clock, plastic, Art Deco style, center round dial surrounds clock, rear grill, two knobs, broadcast, AC/DC, 1939 . . . . **100.00**

Motorola

Model 5X11U, table, plastic, center round dial with inner perforated grill, stand, two knobs, broadcast, AC/DC, 1950 . . . . **40.00**

Model L14E, portable, transistor, plastic, right dial knob, lower horizontal bars, left knob, handle, AM, battery, 1960 . . . . **25.00**

Novelty, figural

Cabbage Patch Kids **15.00**

Coke Bottle **17.50**

Fire Chief **20.00**

Little Orphan Annie **20.00**

Pepsi Cooler, c1960, MIB **320.00**

Olympic, Model LP-163, table, plastic, right front slanted round dial, horizontal wrap-around louvers, two knobs **65.00**

Philco

Model 37-640, console, wood, upper round dial, lower grill with vertical fretwork, seven tubes, broadcast, short wave, AC, 1937 . . . . **135.00**

Model 38-2670, tombstone, wood, center round dial, upper cloth grill with vertical fretwork, eleven tubes, four knobs, 1938 . . . . **150.00**

Model 42-KR5, refrigerator, wood, rounded sides, right dial, left clock, curved base to fit top of refrigerator, 1942 . . . . **60.00**

RCA

Model 9TX23, Little Nipper, table, wood, Art Deco style, right front vertical slide rule "V" dial, left grill, two knobs, AC/DC, 1939 . . . . **75.00**

Model 9X572, table, plastic, thin lower front slide rule dial, bullhorn louvers, side knobs, broadcast, AC, 1949 . . . . **55.00**

Model 87K-1, console, wood, slanted slide rule dial, vertical grill bars, push-button, tuning eye, broadcast, short wave, 1938 . . . . **145.00**

Spartan, Model 309, portable, plastic, left front dial, center lattice grill, handle, broadcast, AC/DC, battery, 1953 . . . . . **35.00**

Stromberg-Carlson, Model 56, console, wood, hinged front door hides controls, Art Deco style fretwork, eight tubes, AC, 1933 . . . . **225.00**

Westinghouse, Model H-397T5, table, clock, plastic, maroon, small tombstone style, slide rule dial, upper alarm clock, lower grill, broadcast, AC, 1953 . . . . **45.00**

Zenith, Model 4-T-26, tombstone, wood, lower black dial, upper cloth grill with Art Deco style fretwork, four tubes, broadcast, short wave, AC, 1935 . . . . . **125.00**

RAILROADIANA

Most individuals collect by railroad, either one near where they live or one near where they grew up. Collectors are split about evenly between steam and diesel. Everyone is saddened by the current state of America's railroads. There are Amtrak collectors, but their numbers are small.

Railroad collectors have been conducting their own specialized shows and swap meets for decades. Railroad material that does show up at flea markets is quickly bought and sent into that market. Collectors use flea markets primarily to make dealer contacts, not for purchasing.

Railroad paper from timetables to menus is gaining in popularity as railroad china, silver-plated flat and hollow wares, and lanterns rise to higher and higher price levels. The key to paper ephemera is

that it bear the company logo and have a nice displayable presence.

Newsletters: *Key, Lock and Lantern*, P. O. Box 15, Spencerport, NY 14559; *U. S. Rail News*, P. O. Box 7007, Huntingdon Woods, MI 48070.

Clubs: Railroad Enthusiasts, 456 Main Street, West Townsend, MA 01474; Railroadiana Collectors Association, 795 Aspen, Buffalo Grove, IL 60089; Railway and Locomotive Historical Society, 3363 Riviera West Drive, Kellseyville, CA 95451.

Berry Dish, Union Pacific Railroad, china, Trenton China Company, $35.00.

Booklet, Santa Fe Railroad, 1927 . . . . **15.00**
Bowl, Union Pacific Railroad, china **35.00**
Butter Pat, 3¼" d, Atchinson, Topeka & Santa Fe Railroad, Sterling China **20.00**
Catalog, Vulcan Gasoline Locomotives, Vulcan Iron Works, Wilkes-Barre, PA, 28 pgs, illus, 1926–1927 . . . . **30.00**
Cup and Saucer, Southern Pacific Railroad, Prairie Mountain Wildflower, Syracuse China **75.00**
Hat, conductor's, Pennsylvania Railroad **60.00**
Lantern, 17½" h, Adlake Non Sweating Lamp, Chicago, yellow, red, blue, and clear lights **150.00**
Match Holder, Burlington Zephyr, stainless steel **22.00**
Napkin, Seaboard Railway, linen, pr **50.00**
Pass, Erie Railroad **8.00**
Plate, New York Central Railroad, veterans, diesel engine dec, 1951 . . . . **29.00**
Playing Cards, California Zephyr, 1950– 1960 . . . . **15.00**
Print, Santa Fe Railroad, pictures Indians, framed, 1949 . . . . **35.00**
Schedule
Pennsylvania Railroad Express, four-page folder, June 21, 1885 . . . . **20.00**

Philadelphia-Erie, framed, 1869 ..... **85.00**
Sugar Bowl, cov, Burlington Railroad, silver, double handles, Reed & Barton **75.00**
Switch Key, Chicago & Northwestern... **13.00**
Tablecloth, Baltimore & Ohio **20.00**
Tape Measure, N & W Railroad, 50 feet........................... **23.00**

RECORDS

Most records are worth between 25¢ and $1.00. A good rule to follow is the more popular the record, the less likely it is to have value. Who does not have a copy of Bing Crosby singing "White Christmas?"

Until the mid-1980s the principal emphasis was on 78 rpm records. As the decade ended, 45 rpm records became increasingly collectible. By 1990 33⅓ rpm albums, especially Broadway show related, were gaining in favor.

To find out what records do have value, check L. R. Dock's *1915–1965 American Premium Record Guide, Third Edition* (Books Americana, 1986) and Jerry Osborne's *The Official Price Guide To Records, Ninth Edition* (House of Collectibles, 1990).

By the way, maybe you had better buy a few old record players. You could still play the 78s and 45s on a 33⅓ machine. You cannot play any of them on a compact disc player.

Newspapers: *Discoveries*, P. O. Box 255, Port Townsend, WA 98368; *Goldmine*, 700 East State Street, Iola, WI 54990.

Children's, Me and My Teddy Bear, Roy Rogers, RCA Victor, dust cover, $8.00.

Children's
Barbie Sings, 45 rpm, Mattel Stock No. 840, 1961 copyright **35.00**
Bugs Bunny in Storyland, 78 rpm, Capitol Records, two record set, 1949 copyright **35.00**
Donald Duck Fire Chief/Donald Duck Song, 78 rpm, yellow plastic, Golden Record, early 1950s............. **15.00**
Mary Poppins, Sidewalk, 1968....... **10.00**
Pink Panther, RCA Victor, 1964...... **12.50**
Popeye the Sailorman, 33⅓ rpm, Rocking Horse Series, Diplomat Records, orig cardboard cov, 1960–70.......................... **20.00**
The Shmoo Club/The Shmoo is Clean, The Shmoo is Neat, 33⅓ rpm, Music You Enjoy, Inc, 7 × 7" paper envelope, 1949 copyright............. **50.00**
Super Heroes Christmas Album, 33⅓ rpm, Peter Pan Label, copyright DC Comics, 1977.................. **35.00**
Top Cat Theme Song, 45 rpm, Little Golden Record, orig paper cov, 1962 Hanna-Barbera copyright........ **15.00**
Movie, 45 rpm
Barbarella, Dyno Voice, 1968........ **22.00**
East of Eden, Columbia, 1957 .... **30.00**
It's A Mad, Mad, Mad, Mad World, United Artists, 1963 .... **18.00**
Lady Sings The Blues, Motown, 1972....................... **10.00**
Pennies From Heaven, Warner Bros, 1981....................... **12.50**
Rosemary's Baby, Dot, 1968 .... **25.00**
To Kill A Mockingbird, Ava, 1962 .... **30.00**
Rock N' Roll, 45 rpm
Beatles, All You Need Is Love, Capitol, 5964........................ **18.00**
Buddy Holly, Peggy Sue, Coral Label, 81191, 1957 .... **25.00**
Jerry Lee Lewis, Great Balls Of Fire, Sun, 281 .... **20.00**
Roy Orbison, Crying, Monument, picture sleeve, 1961............... **15.00**
Three Dog Night, Mama Told Me Not To Come, Dunhill, 1970 .... **5.00**
Television
The Addams Family, The Lurch/Wesley, Ted Cassidy, 45 rpm, Capitol Records, mid-1960s **24.00**
Batman and Robin, 33⅓ rpm, 12 songs including "Batman Theme" and "Joker is Wild," orig cov........ **18.00**
Captain Video and His Video Rangers, 78 rpm, RCA Victor, eight page storybook, punch-out figures, two record set, 1950s............... **80.00**
Dark Shadows, Curtis Records Inc, 11 × 22" poster featuring Barnabas and Quentin, copyright 1969 .... **40.00**
Dragnet, RCA Victor, 1953......... **55.00**
It's Howdy Doody Time, 33⅓ rpm, RCA Victor, TV broadcast record-

ings, orig cardboard sleeve, 1971
copyright **22.00**
Mr Ed Theme Song/Pretty Little Filly,
45 rpm, Golden Record label, copy-
right 1962 The Mr Ed Co. **35.00**
Songs From the Days of Rawhide,
Sheb Wooley, 33⅓ rpm, orig cov . . . **15.00**
Western
The Ballad of Davy Crockett, The
Sandpipers, 78 rpm, Little Golden
Record, orig jacket, 1955 . . . . **20.00**
Square Dance Hold Up, Hopalong
Cassidy, two records **75.00**

RED WING

Red Wing, Minnesota, was home to sev-
eral potteries. Among them were Red
Wing Stoneware Company, Minnesota
Stoneware Company, and The North Star
Stoneware Company. All are equally
collectible.

Red Wing has a strong regional base.
The best buys are generally found at flea
markets far removed from Minnesota.
Look for pieces with advertising. Red Wing
pottery was a popular giveaway product.

Club: Red Wing Collectors Society, Route
3, Box 146, Monticello, MN 55362.

*Vase, light blue glaze, impressed mark and
"#1151," 8⅛" h, $60.00.*

Ashtray, wing shape **35.00**
Bookends, pr, fan and scroll, green **15.00**
Bowl
Bobwhite, 5½" d **7.00**
Lute Song, fruit **7.50**
Plum Blossom, 5½" d **3.00**
Pompeii, cereal **7.00**
Bread Tray
Bobwhite **75.00**
Merrileaf **28.00**
Cup and Saucer
Bobwhite **10.00**
Capistrano **12.00**
Merrileaf **10.00**
Tampico **5.00**
Gravy
Driftwood, blue **15.00**
Merrileaf, cov, handle **20.00**
Plate
Bread and Butter
Bobwhite, 6" d **5.00**
Pompeii, 6½" d **3.00**
Chop, Capistrano, 12" d **15.00**
Dinner
Lotus, 10" d **5.00**
Plum Blossom **5.00**
Two Step **4.50**
Salt and Pepper Shakers, pr
Bobwhite **25.00**
Merrileaf **12.00**
Sugar, cov
Bobwhite **20.00**
Plum Blossom **6.00**
Vegetable Dish, divided
Bobwhite **25.00**
Lute Song **20.00**

ROBOTS

This category covers the friction, windup,
and battery operated robots made after
World War II. The robot concept is much
older, but generated few collectibles. The
grandfather of all modern robot toys is
Atomic Robot Man, made in Japan between 1948 and 1949.

Robots became battery operated by the
1950s. Movies of that era fueled interest in
robots. R2-D2 and C-3PO from *Star Wars*
are the modern contemporaries of Roby
and his cousins.

Robots are collected internationally.
You will be competing with the Japanese
for examples.

When buying at a flea market, take time
to make certain the robot is complete, op-
erates (carry at least two batteries of different sizes with you for testing), and has the
original box. The box is critical.

Great Garloo, battery-operated remote control, plastic, green, fabric waist cloth, Marx, $350.00.

Newsletter: *Robot and Space Toy*, 331 E. 71st St. #1F, New York, NY 10021.

Attacking Martian, 11" h, battery operated, litho tin, marked "made in Japan," 1960s.....................**175.00**

Dalek Money Box, 4" h, plastic, silver, gold, blue, and red accents, three gun attachments, coin slot in back, orig box, marked "Empire Made/copyright Cowan de Groot Ltd," 1965 BBC-TV copyright.......................**125.00**

Ding-A-Lings, 5½" h, plastic, Boxer, orange, black arms, blue legs, Topper Corp, c1970.....................**45.00**

Dr Who Talking K-9, 6" h, battery operated, plastic, gray, BBC, Palitoy, 1978.........................**100.00**

Extracter, 9½" h, plastic, blue, litho tin chest plate, silver accents, marked "Made In Japan," c1970 .....**50.00**

Geag, 8" h, built-in key, litho tin, soft rubber head, blue, green, yellow, and red, orig box, Takara, c1970........**125.00**

The Great Garloo, 18" h, battery-operated, green plastic, black, white, and tan tiger skin waist cloth, medallion, serving tray, Marx, 1960s...........**350.00**

Lost In Space, 12" h, plastic, red, metallic blue arms and legs, clear dome head, claw hands, Remco, copyright 1966 Space Productions................**400.00**

Mr Robot, 11" h, litho tin, silver, red arms, clear plastic head, Cragstan **400.00**

Radar Robot, 6½" h, built-in key, hard

plastic, orig box, S H, marked "Made In Japan," c1980.................**75.00**

Robert The Robot, 14" h, battery-operated, eyes light, orig box, Ideal, 1950s.........................**200.00**

Television, 14½" h, battery-operated, metal, large antenna, gold red eyes spin, screeching sound.............**350.00**

Toto, 8" h, plastic and litho tin, dark gray, orange feet and accents, marked "Made In Japan," c1960 ....**120.00**

Walking Twiki, 7" h, built-in key, plastic, walks forward, grip lock hands, Mego copyright 1979 Robert C Dille **45.00**

Windup Robot, 3½" h, built-in key, litho tin, plastic arms and legs, silver, red, white, blue, and yellow accents, Yone, Japan, 1970s....................**30.00**

ROCK 'N' ROLL

My Dad ought to be forced to do this category. He grew up in the Rock 'n' Roll era, but tuned it out. He claims this is why he can hear, and I cannot. I have heard rumors that he actually went to Bandstand in Philly, but he refuses to confirm them.

Most collectors focus on individual singers and groups. The two largest sources of collectibles are items associated with Elvis and the Beatles. As revivals occur, e.g., the Doors, new interest is drawn to older collectibles. The market has gotten so big that Sotheby's and Christie's hold Rock 'n' Roll sales annually.

Autograph
    Chubby Checker, 8 × 10", glossy black and white photo, black felt tip "It Ain't Over Till It's Over, Keep It Up, Love Chubby Checker 86".........**30.00**
    Fats Domino, 8 × 10", full color photo, sgd "God Bless And Rock Around The Clock"....................**20.00**
Book
    Who's Got The Button, Monkees, Western Publishing Co, copyright 1968 Raybert Productions Inc, 208 pgs...**24.00**
    Woodstock 69, Joseph J Sia, Scholastic Book Services, copyright 1970, 124 pgs..........................**25.00**
Costume, girl's, Davy Jones, molded thin plastic mask, one piece rayon mini dress with Monkees logo, orig box, Bland Charnas Co Inc, copyright 1967 Raybert Productions Inc............**60.00**
Doll
    Diana Ross, 19" h, molded hard plastic body, vinyl face and arms, gold glitter dress, orig box with Supremes

picture, Ideal, copyright 1969 Motown Inc 100.00

Dick Clark, 25" h, plush stuffed body, molded vinyl head and hands, marked "Juro" on back of neck, c1950 .... 150.00

Flasher Ring, Monkees 25.00

Game

Duran Duran Into The Arena, Milton Bradley, copyright 1985 .... 15.00

Kiss On Tour, 1978 copyright Aucoin Management 25.00

Hat

Purple People Eater, 11 × 13½", plastic, two diecut plastic pointed ears, orig display card 50.00

Rock Around The Clock, 9" l, blue felt, removable cardboard record on top, marked "Manufactured by Bing Crosby Phonocards Inc," c1950 .... 60.00

Jacket, tour, silver/gray satin, yellow and white embroidered couple dancing, black "Rock and Roll" above, embroidered 1963, back with gold, black, and white, "The Drifters On Broadway," tag inside marked "Ragtime Collection" 150.00

Magazine

Dick Clark Official American Bandstand Yearbook, 9 × 12", 40 pgs, color and black and white photos, c1950 ..... 25.00

Rock and Roll Songs, 8½ × 11", Vol 3, #11, Dec 1957 .... 15.00

Post Card, Rolling Stones, 4½ × 6½", two, perforated, "The Rolling Stones Exile On Main Street" in red, marked "Scene 1" and "Scene 2," c1972 ..... 15.00

Poster

Doors, 24 × 36", full color, green bottom border, white Doors logo, copyright 1968 Doors Production Corp 20.00

Fleetwood Mac, 33 × 46", full color, Jan 1970 concert, Deutsches Museum, Munich, West Germany 30.00

Grateful Dead Fan Club, 14 × 20", gold and blue, black and white photo, "The Golden Road To Unlimited Devotion," late 1960s 50.00

Jefferson Airplane, 13 × 19", Fillmore, April 11–13, late 1960s 50.00

Moody Blues, 18½ × 25½", stiff paper, April 1, 1970 concert, Terrace Ballroom, Salt Lake City, UT 50.00

Program

Freddie and the Dreamers, 10 × 13", 20 pgs, late 1960s 25.00

Peter and Gordon, 9 × 12", 16 pgs, c1964 .... 18.00

The Dave Clark 5, 10 × 13", 24 pgs, c1965 .... 45.00

Record, Buddy Holly, Peggy Sue/Every Day, 78 rpm, Coral label, 1957 .... 25.00

Sheet Music

Bill Haley and His Comets, *Rock Around the Clock,* 9 × 12", 2 pgs, copyright 1953 Myers Music **18.00**

Paul Anka, *Let The Bells Keep Ringing,* 9 × 12", 2 pgs, copyright 1958 Spanka Music Corp **12.00**

Tour Book, Rod Stewart, 9½ × 13½", 1978–79 World Tour, 96 pgs **15.00**

Yearbook, 8½ × 11", Dick Clark, 42 pgs, 1957 .... **25.00**

NORMAN ROCKWELL

The prices in this listing are retail prices from a dealer specializing in Rockwell and/or limited edition collectibles. Rockwell items are one of those categories for which it really pays to shop around at a flea market. Finding an example in a general booth at ten cents on the dollar is not impossible or uncommon.

When buying any Rockwell item, keep asking yourself how many examples were manufactured. In many cases, the answer is tens to hundreds of thousands. Because of this, never settle for any item in less than fine condition.

Plate, Triple Self Portrait, Gorham, $25.00.

Bell

Chilly Reception, 1980, Gorham **25.00**

Drum For Tommy, 1976, Dave Grossman **28.00**

Figurine

Back To School, Dave Grossman Designs, Inc **45.00**

Country Doctor, Rockwell Museum **35.00**

Music Lesson, Rockwell Museum **40.00**

Wet Sport, Gorham **40.00**

Ingot, Santa Planning A Visit, gold-plated
  silver, Hamilton Mint, 1975 . . . . **45.00**
Magazine Cover
  Colliers, March 1, 1919 . . . . **25.00**
  Family Circle, December, 1967 . . . . **8.00**
  Saturday Evening Post, August 30,
  1952. . . . . **40.00**
  TV Guide, May 16, 1970 . . . . **5.00**
Plate
  Campfire Story, Boy Scout Series, Gor-
  ham, 1978 . . . . **20.00**
  Dear Mother, Mother's Day Series,
  Lynell Studios, 1983 . . . . **25.00**
  Dwight D Eisenhower, Presidential Se-
  ries, Gorham, 1976 . . . . **35.00**
  First Prom, American Family Series,
  Rockwell Museum, 1979 . . . . **30.00**
  Gramps Meets Gramps, Christmas Se-
  ries, Royal Devon, 1980 . . . . **35.00**
  No Kings Nor Dukes, Huckleberry
  Finn Series, Dave Grossman De-
  signs, 1981. . . . . **40.00**
  Santa's Helpers, Christmas Series, Gor-
  ham, 1979 . . . . **20.00**
  Snow Queen, Christmas Series, Lynell
  Studios, 1979. . . . . **30.00**
  Somebody's Up There, Christmas Se-
  ries, Rockwell Society, 1979 . . . . **30.00**
  The Tycoon, Heritage Series, Rockwell
  Society, 1982. . . . . **20.00**
Stein, Pensive Pals, Gorham. **37.50**

ROSEVILLE POTTERY

Roseville rose from the ashes of the J. B.
Owen Company when a group of inves-
tors bought Owen's pottery in the late
1880s. In 1892 George F. Young became
the first of four succeeding generations of
Youngs to manage the plant.

Roseville grew through acquisitions of
another Roseville firm and two in Zanesville. By 1898 the company's offices were
located in Zanesville. Roseville art pottery
was first produced in 1900. The trade
name Rozane was applied to many lines.
During the 1930s Roseville looked for new
product lines. Utilizing several high gloss
glazes in the 1940s, Roseville revived its
art pottery line. Success was limited. In
1954 the Mosaic Tile Company bought
Roseville.

Pieces are identified as early, middle
(Depression era), and late pieces. Because
of limited production, middle period
pieces are the hardest to find. They also
were marked with paper labels that have
become lost over time. Some key patterns
to watch for are Blackberry, Cherry Blos-

Basket, Magnolia, brown tones, 386-12, $95.00.

som, Faline, Ferella, Futura, Jonquil,
Morning Glory, Sunflower, and Windsor.

Basket
  Peony, 10" d, yellow. **65.00**
  Poppy, pink, hanging **45.00**
Bookends, pr
  Bittersweet, green. **125.00**
  Snowberry, blue, 18-E **85.00**
Bowl
  Clematis, blue **50.00**
  Laurel, 9" l, oval, gold. **60.00**
  Snowberry, pink. **50.00**
  Wincraft, blue, 228–12 . . . . **85.00**
Candleholder, pr
  Magnolia, green **35.00**
  White Rose, 2¼" h **30.00**
Compote, Florentine **40.00**
Ewer
  Bushberry, 6" d, blue **65.00**
  Dawn, pink, 834–15. . . . . **450.00**
  Freesia, 6" d, green **35.00**
Jardiniere
  Donatello, 5" h, ivory. **70.00**
  Foxglove, blue, 659-5. . . . . **60.00**
  Poppy, 3" h, green **25.00**
Planter, Velmoss, 16" d **35.00**
Sugar, Snowberry, pink. **20.00**
Teapot, Peony, green **85.00**
Tea Set, Peony. **195.00**
Urn, Wincraft, blue, 256–5 . . . . **60.00**
Vase
  Clematis, green **65.00**
  Donatello, 4" h **45.00**
  Futura, 7" h, pink. **325.00**
  Magnolia, brown **35.00**
  Mostique, 10½" h **60.00**
  Pine Cone II, 8" h, brown. **75.00**
  Snowberry, 9" h, blue **90.00**
  Tuscany, 5" h, urn shape, pink **60.00**
  Wincraft, apricot, 275–12 . . . . **160.00**

Wall Pocket
    Florentine, 9½" l, brown **75.00**
    Tuscany, pink **65.00**
Window Box
    Magnolia, brown **45.00**
    Wincraft, 13×4", blue **55.00**

ROYAL DOULTON

Chances of finding Royal Doulton at flea markets are better than you think. It often is given as gifts. Since the recipients did not pay for it, they often have no idea of its initial value. The same holds true when children have to break up their parent's household. As a result, it is sold for a fraction of its value at garage sales and to dealers.

Check out any piece of Royal Doulton that you find. There are specialized price guides for character jugs, figures, and toby jugs. A great introduction to Royal Doulton is the two-volume videocassette entitled *The Magic of a Name*, produced by Quill Productions, Birmingham, England.

Newsletter: *Jug Collector*, P. O. Box 91748, Long Beach, CA 90809.

Club: Royal Doulton International Collectors Club, P. O. Box 1815, Somerset, NJ 08873.

Figurine, French Peasant, No. 2075, 9¼" h, $395.00.

Ashtray, John Barleycorn	**90.00**
Bowl, 9¼" d, marked "Rosalind"	**70.00**
Candlesticks, 10¼" h, floral, blue ground, pr	**150.00**
Character Jug	
Large, 5¼ to 7" h	
Drake	**120.00**
Pied Piper	**20.00**
Miniature, 2¼ to 2½" h	
Granny	**50.00**
Toby Philpots	**45.00**
Small, 3½ to 4" h	
Mr Micawber	**85.00**
St George	**65.00**
Tiny, 1¼" h	
Gardener	**40.00**
Paddy	**100.00**
Cup and Saucer, hp, c1892	**80.00**
Dickens Ware	
Ashtray, Tony Weller	**35.00**
Demitasse Cup and Saucer, Mr Pickwick on cup, Sam Weller on saucer	**55.00**
Sauce Dish, 5¼" d, Fat Boy	**45.00**
Tray, 4×5⅜", Barnaby Rudge	**50.00**
Figurine	
At Ease, HN2473	**225.00**

Autumn Breezes, HN1934, red dress	**175.00**
Beachcomber, HN2487	**165.00**
Bedtime, HN1978	**80.00**
Biddy Penny Farthing, HN1843	**175.00**
Boatman, HN2417	**165.00**
Bride, HN 2873	**150.00**
Buttercup, HN2309	**155.00**
Charlotte, HN2423	**165.00**
Christmas Morn, HN1992	**155.00**
Coachman, HN2282	**400.00**
Elegance, HN2264	**175.00**
Faith, HN3082	**125.00**
Gentleman from Williamsburg, HN2227	**200.00**
Graduate Male, HN 3017	**150.00**
Innocence, HN2842	**155.00**
Janet, HN1537	**155.00**
Jovial Monk, HN2144	**200.00**
Mandy, HN2476	**95.00**
Michelle, HN2234	**155.00**
Sailor's Holiday, HN 2442	**150.00**
Southern Belle, HN2229	**215.00**
Jug	
Rip Van Winkle	**250.00**
Sairey Gamp, small A mark	**65.00**
Mug, Captain Ahab	**55.00**
Pitcher, 8" h, Old Bob Ye Guard, pinchin type	**95.00**
Plaque, 14" d, Long John Silver	**125.00**
Plate	
6¾" d, Coaching Days	**60.00**

10" d, Shakespeare Plays **45.00**
Tankard, 6" h, Queen Elizabeth at Old
Moreton Hall, c1920 . . . . **20.00**
Tile, Shakespeare Ware, Much Ado
About Nothing **60.00**
Toby Jug
Beefeater, D6233 . . . . **45.00**
Happy John, 5½" h, #6070, c1939 . . . **45.00**
Tray, 5 × 11", Robin Hood Series **85.00**

Penny
Hexagonal, multicolored wool felt on
blue denim ground, green felt bor-
der, 27½ × 61" **205.00**
Runner, diamond design, wool, dark
solid colors and black on pale green
ground, 19 × 120" **375.00**
Rag, multicolored stripes, 72" l **75.00**

RUGS

You have to cover your floors with something. Until we have antique linoleum, the
name of the game is rugs. If you have to
own a rug, own one with some age and
character.

Do not buy any rug without unrolling it.
Hold it up in the air in such a way that
there is a strong light behind it. This will
allow you to spot any holes or areas of
heavy wear.

Braided, felt, alternating gray and blue
squares, red and black squares on bor-
der, 52 × 78" **85.00**
Character
Donald Duck and Nephews, cotton,
marked "Made in Belgium" **35.00**
Mickey Mouse, 22 × 40", Mickey
launching rocket, Thumper watch-
ing, white fringe, c1950 . . . . **50.00**
Snow White, forest scene, 40 × 21" . . . **65.00**
Embroidered, floral design, pastel colors
on light green ground, 48 × 72", 20th
C **125.00**
Hooked
Airedale dog, black and brown, stylized background, maroon trees, partially sheared, worn and repaired,
20 × 32" **95.00**
Barnyard scene, red barn, purple
house, green tree, ducks, chicks, and
birds, 11 × 39", PA, early 20th C **275.00**
Diamond design, multicolored, 17 ×
33½" **95.00**
Floral design, brown ground, 12½ ×
24" **65.00**
Sailing ship, round, zodiac signs, mari-
ner's compass, blue, maroon, yellow, beige, and white yarns, 86" d,
20th C **250.00**
Stag in oval landscape, striped border,
faded, 25 × 39" **95.00**
Sunburst design, yarn, 31 × 86" **200.00**
Tulips, striped ground, bright colors,
crocheted yarn edge, 28 × 52" **65.00**
"Welcome" and floral design on black
ground, 18½ × 24" **70.00**
Machine Woven, kittens on fence, red
poppies in foreground, 37 × 19" **415.00**

SALT AND PEPPER SHAKERS, PAIR

Hang on to your hats. Those great figural
salt and pepper shaker sets from the 1920s
through the 1960s have been discovered
by the New York art and decorator crowd.
Prices have started to jump. What does this
say about taste in America?

When buying a set, make certain it is a
set. Check motif, base, and quality of
workmanship. China shakers should have
no cracks or signs of cracking. Original
paint and decoration should be present on
china and metal figures. Make certain
each shaker has the right closure.

Salt and pepper shaker collectors must
compete with specialized collectors from
other fields, e.g., advertising and black
memorabilia. Dad keeps after me to find
him a pair shaped like jigsaw puzzle pieces.
I have not seen a pair yet nor found a
dealer who has seen one. Do you think
Dad will relent in his quest? Forget it.

Club: Novelty Salt & Pepper Shakers Club,
581 Joy Road, Battle Creek, MI 49017.

Lobsters, china, Japan, 3" h, $15.00.

Aunt Jemima, Uncle Moses, 3½" h, plastic, yellow, black, and white accents on
red ground, F & F Works, c1950 . . . . . **35.00**
Bed and Pillow, ceramic, nester type pattern, white with black trim **10.00**

Black Children, 3 pc set, 3″ high figures in 4″ h yellow and pink nursery basket, sgd ''Betson's Handpainted,'' Japan, 1930s **30.00**

Candelabra, 5½″ h, metal, silvered and black, clear plastic removable candle shakers, orig box, 1950s **18.00**

Captain Midnight and Joyce Ryan, plaster, painted, 1940s **100.00**

Chilly Willy and Charlie Chicken, 4″ h, china, 1958 Walter Lantz copyright . . . **80.00**

Dick Tracy and Tess Trueheart, 3″ h, plaster, painted, Famous Features copyright, 1942 . . . . **65.00**

Donald Duck, 3″ h, china, white glaze, blue, black, red, and yellow, Leeds, 1940s **25.00**

Don Winslow and Red Pennington, 3″ h, plaster, painted, both have blue outfits with white hats and accents, 1940s . . . **40.00**

Dutch Couple, ceramic, sitting on bench, kissing **12.50**

Gay 90's Hat Rack, 6½″ h, plastic and metal rack, yellow straw boater hat salt, black derby pepper, hats hang on rack, base holds toothpicks, orig box, 1954. . . . . **15.00**

Gondola, 3 pcs, 5½″ l, 2″ h, china, detachable shakers form hull of gondola, hp floral pattern on shakers, sgd ''MK,'' Occupied Japan **23.00**

Hammer and Nail, ceramic, gray nail, brown and black hammer **12.00**

Hillbillies in Barrels, yellow, gray, black, and brown, male salt, female pepper **14.00**

Indian and Squaw, 3″ h, composition wood, yellow and green accents on natural brown ground, copyright 1947. . . . . **28.00**

Kitchen Witch, ceramic, blue dress, red hat, one figure has white apron and is holding broom, Taiwan, 1979 . . . . **10.00**

Lobster, red on green base, claws held above head, attached by springs, Japan. **24.00**

Penguin, 3¼″ h, china, glazed, black and white, orange bill and webbed feet, marked Japan, 1930s **19.00**

Pixies, ceramic, blue outfit, yellow hair **10.00**

Smokey the Bear, 4″ h, china, yellow muzzle and hat, blue trousers, brown body, salt holding shovel, pepper holding bucket, 1960s **20.00**

Souvenir, State of Maryland, Parkcraft, 48 state series, figural state and blue clam shell, manufactured by Taneycomo Ceramic Factory, c1957 . . . . **20.00**

Squirrel, brown, ceramic **6.00**

Telephone and Directory, ceramic, black phone, white book with black lettering **8.00**

Television Set, 3″ h, hard plastic, brown, gold accents and legs, black and white picture of Art Linkletter on screen, on/off switch raises and lowers shakers, orig box, 1950s **65.00**

Toonerville Folks, 3½″ h, china, two men, smoking cigars, pepper has brown derby and coat, blue trousers, salt has white shirt and black trousers, marked Japan, 1930s **30.00**

Wrestlers, ceramic, one is held in body slam position above other wrestler's head. **21.00**

World's Fair, 1939 New York World's Fair, 4″ h, Perisphere and Trylon, hard plastic, one piece, orange, dark blue base **30.00**

SCHOOL MEMORABILIA

''School days, school days, good old golden rule days.'' Dad's been singing this refrain since he moved his operation into the former Vera Cruz elementary school in Pennsylvania. If you can't beat 'em, join 'em. Dad, this category is for you.

Alphabet Cards, diecut cardboard, A through Z, circus train theme. **12.00**

Bell, 9″ h, metal, turned wood handle **50.00**

Certificate
  Card of Merit, Model Scholar, attached cut girl scrap, 1889 . . . . **10.00**
  Certificate Of Honor, 60 Merits, printed, red and white, 1877 . . . . . . **20.00**
  Certificate Of Merit, 6¼ × 5⅜″, pen and ink and watercolor, floral border, ''Miss Margaret Ann Matthews has been four days at the head of her class . . . July 8, 1829,'' green, yellow, black, and red **165.00**
  Excelsior, Fifty Merits, white and blue, gold trim, 1866 . . . . **10.00**
  Reward of Merit
    Running zebras illus, printed, multicolored. **8.00**
    Schoolhouse illus, handpainted, reverse with student list, 1862. . . . . **6.00**
  School Card, ''Childhood,'' Longfellow poem, deer in forest illus, purple and white **10.00**

Clock
  Ingraham, 18¾″ h, oak, 8 day time, strike, and calendar movement, c1900. . . . . **325.00**
  Sessions, 27¼″ h, regulator, oak, 8 day time only brass movement, c1910. . . . . **300.00**

Desk
  Student's
    Formica, metal legs, rect top, c1950 . . . . **10.00**

Wood, cherry, top folds up, cast iron scrolled sides 125.00

Teacher's, wood, six drawers 80.00

Diploma, 19½ × 17¼", framed, PA, 1915. . . . . 50.00

Game

College Football, Milton Bradley, c1930. . . . . 45.00

Pinky Lee's Alphabet Game, 1950s . . . 7.00

Magazine, *Collier's*, "School Days" cov, Maxfield Parrish, 1908 . . . . 85.00

Map, wall mount type, United States, orig wood case, varnished 45.00

Penmanship Book, Palmer Penmanship, 135 pgs, 1908 . . . . 28.00

Pin, horseshoe shape, "East Side School, Elk Rapids, Michigan" 25.00

Pinback Button

Bowdoin College, 1¼" d, Elijah Kellogg portrait, "Commencement of 1940," black and white, 1940s 3.00

Gaston Grammar School, 1" d, multicolored, c1915 . . . . 2.00

Yale College, 1¼" d, campus and founder illus, "150 Years Ago," black, white, and blue, 1896–1900. . . . . 5.00

Pointer, wooden 18.50

Post Card

Lincoln Building, Quakertown Schools, PA, black and white 5.00

Pshawbetown School near Suttons Bay, MI, Beebe Photo, Indian children in front of one room school . . . 30.00

Program, Michigan vs Ohio, homecoming, football player illus cov, 36 pgs, 7 × 10", Nov 6, 1920 . . . . 40.00

Report Card, Pupil's Report, neatly filled in, 1900 . . . . 3.00

Sheet Music

Little Old Red Schoolhouse, Wheeler & Durham, 1890. . . . . 12.00

School Bells, Harris, Pfeiffer cov artist 10.00

School Day Sweethearts, Glen Edwards, 1923. . . . . 5.00

School Life, Charles L Johnson, Respectfully Dedicated to All Schools, 1912. . . . . 15.00

The Schoolhouse Blues, Irving Berlin, 1921. . . . . 10.00

Teacher's Pet, Allan Roberts and Jerome Brainin, 1937 . . . . 5.00

SEBASTIAN MINIATURES

Prescott Baston, the originator and first designer of Sebastian figures, began production in 1938 in a plant located in Marblehead, Massachusetts. The handpainted, lightly glazed figures, ranging in size from three to four inches, were usually based on characters from literature and history.

Club: Sebastian Collector's Society, 321 Central Street, Hudson, MA 01749.

Abraham Lincoln, seated 125.00

Betsy Ross, #129 . . . . 85.00

Evangeline, #12 . . . . 125.00

Gabriel #11 . . . . 135.00

Henry Hudson, #311 . . . . 175.00

Kennel Fresh, ashtray, #239 . . . . 300.00

Mark Twain, #315 . . . . 100.00

Parade Rest, #216 . . . . 100.00

Peggotty, #52-A 85.00

Shaker Man, #1 . . . . 150.00

St Joan of Arc, bronzed. 275.00

Thomas Jefferson, #124 . . . . 85.00

SECONDHAND ROSES

This is a catchall category—designed specifically for those items which are bought solely for their utilitarian use. Anyone who regularly attends country auctions, flea markets, or garage sales has undoubtedly seen his or her fair share of "recycled" household goods. Ranging from wringer washers to electronic video games, these products and appliances are neither decorative nor financially lucrative. They are strictly secondhand merchandise.

There is not much reason to focus on brand names, with two exceptions—Maytag and Craftsman. First, Maytag, widely regarded as the Cadillac of washers and dryers, consistently realizes higher prices than any other brand. Second, Craftsman hand tools, distributed by Sears, generally bring higher prices due to the company's generous replacement policy.

As a result of advances in technology and space constraints in modern homes, several larger sized appliances have little or no value on today's market. For example, console stereos and large chest freezers can often be had free for the hauling.

All items listed below are in good, clean condition. All parts are intact and appliances are in working order. The prices are designed to get you in the ballpark. Good luck in getting a hit.

APPLIANCES

Air Conditioner

Purchased in Spring **50–75.00**

Purchased in Fall. **25–40.00**
Dehumidifier **20–30.00**
Dish Washer, portable
  1–5 years old. **50–75.00**
  Over 5 years old **25–50.00**
Dryer
  Maytag
    1–5 years old. **100–150.00**
    Over 5 years old **75–100.00**
  Other Brands
    1–5 years old. **75.00**
    Over 5 years old **50.00**
Floor Polisher **10–20.00**
Freezer
  Chest
    Large Size, less than 5 years old . . .**5–10.00**
    Small Size, less than 5 years old **50.00**
    Over 5 years old, large or small **0–5.00**
  Upright
    Apartment Size
      1–5 years old. **85–100.00**
      Over 5 years old. **50–75.00**
    Full Size
      1–5 years old. **125–175.00**
      Over 5 years old. **75–100.00**
Humidifier **10–20.00**
Iron **2–5.00**
Microwave Oven
  Large, 1–5 years old **75–85.00**
  Small, 1–5 years old **50–60.00**
  With electronic controls or built-in
    turntable, add **5–10.00**
Mixer, counter top, two bowls. **10–12.00**
Refrigerator
  Apartment Size
    1–5 years old. **75–85.00**
    Over 5 years old **35–50.00**
  Full Size
    1–5 years old. **150–175.00**
    Over 5 years old **100–125.00**
  Side-by-Side Model, deduct. **10–20.00**
  With Ice Maker, add **20.00**
Rug Shampooer **15–20.00**
Sewing Machine, modern, electric
  Cabinet Model
    Standard, no frills **25–50.00**
    With assorted attachments and
      stitching variations **50–75.00**
  Portable. **25–30.00**
Small Kitchen Appliances (blender,
  corn popper, electric knife, hand-
  held mixer, toaster) **2–10.00**
Space Heater. **5–15.00**
Toaster/Oven **10–20.00**
Vacuum Cleaner, canister or up-
  right. **15–35.00**
Washer
  Apartment Size, 1–5 years old **50–75.00**
  Full Size
    Maytag
      1–5 years old. **200–225.00**
      Over 5 years old. **150–175.00**
    Other Brands
      1–5 years old. **75–100.00**

Over 5 years old. **50–75.00**
Wringer Washer
  Maytag
    Square aluminum tub. **200–250.00**
    Other models. **50–60.00**
  Other Brands. **25–35.00**

CHILDREN'S ITEMS
Car Seat. **5–10.00**
Crib, wood, mattress **20–30.00**
Highchair, metal, plastic, and vinyl . . **10–15.00**
Playpen, tubular steel frame, mesh
  sides. **10–15.00**
Stroller **10–15.00**

ENTERTAINMENT & RECREATION
Card Table, four chairs **20–25.00**
Entertainment Center, adjustable
  shelves. **20–35.00**
Exercise Equipment
  Bicycle, stationary **15–25.00**
  Rowing Machine **20–30.00**
  Weight Lifting Bench **5–15.00**
  Weights, barbell, two dumbbells,
    and 110 lbs of weights. **25–30.00**
Movie Projector, 8mm or Super 8 . . . **10–25.00**
Projection Screen **10–15.00**
Slide Projector **15–25.00**
Stereo
  Console, wood cabinet, record
    player and radio combination . . **0–25.00**
  Turntable, two speakers, name
    brand. **10–20.00**
Television
  Black and White, console or portable,
    any age **0–5.00**
  Color
    Console
      1–5 years old. **60–70.00**
      Over 5 years old. **30–40.00**
    Portable
      1–5 years old. **50–60.00**
      Over 5 years old. **40–50.00**
    With remote control, add **15.00**
Television Stand, casters **5–10.00**
Television Snack Tables, set of four,
  rack **2–5.00**
VCR
  Beta **0.00**
  VHS
    1–5 years old. **100–125.00**
    Over 5 years old **75–85.00**
Video Game System (Genesis,
  Nintendo, Sega) **40–50.00**

MISCELLANEOUS HOUSEHOLD GOODS
Dinnerware, service for eight **20–25.00**
Flatware, service for eight, stainless
  steel. **15–20.00**
Linens (afghans, bedspreads, blan-
  kets) like-new condition **5–10.00**
Pots and Pans, 8 pc set
  Aluminum **25–30.00**
  Copper Bottom **50–75.00**

Stainless Steel	35–50.00
Stemware, three sizes, 24 pcs.	35–45.00
Wardrobe, metal.	15–20.00
Water Glasses, set of eight	2–5.00

OFFICE EQUIPMENT

Answering Machine	10–15.00
Desk, steel, gray, industrial	5–10.00
Filing Cabinet, metal	
Two Drawer	20–25.00
Four Drawer	40–45.00
Metal Shelving	5–10.00
Telephone	5–10.00
Typewriter	
Electric	35–40.00
Manual	10–12.00

TOOLS AND GARDENING EQUIPMENT

Garden Tools	
Electric Hedge Trimmer, edger, leaf blower	8–15.00
Hoe, rake, shovel	2–5.00
Hand Tools (hammer, pliers, saw, screwdriver, wrench)	
Craftsman	5–8.00
Other Brands.	2–5.00
Ladder	
Extension	
Aluminum	45–50.00
Wood	25–30.00
Step	
4'	8–10.00
6'	12–15.00
Lawn Mower	
Electric	15–25.00
Gas	
Purchased in Spring	35–50.00
Purchased in Fall.	25–40.00
Rotary	0–5.00
Power Tools (drill, grinder, saber saw, sander)	10–20.00
Snow Blower	
Purchased in Spring	35–50.00
Purchased in Fall.	45–60.00
Weed Wacker	
Electric	15–20.00
Gas.	20–30.00
Wheelbarrow	10–20.00

SEWING ITEMS

This is a wide open area. While many favor sterling silver items, only fools overlook objects made of celluloid, ivory, other metals, plastic, and wood. An ideal special collection would be sewing items that contain advertising.

Collecting sewing items has received a big boost as a result of the Victorian craze. During the Victorian era a vast assortment of practical and whimsical sewing devices were marketed. Look for items such as tape measures, pincushions, stilettos for punchwork, crochet hooks, and sewing birds (beware of reproductions).

Modern sewing collectors are focusing on needle threaders, needle holders, and sewing kits from hotels and motels. The general term for this material is "Twenty Pocket" because pieces fit neatly into twenty pocket plastic notebook sleeves.

Box, red leather, paper center medallion of girl in yellow dress, 5$^{1}/_{16}$ × 4 × 1$^{1}/_{2}$", $20.00.

Booklet, *How To Make Children's Clothes,* Singer, 1930	8.00
Bookmark, Merrick Spool Cotton	10.00
Buttonhole Scissors, Germany	12.00
Catalog, McCall's Patterns, costumes for all occasions, 48 pgs, 1904	38.00
Darner	
Egg, black	4.00
Slipper shape, maple wood base, 5$^{1}/_{2}$" l	8.00
Darning Kit, folder, leather, dog on cov	12.00
Manual	
Butterick, needle art, color illus, 1922.	20.00
Singer, #221	35.00
Mending Kit, Bakelite, red and ivory	20.00
Needle Book, A Century of Progress, complete	6.00
Needle Case, bone	
Awl tip, turned	60.00
Brass, top turns	35.00
Parasol, missing Stanhope	55.00
Pincushion	
Advertising, Traveler's Insurance	8.00
Doll, arms at head	10.00
Persian Cat, Victorian, figural, potmetal	52.00
Turtle, nodder type	55.00
Sewing Box, 10$^{3}/_{4}$" d, 6$^{1}/_{2}$" h, wicker, pink	75.00

Tape Measure
   Advertising
      Hoover Vacuum Cleaner, figural,
         canister type **75.00**
      Portland Cement. **25.00**
      Figural, Indian, marked "Japan". **20.00**
      Walnut, squirrel charm pull. **40.00**
Thimble
   Advertising,   Hoover-Home-Happi-
      ness **10.00**
   Child's, pewter, "For A Good Girl" . . . **11.00**
Trade Card, J P Coats, girls with rab-
   bits. **4.00**

SHAWNEE POTTERY

The Shawnee Pottery Company was
founded in Zanesville, Ohio, in 1937. The
plant, formerly home to the American
Encaustic Tiling Company, produced approximately 100,000 pieces of pottery per
working day. Shawnee produced a large
selection of kitchenware, dinnerware, and
decorative art pottery. The company
ceased operations in 1961.

*Teapot, Tom the Piper's Son, yellow hat, pink
pig spout, light blue handle, marked "Pat.
USA," 7" h, 8" w, $38.00.*

Ball Jug
   Flower & Fern **45.00**
   Quill, marked "USA 12" **40.00**
   Valencia, green, marked "USA" **15.00**
Bank, bulldog **90.00**
Butter Dish, cov, King Corn, marked
   "#72" **48.00**
Coffeepot, cov, Sunflower pattern,
   marked "USA" **120.00**
Cookie Jar
   Dutch Girl, cold paint, yellow hair, red
      bows, buttons, and cuffs, marked
      "USA" **50.00**

Fruit Basket, marked "Shawnee
   84". **125.00**
Jo Jo the Clown, marked "Shawnee
   12". **200.00**
King Corn, marked "#66" **135.00**
Sailor, white, marked "USA". **100.00**
Smiley,   shamrocks,   marked
   "USA" **175.00**
Creamer
   Elephant, white, gold trim, marked
      "Pat. USA" **80.00**
   Puss 'n Boots, yellow and green, pink
      bow, marked "Shawnee 85" **40.00**
   Snowflake, marked "USA" **15.00**
Figurine, raccoon, floral decals, gold
   trim **75.00**
Match   Holder,   Fernware,   yellow,
   marked "USA" **25.00**
Mixing Bowl, King Corn, nesting, set of
   three, marked "Shawnee 8, 6," and
   "5". **85.00**
Pie Bird, pink base **28.00**
Pitcher
   Bo Peep, floral decals on dress, gold
      trim and staff, marked "Pat. Bo
      Peep". **150.00**
   Fruits, marked "Shawnee 80" **65.00**
   White Corn, gold trim, marked
      "USA". **95.00**
   Yellow Tilt, marked "USA 10". **35.00**
Salt and Pepper Shakers, pr
   Large
      Blue Jug. **28.00**
      Charlie Chickens, gold trim **55.00**
      Flower and Fern, square, yellow . . . **25.00**
      Muggsy, glue ribbon **50.00**
      Winnie and Smiley, green bibs. **60.00**
   Small
      Ducks. **32.00**
      Flowerpots, gold trim **28.00**
      King Corn **15.00**
      Milk Cans, paper label **12.00**
      Owls, gold trim **38.00**
      Wheelbarrows. **12.00**
Salt Box, cov, Fernware, yellow, marked
   "USA". **32.00**
Sock Darner, blue base, marked
   "USA". **30.00**
Spoon Rest, lobster, red **75.00**
Sugar Bowl
   Bucket, blue trim, marked "Northern
      USA 1042" **38.00**
   Fruit Basket, marked "Shawnee
      83". **32.00**
Sugar Shaker, White Corn, gold trim . . . **85.00**
Syrup Pitcher, Valencia, orange. **12.00**
Teapot, cov
   Cottage, marked "USA 7" **250.00**
   Granny Ann, marked "USA". **65.00**
   Pennsylvania   Dutch,   marked
      "USA" **80.00**
   Rose, emb, gold trim, marked
      "USA" **50.00**
Utility Jar, cov, basketweave, green,
   marked "USA" **60.00**

SHEET MUSIC

Just like post cards, this is a category whose ten cent and quarter days are a thing of the past. Decorators and dealers have discovered the cover value of sheet music. The high ticket sheets are sold to specialized collectors, not sheet music collectors.

You can put a sheet music collection together covering almost any topic imaginable. Be careful about stacking your sheets on top of one another. The ink on the covers tends to bleed. If you can afford the expense, put a sheet of acid free paper between each sheet. Do not, repeat do not, repair any tears with Scotch or similar brand tape. It discolors over time. When removed, it often leaves a gummy residue behind.

Clubs: National Sheet Music Society, 1597 Fair Park, Los Angeles, CA 90041; New York Sheet Music Society, P. O. Box 1214, Great Neck, NY 11023; Remember That Song, 5821 North 67th Avenue, Suite 103-306, Glendale, AZ 85301; The Sheet Music Exchange, P. O. Box 69, Quicksburg, VA 22847.

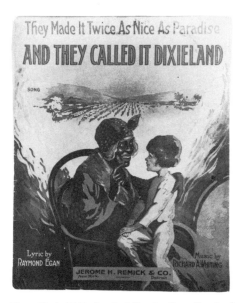

They Made It Twice As Nice As Paradise And They Called It Dixieland, Raymond Egan, 1916, $8.00.

After The War Is Over, 1917 . . . .   5.00
Angel Eyes, Nat King Cole 5.00

As Long As I Have You, 9 × 12", 1957 Gladys Music Inc copyright 15.00
Beyond The Blue Horizon, 1930 . . . .   6.00
By The Old Mill Where Waterlilies Grow, Morgan, 1912 . . . .   2.00
Creeque Alley, Mamas and the Papas, 1967. . . . . 10.00
Cryin' For The Moon, Conley, 1926 . . . .   1.00
Don't Think Twice, It's Alright, Peter, Paul & Mary, 1963 . . . . 12.00
For Me And My Gal, Judy Garland 8.00
Good Bye Broadway Hello France, 1917. . . . .   8.00
Heartbreak Hotel, 9 × 12", bluetone photo, 1956 Tree Publishing Co copyright 25.00
Hinky Dinky Parlay Voo, Ruth Wales and Doris Relyea photos, 1921 copyright 8.00
I'll Meet You In Chicago, 9 × 12" folder, 1933 copyright 15.00
Land Of Long Ago, Charles Knight, 1912. . . . .   2.00
Love Ain't Nothin' But The Blues, Alter, 1929. . . . .   1.00
Military Waltz, 1917 copyright 8.00
Old Black Joe, 1906 . . . .   8.00
Over The Rainbow, Judy Garland 15.00
Over There, George M Cohan, 1917 copyright. 15.00
Panama Canal March, canal photo illus, 1913. . . . . 20.00
Peg O' My Heart, Bryan/Fisher, 1913 . . .   4.00
Roses In The Rain, Frank Sinatra. 5.00
Song Of The South, Disney, 1946 . . . . . . 10.00
Sugar Daddy, The Jackson 5, 1971 . . . . .   5.00
Sunbonnet Sue, Cobb, 1908 . . . .   7.00
Teenage Crush, Tommy Sands, 1956 Central Songs Inc copyright 10.00
That's the Meaning of Uncle Sam, 1916. . . . . 15.00
The Stars And Stripes Forever, John Philip Sousa, 1897 copyright 25.00
Toot Toot Tootsie, Al Jolson, 1922. . . . . . 10.00
When I Lost You, Irving Berlin, 1912 . . .   4.00
Who Will Care For Micky Now?, Eugene T Johnston. 20.00
Why Should I Fall For One Little Girl?, 9 × 12", Fred Fisher Music Co, 1936 copyright. 25.00
You Oughta Be In Pictures, 1934. . . . . . .   4.00
Your Cheatin' Heart, Hank Williams, 1952. . . . .   4.00

SHOE-RELATED COLLECTIBLES

This is a category with sole. Nothing more needs to be said.

Alarm Clock
Peter's Shoes, Art Deco, New Haven Clock Co, c1930 . . . . 50.00

Advertising Whistle, Endicott-Johnson Shoes, tin, yellow and red, $15.00.

Star Brand Shoes, Gilbert	**50.00**
Ball, Poll Parrot Shoes, rubber, 1930s	**20.00**
Baseball Bat, Weatherbird Shoes	**35.00**
Box, Fine Shoes, lithographed	**50.00**
Catalog, Hood Rubber Footwear, 1916	**25.00**

Clicker

Peters Weatherbird Shoes, litho tin, multicolored, c1930	**25.00**
Poll Parrot Shoes	**13.00**

Counter Display

Barton's Dyanshine Shoe Polish, holds twelve tins	**25.00**
Cavalier Shoe Polish, tin, revolving, orange, Cavalier man on top	**90.00**
Marbles and Bag, Weatherbird Shoes	**20.00**

Pinback Button

Battle Axe Shoes, 1¼" d, full color Confederacy flag, black, white, and red logo, white ground, black inscriptions, 1907	**45.00**
Buster Brown Shoes, ⅞" d, multicolored, portrait of Buster and Tige, white ground, black letters, early 1900s	**90.00**
Griffiths Queen City Shoe, ⅞" d, black and white, red logo, 1901–1912	**20.00**
Omaha Made Shoes, 1½" d, black and white high button shoe, blue and white rim, early 1900s	**40.00**
Tennent Shoe Co, multicolored	**25.00**
Top Round Shoe, ⅞" d, multicolored, winged cherubs scaling ladder to place high top shoe on top of world	**22.50**

Pocket Mirror

Buster Brown Shoes, 1¼" h, multicolored portrait of Buster and Tige holding wooden shoe last above inscription, early 1900s	**150.00**
Shoe Worker's Union, c1910	**38.00**
Post Card, Sterling Quality Shoes, Smith Wallace Shoe Co, c1907	**9.50**
Poster, Weatherbird Shoes, multicolored, rooster weathervane	**75.00**
Premium, Poll Parrot Shoes, Howdy Doody Detective Disguises, unused	**70.00**
Puzzle, Red Goose Shoes	**20.00**
Repair Box, wood, dovetailed, tools, soles, heels, and nails	**85.00**

Repair Stand, iron	**32.00**

Shoe Horn

A S Beck Shoes, metal, 1940s	**5.00**
Queen Quality, 2 × 6", celluloid, curled handle, color portrait of lady, c1900, pr	**35.00**
Shoe Polish, American Shoe Polish Co, suede treatment, tin box, paper label	**20.00**
Shoe Shine Kit, child's, Shinola, 1953, MIB	**20.00**
Stickpin, 1" l, Red Fox Shoes, oval, multicolored, hunting dogs chasing fox, brass back with inscription, early 1900s	**40.00**
Store Display, 38 × 23", US Royal Footwear, artist sgd	**85.00**
String Holder, Red Goose Shoes, cast iron	**1,200.00**

Trade Card

A. S. T. Co. Shoe Tips, Father Time, Donaldson Bros	**9.00**
Bixby & Co Shoe Polish, Lady Liberty holding shoe polish	**8.00**
Herrods $5.00 Shoes, drum shape, Bufford Litho	**7.50**

SILVER FLATWARE

Popularity of a pattern, not necessarily age, is the key to pricing silver flatware. Since most individuals buy by pattern, buy only from dealers who have done the research and properly identified each piece that they are selling. Deduct 50 percent from the value if a piece has a monogram.

If you are planning to buy a set, expect to pay considerably less than if you were buying the pieces individually. Set prices should be bargain prices.

Alaska Silver, German Silver, Lashar Silver, and Nickel Silver are alloys designed to imitate silver plate. Do not be fooled.

Asparagus Fork, Lancaster, Gorham	225.00
Asparagus Tongs, Chrysanthemum, Tiffany	850.00
Beef Fork, 5¼" l, Chrysanthemum, Durgin	165.00

Berry Spoon

Isis, Gorham	375.00
Lily, pierced, Whiting	295.00
Bonbon, Pynchon, Lunt	15.00
Butter Knife, Governor, chased, Tiffany	15.00
Butter Pick, Orange Blossom, Alvin	125.00
Carving Set, Cactus, Jensen	300.00
Cheese Knife, Allure, Rogers, 1939	4.50
Cheese Scoop, Cluny, Gorham	195.00
Citrus Spoon, Queen, Howard	25.00

Cocktail Fork
  Blossom, 5½" l, Jensen............. **40.00**
  Lady Sterling, Weidlich **10.00**
Cocktail Stirrer, Royal Danish, International........................ **75.00**
Cold Meat Fork, Repousse, Kirk **125.00**
Cream Soup, Castle Rose, Royal Crest... **15.00**
Croquette Server, 8¾" l, Chrysanthemum, pierced, Durgin............. **575.00**
Demitasse Spoon, Holly, Tiffany **55.00**
Dinner Fork, Chrysanthemum, Tiffany........................... **95.00**
Egg Spoon, Medallion, Gorham....... **65.00**
Fish Knife, 10½" l, Acorn, Jensen...... **115.00**
Fruit Knife, Chrysanthemum, sterling blade, serrated, Tiffany............. **95.00**
Gravy Ladle, Rose, Kirk **85.00**
Hors d'oeuvre Fork, 3¾" l, Acorn, Jensen........................ **40.00**
Ice Cream Knife, Cluny, Gorham **375.00**
Jelly Knife, Lily of the Valley, Whiting........................... **295.00**
Lemon Fork, Normandie, Wallace...... **16.00**
Lettuce Fork, Orange Blossom, Alvin ... **185.00**
Luncheon Fork, Spanish Lace, Wallace **14.00**
Olive Spoon, Chantilly, Gorham **95.00**
Pastry Fork, Cattail, Durgin **75.00**
Pie Server, Blackberry, serrated, Tiffany........................... **850.00**
Poultry Shears, 10¼" l, Blossom, Jensen........................... **300.00**
Ramekin Fork, Chantilly, Gorham **60.00**
Salad Fork, Star, Reed & Barton....... **20.00**
Salad Set
  Fiorito, Shiebler **275.00**
  Grape, gold wash, Dominick & Haff... **450.00**
Sardine Fork, Pynchon, Lunt.......... **15.00**
Serving Spoon, 9¼" l, Blossom, Jensen........................... **300.00**
Soup Ladle, Lotus, Gorham **350.00**
Stuffing Spoon, Georgian, Towle....... **695.00**
Sugar Sifter Ladle, Buttercup, Gorham....................... **75.00**
Tablespoon, Medallion, Duhme **115.00**
Teaspoon
  Chateau Rose, Alvin............... **15.00**
  Formality, State House............. **13.00**
Tomato Server, Edgewood, International........................... **185.00**
Vegetable Fork, large, Queen, Howard **195.00**

SILVER PLATED

G. R. and H. Ekington of England are credited with inventing the electrolytic method of plating silver in 1838. In late nineteenth century pieces, the base metal was often Britannia, an alloy of tin, copper, and antimony. Copper and brass also were used as bases. Today the base is usually nickel silver.

Rogers Bros., Hartford, Connecticut, introduced the silver-plating process to the United States in 1847. By 1855 a large number of silver-plating firms were established.

Extensive polishing will eventually remove silver plating. However, today's replating process is so well developed that you can have a piece replated in such a manner that the full detail of the original is preserved.

Identifying companies and company marks is difficult. Fortunately there is Dorothy Rainwater's *Encyclopedia of American Silver Manufacturers, 3rd Edition* (Schiffer Publishing, 1986).

Mustard Pot, red insert, 4" h, $55.00.

Ashtray, floral dec rim **10.00**
Bowl, figural squirrel perched on fancy rim, Rockford **40.00**
Bread Tray, Daffodil **95.00**
Butter Dish, three pcs, base, lid, and insert, delicate double rows of tiny beading, cut glass drip trap, Meriden Silver Plate Co **50.00**
Cake Basket, swing handle, Tufts **55.00**
Cheese Ball Frame, 5" d, mechanical, elaborate border, E G Webster & Sons...................... **75.00**
Cigar Case, 5" l, scrollwork and leaf dec, holds three cigars **35.00**
Cigar Holder, 10½" h, champagne bottle, beaded trim, engraved "CIGARS," Graham Silver marks **75.00**
Creamer and Sugar, marked "Meriden" **100.00**
Cup, baby's, two handles, monogrammed...................... **20.00**
Flask, 10" h, double, canvas carrying case, England **40.00**
Flatware, luncheon set, service for 12, forks and knives, two crumbers, ser-

ving knife and fork, ivory handles, England **125.00**
Ice Bucket, Baroque pattern, thermos lined, Wallace **225.00**
Knife Rest, dolphin, marked "Pairpoint" **35.00**
Matchsafe, dog and quail dec **25.00**
Salt, ornate, blue ruffled top, liner **25.00**
Syrup, geometric and floral strap work body, figural finial, Meriden, 1865, replated **85.00**
Tea Strainer, wood handle, Hallmark, 1917 .... **30.00**
Toothpick, barrel shape, Aurora **15.00**
Umbrella Stand, 20½″ h, elongated trumpet shape, interlaced flowering branches, H Wilkinson & Co, copper showing **225.00**
Wick Trimmer, floral dec, tray, Hallmark **85.00**

SOAKIES

Soaky bottles are plastic bubble bath containers molded in the shape of popular children's characters. The first Soakies were marketed by the Colgate-Palmolive Company in the 1960s and were an innovative marketing tool designed to convince kids (especially boys) that "Bathtime is Funtime."

As with any profitable idea, copycats soon appeared. One successful line produced by the Purex Company was called the Bubble Club. These containers were fashioned after Hanna-Barbera characters.

The bottles included in this category are all plastic figural containers and range in size from 6″ to 11″ high.

Avon, Superman, 9½″ h, 1978 .... **10.00**
Bubble Fun Bath, baseball player, "Let's Go Mets," 10½″ h, late 1960s **45.00**
Colgate-Palmolive
  Alvin, Chipmunks, 10″ h, mid 1960s **8.00**
  Baloo, The Jungle Book, 7″ h, 1966 .... **15.00**
  Bam-Bam, The Flintstones, 1960s **15.00**
  Batman, 10″ h, 1966 .... **50.00**
  Brutus, 10″ h, 1960s **20.00**
  Bullwinkle, 10½″ h, 1966 .... **25.00**
  Cinderella, 10½″ h, 1960s **15.00**
  Deputy Dawg, 9½″ h, 1966 .... **15.00**
  Dick Tracy, 10¼″ h, 1965 .... **20.00**
  Donald Duck, 9″ h, 1960s **30.00**
  Felix the Cat, 10″ h, 1960s **30.00**
  Mickey Mouse, 7″ h, late 1960s **18.00**
  Mr Magoo, 10″ h, mid 1960s **15.00**
  Mummy, 10″ h, 1960s **60.00**

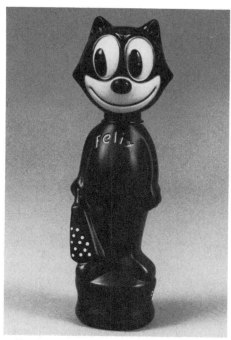

Felix the Cat, Colgate-Palmolive, black, 1960s, 10″ h, $30.00.

  Popeye, 10″ h, 1960s **20.00**
  Robin, 9½″ h, 1966 .... **50.00**
  Rocky Squirrel, 9″ h, 1966 .... **25.00**
  Smokey Bear, 9″ h, mid 1960s **10.00**
  Top Cat, 10″ h, mid 1960s **15.00**
  Tweety, 8½″ h, late 1960s **15.00**
  Wendy, Casper the Friendly Ghost, 10½″ h, 1960s **12.00**
  Wolfman, 10″ h, 1960s **65.00**
Ducair Bioessence Inc, Astrosniks, 1984 .... **25.00**
Purex Corp
  Atom Ant, 9½″ h, 1960s **20.00**
  Augie Doggie, Quick Draw McGraw Show, 10″ h, mid 1960s **35.00**
  Blabber, Quick Draw McGraw Show, 10½″ h, mid 1960s **12.00**
  Breezly, Peter Potamus Show, plastic trap in bottom, 9″ h, 1967 .... **65.00**
  Cecil, Disguise Kit, 8″ h, early 1960s **50.00**
  Droop-A-Long Coyote, Magilla Gorilla Show, 12″ h, mid 1960s **12.00**
  Lippy the Lion, 11½″ h, 1960s **20.00**
  Morocco Mole, Atom Ant Show, 7″ h, late 1960s **20.00**
  Mr Jinks, holding Pixie and Dixie, 10″ h, early 1960s **12.00**
  Mush Mouse, 11½″ h, 1960s **20.00**
  Peter Potamus, 10½″ h, mid 1960s ... **20.00**
  Punkin' Puss, Magilla Gorilla Show, 11½″ h, mid 1960s **30.00**

Ricochet Rabbit, Magilla Gorilla Show, movable arm holds six-shooter, 10½" h, mid 1960s **45.00**

Secret Squirrel, 10" h, 1960s **25.00**

Snagglepuss, 9" h, 1960s **25.00**

Squiddly Diddly, Atom Ant Show, 10½" h, late 1960s **20.00**

Touche Turtle, 10½" h, 1960s **25.00**

Winsome Witch, Atom Ant Show, 10½" h, late 1960s **20.00**

Yakki Doodle, 6" h, 1960s **20.00**

Yogi Bear, 1967 .... **30.00**

SOAP COLLECTIBLES

At first you would not think that a lot of soap collectibles would survive. However, once you start to look around, you'll see no end to the survivors. Many Americans are not as clean as we think.

There is no hotel soap listed. Most survivors sell for 50¢ to $2.00 per bar. Think of all the hotels and motels that you have stayed at that have gone out of business. Don't you wish you would have saved one of the soap packets? You don't? What are you—normal or something?

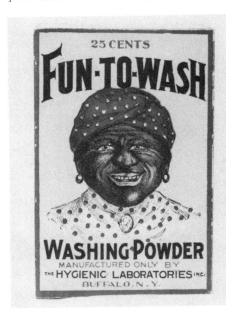

Box, Fun-To-Wash Washing Powder, cardboard, Hygienic Laboratories, Inc., Buffalo, NY, 7¼" h, $15.00.

Bookmark, Dingman's Soap, illus of baby **8.75**

Box

Bee Soap, wood, paper label **65.00**

Capitol Scouring Soap, wood **15.00**

Colgate Fab, sample size, crashing sea scene **8.00**

Daylight Soap, wood **20.00**

Brochure

Bon Ami, The Chick That Never Grew Up **10.00**

Larkin Soap, 1885 .... **15.00**

Pinback Button, 1¼" d, Gold Dust Washing Powder, multicolored, late 1890s **75.00**

Pocket Mirror, 1⅞" d, Dingman Soap, red ground, white letters **30.00**

Poster, 9 × 12", Packer's Tar Soap, barber shaving, c1900 .... **30.00**

Ruler, 5½" l, Glory Soap Chips, celluloid, folding, blue and orange Swift & Co trademark, 1919 calendar **20.00**

Sign, Ideal Soap, diecut, cat scene **110.00**

Soap Dish

Graniteware, hanging, cobalt blue swirl **110.00**

Porcelain, Blue Onion, drain **58.00**

Soap Saver, metal **12.00**

Trade Card

Bells Buffalo Soap, vegetable people, 1887 .... **12.00**

Lainds Bloom of Youth & White Lilac Soap **5.00**

Lautz Bros Master Soap, baby on pillow **7.50**

Wool Soap **3.00**

SODA FOUNTAIN AND ICE CREAM COLLECTIBLES

The local soda fountain and/or ice cream parlor was the social center of small town America between the late 1880s and the 1960s. Ice cream items appeared as early as the 1870s.

This is a category filled with nostalgia—banana splits and dates with friends. Some concentrate on the advertising, some on the implements. It is all terrific.

Club: The Ice Screamer, P. O. Box 5387, Lancaster, PA 17601.

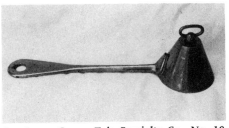

Ice Cream Scoop, Erie Specialty Co., No. 10, $70.00.

ICE CREAM

Brochure, White Mountain Ice Cream, woman making ice cream **25.00**

Carton, Hershey's Ice Cream, one pint, orange and blue **15.00**

Cone Dispenser, glass, copper insert **345.00**

Ice Cream Scoop
  Banana **475.00**
  Magic Ice Cream Sandwich, wafer **395.00**
  Prince Castle Ice Cream, 1½ × 1½" cube size **375.00**

Ice Cream Spoon, tin, set of 24 . . . . **16.00**

Measuring Glass, Sealtest Ice Cream **6.00**

Milk Shaker, Hamilton Beach, green . . . **35.00**

Mold, pewter, star in circle **35.00**

Pinback Button, ⅞" d, Arctic Rainbow Ice Cream Cones, celluloid, multicolored, c1912 . . . . **20.00**

Sign, 9" d, Rich Valley Ice Cream, yellow and red, 1940s **40.00**

Thermometer
  Abbottmaid Ice Cream, 2 × 6¼", 1920–1930, orig label **35.00**
  Harrington's Ice Cream, 12" h, wood **35.00**

Trade Card, Reid's Ice Cream, "She had but one tooth! And that was for Reid's Ice Cream," old lady with one tooth **14.00**

Whistle, Purity Ice Cream, plastic, late 1940s **15.00**

SODA FOUNTAIN

Bottle, Moxie, aqua, 7 oz **7.00**

Candy Scale, Exact Weight, orig weights **75.00**

Catalog, Dean Foster Co, 1908, soda counter goods **48.00**

Dispenser
  Dad's Root Beer, barrel shape, bronze claw feet **250.00**
  Hunter's Root Beer, milk glass **45.00**

Door Push, Whistle Cola, picture of bottle, adjustable, 1940s **55.00**

Funnel, Lash's Bitters, copper **75.00**

Malt Jar, Borden's, aluminum **30.00**

Sign
  Mission Orange Soda, 20 × 26¼", paper, 1940–50 . . . . **50.00**
  Mt Kineo Ginger Ale, 12 × 24", tin, emb, 1940s **30.00**
  Whistle Soda, stand-up, cardboard, diecut, elf and bottle, 1940s **20.00**

Soda Fountain, Pepsi-Cola, 1930s **95.00**

Straw Holder, clear jar, Heisey **135.00**

Syrup Bottle, grapefruit, glass, red script lettering on white enamel label, gold border, plated metal measure cap, FM Williams, 1913 copyright **70.00**

Syrup Dispenser, cherry, 10½" h **25.00**

Thermometer
  Dr Pepper, 20" h, tin, 1960s logo **50.00**
  Royal Crown Cola, 25" h **60.00**

SOFT DRINK COLLECTIBLES

National brands such as Coca-Cola, Canada Dry, Dr. Pepper, and Pepsi-Cola dominate the field. However, there were thousands of regional and local soda bottling plants. Their advertising, bottles, and giveaways are every bit as exciting as those of the national companies. Do not ignore them.

Clubs: The Coca-Cola Collectors Club International, P. O. Box 546, Holmdel, NJ 07733; Pepsi-Cola Collectors Club, P. O. Box 1275, Covina, CA 91722.

Pinback Button, Cherry-Cheer, blue, red, and green lettering, white ground, gold band, Whitehead & Hoag Co., ⅞" d, $20.00.

Bottle, Moxie, porcelain top **18.00**

Bottle Cap, Diet Dad's Root Beer **175.00**

Calendar
  Pepsi, 1941, complete **200.00**
  Sun Crest Cola, 1957 . . . . **28.00**

Chalkboard, A & W Root Beer **110.00**

Door Push
  Grapette, aluminum **145.00**
  Pepsi, wrought iron, 1960s **95.00**
  White Rock Sparkling Water **145.00**

Fan, Dr Pepper, green and red, six pack on reverse **50.00**

Match Dispenser, Dr Pepper, 1930s **65.00**

Mug
  Dad's Root Beer, glass, barrel shape . . . **30.00**
  Graf's Root Beer, ceramic **55.00**

Pencil, Orange Crush, mechanical **20.00**

Sign
  Canada Dry Hi-Spot, tin, 1940s **45.00**
  Dad's Root Beer, 12 × 30", tin, bottle cap illus **45.00**
  Drink R-Pep 5¢ Bottle, tin, 1930s **88.00**
  Nu Icy Soda, 17 × 35" **95.00**
  Orange Crush, 12 × 30", tin, bottle illus **45.00**

Pepsi, tin, "Say Pepsi Please" **85.00**
Royal Crown, tin, 1930s **65.00**
Seven-Up, 33½ × 21", cardboard, girl
  on bike, 1953 . . . . **55.00**
Tap, Pepsi, musical, 1940 . . . . **125.00**
Thermometer
  Dr Pepper Hot & Cold **75.00**
  Nesbitts Orange, bottle illus **65.00**
  Orange Crush, Crushie, tin **95.00**
  Pepsi, 1955 . . . . **60.00**
  Seven-Up, round **125.00**

Tom Corbett, Space Cadet Belt, Yale, copyright Rockhill Productions, $32.00.

SOUTH OF THE BORDER COLLECTIBLES

When you live on the East Coast and do not roam west of Chicago, you are not going to see South of the Border collectibles except for the tourist souvenirs brought home by visitors to Central and South America. However, the growing Hispanic population is beginning to look back to its roots and starting to proudly display family and other items acquired south of the border.

Within the past year there has been a growing interest in Mexican jewelry. In fact, several new books have been published about the subject. Mexican pottery and textiles are also attracting collector attention.

At the moment, buy only high-quality, handmade products. Because of their brilliant colors, South of the Border collectibles accent almost any room. This is an area to watch.

SPACE COLLECTIBLES

This category deals only with fictional space heroes. My grandfather followed Buck Rogers in the Sunday funnies. Dad saw Buster Crabbe as Flash Gordon in the movies and cut his teeth on early television with Captain Video. I am from the Star Trek generation.

Do not overlook the real live space heroes, like the astronauts and cosmonauts who have and are yet to venture out into space. Material relating to these pioneers is going to be very collectible in the year 2091.

Buck Rogers
  Big Little Book, *Buck Rogers In The City Of Floating Globes*, Whitman, Cocomalt premium, 1935 . . . . **75.00**

Book, *The Adventures of Buck Rogers*,
  Whitman, 320 pgs, 1934 . . . . **50.00**
Figure, 1¼" h, silver metal, Tootsietoy,
  1937 . . . . **60.00**
Holster, 9" h, leather, brown, metal
  buckle and rivets, 1930s **75.00**
Mask, 8 × 11", Wilma, paper **65.00**
Rubber Stamp, set of 11, yellow, wood
  back, Wilma, Buddy, Alura, and two
  different Buck Rogers, c1930 . . . . . . **90.00**
Captain Video
  Game, Captain Video Space Game,
    Milton Bradley, early 1950s **75.00**
  Ring, Secret Seal **40.00**
  Watch, orig card **40.00**
Tom Corbett
  Book, *Stand By For Mars*, Grosset &
    Dunlap, 1952 . . . . **12.50**
  Coloring Book, unused, 1952 . . . . **95.00**
  Flashlight, orig box, 1952 . . . . **95.00**
  Lunch Box, 1952 . . . . **120.00**
  Patch, 2 × 4", "Space Cadet," cloth,
    red, yellow, and blue, Kellogg's pre-
    mium **25.00**
  Thermos, 6" h, metal, yellow plastic
    cup, Aladdin Industries, copyright
    1952 Rockhill Radio **45.00**
Flash Gordon
  Costume, space outfit, c1950 . . . . **135.00**
  Game, orig box **25.00**
  Paint Book, 11 × 14", Whitman, 32
    pgs, copyright 1936 King Features
    Syndicate **100.00**
  Toy, Flash Gordon Starship, 5" l, die-
    cast metal and plastic, sticker on
    each wing, Tootsietoy, copyright
    1978 King Features Syndicate **25.00**
  Wallet, faux leather, zipper, 1949 KFS
    copyright **75.00**
Space Cadet, thermos, 1952 . . . . **25.00**
Space Patrol
  Belt Buckle, decoder **110.00**
  Drink Mixer, 8" h, plastic, pink rocket
    ship, marked on side "XY7 Rocket,"
    orig colored carton **35.00**
  Handbook **150.00**
  Projector, Terra V, 5½" h, rocket
    shape, plastic, blue and yellow, orig
    mailing box, Ralston Co premium,
    early 1950s **150.00**

Ring, hydrogen ray gun **200.00**
Wristwatch, silvered metal case, black and red numerals, gray leather straps, US Time, early 1950s **60.00**
Star Trek
Game, Star Trek Phaser II Target Game, orig box **50.00**
Greeting Card, cardboard, Spock photo on front, unfold to 18" l, diecut punch-out Vulcan ears, "I Must Be Hard Of Hearing . . . I Haven't Heard From You Lately," orig envelope, Random House Greetings, copyright 1976 Paramount Pictures Corp **12.00**
Paint Set, 12 × 16" canvas portrait, boxed, slightly used, Hasbro, 1974 copyright **50.00**
Thermos, 6½" h, metal, color illus, white plastic cup, Aladdin Industries, copyright 1968 Paramount Pictures Corp **60.00**
Utility Belt, phaser, tri-corder, and communicator, Remco, 1975 . . . . . . **30.00**
Star Wars
Alarm Clock, talking **25.00**
Book, pop-up **15.00**
Costume, Darth Vadar, orig box, Ben Cooper, copyright 1977 20th Century Fox Film Corp **30.00**
Doll, Chewbacca, 18" h, stuffed, dark brown, plastic eyes and nose, brown vinyl cartridge belt, gray plastic cartridges, orig Kenner tag, 1977 20th Century Fox Film Corp **40.00**
Toy, stuffed, R2-D2, jointed legs, orig Kenner tag, copyright 1977 20th Century Fox Film Corp **25.00**

SPORTS COLLECTIBLES

There has been so much written about sports cards that equipment and other sport-related material have become lost in the shuffle. A number of recent crazes, such as passion for old baseball gloves, indicate that this is about to change.

Decorators have discovered that hanging old sporting equipment on walls makes a great decorative motif. This certainly helps call attention to the collectibility of the material.

Since little has been written outside of baseball and golf collectibles, it is hard to determine what exactly are the best pieces. A good philosophy is to keep expenditures at a minimum until this and other questions are sorted out by collectors and dealers.

Newspaper: *Sports Collectors Digest*, 700 East State Street, Iola, WI 54990.

Cigarette Case, black gun metal, sterling silver relief soccer player, gemstone catch, $150.00.

Club: Golf Collectors' Society, P. O. Box 491, Shawnee Mission, KS 66201.

Award, track
Badge, copper-plated white metal, engraved front "1 Mile Run 1st Prize," reverse "St Patrick's Field Day May 30, 1910" **15.00**
Pin, sterling silver, inscribed "Manual Training school '95," red and blue accents, mid 1890s **18.00**
Book
Guide to Good Golf, James Barnes **25.00**
The Spectacle of Sports from Sports Illustrated, 1957, 320 pgs, dj **25.00**
Boxing Gloves, Jack Dempsey, brown, white vinyl trim, orig box, Everlast, c1950 . . . . **35.00**
Charge Coin, 1¼" d, brass, emb, "Horace Partridge Co/Athletic & Sporting Goods" on one side, other with "Discount & Charge Coin," 1890s **18.00**
Charm, boxing gloves, Benny Leonard, plastic, brassy gold color finish, 1950s **6.00**
Cigarette Lighter, figural, golf bag **45.00**
Dispenser, marbleized plastic bowling ball, chrome push top, six glasses, figural bowler handle **60.00**
Drinking Glass
Kentucky Derby
1959 . . . . **32.50**
1986, 5¼", clear, frosted white panel, red roses and green leaf accents, red and green inscriptions **10.00**
Olympics, 5½" h, clear, frosted white picture, 1932 . . . . **50.00**
Handbook, women's, *Handbook of Light Gymnastics*, Lucy B Hunt, 1887, 92 pgs, hard cover **50.00**
Jug, Who Will Win, made for Michigan-Minnesota football game, Red Wing **195.00**

Pennant, Derby Day, 18" l, felt, red, white lettering, red and white design with pink accents, 1939 . . . . **15.00**
Pin, pennant shape, leather, "Brockton Welcomes Rocky," attached gold plastic boxing gloves **50.00**
Press Badge, Chicago Area Golf Tournament, 1950–1960 . . . . **12.00**
Program
    1948 Summer Olympic Trials, 8 × 10½", weight lifting trials, 20 pgs . . . **15.00**
    1952 Olympic Tryouts, July 3–5, rowing tryouts, 72 pgs **20.00**
    1965 Harlem Globetrotters, 8 × 10½", Magicians of Basketball Tour, 30 pgs **15.00**
Puppet, Joe Louis, 8" h, fabric body, soft rubber boxing gloves and molded head, JV Co **55.00**
Puzzle, 1932 Olympic Games, 10 × 13¼", Toddy Inc, 1932 copyright **30.00**
Score Pad, golf, 2½ × 4", celluloid cov, unused, 1900s **15.00**
Wristwatch
    Boxing, Muhammad Ali, gold colored metal, color photo on dial, black numerals and inscriptions, Depraz-Faure America Corp, c1980 . . . . . . **75.00**
    Football, Pittsburgh Steelers, chrome silver metal case, helmet illus on dial, Lafayette Watch Co, 1960s **30.00**

STANGL POTTERY

Stangl manufactured dinnerware between 1930 and 1978 in Trenton, New Jersey. The dinnerware featured bold floral and fruit designs on a brilliant white or off-white ground.

The company also produced a series of three-dimensional bird figurines that are eagerly sought by collectors. The bird figurines were cast in Trenton and finished at a second company plant in Flemington. During World War II the demand for the birds was so great that over 60 decorators were employed to paint them. Some of the birds were reissued between 1972 and 1977. They are dated on the bottom.

BIRDS

3400, Love Bird, 4" h **50.00**
3401D, Wren, 8" h, pr **90.00**
3402S, Oriole, 3¼" h **40.00**
3406S, Kingfisher, 3½" h **50.00**
3444, Cardinal, 6½" h **55.00**
3447, Yellow Warbler, 5" h **50.00**
3484, Cockatoo, 11⅜" h **190.00**
3491, Hen Pheasant, 6¼ × 11" **155.00**
3492, Cock Pheasant, 6¼ × 11" **150.00**
3582D, Parakeets, pr **145.00**

Plate, Tulip, 9¼" d, $6.00.

3583, Parula Warbler, 4¼" h **50.00**
3585, Rufous Hummingbird, 3" h **50.00**
3594, Red-Faced Warbler, 3" h **55.00**
3597, Wilson Warbler, 3½" h **45.00**
3598, Kentucky Warbler, 3" h **40.00**
3599D, Hummingbird, 8 × 10½", pr **240.00**
3628, Rieffers Hummingbird, 4½" h **125.00**

DINNERWARE

Antique Gold, bowl, 4084 . . . . **28.00**
Blueberry
    Cereal Bowl **4.50**
    Plate, dinner **12.50**
Blue Daisy, plate, 10" d **9.50**
Colonial Green, console set, bowl and two 3" h candlesticks **20.00**
Corn, butter dish, green **15.00**
Country Garden, vegetable bowl, divided **22.50**
Fruit and Flowers, fruit bowl **5.00**
Fruits
    Bean Pot **48.00**
    Teapot, individual size **12.00**
Garden Flower, coaster **5.50**
Garland, creamer **6.00**
Golden Blossom, gravy boat, stand **7.00**
Golden Harvest, coffee warmer **18.00**
Granada Gold, flower bowl, 5139 . . . . . . **20.00**
Holly, punch mug **22.00**
Jonquil
    Bread Tray **10.00**
    Pickle Dish, 10⅜" l **7.50**
Magnolia, egg cup **12.50**
Orchard Song
    Candleholders, round, pr **20.00**
    Server, center handle **15.00**
Red Cherry, casserole, handle **9.00**
Star Flower, cream soup, lug handle **10.00**
Terra Rose
    Butter, cov **20.00**
    Creamer and Sugar, cov **25.00**
    Salt and Pepper Shakers, pr **12.50**

Thistle
Coaster **5.00**
Coffeepot, cov.................... **25.00**
Plate, 6" d, bread and butter......... **6.00**
Sherbet **12.00**
Town and Country, server, 10" d, center
handle, green speckled............ **20.00**
Tulip
Flowerpot, 4" d, yellow **5.00**
Platter, 12½" d, round **20.00**
White Dogwood, cup and saucer....... **10.00**

STAR TREK

In 1966, a new science fiction television show aired that introduced America to a galaxy of strange new worlds filled with new life forms. The voyages of author Gene Roddenberry's starship *Enterprise* enabled the viewing audience to boldly go where no man had gone before.

These adventures created a new generation of collectors: "Trekkies." From posters, costumes, and props to pins, comic books, and model kits, there in no limit to the number of Star Trek collectibles that can be found.

With the release of Paramounts' *Star Trek: The Motion Picture* in 1979, the Star Trek cult grew. The *Enterprise's* new devotees inspired the inevitable new sequels: *Star Trek II: The Wrath of Khan, Star Trek III: The Search for Spock, Star Trek IV: The Voyage Home, Star Trek V: The Final Frontier*, and just last year, *Star Trek VI: The Undiscovered Country*.

In 1988, Trekkies demanded the return of the *Enterprise* to television and were rewarded with *Star Trek: The Next Generation*. A new starship, manned by a new crew, retained the same desire to reach out into the unknown. This television series has generated its own following as well as merchandise.

Whether you are an old Trekkie or a Next Generation Trekkie, keep seeking out those collectibles. May your collection live long and prosper.

TELEVISION SERIES (1966)
Action Figure, Mego, 1974–76
Captain Kirk **25.00**
The Keeper **50.00**
Klingon **30.00**
McCoy.......................... **20.00**
Romulan **100.00**
Activity Book, Punch Out and Play Album, Saalfield, 1975.............. **45.00**

Whiskey Bottle, Grenadier, Mr. Spock, 1979, $20.00.

Belt Buckle, brass, Lee Belts.......... **10.00**
Binoculars. Larami................. **60.00**
Board Game, Hasbro, 1974 .... **30.00**
Book
The Making of Star Trek, Ballantine, 1968..................... **3.00**
Mudd's Angels, Bantam **2.50**
Star Fleet Technical Manual, Ballantine....................... **15.00**
The Trouble with Tribbles, Ballantine, 1973........................ **2.00**
Bop Bag, Spock, inflatable, AHI, 1975... **32.00**
Bottle, Saurian Brandy.............. **100.00**
Calculator, Star Trekulator, Mego, c1975....................... **40.00**
Colorforms **28.00**
Coloring Book, Planet Ecnal's Dilemma, Whitman, 1978.................. **4.00**
Comic Book
Gold Key Enterprise Logs, Gold Key Comics, Vol 1 .... **6.00**
Star Trek, Gold Key Comics
No. 1 .... **45.00**
No. 18 .... **20.00**
Commemorative Coin, Enterprise, 1974......................... **35.00**
Costume
Klingon, 1976................... **50.00**
Mr Spock, Ben Cooper, 1967 .... **90.00**
Freezicle Set, 1975 .... **30.00**
Glass, Enterprise, Dr Pepper, 1978 ..... **40.00**
Lunch Box, Aladdin, 1968........... **200.00**
Model Kit, Klingon Battle Cruiser, lights, AMT, 1967 .... **60.00**
Movie Viewer, 1967................ **15.00**
Phaser Ray Gun **25.00**

Plate, Ernst Enterprises, crew on transporter illus. 25.00
Play Set
   Enterprise Bridge, vinyl, Mego, 1974. . . . . 85.00
   Mission to Gamma VI, Mego, 1976 . . . 225.00
Record, *The Time Stealer*, Power Records, Peter Pan, 1975. . . . . 5.00
Tracer Gun, 1966 . . . . 30.00
Trading Cards, Topps, set of 88, 1976 . . . 30.00
Tribble, stuffed, Mego. 65.00
Tricorder, cassette player, Mego, 1976. . . . . 75.00
Utility Belt, phaser, tricorder, communicator, Remco. 50.00

CARTOON SERIES (1973)

Glass, McCoy, Dr Pepper, 1976 . . . . 25.00
Paper Napkins, Party Creations/Tuttle Press, unopened pkg, 1976. . . . . 3.50
Patch, fabric, Federation emblem, 1975. . . . . 20.00

THE NEXT GENERATION (1987)

Action Figure, Lewis Galoob Toy Co, 1988
   Data. 8.00
   Data, blue skin 30.00
   Ferengi 9.00
   Picard. 4.00
   Q 12.00
Book
   The Children of Hamlin, No. 3. . . . . 2.50
   Metamorphosis 3.00
Costume, Ferengi 8.00
Lunch Box, Halsey Taylor/Thermos 8.00
Model Kit, Enterprise, AMT. 10.00
Pattern, crew jumpsuit, Simplicity 6.00
Phaser, Lewis Galoob Toy Co 18.00
Vehicle
   Ferengi Fighter, Lewis Galoob Toy Co. 12.00
   Shuttlecraft Galileo, Lewis Galoob Toy Co. 15.00
View-Master Packet 5.00

THE MOTION PICTURE (1979)

Action Figure, Mego, 1979
3¾″ h
   Betelgeusian 20.00
   Decker. 15.00
   Scotty. 10.00
   Spock. 10.00
12″ h
   Arcturian. 50.00
   Decker. 75.00
   Spock. 30.00
Activity Book, *Make Your Own Costume*, Wallaby, 1979. . . . . 10.00
Beanbag Chair 25.00
Board Game, Milton Bradley, 1979. . . . . 25.00
Bumper Sticker. 2.00
Coloring Book, Giant Story 12.00

Comic Book, *Motion Picture Magazine*, Marvel Comics, 1979 . . . . 3.00
Costume, Ilia. 15.00
Doll, Kirk, cloth, Knickerbocker 25.00
Dual Phaser II, South Bend, 1979 . . . . . . 35.00
First Aid Kit. 10.00
Glass, Kirk, Spock, and McCoy, Coca-Cola, 1980 . . . . 15.00
Keychain, Spock, lucite 2.00
Play Set, Command Bridge 30.00
Pocket Book, *The Entropy Effect*, No. 2, Simon and Schuster 2.50
Pop-Up Book, Wanderer Books. 10.00
Putty, Larami 10.00
Puzzle, jigsaw, sick bay, Milton Bradley 10.00
Rubber Stamp. 4.00
Trading Cards, Topps, set of 88, 1979 . . . 8.00
Tumbler, plastic, Coca-Cola, 1980. . . . . . 12.00
Wallet 5.00
Wastebasket 20.00
Water Pistol. 30.00
Wrist Communicator 45.00

THE WRATH OF KHAN (1982)

Book and Record Set, Buena Vista Records 3.50
Game Watch 75.00
Model Kit, Enterprise, AMT. 15.00
Mug, Khan 4.00
Photocards, FTCC, 5 × 7″, set of 30. . . . . 25.00
Pinback Button, Enterprise crew, Image Products 2.00
Playing Cards, photo illus backs. 8.00
Pocket Book, *The Trellisane Confrontation*, No. 14, Simon and Schuster. 2.50
Poster 25.00
Vehicle, Klingon ship, Corgi 50.00

THE SEARCH FOR SPOCK (1984)

Action Figure, ERTL, 1984
   Kruge and his dog. 15.00
   Spock. 8.00
Comic Book, *Star Trek III Movie Special*, DC Comics, 1984. . . . . 3.50
Eraser, Excelsior, Diener Enterprises. . . . 5.00
Glass, Fal-Tor-Pan, Taco Bell, 1984 . . . . . 5.00
Kite 15.00
Pinback Button, Chekov, Button-Up Co 2.00
Pocket Book, *The Vulcan Academy Murders*, No. 20, Simon and Schuster 3.00
Post Card Book 4.00
Trading Cards, ship cards, laminated, FTCC, set of 20 . . . . 8.00
Vehicle, Klingon Bird of Prey, diecast . . . 50.00

THE VOYAGE HOME (1986)

Book and Cassette Set, Buena Vista Records 4.00
Comic Book, *Star Trek IV Movie Special*, DC Comics, 1987. . . . . 2.50
Pocket Book, *Star Trek IV: The Voyage Home*, Simon and Schuster. 2.50

Poster 20.00
Program 12.00
Trading Cards, set of 60 .... 8.00

THE FINAL FRONTIER (1989)
Action Figure, Lewis Galoob Toy Co
 Kirk 30.00
 Klaa 32.00
Comic Book, *Star Trek V Movie Special*, DC
 Comics, 1989. .... 3.00
Logbook, *Captain's Log: William Shatner's
 Personal Account of the Making of Star
 Trek V: The Final Frontier* 3.50
Model Kit, Enterprise and shuttle,
 AMT........................... 10.00
Pin, Enterprise in triangle, Collectors
 Classics 6.00
Pocket Book, *Final Frontier*, Simon and
 Schuster 3.00

STAR WARS

It was in a galaxy not so long ago that author and director George Lucas put into motion events that would change the way we think of space. In 1977 a movie was produced that told the story of an evil Empire's tyrannical rule over the galaxy and of the adventures of a young man from a distant world to end this tyranny. Luke Skywalker's aventures became the Star Wars saga and spanned six years and three separate movies: *Star Wars*, *The Empire Strikes Back*, and *Return of the Jedi*.

The enormous success of the Star Wars movies inspired the release of a wide range of movie-related products including toys, games, costumes, records, and comic books. As you travel through the flea market aisles in search of *Star Wars* treasure, "may the Force be with you."

STAR WARS (1977)
Action Figure, Kenner, 1977–1979
 Ben Obi-Wan Kenobi............. 22.00
 Blue Snaggletooth, Sears 42.00
 Boba Fett, rocket launcher, mail of-
 fer........................... 150.00
 Chewbacca 20.00
 Death Star Droid................. 15.00
 Princess Leia Organa.............. 25.00
Activity Book, *Artoo Detoo's Activity Book*,
 Random House, 1979.............. 8.00
Alarm Clock, C-3PO and R2-D2, talking,
 Bradley, 1980 .... 20.00
Bank
 Darth Vader, ceramic, Roman Ce-
 ramics 28.00
 Yoda, litho tin, combination dials 10.00

Beach Towel, Darth Vader 4.00
Belt, stretch, black and white, 1979...... 5.00
Belt Buckle, logo, Leather Shop Inc..... 15.00
Birthday Candle, Chewbacca, Wilton ... 5.00
Board Game, Adventures of R2-D2, Ken-
 ner........................... 12.00
Bop Bag, Jawa, inflatable, Kenner...... 40.00
Cake Decorating Kit, R2-D2, Wilton 15.00
Carrying Case, vinyl................. 20.00
Coloring Set, Star Wars Poster Art, Craft
 Master, 1978.................... 15.00
Comic Book, Marvel Comics Group
 No. 1 .... 8.00
 No. 7 .... 2.00
Cookie Jar, C-3PO, ceramic, Roman Ce-
 ramics Corp..................... 75.00
Glass, Chewbacca, Burger King, Coca-
 Cola 8.00
Han Solo Laser Pistol, *Star Wars* sticker,
 Kenner 35.00
Helmet, Darth Vader, plastic, Don Post
 Studios........................ 100.00
Keychain, Millennium Falcon, metal,
 Adam Joseph Industries............ 6.00
Lightsaber, inflatable, Kenner........ 65.00
Lunch Box, King Seeley Thermos,
 1978.......................... 15.00
Model Kit, Millennium Falcon, lights,
 Modern Plastics Co, 1977 .... 55.00
Movie Viewer, Kenner, 1978.......... 25.00
Night Light, Yoda, Adam Joseph Indus-
 tries 5.00
Pencil Tray, C-3PO 30.00
Pendant, Stormtrooper 10.00
Picture Frame, Darth Vader 35.00
Playset, Land of the Jawas 100.00
Princess Leia's Beauty Bag............ 15.00
Puzzle, jigsaw, Luke, Kenner, #40110,
 500 pcs, purple box............... 5.00
Robot, R2-D2, radio controlled, Ken-
 ner........................... 50.00
Rocket Kit, X-Wing with Maxi-Brutel,
 Estes.......................... 20.00
Roller Skates, Darth Vader and Imperial
 Guard 18.00
Stickpin, Darth Vader............... 5.00
String Dispenser, R2-D2, scissors....... 25.00
Switcheroo, Darth Vader, Kenner...... 8.00
Tankard, Obi-Wan Kenobi, ceramic, Cal-
 ifornia Originals 35.00
Trading Cards, Topps, first series, blue,
 set of 66 .... 18.00
Vehicle
 Death Star Space Station 75.00
 Millennium Falcon Spaceship 80.00
 X-Wing Fighter, battle damage
 stickers....................... 30.00

THE EMPIRE STRIKES BACK (1980)
Action Figure, Kenner, 1980–82
 Bespin Security Guard, white 15.00
 Imperial TIE Fighter Pilot 15.00
 Luke Skywalker, Hoth battle gear 18.00
Arcade Game 500.00

Bulletin Board, glow-in-the-dark, 11 × 17" 10.00
Centerpiece, Designware 8.00
Clock, wall, Bradley 20.00
Coloring Book, Chewbacca, Han, Leia, and Lando on cov, Kenner 4.00
Comic Book, Marvel Special Edition 3.00
Dinnerware Set. 18.00
Glass, Lando Calrissian, Burger King, Coca-Cola 5.00
Han Solo Laser Pistol, *Empire Strikes Back* sticker, Kenner 20.00
Iron-On Transfer, Darth Vader and Stormtroopers.................... 8.00
Medal, X-Wing, W Berrie & Co, Inc. 6.00
Mug, robots, ceramic 8.00
Notebook 4.00
Paint Set, glow in the dark, Darth Vader........................... 12.00
Patch, crew, "Vader in Flames"........ 7.50
Pendant, Darth Vader, W Berrie & Co ... 6.00
Placemats, set 15.00
Playset
    Ice Planet Hoth 80.00
    Turret and Probot, J C Penney....... 90.00
Sketchbook, Ballantine, 1980 .... 12.00
Sleeping Bag 20.00
Toothbrush Holder, Snowspeeder...... 30.00
Trading Cards, Topps, first series, red, set of 132.......................... 10.00
Vehicle
    Rebel Armored Snowspeeder 25.00
    Twin-Pod Cloud Car.............. 30.00

RETURN OF THE JEDI (1983)

Action Figure, Kenner, 1983
    Anakin Skywalker 35.00
    Gamorrean Guard. 15.00
    Han Solo, Carbonite Chamber 50.00
    Lando Calrissian, Skiff Guard disguise........................ 12.00
    Paploo 10.00
    R2-D2, pop-up lightsaber........... 25.00
    Sy Snootles and the Rebo Band, boxed set......................... 28.00
    Weequay....................... 15.00
    Yak Face, with coin 100.00
Activity Book, picture puzzles 3.50
Bank, Emperor's Royal Guard, Adam Joseph Industries 15.00
Belt 2.00
Biker Scout Laser Pistol, Kenner 20.00
Bookmark, Admiral Ackbar, Random House 3.50
Candy Container, Jabba the Hutt, figural, Topps.......................... 1.50
Card Game, Play-for-Power.......... 7.00
Comic Book, Marvel Super Special 3.00
Costume, Klaatu, Ben Cooper, "Revenge of the Jedi" on chestplate.......... 25.00
Curtains 12.00
Doll, Chewbacca, stuffed 10.00

Glass, Emperor's Throne Room, Burger King, Coca-Cola 3.50
Lightsaber, Droid, battery operated..... 30.00
Mask, Gamorrean Guard, soft rubber, Ben Cooper..................... 10.00
Paint Set, figurine, C-3PO, Craft Master 8.00
Patch, crew, "Revenge of the Jedi" 20.00
Pencil, character head 1.00
Picnic Table....................... 55.00
Pinback Button, Heroes in Forest, 2¼" d 2.00
Playset
    Ewok Village 40.00
    Jabba the Hutt................... 45.00
Puzzle, frame tray, Leia and Wicket, Craft Master 3.00
Shoelaces, Stride Rite............... 1.00
Sit 'n Spin, Wicket 12.00
Stickpin, Princess Kneesa, Adam Joseph Industries 5.00
Toothbrush, Jedi Masters, Oral-B 3.00
Toy Chest, bookcase 50.00
Trading Cards, Topps, first series, red, set of 132......................... 8.00
Vehicle
    Speeder Bike.................... 15.00
    TIE Interceptor 25.00

"STRADIVARIUS" VIOLINS

In the late nineteenth century inexpensive violins were made for sale to students, amateur musicians, and others who could not afford an older, quality instrument. Numerous models, many named after famous makers, were sold by department stores, music shops, and by mail. Sears, Roebuck sold "Stradivarius" models. Other famous violin makers whose names appear on paper labels inside these instruments include Amati, Caspar DaSolo, Guarnerius, Maggini, and Stainer. Lowendall of Germany made a Paganini model.

All these violins were sold through advertisements that claimed that the owner could have a violin nearly equal to that of an antique instrument for a modest cost; one "Stradivarius" sold for $2.45. The most expensive model cost less than $15.00. The violins were handmade, but by a factory assembly line process.

If well cared for, these pseudo antique violins often develop a nice tone. The average price for an instrument in playable condition is between $100.00 and $200.00.

298

SUGAR PACKETS

Do not judge sugar packets of the 1940s and 1950s by those you encounter today. There is no comparison. Early sugar packets were colorful and often contained full color scenic views.

Many of the packets were issued as sets, with a variety of scenic views. They were gathered as souvenirs during a vacation travels.

There is a large number of closet sugar packet collectors. They do not write much about their hobby because they are afraid that the minute they draw attention to it, prices will rise. Most sugar packets sell for less than $1.00.

It's time to let the sugar out of the bag. Get them cheap while you can.

Club: Sugar Packet Collectors Society, 105 Ridge Road, Perkasie, PA 18944.

SUPER HEROES

Super heroes and comic books go hand in hand. Superman first appeared in *Action Comics* in 1939. He was followed by Batman, Captain Marvel, Captain Midnight, The Green Hornet, The Green Lantern, The Shadow, Wonder Woman, and a host of others.

The traditional Super Hero was transformed with the appearance of The Fantastic Four—Mr. Fantastic, The Human Torch, The Invisible Girl, and The Thing. The mutant hero lives today with Teenage Mutant Ninja Turtles.

It pays to focus on one hero or a related family of heroes. Go after the three-dimensional material. This is the hardest to find.

Batman and Robin
  Game, Batman and Robin, orig box, 1965 National Periodical Publications Inc copyright **50.00**
  Glass, 5" h, clear, blue and gray illus and text, copyright National Periodical Publications Inc, c1966 . . . . **15.00**
  Helmet, 12" h, molded plastic, diecut mouth and eye openings, black accents on blue ground, gold and black bat symbol, Ideal, copyright National Periodical Publications, 1966 . . . . **100.00**

Superman, wallet, leather and plastic, made in Hong Kong, copyright 1976, $25.00.

Mug, 3½" h, plastic, clear, white insert, multicolored paper illus, copyright National Periodical Publications, 1966 . . . . **30.00**
Pen, 5" l, black and silver, diecast metal Batman figure clip, orig diecut blister card, Empire Pencil Co, copyright 1966 National Periodical Productions Inc **50.00**
Place Mats, 13 × 18", vinyl, foam backing, multicolored, copyright National Periodical Publications, 1966, pr **75.00**
Soaky Bottle, 10" h, soft plastic body, hard plastic head, purple, blue, and yellow, copyright National Periodical Publications, 1966 . . . . **50.00**
Toy
  Batmobile, 8 × 19 × 6½", molded plastic, 3-D figures, red striping, gold and black bat decals, c1966 . . . . **125.00**
  Bat-Ray Gun, 8" l, flashlight, four plastic disks project image, AHI, copyright DC Comics, orig box, 1978 . . . . **35.00**
Captain America
  Badge, Sentinels of Liberty, brass, red and blue accents, 1941–1943 . . . . . . **225.00**

299

Pennant, 6½" l, diecut vinyl, copyright 1966 Marvel Comics Group **20.00**

Captain Marvel

EZ Code Finder, 4" d disk wheel, cardboard, Fawcett Comics premium, mid-1940s **125.00**

Post Card, 3 × 5½", Captain Marvel's Secret Message, blue, dip in water to reveal message, c1940s **75.00**

Puzzle, 13 × 18", Captain Marvel Rides The Engine Of Doom,'' Fawcett Publications Inc, 1941 . . . . **150.00**

Flash Gordon

Lobby Card, 11 × 14", "Flash Gordon Conquers the Universe," Universal Pictures **50.00**

Lunch Box, 7 × 10 × 5", plastic, color decals, Aladdin, copyright 1979 King Features Syndicate **65.00**

Spaceship, 3" l, metal, diecast, blue, white accents, orig display card, LJN Toys, copyright 1975 . . . . **20.00**

Green Hornet

Coloring Book, 8 × 11", Watkins-Strathmore, unused, copyright 1966 . . . . **30.00**

Pinback Button, 4" d, black, red, green, and blue illus, 1966 Greenway Productions Inc copyright on rim **50.00**

Secret Print Putty, secret print book, magic print paper, Colorforms Toy, unopened blister pack, copyright 1966 . . . . **65.00**

Wallet, 3½ × 4½", vinyl, green, Green Hornet on front, Kato on back, Green Hornet insect and logo on both sides, magic slate, pencil, and black and white photo of Kato inside, Mattel, copyright Greenway Productions, 1966 . . . . **60.00**

Spiderman

Bicycle Siren, 4" h, plastic, red and yellow, decals, Empire Toys, copyright Marvel Comics Group, orig box and attachments, unused, 1978 . . . . **40.00**

Doll, 20" h, plush, red, white, and black outfit, orig Knickerbocker tag, copyright Marvel Comics Group, 1978 . . . . **20.00**

Superman

Card Game, plastic case, 45 cards, Whitman, copyright 1966 National Periodical Publications Inc **25.00**

Game, 5 × 6", sliding square puzzle, black and white, Superman flying over buildings, orig display card **70.00**

Glass, 4¼" h, Superman in Action, clear, blue illus, peach color inscriptions, copyright National Periodical Publications Inc, 1964 . . . . **50.00**

Hairbrush, 2½ × 4½", wood, red, white, and blue decal, c1940s **75.00**

Paint Book, Superman To The Rescue,

Western Publishing Co Inc, 24 pgs, unused, copyright 1980 DC Comics Inc **15.00**

Pencil Case, 3½ × 8", vinyl, zippered, red and blue illus and logo on yellow ground, Standard Plastic Products, copyright National Periodical Publications Inc, 1966 . . . . **58.00**

Pennant, 11 × 29", felt, red, white logo, white, pink, and yellow Superman illus, copyright National Periodical Publications Inc, 1966 . . . . **60.00**

Record Player, 1978 . . . . **65.00**

Wonder Woman

Glass, 6¼" h, clear, illus on front, logo and name on back, Pepsi issue, copyright DC Comics, 1978 . . . . **18.00**

Watch, gold case, color illus of Wonder Woman, Dabs, copyright DC Comics, 1977 . . . . **30.00**

SWANKYSWIGS

Swankyswigs are decorated glass containers that were filled with Kraft Cheese Spreads. They date from the early 1930s. See D. M. Fountain's *Swankyswig Price Guide* (published by author in 1979) to identify pieces by pattern.

Most Swankyswigs still sell for under $5.00. If a glass still has its original label, add $5.00 to the price.

Cornflower #2, dark blue, $2.00.

Antique, coal bucket and clock,
  brown **4.00**
Bands, black and red. **3.00**
Bicentennial, yellow, Coin Dot design,
  1975. . . . . **10.00**
Bustling Betsy, brown **2.00**
Carnival, fired-on dark blue. **7.50**
Checkerboard, red **25.00**
Cornflower #2, yellow **1.50**
Daisies, red daisies top row, white daisies
  middle row, green leaves **3.00**
Dots and Circles, green. **3.75**
Forget-Me-Not, light blue **1.50**
Jonquil, yellow, green leaves. **3.00**
Kiddie Kup
  Bird and Elephant, red **2.00**
  Pig and Bear, blue **2.00**
Posy, light blue **3.00**
Sailboat, red **20.00**
Star, black **5.00**
Texas Centennial, dark blue. **10.00**
Tulips, No. 3, yellow, four molded bands
  around top. **3.00**
Violets, blue flowers, green leaves. **2.50**

SWIZZLE STICKS

They just do not make swizzle sticks like they used to. There is no end of the ways to collect them—color, motif, region, time period, and so on.

You can usually find them for less than $1.00. In fact, you can often buy a box or glass full of them for just a few dollars. Sets bring more, but they have to be unusual.

Club: International Swizzlestick Collectors Association, P. O. Box 117, Bellingham, Va 98227-1117.

Advertising, Jack Dempsey Restaurant,
  green and orange **18.00**
American Export Lines, pitch fork
  shape. **4.00**
Bird, Chez **10.00**
Fruit, glass, set of 12, includes stand **55.00**
Penthouse, set of 8 . . . . **20.00**
Piccadilly Circus Bar. **2.00**

TEDDY BEARS

Teddy bear collectors are fanatics. Never tell them their market is going soft. They will club you to death with their bears. Do not tell anyone that you heard it here, but the Teddy Bear craze of the 1980s has ended. The market is flooded with old and contemporary bears.

The name "Teddy" Bear originated with Theodore Roosevelt. The accepted date of its birth is 1902–1903. Early bears had humped backs, elongated muzzles, and jointed limbs. The fabric was usually mohair; the eyes were either glass with pin backs or black shoe buttons.

The contemporary Teddy Bear market is as big or bigger than the market for antique and collectible bears. Many of these bears are quite expensive. Collectors who are speculating in them will find that getting their money out of them in ten to fifteen years is going to be a bearish proposition.

Magazine: *The Teddy Bear And Friends*, Hobby House Press, Inc., 900 Frederick Street, Cumberland, MD 21502.

Club: Good Bears of the World, P. O. Box 13097, Toledo, OH 43613.

Bear
  5" h, plush, swivel head, "Character"
    label. **40.00**
  5½" h, Panda, mohair, black and
    white, googly glass eyes, yarn nose
    and mouth, felt pads, 1950s **95.00**
  6" h, plush, jointed, orig clothes,
    "Berg" label **65.00**
  8" h, mohair, dark brown, excelsior
    stuffed, jointed, black and white
    googly eyes, beige mohair snout
    and inner ears, open felt mouth, red
    felt tongue, beige felt foot pads, tag-
    ged "Fechter Spielwaren" on right
    ear **75.00**
  9" h, plush, blonde, straw filled, black
    shoe button eyes, shoulder hump,
    c1905. . . . . **165.00**
  9½" h, Honey Bear, woolly mohair,
    chocolate brown and beige, kapok
    stuffed, jointed, glass eyes, horizon-
    tal stitched wool floss nose and
    mouth, embroidered tongue, beige
    velveteen pads, 1940 . . . . **80.00**
  10" h, mohair, light gold, rigid neck,
    wire jointed arms and legs, stalk
    eyes, yarn nose and mouth, velvet
    lined ears, squeaker, late 1920s **85.00**
  10½" h, mohair, yellow, jointed, short
    legs, clear glass eyes, vertical
    stitched square floss nose, red velve-
    teen inner ears and pads, 1950–
    1960. . . . . **80.00**
  11" h, cotton plush, gold, jointed
    arms and legs, glass eyes, hemp-
    type floss nose and mouth, stubby
    feet, 1920s. **150.00**
  12" h, plush, white, woolly, clear glass
    eyes, coarse floss nose and mouth,
    worn pads, 1920–1930. . . . . **135.00**

13" h, plush, dark brown, jointed, long nose, felt paws, black sewn nose and mouth **25.00**

14" h, mohair, brown, jointed, inset snout, floss nose and mouth, felt pads, windup music box, Knickerbocker, 1950s **175.00**

16" h, rayon plush, brown-tipped, beige flannel snout and inner ears, papier mache body, amber glass eyes, black floss nose, pink flannel open mouth, felt pads on hands, patterned heavy cotton foot pads, manually swings arms, turns head, and walks, 1950s **165.00**

17" h, Teddy Baby, Steiff **875.00**

18" h, mohair, gold, jointed head, bat shape ears, velveteen snout and pads, flat black eyes, horizontal stitched black floss nose and mouth, red floss tongue, squeaker, 1940s **150.00**

20" h, mohair, brown, jointed, flat face, Knickerbocker **100.00**

21" h, mohair, long pile, gold, excelsior stuffed head and arms, soft stuffed body and legs, jointed arms, clear glass eyes, black yarn nose and mouth, brown velveteen overalls, 1940–50 .... **165.00**

Bear-related Items

Book

Book of Bears, Frank Ver Beck, J B Lippincott Co, 1906, 96 pgs **45.00**

Little Bears Ups & Downs,, Rand McNally, 1936 .... **15.00**

Paddy Paws, Four Adventures, Grace Coolidge, Rand McNally, 1937 ... **20.00**

The Teddy Bears, Bray illustrator, Judge, 1907, set of 8 .... **160.00**

Dish, 6" d, china, full color illus, youngster bear finishing picture on black board, early 1900s **50.00**

Spoon, 5½" l, silver plated, figural handle, enamel dec, Russia **50.00**

TEENAGE MUTANT NINJA TURTLES

It's hard to believe that an independent black and white illustrated comic by Eastman and Laird could cause such a craze. But it's true and they're out there.

Teenage Mutant Ninja Turtles are everywhere and kids love them. Toys, clothes, movies, daily television cartoon shows and even T.M.N.T. cereal are available across the country.

Merchandising of T.M.N.T. began in 1988. The Turtles' popularity demanded a live action movie in 1990. Since then

Teenage Mutant Ninja Turtles have mutated into one of the most popular kids' collectibles of the late twentieth century.

Collecting Turtle items isn't difficult, just take a peek under any plastic manhole cover and you're sure to find Michaelangelo, Donatello, Leonardo, or Raphael staring back at you. Cowabunga Dude!

Action Figures, Playmates, 4½" h

April O'Neil

1988, no stripe, Turtle Force Fan Club Flyer **40.00**

1989, #5055, blue stripe **12.00**

Baxter Stockman, 1988 .... **9.00**

Bebop, 1988

With Turtle Force Fan Club Flyer, 1988 .... **20.00**

Without Flyer **7.50**

Donatello

#5002, 1988 .... **6.00**

#5612, Sewer-swimmin', Wacky Action windup, with Quiz Joke Book, 1989 .... **6.00**

Foot Soldier, #5008, 1988 .... **7.50**

General Traag, #5061, 1989........ **7.50**

Genghis Frog, #5051, 1989 .... **7.50**

Krang, #5056, 1989 .... **12.50**

Leatherhead, 1989 .... **7.50**

Leonardo

#5001, 1988 .... **6.00**

#5181, Talkin' Leonardo, 1991 .... **5.00**

Metalhead, #5053, 1990........... **5.00**

Michaelangelo

#5150, Midshipman Mike, 1991 ... **5.00**

#5614, Rock 'n' Roll Michaelangelo, Wacky Action windup, 1990 .... **6.00**

Mutagen Man, 1990.............. **6.00**

Panda Khan, #5108, 1989 .... **15.00**

Pizzaface, 1990 .... **6.00**

Raphael

#5003, 1988 .... **6.00**

#5144, Grand Slammin' Raph, Sewer Sports All-Stars, 1991 .... **5.00**

Rat King, 1989 .... **7.50**

Ray Filet, #5110, 1990–91

Purple **35.00**

Yellow and Blue **15.00**

Rocksteady, #5009, 1988 .... **7.50**

Scumbug, 1990................. **6.00**

Shredder

#5007, 1988 .... **8.00**

#5617, Slice 'n Dice Shredder, Wacky Action windup, with joke book, 1990.................. **6.00**

Slash, 1990 .... **6.00**

Splinter

1988........................ **8.00**

1991, Creepy Crawlin' Splinter, #5616, Wacky Action windup, with joke book................ **6.00**

Tokka, #5130, 1991 .... **5.00**

Triceraton, #5104, 1990........... **6.00**

Usagi Yojimbo, #5054, 1989........ **8.00**

Wacky Walking Mouser, Wacky Action windup, 1990 . . . .   9.00
Walkabout, #5139, 1991 . . . .   5.00
Wingnut & Screwloose, 1990. . . . . . .   6.00
Comic Book
  Teenage Mutant Ninja Turtles Adventures, second series
    No. 1, Shredder, Bebop, and Rocksteady return to Earth 9.00
    No. 3, Three Fragments, part 1 . . . . .   5.00
    No. 6, introduction to Leatherhead and Mary Bones 3.50
    No. 16, introduction and death of Bubbla the Glubbab 1.50
Doll, Michaelangelo, plush, 13" h 20.00
Game, Subterranean Sewer Hockey, Remco, 39½ × 24½", 1990 . . . . 80.00
Mutant Maker Crazy Character Creation Kit, #5695, Playmates, 1990. . . . . 12.00
Training Manual
  No. 1 . . . .   7.50
  No. 4 . . . .   4.00
Vehicles & Accessories
  Cheapskate Skateboard, 1988 . . . . 11.00
  Don's Sewer Squirter, #5681, 1991 . . .   8.00
  Flushomatic, #5661, 1990 . . . . 15.00
  Foot Cruiser 35.00
  Footski, 1989. . . . . 11.00
  Knucklehead, 1988 . . . . 11.00
  Mega Mutant Killer Bee, #5635, 1990. . . . .   6.00
  Mega Mutant Needlenose, #5634, 1990. . . . . 20.00
  Pizza Thrower, 1989 . . . . 35.00
  Psycho Cycle, #5691, 1990. . . . . 25.00
  Retrocatapult, #5663, 1990 . . . . 11.00
  Retromutagen Ooze, #5531, 4 oz bucket, 1989 . . . .   3.00
  Sewer Playset, #5685, 1990 . . . . 50.00
  Technodrome, 22" h, 1988 . . . . 60.00
  Toilet Taxi, #5552, 1990. . . . .   7.00
  Turtle Blimp, green vinyl, 30" l, 1988. . . . . 30.00
  Turtle Party Wagon, #5622, 1989 . . . . 40.00
  Turtle Trooper Parachute, #5019, 22", 1988. . . . . 10.00
Video Game, talking, handheld, Konami, 1990. . . . . 30.00
Wristwatch, LCD digital, plastic strap, flip-up figure, Hope, 1991 . . . .   9.00

TELEPHONES AND TELEPHONE-RELATED

If you ask a number of people when they think the telephone was invented, most will give you a date in the early twentieth century. The accepted answer is 1876, when Alexander Graham Bell filed his patent. However, crude telegraph and sound-operated devices existed prior to that date.

Beware of reproduction phones or phones made from married parts. Buy only telephones that have the proper period parts, a minimum of restoration, and are in working order. No mass-produced telephone in the United States made prior to 1950 was manufactured with a shiny brass finish.

Concentrating on telephones is only half the story. Telephone companies generated a wealth of secondary material from books to giveaway premiums. Dig around for examples from local companies that eventually were merged into the Bell system.

Clubs: Antique Telephone Collectors Association, Box 94, Abilene, KS 67410; Telephone Collectors International, Inc., 19 North Cherry Dr., Oswego, IL 60543.

Desk Set, Ericsson, metal, rect ivory colored base, marked "Telefon A.-B. L.M. Ericsson, Stockholm 20 48," 10¼" h, 7" w base, $25.00.

Booth, wood, no doors 125.00
Magazine, *Telephony,* 1955 50
Mirror, pocket, adv, 2½" l, blue and white, celluloid, issued for Missouri and Kansas Telephone Co of Bell System and American Telephone & Telegraph, early 1900s 65.00
Notepad, Southern New England Telephone Co, simulated leather, red good luck stamp on cov, black inscription, blue Bell System logo on back 20.00
Paperweight, 3¼" h, figural, bell, glass, dark blue, gold lettering "Bell System, New York Telephone Company, Local and Long Distance Telephone," c1920. . . . . 70.00
Pay Phone, 1950s 165.00

Pin

Ex-Officio, $\frac{1}{2}$" d, Telephone Pioneers
of America, enameled brass, blue
and white, triangular logo and Bell
Telephone symbol, "William J. Denver Chapter, Past Council President," 1950–1951 .... **10.00**

Hanger, 1" l, Bell System, celluloid,
diecut, bell shape, blue, white lettering, "Local Long Distance Telephone" on front, reverse with
"When in Doubt, Telephone and
Find Out, Use the Bell," Whitehead
& Hoag patent, 1905 .... **12.00**

Service, $\frac{1}{2}$" d, octagonal, New England
Telephone & Telegraph, 10K gold,
raised Bell System logo above faux
ruby, 1930s **15.00**

Pinback Button

$\frac{7}{8}$" d, Bell Telephone System, blue let-
tering and logo, white ground, "3
Sale Club" on center bell logo,
"Plant Employee Sales, Go Get 'Em,
Eastern Division" on rim, 1906–
1907....................... **25.00**

1" d

50th Anniversary, white "50" over
black candlestick telephone, dark
blue ground, 1930s **10.00**

New England Telephone & Telegraph Co, Bell System, dark blue
and white, "Our Slogan Service
First," c1933 .... **15.00**

$1\frac{1}{2}$" d, Kansas Independent Telephone
Ass'n, black and white candlestick
telephone standing on brown and
yellow sunflower, early 1900s **45.00**

Sign

American Tissue Mills, $19\frac{1}{2} \times 18\frac{3}{4}$",
cardboard and tissue, standup, Santa
Claus talking on candlestick type
telephone **75.00**

Indiana Telephone Co, 18×18", two
sided, porcelain enamel, black and
white, "Indiana Telephone Corporation, Local & Long Distance Service," late 1940s **65.00**

Stand, gossip bench, mahogany,
1940s....................... **75.00**

Stickpin, 1×1" diecut celluloid hanger,
blue and white, reverse inscribed
"When In Doubt Telephone And Find
Out/Use The Bell," Bell System,
c1905........................ **42.00**

Switchboard, transmitter broom, pre-
1935........................**400.00**

Telephone

Candlestick, straight pipe, dial **185.00**

Desk, rotary dial, black, 1950s **25.00**

Double Box, oak, Stromberg-Carlson
type **350.00**

Field, World War II, US Army **25.00**

Single Box, wood, plain front, 1915–
1920........................**200.00**

Wall, oak, hand crank, 23" l, c1908...**285.00**

TELEVISION CHARACTERS AND PERSONALITIES

The golden age of television varies depending on the period in which you grew
up. Each generation thinks the television
of their childhood is the best there ever
was.

TV collectibles are one category in
which new products establish themselves
as collectible quickly. The minute a show is
canceled, something that happens rather
rapidly today, anything associated with it
is viewed as collectible.

The golden age of TV star endorsements
was the 1950s through the 1960s. For
whatever reason, toy, game, and other
manufacturers today are not as convinced
that TV stars sell products. As a result,
many shows have no licensed products associated with them. Because of the ab-
sence of three-dimensional material, collectors must content themselves with
paper, such as *TV Guide* and magazines.

*Cup, litho tin, Bonanza, Hoss, Ben, and Little
Joe Cartwright, marked "Ponderosa Ranch, Ne-
vada, U.S.A.," $2\frac{5}{8}$" h, $3\frac{1}{2}$" d, 1960s, $15.00.*

Activity Book, *I Love Lucy Golden Fun
Time Tracing Book*, $8\frac{1}{4} \times 11$", 32 pgs,
Golden Press, copyright 1959 Desilu
Productions Inc.................... **50.00**

Big Little Book, *Wyatt Earp*, $4\frac{1}{2} \times 5\frac{3}{4}$",
full color Hugh O'Brien illus on cov,
Whitman #1644, 1958 .... **20.00**

Book

Beverly Hillbillies, 6×8" hard cover,
color photo cover of Clampett Fam-
ily, Whitman #1572 .... **15.00**

*The Mod Squad, Assignment: The Hide-
out*, 212 pgs, hard cov, Western Publishing Co Inc, copyright 1970
Thomas-Spelling Productions **12.50**

The Wild, Wild West, Robert Conrad,
paperback, Signet Books, first printing, 1966 .... **25.00**

Book Cover, Welcome Back Kotter, unused. **12.00**

Charm Bracelet, Ben Casey, orig pkg . . . **60.00**

Coloring Book

Flipper, 8 × 11½", Whitman Publishing Co, copyright 1966 Ivan Tors Films Inc **12.00**

Rin-Tin-Tin, 8¼ × 11", some neatly colored pages, Whitman, #1257, 1955. . . . . **15.00**

Comic Book

Fury, Gold Key Comics, issue #1, Nov 1962, color photo cover and back, costar Bobby Diamond **20.00**

Hogan's Heroes, 7 × 10", #8 Dell Publishing Co, copyright 1967 Bing Crosby Productions. **10.00**

Game

Gunsmoke, 19¼" sq board, 10 × 20 × 2½" slightly scuffed box, Lowell Toy, late 1950s **30.00**

Jackie Gleason's TV Fun Game, 19" sq game board with Gleason illus, orig box, Transogram, copyright 1956 VIP Corp **200.00**

Phil Silvers You'll Never Get Rich Game, 18½ × 19" game board, Silvers photo, four plastic playing pieces, three decks of cards, money, orig box, Gardner Games, 1955–56 . . . . **200.00**

The Fonz, orig box, Milton Bradley, copyright 1976 Paramount Pictures Corp. **25.00**

Welcome Back Kotter Card Game, deck of cards, four score cards, orig box, Milton Bradley, copyright 1976 The Wolper Organization Inc **18.00**

Hand Puppet, Topo Gigio, 11" h, cloth body, molded vinyl head, late 1950s. **50.00**

Lunch Box

Addams Family, 7 × 8½ × 4", litho metal, black trim, full color scenes, King-Seeley, 1974 copyright **30.00**

The Fall Guy, 7 × 8 × 4", metal, emb, color illus, 6½" h plastic thermos, Aladdin Industries, copyright 1981 20th Century Fox Film Corp **30.00**

Hogan's Heroes, 7 × 9 × 4½", metal, dome shape, color illus, Aladdin Industries, copyright 1966 Bing Crosby Productions Inc. **100.00**

Knight Rider, 7 × 9 4", metal, color illus, Thermos co, copyright 1983 Universal City Studios Inc **25.00**

The Waltons, metal, emb, color illus, Aladdin, copyright 1973 Lorimar Productions Inc. **25.00**

Mug, Rocky and His Friends, 4" h, white ceramic, full color Rocky, Mr Peabody, and Bullwinkle carrying signs, 1960 copyright. **75.00**

Paper Dolls, Buffy and Jody, 9" h figures, 32 wardrobe pieces, orig box,

Whitman, copyright 1970 Family Affair Co **28.00**

Pinback Button

Bonanza, 3" d, celluloid, red tone photo of Cartwright family, blue inscriptions, pre-1965 . . . . **35.00**

Fran Allison, 1⅛" d, "Aunt Fanny's Bread/Fran Allison of Radio & TV," litho, full color, 1950s. **20.00**

George Fischbeck, Eye Witness Weather, KOB-TV, 1⅛" d, dark blue and white, Albuquerque, NM station, early 1950s **15.00**

Plate, Davy Crockett, 7" d, milk glass, dark red illus and words "Davy Crockett, Frontier Hero," mid 1950s. **15.00**

Puzzle, Get Smart, 14 × 19", Maxwell Smart and Agent 99, orig box, Jaymar, copyright 1966 talent Associates **25.00**

Sheet Music, *The Waltons*, 8½ × 11", 2 pgs, copyright 1973 Roliram Music . . . **15.00**

Sticker Book, Fat Albert and The Cosby Kids, 8½ × 11", Whitman #2865–66, 1973, unused **17.50**

TV Guide

Lassie, July 4, 1959, full color cov illus of Lassie, Jon Provost, article "The Life and Times of Lassie" with color photos **7.50**

Lucille Ball, April 30, 1966, full color cover art illus, artist Ronald Searle. **10.00**

TELEVISION LAMPS

What 1950s living room would be complete without a black ceramic gondola slowly meandering across the top of the television set? Long before the arrival of VCRs, descramblers, and Nintendo systems, figural lamps dominated the top of televisions. The lamps were made of colorful high gloss ceramics, and the subject matter ranged from the relatively mundane dog statue to the more exotic (tasteless?) hula dancer.

A collection of ten or more of these beauties will certainly lighten up the conversation at your next party. On second thought, it does not take ten. The pink poodle lamp on my television is more than enough to do the job.

Accordion, translucent ceramic, ivory, "Lawrence Welk," gold trim and lettering. **65.00**

Buffalo, ceramic, brown, standing on rocks. **32.00**

Butterfly, ceramic, green, yellow, and black, leafy base **30.00**

Dying Stag, plaster, brown stag, yellow
    flower and base, gold trim **25.00**
Fish, ceramic, white, round metal
    base **18.00**
Flamingos, ceramic, pink, black, and
    white, one with wings spread, planter
    base, Lane & Co, Van Nuys, CA, dated
    1957. . . . . **50.00**
Gazelle, ceramic, black, jumping over
    palm fronds **35.00**
Hearth, ceramic, green, yellow/orange
    screen **28.00**
Horses, ceramic, pair of black racing
    horses, green foliate base **38.00**
Island Girl, ceramic, green, leaning
    against palm tree, screen back-
    ground. **40.00**
Lighthouse and Cottage, ceramic, multi-
    colored. **32.00**
Mallard, ceramic, airbrushed, green and
    brown, wings spread, planter base. . . . **35.00**
Owl, ceramic, brown, green interior, sgd
    "Kron" **20.00**
Panther, ceramic, black, stalking,
    white screen background, green oval
    base **25.00**
Poodles, pr, ceramic, pink and black,
    black oval planter base **30.00**
Rooster, ceramic, crowing, multicolored,
    standing on brown fence, Lane & Co,
    Van Nuys, CA, 13" h. **45.00**
Sampan, ceramic, ivory colored boat . . . **20.00**
Scotty Dog, ceramic, pouncing, gold, . . . **18.00**
Seashells **15.00**

TELEVISIONS

Old television sets are becoming highly
collectible. It is not unusual to see a dozen
or more at a flea market. Do not believe a
tag that says it works. Insist that the seller
find a place to plug it in and show you.

A good general rule is the smaller the
picture tube, the earlier the set. Pre-1946
televisions usually have a maximum of
five stations, 1 through 5. Channels 7
through 13 were added in 1947. In 1949
Channel 1 was dropped. UHF appeared in
1953.

In order to determine the value of a
television, you need to identify the brand
and model number. See *Warman's Antiques
and Their Prices* for a more detailed list.

Newsletter: *Sight, Sound, Style*, P. O. Box
2224, South Hackensack, NJ 07606.

Admiral
    Model 19A11, table, black Bakelite, 7"
        screen, 1948–1949 . . . . **150.00**

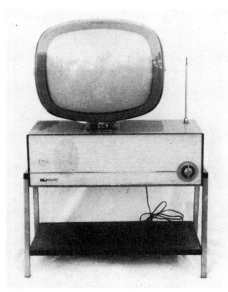

Philco, "Predicta," reconditioned, $250.00.

Model 20X1, console, Bakelite, 10"
    screen, 1947–1948 . . . . **300.00**
Air King, Model A-1001, console, 10"
    screen, twenty tubes, flat front,
    1950. . . . . **85.00**
Automatic, Model TV-707, table, blonde
    wood, 7" screen, 1948 . . . . **150.00**
Bendix, Model 3051, square console, 16"
    screen **35.00**
DuMont, Model RA-101, Revere, con-
    sole, 15" screen, double doors,
    1946. . . . . **125.00**
Fada, Model S-1015, table, wood, Bake-
    lite mask, square lines, 12" screen,
    1949. . . . . **75.00**
General Electric, Model 805, table, Bake-
    lite, 10" screen, streamlined, 1948. . . . **175.00**
Motorola, Model 7-TV5, portable, lea-
    therette cabinet, 7" screen, lid, han-
    dle **150.00**
Philco, Model, 50-701, table, Bakelite, 7"
    screen, 1950 . . . . **200.00**
Pilot, Model TV-37, magnifier, plastic,
    tabs attach to grill, marked "Pilot
    TV" **175.00**
Tele-Tone, Model TV-208, portable, 7"
    porthole screen, handle, 1948 . . . . **150.00**
Westinghouse, Model H-196, table,
    rounded top, 10" screen, 1949 . . . . **125.00**
Zenith, portable, metal, light-weight,
    1950s **35.00**

THERMOMETERS

The thermometer was a popular advertising giveaway and promotional item. Buy

only thermometers in very good or better condition which have a minimum of wear on the visible surface. Remember, thermometers had large production runs. If the first example that you see does not please you, shop around.

Salem Cigarettes, tin, painted, 9¼" h, $12.00.

Advertising

A Tvarosek Oil Co, Berwyn, IL, cardboard, black lettering, 6⅛" h **5.00**
Borden Feed, orig box, 1952 .... **25.00**
Cash Value Tobacco, tin **22.50**
Champion Spark Plugs **20.00**
Coca-Cola, bottle shape, gold, orig box, 1950s **20.00**
Dr Pepper, tin, 1960s logo, 20" h **50.00**
Dr Pierce's Chemical Co, Bakelite, 1931 .... **18.00**
First National Bank, Fremont, OH, wood, orig box **30.00**
Georgia Real Estate Co, wood, 21" h, 1915 .... **70.00**
Happy Jim Chewing Tobacco, 35" h **75.00**
Kendall Oil, round **25.00**
Luminall, 39" h, 1950 .... **60.00**
Naco Fertilizer Co, Charleston, SC.... **22.00**
Nyal Drugstore Service, 38" h **28.00**
Old Dutch Root Beer, 27" h, 1940 .... **65.00**
Old Fashion Moxie, metal **20.00**
Pal Orange Ade, 26" h **40.00**
Rislone **55.00**
Rochester American Insurance Co, NY, porcelain **27.00**
Royal Crown Cola, cardboard, Santa Claus and bottle, 20 × 10", 1950s ... **35.00**
Salem Cigarettes **12.00**
Sauer's Vanilla, wood, 1919 .... **68.00**
Snow Goose Flour, blue trim, white ground, 39" h **50.00**

Standard Oil, tin, orig box **20.00**
Stegmaier Beer, glass, round **43.00**
Switch and Manufacturing Co, Carlisle, PA, frog, dark blue trim, white ground, 36" h **45.00**
Washer Hardware, Sheldon, IA, wood frame **24.00**
Figural
Cat, bisque, 7½" h, Bradly Japan label **22.00**
Negro, 1949 .... **25.00**
Owl, plaster body, 6" h **75.00**
World's Fair, 1934 Chicago World's Fair, octagonal shape, silver and blue dial symbol and lettering, brass rim, black metal back and hanging, 2½ × 2½" ... **50.00**

TINS

The advertising tin has always been at the forefront of advertising collectibles. Look for examples that show no deterioration to the decorated surface and which have little or no signs of rust on the inside or bottom.

The theme sells the tin. Other collectors, especially individuals from the transportation fields, have long had their eyes on the tin market. Tins also play a major part in the Country Store decorating look.

Prices for pre-1940 tins are still escalating. Before you pay a high price for a tin, do your homework and make certain it is difficult to find.

Club: Tin Container Collectors Association, P. O. Box 440101, Aurora, CO 80044.

Bagley's Old Colony, pocket **95.00**
Cadet Condom, round **46.00**
Cavalier **22.50**
Chesterfield Cigarette, cat on lid **38.00**
Cleveland's Superior Baking Powder, lid, label **25.00**
Davis Baking Powder, sample **25.00**
Dining Car Coffee, 1 lb, key wind **58.00**
Educator Cakelets, made in Krackerland, hinged lid, multicolored animal illus, 1920s **145.00**
Epicure Tobacco, pocket **90.00**
Farmer Peet Lard **12.00**
Father Christmas Candy, 1930s **55.00**
Fitch Talc, c1930 .... **10.00**
George Washington Instant Coffee **30.00**
Golden Pheasant Prophylactics **68.00**
Improved Trojans Prophylactics **28.00**
Instant Postum **22.00**
John Orderleys, Owl Drug Co **25.00**
Lucky Strike, flat **8.00**
Maxwell House Coffee, 1 lb, 1909 ...... **20.00**

Royal Baking Powder, paper label, white lettering, red ground, 4" h, 2³⁄₈" d, $25.00.

Monarch Teenie Weenie Popcorn, pail, 1920.	225.00
New Bachelor Cigar, man playing cards and dreaming of woman	100.00
Noonan's Cleansing Cream, 1½" d, lady with mirror	25.00
Old Colony Tobacco, pocket	95.00
Old English Curve Cut	15.00
Philip Morris	22.50
Postmaster Cigar, "2 for 5¢ smokers"	75.00
Red Seal Marshmallow	30.00
Regulax	15.00
Richelieu Tea	12.00
Riley Toffee	15.00
Shedd's Peanut Butter, 5# pail	15.00
Snow Flake Crackers, hinged, 9 × 9"	49.00
Sunshine Biscuit	12.00
Sylae Tooth Powder, sample size	6.00
Type Bar Typewriter	5.00
Union Leader	12.50
US Marine, pocket	140.00
Velvet Night Talcum	24.00
Yellow Bonnet, 1 lb, key wind, unopened.	25.00
ZBT Baby Powder	10.00

TOBACCO-RELATED

The tobacco industry is under siege in the 1990s. Fortunately, they have new frontiers to conquer in Russia, Eastern Europe, Asia, and Africa. The relics of America's smoking past, from ashtrays to humidors, are extremely collectible.

Many individuals are not able to identify a smoking stand or a pocket cigar cutter. I grew up in York County, Pennsylvania, which, along with Lancaster County, was the tobacco center of the East. Today, tobacco growing and manufacturing have virtually disappeared. Is it possible that there will be a time when smoking disappears as well?

Club: International Seal, Label, and Cigar Band Society, 8915 East Bellevue Street, Tuscon, AZ 85715.

Tobacco Jar, terrier, matte finish, blue stamped "R" in diamond and "N588," 5⁵⁄₈" h, $175.00.

Box, 4 × 7 × 12", Old Plug Tobacco, Irvin & Leedys, Henry Country, VA, walnut	20.00
Lunch Box, Patterson Seal Tobacco	18.00
Mirror, Mascot Tobacco	30.00
Oilstone, 2¼" d, Bagley's Tobacco, celluloid, multicolored tobacco can, red ground, mounted on back of emery whetstone, c1900	75.00
Poster, 7 × 13", c1900	
Crusader Tobacco	25.00
Golden Eagle Tobacco	30.00
Pouch, Tiger Chewing Tobacco, black and white, linen, stitched edge, tiger illus on each side, early 1900s	20.00
Sign	
Brown's Mule Tobacco, mule reaching in window pulling cover off man	175.00
Red Jacket Tobacco, 22 × 28", cardboard, baseball scene	125.00

Time Plug Tobacco, 12" sq, card-
board **25.00**
Thermometer
Cash Value Tobacco, tin **22.50**
Happy Jim Chewing Tobacco,
35" h. **75.00**
Tin
Bagdad, pocket **30.00**
Bagley Old Colony, pocket **140.00**
Big Ben Hoby, pocket **25.00**
Blue Heaven Tobacco, beige and
blue **5.00**
Dill's Best, pocket, concave **40.00**
Frishmuth's Whittle Cut Tobacco **15.00**
Half & Half Tobacco, 1926 . . . . **6.00**
Kentucky Club, pocket **15.00**
Obold, pocket, concave **50.00**
Queed Tobacco, pocket. **80.00**
Stag, pocket. **50.00**
Tiger Tobacco, store, round, red. **195.00**
Union Leader Tobacco, red, gold ea-
gle **25.00**
Tobacco Cutter, Enterprise, store type,
1885. . . . . **45.00**

TOKENS

Token collecting is an extremely diverse
field. The listing below barely scratches the
surface with respect to the types of tokens
one might find.

The wonderful thing about tokens is
that, on the whole, they are very inexpensive. You can build an impressive collection on a small budget.

Like match cover and sugar packet collectors, token collectors have kept their
objects outside the main collecting stream.
This has resulted in stable, low prices over
a long period of time in spite of an extensive literature base. There is no indication
that this is going to change in the near
future.

Club: Token and Medal Society, Inc., P. O.
Box 951988, Lake Mary, FL 32795.

Advertising
Fred Biffar & Co, Chicago, "Firearms,
Ammunition, Pocket Cutlery,
Sporting Goods" on front, reverse
with good luck symbols, "Good
Luck," and "Membership Emblem
of the Don't Worry Club," c1930. . . **10.00**
Lion Buggy Co, Cincinnati, OH, brass,
lion's head and company name on
front, reverse with anchor and
rope **5.00**
Remington, 1¼" d, brass, "Shot With
A Kleanbore Remington Cartridge"

on front, reverse with "Shot With A
Remington Rifle" **8.00**
Scranton Stove Works, Scranton, PA,
brass, gear inscribed with company
name and scroll with "Dockash
Medal" on front, reverse with world
globe and "Dockash Range World
Hunt Souvenir 1886". **3.00**
Vaughan's Seed Store, Chicago, copper-nickel alloy, six story building
on front, reverse with inscription
and date "1887" **5.00**
Amusement Park, Applegates Palace
of Flying Animals, brass, two don-
keys, "Then Shall We Three Meet
Again". **12.00**
Barber, Palmer House Barber Shop, cop-
per-nickel alloy, name and "10¢ 66"
on front, blank reverse **15.00**
Billiards, The Garden City Billiard Table
Co, Chicago, IL, brass, inscription on
front, reverse with "Palace/Good For
5¢ in Trade," 1880s **15.00**
Campaign, Horace Greeley, ⅞" d, brass,
portrait and "Sage of Chappaqua" on
front, reverse with eagle and "Greeley,
Brown, and Amnesty 1872" **30.00**
Commemorative
22 Nord-Amer. Sangerfest, Chicago,
IL, woman holding lyre and German
inscription on front, reverse with inscription and date within wreath,
1881. . . . . **5.00**
Baltimore Oriole Celebration, white
metal, memorial statue on front, reverse with oriole, inscription, and
date "Sep 12, 13, 14, 1882" **5.00**
Convention, Women's Relief Corps, Columbus, OH, bronze, female bust portrait and signature "Kate B.
Kenwood" on front, reverse with inscription and date "Sept. 1888". **12.00**
Fraternal
Knights of the Golden Eagle, Washington, D. C., brass, capitol building and
"Annual Convocation of Supreme
Castle, Knights of the Golden Eagle,
Washington, May 22, 1888" on
front, reverse with laurel wreath
around rim and blank center **20.00**
Knights Templars, Easton, PA, gilt
brass, maltese cross and crossed
swords on front, reverse with "36th
Annual Conclave of the Grand
Commandery of K.T. of Pennsylva-
nia Easton May 28, 1889" **15.00**
Insurance, Globe Fire Insurance Com-
pany, NY, copper, eagle holding Liberty Bell and "Centennial 1776 1876"
on front, reverse with world globe and
company name and address **4.00**
Railroad, Michigan Central Railroad,
brass, "M.C.R.R. 50" on front, reverse
with "½ CORD," milled border **75.00**

Saloon
ACME, El Paso, TX, copper-nickel alloy, "N. F. Newland Prop" in oval on front, reverse with "Good For 1 ACME Drink" **12.50**
Pony House, Dayton, OH, brass, name and address on front, reverse with "Good For 5¢ In Trade," c1900 .... **4.00**
State Fair, Pennsylvania State Agricultural Fair, Philadelphia, PA, gilt brass, sheep and inscription on front, reverse with cow and calf above masonry capital and Philadelphia coat of arms, 1880. .... **25.00**

TOOTHPICK HOLDERS

During the Victorian era, the toothpick holder was an important table accessory. It is found in a wide range of materials and was manufactured by American and European firms. Toothpick holders also were popular souvenir objects in the 1880 to 1920 period.

Do not confuse toothpick holders with match holders, shot glasses, miniature spoon holders in a child's dish set, mustard pots without lids, rose or violet bowls, individual open salts, or vases. A toothpick holder allows ample room for the toothpicks and enough of an extension of the toothpicks to allow easy access.

Club: National Toothpick Holder Collector's Society, P. O. Box 246, Sawyer, MI 49125.

Silver Plate, figural, dog dressed as man, holding lantern, basket holder on back, marked "Meriden B #2," c1880, $185.00.

Advertising, Boothby's-Home of Seafood, Phila, celluloid **8.00**
Bisque, piglets..................... **65.00**
Brass, top hat, umbrella **20.00**
China
Barrel Shape, pink roses dec, Bavaria **30.00**
Black Corinthian, Royal Bayreuth.... **85.00**
Egg shape, hp **150.00**
Milk Glass, barrel, metal hoops **25.00**
Opalescent, hobnail, blue............ **28.00**
Pattern Glass
Arched Fleur-De-Lis, clear **30.00**
Beaded Bull's Eye and Drape, clear ... **60.00**
Daisy and Button, ruby stained **28.00**
Galloway, clear................... **30.00**
Loop and Pillar, clear **45.00**
Paneled Zipper, clear **20.00**
Rising Sun **35.00**
Swinger, clear and ruby **22.00**
Souvenir
Belvedere, IL, custard glass **35.00**
Flagstaff Park, Mauch Chunk, PA, custard glass, sawtooth top, gold trim **48.00**
Marshalltown, IA, ruby flashed **18.00**

TORTOISE SHELL ITEMS

It is possible to find tortoise shell items in a variety of forms ranging from boxes to trinkets. Tortoise shell items experienced several crazes in the nineteenth and early twentieth centuries, the last occurring in the 1920s when tortoise shell jewelry was especially popular.

Anyone selling tortoise shell objects is subject to the Endangered Species Act and its amendments. Tortoise shell objects can be imported and sold, but only after adhering to a number of strict requirements.

Bowl
7¼" d, ruffled rim, applied strawberry on pontil, ftd **45.00**
8½" d, folded rim, applied amber foot....................... **85.00**
Box, cov, 4 × 11", fitted int. **150.00**
Bracelet, 3" d, bangle, silver inlay **35.00**
Cigarette Case, brass clips............. **40.00**
Comb, side, applied metallic dec, simulated gemstones **65.00**
Compact, 3" sq, gold frame **115.00**
Hairpin, carved poppy blossoms **140.00**
Humidor, 4½" h, rect, hinged lid.......**150.00**
Match Safe, pocket, emb sides **65.00**
Razor Case, sgd "Jefferson Steel" **15.00**
Salt, sterling silver rivets, orig spoon **25.00**
Shaving Brush, inlaid mother-of-pearl dec handle...................... **40.00**

Stickpin, carved fly perched on coral
branch, gold filled pin **75.00**
Straight Razor, Landers **30.00**

TOURIST SOUVENIRS

This category demonstrates that, given
time, even the tacky can become collectible. Many tourist souvenirs offer a challenge to one's aesthetics. But they are
bought anyway.

Tourist china plates and glass novelties
from the 1900 to 1940 period are one of
the true remaining bargains left. Most of
the items sell for under $25.00. If you really want to have some fun, pick one form
and see how many different places you
can find from which it was sold.

Newspaper: *Travel Collector*, P. O. Box 40,
Manawa, WI 54949.

Clubs: American Spoon Collectors, 4922
State Line, Westwood Hills, KS 66205;
Souvenir China Collectors Society, P. O.
Box 562, Great Barrington, MA 01230.

Ashtray
Empire State Building, marked
"World's Tallest Building" **7.00**
Everett (WA) Yacht Club, brass **20.00**
Bottle Opener, Sequoia National Park,
3⅞" l, cast iron, drunk at sign post **25.00**
Change Tray, Hotel Coronado, china . . . **8.00**
Creamer
Saratoga Springs, 3" h, ruby stained
glass, King's Crown pattern, etched
"Nettie" **36.00**
St James, MN **25.00**
Cup, St Charles Hotel, New Orleans,
2¾" h, china, white **12.00**
Fan, Niagara Falls, silk **8.50**
Hatchet, Hazelton, PA, 6" l, white milk
glass, red lettering **25.00**
Honey Pot, Belleville, KS **10.00**
Jug, miniature, Valley Springs, SD **25.00**
Medallion, Souvenir of Wisconsin, green
with gold, lacy **10.00**
Mug
Colorado Springs, 2¾" h, ruby stained
glass, Button Arches pattern **38.00**
New Rockford, ND, custard glass **330.00**
Paperweight, New Salem State Park,
2¾" d, glass, round **30.00**
Pennant, Kennedy Space Center, 26" l,
red felt, white lettering and Saturn V,
1966–67 . . . . **18.00**
Pinback Button
Carnival Cruises **3.00**
Charleston, SC, 1¼" d, multicolored,
1920s **22.00**
Ontario Beach Park, 2⅛" d, multi-

colored illus, imprinted "Auburn
Day," 1906–07 . . . . **25.00**
Plate
Bridge Over Illinois River, Beardstown **10.00**
Conneaut Lake, 5½" d, milk glass, reticulated border **20.00**
Vanderbilt University, 10" d, rose,
Jonroth **20.00**
Post Card, Main Street, large city **4.00**
Salt and Pepper Shakers, pr
The Baker Hotel, Mineral Wells, TX,
hp **18.00**
Empire State Building, Statue of Liberty, "Souvenir of New York," silvered cast metal **8.00**
Souvenir of Florida, 3" h, hp, pink,
flamingos **6.50**
Shot Glass
Berlin, Germany, clear, multicolored
city illus **5.00**
Virginia Beach, frosted, gold lettering
and shell dec **1.50**
Shovel, Kearney, NE, 6½" l, glass, gold
scoop and lettering, clear handle **20.00**
Snowdome
The American Museum of Natural History, Hayden Planetarium, NY, 2¾ ×
2¼ × 2", plastic dome, printing on
back, camera and city sky line scene,
1980s **4.00**
Disneyland, 2¾ × 2¼ × 2", plastic
dome, Tinkerbell and castle,
1970s **8.00**
Pocono Wild Animal Farm, 2¼ × 2 ×
2", plastic dome, deer and bear on
seesaw, 1960s **7.00**
Spoon
Baltimore, turtle handle, gold wash
bowl, demitasse **20.00**
Golden Gate, San Francisco **30.00**
Teapot, Morrison Hotel, Chicago **25.00**
Tumbler
Saratoga Springs, pewter, 1901 . . . . . . **8.00**
"Souvenir of Buffalo," sepia scenes . . . **12.00**
Vase
Opera House, What Cheer, IA, 4¾" h,
china, colored scene **12.00**
Seven Falls, Cheyenne, cobalt blue,
cannon dec, handled **20.00**

TOYS

The difference between a man and a boy is
the price of his toys. At thirty, one's childhood is affordable, at forty expensive, and
at fifty out of reach. Check the following
list for toys that you may have played
with. You will see what I mean.

Magazine: *Antique Toy World*, P. O. Box
34509, Chicago, IL 60634.

Newspaper: *Toy Shop*, 700 East State Street, Iola, WI 54990.

Club: Antique Toy Collectors of America, Two Wall Street, New York, NY 10005.

Submarine, metal and plastic, black body, red deck, gray conning tower, Tootsietoy, $75.00.

Action Games
    Chinese Checkers, San Loo, includes regular checkers game, 1952 . . . . . . 35.00
    DX Getaway Chase, orig box, 1960s 50.00
    Giant Wheel Cowboys and Indians, orig box, Remco, 1958 . . . . 25.00
    Pick Up Sticks, orig cylinder box, Schoenhut, early 1900s 55.00
    Pinball, orig box, Sears, 1960s 35.00
    Target Game, two guns, Cadaco, 1956 . . . . 40.00
    Tudor True Action Electric Football, orig box, 1949 . . . . 40.00
Baby Toys
    Busy Box, Coleco 6.00
    Musical Humpty Dumpty 15.00
Building Sets
    Architecture Jr, stone blocks, instructions, wood box 75.00
    Erector Set, Gilbert, instruction manual, Gilbert, 1954 . . . . 6.00
    Lincoln Log, #1, orig box 20.00
    Wunder Lumber, interlocking wood blocks, instructions, orig box 25.00
Dime Store Soldiers
    M80, motorized machine gunner 65.00
    M82, motorcycle rider 35.00
    M86, paymaster 185.00
    M115, aviator with bomb sight 48.00
    M142, black 90.00
    M183–184, bazooka team 80.00
Game
    Alfred Hitchcock Game, Milton Bradley, copyright 1958 . . . . 35.00
    Beverly Hillbillies Game, Standard Toykraft, copyright Filmways TV Productions Inc, 1963 . . . . 35.00
    Combat Game, Ideal, copyright Selmur Productions Inc, 1963 . . . . . 30.00
    Mr Potato Head, orig pcs and box, 1965 . . . . 5.00
    Patty Duke Game, Milton Bradley, 1963 . . . . 30.00

    Uncle Wiggily, Milton Bradley, 1954 . . . . 25.00
    The Waltons, Milton Bradley, copyright Lorimar Productions Inc, 1974 . . . . 25.00
Homemaker
    Ironing Board, 20" l, metal, folding legs, Ohio Art, 1958 . . . . 15.00
    Kitchen Set, coppertone, bread box, covered cake, cookie, two covered canisters 15.00
    Sewing Machine, Singer, red "S," orig green box 65.00
Miscellaneous
    Cash Register, Tom Thumb 22.50
    Chicken, clucking, lays marbles, Baldwin 35.00
    Gun, 9" l, sparkler, atomic, litho tin, orig pkg, Japan 28.00
    Fireman's Helmet, gold metal eagle on top, late 1800s 350.00
    Marbles, $5/8$" d, slag, mixed colors, bag of 50 . . . . 30.00
    Morse Code Transmitter, Omnigraph, late 1800s .100.00
    Mr Machine, Ideal, 1977 . . . . 55.00
    Paint and Crayon Set, Scrappy, 1930s 75.00
    Sand Pail, litho tin, girl feeding chickens illus, Ohio Art 28.00
    Troll, Frankenstein, 1960s 55.00
Playset
    Atomic Cape Canaveral 165.00
    Fort Apache 95.00
    Johnny Lightning Fire Leap, orig box 10.00
    Weebles Haunted House, plastic furniture, day glow Ghost Weeble, Witch Weeble, Boy and Girl Weebles 10.00
Pull Toy, 5 × 9 × 5", Little Snoopy, paper on wood, day-glow red vinyl wheels, spring tail, Fisher Price, marked "693," 1965 copyright 20.00
Space Toy
    Flying Saucer, metal, Japan, 1950s . . . 9.00
    Puzzle, Space 1999, orig box 12.00
    US Enterprise, Star Trek, seven 8" action figures, Mego, 1975 . . . . .165.00
Transportation
    Bus, Sun Rubber, 1935 . . . . 8.00
    Catapult Plane, 1950s 10.00
    Dump Truck, 11" l, red and green, Wyandotte 35.00
    Ferrari, 6" l, friction, Japan 75.00
    Fire Engine, 26" l, Texaco Fire Chief tanker, steel, painted, Buddy L 95.00
    Grader, Doepke Adams 95.00
    Hoover Truck, Matchbox 8.00
    Mercedes, convertible, Matchbox, 1982 . . . . 3.00
    School Bus, orig box, Hubley 45.00
    Tractor/Backhoe, battery operated, Ford 350.00

Trolley
Battery Operated, 11" l, tin, Modern
Toy, Japan, 1950s **85.00**
Friction
Tin, San Francisco Trolley, Japan,
1950s **35.00**
Plastic, Ken Kidder, orig box,
1950s **45.00**

TRAINS, TOY

Toy train collectors and dealers exist in a
world unto themselves. They have their
own shows, trade publications, and price
guides. The name that you need to know is
Greenberg Publishing Company, 7566
Main Street, Sykesville, MD 21784. Their
mail order catalog contains an exhaustive
list of their own publications as well as
those by others. If you decide to get involved with toy trains, write for a copy.

The two most recognized names are
American Flyer and Lionel, and the two
most popular gauges are S and O. Do not
overlook other manufacturers and gauges.

The toy train market has gone through a
number of crazes—first Lionel, then
American Flyer. The current craze is boxed
sets. Fortunately, the market is so broad
that there will never be an end to subcate-
gories to collect.

Clubs: Lionel Collector's Club, P. O. Box
479, La Salle, IL 61301; The National
Model Railroad Association, 4121 Crom-
well Rd., Chattanooga, TN 37421; The Toy
Train Operating Society, Inc., 25 West
Walnut Street, Suite 308, Pasadena, CA
91103; The Train Collector's Association,
P. O. Box 248, Strasburg, PA 17579.

Note: The following prices are for equipment in good condition.

AMERICAN FLYER, POSTWAR, S
GAUGE

293, American Flyer/New Haven, steam
locomotive, 4-6-2, black, white lettering, 1953–58 .... **25.00**
322AC, New York Central, steam locomotive, 4-6-4, black, white lettering,
1950. .... **45.00**
479, Silver Flash, Alco, PA diesel locomotive, silver, chocolate brown, and orange, 1955. .... **60.00**
632, Lehigh New England, hopper, gray,
red dot in logo, white lettering, 1946–
53. .... **2.00**
933, Baltimore and Ohio, boxcar, white,

brown roof and ends, black lettering,
1953–54 .... **10.00**
21801-1, Chicago Northwestern,
dummy switcher, green and yellow,
1958. .... **60.00**
24127, Monon, gondola, light gray, dark
red lettering, 1961–65 .... **5.00**
24310, Gulf, tank car, silver, orange logo,
1958–60 .... **8.00**
24626, American Flyer, caboose, yellow,
silver roof and ends, red stripe, black
lettering. **3.00**
24793, Jefferson, pullman, alumunim
finish, 1957–58, 1960–62 .... **30.00**

LIONEL, POSTWAR (1945–69)

45, US, mobile launcher switcher, olive
drab, gray launcher, 1960–62 .... **80.00**
58, Great Northern, snowplow, 2-4-2,
green and white, green logo, 1959–
61. .... **275.00**
71, lamppost, 1949–59. .... **2.00**
145, automatic gateman, 1950–66 ..... **15.00**
167, whistle controller, 1945–46. ...... **1.00**
212T, US Marine Corps, dummy locomo-
tive, blue, white stripes and lettering,
1958–59 .... **175.00**
221, Rio Grande, Alco A unit, yellow, black stripes and lettering,
1963–64 .... **35.00**
239, steam locomotive, 2-4-2, diecast
body, 1964–66 .... **10.00**
419, heliport control tower, 1962 ...... **75.00**
625, Lehigh Valley, GE 44-ton switcher,
red, white stripe and lettering, 1956–
57. .... **75.00**
1063, transformer, 75 watts, 1960–
64. .... **9.00**
1887, flatcar, brown, yellow lettering,
carrying fences and six horses,
1959. .... **60.00**
2257, Lionel, offset-cupola caboose, red,
illuminated, extra details, 1948 ...... **10.00**
2402, Chatham, Pullman, green, gray
roof, 1948–49 .... **25.00**
2431, observation, metal, blue, silver
roof, 1946–47 .... **12.00**
2454, Pennsylvania, boxcar, orange,
brown doors, 1945–46 .... **20.00**
2560, Lionel Lines, crane, eight-wheel,
black boom, 1946–47 .... **20.00**
3366, circus car, white, nine white rubber horses, 1959–62 .... **45.00**
3461, Lionel, operating log car, black,
three logs, 1949. .... **10.00**
3530, searchlight car, pole and base **25.00**
3662-1, automatic milk car, white,
brown roof, 1955–60 and 1964–66... **30.00**
6014, Chun King, boxcar, red, white lettering. **58.00**
6035, Sunoco, single dome tank car,
gray, blue and red lettering, 1952–
53. .... **1.00**

5040, Libby's Tomato Juice, boxcar, white, red and blue lettering, green stems on tomatoes, 1961 . . . . **12.00**

6109, flatcar with logs, gray, 1952. . . . . . **35.00**

6315, Gulf, single dome chemical tank car, 1956–59. **15.00**

6414, Evans Auto Loader, red, black superstructure, four autos with windows, bumpers, and rubber tires, red, yellow, blue, and white cars, 1955–57. . . . . **20.00**

6445, Fort Knox Gold Reserve, silver, clear windows, coin slot, 1961–63. . . . **40.00**

6482, refrigerator car, white, black lettering, 1957. . . . . **20.00**

MARX

112, Lehigh Valley, diesel switcher locomotive, plastic, red, 1974–76. . . . . **15.00**

251, Canadian Pacific "Vancouver," maroon, gold lettering, black frame, four wheel, 6" l. **60.00**

396, Canadian Pacific, steam locomotive, streamlined, sheet metal, electric motor, black cab, copper boiler and sideboards, 1941. . . . . **20.00**

548, Guernsey Milk, gondola, blue, cream int., four silver milk cans, eight wheel, 6" l. **35.00**

551, New York Central, tender for steam locomotive, four wheel, blue, 1934–41 and 1950–55 . . . . **20.00**

554, Northern Pacific, high side gondola, red, yellow int., silver frame, four wheel, 6", 1938–40 . . . . **7.00**

567, New York Central, dump car, yellow, brown interior, red and white frame, four wheel, 6" l. **18.00**

1235, Southern Pacific, caboose, red and silver, 7" l, 1952–55 . . . . **5.00**

1998, Rock Island, S-3 diesel, dummy, red and gray, 1962 . . . . **40.00**

3824, Union Pacific, caboose, yellow and brown, black frame, four wheel, 6" l. **3.00**

5532, Allstate, tank car, plastic, turquoise, eight wheel, 1962. . . . . **5.00**

86000, Lackawanna, hopper, blue, red int., four wheel, 6" l, 1953 . . . . **3.00**

131000, Seaboard Coast Line, gondola, yellow, four wheel, 1973 . . . . **2.00**

738701, Pennsylvania, hopper, brown, white lettering, eight wheel, 6" l **10.00**

TRAMP ART

Tramp art refers to items made by itinerant artists, most of whom are unknown, who made objects out of old cigar boxes or fruit and vegetable crates. Edges of pieces are often chip-carved and layered. When an object was completed, it was often stained.

Tramp art received a boost when it was taken under the wing of the Folk Art groupies. You know what has happened to the Folk Art market. You make a bed, you lie in it.

Box

12" h, 12" w, hanging, bottom crest, old brown paint, black trim **45.00**

13½" l, gilded brass appliques **65.00**

Chest of Drawers, miniature, 10 ½" w, 22" h, Gothic arch mirror, triptych-like back, three drawers, old varnish finish **225.00**

Cosmetic Box, 10½" l, chip carved, mirror and red lined int. **85.00**

Jewelry Box, 10½" h, brass trim and panels, red velvet insert top, lift-out int. tray, hidden drawer, dated 1903. . . . . **95.00**

Magazine Rack, 15", hanging, dark finish, brass tack dec **75.00**

Mirror, 23" h, two birds above horseshoe enclosing date "1914," center heart shaped frame encloses mirror, applied rosettes **220.00**

Picture Frame, 19½ × 17¼", rect, chip carved, diamond shape projections on corners. **45.00**

Rocker, cutout curved sides, lyre-like splat, applied chip carved dec, two porcelain buttons in back, alligatored varnish and brown paint, replaced wooden seat **250.00**

Sewing Box, 9½" l, single drawer, pincushion top, orig finish. **25.00**

Wall Pocket, 11 × 16½", applied strips. . .**125.00**

TRAPS

When the animal rights activists of the 1960s surfaced, trap collectors crawled back into their dens. You will find trap collectors at flea markets, but they are quiet types.

Avoid traps that show excessive wear and pitting. In order to be collectible a trap should be in good working order. Careful when testing one. You may get trapped yourself.

Alligator #1, teeth. **135.00**

Bell Spring, #1¼, single long spring. **175.00**

Catchemalive, mouse, wood and tin **45.00**

C F Orvis, minnow, glass **75.00**

Chasse, mouse, 3 hose choker **35.00**

CM Coghill, mouse, attaches to fruit jar. **15.00**

Elgin, mouse, metal **12.00**

Escape Proof, 7 hole pan. **22.00**

Fly, aqua glass. **32.00**

Fut Set, rat, metal **18.00**
Gibbs, hawk **125.00**
Good Luck #1, Swastika cut in pan, sin-
gle long spring **45.00**
Hotchkiss & Sons #4, double long
spring **135.00**
JVJ, gopher, Crete, NE **30.00**
Klip Trap, mouse, metal **15.00**
Last Word, mouse, wood snap **8.00**
Little Jimmy, rat, wood and tin, live
trap **20.00**
Little Samson, rat, iron, teeth **150.00**
Lomar #3, double coil spring **20.00**
Michigan Wire Goods, mole, spear
type **8.00**
Nash, mole, Kalamazoo, MI **15.00**
Newhouse #150, bear **325.00**
Oberto #200, double coil spring **20.00**
Official Weasel, wood, snap-type, Ani-
mal Trap Co **8.00**
Peerless, mouse, wooden **75.00**
Renkens, gopher **10.00**
Rittenhouse, mole, spear type **15.00**
Runway, mouse **18.00**
Schyler, mouse, folding killer, metal **18.00**
Sears Farm Master, fly **50.00**
Simplex, gopher, self-set **18.00**
S Newhouse, bear, 32" l, wrought iron,
Oneida Community, NY **325.00**
Trailsend #5, double long spring **300.00**
Triumph #115X Triple, clutch, single
long spring **20.00**
Watkins #4, hand forged, double long
spring **125.00**
Wee Stinky, fruit jar, fly **10.00**
Wiggington, mouse, glass **20.00**
Zip, mouse, metal, snap **8.00**

TRAYS

Tin lithographed advertising trays date
back to the last quarter of the nineteenth
century. They were popular at any location where beverages, alcoholic and non-
alcoholic, were served.

Because they were heavily used, it is not
unusual to find dents and scratches. Check
carefully for rust. Once the lithographed
surface was broken, rust developed easily.

Smaller trays are generally tip trays.
Novice collectors often confuse them with
advertising coasters. Tip trays are rather
expensive. Ordinary examples sell in the
$50.00 to $75.00 range.

Advertising
Billy Baxter Ginger Ale, tin **35.00**
Coca-Cola, Betty, tip, 1914 . . . . **65.00**
Cottolene Shortening, 4½" d, litho tin,
multicolored illus, black ground, NK
Fairbank Co **40.00**

*Advertising, Binghamton Ice Cream Co., tip
tray, 6⅛" l, $35.00.*

Evervess Sparkling Water, 10½ ×
14" **35.00**
Falls City Brewing Co, 13" d, topless
girl on horse **250.00**
Fitzgerald Ale Beer **18.00**
Geo Ehret's Hellgate Brewery, NY,
13½ × 16¾", oval, tin **25.00**
Hebburn House Coal, 4" l, eagle in
center, holding banner, wood grain
ground **42.50**
Hopski Soda, litho tin, frog pouring
drinks **50.00**
Miller High Life, girl sitting on
moon **25.00**
Moxie Centennial, 1984 . . . . **35.00**
Old Reading Beer, white lettering, blue
ground, red border **50.00**
Peerless Ice Cream **85.00**
Rockford Watches, 3½ × 5", tin, girl
wearing green dress **115.00**
Ubero Coffee, Boston **60.00**
Character, Pinocchio and Gepetto, 8 ×
10", litho tin, 1940 copyright **20.00**
Political
Taft and Sherman, 4½" d, tip, litho tin,
jugate portraits, rim caption "Grand
Old Party/1856 To 1908," black and
gold border **125.00**
William McKinley, 13 × 16", oval, litho
tin, color portrait, green ground, sig-
nature, c1900 . . . .**100.00**
Souvenir and Commemorative
Chicago World's Fair, 1933, Century
of Progress, 4¾" d, brass, emb,
raised detailed exhibit buildings **25.00**

Gettysburg Battlefield, 16½" l, oval, 1863 . . . . **45.00**
Lindberg Commemorative, 3¼ × 5", china, white, hp, plane, US and French flags on continents illus and "May 21, 1927," Moisy & LeRoi . . . **70.00**
New York World's Fair, 1964, 8 × 11", litho tin, Unisphere and Avenue of Flags, eggshell white rim, gold inscription **15.00**
Queen Elizabeth II Coronation, June 2, 1953, 4¾" d, pin tray, coat of arms, gold trim, Paragon **31.00**
Rochester, MN, 2½ × 6", ruby stained glass, gold trim **10.00**
Washington's Home, Mt Vernon, VA, 7½ × 11", porcelain, portraits of George and Martha Washington and Mt Vernon, multicolored, sq corners, gold trim, marked "Germany" **75.00**
Yellowstone Park, 4" l, oval, copper, silver wash **12.00**

TROPHIES

There are trophies for virtually everything. Ever wonder what happens to them when the receiver grows up or dies? Most wind up in landfills. It is time to do something about this injustice.

Dad has begun collecting them. He is focusing on shape and unusual nature of the award. He has set a $5.00 limit, which is not much of a handicap when it comes to trophy collecting. In fact, most of his trophies have been donated by individuals who no longer want them.

Always check the metal content of trophies. A number of turn-of-the-century trophies are sterling silver. These obviously have weight as well as historic value. Also suspect sterling silver when the trophy is a plate.

TURTLE COLLECTIBLES

Turtle collectors are a slow and steady group who are patient about expanding their collection of objects relating to these funny little reptiles. Don't you believe it! I am one of those collectors, and I'm not at all slow about the expansion of my collection.

I find turtle collectibles everwhere. Like all animal collectibles, they come in all shapes and sizes. Candles, toys, story-

books, jewelry, and ornaments featuring turtles can be found at almost any flea market.

Watch out for tortoise shell items. This material is subject to the provisions of the Federal Endangered Species Act.

Pin, carved tortoise shell, 1½" l, $45.00.

Bank, composition, 5" h, sitting up, holding wrapped baby turtle, green, yellow, and black, mkd "Freddy B. Turtle, copyright Aviva Ent. Inc., Made in Taiwan, Republic of China" on bottom **4.00**
Bottle, figural turtle, 5¼" h, clear, mkd "Merry Xmas" on bottom, tin cap **30.00**
Cookie Jar
McCoy, Timmy Tortoise, brown turtle, green and yellow butterfly finial, mkd "271 McCoy USA" **35.00**
Twin Winton, sitting up, brown, wearing top hat and tie **25.00**
Costume Jewelry
Brooch, sterling silver, thirteen colored stones set in shell **35.00**
Earrings, pr, transparent aqua colored paste stone shells, screw posts **20.00**
Pin, carved clear lucite shell in wooden body frame **50.00**
Covered Dish, glass
Amber, figural, removable shell lid . . . **95.00**
Milk Glass, 7½" l, figural turtle finial, scroll base with tab handles **175.00**
Doll, stuffed, 5" h, mohair, vinyl shell, glass eyes, Steiff **85.00**
Doorstop, 17" l, 4½" h, cast iron, green **300.00**
Figurine
2⅞" h, earthenware, brown, mkd "Japan" **1.00**
3" h, ceramic, orange, sitting up, wearing hat and tie, "E-3425" ink stamped on bottom **2.50**
5½" h, Weller, Coppertone **85.00**
Flower Insert, 5½" l, dark green glaze, Cliftwood Art Potteries, #2, 1920–1940 . . . . **12.00**
Pin Cushion, figural, cast iron body, stuffed velvet shell cushion **25.00**

Planter, green, McCoy 15.00
Pull Toy, Timmie Turtle, musical, litho
   paper on wood head and legs, green
   plastic shell, red wood hat, Fisher Price
   #150, 1953 .... 75.00
Salt and Pepper Shakers, pr, ceramic,
   figural, walking, dark green shell,
   brown body..................... 6.00

TYPEWRITERS

The first commercially produced typewriter in America was the 1874 Shoels and
Gliden machine produced by E. Remington & Sons. The last quarter of the
nineteenth century was spent largely in
experimentation and attempts to make the
typewriter an integral part of every office
environment, something that was
achieved by 1910. Although there were
early examples, the arrival of a universally
acceptable electric typewriter dates from
the 1950s.

The number of typewriter collectors is
small, but growing. Machines made after
1915 have little value, largely because
they do not interest collectors. Do not use
the patent date on a machine to date its
manufacture. Many models were produced for decades. Do not overlook typewriter ephemera. Early catalogs are quite
helpful in identifying and dating machines.

Newsletters: *Typewriter Times*, 1216 Garden Street, Hoboken, NJ 07030; *The Typewriter Exchange*, 2125 Mt. Vernon Street,
Philadelphia, PA 19130.

Clubs: Internationales Forum Historishe
Burowelt, Postfach 500 11 68, D-5000
Koln-50, Germany; Early Typewriter Col-
lectors Association, 2591 Military Ave.,
Los Angeles, CA 90064.

Adler............................125.00
Bing.............................130.00
Corona Folding.................... 60.00
Demountable 80.00
Fox, No. 23 ....140.00
Hammond, Multiplex...............225.00
Harris Visible, No. 4 .... 90.00
L C Smith, No. 3 .... 25.00
Mignon, No. 4.....................150.00
National, No. 2 ....100.00
Noiseless 175.00
Oliver, No. 8 ....100.00
Remington, portable, c1929 .... 25.00
Royal, No. 10 .... 25.00
Smith Premier, No. 2 .... 50.00

Underwood, Standard #5, $25.00.

Standard Folding 250.00
Underwood, portable............... 25.00
Wellington 150.00
Woodstock, No. 5 .... 25.00

UMBRELLAS

Umbrellas suffer a sorry fate. They are
generally forgotten and discarded. Their
handles are removed and collected as separate entities or attached to magnifying
glasses. Given the protection they have
provided, they deserve better.

Look for umbrellas that have advertising
on the fabric. Political candidates often
gave away umbrellas to win votes. Today
baseball teams have umbrella days to win
fans.

Seek out unusual umbrellas in terms of
action or shape. A collection of folding
umbrellas, especially those from the
1950s, is worth considering.

Umbrellas are generally priced low because sellers feel that they are going to
have difficulty getting rid of them. They
probably will. Buy them and put a silver
lining on their rainy cloud.

URINALS

When you have to go, you have to go—
any port in a storm will do. You have been
in enough bathrooms to know that all
plumbing fixtures are not equal.

The human mind has just begun to ex-
plore the recycling potential of hospital
bed pans. Among the uses noted are
flower planters, food serving utensils, and

dispersal units at the bottom of down spouts. How have you used them? Send your ideas and pictures of them in action to the Bedpan Recycling Project, 5093 Vera Cruz Road, Emmaus, PA 18049.

VALENTINES

There is far too much emphasis placed on adult valentines from the nineteenth century through the 1930s. It's true they are lacy and loaded with romantic sentiment. But, are they fun? No!

Fun is in children's valentines, a much neglected segment of the valentine market. If you decide to collect them, focus on penny valentines from the 1920 through 1960 period. The artwork is bold, vibrant, exciting, and a tad corny. This is what makes them fun.

There is another good reason to collect twentieth century children's valentines. They are affordable. Most sell for less than $2.00, with many good examples in the 50¢ range. They often show up at flea markets as a hoard. When you find them, make an offer for the whole lot. You won't regret it.

Club: National Valentine Collectors Association, P. O. Box 1404, Santa Ana, CA 92702.

Diecut, 4³/₈ × 7³/₈″, $10.00.

Art Deco, folder, 1920s	
Heart Shape, 3 × 3″	1.50
Lacy, layered, 6 × 9″	7.50
Art Nouveau, 5 × 7″, folder, lacy, 1900s	7.50
Cameo, 5 × 7″, Berlin and Jones, 1860	35.00
Comic Sheet	
8 × 10″, c1920	5.00
8 × 14″, sgd "CJH"	15.00
Diecut, 4 × 4″, cardboard, hearts and cupids, c1900	4.00
Easel Back, 6 × 9″, fancy cutwork border, 1900	10.00
Embossed, lacy	
Folder, small, c1885	5.00
Hand Made, layered, c1865	7.50
German, pullouts with honeycomb	
Binoculars, large	225.00
Umbrella, pink, fancy	35.00
Honeycomb, pullouts, 1920s	
Car, diecut, 10″ l, black	15.00
Toad Stool, light red	5.00
Mechanical	
Black Boy	10.00
German	
Layered, fancy	12.50
Pulldown, small	4.00
Train, large, 1914	45.00
Paper Doll, large, R Tuck, 1900	25.00
Perforated Lacy, 5 × 7″, hand written verse, Meek, c1850	25.00
Standup, c1895	
Hand Painted, 5 × 5″	12.50
Layered, 8 × 10″, fringed, fancy	9.50
Parchment, fancy center	15.00

VIDEO GAMES

At the moment, most video games sold at a flea market are being purchased for reuse. There are a few collectors, but their number is small.

It might be interesting to speculate at this point on the long-term collecting potential of electronic children's games, especially since the Atari system has come and gone. The key to any toy is playability. A video game cartridge has little collecting value unless it can be put into a machine and played. As a result, the long-term value of video games will rest in collector's ability to keep the machines that use them in running order. Given today's tendency to scrap rather than repair a malfunctioning machine, one wonders if there will be any individuals in 2041 that will understand how video game machines work and, if so, be able to get the parts required to play them.

Next to playability, displayability is important to any collector. How do you display video games? Is the answer to leave the TV screen on 24 hours a day?

Video games are a fad waiting to be replaced by the next fad. There will always be a small cadre of players who will keep video games alive, just as there is a devoted group of adventure game players. But given the number of video game cartridges sold, they should be able to satisfy their collecting urges relatively easily.

What this means is that if you are going to buy video game cartridges at a flea market, buy them for reuse and do not pay more than a few dollars. The closer you try to buy a game to its release, the more you pay. Just wait. Once a few years have passed, the sellers will just be glad to get rid of them.

VIEW-MASTER

William Gruber invented and Sawyer's Inc., of Portland, Oregon, manufactured and marketed the first View-Master viewers and reels in 1939. The company survived the shortages of World War II by supplying training materials in the View-Master format to the army and navy.

Immediately following World War II a 1,000-dealer network taxed the capacity of the Sawyer plant. In 1946 the Model C, the most common of the viewers, was introduced. Sawyer was purchased by General Aniline & Film Corporation in 1966. After passing through other hands, View-Master wound up as part of Ideal Toys.

Do not settle for any viewer or reel in less than near-mint condition. Original packaging, especially reel envelopes, is very important. The category is still in the process of defining which reels are valuable and which are not. Most older, pre-1975, reels sell in the 50¢ to $1.00 range.

Club: National Stereoscopic Association, P. O. Box 14801, Columbus, OH 43214.

Viewer
  Model C, black plastic, reel inserted in
    top, 1946 . . . . **23.00**
  Model D, lighted, focuses **35.00**
  Model H, lighted, round bottom, GAF
    logo on front, 1967–81 . . . . **14.00**
Reel, Packet of 3
  Disneyland, Tomorrowland, SAW, A-
    179 . . . . **4.00**

Emergency, GAF, B-597 . . . . **4.00**
Lost In Space, The Condemned Of
  Space, copyright 1967 Space Pro-
  ductions **75.00**
New York World's Fair, 1964–65,
  General Tour, SAW, A-671 . . . . **25.00**
Star Trek: The Motion Picture, GAF,
  1979, K-57 . . . . **12.50**
Television Shows At Universal City
  Studios, California, copyright 1964
  MCA Enterprises Inc **15.00**
Reel, Single
  Beautiful Caverns of Luray, Virginia,
    white reel, printed titles, blue and
    white envelope, 1946, 195 . . . . **2.00**
  Bible Stories, The Wisemen Find Jesus,
    booklet, white reel, printed titles,
    blue and white envelope, 1947, CH-
    8 . . . . **1.00**
  Making Swiss Cheese, Switzerland,
    white reel, printed titles, blue and
    white envelope, 1948, 2015 . . . . **1.50**
  Mt. Lassen Volcanic National Park,
    California, white reel, hand let-
    tered titles, blue and white enve-
    lope, 256 . . . . **2.00**
  Niagara Falls, NY, white reel, printed
    titles, blue and white envelope,
    1954, 81 . . . . **1.50**
  Phoenix, AZ, gold and blue reel, hand-
    lettered titles, blue and white enve-
    lope, 180 . . . . **3.00**
  Pyramids of Teotihuacan and
    Tenayuca, Mexico, white reel,
    printed titles, blue and white enve-
    lope, 1944, 506 . . . . **4.00**
  The Ugly Duckling, booklet, white re-
    el, printed titles, blue and white en-
    velope, 1948, FT-9 . . . . **4.50**
  Woody Woodpecker in the Pony
    Express Ride, white reel, printed ti-
    tles, blue and white envelope, 1951,
    820 . . . . **1.00**

WADE CERAMICS

Dad has a Wade animal collection because he drinks quantities of Red Rose Tea. Red Rose Tea issued several series of small animals. Like many of his other collections, Dad is not happy until he has multiple sets. "Drink more tea" is the order of the year at his office. How much simpler it would be just to make a list of the missing Wades and pick them up at flea markets where they sell in the $.50 to $1.00 range.

Aquarium Figure
  Lighthouse, 3" h **2.50**
  Mermaid, 2½" h **2.00**

Ashtray
   Panda, black and white, yellow base **3.50**
   Starfish, figural **4.25**
Basket, yellow, basketweave ext. and handle **7.50**
Cigarette Box, cov, copper luster, pastel enameled flower dec **18.50**
Creamer and Sugar
   Bramble ware, raspberry dec **20.00**
   Countryware, Irish Porcelain, emb shamrocks design **40.00**
Key Chain, St Bernard, premium, St Bruno Tobacco adv **5.00**
Miniature
   Elephant, Whoppa, 1976–1981 ...... **10.00**
   Mongrel, 1⅜" h, Whimsies Series, 1971–1984 .... **3.00**
   Three Bears, 1½" w, 1⅜" h, Fairy Tale Series, Red Rose Tea, 1971–1979 .... **15.00**
   Yorkshire Terrier, Dogs and Puppies Series, 1969–1982 .... **14.00**
Pipe Rest, figural, terrier dog, green base **4.50**
Plate, commemorative, Queen Elizabeth II coronation, 1952 .... **25.00**
Teapot, cov, Countryware, Irish Porcelain, emb shamrocks design **60.00**
Vase, 6½" h, Irish Porcelain, Mourne Range, 1970s **35.00**
Wall Pocket, pink tulips **10.00**

WASH DAY COLLECTIBLES

I keep telling my mother that women's liberation has taken all the fun out of washing and ironing. She quickly informs me that it was never fun to begin with. The large piles of unironed clothes she keeps around the house are ample proof of that.

Wash day material is a favorite of advertising collectors. Decorators have a habit of using it in bathroom decor. Is there a message here?

Measuring Cup, litho tin, Hellick's Rain Flakes advertisement, blue and white, $35.00.

Bottle
   Larkin Soap, small **15.00**
   Seabury Laundry Bluing, 4" h, light green **85.00**
Box
   Argo Starch, unopened, 1930s **10.00**
   Armour's Washing Powder **4.00**
   Gold Dust Twins Washing Powder, unopened **55.00**
Brochure, 3⅞ × 6", Gold Dust, Brite Spots, black lettering, yellow ground, 16 pgs **25.00**
Calendar, 1929, Clothesline, full pad ... **60.00**
Catalog, Holland-Rieger Wringer Washing Machines, 12 pgs **8.00**
Clothes Hanger, 17¾" l, turned wood ... **50.00**
Clothes Line Winder, hickory, hand hewn, 18th C **60.00**
Clothespin, carved, late 19th C **10.00**
Clothes Sprinkler
   Chinaman, white and blue **28.00**
   Elephant, ceramic **25.00**
Clothes Wringer, crank turn **20.00**
Drying Rack, 24 × 60", folding, poplar ... **200.00**
Iron
   Blue Enamel, gas **42.00**
   Enterprise, straight back edge, removable handle **15.00**
   Ober, open handle holes, emb, marked "#12 Ober Pat Pend" **15.00**
   Kettle, cast iron, wire bail, marked "Griswold, Erie, PA" **50.00**
Laundry Basket, Shaker, woven splint, bentwood rim handles **100.00**
Pinback Button, 1¼" d, Gold Dust Washing Powder, multicolored, late 1890s **75.00**
Sock Stretcher, wood **30.00**
Trade Card
   Conqueror Clothes Wringer, fold up **12.00**
   Larkin, Ottumwa Starch **3.00**
   Sapolio, Enoch Morgan & Sons, boy wearing fancy clothes **2.50**
Sign
   Borax Dry Soap, metal, red and white **45.00**
   Flame Proof Wax, women ironing clothes, 1890s **875.00**
Wash Board
   National Washboard Co, zinc, wood legs, 1897 .... **18.00**
   The Northern Queen, zinc, wood frame and rollers **25.00**

WATTS POTTERY

Watts Pottery, located in Crooksville, Ohio, was founded in 1922. The company began producing kitchenware in 1935. Most Watts pottery is easily recognized by its simple underglaze decoration on a light tan base. The most commonly found pattern is the Red Apple pattern, introduced in 1950. Other patterns include Cherry, Pennsylvania Dutch Tulip, Rooster, and Star Flower.

Pitcher, rooster dec, 6¼" h, 7" w, $95.00.

Red Apple
Baking Dish, oblong, 1 quart, #85	**55.00**
Bowl, deep, 4 pint, #64	**35.00**
Canister, 6" h, #81	**75.00**
Casserole, 2 quart, #110	**75.00**
Creamer	**35.00**
Drip Jar, #01	**55.00**
Mixing Bowls, nested set of four, #04, 05, 06, and 07	**125.00**
Mug, #121	**95.00**
Pitcher, 2 pint, #16	**60.00**
Pizza Plate, 14½" d, #105	**115.00**
Plate, 8½" d	**20.00**
Salt and Pepper Shakers, pr, hourglass shape, #117 and #118	**75.00**
Sugar, cov, #98	**85.00**
Teapot, 1½ quart, #112	**300.00**

Star Flower
Baking Dish, 7¼" d, #95	**22.00**
Berry Bowl, 5½" d, #4	**10.00**
Bowl, 7½" d, low, banded, #07	**25.00**
Casserole, 1½ quart, oval, #86	**55.00**
Cup	**15.00**
Mug, barrel	**100.00**
Plate	
6½" d	**16.00**
9¾" d	**40.00**
Salad Bowl, 11" d, #106	**80.00**
Spaghetti Bowl, 13" d, #39	**70.00**
Salt and Pepper Shakers, pr, cylinder	**50.00**

WELLER POTTERY

Weller's origin dates back to 1872 when Samuel Weller opened a factory in Fultonham, near Zanesville, Ohio. Eventually, he built a new pottery in Zanesville along the tracks of the Cincinnati and Muskingum Railway. Louwelsa, Weller's art pottery line, was introduced in 1894. Among the famous art pottery designers employed by Weller were Charles Babcock Upjohn, Jacques Sicard, Frederick Rhead, and Gazo Fudji.

Weller survived on production of utilitarian wares, but always managed some art pottery production until cheap Japanese imports captured its market immediately following World War II. Operations at Weller ceased in 1948.

Ewer, Cameo, salmon and white, 10" h, $40.00.

Ashtray, Woodcraft, 3" d	**65.00**
Basket, Cameo, 7½" d, blue	**25.00**
Bowl	
Cornish	**35.00**
Marbleized, 5½" d	**30.00**
Square, 8" w	**65.00**
Candlesticks, pr, Glendale	**150.00**
Child's Mug	**30.00**
Console Set, Blossom, bowl and two candlesticks	**50.00**
Cornucopia, Wild Rose	**25.00**
Ewer, Cameo, 10" h, blue	**30.00**
Figure, boy fishing, Muskota	**215.00**

Flower Frog, Cameo................. **50.00**
Ginger Jar, Greora **175.00**
Hanging Basket, Creamware, 11½" d, re-
   ticulated pattern **45.00**
Jardiniere, Claywood, 8" d, cherries and
   trees.......................... **75.00**
Jug, 6½" h, currants.................**160.00**
Lamp Base, Pelican, multicolored **195.00**
Mug, Claywood, star shaped flowers.... **50.00**
Pitcher, Pansy, 6½" h................ **85.00**
Planter, Woodcraft, 5" h, 11" d, log **50.00**
Teapot, 6" h, pumpkin.............. **75.00**
Vase
   Blossom, 9" h **40.00**
   Cameo, 7" h, blue................ **20.00**
   Darsie, 5½" h, pale blue **32.00**
Delsa **58.00**
   Knifewood, 7" h, low relief molded
     daisies **75.00**
   Manhattan, 6½" h **40.00**
   Oak Leaf **28.00**
   Patricia, white.................. **60.00**
   Roma, 8" h **50.00**
   Wild Rose, 6" h, double bud........ **30.00**
Wall Pocket
   Squirrel.......................**160.00**
   Wood Rose **75.00**
   Woodland, azaleas **135.00**
Window Box, Wood Rose **85.00**

WESTERN COLLECTIBLES

Yippy Kiyay partner, it's time to get a move on and lasso up some of those western goodies. Western yuck has become Western kitsch.

Western collectibles are objects decorated with a Western theme. Some of these ''Western'' collectibles began life on the range in the plants of Eastern manufacturers. Only the truly dedicated have lamps with dried cactus standards.

Actually, Western material can be divided into five groups—American Indian material, cowboy items (boots, saddles, etc.), Mexican collectibles, cowboy kitsch, and movie and T.V. cowboy hero collectibles. Include dude ranch Western under cowboy kitsch.

You will not find Country-Western listed here. There is a big difference between Miss Kitty and Miss Dolly, if you get my drift, partner. Due to its enormous popularity, it has its own category.

Meanwhile, happy trails to you and my hope that you'll be back in the saddle again before too long.

Bookends, pr, Will Rogers, embossed leather, green and gold dec on white ground, marked ''Durand, Chicago,'' $75.00.

Bandanna, West High Cowboys, silk.... **23.00**
Book
   The 2nd William Penn Treating With In-
   dians on the Sante Fe Trail 1860–66, W
     H Ryus, 1913.................. **50.00**
   Woman Trapper, Beadle's Frontier Se-
     ries, pulp novels, 1908–09 .... **20.00**
Catalog, Harness Leather, square rigged
   saddle, copper block plates, Rockford,
   IL, established 1862 .... **50.00**
Cookie Jar, cowboy boots, American
   Bisque **150.00**
Gloves, buckskin, Northern Plains In-
   dian, glass beaded columbines **450.00**
Pin, Texas Cousins Farm and Ranch **30.00**
Print, Northern Pacific North Coast,
   Montana Roundup, orig shipping
   tube **100.00**
Program
   Houston Rodeo Magazine, features
     Gene Autry World Championships,
     1944......................... **50.00**
   Silver Jubilee of Old Trail Driver's Assn
     of Texas, 1940 .... **35.00**
Ribbon
   Fredonia Texas Rodeo, bucking horse
     illus, 1929 .... **42.00**
   Salt Lake City Cattlemen's Conven-
     tion, 1901 .... **85.00**
Saddle, cowboy..................... **40.00**
Saddle Horse Bit **25.00**
Salt and Pepper Shaker, pr, Rod's Steak
   House, Williams, AZ **35.00**
Scarf, silk, cowboy motif **12.50**
Scarf Slide, bronc and cowboy **22.50**
Spur Straps **30.00**
Watch Fob
   Anomous Saddle Co **95.00**
   Bronc with cowboy............... **75.00**
   El Paso Saddlery **140.00**
   Hamley Round-up Saddle **175.00**
   Holster with gun................. **85.00**
   Long horn with saddle **150.00**
   Los Angeles Saddlery & Findings **135.00**
   Star Brand Los Angeles Saddlery **125.00**
   Van Patter's Flying Vee Eff Saddle
     Ranch **140.00**

WESTMORELAND GLASS

Westmoreland Glass Company made a large assortment of glass. Some early pieces were actually reproductions of earlier glass, but have now become legit!

Westmoreland made clear glass in many patterns, some nicely decorated. Its milk glass patterns are becoming quite popular at flea markets.

Be on the lookout for discontinued pieces. They add variety to any Westmoreland setting. Also keep alert at flea markets for pieces that are still in production. Many patterns have remained popular for decades. Flea market prices are generally much lower than contemporary department store prices.

Candlestick, double, Della Robbia, decorated crystal, $35.00.

Ashtray, Old Quilt, milk glass, 4½" sq . . .	12.50
Berry Bowl, Della Robbia, crystal, 5" d . . .	12.00
Bowl	
Beaded Grape, milk glass, 7" d, cov, ftd . . .	35.00
Old Quilt, milk glass, 7" d, skirted, ftd . . .	40.00
Paneled Grape	
9" d, belled, milk glass . . .	45.00
9½" l, oval, milk glass . . .	50.00
Butter Dish, cov, Paneled Grape, milk glass . . .	25.00
Cake Plate, Panel and Grape, milk glass . . .	55.00
Candleholders, pr, English Hobnail, milk glass, two branches . . .	40.00
Candlesticks, pr	
Della Robbia, crystal, 3½" h . . .	22.00
Old Quilt, milk glass, 4" h . . .	25.00
Candy Dish, cov, Old Quilt, milk glass, sq . . .	30.00

Celery Vase	
Old Quilt, milk glass . . .	25.00
Paneled Grape, milk glass . . .	35.00
Cheese Dish, Old Quilt, milk glass, round . . .	45.00
Cigarette Box, cov, Beaded Grape, milk glass . . .	45.00
Cocktail	
English Hobnail, milk glass . . .	7.00
Paneled Grape	
Crystal . . .	15.00
Milk Glass . . .	20.00
Compote, American Hobnail, milk glass, ftd, bell shape . . .	15.00
Cordial, Thousand Eye, crystal . . .	10.00
Creamer	
Beaded Grape, milk glass . . .	15.00
Old Quilt, milk glass, 3½" h . . .	15.00
Cup and Saucer	
English Hobnail, milk glass . . .	7.00
Paneled Grape, milk glass . . .	15.00
Decanter, orig stopper, Paneled Grape, crystal with cranberry stain . . .	195.00
Goblet	
American Hobnail, milk glass . . .	10.00
Della Robbia, milk glass . . .	20.00
Old Quilt, milk glass . . .	15.00
Paneled Grape	
Amethyst . . .	22.00
Milk Glass . . .	15.50
Thousand Eye, crystal . . .	12.00
Honey Dish, cov	
Beaded Grape, milk glass . . .	25.00
Old Quilt, milk glass . . .	28.00
Iced Tea Tumbler, Paneled Grape, milk glass . . .	25.00
Pitcher	
Old Quilt, milk glass, pint . . .	40.00
Paneled Grape, milk glass, quart . . .	40.00
Plate, Paneled Grape, milk glass	
6" d . . .	12.50
8" d . . .	18.50
Puff Box, cov	
American Hobnail, milk glass . . .	20.00
Beaded Grape, milk glass . . .	30.00
Rose Bowl, American Hobnail, milk glass . . .	10.00
Salt and Pepper Shakers, pr	
English Hobnail, milk glass, barrel, pepper mill . . .	20.00
Old Quilt, milk glass . . .	15.00
Paneled Grape, milk glass . . .	25.00
Sauce, English Hobnail, milk glass . . .	4.00
Sauce Boat, Panel and Grape, milk glass . . .	55.00
Sherbet	
American Hobnail, milk glass . . .	10.00
Paneled Grape	
Amethyst . . .	20.00
Milk Glass . . .	18.00
Thousand Eye, crystal, 5" h . . .	10.00
Sugar, cov	
Beaded Grape, milk glass . . .	12.50
Old Quilt, milk glass, 3½" h . . .	15.00

Tumbler, Della Robbia, crystal, 4¾" h,
  ftd **15.00**
Vase, Paneled Grape, golden sunset,
  9" h **35.00**
Wine, Paneled Grape, milk glass **20.00**

WHAT'S IN THE CASE?

A question often heard over and over again while wandering through flea markets is "What's in the case?" It causes casual shoppers to stop, stare, and try to identify what object or objects attracted the speaker's attention. Curiosity may have killed the cat, but it runs rampant at flea markets.

Flea market dealers long ago learned to protect their most delicate and expensive objects, especially smalls, by placing them in locked or hard-to-open cases. Alas, sticky fingers are a part of the flea market scene. Keeping smalls in cases is a plus when it comes to transporting these goods and to setting up and breaking down quickly.

One valuable lesson I have learned over the years is to check these cases carefully. Either through travel or use, they often become disheveled. Some are actually packed to overflowing. Objects are partially covered with other objects, sometimes hidden. Remember, the California 49ers had to prospect for the gold that they found.

On many occasions the cases not only contain material relating to a dealer's specialty, but also objects from a variety of other categories. Often these latter items are priced just above dealer price, but still some distance from full retail. The seller obviously does not want just to pass them along to another dealer, but prefers to make a small profit, though not necessarily a killing.

Flea market etiquette requires that you ask permission before opening one of these cases to remove an object for examination. Also remove and replace objects from a case one at a time. A dealer quickly becomes uncomfortable if you scatter the contents of the case around his or her display space.

"What's in the Case?" has been added as a category as a reminder not to walk nonchalantly past the cases you see in a flea market. Instead, give into temptation

What's In The Case?

and take a peek. One never knows. That prize you have been seeking for the last ten years may well be buried in the next case you check.

WHISKEY BOTTLES, COLLECTORS' EDITIONS

The Jim Beam Distillery issued its first novelty bottle for the 1953 Christmas market. By the 1960s the limited edition whiskey bottle craze was full blown. It was dying by the mid-1970s and was buried sometime around 1982 or 1983. Oversaturation by manufacturers and speculation by non-collectors killed the market.

Limited edition whiskey bottle collecting now rests in the hands of serious collectors. Their Bible is H. F. Montague's *Montague's Modern Bottle Identification and Price Guide* (published by author, 1980). The book used to be revised frequently. Now five years or more pass between editions. The market is so stable that few prices change from one year to the next.

Before you buy or sell a full limited edition whiskey bottle, check state laws. Most states require a license to sell liquor and impose substantial penalties if you sell without one.

Clubs: International Association of Jim Beam Bottle & Specialties Club, 5013 Chase Ave., Downers Grove, IL 60515;

Michter's National Collectors Society, P. O. Box 481, Schaefferstown, PA 17088.

Jim Beam
  Beam Club and Convention
    Blue Hen Club, 1982 . . . . **25.00**
    Convention, third, Detroit, 1973 . . . **25.00**
    Fox Uncle Sam, 1971 . . . . **12.00**
    Twin Bridge Club, 1971 . . . . **55.00**
  Beam on Wheels
    Ernie's Flower Car, 1976 . . . . **35.00**
    Train Baggage Car **50.00**
  Casino Series, Harolds Club, covered
    wagon, green 1969 . . . . **5.00**
  Centennial Series
    Anitoch, arrow, 1967 . . . . **7.00**
    St Louis Arch, 1966 . . . . **18.00**
  Executive Series, Sovereign, 1969 . . . **12.00**
  Foreign Countries, Australia, Kanga-
    roo, 1978 . . . . **15.00**
  People Series, Mortimer Snerd,
    1976 . . . . **30.00**
  Regal China Series, Franklin Mint,
    1970 . . . . **8.00**
  Sport Series, Football Hall of Fame,
    1972 . . . . **8.00**
  States Series, South Dakota, Mt Rush-
    more, 1969 . . . . **6.00**
  Trophy Series, Rabbit, 1971 . . . . **12.00**
Ezra Brooks
  Animal Series, Penguin, 1973 . . . . **10.00**
  Fish Series, Trout and Fly, 1970 . . . . . **10.00**
  Heritage China Series, Telephone,
    1971 . . . . **12.00**
  Institutional Series, Bucket of Blood,
    1970 . . . . **7.00**
  People Series, Dakota Cowgirl,
    1976p **30.00**
  Sports Series, Bareknuckle Fighter,
    1971 . . . . **9.00**
Cabin Still, Gold Coaster, 1955 . . . . **18.00**
Famous Firsts, Animal Series, Tiger, Cir-
  cus, 1980 . . . . **25.00**
Grenadier
  American Revolution Series, Third
    New York, 1970 . . . . **20.00**
  Moose Lodge, 1970 . . . . **14.00**
  Napoleonic Series, Eugene, 1970 . . . . . **20.00**
Hoffman
  Bird Series, Blue Jays, 1979, pr **35.00**
  School Series, Kentucky Wildcats, bas-
    ketball **30.00**
  Wildlife Series, Falcon & Rabbit, min-
    iature, 1978 . . . . **10.00**
Lionstone
  Bicentennial Series, Valley Forge,
    1975 . . . . **22.50**
  Clown Series, Lampy, #6, 1979 . . . . . . **35.00**
Luxardo
  Duck, green **30.00**
  Pheasant, black **125.00**
McCormick
  Bicentennial Series, Paul Revere **45.00**
  Elvis Series, black, #3, 1980 . . . . **50.00**

  Great American Series, Charles Lind-
    bergh, 1977 . . . . **30.00**
Cyrus Noble
  Animal Series, Mountain Lion & Cubs,
    miniature, 1979 . . . . **15.00**
  Mine Series, Landlady, 1977 . . . . **30.00**
  Sea Animals, Seal Family, 1978 . . . . . . **40.00**
Old Commonwealth
  Fireman, Fallen Comrade, #4,
    1983 . . . . **65.00**
  Golden Retriever, 1979 . . . . **25.00**
Ski Country
  Domestic Animal Series, bassett, min-
    iature, 1978 . . . . **20.00**
  Indian Series, End of Trail, miniature,
    1976 . . . . **65.00**
  Waterfowl Series, Pelican, brown,
    1976 . . . . **40.00**
  Wildlife Series
    Coyote Family, 1977 . . . . **45.00**
    Skunk Family, 1978 . . . . **40.00**

WHISKEY-RELATED

Whiskey and whiskey-related items are centuries old. Normally, the words conjure up images of the Western saloon and dance hall. Since the taste of similar whiskeys varies little, manufacturers relied on advertising and promotions to create customer loyalty.

Ashtray, Suntory Whiskey, stone-
  ware **12.00**
Bar Display, figural, camel, Paul Jones
  Whiskey, orig miniature bottle **40.00**
Change Tray
  Bailey's Whiskey **60.00**
  Hyroller Whiskey **25.00**
Display Bottle, 25" h, Old Overholt **60.00**
Fan, Four Roses Whiskey **15.00**
Lamp, oil, Seagram's Whiskey **20.00**
Matchsafe, Old Judson Whiskey **120.00**
Mirror
  Duffy's Malt Whiskey, pocket type . . . **45.00**
  Good Friends Whiskey, pilgrim and In-
    dian shaking hands **125.00**
Pitcher
  G W Seven Star Whiskey, alumi-
    num **5.00**
  Meredith's Diamond Club Whis-
    key **45.00**
Shot Glass
  Bottoms Up, cobalt **8.50**
  Peoria Co Club Whiskey, Peoria, IL,
    etched **25.00**
Sign
  Calvert Whiskey, litho tin **28.00**
  Green River Whiskey, 18 × 22", card-
    board, framed **140.00**
Token, Green River Whiskey **65.00**

Trade Card, Old Kentucky Distillery, monkeys shortening cat's tail, whiskey box chopping block, 1898 . . . . **20.00**

Tray
    Fulton Whiskey, silver plate. **30.00**
    Green River Whiskey, black man and horse **75.00**
    Lord Calvert Whiskey, 23″ d **48.00**

WHISTLES

Webster defines a whistle as an instrument for making a clear, shrill sound. No wonder children love them.

Collectors can whistle a happy tune at virtually every flea market. The most desirable whistles are those associated with well-known characters and personalities. They can command prices that are hardly child's play.

Whistle, pistol shape, litho tin, multicolored, Japan, $6.00.

Advertising
    Benzo-Gas, siren, cylinder, "Blow Out the Carbon," yellow, red, black, and white **18.00**
    Buster Brown Shoes, 1 × 1½″, litho tin, Buster and Tige portrait illus, brown ground, yellow border, green lettering, "With The Tread Straight Feature That Helps You Walk 'Toes Straight Ahead' To Health," 1930s **40.00**
    Keds, Supersonic Space Whistle, 2 × 2¼″, plastic, figural, flat, dark blue space capsule against white cratered moon, secret compartment in back, c1962 . . . . **12.00**
    Oscar Mayer, 2¼″ l, plastic, figural, red wiener, yellow label, c1960 . . . . **15.00**
    Banjo shape, short neck, red, yellow, and blue, Japan **10.00**
Character and Personality
    Jack Armstrong, ring, brass, Egyptian

symbols on sides, built-in siren top, 1938. . . . . **70.00**
Little Orphan Annie, 3¼″ l, brass tube, "Orphan Annie's Sandy Dog Whistle," telescopes to 5¼″ l, flat diecut dog head on end, Ovaltine premium, 1940. . . . . **65.00**
Cracker Jack Prize, paper, cartoon cat on underside, 1930s. **40.00**
Man's Face, emb tin, gold finish **12.00**
Wristwatch shape, litho tin, rect yellow face, red, white, and blue bands, Japan. **15.00**

WICKER

Wicker, or rattan, furniture enjoyed its first American craze during the late Victorian era. It was found on porches and summer cottages across America. It realized a second period of popularity in the 1920s and 30s and a third period in the 1950s. In truth, wicker has been available continuously since the 1870s.

Early wicker has a lighter, more airy feel than its later counterparts. Look for unusual forms, e.g., corner chairs or sewing stands. Most wicker was sold unpainted. However, it was common practice to paint it in order to preserve it, especially if it was going to be kept outside. Too many layers of paint decreases the value of a piece.

Apple Basket, 14″ w, rect, braided handle and rim, two natural shades **20.00**
Armchair, 32″ h, barrel shaped, tightly woven panel on ornately designed back, cushion seat, natural. **325.00**
Birdcage Stand, 74″ h, crescent moon shaped, wrapped pole standard, conical base, white. **175.00**
Creel Basket, center lid hole, early 1900. . . . . **55.00**
Fernery, 25½″ w, 32″ h, rect well, braced legs, white **100.00**
Footstool, 14½″ w, 8″ h, upholstered slip cushion top, tightly woven sides with curlicues **125.00**
Parlor Table, 27½″ d, 30¼″ h, circular top with basketweave pattern, curlicue trim, circular base shelf with cane insert, white **125.00**
Rocker, 33″ h, sqaure back, basket weave pattern, curlicue trim, rect armrests, white **175.00**
Settee, 37″ w, 31″ h, diamond design back, wrap-around sides, upholstered seat cushions, machine woven **350.00**

WILLOW WARE

The traditional willow pattern, developed by Josiah Spode in 1810, is the most universally recognized china pattern. A typical piece contains the following elements in its motif: willow tree, "apple" tree, two pagodas, fence, two birds, and three figures crossing a bridge.

Willow pattern china was made in almost every country that produces ceramics. In the 1830s over 200 English companies offered Willow pattern china. Buffalo China was one of the first American companies to offer the pattern. Japanese production started about 1902, around the same time Buffalo made its first pieces.

Since the Willow pattern has been in continuous production, the term *reproduction* has little meaning. However, the Scio Pottery, Scio, Ohio, is currently producing an unmarked set that is being sold in variety stores. Because it lacks marks, some collectors have purchased it under the mistaken belief that it was made much earlier.

Newsletter: *American Willow Report*, P. O. Box 900, Oakridge, OR 97463.

Plate, Allerton, 9" d, $15.00.

Bowl, blue
    4¾" d, berry, Royal Pottery, Staffordshire, Burslem................. **8.00**
    6" d, Johnson Bros **5.00**
Cream Soup, Buffalo **10.00**
Creamer, 3½" h, blue, Ridgway **12.00**
Cup and Saucer, oversized, brown, Two
    Temples II pattern, England......... **48.00**

Demitasse Set, coffeepot, creamer, six
    cups and saucers, Occupied Japan **100.00**
Dish, 9" d, pea green, Imperial Royal
    Nimy, Belgium, c1920 .... **45.00**
Egg Cup, 5½" h, pink, England **22.00**
Grill Plate, 11" d, blue, Maastricht...... **10.00**
Mug, 3½" h, blue, straight sides **15.00**
Pitcher
    3½" h, pink, Allerton **75.00**
    6½" h, blue **85.00**
Plate
    5¾" d, blue, Allerton **5.00**
    7" d, dark blue, John Steventon &
        Sons, Burslem, England **7.00**
    9½" d, blue, Villery & Boch **8.00**
    10½" d, blue, W A Adderly & Co **25.00**
Platter
    9½" l, blue, W A & Co, Staffordshire......................... **55.00**
    12" l, 9½" w, blue, Johnson Bros, England **35.00**
    13½" l, 11" w, blue, Allerton........ **70.00**
    17¾" l, blue, R H & Co **95.00**
Salt and Pepper Shakers, pr, 4⅝" h, blue,
    England......................... **60.00**
Soup Bowl, 6½" d, blue, underplate...................... **85.00**
Teapot, 5" h, miniature, blue, gold trim,
    gold finial, Sadler, England **125.00**
Vase, 2¼" h, bud, blue **25.00**
Vegetable Bowl, 8½" l, blue, Meakin ... **35.00**
Wash Bowl, 16" d, blue **325.00**

WOOD

There is just something great about the grain, patina, and aging qualities of wood. This is a catchall category for wooden objects that otherwise would not have appeared. The objects are utilitarian, yet classic for their type.

Ballot Box, walnut, orig key, c1860..... **48.00**
Bowl, 6" d, round.................. **50.00**
Bucket, 3⅝" h, stave construction, two
    iron bands, wire bail handle, wood
    hand grip, red and black repaint **135.00**
Butter Paddle, 8¾" l, curly maple, flat
    rounded paddle, long handle **45.00**
Butter Print
    Pineapple, 4¾" d.................. **85.00**
    Swan, 3¾" d, turned handle **125.00**
Candle Box, wall type, early 19th C.... **198.00**
Carrot Slicer, 2½ × 7¾", rect, center hole
    slides over blade, birch tray **75.00**
Chalice, 4½" d, turned, dark finish **10.00**
Cheese Box, 15" d, round **30.00**
Cookie Board, 4 × 7", carved urn of
    fruit **25.00**
Cutting Board, figural
    Elephant, 8 × 13", cherry **85.00**

Pig, 18½" l, maple, dark patina **45.00**
Dough Bowl, 9" d. **12.00**
Dough Box, cov, 16 × 26 × 9", rect, dove-
tailed, canted sides, paneled flat cov
with knob center, painted blue **160.00**
Dustpan, 4 × 6 × 14", pine, lollipop handle, tapered lip, gray-blue paint,
c1840. . . . . **130.00**
Food Mold, 3½ × 8½", cut turtle design,
handle **50.00**
Hat Stand, flapper type, decorated. **30.00**
Herb Drying Tray, wire nail construc-
tion **45.00**
Ladle, 11½" l, burl, shallow bowl, ta-
pered slender pointed handle, old pa-
tina **75.00**
Lemon Squeezer. **35.00**
Pencil Box, tambour cover, Japan **12.00**
Potato Masher, leather strap **15.00**
Pudding Stick, hewn handle, shaped
blade **12.00**
Raisin Seeder, plunger handle, wire grid,
Everett. **48.00**
Rope Bed Tightener, 14¾" l, hewn ma-
ple and hickory, mortised, peg handle,
chamfered shaft, clothespin end,
brown patina, 18th C **50.00**
Seed Box, 25 × 8", stave construction,
divided int. **130.00**
Sieve, 18" l, diamond shape, two
crossbars supporting adjustable
slats **65.00**
Spoon Rack. **25.00**
Towel Rack, 24½ × 32¼", pine, turned,
worn finish **75.00**
Trencher, 9 × 9½", oval, turned detail . . . **145.00**

WORLD'S FAIRS

It says a lot about the status of world's fairs
when Americans cannot stage a fair in
1993–1994 that is even half as good as the
1893 Columbian Exposition in Chicago.
Was the last great world's fair held in New
York in 1964? Judging from recent fairs,
the answer is an unqualified yes.

Although it is important to stress three-
dimensional objects for display purposes,
do not overlook the wealth of paper that
was given away to promote fairs and their
participants.

Magazine: *World's Fair*, P. O. Box 339,
Corte Madera, CA 94925.

Club: World's Fair Collectors' Society,
Inc., P. O. Box 20806, Sarasota, FL 33583.

1876, Philadelphia, Centennial Exposition
Cuff Links, pr, 1⅛" d, tortoise shell,
silver Art Gallery scene and title. . . . **115.00**
Liberty Bell, brass, wood handle, in-

*1964 New York World's Fair, game, Milton
Bradley, $10.00.*

scribed "Proclaim Liberty, 1776–
1876" **85.00**
Memorial Book. **45.00**
Watch Fob, hatchet shape **50.00**
1893, Chicago, Columbian Exposition
Atlas. **30.00**
Change Tray, multicolored. **45.00**
Jigsaw Puzzle, view of Expo, orig
box. **400.00**
Magazine, *Youth's Companion*, illus and
adv. **75.00**
Medal, 2" d, white metal, bust portrait
and inscriptions. **20.00**
Paperweight, ferris wheel. **75.00**
Photo Engravings, *The Vanished City*,
pen and pictures, hard cov, 15 ×
11" **100.00**
Sheet Music, *World's Columbian Exposi-
tion Waltz*, color cover illus **100.00**
Spoon, set of 6, orig box **125.00**
1898, Omaha, Trans-Mississippi Exposi-
tion
Handkerchief, silk, tattered edge **10.00**
Napkin Ring, engraved. **10.00**
1901, Buffalo, Pan-Am Exposition
Letter Opener, brass, figural, buf-
falo. **35.00**
Pin, brass, 1½" w hanger bar, 1½" d
brass mechanical skillet **50.00**
Pinback Button, 1¼" d, "Official But-
ton," multicolored, continental la-
dies shaking hands **20.00**
Purse, small. **13.00**
1904, St Louis, Louisiana Purchase Expo-
sition
Commemorative Coin, elongated **35.00**
Cup, Palace of Manufacturers decal,
Germany **25.00**
Egg, tin **65.00**

Hatchet, 12½" l, cast iron 65.00
Inkwell, porcelain 45.00
Key Chain, 1¼" l, aluminum, emb
Festival Hall and Cascades, blank
back 12.00
Souvenir Spoon 26.00
1915, San Francisco, Panama-Pacific International Exposition
Book, souvenir 30.00
Coin Purse, 2½ × 3½", suede, silvered
brass closure 25.00
1933–34, Chicago, Century of Progress
Ashtray
Kettle, copper, blue glass insert 35.00
Tire, Firestone 55.00
Ashtray and Bookmark, copper, boxed
set 25.00
Atlas, *Century of Progress, Atlas of the World* 30.00
Belt Buckle 45.00
Book, *Chicago 1833–1933 A Century of Progress*, hard cov, pictorial 45.00
Booklet, Alton RR 8.00
Bookmark, set of ten, etched metal . . . 150.00
Bottle, 6½" h 20.00
Bracelet, copper and silver, set of ten
different 150.00
Butter Knife, 7" l, sterling 15.00
Cigarette Case, lady's 35.00
Coasters, set of four 20.00
Commemorative Coin
A & P Foods 25.00
Chrysler 25.00
Ford 25.00
Jewish Day 25.00
Kelvinator 25.00
Mayor Cermack 25.00
Pullman 25.00
Compact, lady's 30.00
Contest Ticket, A & P 10.00
Handkerchief, Japanese silk, set of
3 . . . . 50.00
Jewelry Box, wood 35.00
Jigsaw Puzzle 125.00
Needle Case 12.00
Pinback Button, "I'm From New
York—Visitor—A Century of Progress" 25.00
Poker Chip 15.00
Post Card 15.00
Program, opening week 35.00
Sewing Kit 20.00
Souvenir Spoon, gold plated, set of
6 . . . . 100.00
Vase, 3½" h, blue matte 45.00
1939, New York, New York World's Fair
Booklet, Tony Sarg, 15 pgs, maps 22.00
Locket, mother-of-pearl, bubble
logo 45.00
Place Mat, set of 4, orig pkg 32.00
Plate, Homer Laughlin China 65.00
Playing Cards, one regular deck, one
trick deck 35.00
Salt and Pepper Shakers, pr, orig
box 45.00

1962, Seattle, Century 21 Exposition
Cigarette Lighter, 9¼" h, chromed
metal, tower shape, "Seattle USA
Space Needle," unused 55.00
Tumbler, glass, gold trim, Space Needle, set of 4 . . . . 20.00
View-Master Reels, various outdoor
scenes, set of 5 . . . . 15.00
1964, New York, New York World's Fair
Book, *Official Souvenir book*, 24 pgs, 7 ×
10" 20.00
Key Chain, license plate shape 10.00
Milk Bottle Cap 5.00
Nodder, 3½" d, Unisphere, dark
blue composition base, 1961 copyright 25.00
Plaque 15.00
Salt and Pepper Shakers, pr, glazed ceramic, Unisphere illus 25.00
Tile, 6" sq, ceramic, Unisphere, Statue
of Liberty, and skyline illus, gold accented border 18.00
Tray, 8 × 11", litho tin, Unisphere and
Avenue of Flags, gold inscription . . . 15.00

WRISTWATCHES

The pocket watch generations have been replaced by the wristwatch generations. This category became hot in the late 1980s and still is going strong. There is a great deal of speculation occurring, especially in the area of character and personality watches.

Since the category is relatively new as a collectible, no one is certain exactly how many watches have survived. Dad has almost a dozen that were handed down from his parents. If he is typical, the potential market supply is far greater than anyone realizes. Beware before paying big prices. Many wristwatches are going to be sold five years from now at far less than their 1992 price.

Club: National Association of Watch & Clock Collectors, P. O. Box 33, Columbia, PA 17512.

Character Wristwatch, Hopalong Cassidy, black band, back inscribed "Good Luck from Hoppy," US Time, $85.00.

Advertising
Big Boy, Windert 85.00
Coke, Walt Disney World 15 Year Anniversary 45.00

Nabisco Ritz Crackers **60.00**
Red Goose Shoes, 1½" d, silvered brass
case, inscribed "Friedman Shelby/
All Leather Shoes," orig brown lea-
ther bands, c1930 . . . . **125.00**
Character and Personality
Alice In Wonderland, US Time Watch,
c1951 . . . . **35.00**
Babe Ruth **175.00**
Bambi, birthday series, US Time
Watch, c1949 . . . . **175.00**
Cinderella, Timex, 1958 . . . . **70.00**
Daisy Duck, fluted bezel, birthday se-
ries, US Time Watch, c1948 . . . . **150.00**
Dale Evans and Buttermilk, orig straps,
c1950 . . . . **50.00**
Davy Crockett, silvered metal case,
illus on dial, tan pigskin straps, US
Time Watch, c1950 . . . . **75.00**
Donald Duck, rect face, c1940 . . . . **100.00**
The Fonz, Basis, 1976 . . . . **85.00**
Gene Autry **125.00**
Green Hornet **45.00**
Hopalong Cassidy **150.00**
Little Orphan Annie, New Haven
Clock Co, 1936 . . . . **175.00**
Lone Ranger, metal case, orig tan lea-
ther straps, c1940 . . . . **150.00**
Pluto, birthday series, Ingersoll,
1948. . . . . **200.00**
Richard Nixon. **75.00**
Robin Hood, Viking, c1958 . . . . **75.00**
Space Patrol, silvered metal case, black
inscription, gray leather straps, US
Time Watch Co, early 1950s **75.00**
Tex Ritter. **45.00**
Three Stooges, A & M Hollywood **85.00**
Tom Corbett, orig band. **150.00**
Whoopi Goldberg **50.00**
Yogi Bear, Bradley, c1964 . . . . **45.00**
Lady's
Bulova, Accutron, 14K case, leather
bands **125.00**
Ebel, 17j, 14K case and band,
c1948. . . . . **225.00**
Girod, 14K yg case **150.00**
Illinois
Antoinette, 15j, gold filled,
c1929. . . . . **60.00**
Mary Todd, 16j, 18K, c1929 . . . . . . **175.00**
Longines, 14K yg case, orig box **250.00**
Nicolet, 17j, flexible band, cabochon
crystal, small diamond on each side
of square face. **95.00**
Omega, 17j, silver, wire lugs,
c1925. . . . . **85.00**
Rolex, 17j, gold filled, c1945 . . . . **60.00**
Man's
Angelus, 17j, day, date, and moon
phase, steel, c1949 . . . . **150.00**
Bueche-Girod, 17j, day, date, month,
and moon phase, steel **150.00**
Bulova, Sky Chief, 17j, steel, c1940. . . **225.00**
Elgin
Lord Elgin 680, 21j, 14K gold **100.00**

Sportsman, 17j **25.00**
Hamilton, 17j, gold-filled case, stem
wind, leather band, orig box. **150.00**
Illinois, Aviator, 17j, gold filled **175.00**
Jules Jergensen, quartz, day and date,
leather band **150.00**
Omega, Constellation, 24j, auto-wind,
steel, c1962 . . . . **125.00**

ZOO COLLECTIBLES

Dad has been trying for years to find a "Z"
category to end *Warman's Americana and
Collectibles*. His trouble is he spent too
much of his childhood at the circus and
not enough at the zoo. It's tough to beat
the old man. Gotcha, Pop!

*Game, Fun At The Zoo, Parker Bros., multi-
colored litho board pictures, 20 × 11" wooden
box, c1902, $225.00.*

Ashtray, Denver Zoo, glass, decal cen-
ter **4.50**
Door Hanger, City Zoo, white and yel-
low, "Do Not Disturb" on back **1.00**
Medal, Philadelphia Zoo, silver finish,
c1960. . . . . **10.00**
Pennant, San Francisco Zoo. **5.00**
Pinback Button
American Eagle/Philadelphia Zoo,
1¼" d, black and white, c1930 . . . . . **10.00**
Benson's Wild Animal Farm, Nashua,
NH, Safari, black and white tiger
illus and lettering, 1930s. **5.00**
Columbus Zoo, multicolored, three
monkeys illus, three evil poses,
1950s **4.00**
Junior Naturalist, ⅞" d, black and
white photo of Uncle John, early
1900s **10.00**
The Zoo Babies, black and white tiger
cubs illus, 1896–1900 . . . . **5.00**
The Zoo Nursery, black and white tiger
cub illus, We Love to Be Fondled,
1930s **8.00**
The Zoo, Prince, King of Them All,
black and white lion head, 1901–
10. . . . . **8.00**
Popcorn Box, Cretors Westview Park,
children eating popcorn illus, animal
background, unused, 1929. . . . . **45.00**

Flea Marketeer's Annotated Reference Library

YOU CANNOT TELL THE PLAYERS WITHOUT A SCORECARD

A typical flea market contains hundreds of thousands of objects. You cannot be expected to identify and know the correct price for everything off the top of your head. You need a good, basic reference library.

As a flea marketeer, there are two questions about every object that you want to know: What is it? and How much is it worth? A book that answers only the first question has little use in the field. Titles in the "Books about Objects" list contain both types of information.

The basic reference library consists of fifty titles. I admit the number is arbitrary. However, some limit was necessary. Acquiring all the titles on the list will not be cheap. Expect to pay somewhere between $1,000 and $1,250.

The list contains a few books that are out of print. You will have to pursue their purchase through used-book sources. Many antiques and collectibles book dealers conduct book searches and maintain "wants" lists. It is not uncommon to find one or more of these specialized dealers set up at a flea market. Most advertise in the trade papers, especially *The Antique Trader Weekly*, PO Box 1050, Dubuque, Iowa 52001. One dealer that I have found particularly helpful in locating out-of-print books is Joslin Hall Rare Books, PO Box 516, Concord, MA 01742.

Many reference books are revised every year or every other year. The editions listed are those as of fall 1992. When you buy them, make certain that you get the most recent edition.

One final factor that I used in preparing this list was a desire to introduce you to the major publishers and imprints in the antiques and collectibles field. It is important that you become familiar with Antique Publications, Books Americana, Collector Books, Greenberg Publishing, House of Collectibles, Schiffer Publishing, Wallace-Homestead, and Warman.

GENERAL PRICE GUIDES

Husfloen, Kyle, ed. *The Antique Trader Antiques and Collectibles Price Guide*, 9th ed. Babka Publishing Co., 1992.

There are over a dozen general price guides to antiques and collectibles. Of course, I think my dad's are the best. However, when I want a second opinion or cannot find a specific item in Dad's guides, I use the *Trader's* guide. The descriptions are great and prices are accurate. Most importantly, it is a price guide that focuses on the heartland of America.

Rinker, Harry L., ed. *Warman's Americana and Collectibles*, 5th ed. Radnor, PA: Wallace-Homestead, 1991.

This contains the stuff with which your parents, you, and your children grew up and played. More than any other modern price guide it is a record of what is found in the attics, closets, basements, garages, and sheds of America. It will make you regret everything you ever threw out. It has gone ten years without a rival, which says a great deal about the Warman format that Dad developed for it.

Rinker, Harry L., ed. *Warman's Antiques and Their Prices*, 27th ed. Radnor, PA: Wallace-Homestead, 1993.

This book is more than just a list of objects with prices. It is a user's guide. The introduction to each category contains a brief history, list of reference books, names and addresses of periodicals and collectors' clubs, museums to visit, and information on reproductions. It is the first place to start whenever you need information.

IDENTIFICATION OF REPRODUCTIONS AND FAKES

Hammond, Dorothy. *Confusing Collectibles: A Guide to the Identification of Contemporary Objects*, rev. ed. Radnor, PA: Wallace-Homestead, 1979. Out of print.

This book provides information about reproductions, copycats, fantasy items, contemporary crafts, and fakes from the late 1950s through the 1960s. Much of this material appears in today's flea markets. Some is collectible in its own right. The best defense against being taken is to know what was produced.

Hammond, Dorothy. *More Confusing Collectibles,* vol. II. Wichita, KS: C. B. P. Publishing Company, 1972. Out of print.

Confusing Collectibles took a broad approach to the market. *More Confusing Collectibles* focuses primarily on glass. It contains all new information, so you really do need both volumes.

Lee, Ruth Webb. *Antiques Fakes and Reproductions, Enlarged and Revised.* Published by author: 1938, 1950. Out of print. Note: This book went through seven editions. The later editions contain more information. A good rule is to buy only the fourth through seventh editions.

Dorothy Hammond followed in Ruth Webb Lee's footsteps. Webb Lee's book chronicles the reproductions, copycats, fantasy items, and fakes manufactured between 1920 and 1950. While heavily oriented toward glass, it contains an excellent chapter on metals, discussing and picturing in detail the products of Virginia Metalcrafters.

BOOKS ABOUT OBJECTS

American Manufactured Furniture [actually *Furniture Dealers' Reference Book, 1928–1929, Zone 3*]. West Chester, PA: Schiffer Publishing, 1988.

This reprint covers a wide range of furniture manufacturers whose advertisements often contain important company history. A wide range of styles and forms are illustrated. All illustrations are priced. Ten years ago the furniture pictured was found in secondhand furniture stores or given to the Salvation Army. Now it is in antiques shops.

Barlow, Ronald S. *The Antique Tool Collector's Guide to Value.* El Cajon, CA: Windmill Publishing Company, 1985, revised 1989.

This is *the* book for tools. Barlow has compiled auction and market prices from across the United States. Since this book is organized by tool type, you need to identify the type of tool that you have before you can look it up. There are plenty of illustrations to help.

Bunis, Marty and Sue. *Collector's Guide to Antique Radios,* 2nd ed. Paducah, KY: Collector Books, 1992.

There are a wealth of radio books in the market place. This one is tuned in to a wide band of radios. Organization is by manufacturer and model number. Although heavily illustrated, the book does not picture the majority of the models listed. The book also covers radio parts and accessories.

Carnevale, Diane. *Collectors' Information Bureau's Collectibles Market Guide and Price Index,* 10th ed. Radnor, PA: Wallace-Homestead, 1993.

The best thing about this book is that it covers a wide range of limited edition types, from bells to steins. It serves as a collector's checklist. The worst thing is that it is industry-driven. Important negatives and warnings about the limited edition market are missing. Field-test the prices before paying them.

Cunningham, Jo. *The Collector's Encyclopedia of American Dinnerware.* Paducah, KY: Collector Books, 1982, 1992 price update.

This is a profusely illustrated guide to identifying twentieth-century American dinnerware. In spite of the fact that many new companies and patterns have been discovered since Cunningham prepared her book, it remains a valuable identification tool, especially since its pricing is updated periodically.

Docks, L. R. *American Premium Record Guide: Identification and Value Guide to 1915–1965 78s, 45s, and LPs,* 4th ed. Florence, AL: Books Americana, 1992.

This is an excellent testament to the variety of record-collecting interest in the marketplace. Although a number of new specialized guides, such as Neal Umphred's *Goldmine's Price Guide to Collectible Record Albums* (Krause Publications, 1989), have appeared during the past several years, Docks' remains the best general record price guide in the market.

Duke, Harvey. *The Official Identification and Price Guide to Pottery and Porcelain,* 7th ed. New York, NY: House of Collectibles, 1989.

This is the perfect companion to Cunningham. Duke covers many of the companies and lines of which Cunningham was unaware when she first published her book in the early 1980s. Illustrations are minimal, making it necessary to know the name of your pattern before looking anything up. The book is well-balanced regionally. Many West Coast pottery manufacturers finally receive their due.

Florence, Gene. *The Collector's Encyclopedia of Depression Glass,* 10th ed. Paducah, KY: Collector Books, 1992.

This is the Depression Glass collector's bible. Among its important features are a full listing of pieces found in each pattern and an extensive section on reproductions, copycats, and fakes. One difficulty is that there are hundreds of glass patterns manufactured between 1920 and 1940 that are not found in this book because they do not have the Depression

Glass label. Supplement the book with Gene Florence's *Kitchen Glassware of the Depression Years,* also published by Collector Books.

Foulke, Jan. *10th Blue Book Dolls and Values.* **Cumberland, MD: Hobby House Press, Inc., 1991.**

Foulke is the first place doll collectors turn for information. The book is high-end, turning its back on many of the post-World War II and contemporary dolls. Within the doll field, it sets prices more than it reports them. Cross-check Foulke's prices in Julie Collier's *The Official Identification and Price Guide to Antique and Modern Dolls,* fourth edition (House of Collectibles, 1989) and R. Lane Herron's *Herron's Price Guide to Dolls* (Wallace-Homestead, 1990).

Franklin, Linda Campbell. *300 Years of House-keeping Collectibles.* **Florence, AL: Books Americana, 1992.**

Books Americana split the second edition of *300 Years of Kitchen Collectibles* into two separate volumes, albeit retaining the edition number for one of the spinoffs. Now, instead of paying $10.95 for a handy-to-use single source, you have to pay $45.90 for two volumes at $22.95 each. Hopefully a publisher will see an opportunity and once again put this information in a single volume. Until such time, it makes sense to buy the two Franklin volumes.

Franklin, Linda Campbell. *300 Years of Kitchen Collectibles,* **3rd ed. Florence, AL: Books Americana, 1991.**

The second edition of this book was well organized, had a readable format, and was easy to use. The recently released third edition provides ample proof that bigger is not necessarily better. The new format is incredibly awkward. The wealth of secondary material may be great for the researcher and specialized collector, but it is a pain to wade through for the generalist. Franklin joins the Coca-Cola Company as someone who failed to recognize that they had created a classic. For now this is better than nothing, but it provides a real opportunity for a challenger.

Gibbs, P. J. *Black Collectibles Sold in America.* **Paducah, KY: Collector Books, 1987, 1990 price update.**

Black collectibles have gone through a number of collecting cycles in the past fifteen years. Popular among both white and black collectors, black memorabilia is likely to cycle several more times in the years ahead. Because of this, prices in any black collectibles book have to be taken with a grain of salt.

Giles, Cynthia. *The Official Identification and Price Guide to Vintage Clothing.* **New York, NY: House of Collectibles, 1989.**

While the vintage clothing market has stabilized outside the major metropolitan areas, it still thrives in the big cities. Post-World War II clothing is especially hot right now. Because the market is so large, any book on the subject is merely window dressing. An alternative selection is Maryanne Dolan's *Vintage Clothing: 1880 to 1960: Identification and Value Guide,* second edition (Books Americana, 1987).

Hagan, Tere. *Silverplated Flatware,* **revised 4th ed. Paducah, KY: Collector Books, 1990.**

You do not see a great deal of sterling silver at flea markets because most dealers sell it for weight. Silver-plated items are in abundance. This book concentrates only on flatware, the most commonly found form. You can find information on silver-plated holloware in Jeri Schwartz's *The Official Identification and Price Guide to Silver and Silverplate,* sixth edition (House of Collectibles, 1989).

Hake, Ted. *Hake's Guide to TV Collectibles: An Illustrated Price Guide.* **Radnor, PA: Wallace-Homestead, 1990.**

TV collectibles are hot. They are part of that sizzling topic, post-World War II collectibles. The book, organized by show, utilizes a priced picture format and includes material that Hake sold in Hake's Americana Mail Auction during the past several years. The short history provided for each show is helpful in dating objects.

Hake, Ted. *The Encyclopedia of Political Buttons.* **1896–1972 (1974, 1985); Book II, 1920–1976 (1977); Book III, 1789–1916 (1978); 1991 Revised Prices (1990). York, PA: Hake's Americana & Collectibles Press.**

Do not be confused by the title. These volumes are price guides to all forms of political memorabilia, not just political buttons. Hake is one of the pioneers in the field of political memorabilia. Over the past twenty-five years, he has owned and sold almost every major political item available in the market.

Heacock, William. *The Encyclopedia of Victorian Colored Pattern Glass.* **9 volumes. Marietta, OH: Antique Publications.**

One of the major gaps in the antiques and collectibles literature is a general price guide for glass. On the surface, the subject appears overwhelming. Heacock's nine-volume set covers glass manufactured from the mid-nineteenth through the early twentieth century. Actually, some volumes extended deep into the twentieth century. Book I on tooth-picks, Book II on opalescent glass, and Book 9 on cranberry opalescent glass are among the most helpful.

Huxford, Bob. *Huxfords Old Book Value Guide,* **4th ed. Paducah, KY: Collector Books, 1992.**

There are always piles of old books at any flea market. Most are valued in the twenty-five to fifty cent range. However, there are almost always sleepers in every pile. This book is a beginning. If you think that you have an expensive tome, check it out in the most recent edition of *American Book Prices Current,* published by Bancroft-Parkman.

Klug, Ray. *Antique Advertising Encyclopedia.* **Volume 1 (1978) and volume 2 (1985). West Chester, PA: Schiffer Publishing.**

Klug's is a classic. It is organized by advertising type and follows a priced picture format. It is by no means as encyclopedic as its title suggests. However, it serves as a checklist for many collectors and dealers. Originally published by L-W Book Sales, it was taken over by Schiffer several years ago. Make certain that you get the most up-to-date price list.

Kovel, Ralph and Terry. *The Kovel's Bottle Price List,* **9th ed. New York: Crown Publishers, Inc., 1992.**

This is another category where the best of the mundane wins the prize. The book is organized by bottle type and within each type alphabetically by manufacturer. The quality of pricing is spotty. Totally missing are bottles in the ten cent to four dollar range. This is precisely the range of most bottles found at flea markets. Jim Megura, bottle consultant at Skinner, is taking over authorship of the House of Collectibles bottle guide. Do not look for low-end bottles to appear in this book either.

Kurowski, Jeff, ed. *Baseball Card Price Guide,* **6th ed. Iola, WI: Krause Publications, 1992.**

This is the new kid on the block that has become a superstar. It is more comprehensive and accurate than its competition. James Beckett's *Sports Americana Baseball Card Price Guide,* published by Edgewater Books, has been relegated to bench warmer.

Lane, Kenneth Jay. *The Official Identification and Price Guide to Costume Jewelry.* **New York, NY: House of Collectibles, 1990.**

My heart is breaking. In order to add this book to the list, I had to drop Arthur Buy Kaplan's *The Official Identification and Price*

Guide to Antique Jewelry, sixth edition (House of Collectibles: 1990)—in my opinion, the best of the jewelry price guides. The only problem is that you rarely see antique jewelry at a flea market. On the other hand, costume jewelry exists in abundance.

Mallerich, Dallas J., III. *Greenberg's American Toy Trains: From 1900 with Current Values.* **Sykesville, MD: Greenberg Publishing, 1990.**

When it comes to toy trains, the name to know is Greenberg Publishing, 7566 Main Street, Sykesville, MD 21784. Write for the company's mail order catalog. In addition to their own publications, they also distribute books in the toy train, toy, and military areas from other publishers. Mallerich's book provides an overview that will satisfy most general collectors.

Malloy, Alex. *Comics Values Annual: The Comic Books Price Guide.* **Radnor, PA: Wallace-Homestead, 1992.**

The king has fallen, long live the king. For decades, Robert M. Overstreet's *The Overstreet Comic Book Price Guide,* now in its twenty-second edition (New York: Avon Books, 1992) has dominated the comic book price guide market. Malloy offers more—more accurate listings and prices for modern comics (those you are most likely to find at flea markets), values for European, Pacific Rim, Underground, and Fanzine comics (missing from Overstreet), and quality state-of-the-market information. Try it. You'll like it.

McNulty, Lyndi Stewart. *Wallace-Homestead Price Guide to Plastic Collectibles.* **Radnor, PA: Wallace-Homestead, 1987, 1992 price update.**

The problem with things made of plastic is that they tend to be collected within specialized categories such as kitchen collectibles, advertising, and so on. Plastic as a category has never really caught on. McNulty's book shows the potential. Opportunity awaits.

Morykan, Dana Gehman, and Harry L. Rinker. *Warman's Country Antiques and Collectibles.* **Radnor, PA: Wallace-Homestead, 1992.**

This is the general text-oriented price guide to Country that has long been needed. A special feature is the names and addresses of reproduction craftspersons and manufacturers. For those who still feel the need for a picture-oriented guide, check out Don and Carol Raycraft's *Wallace-Homestead Price Guide to American Country Antiques,* twelfth edition (Radnor, PA: Wallace-Homestead, 1992).

O'Brien, Richard. *Collecting Toys: A Collectors Identification and Value Guide,* 6th ed. Florence, AL: Books Americana, 1992.

The reason that there are no specialized toy or game books on this list is that you have no need for them if you own a copy of O'Brien. The book dominates the field. It is not without its weaknesses, especially in the area of post-World War II toys. However, each edition brings improvement. O'Brien has enlisted the help of specialists to price many of the sections, an approach that greatly strengthens the presentation.

Schiffer, Nancy N. *Costume Jewelry: The Fun of Collecting.* West Chester, PA: Schiffer Publishing Ltd., 1988.

Costume jewelry dominates flea market offerings. The amount of material is so large that it is virtually impossible for one book to do justice to the subject. Nancy Schiffer's book comes the closest. It uses a picture format, something that is essential since word descriptions for jewelry tend to be terribly imprecise.

Shugart, Cooksey, and Tom Engle. *The Official Price Guide to Watches,* 11th ed. Paducah, KY: Collector Books, 1991.

Although this book has been published by three different publishers during the past five years, it has never failed to maintain its high quality. It is the best book available on pocket and wrist watches.

Swedberg, Robert W. and Harriett. *Victorian Furniture: Styles and Prices.* 3 volumes: Book I (1976, 1984), Book II (1983), and Book III (1985). Radnor, PA: Wallace-Homestead.

The Swedbergs write about furniture. Wallace-Homestead published their series on Oak, Pine, Victorian, and Wicker. Collector Books has published their *Collector's Encyclopedia of American Furniture, Volume I—Hardwoods* (1990) and *Furniture of the Depression Era* (1987). All books utilize a priced picture approach. Text information, including descriptions for individual pieces, is minimal. Sources are heavily Midwest. The plus factor is that the books feature pieces for sale in the field, not museum examples.

Tumbusch, T. N. *Space Adventure Collectibles.* Radnor, PA: Wallace-Homestead, 1990.

The TV and toy markets are becoming increasingly sophisticated, *Space Adventure Collectibles* is typical of the wide range of specialized books on toy types (e.g., action figures), individual cartoon characters (e.g., Dick

Tracy), and manufacturers (e.g., Tootsietoy), that are entering the market. It also demonstrates a problem found in many of these books—the use of broad price ranges for individual objects that often verge on being meaningless.

Wellbaum, Bob, ed. *Tomart's Price Guide to Garage Sale Gold.* Radnor, PA: Wallace-Homestead, 1992.

I have included this book because it includes a number of hot contemporary and trendy collectible topics such as Dankin and Pez. However, a word of warning is necessary. The prices were provided by individuals with strong vested interests to prop up and support high market pricing. The information is good; use the prices cautiously.

GENERAL SOURCES

Hyman, H. A. *I'll Buy That Too!* Claremont, CA: Treasure Hunt Publications, 1992.

Tony Hyman is one of the most magnetic radio personalities that I have ever heard. He writes and compiles. Most importantly, he hustles what he has done. This is a list of people who buy things. One good contact pays for the cost of the book. It is also a great place to get your collecting interests listed.

Lehner, Lois. *Lehner's Encyclopedia of U.S. Marks on Pottery, Porcelain, and Clay.* Paducah, KY: Collector Books, 1988.

This is the best reference book for identifying the marks of United States pottery and porcelain manufacturers. It contains detailed company histories and all known marks and trade names used. Whenever possible, marks and trade names are dated.

Kovel, Ralph and Terry. *Kovels' Antiques and Collectibles Fix-It Source Book.* New York: Crown Publishers, 1990.

Many flea market treasures have not withstood the test of time well. While they should probably be passed by, they all too often wind up in the hands of a collector. This book provides the options available to have these objects fixed.

Maloney, David. *1992 Collectors' Information Clearinghouse Antiques and Collectibles Resource Directory.* Radnor, PA: Wallace-Homestead, 1991.

This is the one reference source book to buy when you are only going to buy one. It is a comprehensive directory to the antiques and collectibles field containing approximately, 6,000 entries (names, addresses, telephone numbers, and a wealth of other information) in approximately 1,500 categories. It is fully cross-referenced. It covers buyers, sellers, appraisers, restorers, collectors' clubs, periodicals, museums and galleries, show promoters, shop and malls, and many other specialists.

Manston, Peter B. *Manston's Flea Markets Antique Fairs and Auctions of Britain.* **Travel Keys (PO Box 160691, Sacramento, CA 95816).**

When you are hooked on flea markets, they become part of your blood. Some of the greatest flea markets are in Europe. Peter Manston has written three flea market guides, one each for France, Germany, and Great Britain. Do not go to Europe without them.

Miner, Robert G. *The Flea Market Handbook.* **Radnor, PA: Wallace-Homestead, 1990.**

This book explains how to become a flea market dealer. Collectors should read it to understand the mind-set of the flea market dealer. Understanding the dealer makes doing business easier.

Rainwater, Dorothy T. *Encyclopedia of American Silver Manufacturers,* 3rd ed. **West Chester, PA: Schiffer Publishing, 1986.**

This book focuses on handcrafted and mass-produced factory-manufactured silver and silver plate from the mid-nineteenth century to the present. It is organized alphabetically by company. Each detailed company history is accompanied by carefully drawn and dated marks. A glossary of trademarks is another welcome feature.

Rinker, Harry L. *Rinker on Collectibles.* **Radnor, PA: Wallace-Homestead, 1989. Out of print.**

This book is a compilation of the first sixty test columns from Dad's weekly column, "Rinker on Collectibles." Many are now classics. The book allows you to delve into the mind-set of the collector. It deserves textbook status.

Wanted to Buy, 3rd ed. **Paducah, KY: Collector Books, 1992.**

This is another book listing individuals who want to buy things. If you are a serious collector, write to Collector Books and see if your name and interests can be included in subsequent editions. The book differs from *I'll Buy That Too!* because it contains several dozen listings and prices for most categories.

Werner, Kitty, ed. *The Official Directory to U.S. Flea Markets,* 3rd ed. **New York, NY: House of Collectibles, 1992.**

My opinion of this book is clearly stated earlier. Nothing has changed in my mind since I wrote that section. (see Chapter 2)

JUST FOR THE FUN OF IT

Gash, Jonathan. *The Sleepers of Erin.* **New York: Viking Penguin, 1983.**

If you are unfamiliar with Lovejoy the antiques dealer, it is time you make his acquaintance. You will not regret it. I had a hard time picking a favorite. I could just have easily chosen *The Judas Pair, Gold by Gemini, The Grail Tree, Spend Game, The Vatican Rip,* and *The Gondola Scam,* all in paperback from Viking Penguin. *The Tartan Sell, Moonspender,* and *Pearlhanger* are in hardcover from St. Martin's Press.

Rinker, Harry L. *The Joy of Collecting with Craven Moore.* **Radnor, PA: Wallace-Homestead, 1985. Out of print.**

Try never to become so serious about your collecting or dealing that you forget to laugh and have fun. Find out if you are Craven or Anita Moore or Howie and Constance Lee Bys. You are in *The Joy of Collecting with Craven Moore.* I guarantee it. Dad still sells copies. Send him $6.00 and he will send you one.

WARMAN ENCYCLOPEDIA OF ANTIQUES AND COLLECTIBLES

Chilton Book Company, parent company of Wallace-Homestead, is currently in the process of launching a series of major antiques and collectibles reference books utilizing the Warman format. Dad is in the thick of things acting as series editor. He is rather possessive about the Warman format, and who can blame him. It is a proven winner.

A few of these titles appear among the fifty books listed previously. They are there for emphasis. Actually, you should own all these titles. I strongly recommend buying them.

Bagdade, Susan and Al. *Warman's English and Continental Pottery and Porcelain,* second edition (1991).

Mascarelli, Gloria and Robert. *Warman's Oriental Antiques* (1992).

Morykan, Dana Gehman, and Harry L. Rinker. *Warman's Country Antiques and Collectibles* (1992).

Schroy, Ellen Tischbein. *Warman's Glass* (1992).

Rinker, Harry L., ed. *Warman's Americana and Collectibles,* fifth edition (1991).

Rinker, Harry L., ed. *Warman's Furniture* (1993).

Antiques and Collectibles Trade Newspapers

NATIONAL

American Collector
PO Box 686
Southfield, MI 48037
(313) 351-9910

American Collector's Journal
PO Box 407
Kewanee, IL 61443
(309) 852-2602

Antique Monthly
2100 Powers Ferry Road
Atlanta, GA 30339
(404) 955-5656

The Antique Trader Weekly
PO Box 1050
Dubuque, IA 52004
(319) 588-2073

Antique Week (Central and Eastern Edition)
27 North Jefferson Street
PO Box 90
Knightstown, IN 46148
1-800-876-5133

Antiques & the Arts Weekly
Bee Publishing Company
5 Church Hill Road
Newtown, CT 06470
(203) 426-3141

Collector News
506 Second Street
Grundy Center, IA 50638
(319) 824-6981

Maine Antique Digest
PO Box 645
Waldoboro, ME 04572
(207) 832-4888 or 832-7341

REGIONAL

New England

Cape Code Antiques & Arts
Register Newspaper
PO Box 400
Yarmouth Port, MA 02675
(508) 362-2111

MassBay Antiques
North Shores Weekly
9 Page Street
PO Box 293
Danvers, MA 01923
(508) 777-7070 or (617) 289-6961

New England Antiques Journal
4 Church Street
Ware, MA 01082
(413) 967-3505

Middle Atlantic States

Antique Country
Ultra Graphics
PO Box 649
Berryville, VA 22611
(703) 955-4412

Antiquer's Guide to the Susquehanna Region
PO Box 388
Sidney, NY 13838
(607) 563-8339

Antiques & Auction News
PO Box 500
Mount Joy, PA 17552
(717) 653-9797

Eastern Seaboard Antique Monthly
3611 Autumn Glen Circle
Burtonsville, MD 20866
(301) 890-0214

*The New York Antique Almanac of Art, Antiques,
    Investments & Yesteryear*
The N.Y. Eye Publishing Company
PO Box 335
Lawrence, NY 11559
(516) 371-3300

New York–Pennsylvania Collector
Drawer C
Fishers, NY 14453
(716) 924-4040

Renninger's Antique Guide
PO Box 495
Lafayette Hill, PA 19444
(215) 828-4614 or 825-6392

Treasure Chest
253 West 72nd Street, #211A
New York, NY 10023
(212) 496-2234

South

The Antique Press
12403 North Florida Avenue
Tampa, FL 33612
(813) 935-7577

The Antique Shoppe
2311 63rd Avenue East, Suite F
Bradenton, FL 34203
(813) 753-8354

Antiques & Crafts Gazette
PO Box 181
Cumming, GA 30130
(404) 887-3563

Cotton & Quail Antique Trail
205 East Washington Street
PO Box 326
Monticello, FL 32344
(904) 997-3880

The MidAtlantic Antiques Magazine
Henderson Daily Dispatch Company
304 South Chestnut Street
PO Box 908
Henderson, NC 27536
(919) 492-4001

The Old News Is Good News Antiques Gazette
4928 Government Street
PO Box 65292
Baton Rouge, LA 70896
(504) 923-0575 or 923-0576

Southern Antiques
PO Drawer 1107
Decatur, GA 30031
(404) 289-0054

Midwest

The Antique Collector and Auction Guide
Weekly Section of Farm and Dairy
PO Box 38
Salem, OH 44460
(216) 337-3419

Antique Gazette
6949 Charlotte Pike, Suite 106
Nashville, TN 37209
(615) 352-0941

Antique Review
12 East Stafford Street
PO Box 538
Worthington, OH 43085
(614) 885-9757

The Buckeye Marketeer
PO Box 954
Westerville, OH 43081
(614) 895-1663

Collectors Journal
1800 West D Street
PO Box 601
Vinton, IA 52349
(319) 472-4763

Michigan Antiques Trading Post
132 South Putnam
Williamstown, MI 48895
(517) 655-5621

Yesteryear
PO Box 2
Princeton, WI 54968
(414) 787-4808

Southwest

Antique & Collector's Guide
8510 Frazier Drive
Beaumont, TX 77707
(409) 866-7224

Arizona Antiques News and Southwest Antiques Journal
PO Box 26536
Phoenix, AZ 85068
(602) 943-9137

Rocky Mountain States

Mountain States Collector
PO Box 2525
Evergreen, CO 80439
(303) 987-3994

West Coast

Antique & Collectables
Californian Publishing Co.
1000 Pioneer Way
PO Box 1565
El Cajon, CA 92022
(619) 593-2925

Antique & Collectible Marketplace
Pacific West Publications
18055 Beach Boulevard, Suite 150
Huntington Beach, CA 92648
(714) 847-8500

Antiques Today
Kruse-Arett Publishing
977 Lehigh Circle
Carson City, NV 89705
(702) 267-4600

Antiques West
3315 Sacramento St., #618
San Francisco, CA 94118
(415) 221-4645

Collector
436 West 4th Street, #222
Pomona, CA 91766
(714) 620-9014

West Coast Peddler
PO Box 5134
Whittier, CA 90607
(213) 698-1718

Index